820.8002
OXF

The Oxford book
of late medieval
verse and prose

27217

5/86 $22.46

DATE			

THE
OXFORD BOOK OF
LATE MEDIEVAL
VERSE AND
PROSE

Edited by
DOUGLAS GRAY

With a Note on Grammar and Spelling in the
Fifteenth Century by
NORMAN DAVIS

CLARENDON PRESS · OXFORD
1985

Oxford University Press, Walton Street, Oxford OX2 6DP

Oxford New York Toronto
Delhi Bombay Calcutta Madras Karachi
Kuala Lumpur Singapore Hong Kong Tokyo
Nairobi Dar es Salaam Cape Town
Melbourne Auckland

and associated companies in
Beirut Berlin Ibadan Mexico City Nicosia

Oxford is a trade mark of Oxford University Press

Published in the United States
by Oxford University Press, New York

British Library Cataloguing in Publication Data

The Oxford book of late medieval verse and prose.
1. English literature—Middle English, 1100–1500
I. Gray, Douglas II. Davis, Norman, 1913–
820.8'002 PR1120

ISBN 0–19–812452–X

Set by Hope Services, Abingdon
Printed in Great Britain by
Richard Clay (The Chaucer Press) Ltd
Bungay, Suffolk

PREFACE

WHEN I was completing this book, my eye was caught by a newspaper headline, 'Those Anthology Blues'. Such a title is likely to stir the many and curious anxieties to which an anthologist is prone, and I read on. It was a review written by someone claiming to be a 'founder member of the Society for the Prevention of Anthologists', and it stated flatly: 'we know what's wrong with the whole damned breed: they're as incestuous as used-car salesmen, shifting fifteenth-hand material from one tired lot to the next, and leaving no one but themselves the richer.' While this particular charge does not disturb me, since my lot contains some brand-new material and my older models are of very good quality, the general *cri de cœur* moves me to a brief apologia, or at least a statement of intent (which will no doubt provide ammunition for some other member of the SPA). This anthology contains works written in English from about 1400 (the date of the death of Chaucer) to about 1520. I have rather boldly used the words 'late medieval' to describe this literary tradition, which is a fairly coherent one. That one or two of my authors—notably Skelton and More—are often labelled 'Renaissance' does not worry me overmuch, since it is obviously impossible, even if we wish to restrict the term 'Renaissance' to a chronological period, to fix a starting date. Dates from political history—1485, or even 1509—do not quite fit the slow and complicated development of literature any more than the less precise philological division between 'Middle English' and 'Early Modern English' will. My own final point is also arbitrary, since on the one hand I have ignored it in the case of Lord Berners, whose works are printed after this date, but have in many ways obvious links with earlier literature (although to anyone who knows Tudor books and culture of the period *c.*1525–*c.*1535 he will not seem a totally anomalous figure in his own time), while on the other I have observed it in the cases of Skelton and More, who often, quite rightly, appear in 'Renaissance' anthologies, by representing them here only by their early works. A practical reason for the *terminus* of *c.*1520 is that not only does it remind us that works of a 'medieval' kind were still being written after the accession of Henry VIII, but it excludes the literature (notably the war of books and pamphlets between More and Tyndale) provoked by the Reformation, to do justice to which would have meant lengthening a long book even further.

I have tried to give a sense of the variety and complexity of this long period. To do this I have included much more than well-known authors and works; indeed, these have usually been deliberately under-represented in the form of shorter extracts and, if they are available in good editions, with shorter commentaries. I have avoided the extreme solutions of either not representing these writers at all, which would give 'a body without a head', or of allowing them to extinguish most of the minor, peripheral, but still interesting material. An anthology should encourage its users to read further themselves. And to give a sense of period it must make available many kinds of writing, some of them probably not literary in the narrowest definitions of that term. My aim has been to include the widest variety of texts, and to this aim I have subordinated commentary and critical analysis. I have tried to balance a large number of short extracts with a few complete texts. The arrangement in sections, some of which are devoted to authors, some to genres, some to more loosely grouped miscellanies, has meant a good deal of over-lapping (so that religious lyrics appear in No. 19 as well as in No. 11, and prose romances in No. 25 as well as in Nos. 13 and 14). About this I am unrepentant, being disposed to think that genres in medieval literature are more flexible and less clear-cut than critics would often like them to be, and also disposed to enjoy the opportunity of recreating something of the delightfully miscellaneous quality which some late medieval anthologies themselves have.

The texts have been checked with manuscripts or early printed books wherever possible. The punctuation is editorial, and some spellings þ, 3, u/v, i/j, and Scots ß and initial w/v) have been modernized. Textual emendations are indicated in the Commentary.

I am grateful to a number of libraries for permission to reproduce material in their possession, and to a number of friends for help and advice, in particular to the late Professor J. A. W. Bennett, Professor Norman Davis, Dr J. .D. Fleeman, Mr R. Hamer, Dr A. M. Hudson, Dr I. W. A. Jamieson, Miss E. Mackenzie, Dr N. Mann, Professor J. Norton-Smith, Mr B. O'Donoghue, Miss C. Sisam, Professor J. B. Trapp, Mrs K. Ward-Perkins, and Mr Edward Wilson.

CONTENTS

CONTENTS

ABBREVIATIONS

AL	C. S. Lewis, *The Allegory of Love* (Oxford, 1936)
Archiv	*Archiv für das Studium der neueren Sprachen*
BD	*Book of the Duchess*
BJRL	*Bulletin of the John Rylands Library*
BL	British Library
Bodl.	Bodleian Library
BN	Bibliothèque Nationale
BRUC	A. B. Emden, *A Biographical Register of the University of Cambridge to 1500* (Cambridge, 1963)
BRUO	A. B. Emden, *A Biographical Register of the University of Oxford to AD 1500* (Oxford, 1957)
CA	*Confessio Amantis*
Camb.	Cambridge
CB XV	Carleton Brown, *Religous Lyrics of The Fifteenth Century* (Oxford, 1939)
CCC	Corpus Christi College
COP	W. W. Skeat, *Chaucerian and Other Pieces* (vol. vii of *The Works of Geoffrey Chaucer* [Oxford, 1894–1900])
CR	F. L. Utley, *The Crooked Rib* (Columbus, Ohio, 1949)
CT	*Canterbury Tales*
CUL	Cambridge University Library
DNB	*Dictionary of National Biography*
Dreves	*Analecta Hymnica*, edd. G. M. Dreves and C. Blume (Leipzig, 1886–)
E&S	*Essays and Studies*
EEC	R. L. Greene, *The Early English Carols* (2nd edn., Oxford, 1977)
EEL	E. K. Chambers and F. Sidgwick, *Early English Lyrics* (London, 1921)
EETS	Early English Text Society (ES: Extra Series, SS: Supplementary Series)
EHR	*English Historical Review*
ELH	*Journal of English Literary History*
EMEVP	J. A. W. Bennett and G. V. Smithers, *Early Middle English Verse and Prose* (2nd edn., Oxford, 1968)
ES	*English Studies*
EVCS	E. P. Hammond, *English Verse between Chaucer and Surrey* (Durham, NC, 1927)
facs.	facsimile
Gen. Prol.	*General Prologue of The Canterbury Tales*
HP	R. H. Robbins, *Historical Poems of the Fourteenth and Fifteenth Centuries* (New York, 1959)
Index	C. Brown and R. H. Robbins, *The Index of Middle English Verse* (New York, 1943); *Supplement* by R. H. Robbins and J. L. Cutler (Lexington, Ky., 1965)

JEGP	*Journal of English and Germanic Philology*
Kn. T.	*Knight's Tale*
LGW	*Legend of Good Women*
LSE	*Leeds Studies in English*
M&H	*Medievalia et Humanistica*
M&P	J. Stevens, *Music and Poetry in the Early Tudor Court* (London, 1961)
MÆ	*Medium Ævum*
MC	J. Stevens, *Medieval Carols* (*Musica Britannica*, iv, London, 1952)
MDu.	Middle Dutch
ME	Middle English
MED	*Middle English Dictionary*
MEL	R. T. Davies, *Medieval English Lyrics* (London, 1963)
Merch. T.	*Merchant's Tale*
Met.	*Metamorphoses*
MLN	*Modern Language Notes*
MLR	*Modern Language Review*
MLT	*Man of Law's Tale*
MP	*Modern Philology*
MWME	J. B. Severs and A. E. Hartung, *A Manual of the Writings in Middle English* (New Haven, 1967–)
NLS	National Library of Scotland
NPT	*Nun's Priest's Tale*
NQ	*Notes and Queries*
OBMEV	C. and K. Sisam, *The Oxford Book of Medieval English Verse* (Oxford, 1970)
OE	Old English
OED	*Oxford English Dictionary*
OF	Old French
Pard. T.	*Pardoner's Tale*
Pars. T.	*Parson's Tale*
PBA	*Proceedings of the British Academy*
PF	*Parliament of Fowls*
PL	*Patrologia Latina*, ed. J. P. Migne (Paris, 1844–)
PMLA	*Publications of the Modern Language Association of America*
PPl.	*Piers Plowman*
PQ	*Philological Quarterly*
PRO	Public Record Office
RES	*Review of English Studies*
RS	Rolls Series
SATF	Société des Anciens Textes Français
SL	R. H. Robbins, *Secular Lyrics of the Fourteenth and Fifteenth Centuries* (Oxford, 1952)
SP	*Studies in Philology*
SR	*Studies in the Renaissance*
SRL	D. Gray, *A Selection of Religious Lyrics* (Oxford, 1975)
STC	A. W. Pollard and G. R. Redgrave, *Short-Title Catalogue of*

	English Books . . . 1475–1640 (London, 1926); 2nd rev. edn., edd. W. A. Jackson, F. S. Ferguson, and K. F. Panter, vol. ii (I–Z) (London, 1976)
STS	Scottish Text Society
TC	*Troilus and Criseyde*
TIMERL	D. Gray, *Themes and Images in the Medieval English Religious Lyric* (London, 1972)
TLS	*Times Literary Supplement*
Tr.RHS	*Transactions of the Royal Historical Society*
Vg.	Vulgate
WB Prol.	*Wife of Bath's Prologue*
Whiting	B. J. Whiting, *Proverbs, Sentences and Proverbial Phrases from English Writings Mainly before* 1500 (Cambridge, Mass., 1968)

INTRODUCTION

WRITINGS in English from the period 1400–*c.*1520 offer a fascinating variety of material. For those concerned with the transmission and the re-creation of cultural and literary patterns, this is a period of extraordinary interest, 'an age', in the words of the historian C. L. Kingsford, 'not of stagnation but of ferment'.[1] It demands the attention of students both of earlier medieval and of later Renaissance literature. The general reader will find in it much that is surprising, delightful, and exciting. These claims may seem startling to those whose views have been formed by the older histories of English literature, where misconceptions are to be found which resemble such remarks on the period as 'noticing suddenly that the Middle Ages were coming to an end, the Barons now made a stupendous effort to revive the old Feudal amenities of Sackage, Carnage and Wreckage and so stave off the Tudors for a time' (*1066 and All That*). Two in particular are still widespread: that in the history of English literature there is here a kind of gap, since between Chaucer and Wyatt and Surrey nothing much was written, or, alternatively, that though much was written, it was without question of a consistent and quite extraordinary dullness. The pages of this anthology will, I hope, show the absurdity of these views. It is, to be sure, a period which is not dominated by the towering figure of a single great writer, a Chaucer or a Shakespeare, and only rarely can its literature match contemporary English achievements in the sister arts of music and architecture. Yet it produced much work of distinction. This is especially evident in prose. Here, there is a dominant figure in Sir Thomas Malory, but he is not isolated. Translators can write with style, and sometimes, as in the case of Malory's successor, Lord Berners, with genius. The prose of some devotional and religious works is of the highest quality. Prose is used for controversy, for political theory, for history, and for all kinds of practical instruction. Prose of a more familiar kind is found in the collections of letters. This plain, unadorned, expository prose, close to the syntax and rhythms of contemporary spoken English, is usually more successful and attractive than the more intricate stylistic experiments (necessary though they were), such as Skelton's Diodorus or Berners's *Golden Book*. R. W. Chambers, in a famous essay,[2] insisted on the 'continuity' of English prose, but the variety of our examples from this period suggests that we are not dealing with one single stream, and

---

[1] C. L. Kingsford, *Prejudice and Promise in Fifteenth-Century England* (Oxford, 1925), 66.

[2] R. W. Chambers, *On the Continuity of English Prose from Alfred to More and his School* (part of Introduction to Harpsfield's *Life of More*, edd. E. V. Hitchcock and R. W. Chambers [EETS 186; 1931]; repr. separately 1932, 1957).

certainly not only with one central tradition of religious and devotional prose. One is tempted to recall the sudden revelation that comes to M. Jourdain in *Le Bourgeois Gentilhomme*, that he has been speaking prose all his life. Whatever we think about 'continuity', the diversity and the quality of what was written in this period make it arguable that it is one of the great ages of English prose, as well as one of the most neglected.

In drama, the constraints of space have allowed the inclusion of only two very different examples of the morality play. Much else has survived, and the many references to plays which have not suggest a period of great activity. It is important not to be misled by a pseudo-Darwinian view of the evolution of the drama into thinking that forms which had developed earlier—like liturgical plays, miracle plays, mystery cycles—were superseded by later forms and ceased to exist. The records show quite clearly that the various types continued to coexist: thus at Reading there are references in 1499 and 1539 to the 'Kings of Cologne', which was presumably a miracle play, and the date of its performance 1 May, led E. K. Chambers to suspect some connection with a folk festival.[3] The great mystery cycle at Coventry was seen by kings (Henry V, while he was still Prince of Wales, Richard III, and Henry VII) as well as by commoners.[4] Beside the complete, elaborate cycles, there are references to separate 'parish plays'. The religious drama was clearly deeply embedded in the life of medieval communities (after its suppression or extinction, there are no more charming references in church accounts to 'a pair of gloves for him that played Christ on Corpus Christi day').[5] The secular drama has been almost all lost. The fifteenth-century fragment of a Robin Hood play, and two complete little plays on the outlaw from the early sixteenth century, are certainly only the tip of an iceberg.[6] Among references to minstrels, wrestlers, sword-players, bear-wards, and the like, are references to various forms of semi-dramatic folk festivals involving Lords of Misrule and Mayings. More sedate pageants and political spectacles are used in towns to celebrate the entries or coronations or marriages of kings. From the end of our period some comic interludes and farces survive, and there is every reason to suppose that they existed earlier. There are references to school and college plays, and in the early sixteenth century the printing of *Terens in englysh*[7] gives another hint of developments to come.

The poetry of the period, so often abused in the older histories, shows the same variety. It ranges from genuinely popular kinds like the 'rymes of

[3] E. K. Chambers, *The Medieval Stage* (Oxford, 1903), ii. 392–3.
[4] V. A. Kolve, *The Play Called Corpus Christi* (Stanford, 1966), 6–7.
[5] A. Hanham, *Churchwardens' Accounts of Ashburton 1479–1580* (Devon and Cornwall Record Society, NS 15; Torquay, 1970), 140.
[6] Cf. D. Wiles, *The Early Plays of Robin Hood* (Cambridge: D. S. Brewer, 1981).
[7] *STC* 23894 (*c.*1520?).

Robin Hood' to works in a learned tradition where the influence of Chaucer is often very marked, written not by anonymous craftsmen but by poets whose names are known and who write with some self-consciousness and literary individuality. Alliterative poetry continues to exist (especially in Scotland, where its influence is very strong) alongside the more common metrical verse. Writers of the latter are sometimes still accused (a) of expending much energy in the construction of very intricate stanza forms (at the expense of their matter), and (b) of not being able to scan their verse. In fact, it will be seen that elaborate stanza schemes (as in *The Lovers' Mass* or the Scottish *Buke of the Howlat*) are not really very common, and that most poets are content with couplets, quatrains, rhyme royal, or the simpler French lyric stanza forms. The question of metre is a complicated one, since we have to make allowance for such things as linguistic change, literary convention, and possible scribal corruption, but it might be remarked that a rigid iambic pentameter pattern is not the staple one in late Middle English verse (Scottish verse is notably more strict), and that much of the verse is still close to spoken performance. If it is read as spoken verse with a 'natural cadence' it will not usually cause any difficulty. As in other periods, there is poetry of obviously inferior quality which sometimes, though not in our examples, sounds rather tired. However, although the bold inventiveness of a Skelton is not commonly found, the reader again and again finds that traditional genres and types continue to live on in newly adapted form, often finding a new vitality, and always changing and developing (in No. 12, for instance, we may see how a chronicle of the siege of Belgrade is at the same time a pious romance, and how a long romance in quatrains is beginning to sound like the narrative ballads). The very distinguished achievements of Henryson, Dunbar, and Douglas in Scotland and of Skelton in England are now at last recognised; it is my hope that the unprejudiced reader will find much of value in the other poets represented in these pages.

It is of course in the manner of earlier medieval literature for traditional matter and forms to be accepted and passed on or transformed. In our period a very characteristic and important cultural channel for this process is translation, the extent and quality of which are a clear premonition of the work of the later sixteenth century. The reader with knowledge of that period will at once be aware of a notable absence here of examples of biblical translation. In fact, the earlier Wycliffite versions, the occasion of some official persecution, continue to circulate; late in the period, Murdoch Nisbet 'translates' the Wycliffite New Testament into Scots (*c.*1520),[8] just before the work of the new Reformers, Tyndale and Coverdale, begins to appear. In other areas, however, an amazing amount of material is made available to English readers through translation (and

---

[8] Ed. T. G. Law (STS 46, 49; 1901, 1903)

the coming of printing seems to have intensified the output). As the reader will see, it ranges from fashionable French courtly writings to books of devotion, science, or practical instruction. The nature of the translations varies from what has been called 'stencil translation', the literal Englishing of books for readers with no French or Latin, to a kind of imaginative translation, which can, paradoxically, produce works of genuine originality. As C. S. Lewis very nicely puts it:

The paradox is that it is just this abdication of originality which brings out the originality they really possess. The more devout and concentrated Chaucer's gaze on the *Filostrato* becomes, or Malory's on the 'French Book', the more real the scenes and people become to them. That reality forces them presently to see and hear, hence to set down, at first a little more, and then a good deal more, than their book has actually told them.[9]

More generally, too, although there are many retellings of favourite old stories, the heritage of the past is not simply accepted in a passive way. Henryson's *Testament of Cresseid* is one extreme and fascinating example of the way in which the imagination and creativity of a good writer may be provoked by an earlier work.

The sources of the literary culture of this period are both old and new. There is a clear continuity with the English literary traditions already established in the fourteenth century (most obviously in the case of the 'Chaucerian' poetry). And there are influences from Europe as well. As in previous centuries, Latin is the vehicle for the transmission of works of theology, philosophy, devotion, and for instructional works of various kinds (though one of our prose romances is taken from a Latin source); it may serve also as an intermediary for works in languages not so well known (as in the case of Sebastian Brant's *Narrenschiff*). It seems clear that the English Channel was not so wide—culturally at least—for the actual Henry V as it was for Shakespeare's character of that name. That noble families were related by marriage, and that Englishmen and Frenchmen were brought together by diplomacy or by war, are amply illustrated by the literary history of the period. When Henry VI's bride, Margaret, the daughter of the literary prince René of Anjou, arrived in England, one of the great English 'flowers of chivalry', Sir John Talbot, presented her with a sumptuously produced volume of French romances.[10] The disaster of Agincourt brought Charles d'Orléans, one of the best French poets of the fifteenth century, to England as a prisoner. And at the end of our period we have Lord Berners guarding Calais and occupying himself by translating French chronicles and romances. Close literary contacts with France were of course no new thing. However, in the fifteenth century,

---

[9] C. S. Lewis, *The Discarded Image* (Cambridge, 1964), 211–12.

[10] BL MS Royal E. vi (so that, says Talbot, after she had learnt English she might not forget her mother tongue).

politics and trade brought close relations with the independent and powerful Dukes of Burgundy, whose courts were renowned for their splendid pageantry ('I herd never of non lyek to it save Kyng Artourys cort', says John Paston III in 1468[11]). Artists from Bruges or Ghent illustrated manuscripts and made paintings for rich English clients, and from the Low Countries the art of printing was brought to England by William Caxton. It is possible to exaggerate the importance of Burgundian cultural and literary influence, and indeed it is sometimes difficult to distinguish Burgundian from French, but there are some works—like the translated romance, *The Three Kings' Sons*[12]—which seem certainly to come from a Burgundian milieu. From the close connections with the Low Countries, however, came (through translation) religious and devotional works like *Mary of Nemmegen* or *Everyman*, a version of the beast epic of Reynard the Fox, and merry tales (sometimes of German origin) like those of the Parson of Kalenborowe.

Italy was visited by pilgrims, merchants, and, increasingly in the fifteenth century, by students and scholars. It was already associated with frivolity and luxury: *The Libelle of Englyshe Polycye*, a poem (? *c.*1436–8) which outlines a plan for an English economic policy, grumbles about the deceits practised by Venetian and Florentine traders who bring luxury goods, and spices and medicines which can already be found in England (sugar is the only necessary commodity which they have). Their great galleys are filled

> With swete wynes, all manere of chaffare,
> Apes and japes and marmusettes taylede,
> Nifles, trifles, that litell have availed,
> And thynges wyth whiche they fetely blere oure eye,
> With thynges not endurynge that we bye.[13]

The contrast between the resplendent culture of fifteenth-century Italy and that of the nations to the north, especially the remote England, is a very striking one. Joel Hurstfield puts it vividly:

In reading English history against the background of the Italian Renaissance it is difficult to believe that they belong to the same world. When the battle of Agincourt was fought, Ghiberti was at work on his first doors, Brunelleschi was thirty-eight and Alberti eleven; when Richard III was killed at Bosworth Botticelli, Perugino and Ghirlandaio were at the height of their careers; in 1509 when Henry VII died and when, in England, the last glories of the Perpendicular style were rising at King's College Chapel and Bath Abbey, Michelangelo was painting the Sistine ceiling, Raphael the *Stanze* and Bramante's new St. Peter's had just been started.[14]

---

[11] See No. 2 G.
[12] *The Three Kings' Sons*, ed. F. J. Furnivall, EETS, ES 67 (1895).
[13] Ed. Sir George Warner (Oxford, 1926), 18–19.
[14] J. Hurstfield, in D. Hay (ed.), *The Age of the Renaissance* (London, 1967), 250.

Though it might be said that if we were to move from the visual arts to other aspects of culture, like religious and devotional life (No. 7 J, for instance, shows a sermon of St Bernardino of Siena finding, by an indirect route, a home in English) the contrast would seem less dramatic, nevertheless the differences are certainly great. By the end of the fifteenth century, however, cultural links had been made which were to be immensely important. When Guidobaldo of Urbino was made a member of the Order of the Garter in 1506 by Henry VII, he had Baldassare Castiglione, the author of that influential Renaissance work *Il cortegiano* ('the Book of the Courtier'), take to London the painting of St George by Raphael which still hangs in the National Gallery. More significantly, perhaps, Henry VII himself lies in Westminster Abbey in a chantry which is one of the masterpieces of English Perpendicular art, but the effigy of the King and his wife is done in the newer style by Pietro Torrigiano of Florence. In the case of literature the connections are at first sight less obvious. Chaucer's knowledge of Italian poetry seems to have been unique among the English writers of his time, and there is no one in this period who can emulate him. Petrarch's Latin works are known and some small sections translated, but for translations of his vernacular poetry we have to wait for the generation of Morley (1476–1566),[15] Wyatt (1503–42), and Surrey (1517–47). However, from Italy came the beginnings of the most significant intellectual movement in the literary culture of this period, the growing influence of the new Italian humanism which had been developing from the time of Petrarch. It is marked by an enthusiasm for classical antiquity, its writers and their style, which results in an attempt to recover lost texts, to write Latin in a purer classical style, and to learn Greek. By the end of the fifteenth century this is clearly reflected in English vernacular literature. Although in the literary culture of fourteenth-century England there are a number of strands of what might be called 'medieval humanism', seen for instance in Richard of Bury and his *Philobiblon*, in a number of learned friars interested in classical mythology, or in English poets like Chaucer or Gower who were clearly fascinated by the stories of antiquity, the newer Italian humanism was slow to spread. In 1418 the distinguished scholar Poggio Bracciolini (Caxton's 'Poge the Florentyn') came to England at the invitation of Cardinal Beaufort, but his four-year stay seems to have disappointed him. The 'New Learning' in England begins with the enlightened patronage of Humphrey, Duke of Gloucester (1390–1447), one of the brothers of Henry V. He does not seem to have been a scholar himself, but he collected books (and gave them generously to the University of Oxford), brought Italian scholars to England, and corresponded with humanists, whom he employed to translate Greek classics into Latin. He is certainly the greatest English

---

[15] See Lord Morley's *Tryumphes of Fraunces Petrarcke*, ed. D. D. Carnicelli (Cambridge, Mass., 1971). (The translation was made in the period 1536/7–46.)

literary patron of the period. The contacts he made with humanist scholars were not lost; throughout the fifteenth century a small but growing number of Englishmen went to Italy to study under humanist masters— William Grey (later Bishop of Ely), Robert Flemyng, John Free, and others, mostly ecclesiastics and administrators. The remarkable noble- man, Tiptoft (represented in No. 17 E) is an exceptional layman, who shared the enthusiasms of the others. The Florentine bookseller Vespasiano da Bisticci says that while he stayed in Florence waiting for books to be transcribed, he explored the city and went to hear Giovanni Argiropolo lecture. In Scotland too, although the records are scanty, there seems to have been a gradually growing influence; of the vernacular poets represented here, Gavin Douglas probably received a humanist training in early sixteenth-century Paris. In England, by the time of Henry VII there seems to have been a marked humanist presence at Court, where Carmeliano and Polydore Vergil are to be found, as well as Skelton, who may perhaps be taken as a representative of the first generation of English poets affected in one way or another by the new humanism. As the period continues, the names become more familiar—Grocyn and Linacre (who both visited Italy), the remarkable Colet, who corresponded with Ficino, and who inspired Erasmus with the 'sacred fury' of his disquisition on the story of Cain,[16] and Thomas More, the centre of a newer generation, inspired by Greek and in particular by the wit of Lucian. Yet it must be remembered that this kind of humanism does not happen in isolation, but alongside the older patterns of medieval humanism (and sometimes of medieval obscurantism) together with some curious by-products of the newer, fashionable variety such as Guevara's 'fake' of Marcus Aurelius, Englished by Berners not long before More met his death.

These slow and gradual changes—the appearance of new patterns and modes of thought in the midst of well-established and traditional ones—are profoundly typical of this period of English literature. The conditions in which literature was produced were in many ways similar to those in the days of Chaucer. Patrons (who probably varied in their interest and generosity) could still be found among the nobility, like Duke Humphrey, Talbot, and many others, and among their ladies (who were especially influential in religious literature), among the gentry, and among the merchants. The Church still fulfilled its traditional role as patron, not only in the provision of a market for religious, devotional, or mystical writing, but also by providing a livelihood through ecclesiastical offices of various kinds: in this anthology we find such writer-churchmen or churchmen-writers as Lydgate, Bokenham, Walton, Barclay, Skelton, Henryson (probably), Dunbar, and Bishops Pecock, Alcock, Fisher, and Douglas. Writers in secular life came from the nobility (King James of

---

[16] See J. H. Lupton, *A Life of John Colet D.D.* (London, 1887), 100–1.

Scotland, Charles d'Orléans, John Tiptoft, Lord Berners), the gentry, the ranks of the lawyers (More) or merchants (Caxton), or even the scribes (Hoccleve). The audience envisaged by Caxton later in the century for his Malory, 'alle noble prynces, lordes, and ladyes, gentylmen or gentyl- wymmen', does not sound very different from that of a fourteenth-century courtly romance. But his *Royal Book* is done at the request of a mercer, William Pratt, and the pages of this anthology will suggest from time to time the growing importance of the merchants—although we have to wait for Elizabethans like Deloney to idealize them and their thrifty ways:

> . . . twelve pence a Sunday being spent in good cheare
> To fifty two shillings amounts in the year.[17]

The merchants' wills which we have suggest a rather conservative taste in books; those mentioned are often religious, although one might guess that the solemn moment of making a will might not be the one to record the possession of copies of fabliaux or bawdy tales. A livelier taste is found in the commonplace book of the grocer Richard Hill, which contains that marvellously evocative and mysterious poem the 'Corpus Christi Carol', and has a remarkable range of English poetry, as well as puzzles, riddles, useful information, family records, and a chronicle of public events.

Much more revolutionary changes in the production and dissemination of books, eventually affecting authors and audiences, were to come of course from the invention and rapid spread of printing (Gutenberg's experiments go back to *c.*1436; he was producing printed books at or soon after the middle of the fifteenth century). Yet it is hard to find evidence in contemporary English readers or printers that they sensed that they were seeing a revolution with their own eyes. Later in the period we find remarks like that in the cumbrous style of the preface to the romance *Olyver of Castylle* (1518):

Now it is thus that i[n] this present tyme the scryptures [i.e. writings] by the arte and ingenyous practyke of pryntynge be multeplyed in suche a wy[s]e that dyvers fayre and commodyous ensygnynges and ensamples ben had, of whiche fewe folkes had the bokes and cognyssaunce, and nowe they ben put forth and uttred [put on the market] for so lytell a pryse that it can not be lyghtely lesse . . .[18]

In other words, they are plentiful, available, and cheap. Another point is made rather more succinctly in Horman's Eton *Vulgaria* of 1519: 'pryntynge hath almooste undone scryveners crafte.'[19] In the end it did, but in our period splendid manuscript books were still written. Fifteenth- century readers seem often to have regarded their printed books in much the same way as the manuscript books they resembled so closely,

---

[17] *Jack of Newbury*, ch. 1; *The Novels of Thomas Deloney*, ed. M. E. Lawlis (Bloomington, 1961), 6.

[18] *STC* 18808 (translated by Henry Watson: see No. 7 J, note).

[19] Ed. M. R. James, Roxburghe Club 169 (1926), 125.

sometimes having them illustrated by hand, sometimes having manuscript copies made from them. The early English printers, too, like their audiences apparently, were often conservative in taste, producing books which had begun their life centuries ago. One extreme example of this typically cumulative and traditional aspect of late medieval literature is the *Lucydarye* (printed by Wynkyn de Worde, *c.*1508), a little devotional encyclopaedia, probably taken immediately from a French example of a kind which can be traced back to the *Elucidarium*, a twelfth-century theological work attributed to Honorius of Autun. Other examples can be found in this anthology. Yet at the same time there is a receptiveness to new and even fashionable material. There are, for instance, *two* printed early sixteenth-century English versions of *The Ship of Fools*. It may well be that it took the bitter 'pamphlet war' of the Reformation (particularly in Germany) to bring home the realization of the immense potential for persuasion and for propaganda that the new printing-presses had.

Similar examples of slow but profound changes can be found in almost every area of English culture and society. The English language, for instance, was changing; its status in respect of French and even Latin was rising; one may perhaps detect the development of something like a standard.[20] It would still just be possible to provide for this period a map like that in Sisam's *Fourteenth-Century Verse and Prose* showing the regional and dialectal origins of its texts, but it would be very difficult, and indeed impossible, to place a number of our examples on it. Indeed, apart from some examples from the East Anglian linguistic and cultural area and, notably, in the Scots vernacular of that independent kingdom, literature in regional varieties of English is much less significant than it had been in the fourteenth century. There are some interesting developments in the literary language, too. There is often a rather self-conscious (and not always discriminating) striving for eloquence and 'copiousness' of diction, most obviously expressed in the 'aureate' diction of some poets (the vernacular equivalent of the Latin *florida verborum venustas*). The frequent praises of the eloquence and rhetoric of Chaucer (who is often seen as the father of a poetic tradition) and of the way he has 'illumined' the English language are more than once premonitions of that intense concern with the 'defence' and the 'illustration' of the English vernacular which sixteenth-century writers inherited from fifteen-century Italian discussions of the *questione della lingua*.

Certainly, by 1520 the world would have looked very different to educated eyes from the way it had done in 1400. But even in the case of quite spectacular shifts of knowledge or of feeling, we still have to make allowance for the slow dissemination of knowledge and for the slow movement of cultural change. Like the revolution of the printing-press,

---

[20] See below, pp. 493–508.

the discovery of new lands (and of gold, spices, and souls ripe for salvation) took some time to change old ways of thought. An intellectual like Thomas More makes some use of it, and the new breed of explorers—Vasco da Gama, Columbus, Magellan, and others—attract men of genuine curiosity, like the Italian Pigafetta, who sailed with Magellan in 1519 ('having learnt both by reading of divers books and from the report of many clerks and learned men who discussed the great and terrible things of the Ocean sea . . . I determined . . . to experience and go to see some of the said things').[21] Yet it is possible to find books on geography in the sixteenth century, like the English *Mappa Mundi* printed by Wyer *c.*1550,[22] which make no mention of the new continent of America. Our English travellers in No. 1 go on more traditional routes; one of them, William Wey, sums up the more practical problems of English pilgrims to Compostela in a proverb:

> Be the chorel [churl] nevyr so hard,
> He shall qwake by the berde ar [before] he passe Lyzarde.[23]

But underneath the traditional surface of life, old patterns of thought were being questioned. The results of Luther's dramatic gesture in fixing his 95 theses to the door of the Schlosskirche at Wittenberg in 1517, although they involved a number of authors in this anthology, and indirectly contribute to the deaths of two of them, take us beyond our chronological limits. But throughout the period we find hints of doubts, controversies, and conflicts which sometimes come to the the surface. Traditional Catholic doctrine is still central, and can still, as we see in *Everyman*, produce fine literature, but there is often a sense of unease. There is much satire on ecclesiastical corruption and malpractice; much of the criticism is no doubt exaggerated, but there are still plenty of examples especially from the end of the period where the severity seems to reflect a genuine anxiety—the remarks on bad priests (whose children 'sit by other men's fires') in *Everyman*, for instance, or in Skelton's 'report' in *Collyn Clout* (319–20) of what he hears people say about the princes of the church:

> Theyr moyles [mules] golde dothe eate,
> Theyr neyghbours dye for meate.

Between two extremes—a theology in which the synthesis of faith and reason striven for by the earlier schoolmen is being challenged or abandoned, and a vast, almost hidden, substratum of popular beliefs where magic and religion are totally intermingled—there is a piety of a simple kind, often far removed from intellect, which finds expression in

[21] Antonio Pigafetta, *Magellan's Voyage: A Narrative Account of the First Navigation*, trans. and ed. R. A. Skelton (New Haven, 1969; London 1975) 27.

[22] *STC* 17297.

[23] *Itineraries*, ed. G. Williams, Roxburghe Club, 75 (1857), 155. See No. 1 O.

pilgrimages, in affective devotion, and in a feeling for the 'homeliness' of Christ or the saints. When this fervent piety takes the form of ecstatic practices or such 'enthusiastic' reactions as the 'cryings' of Margery Kempe, one sometimes cannot but feel that in the spiritual life of the community there are powerful emotional forces at work which are barely kept in control by the official organizations and by the traditional vehicles of devotion. Again and again, we are confronted by evidence that this is a period 'not of stagnation but of ferment', of profound change, of apparently contradictory impulses, and sometimes of an acute tension beneath a harmonious surface. For writers living in these times, it was a difficult and a challenging task to come to terms with the demands of the past and of the present.

1

THE MUTABILITY OF WORLDLY
CHANGES

AND MANY MORE DIVERSITIES OF
MANY WONDERFUL THINGS

THIS introductory miscellany drawn from chronicles and other sources does not
pretend to paint a grand historical background, but simply offers a series of
contemporary glimpses of life. The phrase 'the mutability of worldly changes' from
a fifteenth-century poem on those who have suddenly fallen from high estate into
misery sums up a common feeling that the world was in a state of constant flux.
This period, which ends with a Tudor very firmly on the throne, begins with a
spectacular example of the fall of a prince: Richard II, according to one chronicle,
'cursid . . . the untrouthe of Englond, and saide, "Allas! what trust is in this false
worlde?"' There is much talk of war and the rumour of war. The note of English
triumph which rings through the alliterative phrases of a chronicler's verses on the
great victory of Henry V sounds again in another alliterative poem on the defeat of
the Scots at Flodden. Yet the period between these two events saw the loss of
almost all of the English possessions in France, much bitter internal strife
(exemplified here by the invective against Suffolk) which culminated in the Wars of
the Roses, and much social unrest. It is against this background that we have to see
the continuing splendour of royal pageantry. That a number of our scenes take
place in London is a testimony both to that newly popular literary kind, the town
chronicle, and also to the growing importance of the metropolis itself. One of our
pieces shows the tip of the city's criminal underworld (and a story told by Capgrave
in another chronicle has an almost Dickensian flavour: three beggars stole three
children at Lynn and mutilated them so that 'men schuld of pyté gyve hem good';
much later, when the father of one happened to come to London, he was
recognized by his child, who 'cryed loude, "This is my fadir"'). No English poet
could do for London what Villon did for fifteenth-century Paris, but *London
Lyckpeny* at least gives us some sense of the throbbing life of its streets. The
numerous 'heretics' who were put to death in the capital represented for the
chroniclers another kind of disorder. The necessity for continual persecution is,
however, evidence for the continuing presence of religious dissent, and it may be,
as has been suggested, that this is not simply a negative protest, but represents the
groundswell of a popular movement for reformation which preceded the 'State
Reformation' of the 1530s. From this world of dissent we are fortunate to have the
story of Thorpe's interrogation by Arundel, which may well be authentic, and is
certainly told with fine dramatic immediacy. It is impossible not to feel sympathy for
the beleaguered Lollard, but even in his partial account there is a moment when

(for those of a less Puritan turn of mind, at least) the Archbishop scores a point in his defence of the right of pilgrims to solace their 'travail and weariness' with music as they go along.

Our sources, however, do not only record scenes of violence and discord; they contain—in Mandeville's words—'many more diversities of many wonderful things'. They have his curiosity about occurrences 'against kind' and about portents and prophecies. Lands beyond the confines of Western Europe were, as always, particularly associated with 'wonderful things'. Our extracts include the latest news from Rhodes—an impressively realistic description of an actual battle, and a reflection of concern over the contemporary 'Eastern Question', the rapid advance of the Turks. Others illustrate the various delights and dangers of travelling to distant lands. Our English travellers who put pen to paper are still pilgrims. They cannot match the vividness of the loquacious German, Felix Fabri (who warns pilgrims not to chip off fragments from the holy sites and not to carve their names or their coats of arms on the walls), but even the most humdrum will sometimes produce a spark of interest (thus, Robert Langton [1523] in the midst of notes on relics in Italy records under Padua: 'also .ix. myle fro thens lyeth Petrarcha Florentyne, no saynt, but a grete clerke'), and there are some (represented here) who can produce more than that. Towards the end of the period Englishmen began to read of journeys of a more secular and more spectacular kind. References in the chronicles to the voyages of the Cabots are joined by allusions in other literary works to the 'new found isle' (the fullest being in the early sixteenth-century *A New Interlude of the IIII Elementes* by Rastell, a member of the More circle, who tried to visit America), and the discovery of that continent bore its first imaginative fruit in More's *Utopia* of 1516. But to the majority of readers this knowledge did not come as a sudden revelation: our final extract illustrates the rather muddled and undramatic way in which it began to seep through and, eventually, to change men's view of the inhabited world.

A

The Battle of Agincourt (1415)

And in Azyngcorte felde owre kynge faught with the Frensshmen the Fryday tofore the day of Symond and Jude; and ther all the ryall power of Frensshemen come ayenst owre kyng and his litill meyné, save the Frenssh kynge and the Dolfyn, and the duke of Borgoyn, and the duke of Barre;
5 elles all the lordys of Fraunce lay tofore the kynge in his hy way as he schuld passe towarde Calys, embateylyd in .iii. batayles—as the Frensshemen sayde hemsilfe, the nowmbre of .lx m. men of armes, and tho were the fairest men of armys that ever any man saw in any place. And owre kyng with his litell mayné sey well he must nedys fyghte, or he myght not
10 come to Caleys by the hy way. And than he sayde to his lordys and to his mayné: 'Syres and felowes, the yondere mayné thenk to lette us of owre way: and thei wil nat come to us lete every man preve hymsilfe a good man

2

this day, and avant baner in the beste tym of the yere; for as I am trew
kynge and knyht, for me this day schall never Inglonde rawnsome pay;
erste many a wyght man schall leve is weddes, for here erste to deth I wil   15
be dyght, and therfore lordynges, for the love of swete Jesu, helpe
mayntene Inglondes ryght this day. Allso, archers, to yow I pray, no fote
that ye fle away, erste be we alle beten in this felde. And thenke ye be
Englysshemen that never wolde flee at no batelle, for ayenste one of us
thowthe ther be tene, thenke Criste wil help us in owre ryght. Bot I wolde   20
no blood were spilte—Cryste helpe me so now in this case—but tho that
ben cause of this trespase; when thou sittest in jugment, ther holde me
excused tofore thi face, as thou art God omnipotent. But passe we all now
in fere, duke, erle and bachelere! Of all owre synnys he make us seker,
jentil Jesu, borne of Marye; and as for us thou deydyst on Good Fryday, as   25
thi will was, so brynge us to thi blisse an hy, and graunte us ther to have a
place.' 'Do and bete on faste!' owre kynge tho bad wythe full glad chere;
and so thei dyd at that word, lord, knyght, and archere. Ther men myght
see a semblé sade, that turnyd many on to tene and tray; for many a lorde
ther ryght low lay, that commen was of blod full gent, by evensong tym,   30
sothely to say; ther halpe us God omnipotent.

Stedes ther stumbelyd in that stownde,
   That stood stere stuffed under stele;
With gronyng grete thei felle to grownde,
   Her sydes federid whan thei gone fele.   35
   Owre lorde the kynge he foght ryght wele.
Scharpliche on hem his spere he spent,
   Many on seke he made that sele,
Thorow myght of God omnipotent.

The Duke of Glowcestre also that tyde   40
   Manfully with his mayné
Wondes he wroght ther wondere wyde;
   The Duke of Yorke also, perdé,
   Fro his kyng no fote wold he flee,
Til his basonet to his brayn was bent;   45
   Now on his sowle he have peté,
Mersifull God omnipotent.

Hontyngdon and Oxforde bothe,
   Were wonder fers all in that fyght;
That erste was glade thei made ful wrothe;   50
   Thorow hem many on to deth were dight.

3

The erles fowghten with mayn and myght,
Rich hauberke thei rofe and rente;
Owre kyng to helpe thei were full lyght;
55 Now blesse hem, God omnipotent!

The Erle of Suthfolk gan hem assaylle,
And Syr Richarde Kyghlé in that stede,
Here lyves thei losten in that bataile,
With dyntes sore ther were thei dede.
60 Yif eny man byde eny good bede
Unto God with good entent.
To tho two sowles it mote be mede,
Gracius God omnipotent.

Syr William Bowsere, as foule in frith,
65 Preste he ther was upon his pray,
Erpyngham he come hym with;
Her manhode holp us well that day.
Off Frenssh folk in that afray
Thre dukes were dede with doleful dent,
70 And fyve erles—this is no nay;
Ther holpe us God omnipotent. . . .

B

A Royal Entry (1432)

And in this same yere the xxith day of Februaré, Kyng Henry the .vi. come
from his maner of Eltham toward the cité of London; and the maire and
aldermen, with the comynalté of London, roode ayenst the kyng on
horsbak in the best aray that they myght in the reverence of the kyng and in
5 worship and gladnesse of the worthy name of the cité of London,
thurghout the world in worthynesse commended and praysed. For the
maire hymself was clothed in rede crymsyn velwett, and a grete velwet
hatte furred royally, and a girdell of gold aboute his mydell, and a bawdrik
of gold aboute his neck, trillyng doun behynde hym; and his .iii. hensmen
10 on .iii. grete coursoures foloyng hym, in oon sute of a good aray, in rede,
all spangled in silver; and then all the aldermen in gownes of scarlet, with
sangwyn cappes. And all the cominalté of the cité were clothed in white;
bot every crafte with dyvers devices enbrowded upon the white gownes
that every craft myght be knowen oon from another, with scarlet hodes or
15 cappes. And all they hoved still on horsbak on the Blakheth in Kent, on
both sides, as a strete, unto the kynges comyng. And when they sawe the

4

kyng come, the maire with the aldermen rode to the kyng, and welcomed
hym with all reverence, honour, and obeysaunce. And the kyng thanked
hem, and he come ridyng thurgh all the peple; and they obeyed, and seid,
'Welcom oure liege and kyng! Welcom, and thanked be God in all his 20
giftes, that we se you in good quart!' And so the kyng rode streight the high
wey to London. And when the kyng had riden thurgh Suthwerk, and come
to the stulpes without London Brigge, there stode a gyaunt in a toure, with
his swerd drawe in his hande, shewed with countenaunce doth menace all
foreyn enemys to the death without mercy, that seith or doth ayenst the 25
kynges right: 'And y, the kynges champyon, in full myght and power!' And
then the kyng come to London Brigge, and there was made a roiall hevenly
toure; and therein was shewed .iii. ladyes as emperice, worthely
apparaylled in theire aray, which were called by name Nature, Grace, and
Fortune. And theire girdelles were blewe, shynyng like to sapheres, which 30
shewed to the kyng in his comyng all goodnesse and gladnesse in vertuous
lyvyng; and with other .vii. virgynes celestial, in tresses of gold, and with
coronalles on their hedes, all clothed in white, as virgines, with sonnys of
golde on theire garmentes, shewyng as hevenly creatures, mekely salewyng
the kyng, and gaf hym .vii. giftes that were toknes of oure Lord God of 35
heven—that were white dowves, betokenyng the giftes of the Holy Gost, a
spirite of intelligence, a spirite of sapience, and a spirite of strenght and of
connyng, and of consayle, pité, drede, and lowlynesse. And on the lifte
side of these .iii. emperesses were .vii. other virgyns, clothed all in white,
with sterres of gold on theire garmentes, with coronalles on theire hedes, 40
which presented the kyng with royall giftes: first, they endewed the kyng
with the crowne of glorye, and with the septre of mekenesse and of pité; a
swerd of myght and victorie, a mantell of prudence, a shelde of feith, a
helme of helth, a girdell of love and of perfite peas. And all these ladyes
and virgines welcomed the kyng with all honoure and reverence. And then 45
the kyng procedyng forth to the condyte in Cornhill; and there was made
in serkelwyse a trone, and in the myddes sittyng a yonge child arayed as a
kyng, whom to governe were .iii. ladyes, Mercy, Trouthe and the Lady
Clennesse; and .ii. juges of lawe, and .viii. sergeauntes, to shewe the
kyngdom lawe and right. And then the kyng rode forth, and entred into 50
Chepe, and come to the grete conduit, that ranne plenté of good wyne,
bothe white and rede, to all peple that wold drynk. And above, over the
condite, was a royall toure likned to Paradyse, with many dyvers trees
beryng everyche dyvers frutes. And in this same gardeyn was dyvers wells
of dyvers wynes, with bokettes; and .iii. glorious virgines wounde up the 55
wyne, proferyng the kyng there full habundaunce, fulsomnesse, and high
plenté. And the names of these virgines been Mercy, Grace, and Pité. And
in the ende of this gardeyn there appered to the kyng .ii. olde men—that
oon Enok, and that other Ely—that shewed the kyng chere and grete
preysing, ministryng his governance. And the kyng passed forth, and come 60

5

to the crosse in Chepe, and there was made a castell roiall, and on the est
syde stode .ii. grene trees, which bare the armes of England and of
Fraunce, the libardes and the floure-de-lice, which been the kinges right
and trewe armes be lyne. And upon this castell, toward Seint Paules, there
65 was the tree of Jesse, with all the braunches, shewyng the kynrede of oure
Lorde Jesu and of our lady, Seint Marye, to the comfort of the kyng, and
for the grete solempnité of the worthy cité of London. . . .

C

The Arrest of the Duke of Suffolk (1450)

Now is the fox drevin to hole! hoo to hym, hoo, hoo!
For and he crepe out, he will yow alle undo.
Now ye han found parfite, loke well your game;
For and ye ren countre, then be ye to blame.
5   Sum of yow holdith with the fox, and rennyth hare;
But he that tied Talbot oure dog, evyll mot he fare!
For now we mys the black dog with the wide mouth,
For he wold have ronnen well at the fox of the south.
And all gooth bacward, and don is in the myre,
10   As they han deserved so pay they ther hire.
Now is tyme of lent; the fox is in the towre;
Therfore send hym Salesbury to be his confessoure.
Many mo ther ben, and we kowd hem knowe,
But won most begyn the daunce, and all com a-rowe.
15   Loke that your hunte blowe well thy chase;
But he do well is part, I beshrew is face!
This fox at Bury slowe oure grete gandere;
Therfore at Tyborn mony mon on hym wondere.
Jack Napys, with his clogge,
20   Hath tied Talbot, oure gentill dogge.
Wherfore Beaumownt, that gentill rache,
Hath brought Jack Napis in an evill cache.
Beware, al men, of that blame,
And namly ye of grete fame,
25   Spirituall and temperall, beware of this,
Or els hit will not be well, iwis.
God save the kyng; and God forbede
That he suche apes any mo fede!
And of the perille that may befall
30   Beware, dukes, erles, and barons all!

6

D

Jack Cade (1450)

And this same yeer, in the moneth of May, aroos thay of Kent and made thaym a capteyne, a ribaude, an Yrissheman, callid Johan Cade, the whiche atte begynning took on him the name of a gentilmanne, and callid himself Mortymer forto have the more favour of the peple; and he callid himself also John Amende-alle; for forasmuche as thanne and longe 5 before the reme of England hadde be rewlid be untrew counselle, wherfore the comune profit was sore hurt and decresid, so that alle the comune peple, what for taxes and tallages and other oppressions myght not live be thair handwork and husbondrie, wherfore thay grucchid sore ayens thaym that hadde the governaunce of the land.   ·   10

Thanne cam the said capteyn and the Kentisshmen unto the Blakeheth, and there kepte the feld a moneth and more, pilyng alle the cuntré aboute; to whom the cité of Londoun, at that tyme, was fulle favourable and frendly—but it last not longe aftir. In the mene tyme the king sente notable menne to the said capteyn and his feleshippe to knowe thair 15 purpose and the cause of thair insurreccioun. The capteyn was a sotill man, and saide that he and his feleship were assemblid and gadrid there forto redresse and refourme the wrongis that were don in the reme and to withstonde the malice of thayme that were destroiers of the comune profit, and forto correcte and amende the defautis of thaym that were the kyngis 20 chief counselours; and shewde unto thaym the articles of his peticions concernyng and touchyng the myschiefs and mysgovernaunces of the reme, wherynne was nothyng conteyned but that that was rightful and resonable, wherof a copie was sent to the parlement holden that tyme at Westmynstre; wherfore the said capteyne desirid that suche grevaunces 25 sholde be amendid and refourmed be the parlement, and to have answer therof agayne, but he hadde none. Sone aftir the kyng remeved fro Westmynstre unto Grenewich; and while he was ther he wolde have sent certayn lordis with a power forto have distressid the Kentisshmenne, but thair men that sholde have gon with thaym ansuerde to thair lordis and 30 saide that thay wolde not fighte ayens thaym that labourid forto amende and refourme the comune profit; and whanne the lordis herde this, thay lefte thair purpos. Thanne cride the Kentisshmenne and othir ayens the lord Say, the kyngis chamberlayne, that was on of the kyngis fals counselours and holden suspect of tresoun, and the king dredyng the 35 malice of the peple committid him to the tour of Londoun.

Thanne wente the kyng ayen to Londoun, and withynne .ii. daies aftir he wente ayens the Kentisshmenne with .xv m. men wel araid unto the Blakeheth, but the said Kentisshmen heryng how the king wolde come;

40 and fledde the nyght befor his comyng into the wode cuntré to Sevenok.
The kyng thanne retourned to Londoun, and sente out a squier callid
William Stafford, and ser Humfrey Stafford, knyght, his cosyne, forto
aspie where the Kentisshmen were; and whanne they knew that thay were
at Sevenok, thay rood thider hastily with a few menne, wenyng to have
45 gotenne a singular worshippe and laude; but thay were withyn the daunger
of thaym er thay wiste it, and were there bothe yslayne, with the more part
of thair men that abood with thaym. Whanne this was don the king
dissolved the parlement, and remeved unto Kyllyngworth. And whanne
the Kentishmen herde that the kyng was gon fro Londoun, thay cam ayen
50 into Suthwerk, and thair capteyn was loggid atte Hert. And the Thursday
aftir be favour of some of the men of Londoun he came into the cité, but
sone aftir thay repentid, for thay were dividid among thaymself; but the
keies of the cité were delyverid unto the said capteyn, and he kepte thaym
.ii. daies and .ii. nyghtes. And whanne he hadde entrid the cité, anon he
55 and his men fille to roborie, and robbid certayn worthi men of the cité, and
put some of thaym into prison til thay hadde paid notable summes of
money to save thair livis. And the said capteyn rood aboute the cité beryng
a nakid swerd in his hand, armed in a peire of brigaundynes, werying a
peire of gilt sporis, and a gilt salat, and a gowne of blew velvet, as he hadde
60 be a lord or a knyght—and yit was he but a knave—and hadde his swerd
born befor him.
    And the Satirday next the said capteyn commaundid that the lord Say
sholde be brought out of the tour unto Guyldehalle in Londoun, where
that certayn justices sat that tyme; and whanne he was ycome, the
65 Kentisshmen wolde not suffre him forto abide the lawe, but ladde him
unto the Standard in Chepe, and there his hed was smyte of, and his body
was drawe naked at a hors taille upon the pament so that the flesshe clivid
to the stones fro Chepe into Suthwerk, the said capteynes ynne. Also a
squier callid Crowmer that was the shireve of Kent, that hadde weddid the
70 said lord Saies doughtir, be commaundement of the capteyne was
broughte out of Flete, that was committid thider for certayn extorsiones
that he hadde do in his office, and lad to Mile Ende, withoute Londoun,
and there withoute eny othir jugement his hed was smyte of, and the lord
Saies hed and his also were bore upon .ii. long shaftis unto Londoun
75 Brigge, and there set uppe, and the lord Saies body was quartrid.
    On the Sunday next, men of London seyng the tiranny and robory of the
said cursid capteyne and of his men, and whanne it was nyghte thay laide
hand on thayme that were disparblid aboute in the cité, and bet thaym and
droof thaym out of the cité, and shit the yatis. And whanne the capteyn that
80 was in his yn in Suthwerk saw this, anon he with his men made assaut to
Londoun Brigge, and wolde have come yn, and spoylid the cité; and the
lord Scales with his menne and menne of the cité faughte with thayme fro
.ix. of the clocke in the evyn unto .x. of the clocke in the morow, and meny

8

men were slayn on bothe parties, and sore wounded; and there were slayne
Mathew Goghe a squyer of Walis and Johan Sutton an alderman of 85
Londoun. And this skyrmysh endurid til the brigge of tre was set on fire,
betuene thaym of Kent and of Londoun; and thanne thay of Kent
withdrow thaym litille and litille. And thair capteyn put alle his pilage and
the godis that he hadde robbid into a barge, and sente it to Rouchestre be
watir, and he wente be lande and wolde have go into the castel of 90
Queneburghe with a fewe men that were left with himme, but he was let of
his purpos. And anon he fledde into the wode cuntré beside Lewes, and
the shireve of Kent him pursude, and there he was wounded unto the
dethe, and take and caried in a carte toward Londoun, and be the wey he
deide. And thanne his hed was smyte of and set on Londoun brigge, and 95
his body quartrid and sent to dyvers tounes of Englond; whoos tirannye
endurid fro Trinité Sunday unto Saint Thomas eve of Caunterbury: and
thus endid this capteyn of myschief.

E

SCOTISH FEILDE

The Battle of Flodden (1513)

Then the sun full soone shott under the clouds,
And it darkened full dimlie and drew towards night.
Every ryncke to his rest full radlye him dressed;
Beeten fires full fast, and feteled them to sowpe
Besides Barwicke on a banke, within a broad woode. 5
Then dauned the day, soe deere God ordayned;
Clowdes cast up full cleerlye, like castles full hie.
Then Phebus full faire flourished out his beames
With leames full light all the land over.
All was damped with dew the daysies about; 10
Flowers flourished in the feild, faire to behold;
Birrds bradden to the boughes, and boldlye thé songen—
It was solace to heare for any seege living!
Then full boldlye on the broad hills we busked our standards,
And on a soughe us beside there seene we our enemies 15
Were moving over the mountaines—to macch us they thoughten—
As boldly as any bearnes that borne was of mothers.
And we egerlie with ire attilld them to meete.
Then trunmpetts full truly they tryden together,
Many shames in that shawe with theire shrill pipes— 20
Heavenly was theire melody, their mirth to heare,

9

How thé songen with a showte all the shawes over!
There was gurding forth of gunns with many great stones,
Archers uttered out their arrowes, and egerlie they shotten;
25 They proched us with speares, and put many over
That the blood out brast at there broken harnes.
There was swinging out of swords, and swapping of headds;
We blanked them with bills through all their bright armor,
That all the dale dunned of theire derfe strokes . . . .

*   *   *   *   *

30 . . . Then the Scottish king carped these words,
'I will fight with yonder frekes that are soe feirce holden—
And I beate those bearnes the battle is ours!'
Then thé moved towards the mountaines, and manly came
    downwards.
Wee mett him in the midway, and mached him full even—
35 Then there was dealing of dints, that all the dales rangen;
Many helmes with heads were hewd all to peeces!
This layke lasted on the land the length of .iiii. houres.
Yorkshire like yearne men eagerlye they foughten;
Soe did Darbyshire that day—deered many Scotts;
40 Lancashire like lyons laid them about.
All had beene lost, by Our Lord, had not those leeds beene!
But the care of the Scotts increased full sore,
For their king was downe knocked, and killed in there sight,
Under the banner of a bishoppe, that was the bold Standlye.
45 Then they fettled them to flye as fast as they might,
But it serveth not, for sooth, whosoe truth telleth—
Our Englishmen full egerlye after them followed,
And killed them like caitives, in clowes all about.
There were killed of the Scotts, that told were by tale,
50 That were found in the feild .xv. thousand.
Loe, what it is to be false, and the feende serve!
They have broken a book-othe to our blithe kinge,
And the truce that was taken the space of .ii. yeeres.
All the Scotts that were scaped were scattered all assunder,
55 They removed over the more upon the other morning,
And their stode like stakes, and stirr durst no further,
For all the lords of their lande were left them behind.
Besids Brinston in a brynke breathelesse thé lyen,
Gaping against the moone—theire ghostes were away!

F

Heresy and Sacrilege (1466–7)

Alle-soo thys same yere there was an herretyke ibrende at the Towre hyll for he dyspysyd the sacrament of the auter; hys name was William Balowe, and he dwellyd at Walden. And he and hys wyffe were abjuryd longe tyme before. And my lorde of London kepte hym in preson longe tyme, and he wolde not make noo confessyon unto noo pryste, but oonly unto God, and 5 sayde that no pryste had noo more pouer to hyre confessyon thenn Jacke Hare. And he had no consyence to ete flesche aftyr Estyr as welle as thoo that were bothe schryffe and houselyd. At the tyme of hys brennynge a docter, Mayster Hewe Damelet, person of Syn Petrys in the Cornehylle, laboryd him to beleve in the hooly sacrament of the auter. And thys was 10 the herytyke ys sayyng, 'Bawe! bawe! bawe! What menythe thys pryste? Thys I wotte welle, that on Goode Fryday ye make many goddys to be putte in the sepukyr, but at Ester day they can not aryse themselfe, but that ye moste lyfte them uppe and bere them forthe, or ellys they wylle ly stylle yn hyr gravys.' Thys was that tyme of hys departyng from that 15 worschipfulle docter.

Alle-soo that same yere there were many chyrchys robbyd in the cytté of London only of the boxys with the sacrament. And men had moche wondyr of thys, and sad men demyd that there had ben sum felyschippe of heretykys assocyat togederys. But hyt was knowe aftyr that it was done of 20 very nede that they robbyd, wenyng unto the thevys that the boxys hadde ben sylvyr ovyrgylt, but was but copyr. And by a copyrsmythe hit was aspyde of hyr longe contynuans in hyr robbory. At a tyme, alle the hole feleschippe of thevys sat at sopyr togedyr, and had before hem fulle goode metys. But that copyrsmythe sayde, 'I wolde have a more deynty mosselle 25 of mete, for I am wery of capon, conynge, and chekyns, and suche smalle metes. And I mervyl I have ete .ix. goddys at my sopyr that were in the boxys.' And that schamyd sum of them in hyr hertys. Ande a smythe of lokyers crafte, that made hyr instrumentes to opyn lockys, was ther that tyme, for hit was sayde at the sopyr in hys howse. And in the mornynge he 30 went to chyrche to hyre a masse, and prayde God of marcy; but whenn the pryste was at the levacyon of the masse he myght not see that blessyd sacrament of the auter. Thenn he was sory, and abode tylle anothyr pryste wente to masse and helpyd the same pryste to masse, and say howe the oste lay apon the auter and alle the tokyns and sygnys that the pryste made; 35 but whenn the pryste hylde uppe that hooly sacrament at the tyme of levacyon he myght se nothynge of that blessyd body of Cryste at noo tyme of the masse, not so moche at *Agnus Dei*; and thenn he demyd that hit had ben for febyllenys of hys brayne. And he went unto the alehowse and

40 dranke a ob. of goode alle, and went to chyrche agayne, and he helpyd .iii.
moo prystys to masse, and in no maner a wyse he ne myght se that blessyd
sacrament; but then bothe he and hys feleschyppe lackyd grace. And in
schorte tyme aftyr, .iiii. of hem were take, and the same lokyer was one of
the .iiii., and they were put in Newgate. And by processe they were
45 dampnyd for that trespas and othyr to be hangyd and to be drawe fro
Newgate to Tyborne, and soo they were. And the same daye that they
shulde dy they were confessyd. And thes .iiii. docters were hyr
confessourys: Mayster Thomas Eberalle, Mayster Hewe Damylett,
Mayster Wylliam Ivé, and Mayster Wylliam Wryxham. Thenn Mayster
50 Thomas Eberalle wente to masse, and that lokyer aftyr hys confessyon
myght see that blessyd sacrament well inowe, and thenne rejoysyd and was
gladde, and made an opyn confessyon byfore the .iiii. sayde docters of
devynyté. And I truste that hyr soulys ben savyd.

G

William Thorpe, accused of preaching Lollard doctrines, is interrogated by Archbishop Arundel (1407)

. . . And thanne, as if he hadde ben wrooth, the archebischop seide to oon
of his clerkis, 'Take hidir anoon the certificat that cam to me from
Schrouesbirie undir the bailyes seelis, witnessynge the errours and the
eresies whiche this losel hath venymously sowen there!' And anoon the
5 clerke took out and leide forth upon a cupbord dyverse rollis and other
writingis, among which was a litil rolle, which the clerk toke to the
erchebischop. And anoon the archebischop radde this rolle conteynynge
this sentence: 'the thridde Sonedai after Ester in the yeer of Oure Lord a
thousand foure hundrid and sevene, William Thorp cam into the toun of
10 Schrouesbirie, and thorugh leve grauntid to him forto preche, he seide
openli in Seynt Chaddis chirche in his sermoun: that the sacrament of the
auter aftir the consecracioun was material breed; and that ymagis schulden
in noo wyse be worschippid; and that men schulden not goon in
pilgrimage; and that preestis have now no titil to tithis; and that it is not
15 leeful to swere in ony maner.' And whanne the Archebischop hadde rad
this rolle, he rollid it up ayen. And the Archebischop seide to me, 'Is this
holsum loore to teche among the peple?' And I seide to him, 'Ser, I am
bothe aschamed on her bihalve, and right sorouful for hem that have
certified to you these thingis thus untruli, for I prechide never neithir
20 taughte thus, privyli ne apeertly.' And the Archebischop seide to me, 'I
wole yeve credence to these worschipful men which have writun to me and
witnessen undir her seelis that thou prechidest thus openli these forseide

errours and heresies there among hem, though thou denye now this. Gessist thou that I wol yeve credence to thee, thou losel that hast so troublid the worschipful comounté of Schrouesbirie, that the bailies and 25 the comouns of that toun have writun to me, praynge me that am Archebischop of Cauntirbirie, Primate of al Yngelonde and chaunceler, that I wolde vouchesaaf to graunte to hem that if thou schalt be deed, as thou art worthi, and suffre openli thi jewise for thin eresies, that thou maist have thi jewise openli there among hem, so that alle thei whom thou and 30 other suche losels have there pervertid moun thorugh drede of thi deeth be reconseilid ayen to the unyté of holi chirche, and also thei that stoonden in trewe feith of holi chirche moun thorugh thi deeth be the moore stablischid therinne.' And as if this askinge hadde plesid the Archebischop, he seide thanne there, 'Bi my thrifte! This hertli preier and fervent request 35 schal be thought on.' But certis neither this praier of men of Schrouesbiri, neithir the manassynge of the Archebischop ferede me onything, but in the rehersynge of this malice and in the heringe of it myn herte was greetly rejoysid and yit is. . . .

Holy Church and the Sacrament of the Altar

And the Archebischop axid me what I clepid holi chirche. And I seide, 40 'Ser, I toolde to you bifore what was holi chirche, but sith ye axen me yit this demaunde, I clepe Crist and his seintis holi chirche.' And the Archebischop seide to me, 'I wot wel that Crist and his seyntis ben holi chirche in hevene. But what is holi chirche here in erthe?' And I seide, 'Ser, though holi chirche be evere oon in charité, yit it hath two parties. 45 The firste and the principal hath overcomen parfitli al the wickidnes of this lyf, and regneth joifulli in hevene with Crist. And the tother part is here yit in erthe, bisili and contynueli fightinge dai and night ayens temptaciouns of the fend, forsakinge and hatinge the prosperité of this world, dispisinge and withstondinge her fleischli lustis, whiche oonli ben the pilgrymes of 50 Crist, wandrynge towardis hevene bi stable feith, bi stidefast hope, and by parfit charité. For these hevenli pilgrimes moun not neither thei wolen be lettid of her purpos bi the reyne of ony doctrine discordinge from holi writt neither bi the floodis of ony temperal goodis and tribulaciouns neither bi wyndis of ony pride or boost or manasynge of ony creature, for alle thei 55 ben sadli groundid upon the corner-stoon Crist, heerynge his word and lovynge it, bisiinge hem feithfulli and continuelli in alle her wittis to do theraftir.' And the Archebischop seide to hise clerkis, 'Se ye not how his herte is endurid and how it is traveilid with the devel, occupiynge him thus bisili and redili to alegge suche sentencis to maynteyne with hise 60 errours and eresies? Certis, thus he wole occupie us here al dai if we wolen suffre him!'

And oon of the Archebischopis clerkis seide thanne to him, 'Ser, he
seide right now that this certificacioun that cam to you from Schrouesbirie
65 is untruly forgid ayens him. Therfore, ser, appose ye him now here in alle
the poyntis which ben certified ayens him, and so we schulen heere of his
owne mouth his answeringis and wittnesse hem.' And the Archebischop
took thanne the certificacioun in his hond and he lokide therupon awhile,
and so thanne he seide to me, 'Lo, here it is certified and witnessid ayens
70 thee bi worthi men and feithful of Schrouesbirie that thou prechedist there
opinli in Seint Chaddis chirche that the sacrament of the auter was
material breed after the consecracioun. What seist thou? Was this truli
prechid?' And I seide, 'Ser, I telle you truli that I touchide nothing there of
the sacrament of the auter nobut in this wise, as I wol, with Goddis grace
75 schewe here to you. As I stood there in the pulpitte, bisiinge me to teche the
heestis of God, oon knyllide a sacringe-belle, and herfor myche peple
turned awei fersli, and with greet noyse runnen frowardis me. And I,
seynge this, seide to them thus, "Goode men, you were better to stoonden
here stille and to heere Goddis word, for certis the vertu and the mede of
80 the moost holi sacrament of the auter stondith myche moore in the bileve
thereof that ye owen to have in youre soulis than it doith in the outward
sight therof. And therfore you were better to stonde stille quyetefulli and
to heeren Goddis worde, sith thorugh heeringe therof men comen to veri
bileve." And otherwise, ser, I am certeyne I spak not there of the
85 worschipful sacrament of the auter.' And the Archebischop seide to me, 'I
trowe thee not, whatever thou seist, sythe so worschipful men have
witnessid ayens thee. But sith thou denyest that thou seidest not thus
there, what seist thou now? Dwellith ther after the consecracioun of the
oost material breed or nai?' And I seide, 'Ser, I knowe nowhere in holi
90 writt where this terme "material breed" is writun, and therfore, ser,
whanne I speke of this mater I use not to speke of material breed.' And the
Archebischop seide to me, 'How techist thou men to bileve in this
sacrament?' And I seide, 'Ser, as I bileve mysilf so I teche othere men.'
And he seide to me, 'Telle out playnli thy bileve thereof!' And I seide with
95 my forseide protestacioun, 'Ser, I bileve that the night bifore that Crist
Jesu wolde suffre wilfulli passioun for mankynde on the morwe after, hee
took bred in his holi and worschipful hondis, and liftynge up his iyen he
dide thankynges to God his Fadir and blessid breed and brake it, and he
yaf to hise dissciplis, seiinge to hem, "Takith this and etith of this alle.
100 This is my bodi", and that this is, and owith to be to alle mennes bileve, as
Mathew, Mark, Luk and Poul witnessen. Othir bileve, ser, sith I bileve
that this suffisith in this mater, have I noon, neithir wole have, ne teche,
but in this bileve thorugh Goddis grace I purpose to lyve and die,
knowlechinge as I beleve and teche other to beleve, that the worschipful
105 sacrament of the auter is verri Cristis fleisch and his blood in forme of
breed and wyne.' And the Archebischop seide to me, 'It is soth that this

sacrament is Cristis bodi in fourme of breed, but not in substaunce of breed. But thou and thi sect techen it to be in substaunce of breed. Thinke thee this true techinge?'. . .

Pilgrimages

. . . 'I seie now as I seide in Schrouesbirie, though thei that have siche 110 fleischli willis traveilen soore her bodies and spenden myche moneye to sechen and visiten the bones either ymagis—as thei seien thei don—of that seint or of that, siche pilgrymage is neither praisable ne thankful to God neither to ony seint of God; sith in effecte alle siche pilgrymes dispisen God and alle hise seyntis. For the heestis of God thei wolen 115 neither knowen nor kepe, neither thei wolen conforme hem to lyve vertuesly by ensaumple of Crist and of hise seyntis. Wherfor, ser, I have prechid and taughte opinli and privyli, and so I purpose al my lyf-tyme to do, with Goddis helpe, seiinge that siche madde peple wasten blamfulli Goddis goodis in her veyne pilgrymageyng, spendynge these goodis upon 120 vicious hosteleris whiche ben ofte unclene wymmen of her bodies, and at the laste tho goodis of the whiche thei schulden do werkis of mercy aftir Goddis heeste to pore nedi men and wymmen. These pore mennis goodis and her lyflode these renners aboute offren to riche prestis whiche have moche moore lyfelode than thei neden. And thus tho goodis thei wasten 125 wilfulli, and spenden hem unjustli ayens Goddis heeste upon strangeris, with the whiche thei schulden helpe and releeven aftir Goddis wille her pore and nedy neighebores at home. Yhe, and over this foli, oftetymes dyverse men and wymmen of these that rennen thus madly hidir and thidir on pilgrimagynge borowen herto mennys goodis, yhe, and sumtyme thei 130 stelen mennes goodis herto, and thei yelden hem nevere ayen. Also, sire, I knowe wel that whanne dyverse men and wymmen wolen goon thus aftir her owne willis and fyndingis out on pilgrimageyngis thei wolen ordeyne biforehonde to have with hem bothe men and wymmen that kunnen wel synge rowtinge songis. And also summe of these pilgrimes wolen have with 135 hem baggepipis, so that in eche toun that thei comen thorough what with noyse of her syngynge and with the soun of her pipinge and with the gingelynge of her Cantirbirie bellis and with the berkynge out of dogges aftir hem, these maken more noyse than if the king came thereawaye with his clarioneris and manye other mynstrals. And if these men and wymmen 140 ben a monethe oute in her pilgrimage, manye of hem an half yeere aftir schulen be greete jangelers, tale-tellers and lyeris.' And the Archebischop seide to me, 'Lewid losel, thou seest not fer inough in this mateer, for thou considrist not the grete traveile of pilgrymes, and therfore thou blamest that thing that is praisable. I seie to thee that is right wel don that pilgrimes 145 have with hem bothe syngeris and also baggepipes, that whanne oon of

hem that gon barefote and smytith his too ayens a stoon and hurtith him
soore and makith hym blede, it is wel done that he or his felowe take
thanne up a songe either ellis take out of her bosum a baggepipe forto
150 dryve awey with siche myrthe the hurt of his sore. For with siche solace the
traveile and werinesse of pylgrymes is lightli and myrili brought forth.' And
I seide, 'Sere, Seint Poul techith men to wepe with men wepinge.' And the
Archebischop scornede me and seide, 'What janglist thou ayens mennys
devocioun? Whatevere thou or siche other seyen, I seie that the pilgrimage
155 that is now usid is to hem that done it a preparacioun and a good meene to
come the rather to grace. But I holde thee unable to knowe this grace, for
thou enforsist thee to lette the devocioun of the peple, sith by autorité of
Holi Writt men mowen lefulli have and use siche solace as thou reprevest.
For Davith in his laste psalme techith men to usen dyverse instrumentis of
160 musik for to praise with God.' And I seide, 'Sere, by the sentence of
dyverse doctours expownynge the salmes of Davith, the musyk and
minstralcie that Davith and other seyntis of the olde lawe speken of owen
not now to be taken neither usid after the letter, but these instrumentis with
her musyk owen to be interpretid goostly, for alle thei figuren highe
165 vertues and grete, with the whiche vertues men schulden now plese God
and praisen his name. For Seint Poul seith: Alle siche thingis bifallen to
us to figure. And therfore, sere, I undirstonde that Crist appreveth
himself, castynge out mynstrals or that he wolde quyken the dede damysel.'
And the Archebischop seide to me, 'Lewid losel! is it not leful to us for to
170 have orgeynes in the chirche forto herien withal God?' And I seide, 'Yhe,
ser, bi mannes ordinaunce, but bi the ordynaunce of God a good sermoun
to the peples undirstondynge were than moche more plesynge to God.'
And the Archebischop seide that orgeynes goode and delitable songe
175 quykneden and scharpiden ofte more mennys wittis than schulde ony
sermoun.

H

London Lyckpeny

To London once my stepps I bent,
  Where trouth in no wyse should be faynt,
To Westmynster-ward I forthwith went,
  To a man of law to make complaynt.
5   I sayd, 'For Marys love, that holy saynt,
      Pyty the poore that wold proceede'—
    But for lack of mony I cold not spede.

And as I thrust the prese amonge,
  By froward chaunce my hood was gone,
Yet for all that I stayd not longe,   10
  Tyll at the Kynges Bench I was come,
  Before the judge I kneled anon,
    And prayd hym for Gods sake to take heede—
    But for lack of mony I myght not speede.

Beneth them sat clarkes a gret rout,   15
  Which fast dyd wryte by one assent;
There stoode up one and cryed about,
  'Rychard, Robert, and John of Kent!'
  I wyst not well what this man ment;
    He cryed so thycke there in dede—   20
    But he that lackt mony myght not spede.

Unto the Common Place I yode thoo,
  Where sat one with a sylken hoode.
I dyd hym reverence for I ought to do so,
  And told my case as well as I coolde,   25
  How my goodes were defrauded me by falshood.
    I gat not a mum of his mouth for my meed—
    And, for lack of mony I myght not spede.

Unto the Rolls I gat me from thence,
  Before the clarkes of the Chauncerye,   30
Where many I found earnyng of pence,
  But none at all once regarded mee.
  I gave them my playnt uppon my knee,
    They lyked it well, when they had it reade;
    But lackyng mony I could not be sped.   35

In Westmynster Hall I found out one,
  Which went in a long gown of raye.
I crowched and kneled before hym anon—
  For Mayres love, of help I hym praye.
  'I wot not what thou meanest,' gan he say;   40
    To get me thence he dyd me bede—
    For lack of mony I cold not speede.

Within this hall, nether rych nor yett poor
  Wold do for me ought, although I shold dye.
Which seing, I gat me out of the doore,   45
  Where Flemynges began on me for to cry;

'Master, what will you copen or by?
Fyne felt hattes, or spectacles to reede?
Lay down your sylver, and here you may speede.'

50 Then to Westmynster gate I presently went,
When the sonn was at hyghe pryme.
Cookes to me they tooke good entent,
And profered me bread with ale and wyne,
Rybbs of befe, both fat and ful fyne;
55 A fayre cloth they gan forto sprede—
But wantyng mony I myght not speede.

Then into London I dyd me hye,
Of all the land it beareth the pryse;
'Hot pescodes!' one began to crye,
60 'Strabery rype', and 'Cherryes in the ryse!'
One bad me come nere and by some spyce;
Peper and safforne they gan me bede—
But for lack of mony I myght not spede.

Then to the Chepe I gan me drawne,
65 Where mutch people I saw forto stand;
One ofred me velvet, sylke, and lawne;
Another he taketh me by the hande:
'Here is Parys thred, the fynest in the land!'
I never was used to such thynges in dede,
70 And wantyng mony I myght not spede.

Then went I forth by London stone,
Throughout all Canwyke streete;
Drapers mutch cloth me offred anone.
Then comes me one, cryed, 'Hot shepes feete!'
75 One cryde, 'Makerell!'; 'Ryshes grene!' another gan greete.
On bad me by a hood to cover my head—
But for want of mony I myght not be sped.

Then I hyed me into Estchepe,
One cryes, 'Rybbs of befe, and many a pye!'
80 Pewter pottes they clattered on a heape;
There was harpe, pype, and mynstrelsye.
'Yea, by cock!' 'Nay, by cock!' some began crye;
Some songe of Jenken and Julyan for there mede—
But for lack of mony I myght not spede.

Then into Cornhyll anon I yode,   85
    Where was mutch stolen gere amonge;
I saw where honge myne owne hoode,
    That I had lost amonge the thronge.
To by my own hood I thought it wronge—
    I knew it well as I dyd my crede;   90
    But for lack of mony I could not spede.

The taverner tooke me by the sleve;
    'Sir,' sayth he, 'wyll you our wyne assay?'
I answerd, 'that can not mutch me greve;
    A peny can do no more then it may.'   95
I drank a pynt, and for it dyd paye;
    Yet sore a-hungerd from thence I yede,
    And wantyng mony I cold not spede.

Then hyed I me to Belyngsgate,
    And one cryed, 'Hoo! go we hence!'   100
I prayd a bargeman, for Gods sake,
    That he wold spare me my expence.
'Thou scapst not here', quod he, 'under .ii. pence;
    I lyst not yet bestow my almes-dede!'
    Thus lacking mony I could not speede.   105

Then I convayed me into Kent,
    For of the law wold I meddle no more,
Because no man to me tooke entent,
    I dyght me to do as I dyd before.
Now Jesus that in Bethlem was bore,   110
    Save London, and send trew lawyers there mede!
    For whoso wantes mony, with them shall not spede.

I

The Shipman's Vision

The .xxxv. yere of kyng Harry, and the yere of Oure Lorde m.cccc.lvii., a
pylgryme that alle his dayes had be a shipmanne came fro seynt James in
Spayne into Englond aboute Mighelmas, and was loged in the toune of
Weymouthe, in Dorsetshyre, with a brewer, a Duchemanne, the whiche
had be with hym in his seyde pylgremage. And as the sayde pylgryme   5
laye in his bedde waking, he sawe one come into the chambre clothed alle
in whyte having a whyte heede, and sate doune on a fourme nat fer fro hys

bed; and alle the chambre was as lyghte of hym as it had be clere day. The pylgryme was agaste and durst not speke, and anone the seyde spirite
10 vanysshed awey. The secund nyghte the same spyryte came ayene in lyke wyse, and wythoute eny tareyng vanysshed awey. In the morow the pylgrym tolde alle this to his oste, and seyde he was sore afeerde, and wolde no more lye in that chambre. Hys oste counseled hym to telle this to the parysshe preeste, and shryve hym of all his synnes, demyng that he
15 hadde be acombred with some grete dedely synne. The pylgrym sayd, 'I was late shryve at seynt James, and reseved there my Lord God, and sethe that tyme, as fer as I canne remembre, I have nat offended my conscience.' Natheles he was shryvenne, and tolde alle this to the preest; and the preest seyd, 'Sen thow knowest thy selfe clere in conscience, have a good herte
20 and be nat agast, and yef the sayde spirite come ayene, conjure hym in the name of the Fader and of the Sone and of the Holy Goste to telle the what he ys.' The iii^{de} nyghte the spyryte came ayene into the chambre as he had do before, wyth a grete lyghte; and the pylgrym, as the preest had counseled him, conjured the spyryte, and bade hym telle what he was. The
25 spyryte answered and seyde, 'I am thyne eme, thy faderes brother.' The pylgrym seyde, 'How longe ys it ago sen thow deyde?' The spiryte seyde, 'ix. yere.' 'Where ys my fader?' seyde the pylgrime. 'At home in his owne hous,' seyde the spiryte, 'and hath another wyfe.' 'And where ys my moder?' 'In hevene,' seyde the spiryte. Thenne seyde the spiryte to the
30 pylgryme, 'Thou haste be at Seynt James; trowest thou that thow hast welle done thy pylgremage?' 'So I hoope,' saide the pylgryme. Thanne sayde the spiryte, 'Thou haste do to be sayde there .iii. masses, one for thy fader, another for thy moder, and the iii^{de} for thyselve; and yef thou haddest lete say a masse for me, I had be delievred of the peyne that I
35 suffre. But thow most go ayene to Seynt James, and do say a masse for me, and yeve iii.d to .iii. pore men.' 'O', sayde the pylgrime, 'howe shulde I go ayene to Seynt James? I have no money for myne expenses, for I was robbed in the shyppe of .v. nobles.' 'I know welle thys,' sayde the spirite, 'for thow shalt fynde thy purce hanging at the end of the shyp and a stoone
40 therynne; but thow most go ageyne to Seynt James, and begge, and lyve of almesse.' And when the spyryte had thus seyde, the pylgryme saw a develle drawe the same spyryte by the sleve, forto have hym thennys. Thenne saide the spyryte to the pylgryme, 'I have folewed the this .ix. yere, and myghte never speke with the unto now; but blessed be the hous where a
45 spyryte may speke, and farewell, for I may no lenger abyde with the, and therfore I am sory.' And so he vanysshed awey. The pylgryme went into Portyngale, and so forthe to Seynt James, as the spyryte had hym commaunded; wherefore I counseylle every man to worship Seynt James.

J

A Strange Event at Bergamo (1518)

Nat longe agone it hathe bene sene in a felde in londe of Bergame and duryngly preived .iii. or .iiii. tymes in a day out of a certayne wode or forest is come a grete company of men of warre on fote to the nomber of .xii.m. in goodly aray, under the obeysans or commaundement of .v. noble captaynes, of the whiche eche of them ware acompanyed with .v.m. men of war well apoynted, on their right syde, and on their left syde they were accompanyed wyth an innumerable company of men of warre on lyght horses. Betwene these men of warre that be on horsbacke or on fote in goodly aray was a grete nomber of bombardes, courtaus, slyngis, and other great peces of artylery. And agaynst this goodly hooste before named apered another more goodlyer, stronger, rycher, and in noble araye farre passynge and excedynge the other noble company, accompanyed with semely men and noble captaynes rychely besene as noble of birth. The wyche .ii. noble partyes helde speche with eche other, and wythin a lyttel whyle after come out of the wode before named wyth grete triumphe .iii. or .iiii. men on horsbacke, and because that these fornamed personages ware or semed to be apoynted lyke nobell princes, therfore they ware taken in sight as royall kinges. The wyche ware accompanyed wyth one persone ryght triumphantly rydynge before them excellynge all the other and coude nat of no beholders be ymagened what mans persone this myght be, but the other dyd hym grete honour and reverence. This same and selfe parsone went with another personage that abode hym on the waye to speke with hym, the whyche semed to be knouwe for a kynge accompanyed with a grete nomber of many noble princes and lordes rychely besene. But they that semed to be nerre unto his persone they semed better to be embassadours than other men. Within a littel whyle after, this kynge gave a mervelous spytfull regarde, shewynge that he was very angry and unpacyent be his countenans; drawyng of his gauntlet of stele and with an yrful countenance casted it up into the ayre in token of batayle. Whan he had so done, with great haste he retourned unto his armye where he had a mervelous goodly company stondynge in a noble aray redy to embatayle with their ennemys. Than was there herd a great noyse of trompettes, clerons, tromles, with other instrumentes, and an orryble voyse of artelery in suche maner that it semed to be the noyse of helle the whiche was very feerfull. Also there was sene a grete many of baners and standardes pight in the felde, right ryche to beholde, on bothe partyes. And than was there foghten a felde or batayle, the moste cruelle that myght be thought be mannes mynde, the which is nat well to be beleved, so marvelously as it was don. An halfe houre after that all thynges had ben

40 done and everyche departed, there ware of us some bolder one than
another that had beholden this great batayle or foghten felde, and went to
the fornamed place forto beholde and se whether they coude se or fynde
any thynge or token lefte behynd of them that had foghten that mervelous
felde. And whan they come to the place before named there they se so
45 many and innumerable nomber of swyne that they marvayled sore of that
wonderfulle sight. These swyne abode there but a lytell whyle in the place
where the foghten felde had bene, but they departed into the fornamed
wode or forest, and ware no more sene. . . .

K

Prophecia Merlini Doctoris Perfecti

Whane lordes wol leefe theire olde lawes,
And preestis been varyinge in theire sawes,
And leccherie is holden solace,
And oppressyoun for truwe purchace,
5   And whan the moon is on David stall,
And the kynge passe Arthures hall,
Than is the lande of Albyoun
Nexst to his confusyoun.

L

A Prognostication for 1498

. . . The kynge of Englond this yere shall overcome his enmyes, shal be
exalted and fortunate with his childern. He shalbe this yere disposed to
ryde about his realme to sporte hym and to oversee and order his realme;
in whiche journey a knyght or one apte to the warre, a man of grete
5 strength, and a servaunt of the kynges court shall dye. Englonde shall not
be without syknesses and pestylences. Marchantes of Englonde shall
prospere and have wynnynge. The prynce Arthure this yere shal prospere
and encreace his substaunce and honour. My lorde Herry, duke of Yorke,
and my lady Margarete his syster, the whiche shall after this be a quene or
10 elles have some grete honour shall this yere be hole and fortunate. . . .
Novembre shal be very rayny and tempestuous with grete chaungynge of
the ayer with rayne and wynde and happly snowe. Decembre shal be colde,
wyndy, rayny and snowy. . . . Sonnes, childern and messengers shall not do
well this yere, for syknesses and other infortunes. This yere shal be many

22

syknesses, as fevers contynuall and tercyans, pestylence, bledynge at nose, 15
paynes of the heed, the eyes, the bely, and many bytwene the skynne and
the flesshe, carbuncles, pokes, scabbes and suche. But ther shall not many
men dye therof in comparyson of so many and dyverse syknesses, but
yonge folke and very aged shal be moost vexed, and moost wymmen. . . .

M

JOHN KAYE, *THE SIEGE OF RHODES*

The Turks Attack the Tower of St Nicholas (1480)

. . . The Turkes for despyte and grete annoye of the foresayde thynges
whiche were done unto theyme made anone redy a grete ordonnaunce and
came agayne unto the tour of Seynt Nycolas forto have it, and anon with
their bombardes boldely they casted downe the bollewerkes and forslettes.
And as faste as they casted theym downe, the Rhodyans repayred theim 5
agayn. The Turkes also made a long brigge of the lenght of a quarter of a
myle, the whiche recched from the banke thereas the Turkes laye unto the
banke of Seynt Nicolas toure, and was so large that .vi. men on horseback
myghte ryde afronte, and was made with voyded pypes and with bordes
strongly nayled upon them; and purposed to bryng the same brigge by craft 10
into the water. And they fested and knytted strongely to the sayde brigge
grete and myghti ropes whiche had in th'other ende strong ancures,
whiche ancures they fasted with a bote to the nether bank of the tour so
that the brigge with the drawyng of the corde and flotyng shulde have
recched to the sayd banke. Anone after that the Rhodians had knowleche 15
of thees werkes, a shipman wel experte in swymmyng wente by nyghte and
cutted the cordes fro the ancer and knytted theim unto a stone of the
banke, so that lyghtely whenne the Turkes drewe the corde they knewe wel
that they were begyled of the Rhodyans. The lord mayster of Rhodes
understandyng thys noble acte, rewarded the forsayd shypman worshipfully 20
and ryght largely. And so whenne the Turkes sawe and knewe the grete
frawde whyche was done to theym of the Rhodyans, thoughte and
ordeyned that they wold brynge the forsayd brygge theder wyth grete
strenghte and nombre of botes being full of rowers, whyche botes were
conduted and ledded with .xxx. galeyes of grete defence, and with .vii. or 25
.viii. grete and myghty careckes ful of gownes and bombardes forto caste
downe the forsayd tour, and after that to putte in ruyne the haven and
walles of the cytee. And also they ordeyned certayn bargyes to bryng to
lande the moste manly men of werre of the Turke, whiche sholde fyghte
hand for hand with the Rhodyans. In the meane while that they whiche 30
were on the brigge and they of the shippes shulde fyght agaynest the tour

23

and shold araye the brigge and putte their men and instrumentes of werre atte grounde, the lord mayster asked counseyl of all the most proved knyghtes and Crysten men that ther were most manly and most wyse, and

35 of theimselfe of Rhodes whiche were ful of wysedom and bolde manhode. And there was geven counseyl that the tour sholde be strenght with dyches rounde abowte. And because that yt was gravell and stone, the lord mayster with grete costes hyred a thousand laboureurs with pykes and shoules, whiche nyght and daye dyd that they were commanded. And

40 where the toure was feble and in ruyne were ordeyned agaynest the fyrste assaute men of werre, and also were ordeyned men of werre in the netherest dyche to helpe the Rhodyans yf nede were, for they dred that the Turkes shold have assauted the cytee and the tour al at one affray. Therfor the lord mayster putted also strenght of men into the walles of Rhodes

45 whiche were beten downe with bombardes, that ys to saye in the warde of th'Ytalyans and in the warde of the Jues. And for cause that alle the helthe and defence of the cytee was in the welfare of the sayd tour, every man wyth one voys cryed that the toure sholde be dylygentely and manly kepte; where afterward the knyghtes bothe of Latyn tonge and Grekys tonge dyd

50 worshipfully as ever dyd Achylles or Hector. But two yong men soldyers of the sayd toure threwe downe their harnesse in the see to th'entente to be Turkes. And afterward, when thys was knowen, they for their synnes and defawtes were byheded. And so after this, about the .xvi. day of the moneth of July the yere aforsayd, in the tyme of mydnyghte, the Turkes

55 came pryvely by water and by lande forto come to the toure, and with theyre labour and payne broughte the brygge to the fote of the tour, and made thenne a stoute and horryble crye, as they have in theyr guyse afore that they begynne to fyghte. But oure Crysten folke anone herde and perseyved their boldenesse; wherfore wyth crossebowes and bombardes

60 they kepte theym offe, and brake their brigge, where many Turkes were drownyd and four galeyes and careckes were broken with stones and instrumentes of theym that were in Rhodes. And many of the Turkes that were sette a-land by the brygge from the shippes and galeyes anone after were slayne and many wonded, and som of the shyppes were brente, and

65 some of their gables were kytte, so that the shippes were loste in the see. Neverthelesse, the Turkes from th'other banke manly and stoutely faughted and defended their people aforsayd wyth castyng to the cyté and toure grete stones of bombardes and of gonnes, and wyldfyre, and arowes of bowes and balestres. And soo alle the nyght from twelfe the clocke unto .x.

70 in the daye they faught all by derke, but as the fyre of the bombardes and the flammes of the wyldfyre gave lyghte. And so after that the Turkes were put oute with their grete dammage and harme and that the men of Rhodes had the vyctorye, a man myght have seen thre dayes folowyng ded men of the Turkys partye casted and lyyng in the banke of the see toward Rhodes,

75 whiche were fonde arayed wyth golde and sylver and precious clothyng,

and parte of their araye was seen flotyng in the see, whiche geyre and araye
was taken uppe by the Crysten men with grete profyte and wynnyng.

N

By Sea to Santiago

Men may leve alle gamys,
That saylen to seynt Jamys!
For many a man hit gramys,
    When they begyn to sayle.
For when they have take the see,   5
At Sandwyche, or at Wynchylsee,
At Brystow, or where that hit bee,
    Theyr hertes begyn to fayle.

Anone the mastyr commaundeth fast
To hys shypmen, in alle the hast,   10
To dresse hem sone about the mast,
    Theyr takelyng to make.
With 'how! hissa!' then they cry,
'What, howe, mate! thow stondyst to ny,
Thy felow may nat hale the by!'   15
    Thus they begyn to crake.

A boy or tweyn anone up styen,
And overthwart the sayle-yerde lyen.
'Y how! taylia!' the remenaunt cryen,
    And pulle with alle theyr myght.   20
'Bestowe the boote, boteswayne, anon,
That our pylgryms may pley theron;
For som ar lyke to cowgh and grone
    Or hit be full mydnyght.

'Hale the bowelyne! now, vere the shete!—   25
Cooke, make redy anoon our mete!
Our pylgryms have no luste to ete,
    I pray God yeve hem rest!'
'Go to the helm! what, howe! no nere?
Steward, felow! A pot of bere!'   30
'Ye shalle have, sir, with good chere,
    Anon alle of the best.'

'Y howe! trussa! hale in the brayles!
Thow halyst nat, be God, thow fayles!
35   O se howe welle owre good shyp sayles!'
        And thus they say among.
'Hale in the wartake!' 'Hit shal be done!'
'Steward! cover the boorde anone,
And set bred and salt therone,
40   And tary nat to long.'

Then cometh oone and seyth, 'Be mery;
Ye shall have a storme or a pery.'
'Holde thow thy pese! thow canst no whery,
        Thow medlyst wondyr sore.'
45   Thys mene-whyle the pylgryms ly,
And have theyr bowlys fast theym by,
And cry aftyr hote malvesy,
        'Thow helpe for to restore!'

And some wold have a saltyd tost,
50   For they myght ete neyther sode ne rost;
A man myght sone pay for theyr cost,
        As for oo day or twayne.
Som layde theyr bookys on theyr kne,
And rad so long they myght nat se.
55   'Allas! myne hede wolle cleve on thre!'
        Thus seyth another certayne.

Then commeth owre owner lyke a lorde,
And speketh many a royall worde,
And dresseth hym to the hygh borde,
60   To see alle thyng be welle.
Anone he calleth a carpentere,
And byddyth hym bryng with hym hys gere,
To make the cabans here and there,
        With many a febylle celle;

65   A sak of strawe were there ryght good,
For som must lyg theym in theyr hood;
I had as lefe be in the wood
        Without mete or drynk;
For when that we shall go to bedde,
70   The pumpe was nygh oure beddes hede,
A man were as good to be dede
        As smell thereof the stynk!

O

WILLIAM WEY, *ITINERARIES*

Advice for Pilgrims to Jerusalem

A goyd prevysyoun when a man ys at Venyse, and purposyth by the grase of God to passe by the see unto port Jaff in the Holy Londe, and so to the Sepulkyr of Owre Lorde Cryst Jesu in Jerusalem, he most dyspose hym in thys wyse. Furste, yf ye goo in a galey, make yowre covenaunte wyth the patrone by tyme, and chese yow a place in the seyd galey in the overest 5 stage; for in the lawyst under hyt ys ryght smolderyng hote and stynkyng. And ye schal pay for yowre galey and for yowre mete and drynke to port Jaff and ayen to Venyse, .xl. ducatis forto be in a goyd honeste plase, and to have yowre ese in the galey, and also to be cheryschet. Also when ye schal yowre covenant take, take goyd hede that the patron be bounde unto yow 10 afore the duke other lordis of Venyse in an .c. dokettis to kepe al maner covenauntis wyth yow; that ys to say, that he schal conduce yow to certeyne havenys by the wey to refresche yow, and to gete yow fresch water and fresch bred and flesch. And that he schal not tary longer at none havyn than thre days at the most wythowte consent of yow all. And that he schal 15 nat take ynto the vessel nother goyng nother comyng no maner of marchaundyse wythowte yowre wylle, to destresse yow in yowre plasys, and also for taryng of passage by the see. . . .

But make covenaunte that ye com nat at Famagust in Cipres for no thyng, for meny Englysch men and other also have dyde, for that eyre ys so 20 corupte therabowte, and in the water also. Also that yowre patrone yeff yow every day hote mete twyes, at too melys, in the mornynge at dyner, and after none at soper; and the wyne that ye schal drynke be goyd and yowre water fresch, yf ye may com thertoo, and also byscocte. Also ye most ordeyne for yowreselfe and yowre felow, and ye have eny, .iii. barellys eche 25 of a quarte, whyche quarte holdyth .x. galynnys; too of thes barell schal serve for wyne, and the therde for water. In that on barel take rede wyne and kep evyr in store, and tame hyt not yf ye may tyl ye com hamward ayen, withoute syknes cause hyt, other eny other nede. For ye schal thys in specyal note, and ye had the flux, yf ye wold yeff .xx. doketis for a barel, ye 30 schal none have after ye passe moche Venyse; and that othyr barel schal serve when ye have dronke up yowre drynkyng wyne to fyl ageyne at the havyn where ye next come unto. Also ye most by yow a chest to put yn yowre thyngys; and yf ye may have a felow with yow too or thre, y wold then by a chest that were as brode as the barel were long. In that one ende 35 y wolde have loke and key, and a lytyl dore, and ley that same barell that y wold spende frust at the same dore ende; for yf the galymen other

27

pylgremys may come therto, meny wyl tame and drynke therof, and stele
yowre watyr, whyche ye wold nat mysse ofttyme for yowre wyne. And yn
40 the other part of the cheste ye may ley yowre bred, ches, spyses, and al
other thyngis. Also ye most ordeyne yow byscokte to have with yow; for
thow ye schal be at the tabyl wyth yowre patrone, notwythstondyng ye schal
oft tyme have nede to yowre vytelys, bred, chese, eggys, frute, and bakyn,
wyne, and other, to make yowre collasyun: for sum tyme ye schal have
45 febyl bred, wyne, and stynkyng water, meny tymes ye schal be ful fayne to
ete of yowre owne. Also y consel yow to have wyth yow oute of Venyse
confectyunnys, confortatyvys, laxatyvys, restoratyvys, gyngever, ryse, fygys,
reysenes gret and smal, whyche schal do yow gret ese by the wey, pepyr,
saferyn, clowys, masys, a fewe as ye thenge nede, and powder dwke. Also
50 take with yow a lytyl cawdren and fryyng pan, dysches, platerrys, sawserys
of tre, cuppys of glas, a grater for brede, and such nessaryes. Also when
ye com to Venyse ye schal by a bedde by Seynt Markys cherche; ye schal
have a fedyr bedde, a matres, too pylwys, too peyre schetis, and a qwylt,
and ye schal pay .iii. dokettis; and when ye com ayen bryng the same bedde
55 to the man that ye bowt hit of and ye schal have a doket and halfe ayen,
thow hyt be broke and worne. Also make yowre chaunge at Venyse, and
take wyth yow at the leste .xxx. doketis of grotys and grossynes. . . .
       Also by yow a cage for half a dosen of hennys or chekyn to have with yow
in the galey, for ye schal have nede unto them meny tymes; and by yow half
60 a buschel of myle sede of Venyse for hem. Also take a barel wyth you close
for a sege for yowre chambur in the galey; hyt is ful nessessary yf ye be syke
that ye com not in the eyre. Also whan ye com to havyn townys, yf ye wyl ye
may by eggys, yf ye com bytyme to lond, for then ye may have goyd chep,
for they be ful nessessary in the galey, sumtime fryed with oyle olyfe, and
65 sumtyme for a caudel. Also when ye come to havyn townys, yf ye schal tary
there .iii. dayes, go bytyme to londe, for then ye may have logyng byfore
other, for hyt wyl be take up anone, and yf eny goyd vytel be, bee ye sped
afor other. Also when ye com to dyverse havynnys be wel ware of dyverse
frutys, for they be not acordyng to yowre complexioun and they gender a
70 blody fluxe; and yf an Englyschman have that sykenes hyt ys a mervel and
scape hyt but he dye thereof. Also when ye schal com to port Jaff take wyth
yow oute of the galey into the londe too gordys, one with wyne, another
wyth water, eche of a potel at the lest, for ye schal none have tyl ye come to
Ramys, and that ys ryght febyl and dyre; and at Jerusalem hyt ys goyd wyne
75 and dere. Also se that the patron of the galey take charge of yowre harneys
wythyn the galey tyl ye come ayen to the galey. Ye schal tary yn the Holy
Lond .xiii. other .xiiii. days. Also take goyd hede of yowre knyves and other
smal thynges that ye ber apon yow, for the Sarsenes wyl go talkyng wyth
yow and make goyd chere, but they wyl stele fro yow that ye have and they
80 may.

P

THE PYLGRYMAGE OF SIR RICHARDE GUYLFORDE

Bethlehem

At Bethlem comenly be .v. or .vi. freres of Mounte Syon, to kepe the holy places there, which with other freres that come with us from Mounte Syon, dressed them to a solempne procession at our first commyng, whom we folowed to al the holy places within the same monastery, with candles lyght in our handes, as alway used in other places where any processyon 5 was done, etc. And firste the sayde processyon broughte us to a place at an aulter in the southe yle, where our Savyour Criste was circumsised, etc. And from thens we come to another aulter on the northe syde, where the thre kynges made redy their offerynges to present unto our Savyour Criste. And from this place descendyng by certayne stone grees we come into a 10 wonder fayre lytell chapell, at the hyghe aulter wherof is the very place of the byrthe of our Lord, assygned by an hole made lyke a sterre in a fayre whyte marble stone under the myddes of the sayd hygh aulter, whiche byrthe was done in that selfe moste holy place, to the gretest joye and gladnesse that ever come to mankynde, etc. And at this moste holy place is 15 clene remyssyon. And therby is a lytel aulter somwhat under the rok where the thre kynges offered to our blessyd Savyour Criste Jesu gold, myrre, and incence. And there is also clene remyssyon. And a lytel before the sayde hyghe aulter is the cribbe of oure Lorde, where our blessyd Lady her dere sone beforelayde the oxe and the asse, etc. And there is clene 20 remyssyon. And undowted this lytell chapell of the byrthe of our Lorde is the most glorious and devoute place that ever I come in; it is all of tables of fyne whyte marble stone, and the vaughtes be garnysshed with golde, and byset with dyvers storyes of as subtyll musyn worke as maye be, the wallys also of all the body of the churche, from the pyllers to the rooffe, be 25 paynted with storyes from the begynnynge of the worlde of the sayde musyn werke, whiche is the rychest thynge that can be done to any wallys. Howbeit the sayd werkes be gretely defaced, both in the churche and chapell, for very pure age, and the sayd churche, with all the place, falleth in grete dekay, etc. . . . 30

A Storm

. . . And there we laye styll in the sayd haven at Mylo Wednysdaye, Thursday, Fryday, Saterday, Sonday, seynt Nicholas daye, and Mondaye all day. The same nyght there arose a mervaylous grete tempest, with

29

excedynge rayne and with the gretyst rage of wynde that ever I saw in all
35 my lyfe; and so incessantly contynued all that nyghte, insomoche where we
had out .ii. ancres, they helde not fermely, but rasyd and draggyd by
vyolence of that outrageous storme, by force wherof we were almoste
dryven upon the rokky shore there; and great pyté it was to se what
trybulacion and fere the maryners hadde that nyght, and also the
40 pylgrymes, whiche rose out of our lodgynges and drewe us togyther, and
devoutly and ferefully sange *Salve Regina* and other antymes, with versicles
and collettis appropred for suche effecte; and we all yave money and
vowed a pylgrymage in generall to our blessed Lady de Myraculis at
Venyse, besydes other particuler vowes that many pylgrymes made of theyr
45 singuler devocions. And in lyke wyse the maryners made a pylgrymage at
their awne costes and charge. And over this every man, as well pylgrymes
as other, trussed aboute theym suche lyghte geyre as they had, and made
theym redy to shyfte for theyr escape at the fall of the galey to the rok in
suche wyse as the good Lorde wolde yeve theym grace. Howbeit we
50 understode afterwardes by the maryners that all our trussyng and hope to
escape shulde have ben in vayne; for if the galye had ones towched the rok
we had ben all perysshed, as they sayde; and so the best maryners of
them rekenyd none otherwyse for theymselffes. And in this whyle, with
grete devocion and prayer of some well disposed pylgrymes there, and
55 every man hangynge in this grete fere, with outragyous clamours and cryes
of the maryners, they let fall the thyrde ancre, which, thankyd be Almyghty
God, helde faste and kepte oure galye frome dryvyng any further, and so
we rode out the ferse storme for that nyght. The nexte morowe,
Tewysdaye, that was oure Ladyes daye, we were gretely comforted by
60 commynge of the daye lyght and that we myght se aboute us; howbeit the
rage and storme contynued styll all the Tewysdaye and all the nyght
folowynge, and Wednysdaye all daye; so that both nyght and daye we laye
there styll in wondre grete trybulacion and fere, for if our galye had fallen
to rakynge and draggynge ayen, we hadde ben all loste. Thursdaye, that
65 was the .x. daye of Decembre, the tempest began to slake, and the wynde
fell more softe and bycome well in our waye.

Q

Richard Torkington in Venice

The richesse, the sumptuous buyldyng, the religius howses, and the
stabelyssyng of ther justyces and counceylles, with all other thynges that
makyth a cité glorius, surmownteth in Venys above all places that ever I
sawe. And specially at .ii. festis wherat we war present. The on was upon
5 the Assencion Day. The Duke with grett triumphe and solemnyté with all

the senyorye went in ther *archa triumphali*, which ys in maner of a galye of a straunge facion and wonder stately, etc. And the Marchose of Mantua was with them in the forseyd galye. And so they rowed into the see, with the assistens of ther Patriarche, and ther spoused the see with a ryng. The spousall words be *In signum veri perpetuique dominii*. And therwith the Duke lete fall the ryng into the see, the processe and the cerymonyes wherof war to long to wryte. Thanne thaye rode to the Abbey of Seynt Nicholas of blake monkys that stoud by juste be them, and all thaye brake ther fastes, and so retornyd ageyne to Venys, to the Dukys palace, wher they had provyd for them a mervelows dyner, wherat we pilgrymes war present and see them servyd. At which dyner ther wer .viii. corse of soundery metys, and att every corse the trunpettes and mynystrellys com inne afor them. Ther was excedyng myche plate, as basons, ewers, wonders grett and of a straunge facioun. Every .iiii. persons had a bason and ewer to washen ther handes. Also ther was a grett vesell of sylver and gylte, and it was .iiii. cornarde, and it had at every ende .iiii. ryngs that .ii. men myght berè it betwyne them forto cast owt the watyr of ther basons whanne they had wasshed ther handys. Ther dysshys, ther platers, ther sawcers—all was of sylver and gylte. And while they satt at dyner ther was parte of the Dukys chapell singing dyverse balyttys, and sumtyme they song with orgones. And aftyr that ther cam on of the trompetores and he pleyd with the organs all maner of messur, the excellent conyng man that ever I hard, with diverse instruments I hard nor never see afor. And whanne dyner was don, the Duke sent to the pilgryms gret basons full of marchepanys, and also coumfytes and malvysey, and other swete wynys as myche as ony man wold ete and drynke. This don, ther cam on that was disgysyd, and he gestyd afor the Duke and the Marchose and the company and made them very mery. And aftyr that ther cam dauncers and sume of them disgysyd in womens clothes that daunsyd a gret while. And after them come tombelers, both men and children, the marvelows felaws that ever I saw, so myche that I canne nott writt it. . . .

R

Of the Newe Landes and the People found by the Messengers of the Kynge of Portyngale named Emanuel

Here aforetymes in the yere of our Lorde God .m cccc xcvi. and so be, we with shyppes of Lusseboene sayled oute of Portyngale thorough the commaundement of the kynge Emanuel. So have we had our vyage for, by fortune, ylandes over the great see with great charge and daunger. So have we at the laste founde oon lordshyp where we sayled well .ix.c. myles by the cooste of selandes; there we at the laste went a-lande, but that lande is

not nowe knowen, for there have no masters wryten therof nor it knowethe, and it is named Armenica. There we sawe meny wonders of beestes and fowles that we have never seen before. The people of this
10 lande have no kynge nor lorde, nor theyr god, but all thinges is comune. This people goeth all naked, but the men and women have on theyr heed, necke, armes, knees, and fete all with feders bounden for there bewtynes and fayrenes. These folke lyven lyke bestes without any resonablenes, and the wymen be also as comon. And the men hath conversacyon with the
15 wymen, who that they ben or who they fyrst mete, is she his syster, his moder, his daughter, or any other kyndred. And the wymen be very hoote and dysposed to lecherdnes. And they ete also on another. The man etethe his wyfe, his chylderne, as we also have seen; and they hange also the bodyes or persons fleeshe in the smoke, as men do with us swynes fleshe.
20 And that lande is ryght full of folke, for they lyve comonly .iii.c. yere and more, as with sykenesse they dye nat. They take much fysshe, for they can goen under the water, and feche so the fysshes out of the water. And they werre also on upon another, for the olde men brynge the yonge men therto, that they gather a great company therto of towe partyes and come
25 the on ayene the other to the felde or bateyll, and slee on the other with great hepes. And howe holdeth the fylde, they take the other prysoners, and they brynge them to deth and ete them. And as the deed is eten then sley they the rest, and they been than eten also, or otherwyse lyve they longer tymes and many yeres more than other people, for they have costely
30 spyces and rotes, where they themselfe recover with, and hele them as they be seke.

2

LETTERS

READING letters from the past is often a very entertaining as well as an illuminating occupation, and it can be indulged in for the first time in the history of English literature in this period, when correspondence in the vernacular became common, and has survived in bulk. Nor surprisingly, social historians have found a rich quarry especially in the large and varied collection of letters to and from the Pastons, landowners in East Anglia, but also in other collections—of the Stonors in Oxfordshire, the Celys, merchants based in London, the Plumptons from near Harrogate, and of John Shillingford, the Mayor of Exeter up in London on legal business. The letters are concerned with the conduct of everyday affairs—litigation, business and trade, estates and their management, the arranging of marriages and the financial details involved, and a host of personal matters—and give us an extraordinary insight into the way people lived. They are also often written in a vivid and lively style, and it is here probably that their main interest for the literary student lies. Two centuries later, Dorothy Osborne, writing to Sir William Temple (October 1653), remarks shrewdly, 'All letters mee thinks should bee free and easy as ones discourse, not studdyed, as an oration, nor made up of hard words like a charme.' Very many of the best examples from our period are 'free and easy' as discourse, and give a simple, unforced impression which seems to reflect colloquial speech. They are not, however, artlessly naïve. They make use of familiar formulae and stereotyped expressions: forms of address ('Right worshipful/worthy/well-behaved sir/husband/father/mother'), phrases which have their modern equivalents in 'let me know how you are getting on', 'hoping this finds you as it leaves me', or 'I must rush now' ('wretyn in hast . . . be candel lyght'), and so forth. There are pious exclamations, blessings, proverbs, and occasional touches of a more 'literary' style. Our selection attempts to give some idea of the variety of the material. There are factual accounts of great matters of state, such as the death of Suffolk, or the splendours of Continental courtly life, or the movingly simple description of Henry VI's recovery from madness, a description of a meeting with a possible bride, a Valentine, and many requests, especially for money (the unfortunate and battered Thomas Hostelle in his petition essays something like the 'heigh style, as whan that men to kynges write', whereas a later young man's request has a direct and timeless ring—'Modyr, I beseche yow, and ye may spare eny money . . .'). Angry letters are a particular delight: we have Lord Grey so moved by a wicked Welshman and his dirty deeds in the Marches that he bursts out into doggerel invective (later to be called Skeltonics), and a bishop who under the calm surface of pious formulae makes it quite clear to an officious archdeacon that he is likely to get tit for tat.

A

A THIEVING WELSHMAN REFUTED

Lord Grey de Ruthin to Gruffudd ap Dafydd ap Gruffudd

Gruffuth ap David ap Gruffuth,

We send the gretyng welle, but nothyng with goode hert. And we have well understande thy lettre to us sent by Deykus Vaghan, our tenaunt, which maken mencioun and seist that the fals John Weele hath disseyved the. And seist that all men knowen well that thou was under the proteccioun of
5 Mered ap Owyn, and sent to the as thou seist by treté of thy cousynes, Maester Edward, and Edwarde ap David, and asked the if thou woldest come inne, and he wolde gette the thy chartere of the kyng, and that thou sholdest be keyshate in Chirklond; and other thyngis he beheght the, which he fullfylled noght, as thou seiste; and afterwarde asked the whether
10 thou woldest go over the see with him, and he wolde gette the thy chartere of the King, and bryng the to hym sounde and saufe, and thou sholdest have wages as moche as any gentell man that went with hym. And overe thus thou seideist that John Well seide befor the Bishope of Seint Assaph, and befor thy cousynes, that, rather than thou sholdest faile, he wolde
15 spenne of his oun good .xx. marcis. Heerupon thou trusted, as thou seiste, and duddest gete the two men, and boght the armoure for all peces, horsen, and other araie, and comest to Oswaldestree a-nyght befor that thei went; and on the morowe after thou sendest Piers Cambré, the receyvour of Chirklonde, thries to hym, to telle hym that thou was redy,
20 and he seide that thou sholdest speke no worde with hym. And at the last he saide he hadde no wages for the, as thou seiste, and he hadde fully his retenue, and bade the goo to Sir Richarde Laken to loke whether he hadde nede of the other noo, with the which thou, as thou seiste, haddest nevere ado, ne nevere madest covenaunt with. For thou woldest, as thou seiste,
25 have goon for no wages with hym over see, but forto have thy chartere of the kyng, and sume lyvyng that thou myghtest dwelle in pees. And, as thou seist, Sir Richard Laken and Straunge woll berre wittenesse that thou was redy and wylly for to goon with hym giffe he hadde be trewe. And also thou seist he cam to Laken and to Straunge and wolde have made hem to take
30 the, and thou haddest wittyng therof, as thou seiste, and trussed the fro thennes, and knowelechest that thy men cam and breeke our parke by nyght, and tooke out of hyt two of our horses, and of our menis. And, as hit is tolde the, thou seiste, that we ben in pourpose to make our men brenne and slee in whatsoever cuntree thou be inne, and wilt withouten doute, as
35 thou seiste, as many men as we slee and as many housen that we brenne for thy sake, as many brenne and slee for our sake. And, as thou seiste,

thou wilt have bothe breede and ale of the best that is in our lordshipe; and
heerof thou biddest us have no doute, the whiche is agayn our wyll, gife
any thou have breede other ale so, and theras thou berrest upon us that we
sholde ben in pourpose to brenne and sleen men and housen for thy sake,   40
or for any of thyn enclinant to the, or any of hem that ben the kingis trewe
liege men, we was nevere so mysavised to worch agayn the kyng no his
lawes, whiche giffe we dudde, were heigh tresoun; but thou hast hadde fals
messageres and fals reportoures of us touchyng this matere; and that shall
be well knowen unto the king and alle his counsaile. Ferthermore, theras   45
thou knowlechest by thyn oun lettre that thy men hath stolle our horsen
out of our parke, and thou recettour of hem, we hoope that thou and thy
men shall have that ye have deserved. For us thynketh, thegh John Well
hath doon as thou aboven has certefied, us thynketh that that sholde noght
be wroken towarde us.   50

But we hoope we shall do the a pryvé thyng:
a roope, a ladder, and a ryng,
heigh on gallowes for to henge.
And thus shall be your endyng.
And he that made the be ther to helpyng,   55
and we on our behalfe shall be wellwillyng.
For thy lettre is knowlechyng.

B

The Petition of Thomas Hostelle (1429)

To the king oure souverain lorde,

Besechithe mekely youre povere leigemane and humble horatour, Thomas
Hostelle, that, in consideracone of his service doon to youre noble
progenitours of ful blessid memory, kyng Henri the iiiith and kyng Henri
the fift (whoos soules God assoille), being at the siege of Hareflewe there
smyten with a springolt throughe the hede, lesyng his oon eye and his   5
chekboon broken; also at the bataille of Agingcours, and afore at the
takyng of the carrakes on the see, there withe a gadde of yrene his plates
smyten into his body and his hande smyten in sondre, and sore hurte,
maymed and wounded, by mean whereof he being sore febled and
debrused, now falle to greet age and poverté, gretly endetted, and may not 10
help him self, havyng not wherewithe to be susteyned ne relevede, but of
mennes gracious almesse, and being for his said service never yet
recompensed ne rewarded; it plese youre highe and excellent grace, the
premises tenderly considered, of youre benigne pitee and grace to releve
and refresshe your saide povere oratour as it shal plese you with youre   15

most gracious almesse, at the reverence of God and in worke of charitee, and he shal devoutly pray for the soules of youre said noble progenitours and for youre most noble and highe astate.

C

A BISHOP IS OFFENDED

William Grey, Bishop of Lincoln, to Thomas Bekynton

Wele belufede brother, I grete yowe wele, mervaylyng gretely that on Fryday now laste, whan ye had dyned wyth me, and I, as ye saghe, toke myne horse forto ryde, even in my goyng owte, at my yate, come one to me and inhibited me by your auctorytee, and cited me to apere afore yowe
5 wythynne the fourtened day next folowyng; of the whiche inhibicyon I myght neythere hafe syght ne copy at my costes, to suche tyme as I sent fro Colbroke to London for a copye; by the whiche I conceyved wel hit was in the matier of the chapell of Boveney, in the paryssh of Burnham; the whiche matier and all other, as wele spirituell as temporell bytwix thoe
10 partyes, as ye wele knawe, were putte in compromyse. And syth ye be the juge of the hyghest court spirituell in this lande, and to whome all the prelates of this provynce muste hafe recourse, me thynk ye shuld be ryght wele advised what passed under your seal, and in especyall agayns a prelate: and therfore, if ye hafe done me laghe to cite me to so shorte a
15 tyme, wele be hit. Neverthelesse, I wyll not disobey in no kynde, but by the grace of God to apere at my day, and do all that lagh wyll. Wherefore blames me not, if I, anothere day, do as litell favour to yowe, in your jurisdiccyon, if hit lyg in my powere, as hit shall ryght wele, I truste to God, who kepe yow ever. Wryten in my monastery of Eynesham, under my
20 sygnet, the .xvi. day of Feveryer.

D

JOHN SHILLINGFORD PROSPERS, IN SPITE OF THE VENOM OF HIS ENEMIES

John Shillingford, Mayor of Exeter, to his Fellows, from London (1447)

... The morun Tuysday Alhalwyn yeven y receyved the answeris to oure articulis at Westminster of the whiche y sende yow a true copy, yn the whiche articulis as hit appereth they have spatte out the uttmyst and worste venym that they cowde seye or thynke by me; yblessed be God hit is nother

felony, ne treson, ne grete trespas, and thogh hit hadde be, so they wolde 5
have don, and werce yf they cowde: but as for trawthe of the mater that
tocheth me, meny worthy man stondeth on the same cas and have do
moche werce than ever y didde, thogh that be to me none exscuse. As
touchyng the grete venym that they menyth of my lyvyng, y may and
purpose be at my purge, as y may right well apon my sawle of alle wymmen 10
alyve excepte oone, and of hire righte a grete while; therfor y take right
nocht by and sey sadly *si recte vivas etc.*, and am right mery and fare right
well, ever thankyng God and myn awne purse. And y liyng on my bedde
atte writyng of this right yerly, myryly syngyng a myry song, and that ys
this, 'Come no more at oure hous, come, come, come.' Y woll not dye nor 15
for sorowe ne for anger, but be myry and fare right well, while y have
mony; but that ys and like to be scarce with me, considerynge the bisynesse
and coste that y have hadde, and like to have: and yet y hadde with me
.xx. li. and more by my trauthe, wherof of trauthe not right moche y spende
yet, but like etc. Constre ye what ye will. *Item*, Thomas Montagew sholde 20
sende me .xi. li. and odde mony as he wote well and can telle yowe: and y
supposed that John Germyn sholde have broght to me allmost .x. li.—all
this of myne awne gode—wherof cometh to me no peny. Wherfor y sende
home to yow attis tyme William Hampton, berer of this writyng, for this
cause most specially that ye, how that ever ye do, sende me .xx. li. yn hast, 25
as ye wolle the spede of youre mater and welfare of the cité, y not shamed
but pleased attis tyme; and that ye faill yn no wyse, mervaillyng moche, for
as moche as y departed fro yow withoute eny mony of youris, that ye ne
hadde sende to me sithenesse some mony by Germyn, Kyrton, or some
other man. . . .   30

E

THE DEATH OF THE DUKE OF SUFFOLK

William Lomnor to John Paston I (5 May 1450)

Ryght worchipfulle ser, I recomaunde me to yow, and am right sory of
that I shalle sey, and have soo wesshe this litel bille with sorwfulle terys
that onethes ye shulle reede it.

As on Monday nexte after May Day there come tydynges to London
that on Thorsday before the Duke of Suffolk come unto the costes of 5
Kent, full nere Dower, with his .ii. shepes and a litel spynner; the qweche
spynner he sente with certeyn letters, be certeyn of his trustid men, unto
Caleys warde, to knowe howe he shuld be resceyved. And with hym mette
a shippe callyd *Nicolas of the Towre*, with othere shippis waytyng on hym,
and by hem that were yn the spyner the maister of the *Nicolas* hadde 10

37

knowlich of the Dukes comyng. And whanne he espyed the Dukes shepis, he sent forth his bote to wete what they were, and the Duke hym selfe spakke to hem and seyd he was be the kynges comaundement sent to Caleys ward, etc. And they seyd he moste speke with here master; and soo
15 he, with .ii. or .iii. of his men, wente forth wyth hem yn here bote to the *Nicolas*. And whanne he come, the mastere badde hym, 'Wolcom, traitour', as men sey; and forthere, the maister desyryd to wete yf the shepmen woldde holde with the Duke, and they sent word they wold not yn noo wyse; and soo he was yn the *Nicolas* tyl Saturday next folwyng. Soom sey he
20 wrotte moche thenke to be delyverd to the kenge, but that is not verily knowe. He hadde hes confessour with hym, etc. And some sey he was arreyned yn the sheppe, on here maner, upon the appechementes, and fonde gylty, etc. Also he asked the name of the sheppe, and whanne he knew it he remembred Stacy, that seid if he myght eschape the daunger of
25 the Towre he shuld be saffe; and thanne his herte faylyd hym, for he thowght he was dysseyvyd. And yn the syght of all his men he was drawyn ought of the grete shippe ynto the bote, and there was an exe and a stoke; and oon of the lewdeste of the shippe badde hym ley down hys hedde, and he shuld be faire ferd wyth, and dye on a swerd; and toke a rusty swerd,
30 and smotte of his hedde withyn halfe a doseyn strokes, and toke awey his gown of russette and his dobelette of velvet mayled, and leyde his body on the sondes of Dover. And some sey his hedde was sette oon a pole by it, and hes men sette on the londe be grette circumstaunce and preyere. And the shreve of Kent doth weche the body, and sent his undere shreve to the
35 juges to wete what to doo, and also to the kenge. Whatte shal be doo forthere I wotte notte, but thus fer is yt: yf the proces be erroneous, lete his concell reverse it, etc. Asse for alle your othere materes, they slepe; and the freere also, etc. . . .

F

HENRY VI RECOVERS FROM MADNESS

Edmund Clere to John Paston I (9 January 1455)

Right welbiloved cosyn, I recommaund me to you, latyng you wite such tidinges as we have. Blessid be God, the kyng is wel amendid, and hath ben syn Cristesmesday; and on Sent Jones day commaunded his awmener to ride to Caunterbury with his offryng, and commaunded the secretarie to
5 offre at Seint Edward. And on the Moneday after noon the queen come to him and brought my lord prynce with here; and then he askid what the princes name was, and the queen told him Edward; and than he hild up his handes and thankid God therof. And he seid he never knew him til that

tyme, nor wist not what was seid to him, nor wist not where he had be whils he hath be seke til now. And he askid who was godfaderes, and the 10 queen told him; and he was wel apaid. And she told him that the Cardinal was dede, and he seid he knew never therof til that tyme; and he seid oon of the wisist lordes in this land was dede. And my lord of Wynchestre and my lord of Seint Jones were with him on the morow after Twelftheday, and he spake to hem as well as ever he did; and when thei come out, thei wept 15 for joye. And he seith he is in charitee with all the world, and so he wold al the lordes were. And now he seith matyns of Oure Lady and evesong, and herith his masse devoutly; and Richard shal tell yow more tidinges by mouth. . . .

G

THE SPLENDOURS OF THE BURGUNDIAN COURT

John Paston III to Margaret Paston (8 July 1468)

Ryth reverend and worchepfull modyr, I recomand me onto you as humbylly as I can thynk, desyiryng most hertly to her of your welfare and hertys ese, whyche I pray God send yow as hastyly as eny hert can thynk. Ples yt yow to wet that at the makyng of thys byll my brodyr and I and all our felawshep wer in good helle, blyssyd be God. As for the gydyng her in 5 thys contré, it is as worchepfull as all the world can devyse it, and ther wer never Englyshe men had so good cher owt of Inglond that ever I herd of. As for tydyngys her, but if it be of the fest, I can non send yow, savyng that my Lady Margaret was maryd on Sonday last past at a towne that is callyd The Dame, .iii. myle owt of Brugys, at .v. of the clok in the mornyng. And 10 sche was browt the same day to Bruggys to hyr dener, and ther sche was receyvyd as worchepfully as all the world cowd devyse, as wyth presessyon wyth ladys and lordys best beseyn of eny pepyll that ever I sye or herd of. And many pagentys wer pleyid in hyr wey in Bryggys to hyr welcomyng, the best that ever I sye. And the same Sonday my lord the Bastard took 15 upon hym to answere .xxiiii. knytys and gentylmen wythin .viii. dayis at jostys of pese; and when that they wer answeryd they .xxiiii. and hym selve schold tornye wyth othyr .xxv. the next day aftyr, whyche is on Monday next comyng. And they that have jostyd wyth hym into thys day have ben as rychely beseyn, and hym selve also, as clothe of gold and sylk and sylvyr 20 and goldsmythys werk myght mak hem; for of syche ger, and gold and perle and stonys, they of the Dwkys coort, neythyr gentylmen nor gentylwomen, they want non; for wythowt that they have it by wyshys, by my trowthe I herd nevyr of so gret plenté as her is. Thys day my Lord Scalys justyd wyth a lord of thys contré, but nat wyth the Bastard, for they 25

mad promyse at London that non of them bothe shold never dele wyth
othyr in armys. But the Bastard was on of the lordys that browt the Lord
Scalys into the feld; and of mysfortwne an horse strake my lord Bastard on
the lege, and hathe hurt hym so sore that I can thynk he shal be of no power
30 to acomplyshe up hys armys, and that is gret peté, for by my trowthe I trow
God mad never a mor worchepfull knyt. And as for the Dwkys coort, as of
lordys, ladys, and gentylwomen, knytys, sqwyirs, and gentyllmen, I herd
never of non lyek to it save Kyng Artourys cort. By my trowthe, I have no
wyt nor remembrans to wryte to yow halfe the worchep that is her; but that
35 lakyth, as it comyth to mynd I shall tell yow when I come home, whyche I
tryst to God shal not be long to; for we depert owt of Brygys homward on
Twysday next comyng, and all folk that cam wyth my Lady of Burgoyn owt
of Inglond, exept syche as shal abyd her styll wyth her, whyche I wot well
shall be but fewe. We depert the soner, for the Dwk hathe word that the
40 Frenshe kyng is purposyd to mak wer upon hym hastyly, and that he is
wythin .iiii. or .v. dayis jorney of Brugys; and the Dwk rydythe on Twysday
next comyng forward to met wyth hym. God geve hym good sped, and all
hys, for by my trowthe they ar the goodlyest felawshep that ever I cam
among, and best can behave them, and most lyek gentyllmen. . . .

H

THE AFTERMATH OF THE BATTLE OF BARNET

John Paston II to Margaret Paston (18 April 1471)

Moodre, I recomande me to yow, letyng yow wette that, blyssed be God,
my brother John is a-lyffe and farethe well, and in no perell of dethe.
Neverthelesse he is hurt wyth an arow on hys ryght arme benethe the
elbow, and I have sent hym a sorjon, whyche hathe dressid hym, and he
5 tellythe me that he trustythe that he schall be all holl wythin ryght schort
tyme. It is so that John Mylsent is ded, God have mercy on hys sowle, and
Wylliam Mylsent is on lyffe, and hys othere servantys all be askapyd, by all
lyklihod. *Item*, as for me, I ame in good case, blyssyd be God, and in no
joparté off my lyff if me lyst my selffe, fore I am at my lyberté iff nede bee.
10 *Item*, my Lorde Archebysshop is in the Towre. Neverthelesse I trust to
God that he schall do well inoghe. He hathe a saffegarde for hym and me
bothe. Neverthelesse we have ben troblyd syns, but nowe I undrestande that
he hathe a pardon; and so we hope well. There was kyllyd uppon the felde,
halffe a myle from Bernett, on Esterne Daye, the Erle of Warwykk, the
15 Marqweys Montacu, Ser William Terell, Ser Lowes John, and dyverse
other esquierys off owre contré, Godmerston and Bothe. And on the Kyng

Edwardes partye, the Lord Cromwell, the Lorde Saye, Ser Omffrey
Bowghshere off owre contré, whyche is a sore moonyd man here, and
other pepyl off bothe partyes to the nombre off more then a .ml. As for
othere tythynges, it is undrestande here that the Qwyen Margrett is verrély   20
londyd, and hyre sone, in the west contré, and I trow that as tomorow ere
ellys the next daye the Kyng Edwarde wyll depart from hense to hyre-
warde to dryve her owt ageyn. *Item*, I beseche yow that I maye be
recomandyd to my cosyn Lomnore, and to thanke hym fore hys goode wyll
to me-wardes iff I had hadde nede, as I undrestoode by the berer heroff.   25
And I beseche yow on my behalve to advyse hym to be well ware off hys
delyng ore langage as yit, for the worlde, I ensure yow, is ryght qwesye, as
ye schall knowe wythin thys monythe. The peple heere feerythe it soore.
God hathe schewyd hymselffe marvelouslye, lyke hym that made all and
can undoo ageyn what hym lyst; and I kan thynke that by all lyklyod schall   30
schewe hymsylff as mervylous ageyn, and that in schort tyme, and as I
suppose offtere then onys in casis lyke. *Item*, it is soo that my brothere is
onpurveyed off monye. I have holpyn hym to my power and above,
wherffore, as it plesythe yow, remembre hym, for I kan not purveye for
myselffe in the same case. Wretyn at London the Thorysdaye in Esterne   35
weke. I hope hastely to see yow. All thys bylle most be secrett. Be ye nat
adoghtyd off the worlde, for I trust all schall be well. Iff it thusse
contenewe I ame not all undon, nere noon off us; and iff otherwyse, then,
etc.

I

A SON IN DIFFICULTIES

John Paston III to Margaret Paston (30 April 1471)

Aftyr humbyll and most dew recomendacyon, in as humbyll wyse as I can I
beseche yow of your blyssyng, preying God to reward yow wyth as myche
plesyer and hertys ease as I have latward causyd you to have trowbyll and
thowght. And, wyth Godys grace, it shall not be longe to or then my
wrongys and othyr menys shall be redressyd, for the world was nevyr so   5
lyek to be owyrs as it is now; werfor I prey yow let Lomnor no be to besy as
yet. Modyr, I beseche yow, and ye may spare eny money, that ye wyll do
your almesse on me and send me some in as hasty wyse as is possybyll, for
by my trowthe my lechecrafte and fesyk, and rewardys to them that have
kept me and condyt me to London, hathe cost me sythe Estern Day more   10
then .v. li. And now I have neythyr met, drynk, clothys, lechecraft, nor
money but upon borowyng, and I have asayid my frendys so ferre that they
begyn to fayle now in my gretest ned that evyr I was in. Also, modyr, I

beseche yow, and my horse that was at lechecraft at the Holt be not takyn
15 up for the kyngys hawkys, that he may be had hom and kept in your plase,
and not to go owght to watyr nor nowhedyr ellys, but that the gat be shet,
and he to be chasyd aftyr watyr wythin your plase, and that he have as
myche met as he may ete. I have hey inow of myn owne, and as for otys,
Dollys wyll purvey for hym, or who that dothe it I wyll paye. And I beseche
20 yow that he have every wek .iii. boshell of otys, and every day a penyworthe
of bred. . . .

 Item, that Mastress Broom send me hedyr .iii. longe gownys and .ii.
doblettys, and a jaket of plonket chamlett, and a morey bonet, owt of my
cofyr—Ser Jamys hathe the key—as I sent hyr word befor thys. Item, that
25 syche othyr wryghtyngys and stuff as was in my kasket be in your kepyng,
and that nobody look my wryghtyngys. Item, that the horse that Purdy
hathe of myne be put to some good gresse in hast.

 And if it plese yow to have knowlage of our royall person, I thank God I
am hole of my syknesse, and trust to be clene hole of all my hurttys wythin
30 a sevennyght at the ferthest, by wyche tym I trust to have othyr tydyngys.
And those tydyngys onys had, I tryst not to be longe owght of Norffolk,
wyth Godys grace, whom I beseche preserve you and your for my part.

 Wretyn the last day of Apryll. The berer herof can tell you tydyngys
syche as be trew for very serteyn.

35   Your humbylest servaunt, *J. of Gelston*

J

A VALENTINE

Margery Brews to John Paston III (February 1477)

Unto my ryght welbelovyd Voluntyn, John Paston, Squyer, be this bill
delyvered, etc.

Ryght reverent and wurschypfull and my ryght welebeloved Voluntyne, I
recommande me unto yowe full hertely, desyring to here of yowr welefare,
5 whech I beseche Almyghty God long for to preserve unto hys plesure and
yowr hertys desyre. And yf it please yowe to here of my welefare, I am not
in good heele of body ner of herte, nor schall be tyll I here from yowe:

> For ther wottys no creature what peyn that I endure,
> And for to be deede, I dare it not dyscure.

10 And my lady my moder hath labored the mater to my fadure full
delygently, but sche can no more gete then ye knowe of, for the whech
God knowyth I am full sory.

42

But yf that ye loffe me, as I tryste verély that ye do, ye will not leffe me therfor; for if that ye hade not halfe the lyvelode that ye hafe, for to do the grettyst labure that any woman on lyve myght, I wold not forsake yowe.   15

And yf ye commande me to kepe me true whereever I go,
iwyse I will do all my myght yowe to love and never no mo.
And yf my freendys say that I do amys, thei schal not me let so for to
do,
Myn herte me byddys ever more to love yowe   20
truly over all erthely thing.
And yf thei be never so wroth, I tryst it schall be bettur in tyme
commyng.

No more to yowe at this tyme, but the Holy Trinité hafe yowe in kepyng. And I besech yowe that this bill be not seyn of non erthely creature safe   25 only your selfe, etc. And thys lettur was indyte at Topcroft wyth full hevy herte, etc.

Be your own M.B.

K

A GOOD MATCH

Richard Cely to his brother George (13 May 1482)

Riught interly whelbelovyd brother, I recomende me harttely wnto yow, informing yow at the makyng of thys howr mother, brother, my godfather and the howsowlde ar in goode heyll, thankyd be the good Loorde. . . . I hawhe beyn in Cottyssowllde thys .iii. whekys, and packyd wyth Wylliam Mydwyntter .xxii. sarpellys and a poke, wherof be .iiii. mydyll. Wylliam   5 Bretten says hyt ys the fayreste wholl that he saw thys yeyr, and I packyd .iiii. sarpellys at Camden of the same bargen, wherof ar .ii. good, .ii. mydyll. . . . Syr, I whryte to yow a prosses: I pray God sende therof a good heynd. The same day that I come to Norlache, on a Sonday befor mattens frome Burforde, Wylliam Mydwyntter wyllcwmyd me, and in howr   10 comynycacyon he askyd me hefe I wher in any whay of maryayge. I towlde hyme nay, and he informeyd me that ther whos a yeunge genttyllwhoman hos father ys name ys Lemryke, and her mother ys deyd, and sche schawll dyspend be her moter .xl. li. a yer, as thay say in that contré, and her father ys the gretteste rewlar and rycheste mane in that contré, and ther hawhe   15 bene grete genttyllmen to se hyr and wholde hawhe hyr, etc. And hewyr matens wher done, Wylliam Mydwynter had mevyd thys mater to the gretteste mane abot the gentyllman Lemeryke, and he yeyd and informyd

the forsayd of aull the matter, and the yewng gentyllwomane bothe; and
20 the Sattyrday aftyr, Wylliam Mydwyntter whent to London, as aull wholl
getherars wher sent for be wryt be the mene of Pettyt, for inwynde and
grete markyng, and thay hawhe day to cwm agen at Myhellmas. When I
had packyd at Camden and Wylliam Mydwyntter departtyd, I came to
Norlache ageyn to make a nende of packyng, and on the Sonday nexte
25 aftyr, the same mane that Wylliam Mydwynter brake fyrste to cam to me
and telde me that he had brokyn to hys master acordyng as Mydwyntter
desyryde hym, and he sayd hys master whos ryght whell plessyde
therwhothe. And the same mane sayd to me hefe I whowllde tary May Day
I schulde hawhe a syte of the yewnge gentyllwhoman, and I sayd I wholld
30 tary wyth a good wyll, and the same day her father schuld a syttyn at
Norlache for the Kyng, byt he sente whon of hys clarkys and rod hymselfe
to Wynchecwme. And to mattens the same day come the yewnge
gentyllwhoman and her mother-i-law, and I and Wylliam Bretten wher
sayng mattens when thay com into chyrche, and when mattens vhos done
35 thay whente to a kynnyswhoman off the yewnge genttyllwhomane; and I
sent to them a pottell of whyte romnay, and thay toke hyt thankefully, for
thay had cwm a myle afote that mornyng; and when Mes whos done I
come and whellcwmyd them, and kyssyd them, and thay thankyd me for
the whyne, and prayd me to cwm to dyner wyth them, and I ascwysyd me
40 and thay made me promys them to drynke wyth them after dyner. And I
sent them to dyner a galon whyne and thay sent me a heronsew roste, and
aftyr dyner I com and dranke wyth them and toke Wylliam Bretten wyth
me, and whe had ryught gode comynecacyon, and the person plesetheyde
me whell as be the fyrst comynycacyon: sche ys yewnge, lytyll, and whery
45 whellfavyrd and whytty, and the contré spekys myche good bye hyr. Syr,
aull thys matter abydythe the cowmyng of her father to London, that whe
may wndyrstonde what some he wyll departe wyth, and how he lykys me.
He wyll be heyr wythin .iii. whekys. I pray send me a letter how ye thynke
be thys matter. . . .

L

REPAYMENT OVERDUE

Mawd Rose to Sir Robert Plumpton

Sir, after my dowté of comendations remembering, in my most harty
maner I recomend me unto you. Sir, I desire you to beare in remembrance
mony the which you caused to be borowed upon my husband and me; the
which money I dyverse tymes sent for, and ye have dyverse tymes

appoynted me to send for it; and when I send for it at your poyntment, you   5
brak day ever with me, whereby I canot get my money. Therfore I desire
you to send me word how I shal be answered of yt, by this bearer, for if I
may have it, I were loth to troble you. If you will not send me word how I
shall have yt, I wyll take my next remedy; that you shall well know, yt shal
be to your paine and they that borowed yt. No more at this tyme, but Jesu   10
preserve you to his pleasure. Written at Killinghall, by your loving and
frind,

Mawd Rose

M

RECOMMENDATION FOR A GOOD SERVANT

Edward Plumpton to Sir Robert Plumpton (3 January 1489/90)

After the most humble and due recommendation had, please yt your
mastership, that in the most humble lowly wyse I may be recomended unto
my singuler good ladies; praying you to have me excused in that I send no
wyld fole to you afore this tyme, for in all Lancashire cold none be had for
none money. The snaw and frost was so great, none was in the country,   5
but fled away to see; and that caused me that I sent not, as I promysed. Sir,
Robart, my servant, is a true servant to me, neverthelesse he is large to ryde
afore my male, and over weyghty for my horse; wherfore he hartely
desireth me to wryte to your mastership for him. He is a true man of
tongue and hands, and a kind and a good man. If yt please your mastership   10
to take him to your service, I besech you to be his good master, and the
better at the instaunce of my especyall prayer. Sir, I have given to him the
blacke horse that bar him from the feild; and if ther be any service that ye
will comand me, I am redy, and wil be to my lives end at your
comandement, all other lordship and mastership layd aparte. My lord   15
kepeth a great Cristinmas as ever was in this country, and is my especyall
good lord, as I trust in a short tyme your mastership shall know. My simple
bedfelow, your bede-woman and servant, in the most humble wyse
recomendeth hir unto your mastership, and to my ladys good ladyship, and
your servants; as knoweth Jesu, who preserve you. Wrytten at Lathum, the   20
.iii. day of January.

Your most humble servant, *Ed Plompton*
sectory to my lord Straung.

N

SEND HOUNDS AND A HART

Henry Northumberland to Sir Robert Plumpton

Right hartely beloved cosin, I comaund me unto you. And for as much as I am distetute of runyng hounds, I desire and pray you to send me a copple with my servant, this bringer. And of thing like I have fore your pleasure, it shal be redy. Written in my lodging at Spetell of the street, the .xxix. day of
5 October. Over this, Cousin, I pray you to send me your tame haert, for myne dere ar dead.

Your Cousin, Hen: Northumberland.

O

A DAUGHTER IN DIFFICULTIES

Dorothy Plumpton to Sir Robert Plumpton

Ryght worshipfull father, in the most humble manner that I can I recommend me to you, and to my lady my mother, and to all my brethren and sistren, whom I besech almyghtie God to mayntayne and preserve in prosperus health and encrese of worship, entyerly requiering you of your
5 daly blessing; letting you wyt that I send to you mesuage, be Wryghame of Knarsbrugh, of my mynd, and how that he should desire you in my name to send for me to come home to you, and as yet I had no answere agane, the which desire my lady hath gotten knowledg. Wherfore, she is to me more better lady then ever she was before, insomuch that she hath
10 promysed me hir good ladyship as long as ever she shall lyve; and if she or ye can fynd a thing meyter for me in this parties or any other, she will helpe to promoote me to the uttermost of her puyssaunce. Wherfore, I humbly besech you to be so good and kind father unto me as to let me know your pleasure, how that ye will have me ordred, as shortly as it shall like you.
15 And wryt to my lady, thanking hir good ladyship of hir so loving and tender kyndnesse shewed unto me, beseching hir ladyship of good contynewance therof. And therfore, I besech you to send a servant of yours to my lady and to me, and shew now by your fatherly kyndnesse that I am your child; for I have sent you dyverse mesuages and wryttings, and I had never
20 answere againe. Wherfore, yt is thought in this parties, by those persones that list better to say ill than good, that ye have litle favor unto me; the

which error ye may now quench, yf yt will like you to be so good and kynd
father unto me. Also I besech you to send me a fine hatt and some good
cloth to make me some kevercheffes. And thus I besech Jesu to have you in
his blessed keeping to his pleasure, and your harts desire and comforth. 25
Wryten at the Hirste, the .xvii. day of Maye.

By your loving daughter,
Dorythé Plompton.

3

THOMAS HOCCLEVE

HOCCLEVE (born c. 1368, died before 8 May 1426) worked for much of his life in the office of the Privy Seal. One direct result of this is that we have some very valuable autograph manuscript copies of his poems. The poems themselves, however, have been, until recently, poorly thought of, dismissed as lacking distinction and (echoing Hoccleve's own disclaimers) dull. But Hoccleve is a poet of talent, even if his talent shines fitfully and unevenly. He often writes with a directness and a freshness which are immediately engaging. He writes well about London, with its taverns and its boatmen, about his life at the Privy Seal (recording both the names of some of his 'fellawes' and the tribulations they shared: 'we stowpe and stare upon the shepes skyn'), and, most interestingly, about himself. He describes his misspent youth, his financial problems, and in what seem to be genuinely autobiographical passages, his mental breakdown and recovery. In this he is, of course, very unlike his master Chaucer. But though he is never a servile imitator, he did learn from Chaucer rather more than he modestly admits. There are some obvious echoes and, sometimes, a hint of Chaucer's wit and of his characteristic flickering changes of tone. Hoccleve's works include a number of occasional and religious poems, and a spirited version of Christine de Pisan's fervent defence of women, *L'Épistre de Cupide* (which was part of a topical literary argument in France concerning the *Roman de la Rose* and its attitude to love). In *La Male Règle de T. Hoccleve* (? 1405 or 1406) he gives us an account (sometimes wryly comical) of his early 'misrule' and its delights and woes. *The Regement of Princes* (written 1411–12 for the Prince of Wales, during the last years of Henry IV) seems to have been (if we can judge from the number of surviving manuscripts) the poem which was most popular in his own time. It is an example of a very common type, a 'mirror' for a prince. The advice it offers—the need for moral virtue and for the maintaining of order in the realm—is traditional enough, though certainly not without relevance in this period. The poem is not exactly gripping, but neither is it heavy or prolix. Most modern readers, however, will prefer its long introduction, Hoccleve's exchanges with an old man, where the poet's melancholy is felt deeply and where the sombre tone of the writing is sometimes very impressive. From a few years before Hoccleve's death comes an organized 'series' of works—his *Complaint* and his *Dialogue with a Friend* (which provide an autobiographical introduction to the rest), two moral stories from the *Gesta Romanorum*, and a work on 'learning to die'.

A

THE LETTER OF CUPID

Cupid Defends Women

Men beren eek the wommen upon honde,
That lightly, and withouten any peyne,
They wonne been; they can no wight withstonde,
That his disese list to hem conpleyne;
They been so freel, they mowe hem nat restreyne;   5
But whoso lykith may hem lightly have;
So been hire hertes esy in to grave.

To maistir John de Meun, as I suppose,
Than it was a lewde occupacioun
In makynge of *The Romance of the Rose*   10
So many a sly ymaginacioun
And perils for to rollen up and doun;
So long procees, so many a sly cautele,
For to deceyve a cely damoisele.

Nat can we seen ne in our wit conprehende   15
That art and peyne and sotiltee may faille
For to conquere, and soone make an ende,
Whan man a feeble place shal assaille,
And soone also to venquisshe a bataille,
Of which no wight dar make resistence,   20
Ne herte hath noon to stonden at deffense.

Than moot it folwen of necessitee,
Syn art askith so greet engyn and peyne
A woman to deceyve—what shee be—
Of constance they been nat so bareyne   25
As that some of tho sotil clerkes feyne;
But they been—as that wommen oghten be—
Sad, constaunt, and fulfillid of pitee.

How freendly was Medea to Jasoun,
In the conqueryng of the flees of gold!   30
How falsly quitte he hire affeccion,
By whom victorie he gat as he hath wold!
How may this man for shame be so bold

49

To falsen hire that from deeth and shame
35   Him kepte, and gat him so greet prys and name?

Of Troie also the traitour Eneas,
The feithlees man, how hath he him forswore
To Dydo, that queene of Cartage was,
That him releeved of his greeves sore?
40   What gentillesse mighte shee do more
Than shee, with herte unfeyned, to him kidde?
And what mescheef to hire of it betidde!

In our legende of martirs may men fynde,
Whoso that lykith therin forto rede,
45   That ooth noon ne byheeste may men bynde:
Of repreef ne of shame han they no drede;
In herte of man conceites trewe arn dede;
The soile is naght—ther may no trouthe growe:
To womman is hir vice nat unknowe.

50   Clerkes seyn also ther is no malice
Unto wommannes crabbid wikkidnesse.
O womman, how shalt thow thyself chevyce,
Syn men of thee so mochil harm witnesse?
Yee! strah! do foorth! take noon hevynesse!
55   Keepe thyn owne, what men clappe or crake,
And some of hem shuln smerte, I undirtake.

Malice of wommen what is it to drede?
They slee no men, destroien no citees;
They nat oppressen folk ne overlede;
60   Betraye empyres, remes ne duchees;
Ne men byreve hir landes ne hir mees,
Folk enpoysone, or howses sette on fyre,
Ne fals contractes maken for noon hyre.

Trust, parfyt love, and enteer charitee,
65   Fervent wil, and entalentid corage
To thewes goode, as it sit wel to be,
Han wommen ay of custume and usage;
And wel they can a mannes ire asswage
With softe wordes, discreet and benigne;
70   What they been inward, shewith owtward signe.

B

Balade and Roundel to Master Somer

The Sonne, with his bemes of brightnesse,
To man so kyndly is, and norisshynge,
That lakkyng it day nere but dirknesse:
To day he yeveth his enlumynynge,
And causith al fruyt for to wexe and sprynge.   5
Now, syn that sonne may so moche availle,
And moost with Somer is his sojournynge,
That sesoun bounteuous we wole assaille.

Glad cheerid Somer, to your governaille
And grace we submitte al our willynge!   10
To whom yee freendly been he may nat faille
But he shal have his resonable axynge.
Aftir your good lust, be the sesonynge
Of our fruytes this laste Mighelmesse,
The tyme of yeer was of our seed ynnynge,   15
The lak of which is our greet hevynesse.

We truste upon your freendly gentillesse,
Yee wole us helpe and been our suppoaille.
Now yeve us cause ageyn this Cristemesse
For to be glad. O lord, whethir our taille   20
Shal soone make us with our shippes saille
To port salut? If yow list we may synge;
And elles moot us bothe mourne and waille,
Til your favour us sende releevynge.

We, your servantes, Hoccleve and Baillay,   25
Hethe and Offorde, yow byseeche and preye:
'Haastith our hervest, as soone as yee may!'
For fere of stormes our wit is aweye
Were our seed inned wel we mighten pleye,
And us desporte and synge and make game.   30
And yit this rowndel shul we synge and seye
In trust of yow and honour of your name:

Somer, that rypest mannes sustenance
With holsum hete of the Sonnes warmnesse,
Al kynde of man thee holden is to blesse!   35

Ay thankid be thy freendly governance,
And thy fressh look of mirthe and of gladnesse!
    Somer, that rypest mannes sustenance
    With holsum hete of the Sonnes warmnesse,
40   Al kynde of man thee holden is to blesse!

To hevy folk of thee the remembraunce
Is salve and oynement to hir seeknesse,
Forwhy we thus shul synge in Cristemesse,
    Somer, that rypest mannes sustenance
45   With holsum hete of the Sonnes warmnesse,
    Al kynde of man thee holden is to blesse!

C

THE REGEMENT OF PRINCES

Hoccleve meets an old Beggar

. . . Thus ylke nyght I walwyd to and fro,
Sekyng Reste; but, certeynly, sche
Appeeryd nought, for Thoght, my cruel fo,
Chaced hadde hyre and sleepe away fro me;
5   And for I scholde not alone be,
Ageyn my lust, Wach profrid hys servyse,
And I admyttyd hym in hevy wyse.

So long a nyght ne felte I never non
As was that same to my jugement.
10 Whoso that thoughty ys, ys wobegon;
The thoughtful wyght ys vessel of turment;
Ther nys no gref to hym equypolent.
He graveth deppest of seekenesse alle;
Ful wo ys hym that in swyche thought ys falle.

15 What whyght that inly pensyf is, I trowe,
Hys most desyre ys to be solytarie.
That thys is soth in my persone I knowe,
For evere whyl that fretynge adversarie
Myn herte made to hym trybutarie,
20 In sowkynge of the fresschest of my blood,
To sorwe soule me thoughte yt dede me good.

For the nature of hevynesse ys thys:
If yt habunde gretly in a wyht,
The place eischewyt he whereas joye ys,
For joye and he not mow acorde aryght;   25
As discordant as day ys unto nyght,
And honure adversarie is unto schame,
Is hevynes so to joye and game.

Whan to the thoughtful wyght ys tolde a tale,
He herit yt as though he thennes were;   30
Hys hevy thoghtys hym so plukke and hale
Hydyr and thyder, and hym greve and dere,
That hys eres avayle hym nat a pere;
He understondeth nothyng what men seye,
So ben hys wyttys fer gon hem to pleye.   35

The smert of Thought I by experience
Knowe as wel as any man doth lyvynge;
Hys frosty swoot and fyry hote fervence,
And troubly dremes, drempt al in wakynge,
My mazyd hed sleplees han of konnyng   40
And wyt despoylyd, and so me bejapyd,
That after deth ful often have I gapyd.

Passe over whanne thys stormy nyght was gon,
And day gan at my wyndowe in to prye,
I roos me up, for boote fonde I non   45
In myn unresty bed lengere to lye;
Into the felde I dressed me an hye,
And yn my woo y herte-depe gan wade,
As he that was bareyn of thoughtes glade.

By that I walkyd hadde a certeyne tyme   50
(Were yt an oure, y not, or more or lesse)
A pore old hore man cam walkyng by me
And seyde, 'Good day, syre, and God yow blesse!'
But I no word; for my seekly distresse
Forbad myn eres usen hyre offyce,   55
For whyche thys old man helde me lewed and nyce,

Tyl he took hede to my dreré chere,
And to my deedly colour pale and wan.
Thanne thought he thus, 'Thys man that I se here,
Al wrong ys wrestyd, by owght I se can.'   60

53

He sterte unto me, and seyde, 'Sleepstow, man?
Awake!' and gan me schake wonder faste.
And with a sygh I answeered atte laste,

'A! who ys there?' 'I', quod thys olde greye,
65 'Am here,' and he me tolde the maner
How he spake to me, as ye herd me seye;
'O man,' quoth I, 'fore Cristis love dere,
If that thou wolt ought don at my preyere,
As go thi way; talke to me no more.
70 Thy wordes al anoyen me ful sore.

'Voyde fro me—me lyst no compaygnye!
Encresse nought my gref; I have inow!'
'My sone, hast thou good lust thy sorwe drye,
And mayst releved be? what man art thou?
75 Wyrke after me; yt schal be for thy prow.
Thou nard but yong, and hast but lytel seen,
And ful seelde ys that yonge folk wyse ben.

'If that the lyke to ben esyd wel,
As suffre me wyth the talke a whyle.
80 Art thou ought lettred?' 'Ye,' quod I, 'sum del.'
'Blesyd be God! Than hope I, by Synt Gyle,
That God to the thy wyt schal reconsyle,
Whyche that me thynketh ys fer fro the went
Thorgh the assent of thy grevouse tourment.

85 'Lettred folk han gretter discrecion,
And bet conceyve konne a mannes sawe,
And rather wol aplye to reson
And from folye sonner hem withdraw,
Than he that nother can reson ne lawe,
90 Ne lerned hath no maner of lettrure.
Plukke up thyn herte! I hope I schal the cure.'

'Cure, good man? Ye, thow art a fayre leche!
Cure thyself, that tremblest as thow gost,
For al thyn arte wol enden in thi speche.
95 It lyth not in thi powere, pore gost,
To hele me; thow art as seke almost
As I. First on thyself kythe thyn art,
And yf ought leve, let me thanne have part. . . .'

54

Lament for Chaucer

. . . Symple is my goost and scars my letterure
Unto your excellence for to write   100
Myn inward love. And yit in aventure
Wil I me putte, thogh I can but lyte.
My dere mayster—God ys soule quyte!—
And fadir, Chaucer, fayn wolde han me taght;
But I was dul, and lerned lyte or naght.   105

Alas! my worthy mayster honorable,
Thys landes verray tresouur and rychesse,
Deth, by thy deth, hath harme irriparable
Unto us don; hir vengeable duresse
Despoyled hath this land of the swetnesse   110
Of rethorik; for unto Tullius
Was nere man so lyk amonges us.

Also, who was hier in philosophye
To Aristotle, in our tonge but thou?
The steppes of Virgile in poesie   115
Thow filwedist eek, men wot wel inow.
That combre-world that thee, my mayster, slow—
Wolde I slayn were!—deth, was to hastyf
·To renne on the, and reve the thi lyf.

Deth hath but smal consideracion   120
Unto the vertuous, I have espyed,
No more, as schewyth the probacion,
Than to a vycyous mayster losel tried.
Among an heep, every man ys maystried
Wyth here, as wel the poore as ys the ryche;   125
Leered and lewde eek standen al iliche.

Sche myghtte han taried hir vengeance a while
Til that sum man had egal to the be.
Nay, let be that! She knew wel that thys yle
May nevere man forth brenge lyk to the,   130
And hyre office nedes do moot sche;
God bad hire soo, I truste as for thi beste
O maister, maister, God thy soule reste!

D

THE COMPLAINT

Hoccleve Remembers his Madness

Aftir that hervest inned had hise sheves,
And that the broun sesoun of Myhelmesse
Was come, and gan the trees robbe of her leves
That grene had ben and in lusty freisshenesse,
And hem into colour of yelownesse
Had died, and doun throwen undir foote,
That chaunge sanke into myn herte-roote.

For freisshly broughte it to my remembraunce,
That stablenesse in this worlde is ther noon.
Ther is no thing but chaunge and variaunce.
Howe welthi a man be, or wel begoon,
Endure it shal not—he shal it forgoon.
Deeth undir foote shal him thriste adoun;
That is every wightes conclucioun.

Wiche for to weyve is in no mannes myght,
Howe riche he be, stronge, lusty, freissh, and gay.
And in the ende of Novembre, uppon a night,
Sighynge sore as I in my bed lay
For this and othir thoughtis wiche many a day
Byforne I tooke, sleep cam noon in myn ye,
So vexid me the thoughtful maladie.

I sy wel, sithin I with siknesse last
Was scourgid, cloudy hath bene the favour
That shoon on me ful bright in times past.
The sunne abated, and the dirke shour
Hilded doun right on me, and in langour
Me made swymme, so that my spirite
To lyve no lust had, ne no delite. . . .

*   *   *   *   *

. . . Men seiden, I loked as a wilde steer,
And so my looke aboute I gan to throwe.
Min heed to hie anothir seide I beer:
'Ful bukkissh is his brayn, wel may I trowe!'

56

And seyde the thridde—and apt is in the rowe
To site of hem that a resounles reed
Can geve—'No sadnesse is in his heed.'   35

Chaunged had I my pas, somme seiden eke,
For here and there forthe stirte I as a roo,
Noon abood, noon areest, but al brain-seke;
Another spake and of me seide also,
My feet weren ay wavynge to and fro   40
Whanne that I stonde shulde and with men talke,
And that myn yen soughten every halke.

I leide an ere ay to, as I by wente,
And herde al, and thus in myn herte I caste:
'Of longe abidinge here I may me repente;   45
Lest that of hastinesse I at the laste
Answere amys, beste is hens hie faste;
For if I in this prees amys me gye,
To harme wole it me turne and to folie.'

And this I demed wel, and knewe wel eke,   50
Whatso that evere I shulde answere or seie,
They wolden not han holde it worth a leke;
Forwhy, as I had lost my tunges keie,
Kepte I me cloos, and trussid me my weie,
Droupinge and hevy, and all woo-bistad;   55
Smal cause had I, me thoughte, to be glad.

My spirites labouriden evere ful bisily
To peinte countenaunce, chere, and look,
For that men spake of me so wondringly,
And for the verry shame and feer I qwook.   60
Though myn herte hadde be dippid in the brook,
It weet and moist was ynow of my swoot,
Wiche was nowe frosty colde, nowe firy hoot.

And in my chaumbre at home whanne that I was,
Mysilfe aloone, I in this wise wrought: 65
I streite unto my mirrour and my glas,
To loke howe that me of my chere thought,
If any othir were it than it ought;
For fain wolde I, if it not had bene right,
Amendid it to my kunnynge and myght.   70

57

Many a saute made I to this mirrour,
Thinking, 'If that I looke in this manere
Amonge folke as I nowe do, noon errour
Of suspecte look may in my face appere;
75   This countinaunce, I am sure, and this chere
If I it forthe use, is nothing reprevable
To hem that han conceitis resonable.'

And therwithal I thoughte thus anoon:
'Men in her owne cas bene blinde alday,
80   As I have herde seie manie a day agoon,
And in that same plite I stonde may;
Howe shal I do? Wiche is the beste way
My troublid spirit forto bringe in rest?
If I wiste howe, fain wolde I do the best.'

85   Sithen I recovered was, have I ful ofte
Cause had of anger and inpacience,
Where I borne have it esily and softe,
Suffringe wronge be done to me and offence,
And not answerid ayen but kepte scilence,
90   Leste that men of me deme wolde and sein,
'Se howe this man is fallen in ayein' . . .

4

JOHN LYDGATE

LYDGATE (c.1370–1449/50) became a monk (c.1385) at the powerful Benedictine monastery of Bury St Edmunds, Suffolk. His life took him outside the cloister: he seems to have spent two periods of study at Oxford, and his patrons include the King, princes, noblemen and their wives, and rich merchants. Lydgate was a prolific writer—he produced three times as much as Chaucer, the poet whom he most admired and imitated. All the evidence shows that throughout the fifteenth and much of the sixteenth century his poetry was esteemed (his name is regularly linked with those of Chaucer and Gower), and was deeply influential in both England and Scotland, but of all the writers of this period his is the reputation which has suffered the sharpest decline. There is no doubt that Lydgate's long poems can be excessively long (*The Fall of Princes* runs to c.36,000 lines), or that some of his writing is dull and prolix, or that, compared with Chaucer, he is undemanding and lacks subtlety and complexity. It is hard to believe that his contemporary reputation can ever be restored, but though he is not 'original', he is more than simply 'typical of his time'. He has a constant, if not always discriminating, interest in style, which shows itself in a search for eloquence and copiousness of diction, or in experiments with learned 'aureate' words. Sometimes in his rhetorical passages, especially those on his favourite topic of the mutability of worldly things, he can achieve an impressively melancholy sonorousness. And he can write 'felyngly' in moments of pathos, as our extract from the story of Canace shows. There is here a touch of what his eighteenth-century admirer, Thomas Gray, called 'a stiller kind of majesty'. The encyclopaedic range of his work makes it extremely difficult to give a fair representation of it in a short space. Most obviously attractive are his short occasional verses. These are represented here by his elegant poem to Thomas Chaucer, the poet's son. Lydgate's religious poems range from the vast *Life of Our Lady* through saints' lives (of, for instance, St Edmund, King of East Anglia) to simple prayers and the more ambitious, much-anthologized *A Midsummer Rose*. Our extracts from his translation of the Paris *Dance of Death* which was painted at St Paul's will give a taste of that grim monument of the macabre tradition. Space has not allowed the inclusion of examples from his *Temple of Glass* or from the very influential *Troy Book*, which, as John Norton-Smith says, conveyed to 'the Elizabethans (not least to Shakespeare) that complex sense of Troy's perfection which came to symbolize the ·acme of civilization and its tragic vulnerability'. Lydgate's concern with discord and internal strife (as he says— perhaps thinking of the 'untrouthe of England'?—in the *Troy Book*, 'Lo, what meschef lyth in variaunce ǀ Amonge lordis, when thei nat accorde') emerges very clearly in his little-known prose tract *The Serpent of Division*, on the civil war in Rome. To one of the sixteenth-century editions of this was 'annexed the tragedye of Gorboduc', which deals with the horrors of division in Britain. Another

JOHN LYDGATE

sixteenth-century work, *The Mirror for Magistrates*, is in a direct line of descent from *The Fall of Princes* (Lydgate's adaptation of Laurent de Premierfait's version of Boccaccio's *De Casibus Virorum Illustrium*), where yet again the theme of discord is prominent. It contains some fine narrative and lyrical passages, and has an earnestly moral view of Fortune and history. It is a sort of 'mirror for princes', praising order, justice, peace, and the positive value of a ruler's 'virtue'. There is no evidence that Lydgate was touched by the new humanism of Italy, but his evident enthusiasm for the stories of antiquity may perhaps allow us to place him in a wider, older stream of medieval humanism. Lydgate can be tiresome, but at his best there is something in this grave and learned monk which demands respect.

A

On the Departing of Thomas Chaucer

O thow Lucyna, qwene and empyresse
Of waters alle and of floodes rage,
And cleped art lady and goddesse
Of jorneying and fortunate passage,
5   Governe and guye by grace the viage,
Thow hevenly qweene, sith I of herte prey,
My maystre Chaucyer goodely to convey,

Him to expleyten and firtherne on his way
With holsome spede, ay in his journee.
10   And Neptunus, make eke now no delaye
Hym to favour whane he is on the see,
Preserving him frome al adversytee,
Frome al trouble of wynde and eke of wawe:
And lat thy grace so to him adawe

15   That wher to hym may bee the moost plesaunce,
Ther make him lande, he and his meynee.
And God I prey, the whyle he is in France,
To sende him helthe and prosparytee,
Hasty repayre hoom to his cuntree
20   To recomfort ther with this presence
Folkys that mowrne moost for his absence.

For sothely now th'agreable sonne
Of housholding and fulsum haboundaunce
Eclipsid is, as men recorden konne
25   That founden ther so ryche souffisaunce,
Fredam, bountee with gode governaunce,

60

Disport, largesse, joye and al gladnesse,
And passingly good chere with gentylesse.

Ceres also, godesse of welfare,
Was ay present, hir chaare with plentee lade: 30
And Bacus ther ne koude never spare
With his lycour hertes for to glade,
Refresshe folkis that were of colour fade.
Wher his conduyts moost plentyuous habounde
The wellis hed so fulsome ay is founde.   35

His moost joye is innly gret repayre
Of gentilmen of heghe and lowe estate,
That him thenketh, both in foule and fayre,
Withouten hem he is but desolate:
And to be loved the moost fortunate   40
That ever I knewe, with othe of sothefastnesse,
Of ryche and pore, for bounteuouse largesse.

And gentyl Molyns, myn owen lord so der,
Lytel merveyle thoughe thow sighe and pleyne:
Now to forgone thin owen pleying-feere,   45
I wot right wel hit is to the gret peyne.
But have good hope soon for to atteyne
Thin hertis blisse agayne, and that right sone,
Or foure tymes chaunged be the mone.

Lat be your weping, tendre creature,   50
By my sainte Eleyne fer away in Ynde.
How shoule ye the gret woo endure
Of his absence, that been so truwe and kynde?
Have him amonge enprynted in your mynde,
And seythe for him, shortly in a clause,   55
'Goddes soule' to hem that been in cause.

Ye gentilmen dwelling envyroun,
His absence eke ye aught to compleyne,
For farwell now, as in conclusyoun,
Your pleye, your joye, yif I shal not feyne;   60
Farwel huntyng and hawkyng bothe tweyne,
And farewel now cheef cause of your desport,
For he absent, farewel your recomfort.

Late him not nowe out of remembraunce
65   But ever amonge have him in memorye.
And for his saake, as in your dalyaunce,
Saythe every day devotely this memorye:
'Saint Julyan, oure joye and al our glorye,
Come hoome ageyne, lyche as we desyre,
70   To suppowaylen al the hole shyre.'

And for my part, I sey right as I think,
I am pure sory, and hevy is myn hert
More than I expresse can wryte with ink,
The want of him so sore dothe me smert.
75   But for al that, hit shal me nought astert
Daye and night, with herte debonayre,
To prey to God that he soon may repayre.

B

THE SERPENT OF DIVISION

Julius Caesar Crosses the Rubicon

. . . Julius platly enformed of the malicious conspiracie compassid and
wrowght ayens him, anone as in his repeire owte of Albion that he was
passid the bowndes of Almaigne and had atteynd the high Alpies, whiche
bene of autours callid the colde frosty hillis, and the bowndis of
5   Lumbardye, and so holdynge his passage bi the parties of Assoine lyne-
right till he aprochid the rage flode and the sturdy ryvere called of Lucan
Rubicanis, there aperid unto him an olde auncien lady, triste and drery, in
a mantell of blake, wympled hir face toforne in full dolerous wise, the
tresses of her hedde for age full hore and white. And for constreynte of her
10   hertely wo even upon the tyme whan the blake derke nyghte had
oversprad the emysperye with the bordour of her owgly and her clowdie
cope, this wofull ladye toforeseide bigan hir lamentable compleynt to
Julius in this wise: 'O ye noble and worthi knyghtis moste renomed of
fame, alas! whedir purpose ye with soo myghti apparaile of Mars to
15   procede, or where caste ye to ficche youre sturdy standartis or to displey
your dredefull penouns and baners? O alas! ageyns whome have ye caste
finally to execute the mortale hate that brennyth in yowre herte, or ageyne
whome purpose ye in so cruell wise to preve yowre myght. Remembrith in
your thowght that ye bene withholde with the Senat of Rome, and
20   yowreselfe accompted as for noble and full worthi knyghtes of the cité; and
schewe not now yowreselfe enemyes to the empire bi whos worthynes

62

aforetyme hit hathe be sustened and myghtily suppowailled ageyns the assautes of all here foon. O alas! advertith and considerith in youre herte the noble and the prudente statutes of the polecie of Rome, the whiche full pleynely expresse that hit is lefull to no man armed to pas the bondis of this 25 streme but yif he be mortall enmy and rebell to Rome. Alas! ye that have be so longe frendis and so manly mayntened the honour of the cité, withdrawe youre foote and hastith not to faste, but lete good deliberacion restreyne youre reynes, that hasti wilfulnes lede yow not to confusion not onely of youreselfe but into the originall ruyne of the cité bi the 30 habowndawnt schedynge of blod that is likely to sewe.' And sodeynely whan this ladye had brefely expressid the somme of hir sentence, withowte more abode sche disapered.

 This manly man and this fortunate knyght Julius, in partie disamaied of this unkouth apparence, restreyned his oste, and made hem to picche here 35 tentis endelonge the stronde upon the hyndere parties of the ryver; and in his unkouth afraye he sodeynely abreide in this wise: 'O thou myghti Jubiter, undir whos demeyne Wlcanus forgith the dredefull sownes of the thondir and causeth hertis to agrise with the fire levene, and O ye goddes and goddesses that whilom hadde the governance of oure worthi 40 awncestres in Troye, and ye noble goddes Remus and Romulus, the famous fowndours and the myghti protectours and patrons of the cité of Rome, I as an humble soget to yowre deitee full lowly beseche and requyre yow of equité and right to be wellwillid and favourable to promote my trewe querell and cause, and benygngly of your bownteuous goodnesse to 45 favowren and fortune the high emprise, the whiche of juste title I purpose fynallye, for life or dethe, thorowghe your favowre to execute. And not as enemy nor rebell to Rome but as a trewe citesyn and a previd knyght I caste me fully to persevere, with condicion that liche as I have manly deservid I may be resceived, makynge a protestacion that not as enemy but 50 as ful frende and soget to Rome I woll be fownde stedefaste and trewe. Wherefore, ye myghti and ye noble Senatowrs of Rome, I requere yow of right, that ye nothynge arrette nor ascrive to my gilte that I come with stronge and myghti honde, that I entre the bondis of yowre imperiall fraunchise, makynge a full protestacioun that onely with a clene 55 concience and entrikid with none entente of ivell menynge that I come to yow, of full purpose to be resceived as for youre frende and not youre foo, requirynge yow also to holdyn him, whatesoever he be, full enmy to your noble cité, that of wille and entente labowrith to make discorde atwene us tweyne, for so that my meritorie gerdon whiche that I have in my 60 conqueste justely deservid be not denyed me, I am and ever will bene for life or dethe a trewe knyght to the cité to my livis ende.'

 And forthewith, makynge no delay, liche a lion not dismaied nor aferde, firste of all in his owne persone passed the ryver, the whiche ryver, liche as Lucan remembrith, thilke same tyme at the comynge of Cesar ageyne his 65

custumable cours was reised on heighte into a grete flode, and all the white snowes of the Alpyes were resolved with the bemes of Phebus, wherethorowe the rivers in the valis were reised so high that unnethe eny man myght passe over. But Julius, of none unkowthe aventures afraied, but
70 liche a manly man full well assured in hymselfe in the presence of all his worthie knyghtis, seide in this wise: 'Here I leve behynde all the olde consideracions made betwixte Rome and me, and here I leve all the frendschip of olde antiquité and onely folowe the tracis of Fortune, and of hole entente I begyn a rightfull werre, for cause onely that bi mediacion of
75 pees proferid on my side I may not atteyne my title of right!'

And anon withowte more dilacioun, evene upon the sprynge of the day whiche of clerkis is callid Aurora, he unwarely with all the worthye multitude of his knyghtis enterid into the cité of Lucan callid Arymynum, a cité pertynente to Rome, and ther he toke first possession of the empire,
80 none so hardie to resiste nor to withstonde the furie of his swerde. And all this while the Romeyns stondynge in dowte to whiche partie thei schulde enclyne, other the partie of Cesar or of Pompey, for of chierté that thei had to here wivis and here childeryn and to the olde statutes of the cité thei were favowrable to Pompey, and of drede thei had of Cesaris swerde, thei
85 stode in so grete ambiguité that thei cowde not deme whate was beste to do. Lo, how the mortale envie of tweyne was cause and occasion that thilke noble worthi cité, whiche had all the worlde in subjeccion and was callid ladye and emperes of all regions, was browght unto destruccioun. For in this ilke two firste began the devision which never aftir myghte perfitely be
90 restorid nor reconsilid to unyté, whereby as semyth unto men that all prudent prynces whiche have governaunce in provynces and regions schulde take ensample whate harme and damage is and how finall a destruccion is to bene devyded amonge hemselfe.

C

THE FALL OF PRINCES

The Letter of Compleynt of Canace

Out of hir swouh whan she did abraide,
Knowyng no mene but deth in hir distresse,
To hir brother ful pitousli she saide:
'Cause off my sorwe! Roote of myn hevynesse!
5   That whilom were cheeff sours off my gladnesse,
Whan bothe our joies be will were so dysposid
Undir o keie our hertis to be enclosid.

'Whilom thou were support and sekirnesse,
Cheeff rejoisshyng off my wordli plesaunce,
But now thou art the ground off my siknesse,   10
Welle off wanhope off my dedli penaunce,
Which have off sorwe grettest habundaunce
That ever yit hadde any creature
Which mut for love the deth—alas!—endure.

'Thow were whilom my blisse and al my trust,   15
Sovereyn confort my sorwes to appese,
Spryng and well off al myn hertis lust,
And now—alas!—cheeff roote off my disese.
But yiff my deth myht do the any ese,
O brother myn, in remembraunce off tweyne,   20
Deth shal to me be plesaunce and no peyne!

'Mi cruel fader, most onmerciable,
Ordeyned hath—it nedis mut be soo:
In his rigour he is so ontretable,
Al merciles he will that it be doo—   25
That we algate shal deie bothe too.
But I am glad—sithe it may been noon othir—
Thow art escapid, my best beloved brother.

'This is myn ende—I may it nat asterte—
O brother myn, there is nomor to seye,   30
Lowli besechyng with al myn hool herte
For to remembre, speciali I preie,
Yiff it befall my litil sone deie,
That thou maist afftir sum mynde upon us have:
Suffre us bothe be buried in o grave!   35

'I holde hym streihtli atwen myn armys tweyne.
Thow and Nature leide on me this charge—
He, giltles, with me mut suffre peyne—
And sithe thou art at fredam and at large,
Lat kyndnesse our love nat so discharge,   40
But have a mynde, whereever that thou be,
Onys a day upon my child and me.

'On the and me dependith the trespace
Touchyng our gilt and our gret offence,
But—wellaway!—most angelik off face,   45

Our yonge child in his pur innocence
Shal, ageyn riht, suffre dethis violence,
Tendre off lymes—God wot ful giltles—
The goodli faire, that lith heere specheles.

50   'A mouth he hath, but woordis hath he noone,
Can nat compleyne—alas!—for non outrage,
Nor grucchith nat, but lyth heer al aloone,
Stille as a lamb, most meek of his visage.
What herte off steel coude doon to hym damage,
55   Or suffre hym deie, beholdyng the maneer
And look benygne off his tweyne eyen cleer.

'O thou my fader! To cruel is thi wreche,
Hardere off herte than tigre or leoun
To slen a child that lith withoute speche,
60   Void of al mercy and remissioun,
And on his mooder hast no compassioun,
His youthe considred, with lippis softe as silk
Which at my brest lith still and souketh mylk.

'Is any sorwe remembrid be writyng
65   Onto my sorweful sihhes comparable?
Or was ther ever creature lyvyng
That felte off dool a thyng mor lamentable?
For counfortles and onrecuperable
Ar thilke hepid sorwes ful off rage,
70   Which han with wo oppressid my corage.

'Rekne all myschevys in especiall,
And on my myscheeff remembre and ha good mynde!
Mi lord my fadir is myn enmy mortall—
Experience inouh theroff I fynde,
75   For in his pursuit he hath lefft behynde
In destruccioun off the, my child, and me
Routhe and al mercy, and fadirli pité;

'And the, my brother, avoidid from his siht,
Which in no wise his grace maist atteyne.
80   Alas, that rigour, vengaunce and cruel riht
Sholde above merci be lady sovereyne!
But cruelté doth at me so disdeyne
That thou, my brother, my child, and also I
Shal deie exiled—alas—from al mercy.

'Mi fader whilom, be many sundri signe,   85
Was my socour, my supportacioun,
To the and me most gracieux and benygne,
Our wordli gladnesse, our consolacioun,
But love and Fortune ha turned up-so-don
Our grace—alas!—our welfare and our fame   90
Hard to recure, so sclaundrid is our name.

'Spot of diffamyng is hard to wasshe away,
When noise and rumour abrod do folk manace,
To hyndre a man ther may be no delay,
For hatful fame fleeth fere in ful short space—   95
But off us tweyne ther is noon othir grace,
Sauff onli deth, and afftir deth—alas!—
Eternal sclaundre; off us thus stant the cas.

'Whom shal we blame, or whom shal we atwite
Our gret offence, sithe we may it nat hide,   100
For our excus reportis to respite?
Mene is ther noon, except the god Cupide,
And thouh that he wolde for us provide
In this mateer to been our cheef refuge,
Poetis seyn he is blynd to been a juge.   105

'He is depeynt lich a blynd archer,
To marke ariht failyng discretioun,
Holdyng no meseur nouther ferre nor neer,
But lik Fortunys disposicioun,
Al upon happ, void of al resoun,   110
As a blynd archer with arwes sharpe grounde
Off aventure yeveth many a mortal wounde.

'At the and me he wrongli dede marke,
Felli to hyndre our fatal aventures,
As ferre as Phebus shynyth in his arke   115
To make us refus to alle creatures,
Callid us tweyne onto the woful lures
Off diffame, which will departe nevere,
Be newe report the noise encresyng evere.

'Odious fame with swiffte wengis fleeth,   120
But al good fame envie doth restreyne;
Ech man off other the diffautis seeth,
Yit on his owne no man wil compleyne.

But al the world outcryeth on us tweyne,
Whos hatful ire by us may nat be queemyd,
For I mut deie—my fader hath so deemyd.

'Now farwel, brother! To me it doth suffise
To deie allone, for our bothe sake,
And in my moste feithful, humble wise
Onto my deth-ward, thouh I tremble and quake,
Off the for evere now my leve I take—
And onys a yeer forget nat, but take heed
Mi fatal day this lettre for to reed.

'So shaltow han on me sum remembraunce,
Mi name enprentid in thi kalendere,
Bi rehersaile of my dedli grevaunce
Were blak that day, and mak a doolful cheere:
And whan thow comest, and shalt approche neere
My sepulture, I pray the nat disdeyne
Upon my grave summe teris for to reyne.'

Writyng hire lettir, awappid and in dreede,
In hir riht hand hir penne gan to quake,
And a sharp suerd, to make hir herte bleede,
In hir lefft hand hir fader hath hire take,
And most hire sorwe was for hire childes sake,
Upon whos face in hir barm slepyng
Ful many a teer she wepte in compleynyng.

Afftir al this, so as she stood and quook,
Hir child beholdyng, myd off hire peynes smerte
Withoute abood the sharpe suerd she took,
And rooff hirselff evene to the herte.
Hir child fill doun, which myht nat asterte,
Havyng non helpe to socoure hym nor save,
But in hir blood the silff began to bathe. . . .

JOHN LYDGATE

D

The Dance of Death

Deeth to the Emperour:

'Sir Emperour, lorde of al the ground,
Soverein prince, and hiest of noblesse,
Ye must forsake of golde your appil round,
Septre and swerd, and al youre hy prowesse;
Behinde leve your tresour and ricchesse,   5
And with othir to my daunce obeie.
Ayein my myght is worth noon hardinesse—
Adamis children alle thei moste deie.'

The Emperour answerith:

'I note to whom that I may apele,
Touching deth, wiche doth me so constreine.   10
There is no gein to helpe my querele,
But spade and pikois my grave to ateyne,
A simple shete—ther is nomore to seyne—
To wrappe in my body and visage.
Therupon sore I may compleine,   15
That lordis grete have litel avauntage' . . .

Deeth to the Squier:

'Come forth, sir Squier, right fresshe of youre aray,
That can of daunces al the newe gise,
Though ye bare armes, fressh horsed yisterday,
With spere and shelde at youre unkouthe devise,   20
And toke on yow so many hy emprise,
Dnaunceth with us!—it wil no bettir be;
Ther is no socour in no manere wise,
For no man may fro dethes stroke fle.'

The Squier answerith:

'Sithen that dethe me holdith in his lace,   25
Yet shal y speke o worde or y pase:
Adieu, al myrthe! adieu nowe al solace!
Adieu, my ladies, somtime so fressh of face!
Adieu, beuté, plesaunce, and solace!
Of dethes chaunge every day is prime.   30
Thinketh on youre soules, or that deth manace,
For al shal rote, and no man wote what tyme!'

Deeth to the Abbot:

'Come forth, sir Abbot, with youre brood hatte!
Beeth not abaisshed, though ye have right.
Greet is your hood, your bely large and fatte;
Ye mote come daunce, though ye be nothing light.
Leve up youre abbey to some othir wight;
Youre eir is of age youre state to occupie.
Who that is fattest I have hym behight
In his grave shal sonnest putrefie.'

The Abbot answerith:

'Of thi thretis have I noon envie
That I shal nowe leve al governaunce;
But that I shal as a cloistrer dye,
This doth to me passinge grete grevaunce.
Mi liberté nor my greet habondaunce
What may availe, in any manere wise?
Yit axe I mercy, with hertly repentaunce,
Though in diynge to late men hem avise' . . .

Deeth to the Laborer:

'Thou laborer, wiche in sorwe and peine
Hast lad thi life, in ful greet travaile,
Thou moste eke daunce, and therfore not disdeyne,
For if thou do it may thee not availe;
And cause why that I thee assaile
Is oonly this: from thee to dissevere
The fals worlde, that can so folke faile.
He is a fool that weneth to lyve evere!'

The Laborer answerith:

'I have wisshed aftir deeth ful ofte,
Al be that I wolde have fled hym now—
I had levere to have leyn unsofte
In winde and reyn, and have gone at plow,
With spade and pikoys, and labourid for my prow,
Dolve and diched, and at the carte goone—
For I may seie and telle pleinly howe
In this worlde here ther is reste none.' . . .

35
40
45
50
55
60

5

JAMES I OF SCOTLAND: *THE KINGIS QUAIR*

'THE king's little book'—the *kingis quair*, as it is called in the sole surviving manuscript copy—is almost certainly the work of the Scottish King. In March 1406, at the age of eleven, he was captured by the English off Flamborough Head while he was on his way to the French Court; it was not until 1424, after complicated and fitful bargaining, that he was finally released. In that same year he had married Joan Beaufort, the sister of the Earl of Somerset (who himself was in French captivity for over fifteen years). But although Fortune—if we may believe the poem—had smiled on his love, his life was to be tragically short: a vigorous and distinguished reign was brought to an end by his murder in Perth in February 1437.

The scribal ascription of the poem to James has been questioned, but there is nothing which conclusively tells against his authorship. It may very well be that his poem, which like Dante's *Vita nuova* purports to be a 'book of memory', is based on his own experience, though the experience is no doubt heightened and fictionalized, and life is suffused and transfigured by imagination. Certainly, from the time that the poem was rediscovered in the eighteenth century it was taken to be autobiographical; certainly, too, in the nineteenth and early twentieth centuries, this enhanced its emotional appeal. In modern criticism there has been an austere reaction, and the formal, rhetorical, and traditional elements of the poem have been (rightly) stressed; sometimes the reaction has been so extreme that the poem has virtually been turned into a kind of versified Consolation of Philosophy. But it is not a philosophical tract. As in other good medieval love allegories, the 'philosophy' is inherent in the particular emotional experience, and is given both form and force by the poet's passion. *The Kingis Quair* is *both* a moving story of love, *and* a thoughtful poem concerned with the nature of noble love and of fortune.

The poem has much in common with the self-consciously 'Chaucerian' works of the period—some of Hoccleve, some of Lydgate, some of the English pieces illustrated and mentioned in No. 6—but it has an imaginative integrity and boldness of its own. It contains a web of Chaucerian echoes and allusions, but they are most skilfully and sensitively deployed, sometimes deliberately calling up their original contexts (notably in our extract, where memories of the lovesick Troilus are fused with memories of the imprisoned Palamon and Arcite), so that the end result is a poem which is original and distinctive. Not the least of the poem's excellences is its careful construction. A prologue describes how the sleepless poet takes, in good Chaucerian fashion, 'a boke to rede apon a quhile'—it is the *Consolation of Philosophy* of Boethius. The ringing of a matins bell seems to summon him to recount what had befallen him, and he begins the recollection of his 'aventure', how he was imprisoned, and how what he saw from the window brought the sudden shock of love and the beginning of a new 'thraldom' and a new life. The sorrowing prisoner dreams, and his dream brings him illumination: he is carried up in a heavenly journey to visit the goddesses Venus and Minerva (who instruct him that love must be well grounded and virtuous). He is sent down to earth again to ask help from Fortune. He finds this goddess set in a 'round place' in a splendid landscape filled with all the diverse creatures of Nature. Fortune shows him favour, and wakes him up with a mischievous tweak of his ear. A white dove (the bird of Venus) brings him a message of comfort as a sign of the happy conclusion of his 'aventure'. In an epilogue he prays for all lovers and for those dull hearts that have 'no curage at the rose to pull', and blesses the gods, the nightingale, and even the prison walls.

The Imprisoned Poet sees his Lady

Bewailing in my chamber thus allone,
Despeired of all joye and remedye,
Fortirit of my thoght, and wo-begone,
And to the wyndow gan I walk in hye
5   To se the warld and folk that went forby.
As for the tyme, though I of mirthis fude
Myght have no more, to luke it did me gude.

Now was there maid fast by the touris wall
A gardyn fair, and in the corneris set
10   Ane herber grene with wandis long and small
Railit about; and so with treis set
Was all the place, and hawthorn hegis knet,
That lyf was non walking there forby
That myght within scarse ony wight aspye:

15   So thik the bewis and the leves grene
Beschadit all the aleyes that there were.
And myddis every herber myght be sene
The scharpe grene suete jenepere,
Growing so fair with branchis here and there,
20   That—as it semyt to a lyf without—
The bewis spred the herber all about.

And on the smalle grene twistis sat
The lytill suete nyghtingale, and song
So loud and clere the ympnis consecrat
25   Off lufis use, now soft, now lowd among,
That all the gardyng and the wallis rong

Ryght of thair song and of the copill next
Off thair suete armony—and lo the text:

'Worschippe, ye that loveris bene, this May,
For of your blisse the kalendis ar begonne,   30
And sing with us, 'Away, winter, away!
Cum somer, cum, the suete sesoun and sonne!'
Awake for schame, that have your hevynnis wonne,
And amorously lift up your hedis all!
Thank Lufe that list you to his merci call.'   35

Quhen thai this song had song a lytill thrawe,
Thai stent a quhile, and therwith unaffraid
—As I beheld and kest myn eyne a-lawe—
From beugh to beugh thay hippit and thai plaid,
And freschly in thair birdis kynd arraid   40
Thair fetheris new, and fret thame in the sonne,
And thankit Lufe that had thair makis wonne.

This was the plane ditee of thair note,
And therwithall unto myself I thoght:
'Quhat lyf is this, that makis birdis dote?   45
Quhat may this be, how cummyth it of ought?
Quhat nedith it to be so dere ybought?
It is nothing, trowe I, bot feynit chere,
And that men list to counterfeten chere.'

Eft wald I think: 'O Lord, quhat may this be,   50
That Lufe is of so noble myght and kynde,
Lufing his folk? and suich prosperitee,
Is it of him, as we in bukis fynd?
May he oure hertes setten and unbynd?
Hath he upon oure hertis suich maistrye?   55
Or all this is bot feynyt fantasye?

'For gif he be of so grete excellence
That he of every wight hath cure and charge,
Quhat have I gilt to him or doon offense,
That I am thrall, and birdis gone at large,   60
Sen him to serve he myght set my corage?
And gif he be noght so, than may I seyne
Quhat makis folk to jangill of him in veyne?

'Can I noght elles fynd, bot gif that he
65 Be lord, and as a god may lyve and regne,
To bynd and louse and maken thrallis free,
Than wold I pray his blisfull grace benigne
To hable me unto his service digne.
And evermore forto be one of tho
70 Him trewly forto serve in wele and wo.'

And therwith kest I doun myn eye ageyne,
Quhareas I sawe, walking under the tour,
Full secretly new cummyn hir to pleyne,
The fairest or the freschest yonge floure
75 That euer I sawe, me thoght, before that houre.
For quhich sodayn abate anon astert
The blude of all my body to my hert.

And though I stude abaisit tho a lyte,
No wonder was: forquhy my wittis all
80 Were so ouercom with plesance and delyte,
Onely throu latting of myn eyen fall,
That sudaynly my hert became hir thrall
For ever, of free wyll—for of manace
There was no takyn in hir suete face.

85 And in my hede I drewe ryght hastily,
And eftsones I lent it forth ageyne
And saw hir walk, that verray womanly,
With no wight mo, bot onely wommen tueyne.
Than gan I studye in myself and seyne,
90 'A, suete, ar ye a warldly creature,
Or hevinly thing in liknesse of nature?

'Or ar ye god Cupidis owin princesse
And cummyn ar to louse me out of band?
Or ar ye verray Nature the goddesse
95 That have depaynted with your hevinly hand
This gardyn full of flouris, as they stand?
Quhat sall I think, allace, quhat reverence
Sall I minster to your excellence?

'Gif ye a goddesse be, and that ye like
100 To do me payne, I may it noght astert.
Gif ye be warldly wight that dooth me sike

74

Quhy lest God mak you so, my derrest hert,
To do a sely prisoner thus smert,
That lufis yow all and wote of noght bot wo?
And therfore merci, suete, sen it is so.'   105

Quhen I a lytill thrawe had maid my moon,
Bewailling myn infortune and my chance,
Unknawin how or quhat was best to doon,
So ferr I fallyng into lufis dance,
That sodeynly my wit, my contenance,   110
My hert, my will, my nature and my mynd,
Was changit clene ryght in anothir kynd.

Off hir array the form gif I sall write
Toward, hir goldin hair and rich atyre
In fret-wise couchit with perllis quhite   115
And grete balas lemyng as the fyre,
With mony ane emeraut and fair saphire;
And on hir hede a chaplet fresch of hewe,
Off plumys partit rede, and quhite and blewe;

Full of quaking spangis bryght as gold,   120
Forgit of schap like to the amorettis,
So new, so fresch, so plesant to behold;
The plumys eke like to the flour jonettis,
And othir of schap like to the flour burnettis.
And above all this there was—wele I wote—   125
Beautee eneuch to mak a world to dote.

About hir nek, quhite as the fyré amaille,
A gudely cheyne of smale orfeverye
Quhareby there hang a ruby, without faille,
Lyke to ane herte schapin verily,   130
That as a sperk of lowe so wantounly
Semyt birnyng upon hir quhyte throte,
Now gif there was gud partye, God it wote!

And forto walk that fresche Mayes morowe
An huke sche had upon hir, tissew quhite,   135
That gudeliar had noght bene sene toforowe,
As I suppose; and girt sche was a lyte,
Thus halflyng louse for haste, lo, suich delyte
It was to see hir youth in gudelihed
That for rudenes to speke therof I drede.   140

In hir was youth, beautee with humble aport,
Bountee, richesse, and wommanly facture,
—God better wote than my pen can report!—
Wisedome, largesse, estate, and connyng sure.
145 In every poynt so guydit hir mesure,
In word, in dede, in schap, in contenance,
That Nature myght no more hir childe avance.

Throw quhich anon I knew and understude
Wele, that sche was a warldly creature:
150 On quhom to rest myn eye, so mich gude
It did my wofull hert (I yow assure),
That it was to me joye without mesure.
And, at the last, my luke unto the hevin
I threw furthwith and said thir versis sevin:

155 'O Venus clere, of goddis stellifyit,
To quhom I yelde homage and sacrifise,
Fro this day forth your grace be magnifyit,
That me ressavit have in suiche wise,
To lyve under your law and do servise.
160 Now help me furth, and for your merci lede
My hert to rest, that deis nere for drede.'

Quhen I with gude entent this orisoun
Thus endit had, I stynt a lytill stound.
And eft myn eye full pitously adoun
165 I kest, behalding unto hir lytill hound
That with his bellis playit on the ground:
Than wold I say and sigh therwith a lyte,
'A, wele were him that now were in thy plyte!'

Anothir quhile the lytill nyghtingale
170 That sat apon the twiggis wold I chide,
And say ryght thus: 'quhare ar thy notis smale
That thou of love has song this morowe-tyde?
Seis thou noght hir that sittis the besyde?
For Venus sake, the blisfull goddesse clere,
175 Sing on agane and mak my lady chere.

'And eke I pray, for all the paynes grete
That for the love of Proigne, thy sister dere,
Thou sufferit quhilom, quhen thy brestis wete
Were with the teres of thyne eyen clere
180 All bludy ronne—that pitee was to here

76

The crueltee of that unknyghtly dede
Quhare was fro thee bereft thy maidenhede—

'Lift up thyne hert and sing with gude entent,
And in thy notis suete the tresoun telle
That to thy sister trewe and innocent   185
Was kythit by hir husband false and fell;
For quhois gilt (as it is worthy wel)
Chide thir husbandis that ar false, I say,
And bid thame mend, in the .xx^{ti} devil way.

'O lytill wrecche, allace, maist thou noght se   190
Quho commyth yond? Is it now tyme to wring?
Quhat sory thoght is fallin upon the?
Opyn thy throte—hastow no lest to sing?
Allace, sen thou of resoun had felyng,
Now, suete bird, say ones to me "pepe".   195
I dee for wo, me think thou gynnis slepe.

'Hastow no mynde of lufe? quhare is thy make?
Or artow seke, or smyt with jelousye?
Or is sche dede, or hath sche the forsake?
Quhat is the cause of thy malancolye   200
That thou no more list maken melodye?
Sluggart, for schame! lo, here thy goldin hour
That worth were hale all thy lyvis laboure!

'Gyf thou suld sing wele ever in thy lyve
Here is, in fay, the tyme and eke the space.   205
Quhat wostow than? sum bird may cum and stryve
In song with thee the maistry to purchace.
Suld thou than cesse, it were grete schame, allace!
And here, to wyn gree happily for euer,
Here is the tyme to syng or ellis neuer.'   210

I thoght eke thus, gif I my handis clap
Or gif I cast, than will sche flee away.
And gif I hald me pes, than will sche nap,
And gif I crye, sche wate noght quhat I say:
Thus quhat is best wate I noght, be this day,   215
Bot, 'blawe wynd, blawe, and do the levis schake,
That sum twig may wag and mak hir to wake.'

77

With that anonryght sche toke up a sang,
Quhare com anon mo birdis and alight.
220   Bot than, to here the mirth was tham amang,
Over that to, to see the suete sicht
Off hyr ymage my spirit was so light
Me thoght I flawe for joye without arest,
So were my wittis boundin all to fest!

225   And to the notis of the philomene
Quhilkis sche sang, the ditee there I maid
Direct to hir that was my hertis quene,
Withoutin quhom no songis may me glade.
And to that sanct, walking in the schade,
230   My bedis thus with humble hert entere
Devotly I said on this manere:

'Quhen sall your merci rew upon your man
Quhois service is yit uncouth unto yow?
Sen quhen ye go, there is noght ellis than!
235   Bot hert, quhereas the body may noght throu,
Folow thy heuin: quho suld be glad bot thou
That suich a gyde to folow has undertake?
Were it throu hell, the way thou noght forsake!'

And efter this the birdis everichone
240   Tuke up anothir sang full loud and clere,
And with a voce said: 'wele is us begone
That with oure makis ar togider here.
We proyne and play without dout and dangere,
All clothit in a soyte full fresch and newe,
245   In lufis service besy, glad, and trewe.

'And ye, fresche May, ay mercifull to bridis,
Now welcum be ye, flour of monethis all;
For noght onely your grace upon us bydis,
Bot all the warld to witnes this we call,
250   That strowit hath so playnly over all,
With newe, fresche, suete and tender grene,
Oure lyf, oure lust, oure governoure, oure quene.'

This was thair song—as semyt me—full heye,
With full mony uncouth suete note and schill,
255   And therwithall that fair upward hir eye

Wold cast amang—as it was Goddis will—
Quhare I myght se, standing allane full still,
The fair facture that Nature for maistrye
In her visage wroght had full lufingly.

And quhen sche walkit had a lytill thrawe   260
Undir the suete grene bewis bent,
Hir fair fresche face, as quhite as ony snawe,
Scho turnyt has and furth hir wayis went.
Bot tho began myn axis and turment:
To sene hir part, and folowe I na myght.   265
Me thoght the day was turnyt into nyght.

Than said I thus: 'quhareto lyve I langer?
Wofullest wicht and subject unto peyne,—
Of peyne? no—God wote, ya! for thay no stranger
May wirken ony wight, I dar wele seyne.   270
How may this be, that deth and lyf—both tueyne—
Sall bothe atonis in a creature
Togidder duell and turment thus nature?

'I may noght ellis done bot wepe and waile
Within thir calde wallis thus ilokin.   275
From hennesfurth my rest is my travaile,
My drye thrist with teris sall I slokin,
And on myself bene al my harmys wrokin.
Thus bute is none, bot Venus of hir grace
Will schape remede or do my spirit pace.   280

'As Tantalus I travaile ay butles
That ever ylike hailith at the well
Water to draw with buket botemles
And may noght spede—quhois penance is an hell.
So by myself this tale I may wele telle,   285
For unto hir that herith noght I pleyne,
Thus like to him my travaile is in veyne.'

So sore thus sighit I with myself allone
That turnyt is my strenth in febilnesse,
My wele in wo, my frendis all in fone,   290
My lyf in deth, lyght into dirknesse,
My hope in feere, in dout my sekirnesse
Sen sche is gone; and God mote hir convoye
That me may gyde to turment and to joye.

6

'CHAUCERIAN' POEMS

CHAUCER was not only praised and imitated by the better-known poets of this period—Hoccleve, King James, Lydgate, and others; in the manuscript copies of his works and in the printed editions which succeeded them there occur a number of poems not written by him but sometimes attributed to him which were gathered together by his great nineteenth-century editor, Skeat, in a volume called *Chaucerian and Other Pieces*. If we extend the sense of 'Chaucerian poems' to include both apocryphal works and poems which echo, imitate, or are at least similar in some way to Chaucer's, it will serve as a useful label for an attractive group of minor courtly poems—poems such as *The Assembly of Ladies*, *The Court of Love*, *The Book of Cupid*, as well as those represented here. They treat the subject of love with some elegance, and with some attempt at a Chaucerian blend of 'earnest' and 'game'. *The Lovers' Mass* is a splendid example of the long tradition of liturgical parody (cf. the Mass or Office sung by birds, which appears in *The Court of Love* and in Skelton's *Phyllyp Sparowe*). The author's verve and delight in the parody are matched by his dazzling, virtuoso display of intricate metrical forms showing a rhythmical and musical sensitivity rare in the poetry of this period. *La Belle Dame sans mercy* (which gave Keats the title of a famous poem) is translated from the French of Alain Chartier, a learned, skilful, and intelligent poet. Chartier's poem is in the 'courtly' tradition, but, it has been suggested, is in fact a 'subtle and penetrating demolition of it'. Certainly, the lady's wit and good sense is played off against the extravagant eloquence of the lover, and the conclusion in which her 'daunger' causes the death of the woebegone lover was taken by some to be an attack on Love, and was the starting-point of a fashionable literary *querelle*. The translation by Sir Richard Ros (? *c*.1410–82) may well—like Hoccleve's *Letter of Cupid*—reflect an interest in contemporary French literary disputes. It is again technically a highly polished piece of work. Ros writes with ease and assurance (it is, as C. S. Lewis acutely observes, genuine stanzaic writing: 'the last line is felt throughout the whole grave minuet which words and sense go through in order to reach it; and when it comes, there is a full close for ear and mind . . .'); he neatly maintains the dialectic of debate by varying the tone of voice according to the speaker, and continually manages to suggest the strong emotional undertones. *The Floure and the Leafe* (? third quarter of the fifteenth century) seems to be written by a lady (if we take two references to 'my doughter' literally). It describes very elegantly the pageantry and the colourful surface of courtly life, handles its allegory and its 'sentence' lightly and easily. Finally, the lament of Dido (another example of the continuing interest in ancient stories of sentiment) is a bold, if still rather rough, attempt at Ovidian pathos.

A

The Lovers' Mass

Introibo

Wyth all myn hool herte enter,
Tofore the famous riche auter
Of the myghty god of Love,
Whiche that standeth high above.
In the chapel of Cytheron,   5
I will wyth gret devocion
Go knele, and make sacrifyse,
Lyke as the custom doth devyse;
Afor that God preye and wake
Of entent I may be take   10
To hys servyse, and ther assure
As longe as my lyf may dure,
To contune as I best can,
Whil I lyve to ben hys man.

Confiteor

I am aknowe, and wot ryght well   15
I speke pleynly as I fel
Touchynge the grete tendyrnesse
Of my youthe and my symplesse
Of myn unkonying and grene age
Wil lete me han noon avantage.   20
To serve Love I kan so lyte,
And yet myn hert doth delyte
Of hys servauntys forto here.
By exaumple of hem I myghte lere
To folowe the wey of ther servyse,   25
Yif I hadde konnyng to devyse,
That I myght a servant be,
Amongys other in my degré,
Havynge ful gret repentaunce
That I non erste me gan avaunce   30
In Loves court, myselfe to offre
And my servyse forto profre,
For fer of my tender youthe,
Nouther be Est nouther be Southe,

35 Lyst Daunger putte me abake
And Dysdeyn, to make wrake,
Wolde hyndre me in myn entente—
Of all this thyng I me repente,
As my conscience kan recorde:
40 I sey lowly Myserycorde.

Misereatur

By God of Lovys ordynaunce,
Folkys that have repentaunce,
Sorowful in herte, and nothyng lyght,
Whiche ha nat spent hyr tyme aryght,
45 But wastyd yt in ydelnesse,
Only for lake of lustynesse
In slep, slogardye, and slouthe,
Of whom ys pyté and gret routhe;
But when they repente hem ageyn
50 Of al ther tyme spent in veyn,
The God of Love thorgh hys myght,
Syth that mercy passeth ryght
Thé mot acceptyd be to grace,
And pute Daunger out of place—
55 This the wyl of Dame Venus
And of hyr bisshopp Genius.

Officium

In honour of the god Cupide
First that he may be my guyde,
In worshepe eke of the pryncesse,
60 Whyche is lady and maystresse,
By grace they may for me provyde,
Humble of herte, devoyde of pryde,
Envye and rancour set asyde
Withoute change or doubilnesse;
65   In honour of the god Cupide
First that he may be my guyde,
Joye and welfare in every tyde
Be yove to hem wherso they byde,
And yive to hem grace, on my dystresse
70 To have pyté of ther hyghnesse,
For in what place I go or ryde
In honour of the god Cupide
First that he may be my guyde.

Kyrie

Mercy, Mercy,   contynuely   I crye,
In gret disjoynt,   upon the poynt   to deye,   75
For that Pyté   ys unto me   contrayre,
Daunger my fo,   Dysdeyn also,   whylk tweye
Causen myn herte   of mortal smert   dyspeyre,
For she that ys   fayrest ywys   of fayre
Hath gladnesse   of my syknesse   to pleye—   80
Thus my trouble   double and double   doth repayre.

Christe

Repeyreth ay,   which nyght nor day   ne cesseth nought,
Now Hope, now Dred,   now Pensyffhede,   now Thought;
Al thyse yfere   palen myn chere   and hewe.
Yet to hyr grace   ech hour and space   I ha besought;   85
Hyr lyst nat here,   for hyr daunger   doth ay renewe
Towardys me,   for certys she   lyst nat rewe
Upon my peyne;   and thus my cheyne   ys wrought
Which hath me bounde,   never to be founde   untrewe.

Kyrie

Untrewe? Nay!   To se that day,   God forbede!   90
Voyde slouthe,   kepe my trouthe,   in dede,
Eve and morowe,   for joye or sorowe,   I have behyght,
Til I sterve,   evere to serve   hir womanhede;
In erthe lyvynge   ther is no thyng   maketh me so lyght,
For I shal dye,   ne but wer hir mercye   mor than ryght   95
Off no decertys;   but Mercy certys   my journé spede,
Adieu al play,   thus may I say,   I woful wyght.

Gloria in excelsis

Worshyppe to that lord above,
That callyd ys the god of Love;
Pes to hys servantes everychon,   100
Trewe of herte, stable as ston,
    That feythful be;

To hertys trewe of ther corage,
That lyst chaunge for no rage,
But kep hem in ther hestys stylle   105
In al maner wedris ylle,
    Pes, concord, and unyté.

God send hem sone ther desyrs,
And reles of ther hoote fyrs,
110   That brenneth at her herte sore,
And encresseth more and more—
        This my prayere;

And after wynter wyth hys shourys
God send hem counfort of May flourys,
115   Affter gret wynd and stormys kene
The glade sone with bemys shene
        May appere

To yive hem lyght affter dyrknesse;
Joye eke after hevynesse,
120   And after dool and ther wepynge
To here the somer foullys synge
        God yive grace;

For oftesythe men ha seyn
A ful bryght day after gret reyn,
125   And tyl the storme be leyd asyde
The herdys under bussh abyde
        And taketh place.

After also the dirke nyght,
Voyde off the mone and sterre lyght,
130   And after nyghtys dool and sorowe
Folweth ofte a ful glade morowe,
        Of aventure.

Now, lorde, that knowest hertys alle
Off lovers that for helpe calle,
135   On her trouthe, of mercy, rewe;
Namly on swyche as be trewe,
        Helpe to recure.
        Amen. . . .

B

LA BELLE DAME SANS MERCY

The Lady Resists the Lover's Pleas

. . . I herde the lover sighing wondir sore;
For ay the ner, the sorer it hym sought.
His inward payne he couthe not kepe in store,
Nor forto speke, so hardy was he nought.
His leche was nere, the gretter was his thought; 5
He mused sore, to conquere his desire;
For no man may to more penaunce be brought
Then, in his hete, to bryng hym to the fire.

The herte began to swelle withyn his chest,
So sore streyned for anguysh and for payn 10
That all to pecis almost it tobrest,
When bothe at ones so sore it did constrayn:
Desire was bold, but shame it gan refrayn;
The ton was large, the tother was full cloos;
No lyttyll charge was leyd in hym, certeyn, 15
To kepe such ware and have so many foos.

Full oftentyme to speke hymself he payned,
But shamefastnes and drede seid ever 'nay';
Yit at the last so sore he was constrayned,
When he full longe hadde putte it in delay, 20
To his lady right thus then gan he say
With dredfull voys, wepyng, halfe in a rage:
'For me was purveied an unhappy day
Whan y first had a sight of youre vysage!

'I suffre peyne, God wot, full hote burnyng, 25
To cause my dethe, all for my trew service;
And y se wele, ye reche therof nothyng,
Nor take non hede of it, in no kyns wyse.
But when I speke after my best avise,
Ye set it nought, but make therof a game; 30
And though y sue so grete an entirprise,
It peireth not your wurship nor your fame.

'Alas! what shuld be to you prejudice
If that a man do love you faythefully
35   To your wurship, eschuyng every vice?
So am y youres, and will be verély;
I chalange nought of right, and resoun why:
For y am hole submyt to your servyse;
Right as ye lyste it be, right so will y,
40   To bynde myselfe, where y was in fraunchise!

'Though it be so, that y can not deserve
To have youre grace, but ay to leve in drede,
Yit suffre me you forto love and serve
Without magré of youre most goodlyhede;
45   Bothe fayth and trouth y yeve your womanhede,
And my servise, without ayen-callyng.
Love hathe me bounde, withoute wage or mede,
To be your man, and leve all othir thyng.'

When his lady hadde herde all this langage,
50   She yaf answere full softe and demurely,
Without chaungyng of colour or corage,
Nothyng in haste, but mesurabely:
'Me thynketh, sir, your thought is grete foly.
Purpose ye not youre labour forto sees?
55   For thynketh not, whils that ye leve and y,
In this matier to sette youre hert in pees!'

Lamant. 'Ther may non make the pees, but only ye,
Which ar the ground and cause of al this wer;
For with your yen the letters writen be,
60   By which y am defied and put afer,
Your plesaunt looke, my very lodesterre,
Was made heraud of thilke same diffiaunce
Which utterly behight me to forber
My feythefull trust and all myn affiaunce.'

65   La Dame. 'To leve in wo he hathe gret fantasie
And of his hert also hathe sliper hold,
That, only for byholdyng of an ye,
Can not abide in pees, as resoun wolde!
Other or me if ye liste to biholde,
70   Our iyen are made to loke; why shuld we spare?
I take no kepe, nether of yong ne olde;
Who feleth smert, I consayll him by ware!'

86

Lam. 'If it be so one hurt another sore,
  In his defaut that feleth no grevaunce,
  Of very right a man may do namore;   75
  Yit reson wuld it were in remembraunce.
  And, sith Fortune nat only, by her chaunce,
  Hathe caused me to suffre all this payn,
  But your beauté with all the sircumstance,
  Why list you have me in so grete disdeyn?'   80

La D. 'To your persone ne have y non disdeyn,
  Nor never hadde, truly! nor nought will have,
  Nor right gret love, nor hatrede, in certayn;
  Nor youre consayll to knowe, so God me save!
  If such beleve be in your mynde ygrave   85
  That lytell thyng may do you gret plesaunce,
  You to begyle or make you forto rave,
  I will nat cause non such encomberaunce!'

Lam. 'What ever hit be that hath me thus purchacyde,
  Wenyng hath noght deseyved me, sertayne,   90
  But fervent love so sore hath me ychasede
  That I, unware, am casten in your chayne;
  And sith so is, as Fortune lyste ordayne,
  All my welfar is in your handys falle,
  Inn eschewyng of more myschevous payne;   95
  Who sunnest dieth, his care is leste of alle.'

La D. 'This sykenesse is ryght esy to endure—
  But few peple it causeth for to dye;
  But what thei meane, I know hit verey sure,
  Of mor comfort to draw the remedye.   100
  Sych be ther now, playnyng full pytouslye,
  That fele, Gode wote, not althergrettyst payne;
  And ife so be love hurtes so grevously,
  Lesse harm hit were, wone sorouful, then twayn!'

Lam. 'Alas, madame! ife that it myght you please,   105
  Mych better wer, by way of gentyllesse,
  Of won sory, to make twayne wel at ease,
  Then hyme to strye that lyveth in destresse!
  For my desyr is nother mor nor lesse
  But my servysse to do, for your plesaunce,   110
  In eschewyng al maner doublenesse,
  To make too joys in sted of won grevaunce!'

La D. 'Of love I seke nother plesaunce nore ease,
Ne grete desire, nor ryght gret affyaunce;
115   Though ye be seke, hit dothe me no thyng please;
Also, I take none hede to your plesaunce.
Chese whoso wyle thair hertys to avaunce,
Fre am I now, and fre wyll I endure;
To be rulyd by mannys governaunce
120   For erthly gode, nay! that I you ensure!'

Lam. 'Love, which that joy and sorow doth depart,
Hath set the ladyes out of all servage,
And largely doth graunt hem, for thair part,
Lordchip and rule of every maner age.
125   The pore servaunt noght hath of avauntage
But what he may get only of purchace;
And he that ones to love dothe his omage,
Full often tyme der boght is the rechace.'

La D. 'Ladyes beth nat so symple, thus I mene,
130   So dulle of wyte, so sotyd of folye,
That, for wordes which said ben of the splene,
In fayr langage, paynted ful plesantlye,
Which ye and mo holde scolys of dalye,
To make hem all grete wondrys to suppose,
135   But sone thei cane away her hedes wrye,
And to fayr speche lyghtly thair eres close.'

Lam. 'Ther is no man that janglith bysily,
And sette his hert and all his mynd therfor,
That by reason may playn so pytously
140   As he that hath myche hevynesse in store.
Whose hede is hole and saith that it is sore,
His fayned chere is hard to kepe in mewe;
But thoght, which is unfayned evermore,
The wordes preveth, as the warkes sewe.'

145   *La D.* 'Love is sotyle, and hath a grete awayte,
Scharpe in worchyng, in gabbyng gret plesance,
And cane hyme venge of siche as by deceyte
Wold fele and know his secrete governance;
And makyth hem to abey his ordynaunce
150   By cherfull wayes, as in hem is supposed;
But when thei fallen into repentance,
Than, in a rage, his councele is disclosed' . . .

88

C

THE FLOURE AND THE LEAFE

A Courtly Scene and a Sudden Storm

. . . And forth they yede togider, twain and twain,
That to behold it was a worthy sight,
Toward the ladies on the green plain,
That song and daunced, as I said now right.
The ladies, as soone as they goodly might,
They brake of both the song and dance,
And yede to meet hem with full glad semblance.

And every lady tooke ful womanly
By the hond a knight, and forth they yede
Unto a faire laurer that stood fast by,   10
With leves lade, the boughes of great brede.
And to my dome there never was indede
Man that had seen halfe so faire a tre;
For underneath there might it wel have be

An hundred persons at their own plesance,   15
Shadowed from the heat of Phebus bright,
So that they should have felt no grevance
Of raine ne haile, that hem hurt might.
The savour eke rejoice would any wight
That had be sicke or melancolious,   20
It was so very good and vertuous.

And with great reverence they enclined low
To the tree, so soot and faire of hew.
And after that, within a little throw,
They began to sing and daunce of new;   25
Some song of love, some plaining of untrew,
Environing the tree that stood upright,
And ever yede a lady and a knight.

And at the last I cast mine eie aside,
And was ware of a lusty company   30
That came roming out of the field wide,
Hond in hond, a knight and a lady;

The ladies all in surcotes, that richely
Purfiled were with many a rich stone;
35   And every knight of greene ware mantels on,

Embrouded well, so as the surcotes were,
And everich had a chapelet on her hed,
Which did right well upon the shining here,
Made of goodly floures, white and red.
40   The knightes eke, that they in hond led,
In sute of hem ware chapelets everichone.
And before hem went minstrels many one,

As harpes, pipes, lutes, and sautry,
All in greene; and on their heades bare,
45   Of divers floures made full craftely,
All in a sute, goodly chapelets they ware.
And so dauncing into the mede they fare,
In mid the which they found a tuft that was
All oversprad with floures in compas.

50   Whereto they enclined everichon
With great reverence, and that full humbly.
And at the last there began anon
A lady for to sing right womanly
A bargaret in praising the daisie;
55   For, as me thought, among her notes swete
She said, '*Si douce est la Margarete.*'

Then they all answered her in fere
So passingly well and so pleasauntly
That it was a blisful noise to here.
60   But I not how, it happed sodainly,
As about noone, the sonne so fervently
Waxe whote that the prety tender floures
Had lost the beauty of of her fresh coloures,

Forshronke with heat; the ladies eke tobrent,
65   That they ne wist where they hem might bestow.
The knightes swelt, for lack of shade nie shent.
And after that, within a little throw,
The wind began so sturdily to blow
That down goeth all the floures everichone
70   So that in all the mede there laft not one,

Save suche as succoured were among the leves
Fro every storme that might hem assaile,
Growing under hegges and thicke greves,
And after that there came a storme of haile
And raine in feare, so that, withouten faile,   75
The ladies ne the knights nade o threed
Dry on them, so dropping was her weed.

And whan the storm was cleane passed away,
Tho in white, that stood under the tre—
They felt nothing of the great affray   80
That they in greene without had in ybe—
To them they yede for routh and pité,
Them to comfort after their great disease,
So faine they were the helplesse for to ease. . . .

D

The Letter of Dydo to Eneas

'. . . Than in your mynde Dydo ye shall espy,
Whom by disceit ye have caused to dye;
Than shall ye se to make your hert pensyfe
The colde ymage of your disceyved wife,
Hevy, thoughtfull, with heres pulde fro her hed,   5
Spotted with blode, wounded, nat fully ded.
Whan your lyfe fayleth than shall ye sigh sore
And say, "I have deserved this and more."
Ha, my dere frende! Gyve a lytell space
To the sees rage which doth you manace!   10
Tary a whyle; sojourne a space ye may,
Tyll that there come a more goodly day,
And it may be that all these wawes great
Shall well apese, and no more the rockes bete.
And if ye have banysshed fro me pety,   15
Have ye regarde to your sonne Ascany!
Shall your sonne se my sorowfull trespace,
Whom ye have kept in many a divers place?
Saved ye your folke fro fyre of Troy town
To th'ende that the gret see shulde them drown?   20
I am nat the fyrst, I knowe for certayne,
Whom your langage hath caused to complayne!

91

But ye that were well lerned for to lye
Have abused me, alas, through my folly;
25 Your pitous wordes whan I herd with myn eres,
My eyes were moved to stande ful of teres.
After, my hert moche enclyned to pyté
Was holly moved to have your amyté—
That redy wyll and my defaut sodayne
30 Shall nowe be cause of my later payne!
I thynke for trouth that God for your vice
In eche place shal you punishe and chastice.
Sevyn yeres without rest by lande and by see
Ye were in warres and great adversyté;
35 At the last weder driven ye were hyder.
I was content that we shulde lyve togyder
And by payne had of your name knowlege;
My body and landes to you I dyd pledge.
Wolde to God that the fame and yll renowne
40 Of my synne were utterly layde downe!
I was to blame to enclyne and rejoyce
In the swete wordes of your pitous voice,
Trustyng your true spouse to be;
But the fayntnesse of love disceyved me.
45 Pardon ye me of that I was so swyfte—
I dyde it nat for golde nor for no gyfte.
One that semed kynde, lovyng, and honest,
Overcame me to folowe his request;
His noble blode and his swete countenaunce
50 Gave me good hope and of mynde assuraunce.
I knowe no woman so good nor so wyse
That wolde the love of suche one dispice,
For in hym is no defaut but one—
He lacketh pyté, whiche causeth me to mone.
55 Yf Goddes wyll be that ye shall nedes hens,
I wolde he had forbode you my presens.
Allas! ye se and knowe this without fayle
That your people be wery of traveyle,
And to have rest they wolde be very fayne
60 Tyll that they may be esed of their payne.
Also your shippes be nat fully prest,
Your sayles broken, your gables yet unfest.
Yf I of you have ought deserved,
By any thyng wherin I have you served,
65 And ever wyll serve you in my best wyse,
For recompence at lest of that servyce,

I pray you hertely let this be done:
Purpose your mynde nat to go so sone
Tyll the tyme that the see and the rage
Be well apesed and of his wawes aswage,   70
And tyll that I may suffre with good hert
Your departure—sithe ye wyll nedes depart—
And more easely suffre and endure
Thought, traveyle, payne, and displeasure,
For in good faithe I trust of very trothe   75
That ayenst me ye can nat long be wroth!
Yet I pray you—come regarde the ymage
Of her that wrote to you this langage!
Alas, I write—and to encrease my sorowe
There standeth the swerde that shall kyll me tomorowe. 80
With my teres this swerd is spotted,
Whiche in my brest in hast shal be blotted,
And all shal be in stede of teres on the sworde
Spotted with blode—trust me at a worde.
Ha! the swerde ye lefte me whan ye went   85
To my desteny is convenyent.
Of an unhappy offryng and gyfte but small
My sepulture is made great therwithall;
This shall nat be the fyrst glayve or darte
That hath peersed me to the herte,   90
For, afore this, love that setteth folke to scole
Wounded me sore! I se I was more fole!
O suster Anne, ye knewe my hert dyd blede
Or I consented unto this dede!
Whan I am deed and brent to asshes colde,   95
Than shall ye serch and with your handes unfolde
The pouder of my bones, and surely kepe
In your chambre, thereas ye use to slepe.
Fro I be deed, folkes wyll no more call me
Chast Dido, somtyme wyfe to Sechee;   100
On the marble shall stande this scripture,
As an epitaphe upon my sepulture:
"Here lyeth Dido, to whom Enee untrewe
Gave cause of deth and the swerd that her slewe.'"

7

RELIGIOUS PROSE

THERE is a vast amount of religious prose in the manuscripts and the printed books of this period, and some of it is of very high quality. The following pieces will give some idea of its variety of form and content: it ranges from mystical visions to saints' lives that are close to romance, and it can be merry as well as solemn. Reading it may also shake some firmly held prejudices about literary history—the fine prose prayers or the translations of the psalms and canticles in devotional primers make it clear, for instance, that the splendid prose of *The Book of Common Prayer* did not spring up suddenly *ex nihilo*. As in previous centuries, the spiritual tradition of European Christianity is assimilated and made available to less learned readers through translations. Our pieces illustrate also an important element of the literature of medieval spirituality—its traditional and 'cumulative' quality. We have extracts from works written originally in the thirteenth and fourteenth centuries as well as contemporary ones. Some of them appear in the list of pious books read in the household of Cicely, Duchess of York (d. 1495), the mother of Edward IV and Richard III and one of many lay women who made such an important contribution to medieval piety. Besides Hilton on the contemplative and active life, and two fourteenth-century saints, Catherine of Siena and Bridget of Sweden, this household knew 'Bonaventure' (perhaps Nicholas Love's translation of the *Meditationes Vitae Christi*), 'St Maude' (most likely our *Boke of Gostely Grace* from the thirteenth-century Mechtild of Hackeborn), and *The Golden Legend*. At the end of the period we find Thomas More still recommending the old favourites—Hilton's *Scale of Perfection*, the 'Bonaventura' *Meditations*, and *The Imitation of Christ*. A number of these were—deservedly—'best sellers' in medieval Europe. Three of our examples are clearly in this category. The thirteenth-century *Golden Legend* (so called, according to Caxton, because like the metal it is 'holden most noble above all other works'), a wonderful (in all senses of the word) collection of pious stories of the saints in which folklore, romance, and devotion are intermingled, is represented here (from the earlier prose translation to which Caxton himself drew attention) in the stories of St Christopher (that amiable giant of medieval wall-paintings) and of the visionary traveller St Brendan, whose 'land of promise' still fortunately remains as other-worldly as ever, in spite of the efforts of early cartographers and modern enthusiasts. The slightly later *Meditations on the Life of Christ* is a monument of Franciscan piety, intended for the reading of the religious, and immensely influential in both literature and art. Love's free version presents it to a wider audience of devout readers. Finally, the fifteenth century provides another in *The Imitation of Christ*, which, as Dr Johnson said, 'must be a good book, as the world has opened its arms to receive it'. This devotional manual, which instructs the reader on how to seek detachment from the world by the 'imitation' of Christ (a dominant strand in medieval devotion), has been translated into many languages, and read by many kinds of Christians. Late medieval devotion can be highly emotional and even lurid, but its most characteristic qualities (which are abundantly illustrated by these books) are a tender devotion to the humanity and the human sufferings of Christ the lover of mankind, and an intense, simple 'homeliness'. They are found in the most strongly contrasting writers represented here—that simple 'creature' Margery Kempe of Lynn and that eminent figure of State, Bishop John Fisher. Margery's spiritual autobiography gives us in vivid and dramatic scenes an account of her adventures as she wanders through England and on pilgrimage to Rome, Jerusalem, and elsewhere, and of her 'feelings' and visions. Her apprehension of the sufferings of Christ sometimes takes a very emotional form in her 'cryings', but there is as often evidence of a simple humble devotion, and she helps her aged husband 'as she would have done Christ himself'. The reactions of modern readers to this often exasperating but fascinating woman are likely to resemble very closely those of her contemporaries (see D 57–60). With the austere Bishop Fisher, the friend of the humanists Erasmus and More (who said there was 'in this realm no one man in wisdom, learning, and long approved vertue together, mete to be matched and compared with him'), we are in a very different world, but here too in his eloquent sermons, with their learned references to Aristotle, Plato, the 'clerke Orpheus', and the cabbala, and their logical structure which mirrors his strong sense of divine order, we find an inner simplicity of devotion: characteristically, he once remarks that the glory of the Church does not consist in 'sylke copes' and the like, but in 'clennes of consyence'.

A

THE MIRROR OF SIMPLE SOULS

The Ecstasy of Love

'Withouten faile,' seith this soule, 'who that wel loveth, he ne thenketh neithir of takynge ne of askynge but on yevynge withouten anythinge withhaldynge truli forto love. For who that hath two ententis in oon tyme, the toon lassith for the tothir.Therfore trewe love hath but oonli on entente, and that is, that she might alwei love truli, for of the love of hir 5 loved hath she no doute, that he ne doth that best is, and she folwith this that she do that that hir owith to doo, and she willeth not but oon thinge, and that is that, that the wille of God be alwei in hir ydo.'

'She hath right,' seith Love, 'for this is al. She may not wille of hir propre wille, for hir wille is not with hir, but it is withoute mevynge in hym that 10 she loveth, and this is not hir werke, but it is the werk of al the Trinité that werkith in this soule at his wille. This soule', seith Love, 'swymmeth in the see of joie, that is, in the see of delices, stremynge of divine fluences. She felith no joie, for she hirsilf is joie. Sche swymmeth and drenchith in joie, for she ledith in joie withoute felynge ony joie. So is joie in hir, that she 15 hirsilf is joie, bi the vertu of joie that hath hir meved in hym. Now is the wille of the loved and the wille of this soule turned into oon, as fire and flawme, for love hath this soule al ymeved in hym.'

'A! right swete pure divine love,' seith this soule, 'what this is a sweet
20 uniaunce, that I am meved in the thinge that I love more than me! So have I loste my name for lovynge, that so litel may love. Thus am I meved in the thing that I love more than me, this is, in love, for I ne love but love.'

B

NICHOLAS LOVE, *THE MYRROUR OF THE BLESSYD LYF OF JESU CHRIST*

The Nativity

... When tyme of that blessed birthe was come—that is to sey the Soneday at midnight—Goddes son of heven, as he was conceyved in his moder wombe by the Holi Gost without sede of man, so goyng oute of that wombe without travaile or sorowe, sodeynly was upon hey at his moder
5 feet. And anone she, devoutly enclinande, with sovereyn joy toke him in hir armes, and swetly clippyng and kissyng, leide him in hir barme, and with a fulle pap, as she was taght of the Holi Gost, weshe him alle aboute with hir swete milke, and so wrapped him in the kerchif of her hede, and leide him in the crache. And anone the ox and the asse, knelyng doune,
10 leiden hir mouthes on the crache, brething at hir neses upon the child, as thei knewen by resoun that in that colde tyme the child so simply hiled hade nede to be hatte in that maner. And than his moder knelyng doune wirchiped and loued God, inwardly thonkyng, and seying in this maner: 'Lord God, holi fader of heven, I thonke the with al my might that hast
15 yive me thi der sone, and I honour the, almighty God, Goddes son and myn.' Joseph, also honouryng and wirchipyng the child, God and man, toke the sadel of the asse and made thereof a qwischyn Our Lady to sitte on and a suppoyle to leyn to. And so sat the lady of al the worlde in that simple araye byside the cracch, havyng hir mild mode and hir lovely eyene,
20 with her inward affeccioun, upon hir swete derworth child. But in this pore and symple worldly aray what gostly riches and inward counfort and joy she hade may no tonge telle. Wherfore if we wole fele the trewe joy and counfort of Jesu, we most with him and with his moder love poverté, mekenes, and bodily penance, as he yaf us ensaumple of alle these her in
25 this birthe and first comyng into this world. For of the first—that is poverté—seynt Bernard in a sermone of the Nativité of Our Lord, tellyng how he was born to counfort of mankynd, seith in this maner: 'Goddes son counforteth his peple. Wolt thow knawe his peple? That is of whom speketh David in the sauter and seith: Lord, to The is belaft the pore

peple. And he himself seith in the gospel: Wo to yow riche men that haven 30
your counfort here. How suld he counfort hem that haven her hir awne
counfort? Wherfore Cristes innocens and childhode counforteth not
jangelers and gret spekers; Cristes wepyng and teres counforteth not
dissolute laghers; his simple clothing counforteth not hem that gone in
proude clothing; and his stable and crache counforteth not hem that loven 35
first setes and worldly wirchipes. And also the aungeles in Cristes nativité
apperyng to the wakyng shepherdes counforten none other but the pore
travailoures; and to hem tellen thei the joy of newe light, and not to the
rich men that haven hir joy and counfort here.' Also as to the secounde, we
mowen se at this birthe bothe in Crist and in his moder perfite mekenes, 40
for thei wer not sqweymes of the stable, nor of the bestes, nor of hey and
soche other abjecte symplenes. Bot this vertue of mekenes bothe Our
Lord and Our Lady kepten perfitely in alle hir dedes, and commende it
sovereynly to us; wherfore be we aboute with alle our might to gete this
vertue, knawyng that without it is non savacioun, for ther is no werke or 45
dede of us that may pleys God with pride. Also as to the thridde, we maw
se in hem bothe, and namelich in the child Jesu, noght a litel bodily
penaunce; of the whiche seynt Bernarde seith thus: 'Goddes son, whan he
wold be born, that hade in his owne fre wille to chese what tyme he wold
take therto, he chese the tyme that was most noyus and harde, as the cold 50
wyntour, namelich to a yonge childe and a pore wommans sone, that
skarsly hade clothes to wrappe him inne, and a cracche as for a cradile to
lay him inne . . .'

C

THE PYLGREMAGE OF THE SOWLE

Heaven

. . . In this poynt I gan to byholde into the hye hevene, that every dele
schyned as bright burned gold. And there I sawe a merveillous cercle of
syngulere gretnesse conteynyng withynne hitself wonder grete space, and a
ful greet circuite hit made—the grettnesse therof ne couthe I not gesse nor
acounte. This cercle entrid in that oo side of that goldene hevene and 5
come out in that other, in manere of a reynebowe. This cercle in his
bordure was, as me semed, of mesurable brede, of colour saphiryn, and
was redily lyned by ordre, and set ful of sterres wonder bright schynyng
and clerly flawmyng, whiche were sette by thritty and thritty, in suche a
manere wise that in every thritty was a sette a grete sonne, as me semed, as 10
large as the bordure of this cercle. Above this cercle aungels sungen and
maden myche melodie with many dyverse instrumentis, that yif there had

be herd suche a song in erthe, I suppose that stones shulde not have kept
hem fro syngyng, for the passynge joye. There nys no thing in erthe that
15 ne wolde have hasted thider, and have receyved lyf by mevyng of this
forside cercle deferent, so mesurably it turneth aboute. These forseid
aungels led thre spirites whiche were coroned with gold, and clothed to the
foot of the rede blody purpre, gerd with ceyntis of gold wonder bright
schynynge. Withynne this goldene hevene thei entrid. In a litel while thei
20 comyn out ayen, and alle these othre seintes out of here mansiouns
assembled hem redy forto mete with hem. And so thei wenten aboute,
environyng the hevene, and sungen busily, and seide in this wise: 'Blessid
be thou, Lord, oure God and oure sovereigne creatour, Jesu Goddes sone,
that boght us with thi blood, that so honourest oure felawschip, for the
25 good dedes of whiche we ben partiners of thi sovereigne grace!' Than I
bethoght upon the briddes—as thrusshes and throstles and stares—
whiche I have seyn sittynge in assemblé upon an hye tree in a clere day,
singynge so swetly, and preysing the Lord that is her creatour. Right so
dede alle these seintes, ful besily honourynge and praysinge the sovereigne
30 Lord above, ful mekely and devoutly joynenge here hondes.

D

THE BOOK OF MARGERY KEMPE

Margery Comes to Jerusalem

. . . And so thei went forth into the Holy Lond tyl thei myth se Jerusalem.
And, whan this creatur saw Jerusalem, rydyng on an asse, sche thankyd
God wyth al hir hert, preyng hym for hys mercy that lych as he had browt
hir to se this erdly cyté Jerusalem, he wold grawntyn hir grace to se the
5 blysful cité of Jerusalem abovyn, .s. the cyté of Hevyn. Owyr Lord Jesu
Cryst, answeryng to hyr thowt, grawntyd hir to have hir desyr. Than for joy
that sche had and the swetnes that sche felt in the dalyawnce of owyr Lord
sche was in poynt to a fallyn of hir asse, for sche myth not beryn the
swetnesse and grace that God wrowt in hir sowle. Than tweyn pylgrymys
10 of Duchemen went to hir, and kept hir fro fallyng; of whech the on was a
preste, and he put spycys in hir mowth to comfort hir, wenyng sche had
ben seke. And so thei holpyn hir forth to Jerusalem. And whan sche cam
ther, sche seyd, 'Serys, I prey yow beth nowt displesyd thow I wepe sore in
this holy place wher owyr Lord Jesu Crist was qwyk and ded.' Than went
15 thei to the Tempyl in Jerusalem, and thei wer latyn in on the on day at
evynsong-tyme, and abydyn therin til the next day at evynsong-tyme. Than
the frerys lyftyd up a cros and led the pylgrimys abowte fro on place to
another wher owyr Lord had sufferyd hys peynys and hys passyons, every

man and woman beryng a wax candel in her hand. And the frerys alwey, as
thei went abowte, teld hem what owyr Lord sufferyd in every place. And 20
the forseyd creatur wept and sobbyd so plentyvowsly as thow sche had seyn
owyr Lord wyth hir bodyly ey sufferyng hys passyon at that tyme. Befor hir
in hyr sowle sche saw hym veryly be contemplacyon, and that cawsyd hir to
have compassyon. And whan thei cam up onto the Mownt of Calvarye,
sche fel down that sche mygth not stondyn ne knelyn, but walwyd and 25
wrestyd wyth hir body, spredyng hir armys abrode, and cryed wyth a lowde
voys as thow hir hert xulde a brostyn asundyr, for in the cité of hir sowle
sche saw veryly and freschly how owyr Lord was crucifyed. Beforn hir face
she herd and saw in hir gostly sygth the mornyng of owyr Lady, of Sen
John and Mary Mawdelyn, and of many other that lovyd owyr Lord. And 30
sche had so gret compassyon and so gret peyn to se owyr Lordys peyn that
sche myt not kepe hirself fro krying and rorying thow sche xuld a be ded
therfor.

And this was the fyrst cry that evyr sche cryed in any contemplacyon.
And this maner of crying enduryd many yerys aftyr this tyme for owt that 35
any man myt do, and therfor sufferyd sche mych despyte and mech
reprefe. The cryeng was so lowde and so wondyrful that it made the pepyl
astoynd les than thei had herd it beforn and er ellys that thei knew the
cawse of the crying. And sche had hem so oftyntymes that thei madyn hir
ryth weyke in hir bodyly myghtys, and namely yf sche herd of owyr Lordys 40
passyon. And sumtyme, whan sche saw the crucyfyx, er yf sche sey a man
had a wownde er a best, whethyr it wer, er yyf a man bett a childe befor hir
er smet an hors er another best wyth a whippe, yyf sche myth sen it er
heryn it, hir thowt sche saw owyr Lord be betyn er wowndyd lyk as sche
saw in the man er in the best, as wel in the feld as in the town, and be 45
hirselfe alone as wel as among the pepyl. Fyrst whan sche had hir cryingys
at Jerusalem, sche had hem oftyntymes, and in Rome also. And whan sche
come hom into Inglonde, fyrst at hir comyng hom it comyn but seldom, as
it wer onys in a moneth, sythen onys in the weke, aftyrward cotidianly, and
onys sche had .xiiii. on o day, and another day sche had .vii, and so as God 50
wolde visiten hir, sumtyme in the cherch, sumtyme in the strete, sumtym
in the chawmbre, sumtyme in the felde whan God wold sendyn hem, for
sche knew nevyr tyme ne owyr whan thei xulde come. And thei come nevyr
wythowtyn passyng gret swetnesse of devocyon and hey contemplacyon.
And as sone as sche parceyvyd that sche xulde crye, sche wolde kepyn it in 55
as mech as sche myth that the pepyl xulde not an herd it, for noyng of hem.
For summe seyd it was a wikkyd spiryt vexid hir; sum seyd it was a sekenes;
sum seyd sche had dronkyn to mech wyn; sum bannyd hir; sum wisshed
sche had ben in the havyn; sum wolde sche had ben in the se in a
bottumles boyt; and so ich man as hym thowte. Other gostly men lovyd hir 60
and favowrd hir the mor. Sum gret clerkys seyden owyr Lady cryed nevyr

so ne no seynt in hevyn, but thei knewyn ful lytyl what sche felt, ne thei wolde not belevyn but that sche myth an absteynd hir fro crying yf sche had wold. . . .

She Cares for her Old Husband

65 It happyd on a tyme that the husbonde of the sayd creatur, a man in gret age passyng thre scor yer, as he wolde a comyn down of hys chambyr barfoot and bar-legge, he slederyd er ellys faylyd of hys fotyng, and fel down to the grownd fro the gresys, and hys hevyd undyr hym grevowsly brokyn and bresyd, insomeche that he had in hys hevyd .v. teyntys many days whil

70 hys hevyd was in holyng. And, as God wold, it was knowyn to summe of hys neybowrys how he was fallyn downe of the gresys, peraventur thorw the dene and the luschyng of hys fallyng. And so thei comyn to hym, and fowndyn hym lying wyth hys hevyd undir hym, half on lyfe, al rowyd wyth blood, nevyr lyke to a spokyn wyth preyst ne with clerk but thorw hy grace

75 and myracle. Than the sayd creatur, hys wife, was sent for, and so sche cam to hym. Than was he takyn up and hys hevyd was sowyd, and he was seke a long tyme aftyr, that men wend that he xulde a be deed. And than the pepil seyd, yyf he deyd, hys wyfe was worthy to ben hangyn for hys deth, forasmeche as sche myth a kept hym and dede not. They dwellyd not

80 togedyr, ne thei lay not togedyr, for, as it is wretyn beforn, thei bothyn wyth on assent and wyth fre wil of her eithyr haddyn mad avow to levyn chast. And therfor to enchewyn alle perellys thei dwellyd and sojowryd in divers placys wher no suspicyon xulde ben had of her incontinens, for first thei dwellyd togedir aftyr that thei had mad her vow, and than the pepil

85 slawndryd hem and seyd thei usyd her lust and her likyng as thei dedyn beforn her vow makyng. And, whan thei wentyn owt on pilgrimage er to se and spekyn wyth other gostly creaturys, many evyl folke whos tongys wer her owyn hurt, faylyng the dreed and lofe of owr Lord Jesu Crist, demtyn and seydyn that thei went rathar to woodys, grovys, er valeys to usyn the

90 lust of her bodiis that the pepil xuld not aspyin it ne wetyn it. They, havyng knowlach how prone the pepil was to demyn evyl of hem, desiryng to avoydyn al occasyon, inasmech as thei myth goodly, be her good wil and her bothins consentyng, thei partyd asundyr as towchyng to her boord and to her chambrys, and wentyn to boord in divers placys. And this was the

95 cawse that sche was not wyth hym, and also that sche xulde not be lettyd fro hir contemplacyon. And therfor, whan he had fallyn and grevowsly was hurt, as is seyd beforn, the pepil seyd, yyf he deyid, it was worthy that sche xulde answeryn for hys deth. Than sche preyid to owr Lord that hir husbond myth levyn a yer and sche to be deliveryd owt slawndyr yyf it wer

100 hys plesawns. Owr Lord seyd to hir mende, 'Dowtyr, thou xalt have thi bone, for he xal levyn and I have wrowt a gret myrakyl for the that he was

not ded. And I bydde the take hym hom and kepe hym for my lofe.' Sche
seyd, 'Nay, good Lord, for I xal than not tendyn to the as I do now.' 'Yys,
dowtyr,' seyd owr Lord, 'thou xalt have as meche mede for to kepyn hym
and helpyn hym in hys nede at hom as yyf thou wer in chirche to makyn thi 105
preyerys. And thou hast seyd many tymys that thu woldist fawyn kepyn me.
I prey the now kepe hym for the lofe of me, for he hath sumtyme fulfillyd
thi wil and my wil bothe, and he hath mad thi body fre to me that thou
xuldist servyn me and levyn chast and clene, and therfor I wil that thou be
fre to helpyn hym at hys nede in my name.' 'A, Lord,' seyd sche, 'for thi 110
mercy grawnt me grace to obeyn thi wil and fulfille thi wil and late nevyr
my gostly enmys han no powyr to lett me fro fulfillyng of thi wil.' Than
sche toke hom hir husbond to hir and kept hym yerys aftyr as long as he
levyd and had ful mech labowr wyth hym, for in hys last days he turnyd
childisch ayen, and lakkyd reson that he cowd not don hys owyn esement 115
to gon to a sege, er ellys he wolde not, but as a childe voydyd his natural
digestyon in hys lynyn clothys ther he sat be the fyre er at the tabil, whethyr
it wer, he wolde sparyn no place. And therfor was hir labowr meche the
mor in waschyng and wryngyng and hir costage in fyryng, and lettyd hir ful
meche fro hir contemplacyon that many tymys sche xuld an yrkyd hir 120
labowr saf sche bethowt hir how sche in hir yong age had ful many
delectabyl thowtys, fleschly lustys, and inordinat lovys to hys persone. And
therfor sche was glad to be ponischyd wyth the same persone, and toke it
mech the mor esily and servyd hym and helpyd hym, as hir thowt, as sche
wolde a don Crist hymself. 125

E

THE BOKE OF GOSTELY GRACE

Our Lord's Heart

Upon a Sowndaye while the covente song this: *Asperges me Domine*—thys
mayde in her soule seyde to Oure Lorde, 'My lorde, wherin wylt thou now
wasch and clense myn herte?' Oure Lorde anone byclipped here all aboute
all hoole with an unestimable love, and seyde, 'y shall wasch the in the love
of my devyne herte.' And with that he openyd the gate of hys devyne 5
herte, which ys the tresoureye of that swete godhede that passith all the
swetness of any honye. Into the which tresoureye she entred, as it had be
into a vyneyerde, and ther she say a flood of rennyng water fro the este into
the weste, and abowte the flowyng water were .xii. trees which bare .xii.
maner of fruyte. And by tho .xii. maner of fruytes were betokenyd the 10
vertues which Seynt Poule noumbreth in his pistell, that is to say: pees, joy,
cheryté, paciens, longanymyté, goodnes, benignyté, softnes, feith, temper-

aunce, contynence, and chastité. Thys water was clepid the flood of
cheryté. Thys mayd entred into this water, and ther she was all wasch of all
15 fylthes and spottys of synne. In this water ther was a grete multitude of
fyssh, which had skalys all of golde; which multitude betokenyd the lovyng
soulys that were departyd from all erthly delectaciouns, and cast hemself
into the well full of all goodes—and that was into Oure Lorde Jesu. In the
vyneyerd were syonys of the vyne plantyd. Some stode upryght, and sum
20 bowed toward the erth. Thei that stoden upryght ben they which dispysed
the worlde with hys floures, and left up here hertys and thoughtes all to
hevenly thinges. The syones the which bowed downward to the erth beth
such synfull creatures which lyen in the duste of the erth of her synnes.
Thanne, to this maydenes semyng, Oure Lorde dalfe in the erth in the
25 lykenes of a gardener. This mayd seyd thanne to Oure Lorde, 'Lorde,
what is thy dolvyng instrument?' Oure Lorde seyde, 'It is my drede.' In
some places of that vyneyard the erthe was herd, and in som place it was
nesshe. The herd erth bytokenes her hertes which were hardid in synnes,
and kunne nought be amendyd by non amonycioun ne be no blamyng.
30 The nesshe erth betokenith her hertys which be made nesshe by terys and
be verrey contricioun of herte. After thys, Oure Lorde seyde, 'Thys
vyneyerd ys myne holy chyrch, in the which y swat with grete travell .xxxiii.
yere. Travayle thow nowe with me in this vynyard.' She askyd howe, and
Oure Lorde sayde, 'Thy travayle shall be to water it well.' Thys mayd
35 thought in here soule that she ranne anon with a grete fersnesse to the
flowyng water, and brought a cowle full of water on her shulderys, and
gretely was charched with that burden, but oure Lorde cam and bare with
her and than was it to bere but a lyght burden. . . .

F

THE GILTE LEGEND

St Brendan Journeys to the Land of Promise

. . . And then Seint Brandoun made wynde up the sayle, and forthe they
seyled in Goddys name. And the schip seyled forthe as faste as the arowe
fleeth fro the bowe. And when the sunne arose by the morowe, they wist
not where they were, for they myght se no londe; but ther schip was
5 stronge and goode, for they seyled .xl. daies and .xl. nyghtis evyn plat eest.
And then they se an ilelonde in the northe fer fro them, and seilyd
thedirward, and se a greet rocke of stone appere above the watir, and .iii.
dayes they seylid aboute it or they cowde gete ynne. But atte the last,
thorugh the purviaunce of Oure Lorde, they founde a lytil haven, and
10 wente anoon a-londe everychon. And then sodenly come to them a fair

hounde, and fille downe at the feet of Seint Brandon, and made hym goode chere in hys maner. And then he bade his bretheren be of goode chere, for 'Oure Lord Jesu hath sent us his messenger to lede us the weye into summe place ordeyned for us by Oure Lord.' And then the hounde wente foorthe into a ful feyre halle, wherein they founde the tablis spred 15 and set ful of good mete and drynke. And then Seint Brandon with alle his felowis set them to the table and eete and drank and made them mery in the best wise. And also there were beddis ordeyned for them alle wherein they after soper slepte fulle meryly, and toke ther reste aftir ther greet labour. And then on the morowe they wente ayen to ther schip and seiled 20 in the see ful longe aftir or they cowde fynde eny londe. But at the last, by the purvyaunce of oure lord, they se fer fro them a fulle feire ilelonde ful of grene pasture, wherein were the whittist and feyriste schepe that evere they se, and the grettyste, for every schepe was as grete as an oxe. And then there come to them a ful good man, and welcomed them alle and 25 made them ful good chere, and seide, 'This ys the ilelonde of schepe, and in this ilelonde is never colde wedir, but evir feir somer, and that causith the schepe to be so greet and white; and they eetith the beste grasse and erbis that ys in oony londe, wherefor they ben so fair and greet.' And then this good man toke his leve of them, and bad them seile foorthe right eest, 30 and within schorte tyme by Goddis grace they schuld come to a place lyke Paradise where they schulde kepe theyr Eestirtyde. And then they wente to schip ayen, and by the purviaunce of Oure Lorde they came within schort tyme aftir to that ilelonde, and when they come nye thedir they myght not seyle therto for greet rockis of stoon, but abode styl there besyde. And then 35 the monkis wente oute of the schip upon the rocke, and bygan to make a greete fyre on the rocke, and set over a caudron to dight with her mete—but Seynt Brandon abode stylle in the schip. And when the fyre waxid right hoote and ther mete was nye sodyn inough, then this grete rocke lyke an ilelonde bigan to meve, wherfor the monkis were ful sore 40 agast, and lefte ther mete stille in the caudron, and highed hem faste to the schip, for they were ful soore adredde and wist not what it was. But then Seint Brandon comfortid them and seide, 'Be not agast, for it is a greet fissche of the see that is clepid Jasconye; he laborith nyght and daye to put his tayle in hys mouthe, but for greetnes therof he may not.' And then 45 anoon they wounde up the seile and seiled even west .iii. daies and .iii. nyghtis or they se oony londe, wherfor they were right hevy. But within schorte tyme aftir by the purvyaunce of Oure Lord they se a ful feire ilond ful of flouris, trees, and erbes; wherfor they were ful joyful, and thonkid Oure Lord. And as soone as they came thedyr, they wente up into that 50 ilond, and when they hadde longe goon in this ilond they founde a right feyre welle, and thereby stode a ful feire tree ful of feyre bowis, and on every bowe sate a feyre birde. They sat so thycke theron that unnethe a man myght se eny leeff of the tree. And every birde sange so merély that it

55   was an hevenly noyse to here. Wherfor Seynt Brandon knelyd down on his
knees and wepte for joye and made his preyers to Oure Lord to know what
this byrdys mente. And then anoon Oure Lord made oon of the birdis flee
fro the tree toward Seint Brandon, and with the flikerynge of his wynges
he made a noyse lyke a fidill, that hym semyd that he herde never a meryer
60   melodye. And then Seint Brandon commaundid the birde to telle hym
what causith them to sitte so thicke on that tree and synge so merely. And
then the birde seide to hym, 'Sumtyme we were angels in hevyn, but when
oure maister Lucifer fel downe into helle for his hye pride eche of us fyl
with hym aftir oure offence, summe lower than sum after ther trespasse;
65   and for our trespasse was litil, therfor Oure Lorde hath set us here out of
alle peyn in fulle greet joye and myrthe after his plesynge, and to serve hym
thus upon this tree in oure beste maner that we kan. And the Sonday is a
day of reste fro alle worldly ocupacion, and that day alle we ben made as
white as snowe to plese and preyse Oure Lorde in that day in the beste
70   wise we can.'

*   *   *   *   *

    . . . And then they toke theyr leve ther, and wente to there schip ayeen
and seyled foorthe even eest .xl. daies. And at the .xl. daies ende it began
to hayle right faste, and therewith ther come so derke a myst that lastyd
right longe tyme, wherfor Seynt Brandon and hys monkys were ful sore
75   agast. And then anoon come ther procuratour and bad them be of good
cheer, for they were come into the Londe of Beheste. And anoon as the
myst was past, they se the feyrest londe eestward that ever oony man se,
and it was so clere and so bright that it was greet joy to beholde. And every
tree was fulle of frute, and the appyls were rype there thanne lyke as they
80   been here in hervist. And .xl. daies they walkyd aboute in this plesaunt
lond, but they cowthe fynde noon ende of that lond, and there was ever day
and never nyght, and that was a ful menable contrey, neyther to hoote ne
to colde. And at the last they come to a feyr ryver, but they durst not go
overe, and anoon ther come to them a ful feyre yonge man and a ful
85   curteyse, and welcomed theym alle and kussyd them by rowe and callyd
every man by hys name. And he honowred greetly Seynt Brandon and toke
hym by the honde and seid, 'Be mery, for this is the londe that ye have
sought so longe, but Our Lord wylle that ye go hens wythin schort tyme
and he wole schewe yow more of his privitees. When ye come ayen into the
90   see, Owre Lord wylle that ye charge your schip with the frute of this londe,
and hye yow hens for ye may no lenger here abyde; but thou schalt seyle
ayen toward thyn owne contré, and soone aftyr thow comyst hoome, thow
schalt dye. For this water that thow seist here departith the world asondre,
and in the tother syde of this watyr may no man come while he ys here in
95   thys lyfe. And this frute that ye se here is ever thus rype, every tyme of the
yeer, and allwey thys londe is as light as it is nowe, and he that kepith oure

lordis biddingis at alle tyme schalle se this londe or he passe out of the world.' And then Seynt Brandon and hys monkys toke of thys fruyt what they wolde, and also they toke with hem greete plenté of precyous stones, and toke ther leve of this yonge man, and wente to theyr schip with alle 100 theyr stuff with them, but they wepte ful sore that they schuld so soone departe fro thens. And anoon as they come to ther schip they made seyle and come here wey hoom in safté within schort tyme aftyr.

St Christopher Seeks the Mightiest Prince in the World

Seynt Crystofore was of the kynrede of Cananee, and he was of so grete stature that he was .xii. cubytes long, and he had right a dredefull vysage. 105 And yt ys redde in somme gestys that when he hadde servyd a kyng of Cananee yt fyll in hys thought that he wolde seke the grettest prynce of the worlde and dwelle with hym and obey hym. And so longe he sought that he found right a grete kyng, of whom the renowne was that he was the grettest in the worlde. And when the kynge sawe hym, he resseyved hym gladlye, 110 and made hym dwelle wyth hym in hys courte. And, in a tyme, yt fylle that a jugeler sange afore the kynge, and in hys songe he namyd ofte the devylle. And the kyng that was Crysten, whan he herde that, he blessyd hym faste. And when Crystofyr saw hym doo so, he merveyled hym gretly what sygne that was, and why he dyd soo he askyd, and when the kyng 115 wold not telle hym, he seyde but yf that he tolde hym he wolde never do hym service lenger. And then the kynge seyde to hym, 'Every tyme that I here the fende namyd, I drede lest that he take power over me and noye me, and therfor I blesse me with this sygne of the crosse forto defende me fro hys power.' Then seyde Cristofyr. 'Yf thow drede the devyll, then he ys 120 more myghty and gretter lorde then thowe; wherefor I se well that I am dysseyved of myn hope, for I wende to have founde the grettest prynce and the myghtyest of the world. But nowe farewelle, for I wylle go seke hym to be my lorde, and that I bee hys servaunt.' And then he departydd fro the kynge. And then he went in grete haste to seke the devyll, and as he wente 125 by grete deserte he sawe a grete felisschypp of knyghtys, amonge whyche there was oone a cruell and oryble knyght that came to hym and askyd hym whether he went. And Cristofor seyde, 'I go to seke my lorde the devyll, forto have hym to my mayster.' And then the devyll seyde, 'I am he that thowe sekyst!' And then was Cristofer joyfull and glad, and oblegyd hym to 130 be perpetuelly his servaunt. And then as they wente togeder by a grete highwey, they found a crosse sette uppe, and as soone as the fende sawe that crosse, he was aferde, and fledde, and lefte the hyghweye and ledde Cristofor thorowe a scharpe deserte. And when they were passyd the crosse, he brought hym into the highweye ayen. And when Cristofor sawe 135 that, he askyd hym what hym eyled that he was so afreyed. And he wolde

not telle hym. And then seyde Cristofor, 'But yf thowe telle me, I schall anoone parte fro the!' And then the fende was constrayned to telle hym, and seyde a man that ys callyd Cryst was hanged on the crosse, 'and when I
140 se that signe I am soore aferde therof, and flee as ferre as I may.' Then seyde Cristofor, 'Why, ys he myghtyer and gretter then thow that thow art aferde of hym and of hys sygne? Nowe se I well that I have labored in veyne when I have nott sey nor found the grettest lorde. Therfor goo on thy weye, for I wylle no lenger serve the, but I wylle go to seke Crist!' And
145 when he hadde sought longe that Crist, at the laste he came in to the last ende of a deserte, and there he founde an hermyte, the whyche prechyd to hym of Jesu Crist and taught hym dyligentelye in the feythe and seyde to hym, 'This kyng that thowe desyrest forto serve askyth the servyse of ofte fastyng.' And Cristofor seyde to hym, 'Aske somme other thyng of me for
150 that I may not doo.' And the heremyte seyd to hym, 'Then thow must wake and sey many prayers.' And Cristofor seyde, 'I note what that ys. I may do noo suche thynges.' And then the hermyte seyde, 'Knowyst thowe suche a flode?' And Cristofor seyde, 'Yee.' And then the hermyte seyde, 'Moche peple perissche there, and thowe arte of grete stature and strong and
155 myghty. Yf thow woldyst dwelle besyde that ryver and passe over all men that come, yt schulde be ryght plesant to God. And I truste fully that he that thowe desyrest forto serve will apere to the.' And then Cristofor seyd, 'Surely thys servyse may I welle doo, and I behight trewly to Crist that I wylle doo yt!' Then wente Seynt Cristofor to that flode, and made ther an
160 habytacle for hym, and he bare a grete perche in hys hande instede of a staffe, appon the whyche he lenyd in the water, and bare over all men that wolde come without cessyng, and ther he was many a daye. And, in a tyme, as he slepte in hys lytyll howse, he herd the voyse of a lytill chyld that callyd hym and seyde, 'Cristofor, come owte and bere me over!' And then he
165 awooke, and came oute, but he fownde noo creature. And when he was ayen in hys howse, he herde the same voyse, and he ronne owte and fownde noobody. The iii^de tyme he was callyd, and came owte, and then he fownde a chylde besyde the brynke of the ryver, that prayed hym benyngly to helpe hym over. And then Cristofor toke the chylde appon hys nekke,
170 and toke hys staffe in his hande and entred into the water forto passe over. And the water began to encrese lytyll and lytyll, and the chylde began to weye grevously as lede, and the ferther that he wente, the more the water began to encrese, and the chylde to weye more apon hys nekke, so ferforth that Cristofor felte a grete angwyssh, and was in grete dowte to be
175 drowned. And when he was skapyd over with grete peyne, and hadde sette the chylde too the grounde, he seyde to hym, 'Chylde, thowe hast putte me in a grete perylle, and thowe weyed so moche that thowh I hadde bore all the worlde I myght bere no hevyer apon me then I dydde!' And the chylde answeryd and seyd, 'Cristofor, merveyle the not, for thowe hast not oonly
185 bore uppon thy schulder Jesu Crist, thy kyng, that thowe servyst, but also

thow haste borne all the worldys savyowr. And for thowe schalt wete that I
sey sothe, when thowe arte passyd over ayen, pycche thy staffe in the erthe
besyde thy hous, and thowe schalt se tomorowe that he schall bere flowres
and frute.' And anon he vanyssched fro hys syght. And then wente   190
Cristofor, and fycched his staffe into the erthe, and when he arose in the
morowe tyde he founde yt as a palme tree beryng bothe frute and
flowre. . . .

G

DE IMITATIONE CHRISTI

Of Meditacion of Deth

This day a man is, and tomorow he apperith not. Ful sone shal this be
fulfilled in the; loke whether thou canst do othir wise. And whan man is
oute of sight, sone he passeth oute of mynde. O the dulnesse and the
hardenes of mannes herte, that onely thenkith on thinges present, and
providith not more for thinges to come! Thou shuldist have the so in every   5
dede and every thought, as though thou shuldist dye anon. If thou haddist
a gode conscience, thou shuldist not moche drede dethe. It is better to
eschue synnes than to fle dethe. If thou be not redy today, how shalt thou
be redy tomorow? The morwe is a day uncerteyn, and what wost thou if
thou shalt lyve tomorwe? What availith it to lyve longe, when ther ys lytell   10
amendment? A longe lif amendith not at all tyme, but som tyme encrescit
synne. Wolde god that we lyved wel in this worlde o day! Many men
acountin the yeres of her conversion, but oftetymes litel is the fruyt of
amendement. If it be dredful to dye, peraventure it is more perilous to lyve
longe. Blisful is he that hath the houre of his dethe evere before his eyen,   15
and that every day disposeth himself to dye. If thou have seen eny man dye,
thenkith that thou shalt go the same wey. Whan it is mornyng, wene thiself
that thou shalt not come to the even. And whan even cometh be not bolde
to behete thiself the mornyng. Wherfore be evere redy, and lyve so that
dethe finde the never unredy. Many men dien sodenly and unavised; for   20
what houre we wene not the sonne of man shal come. Whan that last houre
cometh, thou shalt begynne to fele all otherwyse of thy lif that is passed,
and thou shalt gretly sorwe that thou hast be so remysse and so negligent.
O hou blessed is he, that laborith to be suche in his lyf as he desirith to be
founde in his dethe! These shul yeve gret trust to dye, parfit contempte of   25
the worlde, fervent desire of profitynge in vertues, love of discipline,
labour of penaunce, promptitude of obedience, denyeng of himself,
beryng of al maner adversité for the love of Crist. While thou art hool, thou

maist do muche good; but whan thou art syke, I wote not what thou maist
30 do. Fewe there bith that are amendid by siknes, as they that gon muche a
pilgrymage are but seldom the holier. Delaie not the helthe of thy soule for
trust of frendes and of neighbours, for men wol foryete the sonner than
thou wenist. It is better now to make provysion by tyme, and sende tofore
som good, than to truste in other mennes helpe. If thou be not besy for
35 thiself now, who shal be besy for the in tyme comyng? Now tyme is right
preciose; but allas that thou spendist it no more profitably, wherein thou
maist deserve whereof everlastingly to lyve. Tyme shal come that thou
shalt desire o day or an houre for thin amendement, and thou wotist not
whethir thou shalt gete it. O my dere frende, of hou gret perel maist thou
40 make the fre, and of hou grete drede delyvere thiself, if thou be now
evermore dredful and suspecte of dethe! Studie to lyve so now, that thou
mowe in the houre of dethe rather joy than drede. Lerne now to dye to the
worlde, that than thou mowe begynne to lyve with Crist. Lerne now to
despice all thinges, that thou mow than go frely to Crist. Chastise now thy
45 body by penaunce, that thou mowe than have certyn confidence. And, thou
fool, wherto thenkist thou thiself to lyve longe, sith thou art sure of no day?
Hou many are deceived, and ayenst all hope drawen oute of the body! Hou
ofte hast thou herde men say, that man was slaien with a swerde, he
drouned, he falling from hye brake his nek, he in etinge sodenly waxid stif,
50 he in pleyeng toke an ende, another with fire, another with yren, another
with pestilence, another slaien amonge theves. And so the ende of all is
dethe, and mannys lif passith awey sodenly as a shadowe. Who shal have
mynde on the after thi dethe, and who shal praie for the? Do, my dere
brother, now what thou maist do, for thou wost not whan thou shalt dye,
55 and thou wost not what shal come to the after thy dethe. Whiles thou hast
tyme, gadre riches immortale; thenke no thinge but thi soule helthe;
charge onely tho thinges that longith to thi soule. Make the now frendes,
worshiping holy seintes, and folowyng her werkes, that whan thou failist in
this lyf, thei receive the into everlastinge tabernacles. Kepe thiself as a
60 pilgrime and a geste upon the erthe, to whom longith nothinge of worldly
besynes. Kepe thin herte fre, and rere it up to thy God, for thou hast here
non abiding cité; thider directe praiers and daily mornynges with teres,
that thy spirit after thi dethe mowe deserve blisfully to come to Our Lorde.

H

PRAYERS AND DEVOTIONS

(i)

Moder of God, wich dyd lappe thy lytel swete babe in clothes, and betwene

two beestes in a crybbe layde hym in hey, pray for me that my naked soul
may be lapped in drede and love of my lorde God and the. *Alleluya. Ave
Maria.*

(ii) *The Psalme of Te Deum*

We prayse the, O God; we knowleage the to be our Lorde. All the erthe   5
do worshyp the, which arte the Father everlastyng. To the crye fourthe all
angelles, the heavens, and all the powers theryn. To the thus cryeth
Cherubyn and Seraphyn contenually: Holy arte thou, holy arte thou, holy
arte thou. Thou arte our lorde God of Sabaoth. Heaven and erthe are
fulfylled with the glorye of thye majestye. The gloryouse company of the   10
apostoles prayseth the. The goodly fellowshypp of the prophetes worshyp
the. The fayre felowshypp of martyrs prayse the. The Holy Churche
throughoute alle the worlde dothe magnifye the. They knowleage the to be
the Father of an infynite majestye. They knowleage the honorable and very
onely sonne. They knowleage the Holy Goost to be a comforter. Thou arte   15
the kynge of glory, O Chryste. Thou arte the everlastynge Sonne of the
Father. Thou, whan thow shuldest take upon the our nature to delyver
man, dedyst not abhorre the Virginis wombe. Whan thou haddest
overcomen the sharpnes of death, thou openest the kyngidome of heavens
to all trew belevers. Thou syttest on the ryght hande of God in the glorye   20
of the Father. Thou arte belevyd to come our Judge. Therefore we praye
the, helpe thy servaunt whome thou haste redemed with thy preciouse
bloude. Make them to be nombred with thy sayntes in joye everlastynge. O
Lorde, save thy people and blesse thy herytage. Governe and also lefte
them up for ever. We prayse the every daye. And we worshyp thy name   25
worlde without ende. O Lorde, let yt be thy pleasure to kepe us thys day
wythoute synne. O Lorde, have mercy on us, have mercy on us. O Lorde,
let thy mercy lyghten on us, even as we truste in the.
  Chryste ys deed for our synnes, and ys rysen agayne for our ryghtuysnes.

(iii) *The Psalme called Benedictus*

Blessed be our Lorde God of Israel, for he hathe vysited and redemed   30
his people, and hathe reysed up an horne of salvacioun unto us in the
howse of hys servaunt David; evyn as he promised by the mouth of hys
holy prophetes, whiche ware syns the worlde beganne, that we shulde be
savyd frome our enemyes, and frome the handes of all them that hate us;
to fulfyll the mercy promised to our fathers, and to remember hys holy   35
testament; to performe the othe whiche he sware to our father Abraham,
that he wolde gyve hymselfe to us; that we delyvered oute of the handes of
oure enemyes might serve hyme without feare, in holynes and ryghtuysnes

before hyme all the dayes of our lyfe. And thou, chylde, shalte be called the
40 prophete of the hyest, for thou shalte go before the face of our Lorde to
prepare hys wayes; to gyve knowlege of salvacion unto hys people for the
remyssion of theyr synnes, through the tender marcye of our God, wherby
the daysprynge frome an hye hath vysited us; to gyve lyght to them that syt
in darkenes and in the shadowe of deathe, and to gyed our feeate into the
45 waye of peace. Glorye be to the Father, to the Sonne, and to the Holy
Goste. As yt was in the begynnyng, as yt ys nowe, and ever shall be. So
be yt.

(iv) *A Meditation after Communion*

    ... Therfor now, my soule, taste and se! For thy Lorde ys swete, softe,
and meke, and delectable to the, that nowe for wondryng of thi goodnes I
50 myght fayle in myselfe ynwardly, cryeng and seyeng: O, the hye myght and
worthynes! O, the hye wysdom and riches! O, the hye grace and goodnes!
O, the hye curtesye and gentilnes! O my Lorde God, that so habundantly
yevest thiself to me in this holy sacrament so that I may seye and desire
with the prophete that my soule in my bodye rejoyseth in allmyghty God
55 lyvyng! My savyour, my hert is enflamed within thy love! Myn eeres be
shadde wyde from fleschly lustes into gostly delites of the! here is my reste
in worlde of worldes! here shall I dwelle, for soveraynly I chese the. For
thou art my lyght and my helth, of whom shulde I drede? Thou art the
defender of my lyfe; whom shulde I fere but the, Lorde? For thou hast not
60 dispised thyn unworthy servaunt, ne thou hast not turned thi face from me;
but of thy pure goodnes hast visited me with thy glorious presence. O thou
endeles Trinité, O glorious Godhed, the which, by unyon of dyvyne
nature, haste made the body and the holy blode of thyn only-begoten Sone
so moche worth in praysyng that it is sufficient to raunsom all mankynde,
65 and this day therwith thou haste fedde my nedy soule, so that I have
receyved all the hole essencial beyng of the holy Trinité. O thou endeles
God! O thou light above all other lightis, of whom commyth all lightes, and
fyer passyng all fyres! For thou art the fyer that brennyth and wasteth not,
but consumest all synne and propre love that thou fyndest in a soule. And
70 yet that thou wastest not peynfully, but thou impreygnest hit with
uncessable love. For thou felest hit, yet hyt ys not so fulfilled, but desireth
evere more and more of thy lovely fyer. O endeles soverayn God, who
stereth the or mevyth thy infinite goodnes to illumyn me, thyne unworthy
creature, with the light of thy trouth? Thou thyself art the same fyer and
75 cause of love that meved the for to doo me mercy, so that on that syde I
turne me, I fynde non other than the depthe and fyre of thy most flamyng
charité. O, thou goodnes above all goodnes! Thou art oonly feyrnes, O
thou endles clennes. O, thou endles swetnes and unspecable bryghtnes!

O, thou endeles lightnes, with myrth and melody! O thou art worthyest, myghtiest, wisest, richest, most bountevous, most homly and curtese, and 80 in love and in goodnes withoute mesure! O, there shulde I have clere sight of the blessid Trinité, beholdyng withoute blynkyngys charité confermed, love delectable, louyng contynual, mekest reverence, wondryng hyest, deppest ransakyng and most plentevous spendyng, myrth withoute mesure, and joye and felicité withoute endyng! To this unspecable joy to 85 com to thou art my verey hope, for thou hast yeven thy only suthfast sone Jesu to me sacramentaly, the swetnes of my salvacioun. O, endles depnes! O endles Godhed! O depe see! ...

(v)

O blessid Jesu, swetenes of hertes and gostely hony of soules, I besiche 90 the for that bitternes of the asell and gall that thou suffred for me in thy passion, graunt me for to receve worthely, holsomly, and devoutely in the houre of my deth thi blessid body in the sacrament of the auter for remedy of my synnes and confort of my soule. Amen. *Pater noster. Ave.*

(vi)

Go, Crysten soule, owte of thys worlde in the name of the Almyghty 95 Fader that made the of nought, in the name of Jesu Cryste hys Son, that suffred hys passyon for the, and in the name of the Holy Gost that was infoundyd into the. Holy angelles and archaungelles, trones and dominacions, pryncehodes, potestates, and vertewes, cherubyn and seraphyn mete with the. Patriarches and profytes, aposteles and evangelystes, martyres 100 and confessoures, monkes, heremytes, maydens and wydows, children and innocentes helpe the. The prayers of all prestys and dekenes and all the degrees of Holy Churche helpe the, that in pease be thy place, and thy dwellyng in hevynly Jerusalem everlasting, by the mediacioun of our Lorde Jesu Criste, that ys medyatour betwene God and man. Amen. 105

I

John Alcock (?): *A Sermon for a Boy Bishop*

... In the begynnynge thenne of this symple exhortacioun, that I a chylde wantynge the habite of cunnynge maye be directyd by hym that gave to that chylde Danyel *sermonem rectum et spiritum deorum* somewhat to say to

his lawde and praysynge, and to alle pure chyldren that ben here present
5 edifyenge. We shal atte this tyme devowtly make our prayers, in the whiche
prayers I recomende unto your devocyons the welfare of all Crystis
chyrche, oure holy fader the Pope, with alle the clergy, my lorde of
Caunterbury, the ryghte reverend fader and worshipfull lord my broder
Bysshop of London, your Dyocesan; also for my worshypful broder Deane
10 of this cathedral chyrche, wyth all residensaries and prebendaries of the
same. And most intierly I pray you to have myself in your speciall
devocioun, that I may contynew in this degree that I now stonde, and never
herafter to be vexyd with Jeroms visyon, the whiche is wryten *Jeremie
primo*, whanne the good Lorde askyd of Jeremy, *'Quid tu vides, Jeremia?'*
15 He answerde and sayd, *'virgam vigilantem ego video.'*: 'a waken rodde I se,'
sayde Jeremy. Truely, thys waken rodde ofte tymes hath troubled me in my
chyldehode, that *lumbi mei impleti illucionibus et non est sanitas in carne mea:
afflictus sum et humiliatus sum nimis*. And therfore, though I be now in hye
dignité, yet whan I se other here my mayster that was, thenne *operuit*
20 *confusio faciem meam; a voce contremuerunt labia mea*. As Nero the emperour
wolde to his mayster Seneca, the same wysshe I wolde to my mayster I love
so well. And for ther true dylygence that al my maysters the whyche
taughte me ony cunnyng in my youthe gave to me, I wolde they were
promyttid to be perpetuall felowes and collegeners of that famouse college
25 of the kynges foundacion in Suthwerk that men calle the Kynges
Benche—gretter worshypp I can not wysshe than forto sytte in the kynges
owne benche. And for bycause charyté is perfyghte yf it be extendyd as
well to th'ende of the lyfe as it is the lyfe self, I wolde they sholde ende ther
lyfe in that holy waye the whyche oftentimes I radde whan I was querester,
30 in the marteloge of Poulis, where many holy bodyes deyed, callyd in Latyn
Via Tiburtina, in Englysshe as moche to saye as the highewaye to
Tiburne. . . .

J

THE CHIRCHE OF THE EVYLL MEN AND WOMEN

Gambling

Fyrst sayd Lucyfer, 'I wyll ordeyne in my chirche the offyces and
benefyces. And even so as in the chirche of Cryst our adversary there is
one chefe that hathe all puyssaunce, that is for to wyte the pope, in lyke
wyse I wyl that there be one heed in my chirche. And that shall be I, that
5 shal be the heed of the players and of the other unhappy dampned.' And
then answered al his supposstes, 'It pleaseth us! It pleaseth us!' After said
Lucyfer, 'I wyl have cardynalles, and ordeyne that they shal be the grete

lordes, the offycers, and all the prelates that taketh awaye these playes wherof procedeth so many evylles and synnes, as bayllyes, the juges, the provostes, the levetenauntes, the mayres, and all them that maye take them 10 awaye, how well that theyrselfe playe not. *Quia qui tacet consentire videtur.* That is for to saye, who that is styll and may punysshe semeth to gyve his consentyng to the thynge that he seeth done. The moost gretest lordes are the cardynalles, the whiche is by my syde. Theyr names are regystred in the boke of the dampned. And then after I wyll have bysshoppes in my 15 chirche. Tho shall be the gentylmen, burgesyse, and marchauntes, that have the great halles, gardyns, and courtes, thereas is tenysplayes, closshe, berlan, fre square, and dyvers other semblable playes that scoles be holden of. *Item*, there is the house episcopall besyde the chirche. And also in this maner I wyll that besyde myne be bordelles, tavernes, sellers, and hote 20 houses dyssolute thereas is commytted so many horryble synnes. After, even so as in the chirche of our adversary there is chanons and curates, I wyll that the hostelers and taverners be oure curates thereas our subgectes may go drynke, laugh, and make good chere. Our chanons shall be they that assyste and beholde the playe, and wage, or lenne mony for to have 25 parte of the butyn or wynnynge that the same unhappy players shall make. *Item*, moreover I wyll have chapelles even so as there is in the chirche of our adversary Cryst, and that shall be the barbers shoppes, and suche maner of folkes, thereas is tables for to passe the tyme whan they have nothynge to do. *Item*, I wyl have oratoryes and places to praye in, for there 30 is in the chirche of our adversary. That shall be the houses of some burgeyses, marchauntes, where as secretely and not openly they resorte and playe togyder, thre or foure or fyve or syxe hasardours and other miserable men and women, and shall be there unto mydnyght playnge at dyce or at cardes. And unto all the abovesaid players for theyr servyce, 35 dystrybucions, and wages we shal receyve them with us, and promyse them the wages of everlastyng dampnacyon. *Item*, yet wyll I that there be dyverse men and women for to come and se the servyce in oure chirche, as at the servyce of oure adversaryes chirche, and that they kepe grete scylence and beholde the players affectuously swere and blaspheme and wronge eche 40 other. It shall be they the whiche beholdeth the players playe at dyce or cardes, the whiche shal be wel by the space of thre or foure houres or more in lokynge and beholdinge the players, indurynge colde, hongre and other necessytees, and shall not anoye and wery them so moche as to be one houre in the chirche of God. Also to the ende that my chirche fayle not, 45 and bycause that dyvers of our offycers maye happen deye, I wyll that the chyldren loke upon theyr faders that playe, and servauntes theyr maysters, and so of other degrees, as well the auncyentes as other, to the ende that they may lerne and contynually byholde it, ryght so as in the chirche of God the chyldren lerne of the auncyent men for to upholde the servyce of 50 Cryst after theyr dethes. And yet better to the ende for to have yonge folke

amonge the olde, I ordeyne that the fyrst day of the newe yere they gyve
unto the chyldren, maydens and bachelers, new yeres gyftes, as pynnes,
poyntes, and moneye for to bye lekerous thynges, for to go to the taverne
55 and other places dyssolute and yll, to the bordelles and other unthrifty
places. By this we may wynne moche.' Unto the whiche answered all the
devylles of hell, his complyces, with one voyce, 'Be it done! Be it done! We
consent therto.'

K

MARY OF NEMMEGEN

Mary Meets the Devil

. . . As Mary had these answeres of hyr aunte, she departed fro hyr with a
hevy harte out of the towne of Nemmegen in the evenyng, and at the laste
she went so longe tyll she cam to a thycke hegge, where that she satt hyr
downe, wepynge and gyvynge hyrselfe unto the dyvell, and sayd, 'Woo be
5 to the, my aunte! This may I thanke the for! Nowe care I nat whether that I
kyll myselfe, or whether that I goo to drowne me, and I care nat whether
the dyvell or God come to me and helpe me—I kare nat whether of them
two it be!'
   The dyvell, that is at all tymes reddy for to hauke after dampned sowles,
10 heryng these wordes of Marye, turned hym into the lekenes of a man, but
he had but one yee, for the dyvell can never turne hym in the lykenes of a
man, but he hathe some faute. And than sayd he to hisselfe, 'Nowe wyll I
goo suger my wordes forto speke unto this mayde that I desplease hyr nat,
for men muste speke swetely to women.' And with those wordes sayde he
15 to Mary, 'O fayer mayde, why syt you here thus wepyng? Hathe there any
man that hathe dyspleased you or done you wronge? If that I knewe hym, I
shulde be awrokyn on hym. Than Mary, herynge his voyce, loked besyde
hyr and sawe a man stande by hyr, wherof she was afrayde, and sayde,
'Helpe God, I am wayted!' The devell sayd unto Mary, 'Fayer mayde, be
20 nat afrayde, for I wyll nat do unto you no maner of harme, but doo you
good. For your fayernes men muste love you, and if that ye wyll consent
unto me, I shall make you a woman above all other women, for I have more
love unto you than I have to any other woman nowe lyvyng.' Than sayde
Mary, 'I syt here halfe mad and in dyspayer. I care nat whether that I gyve
25 myselfe to God or to the dyvyll so that I were out of this thraldome and
mysarye, but I pray you showe unto me who that ye be.' The dyvyll
answered to hyr, 'I am a master of many scyances, for that I take on me to
do I brynge it unto a ende, and if that ye wyll be my paramoure, I shall
teche to you all the forsayde scyances, so that there is no woman in the

worlde shall passe you.' Than sayd Mary to the dyvyll, 'I praye you, showe 30
unto me what ye be, and what youre name is.' Than sayd the dyvell, 'What
recketh you what I be? I am nat the beste of my kynne. And ye wyll nat be
displeased, my name is Satan with the one yee, that is well knowen
amonges good fellowes.' Than sayd Mary, 'Nowe perseyve I well that ye be
the dyvell.' 'That is al one who I be, for I bere unto you good love.' Than 35
sayd Mary, 'I wold nat be afrayd of hym if that it were Lusyfer hymselfe!'
Than sayde the dyvell to Marye, 'Fare mayde, wyll ye be my love? I shall
teche unto you al the scyances aforesayde, and I shall gyve unto you manye
other costely jewelles and also money at youre pleasure, so that ye shall
lacke nothynge at all and you shall have all your owne pleasure to do that 40
thynge that ye wyll desyre, so that there is noo woman shall have the
pleasure that ye shall have.' Than sayde Marye to the dyvyll, 'Or that ye lye
with me, ye shall teche to me the forsayde scyances.' Than sayde the
dyvyll, 'I am contente—aske what that ye wyll, and ye shall have it.' Than
sayde Mary, 'I wyll have nygromancy for one, for I have a unkyll that hathe 45
a boke therof, and when that he lyste, he wyll bynde the fynde therwith.'
Than sayd the dyvell, 'O fayer mayde, what ye desyre ye shal have, but I
occupy nat that scyence myselfe, for it is so daungerouse, for when that ye
begyn forto counger and if ye mysse one letter in redynge, the geste that ye
call for wyll breke your necke, and therfore I counsayll you nat to lerne that 50
scyence.' Than sayd Mary, 'If that it be so, that scyence wyll I nat lerne.'
Than was the dyvyll glad, and sayde to hisselfe, 'Nowe have I turned hyr
mynde fro that scyence, for if that she culde nygromancy, then when she
were angery with me, then wolde she bynde me therwith.' Than sayd the
dyvell to Mary, 'I shall teche to you all the scyences aforesayde, and ye 55
shall speke all maner of langages that ye wyll desyre, wherwith ye shulde
be exalted.' Than sayd Mary, 'Nowe put I away all sorowe thorowght your
wordes, and put me all hole to your wyll.' Than sayde the dyvell, 'O fayer
mayd, I desyre the of one thynge, that ye wyll chaunge your name, for I
love not to here that name, for by one Mary I and all my felashyp fare the 60
worse, and therfore shall I never love that name. And if that ye wyll chonge
your name, I shall make you a woman above all women. And chose you
whether that ye wyll be called Leyskyn, Metken, or Gretenyn.' Then sayde
Mary unto the dyvell, 'What greveth you my name, for Mary cummeth of
Maria, the sweteste name that can be, and for all the good in the worlde 65
wolde nat I chaunge my name nor be called other than Mary, for of Maria
was our Lorde borne.' When the dyvell harde hyr speke in that manere,
than sayde he to hisselfe, 'Nowe is all my laboure loste and caste under the
fote, for I can nat chaunge hyr name!' Than sayde he to Mary, 'My swete
love, if that we two shulde goo togyther, ye muste chaunge youre name, 70
and also whatsoever ye here or se ye muste say nothynge or elles we two
must nedes departe.' Than sayd Mary, 'To kepe your counsayll I am
content, but for to chaunge my name I wyll never whyle I lyve, for Maria is

all my cumforde and helpe in all my nede, and also I serve hyr dayly with a
75 prayer that I dyd lerne in my yongth, and therwith wyll I serve hyr as longe
as I lyve thowghe that I am here nowe in the wylde fylde, syttynge here
cumfordlesse.' Than sayde the dyvell to Mary, 'Whyle that ye be set holy
on that name, I desyre and I am content that ye holde the fyrste letter of
your name that is .M., and ye shall be called Emmekyn, for there be manye
80 women and maydens in your lande that be called so.' Than sayde Mary
unto Satan, 'If that ye wyll nat be contente with my name, yet for all that
wyll nat we two departe, for I am content to be called Emmekyn—yet were
I very loth do it.' Then was the dyvell glad in his mynde that she had
forsake hyr name, and sayde, 'Good love, let us goo to Shertegenbosshe,
85 and from thense we wyll goo to Anwarpe, and or that we come there we
shall have lerned all maner of langages, and also the .vii. free scyences.
And also, if that ye wyll abyde with me any tyme, ye shall see that we two
wyll worke mervayles, and ye shall no other drynke but wyne, bothe
muskeadell, bastard, romney, and all maner of other wynes at your owne
90 wyll.' . . .

Mary and Satan Return to Nijmegen

. . . And when they were come to Nemmegyn, it fortuned on the same
that it was the didycacion of a chyrche. And when they were within the
towne, than sayde Emmekyn to Satan, 'Let us goo see howe my aunte
dothe.' Than sayde Satan, 'Ye nede not to go to hyr, for she is deed more
95 than a yere agoo.' Than seyd Emmekyn to the dyvell, 'What do all yender
folkes that be yender gathered?' Than sayde the dyvell, 'They play a play
that is wont every yere to be played.' Than sayde Emmekyn, 'Good love,
let us goo here it, for I have harde my unkyll say oftentymes that a play
were better than a sermant to some folke.' Than sayde the dyvell to
100 Emmekyn, 'What lye ye on me to see the play? Let us goo to the taverne
and make good chere.' Than sayd Emmekyn, 'Good Satan, let us go here
it.' Than sayde Satan, 'Wyle that ye wolde so fayne here it, go thyder and
here it, but tarry no lenger than I shall call you.' Than went Emmekyn and
harde the playe, and the playe was of synfull lyvynge, and there she sawe
105 hyr lyvyng played before hyr face. Than she began to be sory and take
repentance. Than called the dyvell hyr, for he wolde have hyr here it nat
oute. But she wolde nat come, for by the play she was all hole turned fro
hyr mysselyvynge, and sayde, 'O good Lorde, have mercy on me, pore
wretche and synner! I am nat wordy to trede upon the erthe, and I am
110 afrayde that I have ronne to ferre.' Than sayde the dyvyll to hisselfe, 'All
my laboure is loste! She taketh unto hyr hole repentance', and sayd unto
Emmekyn, 'What ayle ye nowe? Be ye mad? Let be your wepynge and
sorowe, and let us goo to the taverne and make good chere, and put awaye

your sorowe!' Than sayde Emmekyn, 'Go fro me, thou false fynde! Woo
be to the, that ever thou cam to me, and I repente me that ever I chose the   115
for my paramour, for by the I am utterly dampned, without the more mercy
of God.' Than arose the dyvyll fro the grownde, and sayde, 'Holde your
peace and be styll, or elles I shall bere the with me to everlastynge payne!'
Than sayd Emmekyn, 'O good Lorde, have mercy on me, and defende me
from the handes of the dyvell, that he do to me no harme!' Than sayde the   120
dyvell unto hyr, 'I see it wyll be no better!' Than toke he Emmekyn in his
clawes and caryed hyr up into the ayer more hygher than ony stepyll, that
hyr unkyll and al the people mervayled therat howe it cam that she was
caryed so sodenly uppe.

L

JOHN FISHER, *A SERMON ON PSALM 37*

Que est ista que progreditur quasi aurora consurgens?

After the offence of our fyrst faders Adam and Eve, all the worlde was
confounded many yeres by derkenes and the nyght of synne, of the whiche
derkenes and nyght a remembraunce is made in holy scrypture oftentymes.
Notwithstandynge, many that were the very servauntes and worshyppers of
almyghty God, to whome the sayd derknes and nyght of synne was very   5
yrksome and grevous, had monycyon that the very sonne of ryghtwysnes
sholde sprynge upon al the worlde and shyne to theyr grete and synguler
comforte and make a mervaylous clere daye. As the prophete Zacharie
sayd and prephecyed of Cryste, *visitavit nos oriens ex alto, illuminare his qui
in tenebris et in umbra mortis sedent*: our blyssed Lord hath vysyted us from   10
above to gyve lyght unto them whiche syt in derknes and in the shadowe of
deth. Also Cryste in the gospel of Johan sayth: *Abraham vidit diem meum et
gavisus est*. Abraham sawe my daye, wherby he was made gladde and
joyfull. The naturall daye whiche we beholde sholde rather of congruence
be called the daye of the sonne, of whome he hath his begynnynge, than   15
our daye. So this spyrytuall day wherin spyrytually we lyve under the
Crysten fayth, whiche by the sonne of ryghtwysnes hath brought forth Jesu
Cryst, sholde be called more properly the daye of hym than of us. Cryste
our savyour called it his daye, sayenge, *vidit diem meum*: Abraham sawe my
daye. Abraham sawe not the present daye of Cryste as the appostles dyde;   20
he had onely the syght of it in his soule by true hope that it shold come,
notwithstandynge he and many other desyred gretly to se this spiritual
sonne and the clere day of it. Our savyour sayd to his apostles, *multi reges et
prophete voluerunt videre que vos videtis: et non viderunt*: many kynges and
prophetes wolde fayne have seen the mystery of myn incarnacyon whiche   25

ye se, and yet they dyde not, and what mervayle was it yf they that laye in derkenes and in the blynde nyght of synne wherin noo pleasure was to slepe and take rest to desyre fervently and abyde the spryngynge of the bryght sonne, our savyoure. Holy faders before the incarnacyon, whiche
30 mervaylously yrked and despysed the werkes of derkenes and the nyght of synne, everychone of theym dayly and contynually prayed that the very sonne of ryghtwysnes myght sprynge in theyr tyme. Neverthelesse theyr good hope and trust of it was dyfferred many yeres, and at the last, whan tyme was hovable and convenyent in the syght of almyghty God, he caused
35 this clere sonne for to gyve lyght unto the worlde. Nothwithstandynge, it was done in a juste and due ordre. For of a trouth it had not ben semynge and well ordred that after so grete and horryble derkenes of the nyght, the mervaylous clerenes of this sonne sholde have ben shewed immedyatly. It was accordynge of very ryght that fyrst a mornynge sholde come bytwene,
40 which was not so derke as the nyght, neyther so clere as the sonne. This ordre agreeth bothe to nature, scrypture, and reason. Fyrste, by the ordre of nature we perceyve that bytwene the derkenes of the nyght and the clere lyght of the daye, a certayne meane lyght cometh bytwene, the whiche we calle the mornynge. It is more lyghter and clerer than is the nyght, allbeit
45 the sonne is moche more clerer than it. Every man knoweth this thynge well, for dayly we have it in experyence. Holy scrypture also techeth that in the begynnynge of the worlde, whan heven and erth sholde be create, all thynges were covered with derkenes a longe season, and, or ever the sonne in his very clerenes gave lyght to the worlde, a certayne meane lyght was
50 made, whiche had place bytwene derkenes and the very clere lyght of the sonne. This is well shewed by Moyses in the begynnynge of *Genesis*. Reason also, whiche sercheth the knowlege of many causes fyndeth whan one thynge is chaunged into his contrary, as from colde to hete, it is done fyrst by certayne meanes or by certayne alteracyons comynge bytwene.
55 Water, whiche of his nature is very colde, is not sodeynly by the fyre made hote to the uttermost, but fyrste cometh bytwene a lytell warmenes, as we myght saye luke warme, whiche is neyther very hote nor very colde, but in a meane bytwene both. An apple also, whiche first is grene, waxeth not sodeynly yelowe, but fyrste it is somwhat whyte bytwene grene and yelowe
60 indyfferent. Thus we perceyve by reason that it was not convenyent this grete clerenes of the sonne our savyour sholde have ben shewed so soone and immedyatly after so ferefull and the derke nyght of synne, without rysynge of the mornynge whiche is a meane bytwene bothe. Syth it is so than, that juste and ryght ordre wyll it be so, and also it is accordynge for a
65 wyse man soo to ordre it, who wyll doubte but the wysdome of our lorde God, unable to be shewed, kepte this due and reasonable ordre, namely in his werke wherby *salutem operatus est in medio terre*, he wroughte helthe in the myddes of the erth; syth also he kepte the same in all his operacyons, as saynt Poule wytnesseth, sayenge, *quecunque ordinata sunt a deo sunt*: all

thynges well ordred be by the ordynaunce of almyghty God. Ferthermore 70
bycause this mater sholde be expressed more openly we shall endevoyre
ourselfe to shewe by the thre reasons aforerehersed that this blyssed Lady
moder to our savyour, may well be called a mornynge, syth before her none
was without synne. After her the moost clere sonne Cryst Jesu shewed his
lyght to the worlde, expulsynge utterly by his innumerable clerenesse these 75
derkenesses wherin all the worlde was wrapped and covered before.

8

PHILOSOPHY AND POLITICAL THEORY IN PROSE

OUR period offers some interesting examples of this specialized use of prose. Reynold (or Reginald) Pecock (b. 1392–5 in Wales) is an extraordinary and controversial figure, whose brilliant career (after being a fellow of Oriel College, Oxford, he was in 1444 made Bishop of Asaph, and in 1450 Bishop of Chichester) came to a sudden end. In 1457 he was accused of heresy, examined, and given the choice between recantation and death at the stake. He chose (consistently with his view of the ultimate authority of the Church) to abjure, and lived the rest of his life in obscurity and in confinement under the charge of the Abbot of Thorney. The kernel of the dispute is succinctly put in a quatrain which a number of chroniclers attribute to him at the time of his recantation:

> Witte hath wondir that resoun ne telle kan
> How maidene is modir and God is man.
> Leve thy resoun and bileve in the wondir,
> For feith is aboven and reson is undir.

His purpose (embodied in a large number of books in Latin and English, many of which were destroyed) was orthodox enough: the clergy, he thought, should refute the Lollards, and 'bi cleer witt drawe men into consente of trewe feith otherwise than bi fier and swerd or hangement'. It seems to have been the extreme stress he put on reason which was his undoing. By 'cleer witt' he means a rigorous logical argument conducted through syllogisms (as he says, didactically, 'if I be sure in my reason that no man is in the church of St Paul's in London, and that the Bishop of London is a man, I may be sure that the bishop of London is out of the church of St Paul's in London, though all angels in heaven would say the contrary'). For his time he undoubtedly had a sceptical mind: even the writings of the Fathers have to be judged by reason. This 'earnest, humourless, pedantic, but strangely pathetic and engaging figure', as E. F. Jacob describes him, has a number of claims on the attention of literary students. He is something of a linguistic innovator, responsible for some bold coinages—*bigynnyngal* or *sacramenting*—and for some genuine contributions to the development of a philosophical vocabulary (*argumentation*, *conflation*, *derogation*, etc.). He writes a prose which is generally good although it is not always easy to read. It is sometimes prolix, and sometimes nagging and hectoring in tone, but at its best has a simple clarity which is ideally matched to his 'cleer witt' and independent mind.

A general interest in political theory, the 'very and true commonweal of this realm', lies behind the various translated works of counsel for rulers, versions of Aegidius Colonna, the *Secretum Secretorum*, and other traditional writings which deal with order in the body politic and its good governance. An example of these are the translations of Alain Chartier, who speaks here not as a poet of love (cf. 6 B) but from his experience as secretary to the King of France in a period of intense disorder and misery during the wars with the English. His works of advice and consolation are well written, and were well translated (they were obviously thought to be relevant to English readers, who had their own problems of internal dissension). Original works were written by Fortescue and Dudley. The latter is in the eyes of history the better known, since with Sir Richard Empson, his fellow commissioner for forfeitures, he was a notoriously unpopular minister of Henry VII and was quickly committed to the Tower by the new king, Henry VIII, in 1509, where, before his execution in 1510, he wrote *The Tree of Commonwealth*. It is very traditional in matter, but can be eloquent—as it is here on the topic of 'trouthe'. The earlier writer, Sir John Fortescue, also a prominent political personage (he was for many years Chief Justice of the Court of King's Bench), was a more distinguished intellectual figure. In his various works he shows a concern for the continuity of traditional political values and for the need to define them and the institutions in which they took form. *The Governance of England* discusses with clarity and elegance English constitutional principles and suggests some administrative reforms. Fortescue has great faith in the English tradition of 'limited' government by the king (*dominium politicum et regale*) as against the despotic rule of the French king. His view that the test of 'limited monarchy' is in its fruits leads him into an unfavourable discussion of the French system which makes us think of Chartier's lament of the Third Estate. Unlike many other contemporary works, *The Governance of England* shows an awareness of actual political conditions and of the way in which differing economic and social structures are reflected in a country's political institutions.

A

REGINALD PECOCK, *THE REPRESSOR OF OVERMUCH BLAMING OF THE CLERGY*

A Refutation of the Charge that Images are Idolatrous

. . . The .ii. premysse of this now maad argument, as anentis the firste doom, schal be openli proved thus: Peple in havying and using ymagis sett up in the chirche doon noon ydolatrie by hem. Forwhi ydolatrie is nevere doon, save whanne a man takith a creature for his God and worschipith thilk creature as for his God; but so doith no man with eny ymage now in   5 Cristendoom, aftir that the man is come into yeeris of discrecioun and is passid childhode, and which is not a natural fool. Forwhi, if of eny of hem it be askid, whether this ymage is God in heven, which made al thing, and which was ever withoute bigynnyng, and was therfore eer this ymage was maad; he wole seie anoon, that this ymage is not he, but that this ymage is   10 the ymage of him. And thanne, if this man take not this ymage as for his

God, certis he wole not therwith worschipe him as his God; neither he
wole yeve to him the worschip which he knowith to be dew to God oonli;
neither he wole be aknowe that the ymage is his God. Forwhi theryn he dide
15 repugnaunce in sum maner, or ellis certis cause is not likeli to be founde
whi he schulde so do tho thingis togidere. And therfore as for drede of
ydolatrie, that is to seie, lest peple be ydolatreris in having and using
ymagis, doom of resoun hath not forto weerne and reprove ymagis to be
had and usid.
20   The strengthe of this argument stondith upon the very knowing what
ydolatrie is. And sithen ydolatrie is nothing ellis than what is now seid to
be, the argument now maad muste needis have his entent. Ful ofte have y
herd men and wommen unwiseli juge and diffame ful scherpli weelnygh
alle Cristene to be ydolatrers, and al for the havyng and using of ymagis.
25 And yit whanne it hadde be askid of hem what ydolatrie is, forsothe thei
couthe not seie neither feele what it is in his trouthe, though thei schulden
have wonne therbi al the worldis blis or the blis of heven. And whether this
was not an horrible abhomynacioun and a vile stinking presumpcioun hem
forto so sturdili bi manye yeeris juge and diffame bothe the clergi and
30 weelnygh al the lay party of Goddis chirche in so greet a cryme, which thei
couthen neither myghten prove to be doon, (forwhi thei wisten not what
thing thilk cryme is, and therfore thei myghten not knowe whether it was
doon or not doon), and whether such peple be able and worthi to be
admyttid into the homeli reding of Holi Writt, eer thei be weel adauntid
35 and weel schamed of her folie and of her unwisdom and pride, seie
whoevere schal this heere. And y trowe he may not ayens this seie and
holde, if he have eny quantité of discrecioun. Manye lesingis y have herd
hem lie, how thei knowen that persoones reulen hem in amys bilyvyng
fonnedli aboute ymagis; but whanne profris of greet meede (yhe, of .xl.
40 pound and of more) hath be mad to hem forto bringe forth .ii. or .iii. of
suche persoones, thei couthen bringe forth noon of hem.
    Peraventure thei wolen seie thus: Manye hundridis of men clepiden this
ymage the Trinyté, and thei clepen this ymage Crist, and this ymage the
Holi Goost, and this ymage Marie, and this ymage Seint Petir, and this
45 ymage Seint Poul, and so forth of othere; and thei wolden not so clepe but
if thei feeliden and bileeveden withinneforth as thei clepen withouteforth;
for ellis thei weren double. Wherfore alle tho hundridis bileeven amys
aboute tho ymagis. Herto it is ful light forto answere. Whanne y come to
thee in thi parisch chirche thou wolt peraventure seie to me thus, 'Lo here
50 lieth my fadir and there lieth my grauntfadir, and in the other side lieth my
wiif'—and yit thei liggen not there, but oonli her boonys liggen there. If y
come to thee into thin halle or chaumbir thou wolt peraventure seie to me
in descryvyng the storie peintid or wovun in thin halle or chaumbre, 'Here
ridith King Arthir, and there fightith Julius Cesar, and here Hector of
55 Troie throwith doun a knyt', and so forth. For though thou thus seie thou

wolte not holde thee forto seie theryn amys. Schal y therfore bere thee hoond that thou trowist thi fadir and thi grauntfadir and thi wiif for to lyve and dwelle in her sepulcris, or schal y bere thee an hond that thou trowist Artur and Julius Cesar and Hector to be quyk in thi clooth, or that thou were double in this so reuling of speche? Y trowe thou woldist seie y were 60
uncurteis, or ellis unwiis and folisch, if y schulde beere thee so an honde, if it likid thee forto so speke. And, if this be trewe, it folewith that as weel thou art uncurteis, or ellis thou art to be excusid of uncurtesie bi thi greet folie and madnes, if thou bere me an hond that al the world ful of clerkis and of othere lay men weenen summe ymagis to be God, and summe 65
ymages to be quyke seintis; or that thei ben double and gileful, if thei clepen an ymage of God bi the name of God, and an ymage of a seint bi the name of a seint. But (for more clereli this same answere to be undirstonde) it is to wite, that if figuratiif spechis weren not allowid to be had in uce, that the ymage or the likenes of a thing mai be clepid bi the 70
name of the thing of which he is ymage and likenes, and that the parti of a thing mai be clepid under and bi the name of his hool, as that men seien thei han lyved .xl. wynteris, meenyng therbi that thei han lyved forti yeeris, certis thi chalenge myghte weel procede and have his entent; but ayenward it is so that such figuratiif and unpropre speche, forto clepe the ymage of a 75
thing bi and undir the name of the thing of which he is ymage, hath be in famose uce and hath be allowid bothe of Holi Scripture and of alle peplis. And therfore, though men in such woned figuratiif speche seie, 'Here at this autir is the Trinyté, and there at thilk auter is Jesus, and yondir is the Holi Goost, and therbi is Marie with Seint Peter', and so forth, it nedith 80
not that therfore be seid that thei meenen and feelen that this ymage is the Trinyté, or that thilk ymage is verili Jesus, and so forth of othere; but that these ymagis ben the liknessis or the ymagis of hem. . . .

REGINALD PECOCK, *THE FOLEWER TO THE DONET*

Aristotle's Confusion

. . . Also, soon aftir there where in his maner he tretith of involuntari bi ignoraunce, he puttith difference bitwix 'involuntari' and 'not voluntari' or 85
'noon voluntari,' seiyng thus, that it oughte be callid 'involuntari' which nothing moveth the wil, and it oughte be callid 'not voluntari' or 'nooun voluntari' which sumwhat moveth the wil and not parfitli. Of which difference so puttyng semeth to folowe the contrari of what he holdith there a litil bifore. For out of thilk difference semeth to folowe that the seid 90
castyng out of marchaundisis schulde be namyd 'not voluntari' or 'nooun voluntari,' yhe, and schulde not be namyd 'involuntari,' namelich sithen it semeth that he presupposith tho marchaundisis move the wil into her

kepyng, though y so not presuppose. And so hard it wole be to save
95 Aristotil there fro contradiccioun. Whi therfore schulden we algate and for
bettir or wors and uttirli cleve to Aristotil, whatever he teche? What was
Aristotil othir than a lover of trouth, and therfore a laborer bisi forto fynde
the knowyng of treuth, bothe for himsilf and for othire? Many, forsothe, of
oolde philesofris passiden him in the mathamatik sciencis and in
100 astrologie, and many passiden him in methaphisik, and many passiden him
in medicinal philosofie. Oonli in logik and in comoun natural philosofie
and in moral philosofie he passide the othire oolde clerkis. And though
many wolen folewe Aristotil for reverence of Aristotil more than for
reverence of trouth to be defendid and publischid, as ful oft such
105 inparfitnes is wonyd to be usid in scole of philosofie and in scole of
dyvynyté, the more reuth is; yit it likith not to me forto so reverence and
folewe Aristotil ayens treuth, for wel y wote it was nevyr Aristotilis wil that
eny man schulde so do. Forwhi he dide the contrari whanne he varied
from his owen maistir and seide, 'A greet freend is Plato, but a gretter
110 freend is trouth.'

B

SIR JOHN FORTESCUE, *THE GOVERNANCE OF ENGLAND*

The Fruit of jus regale *and of* jus politicum et regale

And howsobeit that the Frenche kyng reignith uppon is peple *dominio
regali*, yet St Lowes sometyme kynge ther, nor eny of his progenitors sette
never tayles or other imposicion uppon the peple of that lande withowt the
assent of the .iii. estates, wich whan thai bith assembled bith like to the
5 courte of the parlement in Ingelonde. And this ordre kepte many of his
successours into late dayes, that Ingelonde men made suche warre in
Fraunce, that the .iii. estates durst not come togedre. And than for that
cause and for gret necessité wich the French kynge hade of good for the
defence of that lande, he toke upon hym to sett tayles and other
10 imposicions upon the comouns withowt the assent of the .iii. estates; but
yet he wolde not sett any such charges, nor hath sette, uppon the nobles of
his lande for fere of rebillion. And bicause the comouns ther, though thai
have grucched, have not rebellid or beth hardy to rebelle, the French
kynges have yerely sithyn sette such charges upon them, and so augmented
15 the same charges, as the same comouns be so impoverysshid and
distroyed, that thai mowe unneth leve. Thai drinken water, thai eyten
apples, with brede right browne made of rye; thai eyten no flesshe but yf it

be right seldon a litle larde, or of the entrales and heydes of bestis slayn, for the nobles and marchauntes of the lande ete suche catalle as thai brede, and the comouns weren no wolen, but yf it be a povere cote undir 20 thair uttermest garnement, made of grete caunvas, and callid a frokke. Thair hausyn beth of lyke caunvas, and passyn not thair kne, wherfore thai beth gartered and ther theis bare. Thair wyfes and childeren gone barefote; thai mowe in non other wyse leve. For somme of thaim that were wont to pay to his lorde for his tenement, wich he hiryth by the yere, a 25 scute, payith nowe to the kyng over that scute .v. scutes. Wherthurgh thai be arted bi necessité so to wacch, labour, and grubbe in the erthe for thair sustenance, that thair nature is wasted, and the kynde of hem broght to noght. Thai gon crokyd, and ben feble, not able to fight, nor to defende the realme; nor thai have wepens, nor money to bie thaim wepen withall. 30 But verély thai liven in the most extreme poverté and miserie, and yet dwellyn thai in on the most fertile reaume of the worlde. Werthurgh the French kyng hath not men of his owne reaume able to defende it, except his nobles, wich beyren non such imposicions, and therfore thai ben right likely of thair bodies; bi wich cause the said kynge is compellid to make his 35 armeys and retenues for the defence of his lande of straungers, as Scottes, Spaynardes, Arrogoners, men of Almeyn, and of other nacions, or ellis all his enymes myght overrenne hym; for he hath no defence of his owne except is castels and fortresses. Lo, this is the frute of his *jus regale*! Yf the reaume of Englonde, wich is an ile, and therfore mey not lyghtly geyte 40 soucor of other landes, were rulid undir such a lawe, and undir such a prince, it wolde be than a pray to all other nacions that wolde conqwer, robbe, or devouir it; wich was well previd in the tyme of the Bretouns, when the Scottes and the Pyctes so bete and oppressid this lande, that the peple therof sought helpe of the Romayns, to whom thai hade be tributori. 45 And when thai coude not be defende be thaym, thai sought helpe of the Duke of litle Bretayn, and grauntid therfore to make his brother Costantyne ther kynge. And so he was made kynge here, and reigned many yeres, and his childirren aftir hym, of wich gret Artour was one of thair issue. But, blessyd be God, this lande is rulid undir a bettir lawe; and 50 therfore the peple therof be not in such peynurie, nor therby hurt in thair persons, but thai bith in welthe, and have all thinges nescessarie to thair sustenance of nature. Wherfore thai ben myghty, and able to resiste the adversaries of this reaume, and to beete other reaumes that do, or wolde do them wronge. Lo, this is the fruyt of *jus polliticum et regale*, undre wich 55 we live. Sumwhat now I have shewid the frutes of both lawes, *ut ex fructibus eorum cognoscetis eos.*

C

Translations of Alain Chartier

THE TREATISE OF HOPE

A Virtuous King

... O Lorde God, how that realme shinith bright where ther regneth a vertuouse and a Catholike kynge. Certainly like as the faire sonne that castith his bright bemes upon th'erthe, through which is voydyd away the derke mystis, and makith the day to shewe more cler, so in lyke wise the
5 rightwise kynge confoundith and destroyeth all maner of wykkednesse through the foresight of his wisedome and dressith all maner of thing to honesté for the honour of his renowm. But O allas, in contrary wise, who that canne ymmagine or thenke the poyson and the venyme that the wicked and the vicwiouse kynge soweth in his realme! For the wickednes
10 descendith from the grette to the smale. Thanne the people sewen the fortune and lyve aftir the patron of their sovereigne. The schrewed kynge makith his subjectis nyce owte of mesure. For looke wher a prince is withowt wisedome there be the people withowte discipline, for and a booke be falsely wretyn it shall make the reders forto erre, and he that
15 wrytith aftir that booke joyneth false upon false. So thanne the kynge is the booke of the people wherein thei shulde lerne to lyve and amende their maners. But and the originall be corrupt thanne by the copyes untrewely wretyn. For the corrupcion that descendith from the hede chavefith the lyvir, chargith the harte and filith the stomacke; it stoppith th'entrailes and
20 alterith all the body. Likewise the vices that rebounden upon the subjectis pervertith the ordir, troublith the offices, and empeirith the condicions of all the estates of his people, for the sekenesse that comyth from the hede causith all the membirs to be troublid. Nowe all kyngys take hede to this, for and thei knewe that in theire wickednesse honged the synne of the
25 people thei wolde enteirly kepe their dignité above all othir, and thei wolde be vertuouse above all othir. ...

THE QUADRILOGUE INVECTIVE

The Lament of the People to France

... O unhappy and soroufull caytif, from whens comyth this false usage that thus turnyth up-so-downe the ordir of justice, which every man hath ovir me as moche power as myght woll geve him? The labour of my hondis

126

norischith the slowthe of idill people, and thei rewarde me ageyn with 30
persecucion of hungir and of sworde. I susteyne their lyf with my swete
and travaile of my body, and thei make me werre with ther outragis, which
hath brought me to lyve as a begger. Thei lyve upon me, and I dey for
them. Thei ought to kepe and diffende me from the enemyes, but, allas,
thei kepe me wele inough from etyng my brede in suerté. O Lord God, 35
hough myght eny man in this werke have perfight pacience whanne to my
persecucion may nothing be joyned but deth? I dey evyn as I go on the
erthe fro defaulte of myn own goodis that I have gotyn. Also I see wele that
Labour hath lost his hoope; Marchaundise canne fynde no redy way to
have his dew course; all goodis ar takyn away save onely suche as is 40
defendid by the spere and the sworde. Wherefor I have non othir of hoope
in my lyve save by dispeyr leve my staate and do as thei do that have
dispoiled me, which lovith bettir the pray than honours of the werre that is
in this realme. But it is a pryvé robbery, a thefte which takith awey by
foorce the comon wele of realme undir the colour of armys, and is 45
ravischid away by violence for defaute of justice and good governaunce.
The werris ben cried and the standardis be reysid on hight ayenst the
enemyes, but the exployt of their dedis be ayeinst me to the distruccion of
my powr sustenaunce and of my wretchid lyfe. Thei feyght with our
enemyes with langage and wordis, but with me thei fyght with dedis. O 50
modir, beholde and avise wele my sorowfull affliccions, and thow shalt
knowe wele that alle comfortis and helpis failyn me. The feldis have no
fredom to kepe me in suerté nor I have nat whereof to labour therinne to
furnisch suche fruytes as shulde be gaderid to the norishyng of my life.
Alle is put in othir mennes handis, closid withinne the wallis and diches 55
that I may nat come ther nygh. And now we must leve the feldis deserte
and abandone them to wylde bestis and to them that be dispurveid and owt
of all confortes, lesing their livis aftir their goodis for hevinesse. The
schare and cultre, which were wont to eary the londe, is turned unto the
mortall sworde, and myne handis that of long tyme have borne the chargis 60
wherof othir men hath gotyn their easis and takyn awey all that I have, and
yet wolde have more thanne I may gete. Wherfor it is force that the body
fall into declyne and myserye for default of good, and so in sorow undir
disperpulid lordeship and charge of household I begge. I live in deying,
seing byfore me the deth of my wyfe and of my powr childern, which daily 65
aschyn me sustenaunce, and liyth nat in my power to confort them, and I
myself as a man lokeing hevyly and sorowfully for hungir and defaulte,
abydyng my last day.

D

SIR EDMUND DUDLEY, *THE TREE OF COMMONWEALTH*

The Root of Truth

Troth is none other but a man to be trew and faithful in all his promisses, couvenantes, and wordes; and the higher in honor the partie is, the more is his shame and rebuke to be provid untrew. If ther be no troth, what avaylyth interchange of marchandize, what availeth cities or townes buylt?
5 If ther be no trothe, what avalith fraternities and felloshipps to be made, and for the more parte, if ther be no troth, what avaleth lawes and ordynances to be made, or to ordeyne parlamentes or courtes to be kept? If there be no trothe, what avalith men to have servantes? Yf ther be no troth, what availyth a king to have subjectes? And so, fynallie, where is no troth
10 can be nether honor nor goodness. Where must this roote fasten hymself? Specially in a king, and in all his trew subjectes, but cheifly in hymself, for in hym hit is most requysyt for his high honour and dignitie, and he most be a great occasioner and helper that it must fasten in his subjectes. The very way must be thus: to ponisshe false men, and to
15 advance and promote trew men. That is the best waie, next to the grace of God, to fastene troth in men, and men in troth. And who can this do? No earthly man, in effect, emong us, but our prince and king. And when a king or a prince in his realme do promote false and subtill men and lett trew men slipp, in that realme or region falshed must encrease, and troth
20 decaie, and thus the tree of comen wealth will in no wyse there stand or growe. But now Englishmen, emongist whome this tree of comen wealth is welnie utterly fayllid and deade, ye have a prince and kinge in whome was never spott or bleamyssche of untroth knowne or found, the which greate vertue and trothe Our Lord, for his passion, daily in hym encrease with
25 profytt and contynewance therin, and that all the nobles in this realme may folloo hym in the same, and so ever one to followe and take example of an other from the highest to the lowest subjectes in his realme. Then how glad shall every noble man be of the company of an other, and one will trust and love an other; what frendship and confydens shall then be
30 betwene man and man, from the highest degré to the lowest; how kyndly and how loveingly will merchauntes and craftysmen of the realme by and sell together, and exchaunge and bargain one thing for another! How diligently and busyly will the artificers and husbondmen occupie ther labor and busynes, and how well content will men be from the highest degré to
35 the lowest, to encrease ther howshold servantes and laborers, wherby all idle people and vagaboundes shalbe sett a worke. And, over this, how glad

shall all strangers and people of outward nacions be to deale and medle with the comodities of this realme! And so shall this roote of trothe and fedelytie roially and mightely supporte and bare uprighte the second quarter of this noble tree of comen wealth.   40

9

THE NATURE OF THINGS:
SCIENCE AND INSTRUCTION

IT IS still a popular fallacy that the 'Renaissance' brought a totally new interest in science, which was reflected in vernacular writings. This section, while it deliberately eschews the tougher 'main-line' scientific vernacular writings, such as the translations of Latin versions of Arabic astronomical works, gives a small selection of the many generally 'scientific' works in English (sometimes translated, sometimes original) which survive in manuscripts and printed books. At the end of the fourteenth century, Trevisa's translation of Bartholomaeus Anglicus's *De Proprietatibus Rerum* gives a clear indication of a developing taste for this material, and during the fifteenth century the demands of a larger reading public are being met. As H. S. Bennett says, 'this century was one which saw knowledge of every kind becoming available to all who could read in their own native tongue'. This is obviously a matter of some moment in the cultural history of the period (though it is still not widely acknowledged), but it is also important in a more narrowly 'literary' way. We find yet again some very accomplished examples of 'practical' prose alongside examples of verse still being used in the old way as a workaday vehicle of instruction. 'Instruction' covers—as will be seen—many areas of knowledge. There are, for instance, many recipes, ranging from the preparation of a peacock to 'how to dyght a crabe'. Our selection ignores those 'sotiltes' intended for the feasts of the great (such as 'custarde royall with a lyoparde of gold syttyng therein and holdynge a floure delyce') in favour of those which are not beyond the scope of an ordinary, curious, household. There is room only for a snippet from the fascinating 'courtesy books' of instructions on serving and on good manners, predecessors of that 'hallowed volume, composed . . . by no less an authority than the wife of a Lord Mayor' from which Rose Maybud in *Ruddigore* learnt: 'the man who bites his bread, or eats peas with a knife I look upon as a lost creature.' Alchemy, which was a 'science' involving the preparation of the substance (the 'Stone') which has the power of transmuting base metal into a precious one, as well as a mystical esoteric art involving symbolic harmonies and the transmuting of sinful man, flourished in this period: the English alchemists Norton (a squire in Edward IV's household) and Ripley were famous throughout Europe. Our less well-known examples, however, attempt to give some idea of the enigmatic, visionary, and imaginative quality of some of this material. We have examples of hunting lore from the very attractive *Master of Game*, and we move from what the *Book of St Albans* calls 'a blast of hunteris' to the quieter world of fishermen, at least one of whose books was read by Izaak Walton. And there is much else besides.

A

The Months

Thirti dayes hath Novembir,
April, June, and Septembir;
Of xxviii^{ti} is but oon,
And all the rememaunt xxx^{ti} and .i.

B

A Prognostication

Her is a goode rewle of the convercioun of Seynte Poule. If Seynte Poules day be fayre and clere, it is tokyn of good tyme of the yer. If hit snowe or rayne, it is tocken of derthe. If it be wynde, it is tocken of batayles. If it be clowde, al bestes shall perishe. And this is of an olde custom among peopill, in olde dayes take for a trouthe.   5

C

Labours of the Months

Januar	By thys fyre I warme my handys;
Februar	And with my spade I delfe my landys.
Marche	Here I sette my thynge to sprynge;
Aprile	And here I here the fowlis synge.
Maii	I am as lyght as byrde in bowe; 5
Junii	And I wede my corne well inow.
Julii	With my sythe my mede I mowe;
Auguste	And here I shere my corne full lowe
September	With my flayll I erne my brede;
October	And here I sawe my whete so rede. 10
November	At Martynesmasse I kylle my swyne;
December	And at Cristesmasse I drynke redde wyne.

D

Of the Ceason of Autumpne, and What he is

Autumpne entreth whan the sonne entreth in the first degree of the Leon,
and lasteth .iiii.^{xx} and .viii. dayes, and .xxvii. houres, that is to sey, from the
.xxiiii. day of Septembre unto the .xxii.^{ti} day of Decembre. In this ceason,
the nyghtes and the daies ben egall of lenght. The aire troubleth, the
5   wyndes entren in thaire region, ryvers and springes discreecyn, the gardyn
drieth, the frutes waxen ripe, the beauté of the erthe fadith, the birdes
seekyn the warme cuntreis, the beestes axen the cavys and warme places,
the serpentes seekyn thaire repaire, where they gete thaire livinge for
wynter. The erthe is as the olde womman that is naked, and passed youthe,
10 and age draweth neere. The tyme is colde and drye. And therfore, this
ceason, eite hoote meytes, as chykenys, lambys, and drinke olde wyne and
eite swete reysons. And beware of all thinges that engendreth blac colour, as
to walke to miche, or to mich leying with womman. And take no bathe, but
yf if be grete nede. . . .

E

WALTER OF HENLEY, *THE BOKE OF HUSBANDRY*

Dung

Nowe shall I tell you what wyning ye shall have by your doung that is
medled withe erthe. The dounge that is rotyn by hymselfe without erth for
it shall laste .ii. yere or .iii. lenger and yet aftur the lond be hote or cold.
And dunge that is medeled withe erthe shall leste double as moche tyme,
5   but it shall not be so sharpe ne so ranke beryng. Ye shall knowe that marle
lastithe lengere then dunge, for dung avastithe and discendith, and marle
mountithe and ascendithe. Dung medled with erthe lastithe lenger then
dung not medled withe erthe for because when dung and erthe medled
togeder is bespred upon the londe, and the lond harowed, the erthe
10 kepithe the dunge, that it may not waste in discendinge as it wold elis do
naturaly, and therfor soyche dunge is beste and moste profetable. And yeff
it rayne a litell when ye lay your doung on your londe, it doithe moche
good, for it cawsithe the dunge and the lond to joyne well togeder. . . .

F

FITZHERBERT'S *BOKE OF HUSBANDRY*

Howe to Sowe both Pees and Beanes

Thow shalt sowe thy pees upon the cley grounde, and thy beanes upon the
barly grounde, for they wolde have ranker grounde than the pees.
Howbeit, some husbandes holde opinyon that byg and styffe grounde, as
clay, wold be sowen with byg ware, as beanes, but me thynke the contrary,
for and a drie somer come, his beanes woll be shorte. And if the grounde   5
be good, put the more beanes to the pees, and the better shall they yelde
whan they be thressed. And if it be very ranke grounde, as is moch at every
towne-syde where catel doth resort, plowe nat that lande tyll ye wyll sowe
it, for and ye do ther wyll come up kedlokes and other wedes. And than
sowe it with beanes, for and ye sowe pees, the kedlokes wyll hurt them.   10
And whan ye se sesonable tyme, sowe both pees and beanes, so that they
be sowen in the begynnynge of Marche. How shall ye knowe seasonable
tyme? Go upon the lande that is plowed, and if it singe or cry, or make any
noyse undre thy fete, then it is to weyt to sowe; and if it make no noyse,
and wyll bere thy horses, than sowe in the name of God. But how to sowe?   15
Put thy pees into thy hopper, and tak a brode thonge of ledder or of garth-
webbe, of an elne longe, fasten it to both endes of the hopper, and put it
over thy heed lyke a lyessh. And stande in the myddes of the land where
the sacke lyeth, the which is most convenient for fyllinge of thy hopper,
and set thy lyft fote before, and take an handefull of pees. And whan thou   20
takest up thy ryght fote, than caste thy pees fro the all abrode, and whan
thy lyft fote ryseth take another handfull, and whan thy ryght fote ryseth
than caste them fro the. And so at every two pases thou shalt sowe an
handfull of pees, and so se that the fote and the hande agré, and than ye
shall sowe evyn. And in your castinge ye must open as well your fyngers as   25
your hand; and the hyer and the farther that ye cast your corne, the better
shall it sprede, except it be a great wynde.

G

Table Manners

. . . Kerve thy brede note to thynne
Ne to thyk, but in twynne.
The mosseylys that thou gynnyst touche,
Cast hem not oute of thy mowthe.

133

5 Put not thy fyngrys in thy dische
 Noydyr in mete of flesche ne fysche.
 Put not thy mete into the salte,
 Into the salere that it halte,
 But ley hit fayre on thy trewnchour
10 Tofor the, and that is thyne honor.
 Pyke not thy erys and thy nostrellys;
 And thou do, men wylle sey thou come of cherlis.
 Sone, whyllys thy mete in thy mowthe is,
 Drynke not; foryete not thys.
15 Ete thy mete be smale mossellys;
 Fill not thy mowthe as do brothelys.
 Pyke note thy teth wyt thy knyff
 Whyle thou etis, be thy lyff.
 And whan thou hast thy potage doon
20 Oute of thy disch put thi spon.
 Ne spit not oure the tabyll
 Ne theron, for hyt is not abyll.
 Ley not thine elbowys ne thy fiste
 Uppon the tabyl whyle thou etist.
25 Bolke note as a bene were in thy throte,
 As a cherle that comyt oute of a cote . . .

H

RECIPES FOR FOOD

Sawmon Irosted in Sauce

Take and cutte a sawmon rownde in peces. Roste hem apon a gredeyrne. And take wyne and poudere of canell, and drawe hit thorowe a streynour; mynce onyons smale, and do togeder, and let boyll. Then take venegur or verjus, and poudere gynger, salte, and do therto. Then ley the sawmon in a
5 dyshe, and poure the seryppe all aboute, and serve it furthe.

Partryche Stewyde

Take fayr myghtye brothe of befe or of moton, and when it is well soden take out the broth of the potte, and strene yt thorowe a strayner, and put it in an erthen potte. And take a good quantité of wyne—as it were halfe—and put therto. And then take partryches, and stoppe hem with
10 hoole pepre and mary, and sewe the wentes of the partryches, and then

take cloves, maces, and hole pepre, and caste into the potte, and latte yt boyll all togeder. And when the partryches be boyllede inowgh, take the potte of the fyr. And when ye schall serve them forthe, caste into the potte pouder of gynger, and salt, and a lytell safferon. And so serve hem forthe.

Capons Stewed

Take percelly, isope, sage, rosemary and tyme. Breke hit betwene thy   15
handes, and stoppe thy capons therwith; and colour them with saferon, and put them yn a erthyn pot or els in brasse (for erth is better), and lay splentys underneth and all aboute the sydes so that the capons tuche not the sydes nother the bottom. And cast of the same herbys into the pot among the capons, and put a quarte or a pynte of the best wyne that thow   20
canste gette, and no other licour, and set a lydde therapon that wyll ly withyn the brym, and make batur of white of eggys and floure, and put betwene the brym a paper lefe or els lyncloth, that the batur may stop hit sowrely that no eyre com oute. Loke that hit be thyke of bature. And set thy pot on a charecole fyre to the mydsyde, and se that the lydde ryse not   25
with the hete, and let hit stew esely and long, and whan thou supposyth hit is enowgh, take hit fro the fyre. Yf hit be a pot of erth, set hit upon a wyspe of straw, that hit toche not the cold grownde. And when the hete is well drawn and overpast, take of the lydde, and take owte thy capons with a stycke, and lay them in another vessell. And make a syrryp of wyne and   30
mynce datys and cannel, drawn with the same wyne. Do therto rasyns of corante, sugur, safferon, and salt. Boyle hit a litill, and cast yn powder of gynger with a litell of the same wyne. Do the sew to the syrruppe above upon the capons, and serve hem furth with a rybbe of beffe, evermore a capon on a dysche.   35

Leche Lumbarde

Take dates, and do awey the stonys, and seth hem in swete wyne, and take hem uppe ageyne. Grynde hem in a morter, and drawe hem in a potte, and lete yt boyll upon the fyre tyll it be styffe, and then take yt uppe and ley hit upon a borde. And then take poudere of gynger and canell, and medele all togeder with thy hande, and make yt so styffe that yt wyll be ilechede.   40
And yf yt be not styff inogh, take harde yolkes of eyren and cryme theron, or els gratede brede, and make yt styffe inogh. And then take clarett and cast therto in maner of syrype when thou serve yt forthe.

For Tartes owte of Lente

Take nesche chese and pare hit, and grynd hit yn a morter, and breke

45 egges and do therto. And then put yn buttur and creme and melk, all well
togethur. Put not to moche buttur theryn if the chese be fatte. Make a
coffyn of dowe, and close hit above with dowe, and collour hit above with
the yolkes of egges, and bake hit well and serve hit furth.

I

MISCELLANEOUS RECIPES

Aqua Aurea ad Scribendum sic fit

Take a quantyté of peyntyd gold and grynde yt with a muller, and in the
gryndyng put therto a penful of the gleyre of an egge. And when yt ys
groundid so small semyng to the that thou seyst noght of the gold, gedyr
yet togedyr of the ston and temper yt with the gleyre of an egge after the
5 quantyté of the gold, and wryte. And when thow hast ywhreton, let stonde
and dreye. And when yt ys drye, take a tothe of a dog oder of a calfe, and
burneseth wel that letter, and thow schalt have feyr gold letter.

To Make a Shyning Water

Take globeris and put them in a glass, and sett it in hores-donge 4 or 5
weakes, and then it will be water. Then put it in a new glasse and hange it
10 in the chamber, and it will shine like a lampe.

To Sle Lyse or Netes

Take thys herbe brome, and stampe hit, and anoynte the with the juse,
and hit wyll sley them.

To Make a Wyld Hors Tame

Set on hym a sadell and a brydell—and streyn the rayn on the sadell
bow—and a dowblet full of straw, and a peyr off hosyn, and fyll them full
15 of sand, and set a peyr of spores on them, and fest them to the doblet, and
the dubelet to the sadell, and the steroppe to the hosyn. And put the hors
in close feld, and lett hym renne. And as he rennyth, the spores wole dasch
hym in the syd. And he wole renne tyll he be wery, and then he wole stond
styll. And then leed hym into a stable, and ley leter ynow undere hym, and
20 clothys ynow uppon hym with a stone on every fotte, and kep hym with a
lytell mette .iii. daye affter, and cum to hym every day .ii. or .iii. tymes and

loke on his fette, and cory hym well. And he wole be tame ynow of hys awn kynd.

J

A Charm to Stop Bleeding

I hot and halson that this blod mot stop and stanch by the vertu of the Fader, Son, and Holi Gost, 3 persons and o God in Trinité.

As wyshly and so sothli as Crist hymself was bar in the borh of Bedlehem,
yfollid in the water of flum Jordan;
that water was wild and wod,   5
The child was mek and gud.
He het it stond, and it stod—

and so mot this sam blod of this man, woman, or child, in the nam of the Fader, and of the Son, and of the Holy Gost, 3 persons and o God in Trinité.   10
And say this charm 3, with 3 *pater noster*, 3 *ave*, and o cred, and crosse it with thi hand.

K

Treatment for a Broken Skull

. . . Paraventur the sckoll is broke, and thou meyst not see it for smalnes of the breche. Make the man than holde his mouthe and his nostrelle close and blowe faste, and if the skolle be broke, ther woll come upp wynde at the breche. And than if the wounde be to narow above, make it larger as I have tolde befor. At the bothe endes of the wounde of the sckoll make twey   5
holys as thou seyste that it nedythe after the mochulnes of the breche, and kute awey as moche as is betwene tho .ii. holys, and than hell it upp as is tolde befor. Bout if a pece of the sckull be kute awey and hong by the skynne and commethe not at the brayne, departe the bone from the skynne that hangythe and sew hit up to the other skyne and benethe ordeyne a   10
voyde place that the quytter may have his issew out, and straw theron the rede poudyr, for that shall sowde him togedyr, and hele it upe with som of the oynemente—but ley thi pouder therto but .ix. dayes or .xii. But if the skull be kut thorowoute and the pece hang besyde on the skynne, than slyte the skynne evyn a-too and kute aweye the skyn from the bone, and   15

than sowe tho .ii. peces to the skynne of the heede, and let thy nedyll be
opyn betwene hem too to ley in lynen clothe apon the brayne and than hele
up the skull as I tolde the befor, and sowde the sydes of the 2 skynnes to
the heede with the rede poudyr, and if the skyne be howede in with a
20 stroke, as moche as is aperyd therof most be kute awey and helyde upp as I
seyde befor . . .

L

Mania

Mania is another siknesse of the middel part of the brayne, and cometh of
a postum in that party; bote otherwhyles hit is a sikenesse himself, and
otherwhile hit folweth another sikenesse. And som cometh of blod, and
som cometh of colour, and som cometh of malencolye; bote of clene
5 flemne hit cometh never, for flemne is whit as the brayn is and therfore hit
may noght apeyre hit. And hit cometh of blod, the grevaunce is with
lawghinge; and yef hit cometh of colour hit is with a fers wodnesse; and yef
hit be of malencolie hit is with moche drede; yef hit is of blod and colowre
ymened togeder, he lawghth and fighteth togeder; and yef hit is of other
10 humeres hit hath the properteiis of thilke humores. Bote cominliche thilke
that hath this sikenes of malencolye he haveth moche sorwe, and dredeth
moche of thyng that is no drede of, and thenketh moche of thing that is
noght for to thenk on. And him semeth that they seth dredful thyng, when
they seth nothyng; and they semeth that they seith blak men, as monkes,
15 that wol sle hem; and som weneth that heven wol falle undir hem. And
moche desyre they have to leches and after medecines, and when they
haveth hem they taketh but litel kepe of her wordes; and they desiren to be
in derk places and by hemselfen. Bote thilke that haveth this sekenesse of
blod loveth to walken abowten revers and in feldes and in feyre gardinys
20 and in light places, and they loveth company and mirthe. And hem lakketh
seche thinges hem semeth they beth neyghe dede. But thilke that haveth
hit of colour loveth wraxlynges and fighttynges and lepynges and other
doynges of hardenis, and cryyng, and moche noyse, and seche other
doyinges . . .

M

Medical Recipes

For sore teeth: Take horsgrece, and bawme therwith thy teeth and thy
cheke. Thy medicyn ys preved for soth.

For cornus that waxith in mannes foot: Take gander dryt and eysel, and hete hem togeder, and ley therto, and hit schal hele.

For a man that may not hold hys pisse: Tak gose clawes, and brenne hem in a 5 new pot to pouder, and ete therof in thy potage, and thou schalt be al hole.

Forto make heer to growe: Seth the leves of whyt wethy in oyle, and anoynte hyt ther the her ys aways. *For the same*: Schaf the hed clene of fyrst wyth the heer, and aftur agayn the heer, and anoynte hyt ofte wyth hony; and 10 loke that hyt be eche wyke onys yshave, and eche day twyez anoynted, and hyt schal helpe wythowten fayle.

For the totheache: Take grene berke of elder tre, and bruse it, and a quantité of gret salt, and 3 droppes of triacle, and bynd it in a clothe with a thred, and ley betwene the cheke and soore tothe. 15

Forto staunche blode withouten charme: When a master-veayne is forcorven, and woll not gladly staunche with charme, and ife the wounde be large, take a pece of salt beffe, bothe fatte and lene togeder, as moche as thou hopyste woll in the hoole, and ley it on the hote colys, and let it roste tyll it be thoroughe hote, and all hote thruste it in the wounde, and bynd it 20 fast to, and it shall stanche anon, and never ren after, on warantyse.

Forto gette a man chylde: For to gette a man childe, take the henge of hare and the modir, and bren hem and make pouder therof, and yeve the man and the woman to drynke with wyne or ale or they go to bedde. *Anoder*: Take the blake of an hare, and lat a woman swalow hit al hole. 25 *Anoder*: Tak on waschyn wolle, and weet it in marres mylke, and bynd it to her navyll whille the man lythe be here.

N

Seven Signs of the Plague

The fyrste is whan in a sommers day the weder oftentymes chaungeth—as in the mornyng when the weder appereth to reyn, afterward it aperyth clowdy, and at the last wyndy in the sowth. The second token is when in somer the deye apperyth all derke and lyke to reyn, and yet it rayneth not—and if many deys so contynue, yt is to drede of greate pestylence. 5 The .iii. token is whan grette multitude of fleys ben upone the erthe—thenne it is a sygne that the ayer is venemous and infecte. The .iiii.te token is whan the sterres semen oftetymes to fall—than it is token

that the eyer is infecte with moche venemous vapours. The .v. token is
10 when a blasyng sterre is sene in the element—then it is sygne to be sone
aftyr grete pestylence or grete manslagthter in batayle. The .vi. token is
when ther is grete lyghtnyng and thunder, namely owte of the sowthe. The
.vii. token is when grete wyndys passyn owte of the sowthe: they ben fowle
and onclene. Therfor when thes tokenes appere, it is to dred gret
15 pestelence but God of hys gret mercy wyll remeve it.

O

Dew, Snow, Lightning

. . . The mater of dew is a watery vapour assendyng to the firste regioune
of the eyer, or ever it mey com to the seconde regioun taken with colde, the
wiche colde tackithe awey the heet of the seide vapour and also causithe
hit to fall downe; and so ther aperithe apone herbis a stillid water, wiche
5 water, whan it is drey, apperithe lyyng uppon herbis licke flour; of the
wiche, sheepe if they ete therof they shall dey sone after of the rote, for hit
is evyr swete, and causithe hem to have the flixe (and this is callyd
mylldew).
. . . Snowe is causide of grose vapours lickewise as the rayne, wiche
10 vapour in the myddill part of the eyer is turned into a rawe clowde, and
afterwarde be excesife colde ther is congelide; the seide clowde aperyng
unto us scaturyd abrode, and hathe a whight colour. Wiche clowde after
the cause of the resistence that it makithe ageyne the sone is dissolvyde,
and fallethe doune unto the erthe in the same forme that it was in the
15 cloude. . . .
. . . The sone bi his vertu pullethe up vapours bothe hote and dry and
also wete vapours otherwhile. Thes .ii. vapours assend, the on afore and
the odir of hem after, and as the moyste assendeth afor, the dry vapours
after, and this dry vapour resceyveth into hym; wiche moyste vapour, after
20 that he hathe this vapour resceyved, gothe abrode as all watery thynges
woll and keepeth this dry vapour within him, that no wey he may passe
esily. Then this vapour thous encludet within assendithe with this moyste
vapour, and after that hit come unto the seconde regioun of the eyer ther
for the coldnes of the place to a cloude is congelid, and than this dry
25 exaltacioun includit within this cloude resistithe inasmoche as he can for
he is of a contrary disposicioun, and wolde go owte, so that be the labur
that he hathe within this cloude this cloude is set on fyre and then this fyre
thus fightyng within the cloude, at some place theras he may best brekithe

oute and this brekyng oute of the fyre causithe this excelent and ferfull
30 noyse that is callid the thonder, so that the more difficulté that it be to the
fyre to gete oute the more is the thondir clappe; and the fyre thus brekyng
out is callid lightenyng.

P

The Philosopher's Stone

I schal yow tel wyth hert and mode,
Of thre kynggys that ben so goud,
And how thaye cam to God almyght,
The wych was ther a swete syght.
I figure now owr blesset Stone,   5
Fro heven wase sende downe to Salomon:
By ane angele bothe goud and stylle,
The wych wase than Crysstis wylle.
The present of hem in Bedlem than,
To Cryst brwght *Aurum, Tus, et Myram*   10
Owre Sol and Sulphir wyth hys Mercuri,
Bothe bodi and soule wyth oure luneyré.
Aurum betokeneth her owre bodi than,
The wych was brwght to God and Man.
And *Tus* alleso owre soule of lyfe,   15
Wyth *Myram* owre Mercurye that ys hys wyfe.
Here bethe thre namys fayre and good,
And alle thaye ben but on in mode,
Lyke as the Trenité ys but on,
Ryght so conclude the Phylosofirs Ston.   20
Thow mayst a se her now in syght,
Off owre Ston ifiguriet aryght;
How sende he wase out of heven,
By an angele wyth mylde stefyn.
And by thys fygure thow mayst se   25
That hyt ys lyke to personis thre;
To Fader and Sonne and Holi Gost,
The wych ys than of mytis most;
Into hys blyse now come wee,
Amen, goud Lord, for cheryté.   30

Q

THE MIRROR OF LIGHT

The Making of the Stone

Our medisyn is a ston that is no ston, and a thyng in kende and not diverse thynges, of whom all metalles beth made. And so it is no salte, nother water, nor oyle, ne mannys here, ne mannys blode, ne uryne, eyrine, ne erbe, ne gottes blode, ne gottes hornys, ne no such other thynges that
5 dyscordeth fro metals as ydyottes wenyth. But he is 2 thynges: s. water and erth. No water of welles, ne of clowdes, ne of saltes. But water of the sonne and of the mone, that brennyth our erth more than ony fyer. And it is 3 thynges: body, spirit, and saule. And it is 4 thynges: water, erth, eyr and fyer. And therfor he is a ston in every place in every tyme, and he is all
10 ownestabell of colour, as a schamfaste woman that changith hyr colour for drede of her love that repreveth her of untrowth, for sche is now pale, now grene, now rede. Ryght so our ston turneth to all colours, for he is blake, whyete, and pale grene, blewe, rede. But he ne hath no stabyll colour save whyete and rede, and his water we call Elexer, that is the phelisopheris
15 ston. Take this ston and put hym in a well closede vessell and clere, that thou may seen it in werchyng. And wan thou haste water of erth and eyre of fyer then it is made. For then is the spirite departed fro the body and levethe the body dede and blake, but yyt yyf the sepulcour be well closede above he wull come doune ayeyn unto the bodye and make hym ryse ayeyn
20 and lyve, and then the body and the soule wull nevere be departed; for hyr resurrexioun thei schall evere be togeder. Nowe understonde what is thy ston. Take a rede man and a whyet woman and wede them togeder, and let hem go to chambour, and schette faste the dor and the wyndowes, for els the woman wull go from her husbonde. Yyf sche lye warme with hym in
25 bedde, then be war that sche go nowhere oute, for yyf sche doo, hyr husbonde schall nevere after take her, thowh he were as swyfte as a facoun. And yyff sche may noght oute, sche wyll come unto hym agayn and be with hym in bedde. And then sche schall conseyve and ber a sone that schall worshype all kyne, and after that sche wyll nevere go fro hyr
30 husbonde, for this man and this woman getten our ston. . . .

R

Visio Johannis Dastyne

. . . We thowght that we were ravysched before the syght of the olde

goddes, and ther beholdyng the 7 planettes cummyng. They have chosyne
by nature ther elder brother unto ther kyng, and crownyd hym with a
dyadem, and also dyd worschype hyme as a god. Unto whom they dyd
schewe all ther infeccions, for they wer almoste all infectyd with the   5
leperus scab with gret deformité. The kyng wyllyng to comforte hys
bretherne sayd thus, 'It is expedyent suerly that on of youe beyng withoute
spot or defaute dye for the people, and that all the people perysche not,
and youe anoyntyd with the newe warme blode of hym schall get helthe of
youer dyssesys, for after the meryte or goodnes of the mater the forme is   10
made. (Note thys sentens well). The other planettes, heryng the kyng,
sayd, 'And wyche of us is withoute spot? For we be borne in syns, and in
syne our mother conceyved us. Whoo is he then that cane make on clene
conceyvyd of unclene sede? Nothyng cane be fownde in the thyng that is
not in the thyng selfe.' Unto whom Mercury ther mother answeryd sayeng,   15
'Chylderne, I have gotyne 6 bodys, of whome on is clene, clere, schynyng
and immaculate, kyng and hed and beste of all the planettes. Nothyng is
superfluus in hyme, nor nothyng lackythe; he is all perfyte, whose
complexioun is temperate in hete, colde, moyste, and drye, wherfore in
fyer he byrnythe not, nor by corrupcioun corruptythe not, nother fyer nor   20
water alterythe hyme. Therfore by hyme we schall all be made perfyte, but
perfyte he hymselfe in maners cannot dye.' Then all the bretherne wept
and waylyd, sayng, 'Alas, mother, why haste thowe goten us so unclene,
and hyme so perfyte? Alas, why haste thou browght up us chylderne of
sorowe? Why dyed we not in our mothers bely when we were borne? Alas,   25
why dyd we not perysche? Why dyd we syt uppon our mothers knes,
norysched with her mylke, borne to be burnt, and met for the fyer?' Then
the olde god sayd, 'I have creatyd all thynges in wysdom and mesure. He
that hathe gevyne the councell, he muste fynde the remedye, for a good
scheperde wyll dye for hys schepe. Therfore, thowe kyng, it behovythe the   30
to be borne agayne, for els otherwysse thowe canst not dye nor make
perfyte thy bretherne.' And the kyng brake owght a-lawyng, and thus sayd,
'How can a man be borne when he is olde? Maye a mane enter into hys
mothers bely agayne, or . . .'

S

Heraldic Creatures

. . . The herte, as Aristotle saith in the .viii. boke of bestes, hath no galle.
And among all unresonable bestes he is moost wysest and full strong, for
of his wysdome he maketh his hynde to calve beside the way, where other
bestes dare not come for comers-bye. Also after the calvyng of hyre calve,
he ledeth hem into smale caves, the which have but oon entree, for there   5

he may withstande all beestes. Also his age is knowen by the braunches of his hede or hornes, for every yere ther groweth a newe braunche of his hede, as Isodre saith in the .xii. boke. Also his age is knowen by the falling of his hornys; and than he is in wildernesse, but of his owne wysdome and discrecion he desireth not to fyght til that his hornys be growen ayen, and 10 that he have a newe armour (for this is Isodre in the place above legged, and the philosopher accordeth as it is abovesaid). To bere an herte in armys is a tokyn that the berer or, at the leest wey, the first taker, was pouere in his first age, whos substaunce litil and litill somdell encreessed. Hit semeth also that the berer was wyse in dedes of batell and sotil in 15 armys how he shuld assaile his enemyes and with sufficiant defence. But he abideth til that his hornys and power growe and encrese. . . . To bere a luce in armys betokenyth a ravenous man and an oppressour of such that be truer and lower than he, for a luce hath a propreté that he wole ete and devoure tho that been lesse than hee, as it is sufficiently knowen. But note 20 and beware, for the rule is not alwey generall that who that bereth such a tokyn or such a beste is of the same condicions that the tokyn signyfieth or that the beste is of, for sumtyme hit falleth as peraventure a man that is called Luce of good condicions and gentil birthe berith in his armys a luce. This wyse sumtyme a man may take to hym his armys of hys name of ellis 25 of the cuntré that he was borne yn. And happely a Cornyssh man assigneth to hym a chough in his armys, and yit it foloweth not that he hath a crowes condicions. . . .

T

THE BOKE OF ST ALBANS

Compaynys of Beestys and Fowlys

A mustre of pecockys. An exaltyng of larkis. A wache ỏf nyghtingalis. A cherme of goldefynches. An unkyndenes of ravenes. A clateryng of choughes. A pride of lionys. A besynes of ferettis. A noonpaciens of wyves. A doctryne of doctoris. A sentence of juges. A glosyng of taverneris. A melody of harpers. A tabernacle of bakers. A rage of maydenys. An 5 uncredibilité of cocoldis. A skulke of foxis. A gagle of women. A pepe of chykennys. An eloquens of laweyeris. A blast of hunteris.

U

EDWARD, DUKE OF YORK, *THE MASTER OF GAME*

The Joy of the Hunter

Now shall I preve how hunters lyven in this world most joyfully of eny
other men. For whan the hunter ryseth in the mornyng, he seeth a swete
and fayr morow and the clere wedir and bryght, and hereth the songe of
the smale fowles, the which syngen swetely with grete melodye and ful of
love, everich in his langage in the best wyse that he may aftir that he lereth   5
of his owyn kynde. And whan the sonne is arise, he shall see the fressh
dewe uppon the smale twygges and grasse, and the sunne which by his
vertu shal make hem shyne. And that is grete lykeng and joye to the
hunters hert. After, whan he shal be on his quest or serching and he shal
se other mete anoon with the hert without grete sekyng, and he shal   10
harbour hym wel and redily withinne a litil compas, it is a gret joie and
lykeng to the hunter. Aftir, whan he shall come to the semblé or gaderyng,
and he shall report byfore the lord and his company either that he hath
seye with his eyne, or by the scantiloun of the trace, the which hym oweth
algate of ryght for to take, either by the fumes that he shal have in his horn   15
or in his lappe, and every man shal say, 'Lo, here a gret hert and is a dere
of hye metyng or pasturyng; go we meve hym'—the whiche thingges I shal
declare hereafter what it is to say—than hath the hunter gret joye. Aftir
when he bygynneth to sewe, and he hath sued but a lytel, and he shal here
or see stert the hert byfore him and shal wel knowe that it is ryght, and his   20
houndes that shul this day be fynders shal come to the leire or to the fewes,
and shul there be uncoupled without that eny go coupled, and alle thei
shul wel renne and enchace, than hath the hunter gret joy and grete likyng.
After, he leppeth on an hors bak, yif he be of that astate, and ellis on foote
with a grete hast forto folow his houndes. And bycause that by aventure his   25
houndes shul be goon fer from thennes where he uncoupled, he secheth
some avauntage forto come byfore his houndes. And than he shal se the
hert passe byfore hym, and shal halowe and rout myghtily, and he shal se
whiche houndes cometh in the vaunchace, and in the middel, and which
bene parfitours, after that thei shul come. And than, whan his houndes byn   30
passid bifore hym, than he shal ryde after hem and he shal route and blowe
as lowde as he may with gret joye and grete likynge, and I assure yow that
he ne thenketh to noon other synne ne to noon other evel. Aftir, whan the
hert shal be ovyrcome and shal be at abay, he shal have gret lykynge. And
aftir, whan the herte is spaied and dede, he undoth hym, and maketh his   35
kyrré and enquirreth or rewardeth his houndes, and so he hath gret likyng;
and whan he cometh home he cometh joyfully, for his lord hath yeve hym

to drynk of his good wyne at kyrré, and whan he is comen home, he shal
doon of his clothes and he shal doon of his shoon and his hosen, and he
40 shal wassh his theyes and his legges and peraventure alle his body. And in
the mene while he shal lat ordeyn wel his soper with wortes of the nek of
the hert and of other good metis, and of good wyne or ale. And whan he
hath wel ete and wel dronke, he shal be al glad and wel at his eese. Than
he shal goo to take the eyre in the evenyng of the nyght, for the gret hete
45 that he hath had. And than he shal goo drynk and goo lye in his bed in faire
fressh clothes, and shal slepe wel and stedfastly al the nyght without eny
evel thought of eny synne. Wherfore I say that hunters goon into Paradise
whan thei dey, and lyven in this world most joiful of eny other men. . . .

The Boar

. . . A boor hereth wondir wel and cleerly, and whan he is hunted and
50 commeth out of the forest or of the bussh, and he is so huntyd that he must
voyde the contré, than he is ful sore adrad to take the playn contré and leve
the forest, and therfore he putteth his heved out of the woode or he putte
out his body. And than he abydeth there and harkeneth and loketh about
and taketh the wynde in every side. And yif that tyme he seeth ony thing
55 the whiche myght lette hym of his way that he wold go, than he turneth
hym agayn to the wode, and than wil he never more come out thoo al the
hornes and al the holowyng of the world were there. But whan he hathe
undirtake the way to go out he wil spare for no thing that he ne shuld holde
his way thorghout. Whan he fleeth he maketh but fewe turnynges, but it be
60 whan he wil turne to abay—and than he renneth upon the houndis and
upon the men. And for no strooke ne for wounde that men doon to hym he
playneth nat ne crieth not, but whan he renneth upon the men he
manesseth, strongly gronyng. . . .

The End of the Hunt

. . . And than the lord shuld take a faire smalle rodde in his honde, the
65 which oon of the yemen or oon of the gromys shuld kitte for hym, and the
Maister of the Game another, and the sergeant, and the yemen at hors,
and other, and than the lord shuld take up the hertis hede bitwyne the
susreal and the fourche or troche, whedir it be that he bere, and the
Maister of the Game the lift side in the same wise, and holde the hede
70 upright that the nose touch the erth. And than every man that is ther, save
the beornors on foot and the chacechiens and the lymners, the which
shuld be with her houndes and waite upon hem in a faire grene there as a
cold shadow were, shuld stonde on fronte in either side the hede, with
roddes, that noon hounde come about nor on the sydes, but that alle

stonde afore. And whan this is redy, the Maister of the Game or the 75
sergeant shuld bidde the beerners bryng forth her houndes and stonde
stille afore hem, a smal cotes cast from thennes, as the abay is ordeyned.
And whan thei be ther, the Maister of the Game or the sergeant shuld cry
skilfully loude, 'Devour!', and than halow every wight, and every hunter
blowe the deeth. And whan the houndes ben comyn and abaien the 80
heede, the beernours shuld pulle of the couplys as fast as thei mowen. And
whan the lord thenketh that the abay hath lasted longe ynow, the Maister of
the Game shuld pulle away the hede and anoon other shuld be redy
behynde and pulle away the skyn and lat the houndes come to the reward.
And than shuld the lord, and Maister of the Game, and alle the hunters 85
stonde a-rome all about the reward, and blow the deeth. As oft as eny of
hem bygynneth, every mane shulde bere him felaushipe, to the houndes
ben wel rewardid, and that thei have nought left. And right thus shal be do
whan the houndes shul byn enquyrreide of the hoole deer. And whan ther
nys nought ylaft, than shuld the lorde, if hym list, and ellis the Maister of 90
the Game, or in his absence whoso is grettest next hym, strake in this wise,
that is to say blow .iiii. moot and stintte not half an Ave Marie while, and
blow other .iiii. mootis a litil lenger than the first four moot. And thus
shuld no wight strake but whan the hert is slayn with strength. And whan
oon of the forsaide hath thus blowen, than shulde the gromys couple up 95
the houndes and draw homward faire and soft. And alle the remenaunte of
the hunters shuld strake in this wise, *trut*, *trut*, *trororow*, *trororow*, and .iiii.
moot withal of on length, not to longe, not to short. And otherwise shuld
non hert hunter strake fro thenforth til thei go to bedde. And thus shuld
the beerners on foot and the gromes lede home the houndes, and sende 100
afore that the kenel be clene and the trought filled with clene water and
than the couch renewid with fresh strawe. And the Maister of the Game
and the sergeant and the yeman at hors shuld comen home and blow the
meené att the halle door or at the celer dore as y shal thon devyse: first the
Maister, or whoso is grettest next hym, shalle begynne and blowe .iii. mote 105
allone, and at the third moot the remenaunte of the forsaid shuld blowe
with hym, and be ware that noon blow lenger than other. And after the
thre moot, even forthwith thei shuld blow the recopes as thus, *trut*, *trut*,
trorororot, and that thei be avised that from that tyme that thei falle inne to
blowe togedir that none of hem begynne afore other ne ende after other. 110
And if it be the first hert slayn with strength in the seson, or the last, the
sergeaunt or the yemen shul goo on theire offices bihalfe and axe theire
fees, the which I reporte me to the olde statutis and custumes of the
kyngges hous. And this do, the Maister of the Game ought to speke to the
officers that alle the hunters soper be well ordeyned, and that thei drynk 115
non ale for nothing, but alle wyne that nyght for the good and grete labour
that thei have had for the lordes game and disport, and for the exploit and
makyng of the houndes. And also that thei the more merily and gladly telle

what ech of hem hath don of alle the day, and which houndes have best
120 ronne and boldliest.

V

Anglers' Notes

In the monethe of Marche begyn to angle—on Seynt Valentynnes day and
the water be clene—for the pyke, the perche, the trowte, and the roche,
the dare, and the bleyke. For the peke, take a feyr bleyke or a roche, and
ley it on a drye lynene clothe, that non scales go from yt; and loke that thi
5 hoke be well enermede with wyer for byttyng of the lyn, and put yt on or in
the mowthe tyll yt come oughte at the tayll, for slyppyng too and froo.
Another for the same: Take a paddoke and put hym in a pote with hony 5
dayes, then take hym out and weshe hym in feyr water, and put hym in oyle
benedictum the space of an hour. Then take him oughte and put hym an the
10 hoke. Thes beyttes be ryghte good for the peke all tymes of the yer. . . .
    In the monethe of Maye: In Maye, for the chevyn, take the angyll-pertes
that lyeth in the felde knyte togeder, slete hem and put ought the erthe of
hem, and caste hem in venegar tyll wex blewe; then washe hem in a lytell
hony with water of valeryane. Bayte the hocke with on of them and depe yt
15 in oyle benedictum. Or els take slo-worme that lyeth in the webbes of the
same tre, of the whyght canker that lyeth in water-sokkels outher pagelles;
or the may-fley that hath a blake cape on his hedde lyke a fryer (his erys
arne yelowe and blake) . . .

W

The Treatyse of Fysshynge wyth an Angle

. . . Thys me semyth that huntyng, haukyng, and fowlyng be so laborous
and grevous that non of them may performe to enduce a man to a mery
spryght the wyche is cause of longe lyfe acordyng to the seyd parabul of
Salomon. Dowtles then folowyth it that it must nedys be the disporte and
5 game of fyschyng with an angul-rode—for all other maner of fyschyng is
also ryght laburus and grevous, often causyng men to be ryght weyth and
colde, wyche mony tymes hathe be seyn the cheyf cause of infyrmyté and
sum tyme deythe. But the angleer may have no colde ne no disese ne angur
but he be causer hymselfe, for he may not gretly lose by a lyne or an hoke,
10 of wyche he may hayf plenté of hys owyne makyng or of other mens, as thys
sympul tretes schall teche hym, so then hys loste ys no grevous. And other

148

grevous may he have non, but yf any fysche breke awey from hym wen he is
upon hys hoke in londyng of the same fych, or els that ys to sey that he
cache not, the wich be no greyt grevous. For yf he fayl of on, he may not
faylle of another yf he do as thys tretes folowyng schall ynforme hym, but yf 15
ther ben non yn the watur wer he schall angul. And yet at the leste, he
schall have hys holsom walke and mery at hys own ease, and also meny a
sweyt eayr of dyvers erbis and flowres that schall make hym ryght hongré
and well disposud in hys body. He schall heyr the melodyes melodious of
the ermony of brydes. He schall se also the yong swannys and signetes 20
folowyng her eyrours, duckes, cootes, herons, and many other fowlys with
ther brodys, wyche me semyt better then all the noyse of houndes and
blastes of hornes and other gamys that fawkners and hunters can make, or
els the games that fowlers can make. And yf the angler take the fysche,
hardly then ys ther no man meryer then he is in hys spirites. . . .   25

In Wat Place is Best Angleyng

Her y wyll declar in wat places of the watur ye schall angle to yowr best
spede. Ye schall angle yn a pole or yn a stondyng watur, yn every place ther
it is anythyng depe. Ther is no grete choyse in a pole, for it is but a pryson
to fysche, and thei lyve moste parte in pryson and hungré as a prisoner.
Therfor it is the lesse mastry to take hym. But in rewares ye schall angle 30
every place wher it is depe and clere by the grounde, as gravel or clay
withowten mudde or wedes; and especiall yf ther be a werly wherly pyt of
watur or a coverte, as an holow banke or greyt rottes of treys or long wedys
flotyng above the watur wher the fysche may cover hym at dyverse tymes;
also in depe stiff stremys, and yn falles of watur, and weeres, flode-gates, 35
and mylle-pittes, and weyr the watur restith by the banke and the streme
renneyth nye therby, and ys dep and clere by the grounde, and yn other
places wher ye may se any fyche howvyng and fede above. . . .

Bayt for the Samonde

And for because the samond ys the most goodly fyche that man may
angle to in fresche watur therfor I porpos to begynne with hym. The 40
samond ys a gentyl fyche, but he ys cumburus to take, for commynly he ys
but yn ryght dep waturs and greyt ryveres, and for the moyr parte he holdet
the mydul of the streym, that a man may not cum to hym easly. And he ys
in season from the moneth of Marche unto Mychelmas, in wyche seson ye
schall angul to hym with thys baytes when they may be had: fyrst with a 45
bleke, like as ye do to the trowt, with a menowe, and with a red worme in
the begynnyng and the endyng of the seyde season, and also with a worme
that bredyt yn a donghyll and especially with a soverent bayt that bredyt yn

the watur-sokul, but he bytyt not at the grounde but at the floot. Also ye
50 may hap to take hym (but hyt ys seldim seyn) with a dub at hys leping lyke
as ye do a trowyt or a gralynge. . . .

The Chevyn

The chevyn is a stately fysshe, and his heed is a deynty morsell. There is
noo fysshe soo strongly enarmyd wyth scalys on the body. And bicause he
is a stronge byter he hathe the more baytes, whiche ben thyse: In Marche,
55 the redde worme at the grounde, for comynly thenne he woll byte there at
all tymes of the yere yf he be onythinge hungry. In Apryll, the dyche canker
that bredith in the tree; a worme that bredith betwene the rynde and the
tree of an oke; the redde worme, and the yonge frosshys whan the fete ben
kyt of; also the stone-flye, the bobbe under the cowe torde, the redde
60 snaylle. In May the bayte that bredyth on the osyer leyf and the docke-
canker togyder upon your hoke; also a bayte that bredyth on a fern leyf, the
cod-worme, and a bayte that bredyth on an hawthorn; and a bayte that
bredyth on an oke leyf, and a sylkeworme and a codworme togyder. In
June, take the creket and the dorre, and also a red worme, the heed kytte
65 of, and a codworme before, and put theym on the hoke; also a bayte in the
osyer leyf; yonge frosshys, the thre fete kitte of by the body, and the fourth
by the knee; the bayte on the hawthorn and the codworme togyder and a
grubbe that bredyth in a dunghyll, and a grete greshop. In Juyll, the
greshop and the humbylbee in the medow; also yonge bees and yonge
70 hornettes; also a grete brended flye that bredith in pathes of medowes, and
the flye that is amonge pysmeers hyllys. In August, take wortwormes and
magotes unto Myghelmas. In Septembre, the redde worme; and also take
the baytes whan ye may gete theym: that is to wyte, cheryes, yonge myce
not heeryd, and the house-combe.

10

A SCOTTISH MISCELLANY

THIS period deserves to be called the golden age of Scottish poetry, and not simply because of the great achievements of the famous 'makars'—James I, Henryson, Dunbar, and Douglas. Its 'minor' poetry also deserves the attention of the modern reader. A glance at Dunbar's list of writers (19 F) will show how much of the poetry of the time has not survived, and in the records of the Kirk and the burghs there are many references which bear witness to the existence of a thriving, but now vanished, dramatic tradition. Fortunately, however, enough has survived to enable us to construct at least a partial picture. The scope is impressive—there are romances, chronicles, comic and satiric tales, and lyrics both devotional and secular—and the quality is often high. Narrative verse is especially impressive (besides the examples represented here, there are such fine works as *Rauf Coilyear* and *The Three Prestis of Peblis*) and cautions us against seeing Henryson's superb mastery of this art in isolation. Alliterative poetry survived and flourished, and we have a fine example of it in the intricate stanzas of *The Buke of the Howlat* (? 1448) by Sir Richard Holland, possibly a native of Orkney, who was for a time the cantor of Moray Cathedral. The parliament of birds which is at its centre has some clear contemporary references; Holland's approbation of the cause of the Douglas family is clearly reflected in this little narrative digression on how the Black Douglas, bearing the heart of Robert the Bruce to the Holy Land, met his end surrounded by Saracens 'whereas' (says Froissart) 'he did marvels in arms, but finally he could not endure, so that he and all his company were slain'. *The Wallace* (? *c.*1474–9), attributed to 'blind Hary', is in the tradition of Barbour's *Bruce* from the preceding century. It treats the deeds of the Scottish patriot, Sir William Wallace against 'our ald ennemys cummyn of Saxonys blud' in a narrative which is always exciting and passionate, and sometimes genuinely heroic. Hary handles both story line and dialogue with skill; he has an eye for a good 'scene', and can treat it (as he does here) with a grim realism which brings us close to the ruthlessness of a real war. Finally, we have an example of a beast tale, which, in its handling of the story at least, is not totally put to shame by Henryson's *Fables*.

A

HOLLAND, *THE BUKE OF THE HOWLAT*

Douglas and the Bruce's Heart

The roye Robert the Brus to rayke he awowit
With all the hart that he had to the haly graif.

Syne quhen the dait of his deid derfly him dowit,
With lordis of Scotland lerit and the laif
As worthy wysest to waile in worschipe allowit
To James Lord Dowglas thay the gré gaif
To ga with the kingis hart. Thairwith he nocht growit,
Bot said to his soverane, 'So me God saif
   Your gret giftis and grant ay gracious I fand,
     Bot now it movis allther maist
     That your hart nobillast
     To me is closit and cast,
   Throw your command!

'I love you mair for that lois ye lippyn me till
Than ony lordschipe or land, so me our Lord leid.
I sall waynd for no wye to wirk as ye will
At wis gif my werd wald with you to the deid.'
Tharwith he lowtit full lawe. Tham lykit full ill
Baith lordis and ladyis that stude in the steid
Off commoun nature the cours be kynd to fulfill.
The gud king gaif the gaist to God for to reid
   In Cardros, that crownit closit his end.
     Now God for his gret grace
     Set his saull in solace
     And we will speike of Dowglace
   Quhat way he couth wend.

The hert costlye he couth clos in a clere cace,
And held all hale the behest he hecht to the king—
Come to the haly graf throw Goddis gret grace,
With offerandis and urisonnis and all uthir thing,
Our salvatouris sepulture and the samyn place
Quhar he rais, as we reid, richtuis to ryng.
With all the relykis raith that in that roume was
He gart hallowe the hart, and syne couth it hyng
   About his hals full hende and on his awne hart.
     Oft wald he kis it and cry,
     'O flour of all chewalry!
     Quhy leif I, allace! quhy,
   And thow deid art?'

'My deire,' quod the Douglas, 'Art thow to deid dicht,
My singuler soverane, of Saxonis the wand?
Now bot I semble for thi saull with Sarazenis mycht
Sall I never sene be into Scotland.'

Thus in defence of the faith he fure to the fecht
With knychtis of Cristindome to kepe his command,   45
And quhen the battallis so brym brathly and bricht
War joyned thraly in thrang mony thousand,
   Amang the hethin men the hert hardely he slang,
     Said, 'Wend on, as thou was wont
      Throw the batell in bront   50
      Ay formast in the front
     Thy fays amang!'

'And I sall followe the in faith or feye to be fellit;
As thi lege man leile my lyking thow art!'
Tharwith on Mahownis men manly he mellit,   55
Braid throw the batallis in bront and bur thaim bakwart.
The wyis quhar the wicht went war in wa wellit;
Was nane so sture in the steid micht stand him a start
Thus frayis he the fals folk, trewly to tell it,
Aye quhill he cowerit and come to the kingis hart.   60
   Thus feile feildis he wan aye worschipand it;
     Throwout Cristendome kid
     War the deidis that he did
     Till on a tyme it betid,
    As tellis the writ,   65

He bownyt till a batall and the beld wan,
Ourset all the Sathanas syde Sarazenis mycht,
Syne followit fast on the chace quhen thai fle can;
Full ferly feile has he feld and slane in the flicht.
As he relevit iwis, so was he war than   70
Of ane wy him allane worthy and wicht,
Circulit with Sarazenis mony sad man
That tranoyntit with a trayne apon that trewe knycht.
   'Thow sall nocht de the allane!' quod the Dowglas,
     'Sen I se the ourset   75
      To fecht for the faith fete,
      I sall devoid the of det
     Or de in the place!'

He ruschit in the gret rowte the knycht to reskewe;
Feile of the fals folk that fled of before   80
Relevit in on thir twa, for to tell trewe,
That thai war samyn ourset—thairfor I murn sore.
Thus in defence of the faith, as fermes ynewe,
And pité of the prys knycht that was in thore,

153

85 The douchty Dowglas is deid and adewe.
With los and with lyking that lestis evirmore
His hardy men tuke the hart syne upon hand.
Quhen thai had beryit thair lord
With mekle mane to remord,
90 Thai maid it hame be restord
Into Scotland.

Be this ressoun we reid and as our roy levit
The Dowglas in armes the bludy hart beris.
For it bled he his blud as the bill brevit
95 And in battallis full braid under baneris
Throw full chevalrus chance he this hert chevit
Fra walit wyis and wicht worthy in weris
Mony galiard gome was on the ground levit
Quhen he it flang in the feld felloun of feris,
100 Syne reskewand it agane the hethin mennis harmes.
This hert, red to behald,
Throw thir ressonis ald
The bludy hart it is cald
In Dowglas armes.

B

HARY, *THE WALLACE*

The Burning of the Barns of Ayr

Wallace commaunde a burges for to get
Fyne cawk eneuch, that his der nece mycht set
On ilk yeit quhar Sotheroun wer on raw.
Than xx^{ti} men he gert fast wetheis thraw,
5 Ilk man a pair, and on thar arme thaim threw.
Than to the toune full fast thai cuth persew.
The woman past befor thaim suttelly,
Cawkit ilk yett that thai neid nocht gang by.
Than festnyt thai with wetheis duris fast,
10 To stapill and hesp with mony sekyr cast.
Wallace gert Boid ner-hand the castell ga
With fyfté men a jeperté to ma.
Gyff ony ischet, the fyr quhen that thai saw,
Fast to the yett he ordand thaim to draw.

The laiff with him about the bernys yheid.   15
This trew woman thaim servit weill in deid
With lynt and fyr that haistely kendill wald.
In euirilk nuk thai festnyt blesis bald.
Wallace commaund till all his men about,
Na Sotheron man at thai suld lat brek out;   20
'Quhateuir he be reskewis off that kyn
Fra the rede fyr, himselff sall pas tharin!'
The lemand low sone lanssyt apon hycht.
'Forsuth,' he said, this is a plessand sicht;
Till our hartis it suld be sum radres.   25
War thir away thar power war the les!'
Onto the Justice himselff loud can caw:
'Lat ws toborch our men fra your fals law
At leyffand ar, that chapyt fra your ayr.
Deyll nocht thar land, the wnlaw is our sayr.   30
Thou had no rycht—that sall be on the seyne!'
The rewmour rais with cairfull cry and keyne.
The bryme fyr brynt rycht braithly apon loft.
Till slepand men that walkning was nocht soft!
The sycht without was awfull for to se.   35
In all the warld na grettar payne mycht be
Than thai within insufferit sor to duell,
That euir was wrocht bot purgatory or hell—
A payne off hell weill-ner it mycht be cauld,
Mad folk with fyr hampryt in mony hauld.   40
Feill byggyns brynt that worthi war and wicht;
Gat nane away, knaiff, captane nor knycht.
Quhen brundis fell off ruf-treis thaim amang
Sum rudly rais in byttir paynys strang;
Sum nakyt brynt bot belches all away;   45
Sum nevir rais bot smoryt quhar thai lay;
Sum ruschit fast till Ayr gyff thai mycht wyn.
Blyndyt in fyr thar deidis war full dym.
The reik mellyt with fylth off carioune
Amang the fyr, rycht foull off offensioune.   50
The peple beryt lyk wyld bestis in that tyd
Within the wallis rampand on athir sid,
Rewmyd in reuth with mony grysly grayne.
Sum grymly gret quhill thar lyff-dayis war gayne;
Sum durris socht the entré for to get,   55
Bot Scottismen so wysly thaim beset,
Gyff ony brak be awnter off that steid
With suerdis sone bertnyt thai war to dede,

Or ellys agayne be force drewyn in the fyr.
60   Thar chapyt nayne, bot brynt wp bayne and lyr.
The stynk scalyt off ded bodyis sa wyde
The Scottis abhord ner-hand thaim for to byd,
Yeid to the wynd and leit thaim ewyn allayne
Quhill the rede fyr had that fals blude ourgayne. . . .

C

THE TALIS OF THE FYVE BESTIS

The Unicornis Tale

Before this tyme in Kentschire it befell,
A bonde thar was, his name I can nocht tell,
Gundulfus was his sonis name I ges,
Of tender age of nyne yeris ald he wes,
5   And wele he usit for to rys at mornys
To kepe the grange and his faderis cornis
Fra cokis, crawis, and uther foulis wyld.
So on a day this litill prety child
Seand thir birdis lukand our the wall
10   Toward the grangis, Gundulfus gois withall,
And with the casting of a litill stone,
Of ane littil bird the theis bone
Brokin he has in sounder at a cast,
And sone the fowlis flokit about him fast.
15   Quhat will ye mare, he was bot slane or schent,
Sore for him wepit all the hennis of Kent.
Wp was he takin, and in a garding led,
Amang thir herbes thai haf maid him a bed,
And quhat throu comfort and throu medecyne,
20   Within the space of days .viii. or nyne,
This bird was mendit hale and sound,
Of all the panys of his bludy wound.
And Gundulfus, with his frendis assent,
To Oxinfurd to study is he went.
25   Sone efter this, this yong bird wox a cok,
The gudliest and farest of the flok,
Clerast of voce and wysest in his entent,
The cruellest of all the cokis of Kent;
And he had Coping to be his wyf,
30   And he had chosyn hir for term of lyf,

And scho agane till him hire treuth plicht,
To luf him best of ony erdly wicht.
And so at evyne apon his perke he gat,
On his richt hand dame Copok nixt him sat;
And quhill he clapit durst thar na cok craw,   35
Quhen he had clapit than crau thai all on raw.
So wele he had the houssis observance,
That of the flok he baire the governans.
Thus was he cheif cok of the bondis place,
And baire he rewle threttene yeris space.   40
And all this tyme he had this child in thocht
That brak his leg quhen he trespassit nocht.

                    *   *   *   *   *

He was na master in divinité
Bot he wald preche into that science hie.
Weile couth he cast the bukis of decres,   45
Bot tharin nothing had he of his greis.
Prentis in court he had bene for a yere;
He was a richt gud syngare in the quere.
He couth wele reid and sumpart write and dyte,
And in his grammere was he wele perfyte.   50
He was na gret bachillare in sophistry,
With part of pratik of nygramansy,
Of phesik he baire ane urinale,
To se thire folk gif thai war seike or hale.
And in his clething was he wele besene,   55
For goune and hude was all of Lyncome grene.
Gret was the joy that in the place was than,
To se the meting of that noble man.
In come his frendis till him fast anone,
And notwithstanding that the day was gone,   60
'Fader,' he said, 'I can nocht byde this nycht,
To Rochister I mon thir wayis richt,
Tomorne is the day of my promocioun,
Of haly ordour to resaif the croune,
And tharin standis myne awansing hale,   65
Unto ane benefice perpetuale,
And falye this, the kirk gais to ane nothir.'
Than spak our dame that was the childis modir,
'Son, for my blissing, this nycht with ws abyde,
And all at eis tomorne son sall ye ryd,   70
Oure hous cok sall the houris of the nycht
Als wele devyde as ony orlage richt,

And at the first cok walkinnit sall ye be,
And at your hors sone be the houre of thre,
75   Ye have bot nyne myle of the farest way,
At Rochister ye sall be sone be day,
And haf your tonsour be the houre of nyne.'
And so he baid, and drank with thaim the wyne.
Quhen thai war full of mychti ale and wyne,
80   Thai gat to rest and slepis as ony swyne.
The nycht yeid oure, the freindis thocht nocht lang,
For all thare trast was on the cokis sang.
And all this sawe the cok apon the balk,
And quhen he hard the matir of thair talk,
85   And on the breking of this theis bone
This cok had mynd, Gundulfus he had none.
Sone come the tyme that he suld say his voce,
The houre yeid oure, the cok he held him clos:
With that dame Coppok putis on hir maik,
90   Said, 'Slepe ye schir! get wp for Cristis saik,
Your houre is gone, quhy syng ye nocht, for schame!
Wait ye nocht weile yone clerk suld ryde fra hame.
And all thare trast apon your sang thai lay,
Schir! syng ye nocht, yone clerk sall slepe quhill day.
95   And so in vane is all thing that thai wirk,
It war gret peté he suld tyne his kirk,
And of the tynsall ye sall haf the blame.'
Syng wald he nocht, bot schrewitly said, 'Madame,
Wysest ye are quhen that ye hald yow still,
100   And yit ye wyffis evir speike ye will.
Dame, intromet yow in your wyfis deid,
Lytill ye wist quhen that my lege couth bleid,
And yone is he that brak my leg in sounder,
Gif I suld crawe, madame, it ware gret wounder,
105   For thocht my leg be werray haile outwart,
Quhen I him se, it bledis at my hart.'
As thai ware talkand this fer thaim amang,
Lang efter that the cok tuke wp a sang,
And all the birdis with ane woce thai cry,
110   'Get wp! get wp! we se the dayis sky!'
And wp he gat and saw that it was day.
Said kirk and worshipe fastly war away.
On hors he gat, fast throw the toune he raid,
And all the doggis intill his tale he had;
115   Quhill at ane stone he styntit with sic fors,
That to the erd yeid baith the man and hors.

This hors gat wp and ran oure to the hill,
And in the myre this worthy clerk lay still.
And still he lay quhill it was tyme of none,
The kirk disponit, and all the service done.   120
Than wp he gat, and hame agane is went,
Ane hevy man forsuth in his entent.
His garment grene that was of colour gud
Was sa mismaide in the myre and mude;
And quhat for schame he was so pale of hewe,   125
Quhen he come hame, thar was no man him knewe.
So quhen this clerk with schame come hame agane,
Than was this cok quyt of his legis pane,
And said, 'Madame Coppok, mak gud cheire,
Now wepis he that leuch this hender yeire   130
Quhen with ane stone my thees bone he brak,
Bot for I lukit till his faderis stak,
And quhen I bled he said the feild was his,
Now, God I loif this day has send ws this.'

135

Now be this tale ye sall wele wnderstand,
Gif ye be lord and rewlare of this land,
Ye schape yow nocht for till oppres the pure;
For and ye do, forsuth I yow assure
The tyme may cum that your awentour standis   140
Perawenture into sic mennis handis.
Quha schapis him the pure for to oppres,
At Goddis hand the mater has to addres.
Quhill that ye haf space tharfor ye suld amend,
Byde nocht the straik of vengeans at your end,   145
For till amend als oft as ye do mys,
And we beseke Jesu of his bliss.

11

LYRICS

THE best of the surviving lyric poetry of this period is immediately attractive and needs no apology. The music has often (but not always) survived as well, and we must remember that these poems were usually intended for performance. Fortunately there are now some good recordings available of a number of them (see the Commentary). Our selection presents a mélange of the kind often found in medieval manuscripts. Religious lyrics exist in large numbers. The finest are marked by an exquisite simplicity, in which a traditional diction may be used (as in the well-known 'I syng of a mayden') to crystallize a range of undertones or allusions. Yet there is variety—besides the excitement of the news of the Incarnation which is so memorably caught in 'Owt of your slepe aryse and wake' (a carol, i.e. a poem with a 'burden' at the head which is repeated after each stanza), we have a dying man's farewell to the world (O), a dramatic monologue which conveys a genuine pathos, or the infinitely suggestive and mysterious 'Corpus Christi Carol' (R). Secular lyrics (though less numerous) are even more varied. There are drinking-songs, nonsense songs (cf. S), merry pieces like the schoolboy's lament (Q), or various bawdy and fabliau-like lyrics. Of the latter, the most successful is probably our piece C, where the 'lovers' meeting' takes place in the setting of procession and Mass (the refrain *Kyrie eleyson* 'Lord, have mercy' not only plays on the girl's name 'Alison', but also—paradoxically—suggests the conventional lover's cry for 'mercy') and is seen through the girl's eye and thoughts (often of a less than solemn kind: 'I payid for his cote').The more 'courtly' lyrics are a highly formal type of poetry, with its own traditional commonplaces and an almost technical vocabulary. That this again can be transformed by a poet of talent into a suggestive and flexible style is shown especially by pieces I–N, English poems which may very well be by the distinguished French poet, Charles d'Orléans, the nephew of King Charles VI, who was captured at Agincourt and had to remain in England for over twenty years. The collection of poems is arranged in two sequences, the first addressed to a Lady Beauty, whose death (cf. Nos. I, J) leads the lover to renounce love in despair, and, after an interlude, another in which the poet is introduced to another lady. The poems show not only an easy mastery of two favourite courtly forms, the ballade and the rondeau, but a very distinctive and interesting poetic voice. Charles can create an exquisite melancholy, and can handle with confidence the allegorical landscape of love deriving ultimately from the *Romance of the Rose*, but is equally at home in witty games with the 'religion of love'. Our period—which shows no sign of tiredness or degeneration—comes to a brilliant close with the lyrics from Tudor manuscripts, which continue, and sometimes transform, earlier forms and techniques. We end with a poem of deceptive simplicity which is surely one of the best love lyrics in the whole of English literature.

A

Adam Lay Ibounden

Adam lay ibowndyn, bowndyn in a bond,
Fowre thowsand wynter thowt he not to long.

And al was for an appil, an appil that he tok,
As clerkes fyndyn wretyn in here book.

Ne hadde the appil take ben, the appil take ben,   5
Ne hadde never our Lady a ben hevene qwen.

Blyssid be the tyme that appil take was,
Therfore we mown syngyn 'Deo gracias!'

B

I Sing of a Maiden

I syng of a mayden that is makeles,
Kyng of alle kynges to here sone che ches.

He cam also stylle ther his moder was
As dew in Aprylle that fallyt on the gras.

He cam also stylle to his moderes bowr   5
As dew in Aprille that fallyt on the flour.

He cam also stylle ther his moder lay
As dew in Aprille that fallyt on the spray.

Moder and maydyn was never non but che—
Wel may swych a lady Godes moder be!   10

C

Jolly Jankin

'Kyrie, so kyrie,'
Jankyn syngyt merie,
With 'aleyson'.

As I went on Yol Day in owre prosessyon,
5   Knew I joly Jankyn be his mery ton.
Kyrieleyson.

Jankyn began the Offys on the Yol day,
And yyt me thynkyt it dos me good, so merie gan he say,
'Kyrieleyson.'

10   Jankyn red the pystyl ful fayre and ful wel,
And yyt me thinkyt it dos me good, as evere have I sel.
Kyrieleyson.

Jankyn at the Sanctus crakit a merie note,
And yyt me thinkyt it dos me good—I payid for his cote.
15   *Kyrieleyson.*

Jankyn crakit notes an hunderid on a knot,
And yyt he hakkyt hem smaller than wortes to the pot.
Kyrieleyson.

Jankyn at the Angnus beryt the pax-brede;
20   He twynkelid, but sayd nowt, and on myn fot he trede.
Kyrieleyson.

Benedicamus Domino: Cryst fro schame me schylde;
Deo gracias therto: alas, I go with chylde!
Kyrieleyson.

D

The Rose that bore Jesu

Ther is no rose of swych vertu
As is the rose that bare Jesu.

Ther is no rose of swych vertu
As is the rose that bar Jesu;
   Alleluya!   5

For in this rose conteynyd was
Heven and erthe in lytyl space,
   Res miranda!

Be that rose we may weel see
That he is God in personys thre,   10
   Pari forma.

The aungelys sungyn the sheperdes to,
'*Gloria in excelcis Deo.*'
   Gaudeamus.

Leve we al this wordly merthe,   15
And folwe we this joyful berthe;
   Transeamus.

E

Out of your Sleep arise and wake!

Nowel, nowel, nowel,
Nowel, nowel, nowel!

Owt of your slepe aryse and wake,
For God mankynd nowe hath ytake
Al of a maide without eny make;   5
   Of al women she bereth the belle.
      Nowel!

And thorwe a maide faire and wys
Now man is made of ful grete pris;
Now angelys knelen to mannys servys,   10
   And at this tyme al this byfel.
      Nowel!

Now man is brighter than the sonne;
Now man in heven an hye shal wone;
Blessyd be God this game is begonne,   15
   And his moder emperesse of helle.
      Nowel!

That ever was thralle, now ys he fre;
That ever was smalle, now grete is she;
20 Now shal God deme bothe the and me
   Unto his blysse yf we do wel.
      Nowel!

Now man may to heven wende;
Now heven and erthe to hym they bende;
25 He that was foo now is oure frende;
   This is no nay that y yowe telle.
      Nowel!

Now, blessyd brother, graunte us grace
A Domesday to se thy face
30 And in thy courte to have a place,
   That we mow there synge nowel.
      Nowel!

F

The Virgin's Lullaby

'Lullay, lullow, lully, lullay,
Bewy, bewy, lully, lully,
Bewy, lully, lullow, lully,
Lullay, baw, baw, my barne,
5 *Slepe softly now.'*

I saw a swete semly syght,
A blisful birde, a blossum bright,
That murnyng made and mirth of-mange;
A maydin moder, mek and myld,
10 In credil kep a knave child
That softly slepe; scho sat and sange.

G

The Fox and the Goose

'Pax vobis,' quod the fox,
'For I am comyn to toowne!'

It fell ageyns the next nyght,
The fox yede to with all his myghte,
Withouten cole or candelight,   5
   Whan that he cam unto the toowne.

Whan he cam all in the yerde,
Soore the geys wer ill aferde;
'I shall macke some of yow lerde,
   Or that I goo from the toowne!'   10

Whan he cam all in the croofte,
There he stalkyd wundirfull soofte;
'For here have I be frayed full ofte
   Whan that I have come to toowne.'

He hente a goose all be the heye;   15
Faste the goos began to creye!
Oowte yede men as they myght heye,
   And seyde, 'Fals fox, ley it doowne!'

'Nay,' he saide, 'soo mot I the—
Sche shall goo unto the wode with me;   20
Sche and I wnther a tre,
   Emange the beryis browne.

'I have a wyf, and sche lyeth seke;
Many smale whelppis sche have to-eke—
Many bonys they muste pike   25
   Will they ley adowne!'

H

Go, Heart, Hurt with Adversity

Go hert, hurt with adversité,
And let my lady thi wondis see!
And sey hir this, as y say the:
   Farwel my joy, and welcom peyne,
   Til y se my lady agayne.   5

I

Charles of Orléans, *Alas, Death*

Allas, deth! Who made thee so hardy
To take awey the most nobill princesse,
Which comfort was of my liif and body—
Mi wele, my joy, my plesere and ricchesse?
5 But syn thou hast biraft me my maystres,
Take me, poore wrecche, hir cely serviture,
For levyr had y hastily forto dy
Than langwysshe in this karfull tragedy
In payne, sorowe, and woofull aventure!

10 Allas! Nad she of eche good thing plenté,
Flowryng in youthe and in hir lustynes?
I biseche God, acursid mote thou be,
O false Deth, so full of gret rudenes!
Had thou hir taken in unweldynes,
15 As had thou not ydoon so gret rigure;
But thou, alak, hast take hir hastily,
And, welaway! this left me pitously
In payne, sorow, and wooful aventure.

Allas! alone am y out compané!
20 Fare well, my lady, fare well, my gladnes!
Now is the love partid twix yow and me—
Yet, what for then, y make yow here promes
That with prayers y shall of gret larges
Here serve yow ded while my liif may endure,
25 Out forgetyng in slouthe, or slogardy,
Biwaylyng oft yowre deth with wepyng ey,
In payne, sorow, and wofull aventure.

O God, that lordist every creature,
Graunt of thi grace thi right forto mesure
30 On alle the offens she hath doon wilfully,
So that the good sowle of hir now not ly
In payne, sorow, and wofull aventure.

J

Charles of Orléans, *The Whole Treasure of All Worldly Bliss*

I have the obit of my lady dere
Made in the chirche of Love full solempnely,
And for hir sowle the service and prayere
In thought waylyng have songe hit hevyly;
The torchis sett of sighis pitously,   5
Which was with sorow sett aflame;
The toumbe is made als to the same
Of karfull cry, depáyntid all with teeris,
The which richely is write abowt:
That here, lo! lith withouten dowt   10
The hool tresoure of all worldly blys.

Of gold on hir ther lith an ymage clere,
With safyr blew ysett so inrichely,
For hit is write and seide how the safere
Doth token trouthe, and gold to ben happy;   15
The which that wel bisettith hir hardily,
Forwhi hit was an ewrous trewe madame,
And of goodnes ay flowren may hir name,
For God the which that made hir, lo ywys,
To make such oon me thynke a myght ben prowt   20
For, lo, she was, as right well be she mowt,
The hool tresoure of all worldly blys!

O pese! no more myn hert astoneth here
To here my prayse hir vertu so trewly
Of hir that had no fawt withouten were,   25
As all the world hit saith, as well as y,
The whiche that knew hir deedis inthorowly.
God hath hir tane, y trowe, for hir good fame,
His hevene the more to joy with sport and game,
The more to plese and comfort his seyntis;   30
For, certis, well may she comfort a rowt—
Noou is she saynt, she was here so devowt,
The hool tresoure of all worldly blys!

Not vaylith now though y complayne this—
Al most we deye, therto so let us lowt;   35
For ay to kepe ther is no wight so stowt
The hool tresoure of all worldly blys!

K

Charles of Orléans, *In the Forest of Noyous Heaviness*

In the forest of Noyous Hevynes
As y went wandryng in the moneth of May,
I mette of Love the myghti gret goddes,
Which axid me whithir y was away.
I hir answerid, 'As fortune doth convey
As oon exylid from joy, al be me loth,
That passyng well all folke me clepyn may
The man forlost that wot not where he goth.'

Half in a smyle ayen of hir humblesse
She seide, 'My frend, if so y wist, mafay,
Wherfore that thou art brought in such distresse,
To shape thyn ese y wolde mysilf assay,
For heretofore y sett thyn hert in way
Of gret plesere. Y not whoo made thee wroth;
Hit grevith me thee see in suche aray,
The man forlost that wot not where he goth.'

'Allas!' y seide, 'Most sovereyne good princesse,
Ye knowe my case, what nedith to yow say?
Hit is thorugh Deth that shewith to all rudesse
Hath fro me tane that y most lovyd ay,
In whom that all myn hope and comfort lay,
So passyng frendship was bitwene us both
That y was not—to fals Deth did hir day—
The man forlost that wot not where he goth.'

'Thus am y blynd, allas and welaway!
Al fer myswent with my staf grapsyng wey,
That no thyng axe but me a grave to cloth,
For pité is that y lyve thus a day
The man forlost that wot not where he goth!'

L

Charles of Orléans, *Your Mouth says, Kiss me*

Yowre mouth hit saith me, 'Bas me, bas swet!'
When that y yow bihold this semeth me,
But Daunger stant so nygh hit may not be,
Which doth me sorow gret, y yow bihet!
But bi yowre trouth gefe me hit now we mete,   5
A pryvé swet swete cosse two or thre!
    Yowre mouth hit saith me, 'Bas me, bas swet!'
    When that y yow bihold this semeth me.
Daunger me hatith—whi y kan not wet—
And labourith ay my gret adversité,   10
God graunt me onys forbrent y may him se,
That y myght stampe his asshis with my feet!
    Yowre mouth hit saith me, 'Bas me, bas swet!'
    When that y yow bihold this semeth me.

M

Charles of Orléans, *The Lover's Confession*

    My gostly fadir, y me confesse
    First to God and then to yow
    That at a wyndow, wot ye how,
    I stale a cosse of gret swetnes;
    Which don was out avisynes—   5
    But hit is doon, not undoon now.
        My gostly fadir y me confesse
        First to God and then to yow.
    But y restore it shall, dowtles,
    Ageyn, if so be that y mow—   10
    And that, God, y make avow—
    And ellis y axe foryefnes.
        My gostly fadir y me confesse
        First to God and then to yow.

N

Charles of Orléans, *Wanton Eye*

Wel, wanton ey, but must ye nedis pley;
Yowre lokis nyse ye let hem renne to wide!
I drede me sore if that ye ben aspide,
And then we must hit bothe right dere abey!
5   Take sum and leve sum to an othir day,
And for oure ese swift from yowre theftis glide!
    Wel, wanton ey, but must ye nedis pley;
    Yowre lookis nyse ye let hem renne to wide!
For myght onys Sklaundir gete yow undir key,
10   Ye shulde ben then from alle suche theftis tide—
So, fy, for shame! lete Reson be yowre gide,
And stele—spare not!—when ye se tyme and may!
    Wel wanton ey, but must ye nedis pley;
    Yowre lokis nyse ye let hem renne to wide!

O

Farewell this World

Farewell, this world! I take my leve for evere;
I am arested to apere at Goddes face.
O myghtyfull God, thou knowest that I had levere
Than all this world to have oone houre space
5   To make asythe for all my grete trespace.
My hert, alas, is brokyne for that sorowe—
Som be this day that shall not be tomorow!

This lyfe, I see, is but a cheyré feyre;
All thyngis passene and so most I algate.
10   Today I sat full ryall in a cheyere,
Tyll sotell Deth knokyd at my gate,
And onavysed he seyd to me, 'Chek-mate!'
Lo, how sotell he maketh a devors!
And, wormys to fede, he hath here leyd my cors.

Speke softe, ye folk, for I am leyd aslepe!   15
I have my dreme—in trust is moche treson.
Fram Dethes hold feyne wold I make a lepe,
But my wysdom is turnyd into feble resoun:
I see this worldis joye lastith but a season—
Wold to God I had remembyrd me beforne!   20
I sey no more, but be ware of ane horne!

This febyll world, so fals and so unstable,
Promoteth his lovers for a lytell while,
But at the last he yeveth hem a bable
When his peynted trowth is torned into gile.   25
Experyence cawsith me the trowth to compile,
Thynkyng this, to late, alas, that I began,
For foly and hope disseyveth many a man.

Farewell, my frendis! the tide abidith no man:
I moste departe hens, and so shall ye.   30
But in this passage, the beste song that I can
Is *Requiem eternam*—I pray God grant it me!
Whan I have endid all myn adversité,
Graunte me in Paradise to have a mancyon,
That shede his blode for my redempcion.   35

P

The Friar and the Nun

Inducas, inducas,
In temptacionibus.

Ther was a frier of order gray,
Inducas,
Which loved a nunne full meny a day   5
In temptacionibus.

This fryer was lusty, proper, and yong,
Inducas,
He offerd the nunne to lerne her syng
In temptacionibus.   10

Othe re me fa the frier her tawght,
Inducas.
Sol la, this nunne he kyst full oft
In temptacionibus.

15   By proper-chaunt and Bequory,
Inducas.
This nunne he groped with flattery
In temptacionibus.

The fryers first lesson was '*Veni ad me*',
20   *Inducas,*
'*Et ponam tollum meum ad te*'
In temptacionibus.

The frier sang all by *bemoll*,
Inducas,
25   Of the nunne he begate a cristenyd sowle
In temptacionibus.

The nunne was taught to syng '*Sepe*',
Inducas,
'*Lapides expungnaverunt me*'
30   *In temptacionibus.*

Thus the fryer lyke a prety man,
Inducas,
Ofte rokkyd the nunnys quoniam
In temptacionibus.

Q

The Schoolboy's Lament

Hay, hay, by this day,
What avayleth it me thowgh I say nay?

I wold fayn be a clarke,
But yet hit is a strange werke;
5   The byrchyn twygges be so sharpe
Hit makith me have a faynt harte;
     What avaylith it me thowgh I say nay?

On Monday in the mornyng whan I shall rise,
At .vi. of the clok, hyt is the gise,
To go to skole withowt avise,   10
I had lever go xx^{ti} myle twyse;
   What avaylith it me thowgh I say nay?

My master lokith as he were madde:
'Wher hast thou be, thow sory ladde?'
'Milke dukkes my moder badde.'   15
Hit was no mervayle thow I were sadde;
   What vaylith it me thowgh I say nay?

My master pepered my ars with well good spede;
Hit was worse than fynkyll sede;
He wold not leve till it did blede;   20
Myche sorow have he for his dede!
   What vayleth it me thowgh I say nay?

I wold my master were a watt,
And my boke a wyld catt,
And a brase of grehowndes in his toppe;   25
I wold be glade for to se that.
   What vayleth it me thowgh I say nay?

I wold my master were an hare,
And all his bokes howndes were,
And I myself a joly hontere;   30
To blow my horn I wold not spare,
For if he were dede I would not care.
   What vaylith me thowgh I say nay?

R

The Corpus Christi Carol

Lully, lulley; lully, lulley;
The fawcon hath born my mak away.

He bare hym up, he bare hym down;
He bare hym into an orchard brown.

In that orchard ther was an hall,   5
That was hangid with purpill and pall.

And in that hall ther was a bede;
Hit was hangid with gold so rede.

And yn that bed ther lythe a knyght,
His wowndes bledyng day and nyght.

By that bedes side ther kneleth a may,
And she wepeth both nyght and day.

And by that beddes side ther stondith a ston,
'*Corpus Christi*' wretyn theron.

S

A Nonsense Song

My harte of golde as true as stele,
  As I me lened to a bough,
In fayth, but yf ye love me well,
  Lorde, so Robyn lough!

My lady went to Caunterbury,
  The Saynt to be her bothe;
She met with Cate of Malmesbery;
  Why wepyst thou in an apple rote?

Nyne myle to Mychelmas,
  Our dame began to brew;
Mychell set his mare to gras;
  Lorde, so fast it snew!

For you, love, I brake my glasse;
  Your gowne is furred with blew;
The devyll is dede, for there I was;
  Iwys, it is full trew.

And yf ye slepe, the cocke wyll crow;
  True hart, thynke what I say;
Jacke Napes wyll make a mow,
  Loke who dare say hym nay.

I pray you, have me now in mynde;
   I tell you of the mater:
He blew his horne agaynst the wynde;
   The crow gothe to the water.

Yet I tell you mekyll more: 25
   That cat lyeth in the cradell;
I pray you, kepe true hart in store,
   A peny for a ladell.

I swere by Saynt Katheryn of Kent,
   The gose gothe to the grene;   30
All our dogges tayle is brent;
   It is not as I wene.

'Tyrlery lorpyn', the laverocke songe;
   So meryly pypes the sparow;
The cow brake lose; the rope ran home;   35
   Syr, God gyve yow good morow!

T

Green Groweth the Holly

Grene growith the holy,
So doth the ivé,
Thow wynter blastys blow never so hye,
Grene growth the holy.

As the holy grouth grene   5
   And never chaungyth hew,
So I am, ever hath bene,
   Unto my lady trew.

As the holy grouth grene
   With ivé all alone   10
When flowerys cannot be sene,
   And grenewode levys be gone.

Now unto my lady
   Promyse to her I make,
Frome all other only   15
   To her I me betake.

Adew, myne owne lady,
Adew, my specyall,
Who hath my hart trewly,
20 Be suere, and ever shall.

U

Blow Thy Horn, Hunter

Blow thi horne, hunter, and blow thi horne on hye!
Ther ys a do in yonder wode; in faith, she woll not dy:
Now blow thi horne, hunter, and blow thi horne, joly hunter!

Sore this dere strykyn ys,
5 And yet she bledes no whytt;
She lay so fayre, I cowde nott mys;
Lord, I was glad of it!

As I stod under a bank
The dere shoffe on the mede;
10 I stroke her so that downe she sanke,
But yet she was not dede.

There she gothe! Se ye nott,
How she gothe over the playne?
And yf ye lust to have a shott,
15 I warrant her barrayne.

He to go and I to go,
But he ran fast afore;
I bad hym shott and strik the do,
For I myght shott no more.

20 To the covert bothe thay went,
For I fownd wher she lay;
And arrow in her hanch she hent;
For faynte she myght nott bray.

I was wery of the game,
25 I went to tavern to drynk;
Now the construccyon of the same—
What do yow meane or thynk?

Here I leve and mak an end,
  Now of this hunters lore;
I thynk his bow ys well unbent,   30
  Hys bolt may fle no more.

V

The Knight Knocked at the Castle Gate

Yow and I and Amyas,
  Amyas and yow and I,
To the grenewode must we go, alas!
  Yow and I, my lyff, and Amyas.

The knyght knokett at the castell gate;   5
The lady mervelyd who was therat.

To call the porter he wold not blyn;
The lady said he shuld not com in.

The portres was a lady bryght;
Strangenes that lady hyght.   10

She asked hym what was his name;
He said, 'Desyre, your man, madame.'

She said, 'Desyre, what do ye here?'
He said, 'Madame, as your prisoner.'

He was cownselled to breffe a byll   15
And shew my lady hys oune wyll.

Kyndnes said she wold yt bere,
And Pyté said she wold be ther.

Thus how that dyd we cannot say—
We left them ther and went ower way.   20

W

Western Wind

Westron wynde when wyll thow blow,
The smalle rayne downe can rayne—
Cryst, yf my love wer in my armys
And I yn my bed agayne!

12

BALLADS AND VERSE ROMANCES

THE 'traditional ballads', as collected in the great nineteenth-century anthology of F. J. Child, have been by convention associated with this period, but in fact very few can be definitely placed within its chronological limits, although there are certainly some 'ballads' in later manuscripts—on the battle of Otterburn or on the outlaw Adam Bell—which are probably of fifteenth-century origin. Poems from our period which are described by modern editors as 'ballads' range from short pieces ('St Stephen', 'Robin and Gandelyn', etc.) to more expansive examples of narrative which seem to have some relationship with popular verse romance. The 'rymes' of Robin Hood, which, to judge from the many (and usually slighting) references to them, were immensely popular, are represented here by an extract from the third 'fit' of the *Gest of Robin Hood*, a long poem of uncertain date (? first half of the fifteenth century), which may be based on earlier separate ballads. Robin Hood in the popular drama (of which only a fragment remains) seems to have been a Lord of Misrule, and something of the spirit of carnival 'inversion' is present in the poems about him or—as here—his boisterous follower, Little John. There are many unanswered questions about 'Robin Hood'. It is still uncertain whether he is based on a real outlaw or highwayman, or whether the songs about him go back beyond the fourteenth century. In the early poems his 'kingdom' in the greenwood (in Barnsdale or Sherwood) offers an alternative world to that of the Sheriff of Nottingham (and, sometimes, to that of the king) where true 'fellowship' and 'courtesy' can be found, yet it is a world marked by violence and robbery. An old proverb neatly sums up the mystery and fascination of the outlaw hero: 'many men speak of Robin Hood that never bent his bow.'

Verse romances continued to flourish beside their equivalents in prose. Old favourites (such as *Guy of Warwick*) were recopied and sometimes revised, and some of them eventually found their way into print. Others—like *The Squyer of Lowe Degre*, or some popular Gawain romances like *The Turke and Gowin*—were probably composed in this period. We have the complete text of *The Knight of Curtesy and the Fair Lady of Faguell*, a grim and pathetic story of doomed love, based on the widespread legend of the 'eaten heart', and an extract from the almost unknown *Capistranus*, an interesting example of how contemporary history could be transformed into a hagiographical romance in the popular style. With vigour and enthusiastic piety it sets about telling the story of what one chronicler describes as 'the batayll of Seint John Capistrane, a frere, which destroyed an innumerable number of Turkes'.

A

A GEST OF ROBYN HODE

Little John Tricks the Sheriff of Nottingham

It fell upon a Wednesday
The sherif on huntynge was gone,
And Litel John lay in his bed,
And was foriete at home.

5   Therfore he was fastinge
Til it was past the none;
'Gode sir stuarde, I pray to the,
Gyve me my dynere,' saide Litell John,

'It is longe for Grenelefe
10   Fastinge thus for to be;
Therfor I pray the, sir stuarde,
Mi dyner gif thou me.'

'Shalt thou never ete ne drynke,' saide the stuarde,
'Tyll my lorde be come to towne':
15   'I make myn avowe to God,' saide Litell John,
'I had lever to crake thy crowne!'

The boteler was full uncurteys,
There he stode on flore;
He start to the botery
20   And shet fast the dore.

Lytell John gave the boteler suche a tap
His backe went nere in two;
Though he lived an .c. ier,
The wors shuld he be go.

25   He sporned the dore with his fote;
It went open wel and fyne;
And there he made large lyveray,
Bothe of ale and wyne.

'Sith ye wol nat dyne,' sayde Litell John,
'I shall gyve you to drinke;   30
And though ye lyve an hundred wynter,
On Lytel John ye shall thinke!'

Litell John ete, and Litel John drank,
The while that he wolde;
The sherife had in his kechyn a coke,   35
A stoute man and a bolde.

'I make myn avowe to God,' saide the coke,
'Thou arte a shrewde hynde
In ani hous for to dwel,
For to aske thus to dyne!'   40

And there he lent Litell John
God strokis thre;
'I make myn avowe to God,' sayde Lytell John,
'These strokis lyked well me.

'Thou arte a bolde man and hardy,   45
And so thinketh me;
And or I pas fro this place
Assayed better shalt thou be.'

Lytell John drew a ful gode sworde,
The coke toke another in hande;   50
They thought nothynge for to fle,
But stifly for to stande.

There they faught sore togedere
Two myle way and well more;
Myght neyther other harme done,   55
The mountnaunce of an owre.

'I make myn avowe to God,' sayde Litell John,
'And by my true lewté,
Thou art one of the best swordemen
That ever yit sawe I me!   60

'Cowdest thou shote as well in a bowe,
To grene wode thou shuldest with me,
And two times in the yere thy clothinge
Chaunged shulde be;

65 'And every yere of Robyn Hode
Twenty merke to thy fe':
'Put up thy swerde,' saide the coke,
'And felowes woll we be.'

Thanne he fet to Lytell John
70 The nowmbles of a do,
Gode brede, and full gode wyne;
They ete and drank theretoo.

And when they had dronkyn well,
Theyre trouthes togeder they plight
75 That they wolde be with Robyn
That ylke same nyght.

They dyd them to the tresoure-hows,
As fast as they myght gone;
The lokkes, that were of full gode stele,
80 They brake them everichone.

They toke away the silver vessell,
And all that thei migt get;
Pecis, masars, ne sponis,
Wolde thei not forget.

85 Also they toke the gode pens,
Thre hundred pounde and more,
And did them streyte to Robyn Hode,
Under the grene wode hore.

'God the save, my dere mayster,
And Criste the save and se!'
90 And thanne sayde Robyn to Litell John,
'Welcome myght thou be!

'Also be that fayre yeman
Thou bryngest there with the;
95 What tydynges fro Notyngham?
Lytill John, tell thou me.'

'Well the gretith the proude sheryf,
And sende the here by me
His coke and his silver vessell,
100 And thre hundred pounde and thre.'

'I make myne avowe to God,' sayde Robyn,
'And to the Trenyté,
It was never by his gode wyll
This gode is come to me.'

Lytyll John there hym bethought   105
On a shrewde wyle;
Fyve myle in the forest he ran,
Hym happed all his wyll.

Than he met the proude sheref,
Huntynge with houndes and horne;   110
Lytell John coude of curtesye,
And knelyd hym beforne.

'God the save, my dere mayster,
And Criste the save and se!'
'Reynolde Grenelefe,' sayde the shryef,   115
'Where hast thou nowe be?'

'I have be in this forest;
A fayre syght can I se;
It was one of the fayrest syghtes
That ever yet sawe I me.   120

'Yonder I sawe a ryght fayre harte,
His coloure is of grene;
Seven score of dere upon a herde
Be with hym all bydene.

'Their tyndes are so sharpe, maister,   125
Of sexty and well mo,
That I durst not shote for drede,
Lest they wolde me slo.'

'I make myn avowe to God,' sayde the shyref,
'That syght wolde I fayne se':   130
'Buske you thyderwarde, mi dere mayster,
Anone, and wende with me.'

The sherif rode, and Litell John
Of fote he was full smerte,
And whane they came before Robyn,   135
'Lo, sir, here is the mayster-herte.'

Still stode the proude sherief,
A sory man was he;
'Wo the worthe, Raynolde Grenelefe,
140   Thou hast betrayed nowe me!'

'I make myn avowe to God,' sayde Litell John,
'Mayster, ye be to blame;
I was mysserved of my dynere
Whan I was with you at hame.'

145   Sone he was to souper sette,
And served well with silver white,
And whan the sherif sawe his vessell,
For sorowe he myght nat ete.

'Make glad chere,' sayde Robyn Hode,
150   'Sherif, for charité,
And for the love of Litill John
Thy lyfe I graunt to the.'

Whan they had souped well,
The day was al gone;
155   Robyn commaunde Litell John
To drawe of his hosen and his shone;

His kirtell, and his cote-of-pie,
That was fured well and fine,
And toke hym a grene mantel,
160   To lap his body therin.

Robyn commaundyd his wight yonge men,
Under the grenewode tree,
They shulde lye in that same sute,
That the sherif myght them see.

165   All nyght lay the proude sherif
In his breche and in his schert;
No wonder it was, in grene wode,
Though his sydes gan smerte.

'Make glade chere,' sayde Robyn Hode,
170   'Sheref, for charité;
For this is our ordre iwys,
Under the grenewode tree.'

184

'This is harder order', sayde the sherief,
'Than any ankir or frere;
For all the golde in mery Englonde   175
I wolde nat longe dwell her.'

B

The Knight of Curtesy

In Faguell, a fayre countré,
A great lord somtyme dyd dwell,
Which had a lady so fayre and fre
That all men good of her dyd tel.

Fayre and pleasant she was in sight,   5
Gentyl and amyable in eche degré,
Chaste to her lorde, bothe day and nyght,
As is the turtyll upon the tre.

All men her loved, bothe yonge and olde,
For her vertue and gentylnesse.   10
Also in that lande was a knight bolde,
Ryght wyse and ful of doughtinesse.

All men spake of his hardynesse,
Ryche and poore of eche degré,
So that they called him, doutlesse,   15
The noble Knyght of Curtesy.

This knight so curteys was and bolde
That the lorde herde therof anone.
He sayd that speke with him he wolde—
For hym the messengere is gone   20

Wyth a letter unto this knight
And sayd, 'Syr, I pray God you se.
My lorde of Faguell you sendeth right
And hundredfolde gretynge by me.

'He praieth you in all hastynge   25
To come in his court for to dwell;
And ye shal lake no maner of thynge,
As townes, towres, and many a castell.'

The curteyse knight was sone content;
And in all dilygence that might be
Wyth the messyngere anone he went
This lorde to serve with humylité.

Fast they rode bothe day and nyght
Tyll he unto the lorde was come;
And whan the lorde of hym had a sight,
Right frendly he did him welcome.

He gave hym townes, castelles, and towres,
Whereof all other had envye;
They thought to reve him his honoures
By some treason or trechery.

This lady, of whome I spake before,
Seyng this knight so good and kynde,
Afore all men that ever were bore
She set on hym her herte and minde.

His paramour she thought to be,
Hym for to love wyth herte and minde,
Nat in vyce but in chastyté,
As chyldren that together are kynde.

This knight also, curteyse and wyse,
With herte and mynde bothe ferme and fast,
Lovyd this lady wythouten vyse,
Whyche tyll they dyed dyd ever laste.

Both night and day these lovers true
Suffred great paine, wo, and grevaunce,
How eche to other theyr minde might shewe,
Tyll at the last by a sodaine chaunce

This knight was in a garden grene
And thus began him to complayne;
'Alas!' he sayd with murnynge eyen,
Now is my herte in wo and paine!

'From mournynge can I nat refrayne,
This ladyes love dothe me so wounde,
I feare she hath of me disdayne.'
With that he fell downe to the grounde.

30
35
40
45
50
55
60

The lady in a windowe laye,   65
With herte colde as any stone;
She wyst nat what to do nor saye
Whan she herde the knightes mone.

Sore sighed that lady of renowne,
In her face was no colour founde;   70
Than into the gardein came she downe
And sawe this knight lye on the grounde.

When she sawe hym lye so for her sake,
Her hert for wo was almoost gone;
To her comforte coude she none take,   75
But in swoune fell downe hym upon,

So sadly that the kynght awoke;
And whan that he sawe her so nere,
To hym comforte anone he toke
And began the lady for to chere.   80

He sayd, 'Lady and love, alas!
Into this cure who hath you brought?'
She sayd, 'My love and my solas,
Your beauté standeth so in my thought

'That, yf I had no worldly make,   85
Never none should have my herte but ye.'
The knyght sayd, 'Lady, for your sake,
I shal you love in chastyté.'

'Our love,' he sayde, 'shal be none other
But chaste and true as is betwene   90
A goodly syster and a brother,
Fro luste our bodyes to kepe clene.

'And wheresoever mi body be,
Bothe day and night, at every tyde,
My simpele herte in chastité   95
Shall evermore, lady, with you abide.'

This lady, white as any floure,
Replete with feminine shamefastnesse,
Begayne to chaunge her fare coloure
And to him sayd, 'My love, doubtelesse,   100

'Under suche forme I shal you love
With faythful herte in chastité,
Next unto God that is above,
Bothe in welthe and adversyté.'

105   Eche of them kyssed other truely;
But ever, alas! ther was a fo
Behynde the wall, them to espye,
Which after torned them to muche wo.

Out of the garden whan they were gone,
110   Eche from other dyd departe;
Awaye was all theyr wofull mone,
The one had lyghted the others herte.

Than this spye of whome I tolde,
Whyche stode behinde the garden wall,
115   Wente unto his lorde ful bolde
And sayd, 'Syr, shewe you I shall:

'By your gardyn as I was walkynge,
I herde the Knight of Curtesye,
Which with your lady was talkinge
120   Of love unlaufull pryvely;

'Therfore yf ye suffre him for to procede,
Wyth your lady to have his joye,
She shal bee lede fro you in dede,
Or elles they bothe shal you distroye.'

125   Whan than the lorde had understande
The wordes that the spye him tolde,
He sware he wolde rydde him fro that lande
Were he never so stronge and bolde.

He sware an othe, by God Almyght,
130   That he should never be glade certayne
While that knight was in his sight,
Tyl that he by some meane were slaine.

Than let he do crye a feest
For every man that thider wolde come,
135   For every man bothe moost and leest;
Thyder came lordes bothe olde and yonge.

The lorde was at the table set
And his lady by him that tide;
The Knight of Curtesy anone was fet
And set downe on the other syde.   140

Theyr hartes should have be wobegone,
If they had knowen the lordes thought;
But whan that they were styll echone,
The lorde these words anone forth brought:

'Me thinke it is syttinge for a knight   145
For aventures to enquyre,
And nat thus, bothe day and night,
At home to sojourne by the fyre.

'Therfore, Syr Knight of Curtesye,
This thinge wyl I you counseyll,   150
To ryde and go throughe the countré
To seke adventures for your avayle—

'As unto Rodes, for to fight,
The Christen fayth for to mayntayne,
To shewe by armes your force and myght,   155
In Lumbardy, Portyngale, and in Spayne.'

Than spake the knyght to the lorde anone:
'For your sake wyl I aventure my lyfe,
Whether ever I come agayne or none,
And for my ladyes sake, your wyfe;   160

'If I dyd nat, I were to blame.'
Than sighed the lady with that worde;
In dolour depe her herte was tane
And sore wounded as wyth a sworde.

Than after dyner the knight did go   165
His horse and harneyse to make redy;
The woful lady came him unto
And to him sayd right pyteously:

'Alas! yf ye go, I must complayne
Alone as a wofull creature;   170
If that ye be in batayle slayne,
On lyve may I not endure.

189

'Alas! unhappy creature,
Where shal I go, where shal I byde?
175   Of dethe, sothely, nowe am I sure;
And all worldly joye I shal set asyde!'

A payre of sheres than dyd she take
And cut of her here bothe yelowe and bright.
'Were this', than sayd she, 'for my sake,
180   Upon your helme, moche curteyse knight.'

'I shall, dere lady, for your sake,'
This knyght sayd with styl morninge;
No comforte to him coude he take
Nor absteine him fro perfounde syghinge.

185   For grete pyté I can not wryte
The sorowe that was betwene them two;
Also I have to smal respyte
For to declare theyr payne and wo.

The wofull departinge and complaynt
190   That was betwene these lovers twayne,
Was never man that coude depaynt,
So wofully did they complayne.

The teres ran from theyr eyen twayne
For doloure whan they did departe;
195   The lady in her castell did remayne,
Wyth langour replenysshed was her herte.

Now leve we here this lady bryght
Wythin her castel makinge her mone,
And tourne we to the curteys knyght
200   Whyche on his journey forth is gone.

Unto hymselfe this knight sayd he,
'Agaynst the Chrysten I wyl not fyght;
But to the Rodes wyl I go
Them to susteyne with all my myght.'

205   Than did he her heere unfolde
And one his helme it set on hye
Wyth rede thredes of ryche golde
Whiche he had of his lady

Full richely his shelde was wrought
Wyth asure stones and beten golde;   210
But on his lady was his thought
The yelowe heare whan he dyd beholde.

Than forth he rode by dale and downe,
After aventures to enquyre,
By many a castel, cyté, and towne;   215
All to batayl was his desyre.

In every justyng where he came
None so good as he was founde;
In every place the pryce he wan
And smote his adversaryes to the grounde.   220

So whan he came to Lumberdye,
Ther was a dragon theraboute
Whyche did great hurt and vylanye;
Bothe man and beste of hym had doubte.

As this knight rode there alone,   225
Save onely his page by his syde,
For his lady he began to mone,
Sore syghynge as he did ride.

'Alas!' he sayd, 'my lady swete,
God wote in what case ye be!   230
God wote whan we two shal mete;
I feare that I shal never you se.'

Than as he loked hym aboute
Towarde a hyll that was so hye,
Of this dragon he harde a shoute;   235
'Yonder is a feast,' he sayd, 'truly.'

The knight him blessyd and forthe dyd go
And sayd, 'I shal do my travayle!
Betyde me well, betyde me wo,
The fyers fynde I shal assayle.'   240

Than wyth the dragon dyd he meate;
Whan she him sawe, she gaped wyde;
He toke good hede, as ye may wete,
And quyckely sterte a lytle asyde.

245 He drewe his swerde like a knyght,
This dragon fyersly to assayle;
He gave her strokes ful of myght;
Stronge and mortall was the batayle.

The dragon gave this knight a wounde
250 Wyth his tayle upon the heed
That he fell downe unto the grounde
In a sowne as he had ben deed.

So at the last he rose agayne
And made his mone to God Almyght,
255 And to Our Lady he dyd compleyne,
Theyr helpe desyrynge in that fyght.

Than sterte he wyth a fayrse courage
Unto the dragon without fayle;
He loked so for his advauntage
260 That he smote of her tayle.

Than began the dragon for to yell
And tourned her upon her syde;
The knight was ware of her right well
And in her bodi made his sworde to slyde,

265 So that she coud nat remeve scarcely.
The knight, that seinge, approched nere
And smote her heed of lyghtly;
Than was he escaped that daungere.

Than thanked he God of his grace,
270 Whiche by his goodnes and mercye
Hym had preserved in that place
Through vertue of hys deyté.

Than went he to a nonrye there besyde,
And there a surgeand by his arte
275 Heled his woundes that were so wyde;
And than fro thens he dyd departe

Towarde the Rodes for to fyght
In bataill, as he had undertake,
The fayth to susteyne with all his might;
280 For his promysse he will not breke.

Than of Sarazyns there was a route,
All redy armed and in araye,
That syeged the Rodes round aboute
Fyersly agaynst the Good Fredaye.

The knight was welcomed of echone   285
That within the cyté were;
They provided forth batayle anone;
So for this time I leve them there

And tourne to his lady bryght
Which is at home wyth wofull mone.   290
Sore morned she both day and night,
Sayenge, 'Alas! my love is gone!'

'Alas!' she sayd, 'my gentyl knight,
For your sake is my herte ful sore;
Myght I ones of you have a syght   295
Afore my dethe, I desyre no more.

'Alas! what treson or envye
Hath made my love fro me to go?
I thynke my lorde for ire truley
By treason him to deth hathe do.   300

'Alas! my lorde, ye were to blame
Thus my love for to betraye!
It is to you a right great shame,
Sythe that our love was chast alwaye.

'Our love was clene in chastyté,   305
Without synne styl to endure.
We never entended vylanye.
Alas, moost curteyse creature,

'Where do ye dwell? where do ye byde?
Wold God I knewe where you to fynde!   310
Wherever ye go, whereever ye ride,
Love, ye shal never out of my mynde!

'A deth! where art thou so longe fro me?
Come and departe me fro this paine;
For dead and buried til I be   315
Fro morning can I nat refrayne.

'Farewel, dere love, wherever ye be!
Bi you pleasure is fro me gone;
Unto the time I may you se
320   Withoute comforte still must I mone.'

Thus this lady of coloure clere
Alone mourninge did complaine;
Nothinge coulde her comforte ne chere
So was she oppressed with wo and paine.

325   So leve we her here in this traine,
For her love mourning alwaye,
And to the knight tourne we againe,
Which at Rodes abideth the day

Of bataile. So whan the daie was come,
330   The knightes armed them echeone,
And out of the citie wente all and some,
Strongly to fight with Goddes fone.

Faire and semely was the sight,
To se them redy unto the warre!
335   There was many a man of might
That to that bataile was come full farre.

The Knight of Curtesy came into the felde,
Well armed, right fast did ride;
Both knightes and barans him behelde,
340   How comely he was on eche side.

Above the helme upon his hede
Was set, with many a precious stone,
The comely heare as golde so rede;
Better armed than he was none.

345   Than the trumpettes began to sounde;
The speres ranne and brake the raye;
The noise of gonnes did rebounde;
In this metinge there was no plaie!

Great was the bataile on everi side;
350   The Knight of Curtesy was nat behinde;
He smote all downe that wolde abide;
His mache coulde he nowhere finde.

There was a Sarazin stronge and wight
That at this knight had great envye;   355
He ran to him with all his might
And said, 'Traitour, I thee defie!'

They ranne together with speres longe;
Anone the Sarazin lay on the grounde.
The knight drew out his sworde so stronge   360
And smote his head of in that stounde.

Than came twelve Sarazins in a rought
And the knight did sore assaile;
So they beset him rounde aboute;
There began a stronge bataile.

The knight kest foure unto the grounde   365
With four strokes by and by;
The other gave him many a wounde;
For they did ever multeplie.

They laide on him on every side
Wyth cruell strokes and mortall;   370
They gave him woundes so depe and wide
That to the grounde downe he did fall.

The Sarazins went and let him lye
With mortall woundes piteous to se;
He called his page hastely   375
And said, 'My time is come to die.

'In mi herte is so depe a wounde
That I must dye withouten naye;
But or thou me burye in the grounde,
Of one thinge I thee praie: 380

'Out of mi body to cut my herte
And wrappe it in this yelowe here;
And whan thou doest from hence departe,
Unto my lady thou do it bere.

'This promisse thou me without delay,   385
To bere my lady this present;
And burie mi body in the crosse-waie.'
The page was sory and dolent.

The knight yelded up the goost anone;
390   The page him buried as he had him bad;
And towarde Faguell is he gone—
The herte and here with him he had.

Sometime he went, sometime he ran,
With wofull mone and sory jest,
395   Till unto Faguell he came,
Nere to a castell in a forest.

The lorde of Faguell without let
Was in the forest with his meyné;
With this page anone he met;
400   'Page,' he said, 'what tidinges with thee?

'With thi maister how is the case?
Shew me lightli or thou go,
Or thou shalt never out of this place!'
The page was afearde whan he said so.

405   The page for feare that he had
The herte unto the lorde he toke tho—
In his courage he was full sad—
He toke the here to him also.

He tolde him trothe of everi thinge,
410   How that the knight in bataile was slaine,
And howe he sent his lady that thinge
For a speciall token of love certaine.

The lorde therof toke good hede
And behelde the herte, that high presente.
415   'Their love', he said, 'was hote indede!
They were bothe in great torment.'

Than home is he to the kechin gone;
'Coke,' he said, 'herken unto me.
Dresse me this herte, and that anone,
420   In the deintiest wise that may be.

'Make it swete and delycate to eate;
For it is for my lady bryght.
If that she wyst what were the meate,
Sothely her hert wolde not be lyght!'

Therof sayd the lorde full trewe—   425
That meat was doleful and mortall,
So thought the lady whan she it knewe.
Than went the lorde into the hall.

Anone the lorde to meate was set
And this lady nat farre him fro.   430
The hert anone he made be fet,
Wherof proceded muche wo.

'Madame, eate herof,' he sayd,
'For it is deynteous and plesaunte.'
The lady eate and was not dismayde;   435
For of good spyce there dyd none wante.

Whan the lady had eaten wele,
Anone to her the lorde sayd there,
'His herte have ye eaten, every dele,
To whome you gave your yelowe here.   440

'Your knight is dead, as you may se;
I tell you, lady, certaynly,
His owne herte eaten have ye.
Madame, at the last we all must dye.'

Whan the lady herde him so say,   445
She sayd, 'My herte for wo shall brast!
Alas! that ever I sawe this day!
Now may my lyfe no lenger last!'

Up she rose wyth hert full wo,
And streight up into her chambre wente;   450
She confessed her devoutly tho
And shortely receyved the sacrament.

In her bed mournyng she her layde—
God wote ryght wofull was her mone!
'Alas! myne owne dere love,' she sayd,   455
'Syth ye be dead my joye is gone!

'Have I eaten thy herte in my body?
That meate to me shal be full dere;
For sorowe, alas, now must I dye,
A, noble knight withouten fere!   460

'That herte shal certayne with me dye;
I have recived theron the sacrament.
All erthly fode here I denye—
For wo and paine my life is spente!

465 'My lorde and husbande, full of cruelté,
Why have you done this cursed dede?
Ye have him slaine, so have ye me—
The hie God graunte to you your mede!'

Than sayd the lorde, 'My lady fayre,
470 Forgive me if I have misdone;
I repent I was nat ware
That ye wolde your herte oppresse so sone!'

The lady sayd, 'I you forgive;
Adew, my lorde, for evermore!
475 My time is come, I may not live.'
The lorde sayd, 'I am wo therfore!'

Great was the sorowe of more and lesse,
Bothe lordes and ladyes that were there;
Some for great wo swouned doubtelesse;
480 All of her dethe full wofull were.

Her complaynt pyteous was to here:
'Adieu, my lorde! Nowe muste we discever;
I dye to you, husbande, a true wedded fere,
As any in Faguell was found ever.

485 'I am clene of the Knight of Curtesy,
And wrongfully are we brought to confusion;
I am clene for hym, and he for me,
And for all other save you alone.

'My lorde, ye were to blame truely
490 His herte to make me for to eate;
But sythe it is buryed in mi body,
On it shall I never eate other meate.

'Theron have I recyved eternall fode;
Erthly meate wyll I never none.
495 Now Jesu, that was don on the rode,
Have mercy on me! My lyfe is gone.'

198

Wyth that the lady in all theyr syght
Yelded up her spyrit, makinge her mone.
The hyghe God, moost of myght,
On her have mercy and us echone!   500

And brynge us to that gloryous trone
To se the joye of Paradyse,
Whyche God graunte to us echone,
And to the reders and herers of this treatyse.

C

CAPYSTRANUS

The Relief of Belgrade

There .xx. thousande met in fere
With Obedyanus and the frere,
In helme and hauberke bryght.
To Grecuswyssynburgh he toke the waye,
There the Turke at syege laye,   5
With many a knyght.
Fourtene wekes the Turke had ben there
And put the Crysten to moche fere;
To hym they had no myght.
Fyve .c. gonnes he lete shote at ones,   10
Brake doune the walles with stones;
The wyldefyre lemed lyght.

To here it was grete wonder
The noyse of gonnes moche lyke the thonder—
That was a fereful dynne!   15
The noyse was herde many a myle.
Obedyaunce the meane whyle
Entred the towne within,
At .vi. of the clocke, the sothe to saye,
After noone on the Maudeleyne daye,   20
And neyther lesse ne mo.
And Capystranus, good frere Jhon
Assoyled our men everychone
To batayll or they dyde go;

199

25 And cryed loude with voyce clere,
'Lete us fyght for our soupere
In heven is redy dyght!
Our baner shall I bere todaye,
And to Jesu fast shall praye
30 To spede us in our ryght!'
Anone they togyder mette—
Fyve .m. deed withouten lette,
In helme and hauberke bryght.

Obedianus, that noble man,
Slewe them fast that served Sathan—
35 Thorowe Cryst theyr crownes had care!
All that he with his faucon hyt
There was no salve, I lette you wyt,
That ever myght hele that sare!
There was no Turke that he with met
40 But he had suche a buffet
That he greved never Crysten man mare.
He was a doughty knyght;
The fals he felled for Goddes ryght—
45 I praye God wele myght he fare!

Morpath and blacke Johan
That daye kylled Turkes many one,
Certayne withouten lette.
There was none so good armoure
50 That theyr dyntes myght endure,
Helme nor bryght baysnet.
They hewe upon the hethen on hye;
The fyre out of every syde gan flye—
So boldely on they bette!
55 Many a Turke there was cast,
Beten tyll the braynes brast—
Theyr maysters there they mette!

Many a .m. of preestes there was—
The Turkes herden never suche a masse
60 As they herde that daye.
Our preestes *Te Deum* songe;
The hethen fast downe they donge—
Then *pax* was put awaye.
There was scolemaysters of the best—
65 Many of them were brought to rest

That wolde not lere theyr laye.
Thus our Crysten people dyde fyght
From .v. of the clocke on Maudeleyne nyght
Tyll .x. on the other daye.

Then came the Turkes with newe batayll,   70
Clene clad in plate and male,
A .c. thousande and mo;
On dromydaryes gan they ryde,
And kylled our men on every syde—
Two .m. were there sloo.   75
Our men to stande they had no mayne,
But fledde to the towne agayne,
With woundes wyde and bloo.
Twenty thousande of our men
Were borne doune at the brydge ende—   80
The Turkes were so thro.

Dromydaryes over them ranne,
And kylled downe bothe horse and man—
In the felde durst none abyde.
Obedianus had many a wounde   85
Or he wolde flee the grounde,
For all the Turkes pryde.
Morpath and blacke Johan
Had woundes many one,
That blody were and wyde.
To the towne they fledde on fote;   90
They sawe it was no better bote—
Theyr stedes were slayne that tyde.

The Turkes folowed into the toune,
And kylled all before them downe—   95
Grete doyll it was to see.
Into the toune the grete Turke wanne,
And kylled wyfe, chylde, and man—
The innocentes thycke gan dye.
Johan Capystranus se that it was thus,   100
And hent a crucyfyxe of Cryst Jesus,
Ranne up tyll a toure on hye;
The halowed baner with hym he bare,
In the top of the toure he set it there,
And cryed full pytefully.   105

He sayd, 'Lorde God in heven on hyght,
Where is become thyn olde myght,
That men were wonte to have?
O my lord, Cryste Jesus,
110 Why hast thou forgoten us?
Now helpe of the we crave.
Loke on thy people that do thus dye—
Lorde, ones cast downe thyn eye
And helpe thy men to save.
115 Now, Lorde, sende downe thy moche myght
Agaynst these fendes for to fyght
That so thy people dysprave.

'Thynke, Lorde, how I have preched thy lawe,
Gone barefote bothe in frost and snawe,
120 To plese the to thy paye.
I have fasted and suffred dysease,
Prayed all onely the to please,
The psalmes ofte I saye—
For all my servyse I have done the
125 I aske no more to my fee
But helpe thy men today,
For and thou lette them thus spyll,
I am ryght in good wyll
Forever to forsake thy laye.

130 'Now, Mary, mayden, helpe me todaye,
Or elles thy matyns shall I never saye
Dayes of all my lyve,
Ne no prayer that the shall please
But yf thou helpe now our desease,
135 Ne menye thy joyes fyve.
Apoynt is for thy maydenhede
That all this people suffreth dede—
Now helpe to stynte our stryve!
Now, lady, of thy men have pyté,
140 Praye for them to thy sone on hye,
As thou arte mayden and wyfe!

'O Lorde, fader omnypotent,
Thynke on the myracle that thou Charles sent,
That for the dyde fyght.
145 Thrughe his prayer and grace
The sone stode styll thre dayes space,

202

And shone with beames bryght.
Pharao thou drowned in the see—
Tho that thou lete go free,
Awaye thou ledde them ryght.   150
This daye, Lorde, thou helpe thy men—
Thou art also bygge now as thou was then,
And of as moche myght!'

The frere loude on God cryed,
A longe myle on every syde;   155
The people herde his voyse.
Twenty .m. dede for to see
Within the twynclyn of an eye
To lyfe agayne they rose.
Echone a wepyn in hande hente,   160
And frely began to fyght
And felde downe fast theyr foes. . . .

13

SIR THOMAS MALORY

THE best and the most famous of all the Arthurian books in the English language was finished in prison in 1469–70. Sir Thomas Malory, probably of Newbold Revel in Warwickshire (d. 1471), had been imprisoned before: in 1451 he was held to await trial on a number of charges, including plotting to murder, felonious rape, extortion, and robbery (sometimes with numerous accomplices). He remained in prison for the rest of the decade. It may not simply be a case of a respectable citizen suddenly turning into a picturesque ruffian. There is much that is unknown about Malory's life, but the researches of Dr Peter Field have suggested that political matters were involved. Malory (like others) seems to have followed various lords, whose fortunes fluctuated. He may well have been a Yorkist man of some consequence, perhaps a follower of Richard Neville, Earl of Warwick, who subsequently became estranged from Edward IV. The reasons for his later imprisonment by the Yorkists remain obscure—possibly he had been caught up in a Lancastrian plot—but the imprisonment seems to have been an honourable one, which allowed Malory access (perhaps through royal generosity) to a large library. His own book was for centuries known only in Caxton's print of 1485, but in 1934 there was discovered in the Fellows' Library of Winchester College a manuscript, closely related but not identical with it, which has formed the basis of the modern editions. Caxton's title, *Le Morte Darthur*, has been universally accepted, but Malory himself calls it in the text 'The Hoole Book of Kyng Arthur and of his Noble Knyghtes of the Rounde Table', and this gives a much better idea of its content, for it tells the stories of the coming of Arthur, the founding of the fellowship of the Round Table, and its final destruction, when 'the noble knights were laid to the cold earth', with those of Tristram and Iseult, the quest of the Holy Grail, the love of Lancelot and Guinevere,and others. The book is both profoundly traditional (consisting indeed of translations or adaptations of French and English romances) and very original and distinctive. Its various stories are shaped into a coherent imaginative unity, but they give it an 'encyclopaedic' quality, an extraordinary range of incident and emotion. Comic scenes (like our example with the mocking Sir Dinadan) are found as well as scenes of pathos and violence, and strange supernatural events are found side by side with scenes of grim realism. Malory is a dramatic writer rather than a self-consciously 'philosophical' one; he does not usually analyse characters, behaviour, or ideas, but presents us with a series of vivid scenes which show them in action. He has a brilliant gift for dialogue and direct speech. There is no doubt that he is the greatest prose stylist of this period: he developed a style of outstanding flexibility and variety, which plays intricate variations on an underlying simplicity of pattern, and derives great power from a relatively narrow range of vocabulary. It often has a very distinctive rhythm of quite uncanny power. Malory takes an obvious delight in 'mervillous dedes of armes' and in knightly 'worship' and ideals, but at the same time he makes us feel very close to the actualities of warfare (here, for instance, in the descriptions of the death of Mordred, or of how Sir Lucan 'lay fomyng at the mouth and parte of his guttes lay at hys fyete', or of the scene of the pillagers on the battlefield in the moonlight), and he has an awareness of the strains and tensions within the group and within its patterns of behaviour. Once or twice he is moved to think of the instability of contemporary Englishmen and of the 'untrouthe of Englond'. The phrase 'the noble felyshyp of the Rounde Table is brokyn for ever' recurs like an elegiac refrain as the tension rises steadily and inevitably before the final scenes, which achieve an immense power and pathos. Malory's book presents the fall of this noble fellowship as an intensely *human* tragedy, which he sees with clear-sightedness and compassionate understanding. Caxton presented the book as a 'mirror' of chivalry, but he also drew attention to the great variety of human conduct and emotion that it contains: 'herein may be seen noble chivalrye, curtosye, humanyté, frendlynesse, hardynesse, love, frendshyp, cowardyse, murdre, hate, vertue, and synne.'

A

Tristram and Dinadan

Now turne we unto sir Trystram, that as they rode an-huntynge he mette wyth sir Dynadan, that was commyn into the contrey to seke sir Trystram. And anone sir Dynadan tolde sir Trystram his name, but sir Trystram wolde nat tell his name, wherefore sir Dynadan was wrothe. 'For suche a folyshe knyght as ye ar,' seyde sir Dynadan, 'I saw but late this day lyynge 5 by a welle, and he fared as he slepte. And there he lay lyke a fole grennynge and wolde nat speke, and his shylde lay by hym, and his horse also stood by hym. And well I wote he was a lovear.' 'A, fayre sir,' seyde sir Trystram, 'ar nat ye a lovear?' 'Mary, fye on that crauffte!' seyde sir Dynadan. 'Sir, that is yevell seyde,' seyde sir Trystram, 'for a knyght may 10 never be of proues but yf he be a lovear.' 'Ye say well,' seyde sir Dynadan, 'Now I pray you telle me youre name, syth ye be suche a lovear; othir ellys I shall do batayle with you.' 'As for that,' seyde sir Trystram, 'hit is no reson to fyght wyth me but yf I telle you my name. And as for my name, ye shall nat wyte as at this tyme for me.' 'Fye for shame! Ar ye a knyght and 15 dare nat telle youre name to me? Therefore, sir, I woll fyght with you!' 'As for that,' seyde sir Trystram, 'I woll be avysed, for I woll nat do batayle but yf me lyste. And yf I do batayle wyth you,' seyde sir Trystram, 'ye ar nat able to withstonde me.' 'Fye on the, cowarde!' seyde sir Dynadan.

And thus as they hoved stylle they saw a knyght com rydynge agaynste 20 them. 'Lo,' seyde sir Trystram, 'se where commyth a knyght rydynge whyche woll juste wyth you.' Anone as sir Dynadan behylde hym he seyde, 'Be my fayth! That same is the doted knyght that I saw lye by the welle,

nother slepynge nother wakynge.' 'Well,' seyde sir Trystram, 'I know that
25 knyght well wyth the coverde shylde of assure, for he is the kynges sonne
of Northumbirlonde. His name is sir Epynogrys, and he is as grete a lover
as I know, and he lovyth the kynges doughter of Walys, a full fayre lady.
And now I suppose,' seyde sir Trystram, 'and ye requyre hym, he woll
juste wyth you, and than shall ye preve whether a lover be bettir knyght or
30 ye that woll nat love no lady.' 'Well,' seyde sir Dynadan, 'now shalt thou se
what I shall do.'

And therewythall sir Dynadan spake on hyght and sayde, 'Sir knyght,
make the redy to juste wythe me, for juste ye muste nedis, for hit is the
custom of knyghtes arraunte forto make a knyght to juste, woll he othir nell
35 he.' 'Sir,' seyde sir Epynogrys, 'ys that the rule and custom of you?' 'As for
that,' seyde sir Dynadan, 'make the redy, for here is for me!' And
therewythall they spurred their horsys and mette togydirs so harde that sir
Epynogrys smote downe sir Dynadan. And anone sir Trystram rode to sir
Dynadan and sayde, 'How now? Me semyth the lover hath well sped.' 'Fye
40 on the, cowarde!' seyde sir Dynadan. 'And yf thou be a good knyght,
revenge me!' 'Nay,' seyde sir Trystram, 'I wol nat juste as at this tyme, but
take youre horse and let us go hens.' 'God defende me,' seyde sir
Dynadan, 'frome thy felyshyp, for I never spedde well syns I mette wyth
the.' And so they departed. 'Well,' seyde sir Trystram, 'peraventure I
45 cowde tell you tydynges of sir Trystram.' 'Godde save me,' seyde sir
Dynadan, 'from thy felyshyp! For sir Trystram were mykyll the warre and
he were in thy company.' And they departed. . . .

. . . And so sir Trystram rode unto Joyus Garde, and there he alyght and
unarmed hym. So sir Trystram tolde la beall Isode of all this adventure as
50 ye have harde toforne, and whan she harde hym tell of sir Dynadan, 'Sir,'
she seyde, 'is nat that he that made the songe by kynge Marke?' 'That
same is he,' seyde sir Trystram, 'for he is the beste bourder and japer that I
know, and a noble knyght of his hondis, and the beste felawe that I know,
and all good knyghtis lovyth his felyship.' 'Alas, sir,' seyde she, 'why
55 brought ye hym nat wyth you hydir?' 'Have ye no care,' seyde sir Trystram,
'for he rydyth to seke me in this contrey, and therefore he woll nat away tyll
he have mette wyth me.' And there sir Trystram tolde la beall Isode how
sir Dynadan hylde ayenste all lovers.

Ryght so cam in a varlette and tolde sir Trystram how there was com an
60 arraunte knyght into the towne wyth suche a coloures upon his shylde.
'Be my fayth, that is sir Dynadan!' seyde sir Trystram, 'Therefore,
madame, wote ye what ye shall do: sende ye for hym, and I woll nat be
seyne. And ye shall hyre the myrryeste knyght that ever ye spake wythall,
and the maddyst talker. And I pray you hertaly that ye make hym good
65 chere.' So anone la beall Isode sente unto the towne and prayde sir
Dynadan that he wolde com into the castell and repose hym there wyth a
lady. 'Wyth a good wyll!' seyde sir Dynadan. And so he mownted upon

his horse and rode into the castell, and there he alyght and was unarmed
and brought into the halle. And anone la beall Isode cam unto hym and
aythir salewed other. Than she asked hym of whens that he was. 70
'Madame,' seyde sir Dynadan, 'I am of the courte of kynge Arthure, and a
knyght of the Table Rounde, and my name is sir Dynadan.' 'What do ye in
this contrey?' seyde la beall Isode. 'For sothe, madame, I seke after sir
Trystram, the good knyght, for hit was tolde me that he was in this
contrey.' 'Hit may well be,' seyde la beall Isode, 'but I am nat ware of hym.' 75
'Madame,' seyde sir Dynadan, 'I mervayle at sir Trystram and mo other
suche lovers. What aylyth them to be so madde and so asoted uppon
women?' 'Why,' seyde la beall Isode, 'are ye a knyght and ar no lovear? For
sothe, hit is grete shame to you, wherefore ye may nat be called a good
knyght be reson but yf make a quarrell for a lady.' 'God deffende me!' 80
seyde sir Dynadan, 'for the joy of love is to shorte, and the sorow thereof
and what cometh therof is duras over longe.' 'A!' sayde la beall Isode, 'say
ye nevermore so, for hyre faste by was the good knyght sir Bleoberys de
Galys that fought wyth .iii. knyghtes at onys for a damesell, and he wan her
afore the kynge of Northumbirlonde. And that was worshypfully done,' 85
seyde la beall Isode. 'For sothe, hit was so,' seyde sir Dynadan, 'for I
knowe him well for a good knyght and a noble, and commyn he is of noble
bloode; and all be noble knyghtes of the blood of sir Launcelot de Lake.'
'Now I pray you, for my love,' seyde la beall Isode, 'wyll ye fyght for me
wyth .iii. knyghtes that doth me grete wronge? And insomuche as ye bene a 90
knyght of kynge Arthurs, I requyre you to do batayle for me.' Than sir
Dynadan seyde, 'I shall sey you ye be as fayre a lady as evir I sawe ony, and
much fayrer than is my lady quene Gwenyver, but wyte you well, at one
worde, I woll nat fyght for you wyth .iii. knyghtes, Jesu me defende!' Than
Isode lowghe, and had good game at hym. 95

B

The Death of Arthur

And anone kynge Arthure drew hym wyth his oste downe by the seesyde
westewarde, towarde Salusbyry. And there was a day assygned betwyxte
kynge Arthur and sir Mordred, that they shulde mete uppon a downe
bysyde Salesbyry and nat farre frome the seesyde. And thys day was
assygned on Monday aftir Trynyté Sonday, whereof kynge Arthur was 5
passyng glad that he myght be avenged uppon sir Mordred. Than sir
Mordred arraysed muche people aboute London, for they of Kente,
Southsex and Surrey, Esax, Suffolke and Northefolke helde the moste
party with sir Mordred. And many a full noble knyght drew unto hym and
also the kynge; but they that loved sir Launcelot drew unto sir Mordred. 10

So uppon Trynyté Sunday at nyght kynge Arthure dremed a wondirfull dreme, and in hys dreme hym semed that he saw uppon a chafflet a chayre, and the chayre was faste to a whele, and theruppon sate kynge Arthure in the rychest clothe of golde that myght be made. And the kynge thought

15 there was undir hym, farre from hym, an hydeous depe blak watir, and therein was all maner of serpentis and wormes and wylde bestis fowle and orryble. And suddeynly the kynge thought that the whyle turned up-so-downe, and he felle among the serpentis, and every beste toke hym by a lymme. And than the kynge cryed as he lay in hys bed, 'Helpe! Helpe!'

20 And than knyghtes, squyars and yomen awaked the kynge, and than he was so amased that he wyste nat where he was. And than so he awaked untylle hit was nyghe day, and than he felle on slumberynge agayne, nat slepynge nor thorowly wakynge. So the kyng semed verryly that there cam sir Gawayne unto hym with a numbir of fayre ladyes wyth hym. So whan kyng

25 Arthur saw hym he seyde, 'Wellcom, my systers sonne, I wende ye had bene dede! And now I se the on lyve, much am I beholdyn unto Allmyghty Jesu. A, fayre, nevew, what bene thes ladyes that hyder be com with you?' 'Sir,' seyde sir Gawayne, 'all thes be ladyes for whom I have foughten for, whan I was man lyvynge. And all thes ar tho that I ded batayle fore in

30 ryghteuous quarels, and God hath gyvyn hem that grace at their grete prayer bycause I ded batayle for them for their ryght, that they shulde brynge me hydder unto you. Thus much hath gyvyn me leve God forto warne you of youre dethe: for and ye fyght as tomorne with sir Mordred as ye bothe have assygned, doute ye nat ye shall be slayne, and the moste

35 party of youre people on bothe partyes. And for the grete grace and goodnes that Allmyghty Jesu hath unto you, and for pyté of you and many mo other good men there shall be slayne, God hath sente me to you of hys speciall grace to gyff you warnyng that in no wyse ye do batayle as to-morne but that ye take a tretyse for a moneth-day. And proffir you largely, so that

40 to-morne ye put in a delay. For within a moneth shall com sir Launcelot with all hys noble knyghtes, and rescow you worshypfully, and sle sir Mordred and all that ever wyll holde wyth hym.'

Than sir Gawayne and all the ladyes vanysshed, and anone the kynge called uppon hys knyghtes, squyars, and yomen, and charged them wyghtly

45 to fecche hys noble lordis and wyse bysshoppis unto hym. And whan they were com the kynge tolde hem of hys avision, that sir Gawayne had tolde hym and warned hym that and he fought on the morn, he sholde be slayne. Than the kynge commanded sir Lucan the Butlere and hys brothir sir Bedyvere the bolde, with .ii. bysshoppis wyth hem, and charged them in

50 ony wyse to take a tretyse for a moneth-day wyth sir Mordred: 'And spare nat, proffir hym londys and goodys as much as ye thynke resonable.'

So than they departed and cam to sir Mordred where he had a grymme oste of an .c.ml., and there they entretyd sir Mordred longe tyme. And at the laste sir Mordred was aggreed for to have Cornwale and Kente by

kynge Arthurs dayes; and afftir that all Inglonde, after the dayes of kynge 55
Arthur. Than were they condescende that kynge Arthure and sir Mordred
shulde mete betwyxte bothe their ostis, and everych of them shulde brynge
.xiiii. persons. And so they cam wyth thys worde unto Arthur. Than seyde
he, 'I am glad that thys ys done,' and so he wente into the fylde. And whan
kynge Arthur shulde departe he warned all hys hoost that and they se ony 60
swerde drawyn, 'loke ye com on fyersely and sle that traytoure, sir
Mordred, for I in no wyse truste hym.' In lyke wyse sir Mordred warned
hys oste, 'that and ye se ony maner of swerde drawyn, loke that ye com on
fyersely and so sle all that ever before you stondyth, for in no wyse I woll
nat truste for thys tretyse'. And in the same wyse seyde sir Mordred unto 65
hys oste: 'for I know well my fadir woll be avenged uppon me.'

And so they mette as their poyntemente was, and were agreed and
accorded thorowly. And wyne was fette, and they dranke togydir. Ryght so
cam oute an addir of a lytyll hethe-buysshe, and hit stange a knyght in the
foote. And so whan the knyght felte hym so stonge, he loked downe and 70
saw the adder; and anone he drew hys swerde to sle the addir, and thought
none othir harme. And whan the oste on bothe partyes saw the swerde
drawyn, than they blewe beamys, trumpettis, and hornys, and shoutted
grymly, and so bothe ostis dressed hem togydirs. And kynge Arthur toke
hys horse and seyde, 'Alas, this unhappy day!' and so rode to hys party, and 75
sir Mordred in lyke wyse.

And never syns was there never seyne a more dolefuller batayle in no
Crysten londe, for there was but russhynge and rydynge, foynynge and
strykynge, and many a grym worde was there spokyn of aythir to othir, and
many a dedely stroke. But ever kynge Arthure rode thorowoute the batayle 80
of sir Mordred many tymys and ded full nobely, as a noble kynge shulde
do, and at all tymes he faynted never. And sir Mordred ded hys devoure
that day and put hymselffe in grete perell. And thus they fought all the
longe day, and never stynted tylle the noble knyghtes were layde to the
colde erthe. And ever they fought stylle tylle hit was nere nyght, and by 85
than was there an .c.ml. leyde dede uppon the erthe. Than was kynge
Arthure wode wrothe oute of mesure, whan he saw hys people so slayne
frome hym. And so he loked aboute hym and cowde se no mo of all hys
oste and good knyghtes leffte,no mo on lyve but two knyghtes: the tone was
sir Lucan de Buttler and hys brother, sir Bedwere; and yette they were full 90
sore wounded. 'Jesu mercy!' seyde the kynge, 'where ar all my noble
knyghtes becom? Alas, that ever I shulde se thys doleful day! For now',
seyde kynge Arthur, 'I am com to myne ende. But wolde to God', seyde
he, 'that I wyste now where were that traytoure sir Mordred that hath
caused all thys myschyff.' 95

Than kynge Arthur loked aboute and was ware where stood sir
Mordred leanyng uppon hys swerde amonge a grete hepe of dede men.
'Now, gyff me my speare,' seyde kynge Arthure unto sir Lucan, 'for yondir

I have aspyed the traytoure that all thys woo hath wrought.' 'Sir, latte hym
100 be,' seyde sir Lucan, 'for he ys unhappy. And yf ye passe this unhappy day
ye shall be ryght well revenged. And, good lord, remembre ye of your
nyghtes dreme and what the spyryte of sir Gawayne tolde you tonyght, and
yet God of Hys grete goodnes hath preserved you hyddirto. And for
Goddes sake, my lorde, leve of thys, for, blyssed be God, ye have won the
105 fylde; for yet we ben here .iii. on lyve, and with sir Mordred ys nat one on
lyve. And therefore if ye leve of now, thys wycked day of desteny ys paste!'
'Now tyde me dethe, tyde me lyff,' seyde the kyng, 'now I se hym yondir
alone, he shall never ascape myne hondes! For at a bettir avayle shall I
never have hym.' 'God spyede you well!' seyde sir Bedyvere.
110   Than the kynge gate his speare in bothe hys hondis, and ran towarde sir
Mordred, cryyng and saying, 'Traytoure, now ys thy dethe-day com!' And
whan sir Mordred saw kynge Arthur he ran untyll hym with hys swerde
drawyn in hys honde, and there kyng Arthur smote sir Mordred undir the
shylde, with a foyne of hys speare, thorowoute the body more than a
115 fadom. And whan sir Mordred felte that he had hys dethys wounde he
threste hymselff with the myght that he had upp to the burre of kyng
Arthurs spear, and ryght so he smote hys fadir, kynge Arthure, with hys
swerde holdynge in both hys hondys, uppon the syde of the hede, that the
swerde perced the helmet and the tay of the brayne. And therewith
120 Mordred daysshed downe starke dede to the erthe. And noble kynge
Arthure felle in a swoughe to the erthe, and ther he sowned oftyntymys,
and sir Lucan and sir Bedwere offtetymys hove hym up. And so waykly
betwyxte them they lad hym to a lytyll chapell nat farre frome the see, and
whan the kyng was there, hym thought hym resonabely eased.
125   Than harde they people crye in the fylde. 'Now go thou, sir Lucan,'
seyde the kyng, 'and do me to wyte what betokyns that noyse in the fylde.'
So sir Lucan departed, for he was grevously wounded in many placis; and
so as he yode he saw and harkened by the moonelyght how that pyllours
and robbers were com into the fylde to pylle and to robbe many a full noble
130 knyght of brochys and bees and of many a good rynge and many a ryche
juell. And who that were nat dede all oute, there they slew them for their
harneys and their ryches. Whan sir Lucan undirstood thys warke he cam to
the kynge as sone as he myght, and tolde hym all what he had harde and
seyne. 'Therefore be my rede,' seyde sir Lucan, 'hit ys beste that we
135 brynge you to som towne.' 'I wolde hit were so,' seyde the kynge, 'but I
may nat stonde, my hede worchys so. A, sir Launcelot!' seyde kynge
Arthure, 'thys day have I sore myssed the! And alas, that ever I was ayenste
the! For now have I my dethe, wherof sir Gawayne me warned in my
dreame.'
140   Than sir Lucan toke up the kynge the tone party and sir Bedwere the
othir parté, and in the lyfftyng up the kynge sowned, and in the lyfttynge sir
Lucan felle in a sowne, that parte of hys guttis felle oute of hys bodye, and

therewith the noble knyght hys harte braste. And whan the kynge awoke he
behylde sir Lucan, how he lay fomyng at the mowth and parte of his guttes
lay at hys fyete. 'Alas,' seyde the kynge, 'thys ys to me a fulle hevy syght to 145
se thys noble deuke so dye for my sake, for he wold have holpyn me that
had more nede of helpe than I! Alas, that he wolde nat complayne hym, for
hys harte was so sette to helpe me. Now Jesu have mercy uppon hys soule!'
Than sir Bedwere wepte for the deth of hys brothir. 'Now leve thys
mournynge and wepyng, jantyll knyght!' seyde the kyng, 'for all thys woll 150
nat avayle me. For wyte thou well, and I myght lyve myself, the dethe of
sir Lucan wolde greve me evermore. But my tyme hyeth faste,' seyde the
kynge. 'Therefore,' seyde kynge Arthur unto sir Bedwere, 'take thou here
Excaliber, my good swerde, and go wyth hit to yondir watirs syde; and
whan thou commyste there, I charge the throw my swerde in that water, 155
and com agayne and telle me what thou syeste there.' 'My lorde,' seyde sir
Bedwere, 'youre commaundement shall be done, and lyghtly brynge you
worde agayne.'

So sir Bedwere departed. And by the way he behylde that noble swerde,
and the pomell and the hauffte was all precious stonys. And than he seyd 160
to hymselff, 'If I throw thys ryche swerde in the water, thereof shall never
com good, but harme and losse.' And than sir Bedwere hyd Excalyber
undir a tre, and so as sone as he myght he came agayne unto the kynge and
seyde he had bene at the watir and had throwen the swerde into the watir.
'What sawe thou there?' seyde the kynge. 'Sir,' he seyde, he saw nothyng 165
but wawis and wyndys. 'That ys untruly seyde of the,' seyde the kynge.
'And therefore go thou lyghtly agayne, and do my commaundemente; as
thou art to me lyff and dere, spare nat, but throw hit in.'

Than sir Bedwere returned agayne and toke the swerde in hys honde;
and yet hym thought synne and shame to throw away that noble swerde. 170
And so efte he hyd the swerde and returned agayne and tolde the kynge
that he had bene at the watir and done hys commaundement. 'What sawist
thou there?' seyde the kynge. 'Sir,' he seyde, 'I sy nothynge but watirs wap
and wawys wanne.' 'A, traytour unto me and untrew,' seyde kynge
Arthure, 'now hast thou betrayed me twyse! Who wolde wene that thou 175
that hast bene to me so leve and dere, and also named so noble a knyght,
that thou wolde betray me for the ryches of thys swerde? But now go agayn
lyghtly; for thy longe taryynge puttith me in grete jouperté of my lyff, for I
have takyn colde. And but if thou do now as I bydde the, if ever I may se
the, I shall sle the myne owne hondis, for thou woldist for my rych swerde 180
se me dede.'

Than sir Bedwere departed and wente to the swerde and lyghtly toke hit
up, and so he wente unto the watirs syde. And there he bounde the gyrdyll
aboute the hyltis, and threw the swerde as farre into the watir as he myght.
And there cam an arme and an honde above the watir, and toke hit and 185
cleyght hit, and shoke hit thryse and braundysshed, and than vanysshed

with the swerde into the watir. So sir Bedyvere cam agayne to the kynge and tolde hym what he saw. 'Alas,' seyde the kynge, 'helpe me hens, for I drede me I have taryed over longe.'

190 Than sir Bedwere toke the kynge uppon hys bak, and so wente with hym to the watirs syde. And whan they were there, evyn faste by the banke hoved a lytyll barge wyth many fayre ladyes in hit, and amonge hem all was a quene, and all they had blak hoodis. And all they wepte and shryked whan they saw kynge Arthur. 'Now put me into that barge,' seyde the 195 kynge. And so he ded sofftely, and there resceyved hym three ladyes with grete mournyng. And so they sette hem downe, and in one of their lappis kyng Arthure layde hys hede. And than the quene sayde, 'A, my dere brothir! Why have ye taryed so longe frome me? Alas, thys wounde on youre hede hath caught over-much coulde!' And anone they rowed 200 fromward the londe, and sir Bedyvere behylde all tho ladyes go frowarde hym. Than sir Bedwere cryed and seyde, 'A, my lorde Arthur, what shall becom of me, now ye go frome me and leve me here alone amonge myne enemyes?' 'Comforte thyselff,' seyde the kynge, 'and do as well as thou mayste, for in me ys no truste for to truste in. For I wyl into the vale of 205 Avylyon to hele me of my grevous wounde. And if thou here nevermore of me, pray for my soule!' But ever the quene and ladyes wepte and shryked, that hit was pité to hyre. And as sone as sir Bedwere had loste the syght of the barge he wepte and wayled, and so toke the foreste and wente all that nyght.

14

PROSE ROMANCES

FOR modern readers, 'late medieval prose romance' simply means Malory, but although his achievement in the genre is overwhelmingly superior, it ought not to be forgotten that there are other worthy examples, and not only those written by Caxton or Malory's talented successor, Lord Berners (see No. 25 B and C). English prose romances are usually translated or adapted from French originals, sometimes closely (as in the *Prose Merlin* of *c.*1450), but sometimes more freely and imaginatively. Our three examples illustrate very different kinds of story material. The *Prose Alexander* (translated from Latin) treats with clarity and elegance one of the most popular exotic 'wonders' of the Alexander legend. From *Melusine* (based on a French prose romance) we have the pathetic leave-taking of the fairy from her mortal husband Raymondin, Count of Lusignan, who has broken the taboo imposed on him against visiting her on a Saturday and has seen her transformed into a serpent from the waist down (this metamorphosis was itself a punishment imposed by Melusine's fairy mother because of her daughter's treatment of their father, who had also broken a vow). In consequence, Melusine has to leave her castle and wander in torment. Our final scene is also treated with feeling. It is from *Valentine and Orson*, well translated by Henry Watson, the story of which, full of folk-tale motifs and marvellous enchantments, was still widely read by the authors of the later sixteenth and seventeenth centuries, and survived even longer in inexpensive chap-book form. Bellyssant, the sister of King Pepin, married to the Emperor of Constantinople, is falsely accused of adultery by a wicked archbishop. The pregnant lady is banished, and pursued into the forest.

A

THE THORNTON *PROSE ALEXANDER*

The Trees of the Sun and Moon

Fra theine thay went till they come to the ferreste of that waye; and ferrere myghte thay noghte wynn, for thare ware so hye mountaynes agaynes tham and cragges like walles that they myghte passe no forther. And than thay turned agayne, and come to the forsaide playne, and went by that way that streched towarde the weste fyvftene days. And than thay lefte that way and 5 turnede on the lefte hande. And so thay went four score days, and at the laste thay come till a mountayne of adamande, and at the fute thareoffe thare hange chynes of golde. This mountayne hadd made of saphyres twa

thowsande grees and a halfe, by the whilke men ascendid to the summit of
10 the mountayne. And thare Alexander and his oste luged tham. And on the
morne Alexander offerd sacrafice till his goddes. And than he tuk with
hym .xii. prynces of the wyrchipfullest that he hade, and went up bi the
forsaid grees till he come aboun on the mountayne. And thare he fande a
palace wonder faire and curiously wroghte; and it hade twelve yates and
15 thre score and ten wyndows. And the lyntalls bathe of the durs and of the
wyndows ware of fyn golde, wele burnescht, and that palace was called the
Howse of the Son. Thare was also a temple all of golde and of precious
stanes; and bifore the dores thareoffe thare was a vyne of golde, berande
grapes of charbuncles, of rubyes, dyamandes, and many other maneres of
20 precyous stanes. Than kyng Alexander and his prynces went into the
palace, and fande thare a man liggand in a bedd of golde, and coverd with
a riche clathe of golde. And he was righte a mekill man and a faire, and his
berde and his heved were als whitt als any wolle; and hym semed lyke a
bischoppe. Als son als Alexander and his prynces saw this alde man thay
25 knelid doune on thaire kneess and saluste hym. And he ansuerd and
saide, 'Welcom, Alexander,' quod he, 'I telle the thou sall see that never
flescly man bifore this tyme sawe, and thou sall here that never erthly man
herde are.' And Alexander ansuerd and sayd, 'Maste blyssed alde man,'
quod he, 'how hase thou knowyng of me?' 'For soth,' quod he, 'bifore Noy
30 flode coverde all the erthe knewe I bathe the and thi dedis. I wate wele
thou desyres forto see the haly trees of the Son and the Mone, the whilke
telles thynges that ere to come.' 'Yaa for sothe,' quod Alexander, 'ther es
nathynge that I desyre mare than for to see tham.' And he was right gladd.
Than saide the alde man till hym, 'And ye be clene of flescly dede with
35 women, than es it leefull to yow to see tham and to entir into that haly
place that es a sette of Godd. And if ye be noghte clene, it es noghte leefull
to yow.' 'Yis, sir, sothely,' quod Alexander, 'we ere clene.' Than raise the
alde man up of the bedd that he lay in, and said to tham, 'Puttes offe your
rynges,' quod he, 'and youre clathes, and your schone, and folowes me.'
40 And thay dyd so. And then Alexander tuk with hym Tholomeus and
Antiochus, and folowed the alde man, and went thurgh the wodd that was
aboun on the mountayne closed with mannes handes. The trees of that
wodd ware an hundreth fote lange and hye, and thay ware lyke lorers or
olyve trees; and out of tham thare ran rykyles and fynne bawme. And as
45 thay went thurgh that wodd thay saw a tree wondere hye, in the whilke
thare satt a mekill fewle. That tree hadd nother thareon lefes ne fruyte.
The fewle that satt thareon hadd on his heved a creste lyk till a pacokke,
and his beeke also crested; abowte his nekke he hadd fethers lyke golde.
The hynder of hym was lyk purpure; and the tayle was ownded overthwert,
50 with a colour reede as rose and with blewe. And his fethers ware righte
faire schynand. When Alexander saw this fewle he was gretely mervailled
of the faired of hym; than saide the alde man, 'Alexander,' quod he, 'this

214

ilke fewle that thou here seese es a fenix.' And than thay went forther
thurgh the forsaid wodd, and come to thiese haly trees of the Son and the
Mone that growed in myddes of the wodde. And than the alde man saide 55
till Alexander, 'Luke up', quod he, 'to yone haly trees, and thynke in thi
hert what prevatee so the liste, and thou sall hafe a trewe ansuere. Bot luke
that thou speke na worde in opyn. And thareby sall thou witt that it es a
gude spiritt, that knawes thi thoghte.' Thir twa trees were wonder hye.
And the tree of the Son had leves lyk fyne golde, reed and faire schynande. 60
And the tree of the Mone had lefes whitt als sylver and faire schynande.
And than walde Alexander hafe offrede sacrafyce to thir trees. Bot the alde
man walde noghte suffre hym, bot said, 'It es noghte levefull', quod he, 'in
this haly place, nowther to offre encense, ne to slaa na bestes, bot to knele
doun to the boles of thir trees and kysse tham and pray the Son and the 65
Mone to giffe trew ansuers.' And than Alexander spirred the alde man in
what langage the trees sulde giffe thaire answers. And the alde man
ansuerd and said, 'The tree of the Son', quod he, 'answers owther all in
the langage of Inde or ells of Grewe. And the tree of the Mone begynnes
with the langage of Grewe and endes with the langage of Inde.' And as 70
thay stode thus spekande sudaynly thare come a bryghte beme fra the
weste that schane over all the wodde. And then Alexander kneled doun,
and kyssede the trees, and thoght thus in his hert: 'Sall I conquere all the
werlde, and efterwardes with the victorye wende hame to Macedoyne till
my moder Olympias and my sisters?' And than the tree of the Son ansuerd 75
softly in the langage of Inde, and said thir verses:

> 'Tu dominator orbis dominus simul et pater extas,
> Set patrium rignum per tempora nulla videbis'

—that es at say, 'thou ert bathe lorde and fader of all the werlde, bot the
rewme of thy fadyrs sall thou never see with thyn eghne.' Than bygan 80
Alexander to thynke how lange he sulde lyffe, and whate dedd he sulde
dye. And the tree of the Mone ansuerd by thir twa verses:

> 'Anno completo vives et mensibus octo,
> De quo confidis tibi mortis pocula dabit'

—that es at saye, 'A twlvemonthe and aughte monethes sall thou lyffe, and 85
than he that thou traistes on sall giffe thee a drynke of dedd.' Than bigan
Alexander to thynke in his hert on this wyse:

> 'Telle me now, haly tree,
> Wha he es that sall slaa mee.'

And than the tree of the Son ansuerd by thir twa verses: 90

> 'Si tibi pandatur vir qui tua facta resolvet,
> Illum confrynges et sic mea carmina fallent'

—that es at say, 'And I schew the the manes name that sall undo thi dedis thou will slaa hym, and so sall my prophycye fayle.' And than the forsaide
95 ald man sayd till Alexander, 'Disese na mare thir trees', quod he, 'with thyne askynges. Bot tourne we agayne as we come hedir.' And than Alexander and his twa prynces with hym tourned agayne with the alde man. And ay as he went, he weped bitterly bicause of his schorte tyme; and his prynces also weped righte sare. Bot he commanded tham that thay
100 schulde noghte telle to na man of his oste that that thay hadd herde and sene.

B

MELUSINE

Melusine's Farewell

And with thoo wordes Melusyne toke up Raymondyn her lord, and thenne, as they wold have embraced and kyssed eche other, they fell both at ones in a swoune, so that almost theire hertes brake for grete douleur. Certayn, there was a pyteous syght! There wept and bewaylled barons,
5 ladyes, and damoyselles, sayeng in this manere: 'Ha, fals Fortune! We shal lese this day the best lady that ever governed ony land, the moost sage, most humble, moost charytable and curteys of all other lyvyng in erthe.' And they al lamented and bewaylled so pyteously, and rendred teerys in habundaunce in so moche that it was a pyteous syght. Thenne retourned
10 Melusyne to herself out of swounyng, and herd the hevynes and dolour that the baronnye made for her departyng, and cam to Raymondyn, that yet laye on the grounde, and toke hym up, and thenne to hym, in heryng of th'assistaunce, she said in this manere: 'My lord and swete frend Raymondyn, impossible is my lenger taryeng with you; wherfore lyst, and
15 herke, and putte in mynde that I shal saye. Wete it, Raymondyn, that certayn after your lyf naturel expired, no man shal not empocesse nor hold your land so free in peas as ye now hold it, and your heyres and successours shal have moche to doo, and wete it shal be overthrawen and subdued thrugh theire foly from theire honour and from theire ryght
20 enherytaunce; but doubte you not, for I shal help you duryng the cours of your lyf naturel. And putte not Geffray, oure sone, fro your court. He is your sone, and he shal preve a noble and valyaunt man. Also we have two yong children male, Raymond and Theoderyk—of them I shal take good heede, how be it aftir my departyng, that ryght soone shal be, ye shal never
25 see me in no womans fourme. And I wyl and bequethe to Theodoryk, yongest of all our children, the lordshipes with al th'appurtenaunces of Partenay, Vernon, Rochelle, and the port there. And Raymond shal be

Erle of Forestz. And, as touching Geffray, he shal wel purveye for hymself.' Thenne drew she Raymondyn and hys counseyll apart, and sayd to them in this wyse: 'As touching our sone that men calle Horryble, that 30 hath thre eyen, wete it for certayn, yf he be lefte alyve, never man dide nor never shal doo so grete dommage as he shall. Wherfore I pray and also charge you that anoone aftir my departyng he be put to deth. For yf ye doo not soo, his lyf shall full dere be bought, and never ye dide so grete folye.' 'My swete love,' sayd Raymondyn, 'there shal be no fawte of it, but, for 35 Goddis love, have pyté on yourself, and wyl abyde with me.' And she said to hym: 'My swete frend, yf it were possyble, soo wold I fayne doo, but it may not be. And wete it wel that my departyng fro you is more gryevous and doubtous a thousand tymes to me than to you, but it is the wyll and playsire of hym that can do and undoo al thinges.' And, with these wordes 40 she embraced and kyssed hym full tenderly, sayeng, 'Farwel, myn owne lord and husbond! Adieu, myn herte, and al my joye! Farwel, my love, and al myn wele!—and yet as long as thou lyvest, I shal feed myn eyen with the syght of the, but pyté I have on the of this, that thou mayst never see me but in horryble figure.' And therwith she lept upon the windowe that was 45 toward the feldes and gardyns ayenst Lusynen.

In this partye saith th'istorye that whan Melusyne was upon the wyndowe as before is said, she toke leve sore wepyng, and her commanded to all the barons, ladyes, and damoyselles that were present, and after said to Raymondyn, 'Here be two rynges of gold that be bothe of one vertue, 50 and wete it for trouth that as long as ye have them, or one of them, you nor your heyres that shal have them after you shal never be dyscomfyted in plee nor in batayll, yf they have good cause, nor they that have them shal not dey by no dede of armes.' And immedyatly he toke the rynges. And after bygan the lady to make pyteous regrets and grevouse syghynges, 55 beholdyng Raymondyn right pyteously. And they that were there wept alway so tenderly that everyche of them had grete pyté, they syghyng full pyteously. Thenne Melusyne in her lamentable place, where she was upon the wyndowe havyng respection toward Lusynen, sayd in this wyse: 'Ha, thou swete countré, in the have I had so grete solas and recreacion, in the 60 was al my felicité! Yf God had not consented that I had be so betrayed, I had be full happy. Alas! I was wonnt to be called lady, and men were redy to fulfylle my commandementes, and now not able to be alowed a symple servaunt, but assygned to horryble peynes and tourments unto the day of fynal jugement. And al they that myght come to my presence had grete 65 joye to behold me, and fro this tyme foorth they shal dysdayne me and be ferefull of myn abhomynable figure; and the lustes and playsirs that I was wonnt to have shal be revertid in tribulacions and grievous penitences.' And thenne she bygan to say with a hye voyce: 'Adieu, my lustis and playsirs! Farwel, my lord, barons, ladyes, and damoyselles! And I beseche 70 you in the moost humble wyse that ye vouchesauf to pray to the good Lord

devoutely for me, that it playse hym to mynusshe my dolorous peyne.
Notwithstanding I wyl lete you knowe what I am and who was my fader, to
th'entent that ye reproche not my children, that they be not borne but of a
75 mortal woman, and not of a serpent, nor as a creature of the fayry, and that
they are the children of the doughter of kynge Elynas of Albanye and of
the queene Pressyne; and that we be thre sustirs that by predestinacion are
predestynate to suffre and bere grievous penaunces, and of this matere I
may no more shew, nor wyl.' And therwith she said, 'Farwel, my lord
80 Raymondyn, and forgete not to doo with your sone called Horryble this
that I have you said, but thinke of your two sones Raymond and
Theodoryk.' Thenne she bygan to gyve a sore syghe, and therwith flawgh
into th'ayer out of the wyndowe, transfigured lyke a serpent grete and long
in .xv. foote of length. And wete it wel that on the basse stone of the
85 wyndowe apereth at this day th'emprynte of her foote serpentous. Thenne
encreaced the lamentable sorowes of Raymondyn, and of the barons,
ladyes, and damoyselles, and moost in especial Raymondyns hevynes
above al other. And foorthwith they loked out of the wyndowe to behold
what way she toke. And the noble Melusyne so transfygured, as it is
90 aforsaid, flyeng thre tymes about the place, passed foreby the wyndow,
gyvyng at everyche tyme an horryble cry and pyteous, that caused them that
beheld her to wepe for pyté. For they perceyved wel that loth she was to
departe fro the place, and that it was by constraynte. And thenne she toke
her way toward Lusynen, makyng in th'ayer by her furyousnes suche
95 horryble crye and noyse that it semed al th'ayer to be replete with thundre
and tempeste.

Thus, as I have shewed, went Melusyne, lyke a serpent, flyeng in th'ayer
toward Lusynen, and not so hygh but that the men of the countré might
see her. And she was herd a myle in th'ayer, for she made suche noyse that
100 al the peple were abasshed. And so she flawgh to Lusynen thre times about
the fortres, cryeng so pyteously and lamentably, lyke the voyce of a
mermayde. Wherof they of the fortresse and of the toun were gretly
abasshed, and wyst not what they shuld thinke, for they sawe the fygure of
a serpent, and the voyce of a woman that cam fro the serpent. And whan
105 she had floughe about the fortresse thre tymes, she lyghted so sodaynly
and horrybly upon the toure called Poterne, bryngyng with her such
thundre and tempest, that it semed that bothe the fortres and the toun
shuld have sonk and fall. And therwith they lost the syght of her, and wyst
not where she was becom.

C

VALENTINE AND ORSON

How Bellyssant was Delivered of Two Fair Sons

Bellyssant was ryding within the forest, the which was with chylde as you
have heard recyted before. It happened that her bodye had determined
and fulfilled her time, that constrayned her forto descende of her horse
and complayne her tenderly. Blandimain demaunded her what she ayled
that she complayned her soo. 'Alas! Blandymayn,' sayde the lady, 'lyght   5
downe of thy horse and helpe that I were layde under yonder great tree,
and thynke diligently forto seke me some wife. For the tyme is come that I
must nedes be delivered without any lenger delaye.' Blandymayne
descended quickely and laid her upon a fayre grene place under a tree, the
which he did chose and marke forto knowe it the better. And then he lept   10
on horsebacke, and rode also fast as he might forto seke some wyfe to
helpe and sucoure the lady. The noble lady Bellyssant abode there all
alone without any company, save God and the blessed Virgyn Mary, that
did helpe her and succoured her in such maner that she was delivered of
twoo fayre sonnes in the forest. But they were not so sone come upon the   15
earthe, but that the good lady suffred muche payne and anguyshe as you
shall heare. So as the lady was delivered of the fruyte of her wombe, and
that she laye under the tree, ther came unto her a beer, the which was
marveilously great and horrible, and toke one of her children in his
mouthe, and wente his waye into the thycke of the forest also faste as he   20
myght. Then was the gracious lady sorowfull—and not without a
cause—for the perdiction of her chylde, and began forto crye with a feable
voyce muche pyteously. And upon bothe her fete and handes she wente
after the beer in the forest, that was anone out of her syght. Alas! to lytle
avayled her the pursuyte. For she shal never se her chyld unto the tyme   25
that by myracle he be yelded unto her agayne. So longe went the lady
through the forest wepyng for her child, and travaylled her so sore to goo
after, that a stronge sicknes toke her, in suche wise that she fel in a swoune
upon the colde earth as it had bene a dead woman. I wyll leve here to
speake of her, and wyll tell you of the other childe that was left all alone.   30
    It happened the same daye that the kynge Pepyn was departed out of
Parys, accompanyed wyth divers great lordes and barons, forto go unto
Constantinoble to se his sister Bellyssant; and toke his way toward
Orleaunce, and he rode so faste that he entred into the forest whereas his
syster Bellyssant was delivered, but he knew nothyng therof at that tyme.   35
Now it is true as it was the pleasure of God that as the kynge Pepyn passed
throughe the forest, he espyed under the hye tree the other sonne of

Bellyssant all alone, that lay upon the earth, soo he rode that waye and sayd
unto hys barons, 'Lordes, by the God that created all thynges I have
40 founde here a muche fayre encountre. Se what a fayre chylde I have
founde here!' 'By Jesus,' sayd the lordes, 'syr kynge, you say true.' 'Nowe,'
sayd the kynge Pepyn, 'I wyll that it be nourysshed at myne expenses also
longe as God shall give it lyfe, and wil that it be kept ryght tenderly and
nobly as if it were myne owne propre chylde. For yf that God sende hym
45 lyfe untyll the tyme that he be a man I shal gyve hym great landes and
tenementes for to live upon.' Then the kynge Pepyn called unto hym one
of hys squyers, and gave hym the charge of the chyld, sainge to him, 'Bere
this child to Orleaunce and make it be baptyzed, and seke him a good
nouryce, and make that he be nourysshed also well as is possible.' Good
50 ryght had kyng Pepyn to love the chylde, for he was hys nevewe, but he
knewe it not. The squyer toke the childe as kyng Pepyn badde hym and
bare it into Orleaunce, and after made it to be baptised and gave it his
name, for he made it to be named Valentine, for suche was the name of the
sqyer. After, he sought a nouryce and made the chylde to be well kept as
55 he was commaunded.

The kynge roode in the forest, alwaye holdynge his journaye, for he had
great desyre to be in the cytie of Constantinoble to se his syster Bellyssant
that he loved so muche. And even so as he passed through the forest, he
recountred Blandymayn that led a wife with hym. Blandymain knewe the
60 kyng, and anone lyghte of his horse and salwed him. After the salute done,
the kynge sayde unto him, 'Blandymayn, fayre syr, tell us tidinges of
Constantinoble. And among other thinges tell us howe oure syster
Bellyssant doth.' 'Dere syr,' said Blandymayn, 'as to the regarde of
tidinges, with payne can I tel you any that is good; for your syster
65 Bellyssant hath to muche evil by the treason and false language of the
cursed Archebisshop, for she is banisshed from the Emperoure, and
chased out of the country. And the Archebysshop made him beleve so
many false wordes, that if the lordes of his court had not bene, the whiche
fered your furoure, he wold have made her be brente in a fyre afore all the
70 worlde.' 'Blandymayn,' said the kynge Pepyn, the whiche was tryst and
sorowfull, 'Of as muche holde I the Emperoure more folysher because he
made not my syster dye, for by the God almighty, if I had her here at this
present time, I should never reste til that I hadde made her dye an evil
death. Nowe forwarde, lordes!' saide kynge Pepyn, 'for oure vyage is done.
75 Retorne we unto Paris, for I will go no ferder. I knowe to muche tydinges
of my sister without demaundinge or enquiryng any more!' At these
wordes he torned the bridle of his horse for to retorne, making great
sorowe in his courage, and beganne to saye unto himselfe. 'Ha, veray God
almighty,' sayd he, 'howe often is man deceived by woman! Nowe am I
80 come to the clene contrary of mine entencion, for I purpensed to have had
once of my syster Bellyssant in my lyfe joye and pleasure, and to have had

the Emperoure Alexander for my frende, to succoure me in all my
necessities. And by her I am greatly diffamed, and put unto a great
dishonour.' In that distresse and melancholy rode the king Pepyn a great
whyle, so longe he rode so that he arived at Orleaunce.   85
    Then Blandimain, that sawe wel and knewe well the courage of the king
Pepyn, durste declare no more unto him of the lady Bellyssant. So he
retourned towarde the tre where as he had left her, but he founde her not,
wherfore he was angry and ryght sorowefull. He discended, and fastened
his horse, and began to serche her thorough the wodde; and he didde so   90
muche that he founde her lyeng upon the earth, the whiche had wepte so
muche for her chylde that she might not speake but with great payne.
Blandimayn embraced her and set her on her fete, and then saide unto
her, 'Alas! who may have brought you hether?' 'Ha, Blandymayn,' said she,
'ever encreaseth my doloure and dystresse. It is true that whan you were   95
departed there came a beer to me and bare awaye one of my chyldren. And
I put myselfe on the waye after, thinkyng to have taken it from hym, but I
coude not retorne unto the tree whereas I left mine other childe.' 'Lady,'
sayd he, 'I come from the fote of the tree, but I have founde no chyld, yet
have I well loked on every syde.' Whan the lady heard Blandymayne, she   100
was more sorwfull than before, and yet agayne she fell in a swone.
Blandymayn toke her up, and wepte full hertely for the ladies sake. He
ledde her towarde the tree whereas she had left the chylde, but whan she
founde it not, she discharged so great sighes, and so pyteous, that it semed
that the hert in her bely wolde depart in sunder. 'Alas,' said she, 'there is   105
not in the world a more discomforted lady than I am, for from syde to side
I am devoyde of joye, of pleasure, of myrthe, and am replete wyth doloure
and misery, and of intollerable dystresse, greved wyth all trybulacyons, and
amonge all desolates the moost desolate. Alas, Emperour, you are the
cause to avaunce my death wrongfully, and without cause and by evyl   110
counsell have depryved me from your company, for on my soule never the
dayes of my life dydde I faute wyth my body. I have nowe loste by you your
propre chyldren legityme, yssued out of bloud ryall, by whom I trusted
ones to be venged. Come, death, unto me for to finisshe my dolour, for the
death shall be more agreable unto me, than to live in this martyre!'   115
    Whan Blandymaine sawe the lady so inwardly discomforted, the best
wyse that he might he comforted her, wyth the woman, and lead her into a
litle village whereas she was bayned, kepte, and cherisshed, tyll that she was
well healed, and in good poynt, and that of her greate sorowes she was a
litle appeased, for there is no dole but that it is forgotten by processe.   120
Than Blandimain began for to tell and recyte unto the lady howe he had
encountred the kyng Pepyn her brother, the whiche had demaunded him
tidinges, and how he was angry against her. And sayde, 'By God, madame,
I have greate feare that ye shall not be welcome to the kynge your brother,
for also soone as he knewe that the Emperoure had expulsed you from   125

him, he shewed the semblaunt that he was muche angry against you, as he
the whiche will beleve lightly that the faute is in you.' 'Ha, God!' sayde the
lady, 'Now is come unto me the thing that I moste doubted; at this houre
maye I well saye that I from al sydes have adversities. For I am expulsed
130 from my lord and husbande the Emperoure without ryght or reason. Never
shall I retourne unto Paris, but will go into a straunge countrey, so farre
that never man nor woman shall have knowledge of my faute, nor know
where I am. If my brother the king Pepyn helde me, he would make me
dye. Now it is better for to eschewe his ire and furoure, then for to abyde
135 the death!' And Blandymayne sayde unto her, 'Lady, wepe no more, for ye
be sure that I shall never leve you unto the deathe, and am delibered to live
and dye with you, and to kepe you company whethersoever you will go.'
'Blandymayn,' sayd the lady, 'let us go at our adventure, and I thanke you
hartely for your good wil, for my truste is hole on you.' Thus is the lady
140 Bellyssant and Blandymayn on their waye muche pensyfe and sorowfull,
all charged with anguysshes. Here wil I leve for to speake of them and will
tell you of the beer that bare awaye the chylde through the wodde.

The beer that had taken one of the chyldren of Bellyssant devoured it
not, but bare it in to his caverne that was profounde and obscure, in the
145 whiche was foure yonge beers stronge and puyssaunt. The beer caste the
chylde amonge hys whelpes to be eaten, but God that never forgeteth his
frendes shewed an evydent myracle. For the young beeres dydde it no
harme, but with theyr roughe pawes strooked it softelye. When the beer
sawe that her lytle whelpes would not devoure it, she was right amerous of
150 the chylde, so muche that she kepte it and gave it souke a hole yeare. The
chylde was all roughe, because of the neutrifaction of the beer, as a wilde
beest. So he began to go in the woode, and became great within a while
and began forto smyte the other beastes of the forest, in suche wyse that
they all douted hym, and fledde before him. For he fered nothyng in the
155 worlde. In suche estate was the chylde ledyng a beastes lyfe the space of
.xv. yeare. He became so great and strong, that none durste passe through
the forest for hym, for bothe men and beastes he put unto death, and eate
their flesh al raw as the other beastes did, and lived a beastual life and not
humayne. He was called Orson because of the beere that had nouryshed
160 hym, and he was also rough as a beere. He dyd so muche harme in the
forest, and was so sore redoubted, that there was none, were he never so
valiaunt and hardy, but that he had great fere to encountre the wylde man.
The renowne sprange so of hym, that all they of the countrey aboute
chaced and hunted him with force and strength, but nothynge avaylled all
165 their deade, for he fered neyther gynnes nor weapons, but brake al in
peces. Now he is in the forest leding the life of a wilde beast, without
wering of any cloth, or any worde speaking. And the mother Bellyssant
that thought that she had lost him, goeth as a woman discomforted through
the countrey at adventure, and Blandymayne conduyted her, and
170 comforteth her also well as he maye.

15

WILLIAM CAXTON

THE merchant and printer Caxton (*c.*1422–?1492) is a figure of great importance in the cultural history of this period. He was apprenticed to a mercer in London, but went (? *c.*1445) to Bruges, the centre of the Guild of the Merchant Adventurers, the main English wool-trading company. Caxton spent some thirty years in the Low Countries, and rose high in the world of the merchants, becoming in 1462 the governor of the English 'nation' at Bruges. In 1471 he went to Cologne for eighteen months, and it was there that he learnt the art of printing. When he returned to Bruges he began printing himself (producing his first translation, *The Recuyell of the Historyes of Troye*), and by September 1476 was back in London, installed at Westminster (a later printed advertisement for an *Ordinale* instructs any man who wishes to buy copies 'enpryntid after the forme of this present lettre whiche ben wel and truly correct' to 'come to Westmonester in to the Almonesrye at the Reed Pale ... and he shal have them good chepe'). He published about a hundred books (and translated about twenty); he was clearly a very successful merchant printer, who gauged very precisely the tastes of his reading public and of his various patrons, who included kings and noblemen (like Earl Rivers, or the Earl of Arundel, at whose request he did the *Golden Legend* and who promised him a yearly fee—'that is to wit a buck in summer and a doe in winter, with which fee I hold me well content') as well as merchants. As a publisher's list, Caxton's is remarkable for its variety (in it are found most of the English literary 'kinds' represented in this anthology). It is true that he was not an intellectual innovator, nor a humanist scholar-printer of the Continental variety, but he clearly had a taste for books and an urgent desire to pass on the knowledge he had acquired. Moreover, he made a contribution both to English printing and to English letters which is quite unique. His output consists almost exclusively of works in the vernacular, and in this he set a pattern for later English printers. Books written in Latin could be—and were—imported; Caxton concentrated on what could not be found ready-made abroad. But what is even more distinctive is the dominant—and equally influential—part he gave to the English *literary* tradition. Recent research has suggested strongly that at Westminster his publication of *The Canterbury Tales* preceded his translations. He printed Chaucer *in extenso*, beginning a stream of editions of the poet's works; he printed Gower and Lydgate (though not Langland); he printed the finest contemporary prose stylist, Malory. Our extracts give some idea of his own translations: from a French moralized Ovid we have a couple of those stories from antiquity which never seem to have lost their popularity; from a Dutch *Reynard*, one of the famous exploits of that disreputable 'anti-hero'; from a French translation of a great encyclopaedic collection of fables another animal story that is more moral in its import, together with one of the 'many mad tales' (as Skelton calls them) of Poggio, which—like the fabliau from *Caton*—shows that Caxton's taste was not always solemn. His style (constricted by his originals) sometimes seems to us awkward and stiff—we find it hard to admire the sonorous 'doublets' he uses—but more often than not it is clear, steady, and workman-like. Finally, we have one of his prefaces which shows his genuine humility and sense of decorum as well as the direct and sensible way he discusses linguistic or stylistic questions. His interest in the English vernacular runs throughout his work, and it is not surprising that historians of our language have often quoted the striking passage on dialectal variations (a topic of obvious interest to a printer). It is not so often pointed out how clearly his discussion of the problems of diction—'over-curyous termes' and 'olde and homely termes'—foreshadows the arguments about the defence and the embellishment of the vernacular which are so prominent in the sixteenth-century English treatments of the *questione della lingua*.

A

OVYDE HYS BOOKE OF METHAMORPHOSE

The Golden Age (i. 6)

Thus the erthe that somtyme was rude and withoute culture was clothed of straunge vestures and receyved ymages humaines. Tho began the eage and worlde of golde. Peple assewred with fayth and trouth; thenne withoute constraynt ne establysshement of lawes they lyved withoute payne, without
5   drede, and also withoute covetyse. Yet that tyme was not founden shippes forto sayle by the see; men went not forto serche other ryvage ne vysyte other landes. Tho was not knowen the feat of warre ne for to bere armures; tho were not fortresses ne engyns. The erthe withoute culture of eerynge or sowynge gaf to every man that hym neded; and that they had
10 suffysed to them. They ete rotes, knoppes of herbes, akehornes, strawberys, and other fruytes, for they savourd better thenne than now doth venyson or other dyverse browesses. Thenne ran grete ryvers full of hony, of mylke, and of pyment. Of the fruytes that of the erthe yssued men fedde and norysshid them to their fylle; and dronke of the waters of
15 whiche they had more delyte than they have now of the stronge wyns and other bevrages. They lyved thenne right joyously withoute travayl. Tho was the erthe full of plentyvousnes, for tho was neyther wynter ne somer. The tyme was attempred withoute overmoch heet or colde; prymetemps was tho pardurably, and wynter delectable, and the plesant Zephirus made
20 the floures of all colours without sowynge of eny seed.

Phoebus and Daphne (i. 17)

The first love that ever Phebus hade was unto a damoysel named Daphne. Phebus loved this lady by aventure and movynge love, which came and was caused by the anger of Cupido, as I shall reherce to you. On a tyme, Cupido wente lepyng and playnge as a yong chylde, ryghtynge and appoyntynge hys arowes and dartes. Phebus, that newly had slayne Phiton the grete serpente, wherof he helde hymself over proude and fiers, cam to Cupido, and sayd to hym thus, as in mokkerye, 'This bowe and arowes ben not convenable to the, ne thou oughtest not to bere them. Gyve them to me, which am gret and stronge, that have slayne the serpent. I oughte better to bere them than thou ner—also thou oughtest not to compare unto me.' Cupido was thenne gretely wroth and angry agaynst Phebus. And Cupido sayd to hym, 'Knowe thou for trouthe that I shall make the knowe and apperceyve my strengthe and also yf myn arowes have eny force and vertu. For I wene that I shal so grevously hurte the that withoute payn the wounde shal not be heled!' With that, Cupido, which was right wrothe on Phebus, flewe his waye unto the hyll of Pernasus, and satte on it, and after bent hys bowe, and drew out two arowes, that one dyverse fro that other. That one hade the poynte of fyn gold, and whosomever was smetton therwith, he muste nedes love. And that other was poynted with leede, and whoso that was hurt with that, he was anone full of desdayn and hate. Cupido, for t'avenge hyme of Phebus, toke the arowe of golde, and smote hym through the herte. And Phebus anone was esprysed of love to Daphne, in such wyse that withoute her he myght not lyve. And after this, Cupydo toke the arowe of leede, and smote it throughe the herte of Daphne, and she after this coude not but hate Phebus.

This Daphne was the fayrest mayde that was tho in alle the worlde, but she recched not ce sette by ony man ne by maryage, but alle her corage was sette in huntynge and in servyse of Diane the goddesse of the wodes, which was a virgyn. Phebus brende and was afflamed; he was so moche surprysed with the love of the fayre Daphne that he coude not maynteyne hymself, but poursyewed alwey her in wodes and forestis. But this was alle for nought, and withoute rayson, for she sette nought by hym. Oftentymes Phebus wolde saye thus to her, 'Alas, my right swete love Daphne, have mercy on me as on hym that for youre love can not endure ne lyve. Beholde, my love, am I a man to be despysed? I am kynge of Cloros, of Delphé, of Phateros, and of Thenedos, and am son to Jupiter, the soverayne god, and am the sonne that enlumyneth alle the worlde. I have fonde the arte of medycyne, of physyque, and of musyque, but alle my connynge ne my puissance ne my crafte may not help me of the ryght grevous and importable maladye that love hath gyven me, of whiche maladye I can have none other guaryson ne helthe but onely by you.'

The fayre Daphne, that had sette her love and entente otherwyse, made no compte, ne sette by the wordes ne prayers of Phebus ner to ony thynge that he sayd or requyred. She lent not only her eeres to here it, for she wolde kepe her virgynyté. Phebus, that alway abode and hoped for to have ben heeled of his maladye by hys love, and sawe that by prayer ne by yefte

or promesse myght not converte her ne have, wolde have enforced her. Daphne, that apperceyved this, sette her to flight forto save her. And Phebus began to renne after her, and overtoke and approched her so
70 nyghe that the mayde wist not what to do, but forto crye and calle her maistresse Dyane that she wold com helpe her at this extreme nede. And anone the goddesse herde her prayer, and converted and transformed her into a laurer tree. And whan Phebus sawe her so chaunged and transformed, he embraced and kyssed her, and gafe her suche dyvynyté
75 that ever after in all seasons she sholde be grene. And after this, Phebus made of her grene bowes a chapellet. . . .

B

THE HISTORYE OF REYNART THE FOXE

How Bruin ate the Honey

Thenne spacke the rede Reynart, 'Is it thenne ernest that ye love so wel the hony? I shal do late you have so moche that ten of yow shold not ete it at one mele, myght I gete therwith your friendship.' 'Not we ten, Reyner neve,' sayd the bere, 'How shold that be? Had I alle the hony that is
5 bytwene this and Portyngale, I shold wel ete it allone.' Reynard sayde, 'What say ye, eme? Hierby dwelleth an husbondman named Lantfert, whiche hath so moche hony that ye shold not ete it in .vii. yere; whiche ye shal have in your holde yf ye wille be to me friendly and helpyng ayenst myn enemyes in the kynges court.' Thenne promysed Bruyn the bere to
10 hym that yf he myght have his bely full, he wold truly be to hym tofore alle other a faythful frende. Herof laughed Reynart the shrewe, and sayde, 'Yf ye wolde have .vii. hamber barelis ful, I shal wel gete them, and helpe you to have them.' These wordes plesyd the bere so wel, and made hym so moche to lawhe that he coude not wel stande. Tho thought Reynart, 'This
15 is good luck; I shal lede hym thyder that he shal lawhe by mesure.'
Reynart sayd thenne, 'This mater may not be longe taryed. I muste payne myself for you. Ye shal wel understande the very yonste and good wyl that I bere to you ward. I knowe none in al my lygnage that I nou wolde laboure fore thus sore.' That thanked hym the bere, and thought he taryed
20 longe. 'Now, eme, late us goo a good paas, and folowe ye me. I shal make you to have as moche hony as ye may bere.' The foxe mente of good strokes, but the caytyf markyd not what the foxe mente, and they wente so longe togydre that they cam unto Lantferts yerde. Tho was Sir Bruyn mery. Now herke of Lantfert. Is it true that men saye, so was Lantfert a
25 strong carpenter of grete tymbre, and had brought that other day tofore into his yerde a grete oke, whiche he had begonne to cleve. And as men be

226

woned, he had smeten two betels therin, one after that other, in suche
wyse the oke was wyde open, wherof Reynart was glad, for he had founde
it right as he wisshed, and sayde to the bere all lawhyng, 'See nou wel
sharply to! In this tree is so moche hony that it is without mesure. Asaye yf   30
ye can come therin, and ete but lytil, for though the honycombes be swete
and good, yet beware that ye ete not to many, but take of them by mesure,
that ye cacche no harme in your body, for, swete eme, I shold be blasmed
yf they dyde you ony harme.' 'What, Reynart cosyn, sorowe ye not for me.
Wene ye that I were a fole? Mesure is good in alle mete.' Reynart sayde,   35
'Ye saye trouthe. Wherfore shold I sorowe? Goo to th'ende, and crepe
theryn.' Bruyn the bere hasted sore toward the hony, and trad in wyth his
two formest feet, and put his heed over his eeris in to the clyft of the tree.
And Reynart sprang lyghtly, and brak out the betle of the tree. Tho helped
the bere nether flateryng ne chydyng: he was fast shette in the tree. Thus   40
hath the neveu wyth deceyte brought his eme in prysoun in the tree, in
suche wyse as he coude not gete out wyth myght ne wyth crafte, hede ne
foote.

What prouffyteth Bruyn the bere that he stronge and hardy is? That may
not helpe hym. He sawe wel that be begyled was. He began to howle and to   45
braye, and cratched wyth the hynder feet, and made suche a noyse and
rumour that Lantfert cam out hastely, and knewe nothyng what this myght
be, and brought in his hand a sharp hoke. Bruyn the bere laye in the clyfte
of the tree in grete fere and drede, and helde faste his heed, and nyped
both his fore feet. He wrange, he wrastled, and cryed, and all was for   50
nought. He wiste not how he myght gete out. Reynar the foxe sawe fro
ferre how that Lantfert the carpenter cam, and tho spack Reynart to the
bere, 'Is that hony good? How is it now? Ete not to moche—it shold do you
harme; ye shold not thenne wel conne goo to the court. Whan Lantfert
cometh, yf ye have wel eten, he shal yeve you better to drynke, and thenne   55
it shal not styke in your throte.'

After these wordes, tho torned hym Reynart toward his castel, and
Lantfert cam, and fonde the bere fast taken in the tree. Thenne ranne he
faste to his neyghbours and sayde, 'Come alle in to my yerde! Ther is a
beere taken!' The worde anone sprange overal in the thorpe. Ther ne   60
bleef nether man ne wyf, but alle ranne theder as fast as they coude,
everyche wyth his wepen—some wyth a staf, some with a rake, some with a
brome, some with a stake of the hegghe, and some wyth a flayel, and the
preest of the chirche had the staf of the crosse, and the clerk brought a
vane. The prestis wyf Julok cam with her dystaf (she sat tho and spanne);   65
ther cam olde wymen that for age had not one toeth in her heed. Now was
Bruyn the bere nygh moche sorowe, that he allone muste stande ayenst
them alle. Whan he herde alle this grete noyse and crye, he wrastled and
plucked so harde and so sore that he gate out his heed, but he lefte
behynde all the skyne and bothe his eeris, in suche wyse that never man   70

sawe fowller ne lothlyer beest, for the blode ran over his eyen. And or he coude gete out his fete, he muste lete there his clawes or nayles and his roughe hande. This market cam to hym evyl, for he supposed never to have goon, his feet were so sore, and he myght not see for the blode
75 whiche ran so over his eyen. Lantfert cam to hym wyth the preest and forthwith alle the parysshe, and began to smyte and stryke sore upon his heed and visage. He receyved there many a sore stroke. Every man beware hierby: who hath harme and scathe, every man wil be therat and put more to. That was wel seen on the bere, for they were alle fiers and wroth on the
80 bere, grete and smal. Ye Hughelyn wyth the croked lege, and Ludolf with the brode longe noose, they were booth wroth. That one had an leden malle, and that other a grete leden wapper, therwyth they wappred and al forslyngred hym. Syr Bertolt with the longe fyngers, Lantfert, and Ottram the longe, thyse dyde to the bere more harme than al the other; that one
85 had a sharp hoke, and that other a croked staf wel leded on th'ende for to playe at the balle. Baetkyn ende Ave Abelquak, my dame Bave, and the preest with his staf, and dame Julok his wyf, thise wroughten to the bere so moche harme that they wold fayn have brought hym fro his lyf to deth; they smote and stacke hym al that they cowde. Bruyn the beere satte and
90 syghed and groned, and muste take such as was gyven to hym. But Lantfert was the worthiest of byrthe of them alle, and made moste noyse—for dame Pogge of Chafporte was his moder, and his fader was Macob the stoppelmaker, a moche stowte man thereas he was allone. Bruyn receyved of hem many a caste of stones. Tofore hem alle sprang
95 Forst, Lanteferts brother, with a staf, and smote the bere on the heed that he ne herde ne sawe, and therewith the bere sprange up bytwene the bushe and the ryver emonge an heep of wyvis, that he threwe a deel of them in the ryver, whiche was wyde and depe. Ther was the persons wyf one of them, wherfor he was ful of sorow. Whan he sawe his wyf lye in the
100 water, hym lusted no lenger to smyte the bere, but called, 'Dame Juloke in the water! Now every man see to! Alle they that may helpe her, be they men or wymen, I gyve to hem alle pardon of her penance, and relece alle theyr synnes!' Alle they thenne lefte Bruyn the bere lye, and dyde that the preest badde.
105 Whan Bruyn the bere sawe that they ranne alle fro hym and ranne to save the wymen, tho sprange he into the water, and swame alle that he coude. Thenne made the preest a grete showte and noyse, and ran after the bere wyth grete anger, and said, 'Come and torne agayn, thow false theef!' The bere swame after the beste of the streme, and lete them calle
110 and crye, for he was glad that he was so escaped from them. He cursed and banned the hony tree, and the foxe also that had so betrayed hym, that he had cropen therin so depe that he loste boothe his hood and his eeris. And so forth he droof in the streem wel a .ii. or .iii. myle. Tho waxe he so wery that he wente to lande for to sitte and reste hym, for he was hevy; he

groned and syghed, and the blode lepe over his eyen: he draugh his breth
lyke as one sholde have deyde.

Now herke how the foxe dyde. Er he cam fro Lantferts hows, he had
stolen a fatte henne, and had leyde her in his male, and ran hastely away by
a by-path were he wende that noman shold have comen. He ranne toward 115
the ryver, that he swette; he was so glad that he wist not what to do for joye,
for he hoped that the bere had be dede. He sayd, 'I have now wel spedde,
for he that sholde moste have hyndred me in the court is now dede, and
none shal wyte me therof. May I not thenne by right be wel glad?' With
thise wordes the foxe loked to the ryver-ward, and espyed where Bruyn the 120
bere laye and rested hym. Tho was the foxe sorier and hevyer than he
tofore was mery, and was as angry, and sayde in chydyng to Lantfert, 'Alas,
Landfert, lewde fool! God gyve hym a shames deth that hath loste suche
good venyson, whiche is good and fatte, and hath late hym goo whiche was
taken to his hande! Many a man wolde gladly have eten of hym. He hath 125
loste a riche and fatte bere.' Thus al chydyng, he cam to the ryver, where
he fonde the beere sore wounded, bebled, and right seke, whiche he
myght thanke none better therof than Reynart, whiche spack to the bere in
skorne, '*Chiere priestre, Dieu vous garde!* Wylle ye se the rede theef?' Sayde
the bere to hymself, 'The rybaud and the felle diere! Here I se hym 130
comen.' Thenne sayd the foxe, 'Have ye ought forgotten at Lantferts?
Have ye also payd hym for the honycombes that ye stale fro hym? Yf ye
have not, it were a grete shame, and not honeste; I wyl rather be the
messager myself forto goo and paye hym. Was the hony not good? I knowe
yet more of the same prys. Dere eme, telle me er I goo hens, into what 135
ordre wille ye goo that were this newe hode? Were be ye a monke or an
abbot? He that shoef your crowne hath nyped of your eeris: ye have lost
your toppe and don of your gloves—I trowe veryly that ye wyl go synge
complyn.' Alle this herde Bruyn the bere, and wexe alle angry and sory, for
he myght not avenge hym. He lete the foxe saye his wylle, and wyth grete 140
payne suffred it, and sterte agayn in the ryver, and swam doun wyth the
streem to that other syde.

C

CATON

Meretricem Fuge: Flee the Harlot

Peter Alphons rcherceth in his book that in Spayne wythin the cyté of
Hyspalensy was a moche fayre and a good bourgeys wyf and wel beloved of
her husbond. It happed that a yonge clerke was enamowred of hyr, and

many tymes prayed and requyred hir of love, but for no thynge she wolde
5 never consente to hit. Thenne, whan the clerke sawe that he was refused,
he entred into suche a malencolye that better he semed to be deed thenne
on lyve. But nyghe his hows dwellyd a maquerel or bawde, whiche had
grete acqueyntaunce wyth the sayd bourgeyse. And whan the sayd bawde
knewe that the sayd clerke was in suche poynte, she came forto speke wyth
10 hym, and demaunded of hym what he eyled, and why he was in so grete
malencolye, and comforted hym, and dyd so moche that she knewe al his
fayte. And indede the clerke made bargeyn with the sayd olde bawde forto
fynde the meanes that he myght have his plesure of the sayd bourgeys wyf,
and forto fulfylle his wylle and his entencion. This olde bawde had a lytel
15 catte whiche she named Pasquette, the which she kepte wythout ony mete
or drynke the space of thre dayes, and after she gave to the catte a lytel
flesshe with right stronge mustard. And after, she wente forto speke wyth
the sayd bourgeys wyf, and ledde with hir her lytel catte, but bycause that
she had eten the sayd mustard she dyd none other but wepte ever. And
20 thenne the good wyf demaunded of the bawde why her catte wepte and
syghed so sore. And she, syghyng and wepyng, answerd, 'Helas, my lady,
my catte whiche ye see, and I, have cause ynough forto wepe.' 'Wherfore?'
sayd the wyf, 'I praye you that ye wyl telle to me the cause.' 'Helas,' sayd
the olde bawde, 'My lady, I dar not telle hit to you.' Neverthelesse, the
25 bourgeys wyf prayed hyr so moche, that she tolde hit to hir, sayeng,
'Madame, sythe hit pleseth to you, I shal telle hit to you. This catte whiche
ye now see here is myn owne doughter, the whiche by the wylle and
plesure of God hath ben transfourmed into a catte, bycause that a yonge
man loved hir, but never for no thynge she wold not accorde forto doo his
30 plesure and wylle, wherfore the goddes were wroth and torned hir into a
catte, as ye may see. And therfore she wepeth thus contynuelly, and whan
she wepeth, I can not holde me but that I must wepe.' 'How?' sayd the
bourgeys wyf, 'Ye say wonder! Is hit trouthe that ye say?' The whiche
sware that hit was veray trouthe. 'Helas!' sayd the bourgeys wyf, whiche
35 belevyd lightly, 'Knowest thou not suche a yonge clerke?' 'Yes, my lady, I
knowe hym ful wel.' 'Certeynly,' sayde the bourgeys wyf, 'he hath prayed
me of love, and hathe offred to me many grete yeftes, but never for no
thynge I ne wold consente ne graunte hys plesure, wherfore, as I suppose,
he is in grete thought and malencolye. And therfore, yf hit were sothe that
40 thou sayest, I sholde be torned into a catte as thy doughter is, yf the goddes
ben wrothe with me.' 'Certeynly,' said the bawde, 'yf ye holde thus longe
the sayd clerke in that payne and langour, ye are in grete parelle for to be
transformed from your fayre fourme into the lykenesse and fourme of a
catte, and ye shal therfore wepe al the tyme of your lyf. Wherfore, my dere
45 lady, I counceyl you, or the goddes be wrothe upon you, that ye doo after
the wylle of the sayd clerke. For yf ye were torned into a lityl catte, ye shold
be dyshonoured, and ye sholde be cause of the shame and dyshonoure

perpetuell of al your lynage.' Thus the sayd bourgeys wyf, whiche doubted the furour and wrath of the goddes, and the shame and dyshonour bothe of hirself and of her parentes, bylevyng the wordes of the forsayd olde 50 bawde, consented wythin her herte to doo the wylle and plesure of the sayd clerke. And thenne, with grete sygheng and malencolyes, for doubte that wors shold come to hir, sayd to the sayd olde woman that she wold goo toward the sayd clerke, and that she shold telle to hym that he wold come forto speke with hir, and that of hyr he shold have his plesure. Thenne was 55 the olde bawde joyeful and gladde, and after wente to the sayd clerke, and said to hym that he shold make good chere, and that incontynente he shold goo toward the bourgeys wyf, and that of hir he shold have al that shold please to hym. The whiche clerke wente incontynent thyder, and payed the bawde as he had promysed to hyr. And thus he had hys wylle of the sayd 60 bourgeys wyf.

D

THE BOOK OF THE SUBTYL HISTORYES AND FABLES OF ESOPE

The Dog, the Wolf, and the Wether

Grete folye is to a fool that hath no myght that wylle begyle another stronger than hymself, as reherceth this fable of a fader of famylle, whiche had a grete herd or flock of sheep, and had a grete dogge forto kepe them, which was wel stronge, and of his voys all the wolves were aferd, wherfore the sheepherd slepte more surely. But it happed that this dogge for his 5 grete age deyde, wherfore the sheepherdes were sore troubled and wrothe, and sayd one to other, 'We shall nomore slepe at oure ease bycause that our dogge is dede, for the wulves shall now come and ete our sheep.' And thenne a grete wether fyers and prowd, whiche herd alle these wordes came to them, and sayd, 'I shall gyve yow good counceylle. Shave me, and 10 put on me the skynne of the dogge, and whanne the wulves shalle see me, they shalle have grete fere of me.' And whanne the wulves came and sawe the wether clothed with the skynne of the dogge they began all to flee, and ranne away. It happed on a day that a wulf whiche was sore hongry came and toke a lambe, and after ran awaye therwith. And thenne the sayd 15 wether ranne after hym. And the wulf, whiche supposed that it had ben the dogge, shote thryes by the waye for the grete fere that he had, and ranne ever as fast as he coude. And the wether also ranne after hym withoute cesse, tyl that he ranne thurgh a busshe full of sharp thornes, the whiche thornes rente and brake alle the dogges skynne whiche was on hym. And 20

as the wulf loked and saw behynde hym, beynge moche doubtous of his dethe, sawe and perceyved alle the decepcion and falshede of the wether, and forthwith retorned ageynste hym, and demaunded of hym, 'What beest arte thow?' And the wether ansuered to hym in this maner, 'My lord,
25 I am a wether whiche playeth with the.' And the wulf sayd, 'Ha, mayster, ought ye to playe with your mayster and with your lord? Thow hast made me so sore aferd that by the weye as I ranne before the I dyde shyte thre grete toordes.' And thenne the wulf ledde hym unto the place whereas he had shyte, sayenge thus to hym, 'Loke hyther—callest thow this a playe? I
30 take hit not for playe, for now I shalle shewe to the how thow oughtest not to playe so with thy lord.' And thenne the wulf took and kylled hym, and devoured and ete hym. And therfore he that is wyse muste take good hede how he playeth with hym whiche is wyser, more sage, and more stronge than hymself is.

The Subtylté of the Woman forto Deceyve her Husbond

35   The cautele or falshede of the woman is wonder merveyllous, as it appiereth by this fable of a marchaunt, whiche was wedded of newe unto a fayre and yong woman, the whiche marchaunt wente over the see forto bye and selle, and forto gete somewhat forto lyve honestly. And bycause that he dwellyd to longe, his wyf supposed that he was dede. And therfore she
40 enamoured herself with another man, whiche dyd to her mykle good, as forto have doo make and bylde up his hows of newe, the whiche had grete nede of reparacion, and also he gaf to her all newe utensyles to kepe a houshold. And within a long tyme after the departyng of the marchaunt, he came ageyne into his hows, whiche he sawe new bylded, and sawe dysshes,
45 pottes, pannes, and suche other houshold, wherfore he demaunded of his wyf how and in what manere she had founde the facion and the meane forto have repayred so honestly his hows. And she ansuerd that it was by the grace of God. And he ansuered, 'Blessyd be God of hit!' And when he was within the chambre, he sawe the bedde rychely coverd, and the walles
50 wel hanged, and demaunded of his wyf as he had done before. And she thenne ansuerd to hym in lyke maner as she dyd before. And therfore he thanked God as he had done tofore. And as he wold sette hym at his dyner, there was brought before hym unto his wyf a child of thre yere of age or thereaboute, wherfore he demaunded of his wyf, 'My frend, to whome
55 belongeth this fayre child?' And she ansuerd, 'My frend, the holy ghoost of his grace hath sente hit to me.' Thenne ansuerd the marchaunt to his wyf in this manere, 'I rendre not graces ne thankes not to the holy ghoost of this, for he hath taken to moche payne and labour forto have it made up myn owne werke, and I wyll that in no maner wyse he medle no more
60 therwith, for suche thynge belongeth to me forto doo hit, and not to the holy ghoost.'

E

The Prologue to *The Boke of Eneydos*

After dyverse werkes made, translated, and achieved, havyng noo werke in hande, I, sittyng in my studye whereas laye many dyverse paunflettis and bookys, happened that to my hande came a lytyl booke in Frenshe, whiche late was translated oute of Latyn by some noble clerke of Fraunce, whiche booke is named *Eneydos*, made in Latyn by that noble poete and grete   5 clerke Vyrgyle; whiche booke I sawe over, and redde therin how, after the generall destruccyon of the grete Troye, Eneas departed, berynge his olde fader Anchises upon his sholdres, his lityl son Yolus on his honde, his wyfe wyth moche other people folowynge, and how he shypped and departed, wyth alle th'ystorye of his adventures that he had er he cam to the   10 achievement of his conquest of Ytalye, as all alonge shall be shewed in this present boke. In whiche booke I had grete playsyr, bycause of the fayr and honest termes and wordes in Frenshe, whyche I never saw to-fore lyke, ne none so playsaunt ne so wel ordred; whiche booke, as me semed, sholde be moche requysyte to noble men to see, as wel for the eloquence as the   15 historyes; how wel that many honderd yerys passed was the sayd booke of *Eneydos*, wyth other werkes, made and lerned dayly in scolis, specyally in Ytalye and other places, whiche historye the sayd Vyrgyle made in metre. And whan I had advysed me in this sayd boke, I delybered and concluded to translate it into Englysshe, and forthwyth toke a penne and ynke, and   20 wrote a leef or tweyne, whyche I oversawe agayn to corecte it. And whan I sawe the fayr and straunge termes therin, I doubted that it sholde not please some gentylmen whiche late blamed me, sayeng that in my translacyons I had over-curyous termes whiche coude not be understande of comyn peple, and desired me to use olde and homely termes in my   25 translacyons. And fayn wolde I satysfye every man, and so to doo, toke an olde boke and redde therin, and certaynly the Englysshe was so rude and brood that I coude not wele understande it. And also my lorde abbot of Westmynster ded do shewe to me late certayn evydences wryton in olde Englysshe, forto reduce it into our Englysshe now usid. And certaynly it   30 was wreton in suche wyse that it was more lyke to Dutche than Englysshe. I coude not reduce ne brynge it to be understonden. And certaynly our langage now used varyeth ferre from that whiche was used and spoken whan I was borne. For we Englysshe men ben borne under the domynacyon of the mone, whiche is never stedfast, but ever waverynge,   35 wexynge one season and waneth and dyscreaseth another season. And that comyn Englysshe that is spoken in one shyre varyeth from another. Insomuche that in my dayes happened that certayn marchauntes were in a shippe in Tamyse, forto have sayled over the see into Zelande, and for

40 lacke of wynde, thei taryed atte forlond, and wente to lande forto refreshe
them. And one of theym named Sheffelde, a mercer, cam into an hows and
axed for mete; and specyally he axyd after eggys. And the goode wyf
answerde that she coude speke no Frenshe. And the marchaunt was angry,
for he also coude speke no Frenshe, but wolde have hadde egges, and she
45 understode hym not. And thenne at laste another sayd that he wolde have
eyren. Then the good wyfe sayd that she understood hym wel. Loo, what
sholde a man in thyse dayes now wryte—egges or eyren? Certaynly it is
harde to playse every man, bycause of dyversité and chaunge of langage.
For in these dayes every man that is in ony reputacyon in his countré wyll
50 utter his commynycacyon and maters in suche maners and termes that
fewe men shall understonde theym. And som honest and grete clerkes
have ben wyth me, and desired me to wryte the moste curyous termes that
I coude fynde. And thus bytwene playn, rude, and curyous, I stande
abasshed. But in my judgemente, the comyn termes that be dayli used ben
55 lyghter to be understonde than the olde and auncyent Englysshe. And
forasmoche as this present booke is not for a rude uplondyssh man to
laboure therin ne rede it, but onely for a clerke and a noble gentylman that
feleth and understondeth in faytes of armes, in love, and in noble
chyvalrye, therfor in a meane bytwene both, I have reduced and
60 translated this sayd booke into our Englysshe, not over-rude ne curyous,
but in suche termes as shall be understanden by Goddys grace,
accordynge to my copye. And yf ony man wyll entermete in redyng of hit,
and fyndeth suche termes that he can not understande, late hym goo rede
and lerne Vyrgyll, or the pystles of Ovyde, and ther he shall see and
65 understonde lyghtly all, yf he have a good redar and enformer. For this
booke is not for every rude and unconnynge man to see, but to clerkys and
very gentylmen that understande gentylnes and scyence. Thenne I praye
alle theym that shall rede in this lytyl treatys to holde me for excused for
the translatynge of hit. For I knowleche myselfe ignorant of connynge to
70 enpryse on me so hie and noble a werke. But I praye mayster John Skelton,
late created poete laureate in the unyversité of Oxenforde, to oversee and
correcte this sayd booke, and t'addresse and expowne whereas shalle be
founde faulte to theym that shall requyre it. For hym I knowe for
suffycyent to expowne and englysshe every dyffyculté that is therin. For he
75 hath late translated the epystlys of Tulle, and the boke of Dyodorus
Syculus, and diverse other werkes oute of Latyn into Englysshe, not in
rude and olde langage, but in polysshed and ornate termes craftely, as he
that hath redde Vyrgyle, Ovyde, Tullye, and all the other noble poetes and
oratours to me unknowen: and also he hath redde the .ix. muses, and
80 understande theyr musicalle scyences, and to whom of theym eche scyence
is appropred. I suppose he hath dronken of Elycons well. Then I praye
hym, and suche other, to correcte, adde or mynysshe whereas he or they
shall fynde faulte, for I have but folowed my copye in Frenshe as nygh as

me is possyble, and yf ony worde be sayd therein well I am glad; and yf
otherwyse, I submytte my sayd boke to theyr correctyon. Whiche boke I 85
presente unto the hye born my to-comynge naturell and soverayn lord,
Arthur, by the grace of God, Prynce of Walys, Duc of Cornewayll, and
Erle of Chester, fyrst bygoten sone and heyer unto our most dradde
naturall and soverayn lorde, and most Crysten kynge, Henry the .vii. by the
grace of God, kynge of Englonde and of Fraunce, and lord of Irelonde, 90
bysechyng his noble grace to receyve it in thanke of me, his moste humble
subget and servaunt. And I shall praye unto almyghty God for his
prosperous encreasyng in vertue, wysedom, and humanyté, that he may be
egal wyth the most renommed of alle his noble progenytours; and so to
lyve in this present lyf that after this transitorye lyfe he and we alle may 95
come to everlastynge lyf in heven. Amen.

16

MANKIND

AFTER much neglect and misrepresentation, the morality play is at last being studied with some insight and respect—and not least because the best examples of the genre have proved to be effective in performance. It is unusual in this kind of play to find the subtlety we associate with modern 'psychological' drama. Like much early Western—and much modern non-Western—drama, it prefers strongly 'typed' characters and large expressive or 'emblematic' scenes (sometimes, as here, involving symbolic dress and changes of dress). In its two most distinctive characteristics—allegory, and a didactic, exemplary narrative structure—the best practitioners discover a surprising variety of dramatic possibilities. Most examples have a basic story pattern like a folk-tale or a parable (here, of the Prodigal Son). Underneath this, perhaps, lie what might be termed 'deep structures'—characteristically a spiritual war or *psychomachia* (affording possibilities not only of direct conflict, but also of deceit, disguise, and comedy) and a journey or quest, a kind of pilgrimage of life (both later powerfully used by Spenser and Bunyan). The plays survive in various shapes and forms, ranging from the long *Castle of Perseverance*, requiring a large-scale open-air performance, to much shorter pieces which could have been presented by small groups of players in inn-yards or halls. *Mankind* (? 1465–70; probably from East Anglia) clearly falls into the latter category. In some ways it seems close to popular drama (the collection of money and the great mask worn by Titivillus have, for instance, been compared with similar features in mumming-plays). It certainly makes the most of the rough comedy of the vices and Titivillus; their abrasive mockery in language and behaviour becomes a kind of carnivalesque inversion or misrule (parallel, perhaps, to some uses of comedy in the mystery plays). One of the things they guy is the learned language of Mercy and Mankind early in the play, which they call 'English Latin'. These exchanges present us with something that is probably a little more complicated than the simple alternatives suggested by some commentators—e.g. *either* that the mockery destroys totally the dignity and the credibility of the 'virtuous' figures *or* that it is a total indictment of the ignorance and wickedness of the vices. The contrary 'tones' are held in tension. Perhaps too, the rather abstract terms might have sounded less inflated and 'over-curyous' to contemporary educated ears, and might have suggested the language of 'clerks' (certainly New Gyse's response in lines 124–8 has a distinctly anti-intellectual ring). Furthermore, in this play language—like clothes—shows the man. Mercy (cf. line 102) does not use many words, and they embody sober traditional values, whereas the vices are fashionable dandies ('nyse in ther aray, in language thei be large') and their 'many wordys and schortely sett' perhaps represent the 'new guise' with its lack of 'measure'. At the same time, the central dramatic narrative is skilfully handled. A number of essential *données* are economically introduced: the intense and pathetic vulnerability of Mankind (cf. lines 194–216), the spiritual power of his enemies. The idea that mortal life is a battleground is made explicit (cf. lines 226–31) by Mankind's spiritual guide and counsellor, Mercy. The father–son relationship established so soon is of course necessary for the Prodigal Son parable underlying the morality, and also allows the author scope for the development of its emotional ties (the 'kindness' and 'unkindness' of family life). The plot moves steadily through its four stages—the state of innocence, temptation and fall, life in sin, and repentance—by means of a series of splendidly expressive visual scenes (cf. e.g. the episode of Mankind digging with his spade, or that in which he is given 'a fresh jakett after the new gyse'). As the climax approaches, the emotional undertones increase—the fine scene in which Mercy is rejected is pointed by his speech (lines 734–77), which is full of pathos and 'kindly' emotion—and the dramatic rhythms become tense, as the two opposing 'forces', one moving 'upwards' to repentance and grace, the other 'downwards' to despair and damnation, pull harder and harder. The final scenes are especially well done. We abruptly move to the point at which Mankind's despair leads him to call for a rope to hang himself and the scene is at the same time full of gruesome comedy. Some readers have thought Mankind rather lucky to find rescue so close at hand, but in the dramatic movement of the play it comes as no surprise. From the point of view of doctrine, and of drama, the power of mercy and grace has been shown to be stronger than these particular agents of wickedness. Mercy is not only a 'guide' but a source of spiritual power, yearning to bring help to his 'son'. Moreover, the underlying story pattern is not unlike that type of folk-tale in which the well-meaning but vulnerable hero is rescued by a magical helper. In fact, the dramatist's eye was on the scene of forgiveness which follows. Omitting any psychological analysis of the process of repentance (for which perhaps he might not have had an adequate language), he simply leaves Mankind's despairing cry—'a rope, a rope, a rope! I am not worthy'—reverberating, and very dramatically moves straight on to a fine and emotional scene of reunion, in which the intellectual content—the question of mercy and justice—is effortlessly fused with the language of paternal and filial 'kindness'. It is a scene which, as Emrys Jones says, 'momentarily foreshadows the reunion of Lear and Cordelia'.

DRAMATIS PERSONAE

MANKIND	MISCHIEF
MERCY	NEW-GUISE
TITIVILLUS	NOW-A-DAYS
NOUGHT	

[Enter Mercy]

Mercy. The very fownder and begynner of owr fyrst creacyon
Amonge ws synfull wrechys he oweth to be magnyfyede,
That for owr dysobedyenc he hade non indygnacyon
To sende hys own son to be torn and crucyfyede.

5   Owr obsequyouse servyce to hym xulde be aplyede,
     Where he was lorde of all and made all thynge of nought,
     For the synnfull synnere to have hade hym revyvyde
     And for hys redempcyon sett hys own son at nought.

     Yt may be seyde and veryfyede, mankynde was dere bought.
10   By the pytuose deth of Jesu he hade hys remedye.
     He was purgyde of hys defawte that wrechydly hade wrought
     By hys gloryus passyon, that blyssyde lavatorye.
     O soverence, I beseche yow yowr condycyons to rectyfye
     Ande wyth humylité and reverence to have a remocyon
15   To this blyssyde prynce that owr nature doth gloryfye,
     That ye may be partycypable of hys retribucyon.

     I have be the very mene for yowr restytucyon.
     Mercy ys my name that mornyth for yowr offence.
     Dyverte not yowrsylffe in tyme of temtacyon,
20   That ye may be acceptable to Gode at yowr goyng hence.
     The grett mercy of Gode, that ys of most preemmynence,
     Be medyacyon of Owr Lady that ys ever habundante
     To the synfull creature that wyll repent hys neclygence.
     I prey Gode at yowr most nede that mercy be yowr defendawnte.

25   In goode werkys I awyse yow, soverence, to be perseverante
     To puryfye yowr sowlys, that thei be not corupte;
     For yowr gostly enmy wyll make hys avaunte,
     Yowr goode condycyons yf he may interrupte.

     O ye soverens that sytt and ye brothern that stonde ryght wppe,
30   Pryke not yowr felycytés in thyngys transytorye;
     Beholde not the erth, but lyfte yowr ey wppe.
     Se how the hede the members dayly do magnyfye.
     Who ys the hede forsoth I xall yow certyfye—
     I mene Owr Savyowr, that was lykynnyde to a lambe;
35   Ande hys sayntys be the members that dayly he doth satysfye
     Wyth the precyose rever that rynnyth from hys wombe.

     Ther ys non such foode, be water nor by londe,
     So precyouse, so gloryouse, so nedefull to owr entent,
     For yt hath dyssolvyde mankynde from the bytter bonde
40   Of the mortall enmye, that venymousse serpente,
     From the wyche Gode preserve yow all at the last jugement!
     For sekyrly ther xall be a streyt examynacyon,
     The corn xall be savyde, the chaffe xall be brente.
     I besech yow hertyly, have this premedytacyon.

[Enter Mischief]

Myscheffe. I beseche yow hertyly, leve yowr calcacyon.   45
Leve yowr chaffe, leve yowr corn, leve yowr dalyacyon.
Yowr wytt ys lytyll, yowr hede ys mekyll, ye are full of predycacyon.
But, ser, I prey this questyon to claryfye:
Mysse-masche, dryff-draff,
Sume was corn and sume was chaffe,   50
My dame seyde my name was Raffe;
Onschett yowr lokke and take an halpenye.

Mercy. Why com ye hethyr, brother? Ye were not dysyryde.
Myscheffe. For a wynter corn-threscher, ser, I have hyryde,
Ande ye sayde the corn xulde be savyde and the chaff xulde be
  feryde,   55
Ande he provyth nay, as yt schewth be this werse:
'*Corn servit bredibus, chaffe horsibus, straw fyrybusque.*'
Thys ys as moche to say, to yowr leude wndyrstondynge,
As the corn xall serve to brede at the nexte bakynge;
'*Chaff horsybus et reliqua,*'   60
The chaff to horse xall be goode provente,
When a man ys forcolde the straw may be brent,
And so forth, *et cetera.*

Mercy. Avoyde, goode brother! Ye ben culpable
To interrupte thus my talkyng delectable.   65
Myscheff. Ser, I have nother horse nor sadyll,
Therfore I may not ryde.
Mercy. Hye yow forth on fote, brother, in Godys name!
Myscheff. I say, ser, I am cumme hedyr to make yow game.
Yet bade ye me not go out in the Deullys name   70
Ande I wyll abyde.

[one leaf of MS missing]

[Enter New Guise, Now-a-days, and Nought, with minstrels]

New Gyse. Ande how, mynstrellys, pley the comyn trace!
Ley on wyth thi ballys tyll hys bely breste!
Nought. I putt case I breke my neke: how than?
New Gyse. I gyff no force, by Sent Tanne!   75
Nowadays. Leppe about lyvely—thou art a wyght man!
Lett ws be mery wyll we be here!
Nought. Xall I breke my neke to schew yow sporte?
Nowadays. Therfor ever be ware of thi reporte.
Nought. I beschrew ye all—her ys a schrewde sorte.   80
Have theratt then wyth a mery chere!

Do wey, do wey this reull, sers! do wey!
Nowadays. Do wey, goode Adam? do wey?
Thys ys no parte of thi pley.
85   *Nought.* Yys, mary, I prey yow, for I love not this rewelynge.
Cum forth, goode fader, I yow prey!
Be a lytyll ye may assay.
Anon of wyth yowr clothes, yf ye wyll play.
Go to! for I have hade a praty scottlynge.

90   *Mercy.* Nay, brother, I wyll not daunce.
New Gyse. Yf ye wyll, ser, my brother wyll make yow to prawnce.
Nowadays. Wyth all my herte, ser, yf I may yow avaunce.
Ye may assay be a lytyll trace.
Nought. Ye, ser, wyll ye do well,
95   Trace not wyth them, be my cownsell,
For I have tracyed sumwhat to fell;
I tell yt ys a narow space.

But, ser, I trow of ws thre I herde yow speke,
New Gyse. Crystys curse hade therfor, for I was in slepe.
100   *Nowadays.* And I hade the cuppe in my honde, redy to goo to met.
Therfor, ser, curtly, grett yow well.
Mercy. Few wordys, few and well sett!
New Gyse. Ser, yt ys the new gyse and the new jett:
Many wordys and schortely sett,
105   Thys ys the new gyse, every-dele.

Mercy. Lady, helpe! how wrechys delyte in ther synfull weys!
Nowadays. Say not ageyn the new gyse nowadays!
Thou xall fynde ws schrewys at all assays.
Beware, ye may son lyke a bofett.
110   *Mercy.* He was well occupyede that browte yow brethern.
Nought. I harde yow call 'New Gyse, Nowadays, Nought,' all thes
    thre togethere.
Yf ye sey that I lye, I xall make yow to slyther.
Lo, take yow her a trepett!

Mercy. Say me yowr namys, I know yow not.
New Gyse. New Gyse, I.
Nowadays.   I, Nowadays.
115   *Nought.*   I, Nought.
Mercy. Be Jesu Cryst that me dere bowte
Ye betray many men.

New Gyse. Betray! nay, nay, ser, nay, nay!
We make them both fresch and gay.
But of yowr name, ser, I yow prey,   120
That we may yow ken.

Mercy. Mercy ys my name by denomynacyon.
I conseyve ye have but a lytyll favour in my communycacyon.
New Gyse. Ey, ey! yowr body ys full of Englysch Laten.
I am aferde yt wyll brest.   125
'*Pravo te*', quod the bocher onto me
When I stale a leg a motun.
Ye are a stronge cunnyng clerke.
Nowadays. I prey yow hertyly, worschyppull clerke,
To have this Englysch mad in Laten: 130

I have etun a dyschfull of curdys,
Ande I have schetun yowr mowth full of turdys.'
Now opyn yowr sachell wyth Laten wordys
Ande sey me this in clerycall manere!
Also I have a wyf, her name ys Rachell;   135
Betuyx her and me was a gret batell;
Ande fayn of yow I wolde here tell
Who was the most master.

Nought. Thy wyf Rachell, I dare ley xx^ti lyse.
Nowadays. Who spake to the, foll? Thou art not wyse!   140
Go and do that longyth to thin offyce:
Osculare fundamentum!
Nought. Lo, master, lo, here ys a pardon bely-mett.
Yt ys grawntyde of Pope Pokett,
Yf ye wyll putt yowr nose in hys wyffys sokett,   145
Ye xall have xl^ry days of pardon.

Mercy. Thys ydyll language ye xall repent.
Out of this place I wolde ye went.
New Gyse. Goo we hens all thre wyth on assent.
My fadyr ys yrke of owr eloquence.   150
Therfor I wyll no lenger tary,
Gode brynge yow master, and blyssyde Mary
To the number of the demonycall frayry!

Nowadays. Cum wynde, cum reyn,
Thow I cumme never ageyn!   155
The Deull put out both yowr eyn!
Felouse, go we hens tyght.

Nought. Go we hens, a deull wey!
Here ys the dore, her ys the wey.
160 Farwell, jentyll Jaffrey,
I prey Gode gyf yow goode nyght!

> *Exiant simul. Cantent* [*Let them go out together.*
> *Let them sing*]

Mercy. Thankyde be Gode, we have a fayer dylyverance
Of thes thre onthryfty gestys.
They know full lytyll what ys ther ordynance.
165 I preve by reson thei be wers then bestys:

A best doth after hys naturall instytucyon;
Ye may conseyve by there dysporte and behavour,
Ther joy ande delyte ys in derysyon
Of her owyn Cryste to hys dyshonur.

170 Thys condycyon of levyng, yt ys prejudycyall;
Beware therof, yt ys wers than ony felony or treson.
How may yt bé excusyde before the Justyce of all
When for every ydyll worde we must yelde a reson?

They have grett ease, therfor thei wyll take no thought.
175 But how then when the angell of hewyn xall blow the trumpe
Ande sey to the transgressors that wykkydly hath wrought,
'Cum forth onto yowr Juge and yelde yowr acownte'?

Then xall I, Mercy, begyn sore to wepe;
Nother comfort nor cownsell ther xall non be hade;
180 But such as thei have sowyn, such xall thei repe.
Thei be wanton now, but then xall thei be sade.

The goode new gyse nowadays I wyll not dysalow.
I dyscomende the vycyouse gyse; I prey have me excusyde,
I nede not to speke of yt, yowr reson wyll tell it yow.
185 Take that ys to be takyn and leve that ys to be refusyde.

> [*Enter Mankind*]

Mankynde. Of the erth and of the cley we have owr propagacyon.
By the provydens of Gode thus be we deryvatt,
To whos mercy I recomende this holl congrygacyon:
I hope onto hys blysse ye be all predestynatt.

Every man for hys degré I trust xall be partycypatt,   190
Yf we wyll mortyfye owr carnall condycyon
Ande owr voluntarye dysyres, that ever be pervercyonatt,
To renunce them and yelde ws wnder Godys provycyon.

My name ys Mankynde. I have my composycyon
Of a body and of a soull, of condycyon contrarye.   195
Betwyx them tweyn ys a grett dyvisyon;
He that xulde be subjecte, now he hath the victory.
Thys ys to me a lamentable story
To se my flesch of my soull to have governance.
Wher the goodewyff ys master, the goodeman may be sory.   200
I may both syth and sobbe, this ys a pytuose remembrance.

O thou my soull, so sotyll in thy substance,
Alasse, what was thi fortune and thi chaunce
To be assocyat wyth my flesch, that stynkyng dungehyll?
Lady, helpe! Soverens, yt doth my soull myche yll   205
To se the flesch prosperouse and the soull trodyn wnder fote.
I xall go to yondyr man and asay hym I wyll.
I trust of gostly solace he wyll be my bote.

[*He approaches Mercy and kneels*]

All heyll, semely father! Ye be welcom to this house.
Of the very wysdam ye have partycypacyon.   210
My body wyth my soull ys ever querulose.
I prey yow, for sent charyté, of yowr supportacyon.

I beseche yow hertyly of yowr gostly comforte.
I am onstedfast in lywynge; my name ys Mankynde.
My gostly enmy the Deull wyll have a grett dysporte   215
In synfull gydynge yf he may se me ende.

   Mercy. Cryst sende yow goode comforte! Ye be welcum, my
      frende.
Stonde wppe on yowr fete—I prey yow aryse.
My name ys Mercy. Ye be to me full hende.
To eschew vyce I wyll yow avyse.   220

   Mankynde. O Mercy, of all grace and vertu ye are the well!
I have herde tell of ryght worschyppfull clerkys,
Ye be aproxymatt to Gode and nere of hys consell.
He hat instytut you above all hys werkys.

243

225 O, yowr lovely wordys to my soull are swetere then hony.
    Mercy. The temptacyon of the flesch ye must resyst lyke a man,
For ther ys ever a batell betwyx the soull and the body:
Vita hominis est milicia super terram.

Oppresse yowr gostly enmy and be Crystys own knyght.
230 Be never a cowarde ageyn yowr adversary.
Yf ye wyll be crownyde, ye must nedys fyght.
Intende well and Gode wyll be yow adjutory.

Remember, my frende, the tyme of contynuance,
So helpe me Gode, yt ys but a chery tyme.
235 Spende yt well; serve Gode wyth hertys affyance.
Dystempure not yowr brayn wyth goode ale nor wyth wyn.

Mesure ys tresure. Y forbyde yow not the use.
Mesure yowrsylf ever—beware of excesse.
The superfluouse gyse I wyll that ye refuse,
240 When nature ys suffysyde, anon that ye sese.

Yf a man have an hors and kepe hym not to hye,
He may then reull hym at hys own dysyere.
Yf he be fede overwell he wyll dysobey
Ande in happe cast his master in the myre.

                 [Enter New Guise, behind]

245   *New Gyse.* Ye sey trew, ser, ye are no faytour.
I have fede my wyff so well tyll sche ys my master.
I have a grett wonde on my hede, lo, and theron leyth a playster,
Ande another ther I pysse my peson.
Ande my wyf were yowr hors, sche wolde yow all tobanne.
250 Ye fede yowr hors in mesure, ye are a wyse man.
I trow, and ye were the kyngys palfreyman,
A goode horse xulde be gesonne.

    Mankynde. Wher spekys this felow? Wyll he not com nere?
    Mercy. All to son, my brother, I fere me, for yow.
255 He was here ryght now, by hym that bowte me dere,
Wyth other of hys felouse—thei kan moche sorow.

They wyll be here ryght son, yf I owt departe.
Thynke on my doctryne; yt xall be yowr defence.
Lerne wyll I am here, sett my wordys in herte.
260 Wythin a schorte space I must nedys hens.

244

[*Enter Now-a-days and Nought, behind*]

Nowadays. The sonner the lever, and yt be ewyn anon!
I trow yowr name ys Do Lytyll, ye be so long fro hom.
Yf ye wolde go hens, we xall cum everychon,
Mo then a goode sorte.
Ye have leve, I dare well say,   265
When ye wyll, go forth yowr wey.
Men have lytyll deynté of yowr pley
Because ye make no sporte.

Nought. Yowr potage xall be forcolde, ser—when wyll ye go dyn?
I have sen a man lost xx^{ti} noblys in as lytyll tyme;   270
Yet yt was not I, be Sent Qwyntyn,
For I was never worth a pottfull a wortys sythyn I was born.
My name ys Nought. I love well to make mery.
I have be sethen wyth the comyn tapster of Bury
And pleyde so longe the foll tht I am ewyn wery.   275
Yyt xall I be ther ageyn tomorn.

Mercy. I have moche care for yow, my own frende.
Yowr enmys wyll be here anon—thei make ther avaunte.
Thynke well in yowr hert, yowr name ys Mankynde;
Be not wnkynde to Gode—I prey yow be hys servante.   280

Be stedefast in condycyon; se ye be not varyant.
Lose not thorow foly that ys bowte so dere.
Gode wyll prove yow son; ande yf that ye be constant,
Of hys blysse perpetuall ye xall be partener.

Ye may not have yowr intent at yowr fyrst dysyere.   285
Se the grett pacyence of Job in tribulacyon;
Lyke as the smyth trieth ern in the feere,
So was he triede by Godys vysytacyon.

He was of yowr nature and of yowr fragylyté;
Folow the steppys of hym, my own swete son,   290
Ande sey as he seyde in yowr trobyll and adversyté:
Dominus dedit, Dominus abstulit; sicut sibi placuit; sit nomen Domini
    benedictum!

Moreover, in specyall I gyve yow in charge,
Beware of New Gyse, Nowadays, and Nought.
Nyse in ther aray, in language thei be large—   295
To perverte yowr condycyons all ther menys xall be sowte.

Gode son, intromytt not yowrsylff in ther cumpeny.
Thei harde not a masse this twelmonyth, I dare well say.
Gyff them no audyence; thei wyll tell yow many a lye.
300   Do truly yowr labure and kepe yowr halyday.

Beware of Tytivillus, for he lesyth no wey,
That goth invysybull and wyll not be sen.
He wyll ronde in yowr ere and cast a nett befor yowr ey.
He ys worst of them all; Gode lett hym never then!

305   Yf ye dysples Gode, aske mercy anon,
Ellys Myscheff wyll be redy to brace yow in hys brydyll.
Kysse me now, my dere darlynge! Gode schelde yow from
        yowr fon!
Do truly yowr labure and be never ydyll.
The blyssynge of Gode by wyth yow and wyth all these
        worschyppull men!

                                                                    [*Exit*]

310   *Mankynde.* Amen, for sent charyté, amen!

Now blyssyde be Jesu! my soull ys well sacyatt
Wyth the mellyfluose doctryne of this worschyppfull man.
The rebellyn of my flesch now yt ys superatt,
Thankynge be Gode of the commynge that I kam.

315   Her wyll I sytt and tytyll in this papyr
The incomparable astat of my promycyon.
Worschypfull soverence, I have wretyn here
The gloryuse remembrance of my nobyll condycyon.

To have remos and memory of mysylff thus wretyn yt ys,
320   To defende me from all superstycyus charmys:
Memento, homo, quod cinis es et in cinerem reverteris.
Lo, I ber on my bryst the bagge of myn armys.

    New Gyse. The wether ys colde, Gode sende ws goode ferys!
Cum sancto sanctus eris et cum perverso perverteris.
325   '*Ecce quam bonum et quam jocundum*', quod the Deull to the frerys,
'*Habitare fratres in unum.*'

    Mankynde. I her a felow speke; wyth hym I wyll not mell.
Thys erth wyth my spade I xall assay to delffe.
To eschew ydullnes I do yt myn own selffe.
330   I prey Gode sende yt hys fusyon!

Nowadays. Make rom, sers, for we have be longe!
We wyll cum gyf yow a Crystemes songe.
  Nought. Now I prey all the yemandry that ys here
To synge wyth ws wyth a mery chere:

[*He sings*]

Yt ys wretyn wyth a coll, yt ys wretyn wyth a cole,   335
  New Gyse and Nowadays. Yt ys wretyn wyth a colle, yt ys wretyn
    wyth a colle,
  Nought. He that schytyth wyth hys hoyll, he that schytyth wyth
    hys hoyll,
  New Guyse, Nowadays. He that schytyth wyth hys hoyll, he that
    schytyth with his hoyll,
  Nought. But he wyppe hys ars clen, but he wyppe hys ars clen,
  New Gyse, Nowadays. But he wype his ars clen, but he wype his
    ars clen,   340
  Nought. On hys breche yt xall be sen, on hys breche yt xall be
    sen!
  New Gyse, Nowadays. On hys breche yt xall be sen, on hys breche
    yt xall be sen!
Cantant Omnes [*They all sing*]. Hoylyke, holyke, holyke! holyke,
    holyke, holyke!

  New Gyse. Ey, Mankynde, Gode spede yow wyth yowr spade!
I xall tell yow of a maryage: 345
I wolde yowr mowth and hys ars that this made
Wer maryede junctly together.
  Mankynde. Hey yow hens, felouse, wyth bredynge.
Leve yowr derysyon and yowr japyng.
I must nedys labure—yt ys my lyvynge.
  Nowadays. What, ser, we cam but lat hethyr.   350

Xall all this corn grow here
That ye xall have the next yer?
Yf yt be so, corn hade nede be dere,
Ellys ye xall have a pore lyffe.   355
  Nought. Alasse, goode fadere, this labor fretyth yow to the bon.
But for yowr croppe I take grett mone.
Ye xall never spende yt alonne;
I xall assay to geett yow a wyffe.

How many acres suppose ye here by estymacyon?   360
  New Gyse. Ey, how ye turne the erth wppe and down!
I have be in my days in many goode town
Yett saw I never such another tyllynge.

Mankynde. Why stonde ye ydyll? Yt ys pety that ye were born!
365   *Nowadays.* We xall bargen wyth yow and nother moke nor scorne.
Take a goode carte in herwest and lode yt wyth yowr corne,
Ande what xall we gyf yow for the levynge?

   Nought. He ys a goode starke laburrer, he wolde fayn do well.
He hath mett wyth the goode man Mercy in a schroude sell.
370   For all this he may have many a hungry mele.
Yyt woll ye se he ys polytyke.
Here xall be goode corn, he may not mysse yt.
Yf he wyll have reyn he may overpysse yt;
Ande yf he wyll have compasse he may overblysse yt
A lytyll wyth hys ars lyke.
375

   Mankynde. Go and do yowr labur! Gode lett yow never the!
Or wyth my spade I xall yow dynge, by the Holy Trinyté!
Have ye non other man to moke, but ever me?
Ye wolde have me of yowr sett?
Hye yow forth lyvely, for hens I wyll yow dryffe.
380   *[He beats them with his spade]*
   New Gyse. Alas, my jewellys! I xall be schent of my wyff!
   Nowadays. Alasse! and I am lyke never for to thryve,
I have such a buffett.

   Mankynde. Hens I sey, New Gyse, Nowadays, and Nowte!
385   Yt was seyde beforn, all the menys xuld be sought
To perverte my condycyons and brynge me to nought.
Hens, thevys! Ye have made many a lesynge.
   Nought. Marryde I was for colde, but now am I warme.
Ye are ewyll avysyde, ser, for ye have don harme.
390   By cokkys body sakyrde, I have such a peyn in my arme
I may not chonge a man a ferthynge.

   Mankynde. Now I thanke Gode, knelynge on my kne.
Blyssyde be hys name, he ys of hye degré!
By the subsyde of hys grace that he hath sente me
395   .iii. of myn enmys I have putt to flyght.
Yyt this instrument, soverens, ys not made to defende.
Davide seyth, '*Nec in hasta nec in gladio salvat Dominus.*'
   Nought. No, mary, I beschrew yow, yt ys *in spadibus.*
Therfor Crystys curse cum on yowr *hedybus*
To sende yow lesse myght!   *Exiant*

Mankynde. I promytt yow thes felouse wyll no more cum here,
For summe of them, certenly, were summewhat to nere.
My fadyr Mercy avysyde me to be of a goode chere
Ande agayn my enmys manly for to fyght.

I xall convycte them, I hope, everychon.   405
Yet I say amysse—I do yt not alon;
Wyth the helpe of the grace of Gode I resyst my fon
Ande ther malycyuse herte.
Wyth my spade I wyll departe, my worschyppull soverence,
And lyve ever wyth labure to corecte my insolence.   410
I xall go fett corn for my londe—I prey yow of pacyence;
Ryght son I xall reverte.   *Exit*

[*Enter Mischief*]

Myscheff. Alas, alasse, that ever I was wrought!
Alasse the whyll, I wers then nought!
Sythyn I was here, by hym that me bought,   415
I am wtterly ondon!
I, Myscheff, was here at the begynnynge of the game
Ande arguyde wyth Mercy, Gode gyff hym schame!
He hath taught Mankynde wyll I have be vane
To fyght manly ageyn hys fon.   420

For wyth hys spade, that was hys wepyn,
Neu Gyse, Nowadays, Nought hath all tobeton.
I have grett pyté to se them wepyn.
Wyll ye lyst? I here them crye.   *Clamant* [*They cry out*]
Alasse, alasse! cum hether, I xall be yowr borow.   425
Alac, alac! ven, ven! cum hethere wyth sorowe!
Pesse, fayer babys, ye xall have a nappyll tomorow!
Why grete ye so, why?

[*Enter New Guise, Now-a-days, and Nought*]

New Gyse. Alasse, master, alasse, my privyté!
Myscheff. A, wher? alake! fayer babe, ba me!   430
Abyde! to son I xall yt se.
Nowadays. Here, here, se my hede, goode master!
Myscheff. Lady, helpe! sely darlynge, ven, ven!
I xall helpe the of thi peyn;
I xall smytt of thi hede and sett yt on agayn.   435
Nought. By owr Lady, ser, a fayer playster!

249

Wyll ye of wyth hys hede! Yt ys a shreude charme!
As for me, I have non harme.
I were loth to forbere myn arme.
440 Ye pley *in nomine patris*, choppe!
    New Gyse. Ye xall not choppe my jewellys, and I may.
    Nowadays. Ye, Cristys crose, wyll ye smyght my hede awey?
Ther wer on and on! Oute! Ye xall not assay.
I myght well be callyde a foppe.

445   *Myscheff.* I kan choppe yt of and make yt agayn.
    New Gyse. I hade a schreude recumbentibus but I fele no peyn.
    Nowadays. Ande my hede ys all save and holl agayn.
Now towchynge the mater of Mankynde,
Lett ws have an interleccyon, sythen ye be cum hethere.
450 Yt were goode to have an ende.

    Myscheff. How, how, a mynstrell! Know ye ony out?
    Nought. I kan pype in a Walsyngham wystyll, I, Nought, Nought.
    Myscheff. Blow apase, and thou xall bryng hym in wyth a flowte.
    Tytivillus [*Shouts from off-stage*]. I com wyth my leggys wnder me.
455   *Myscheff.* How, New Gyse, Nowadays, herke or I goo!
When owr hedys wer togethere I spake of *si dedero*.
    New Gyse. Ye, go thi wey! We xall gather mony onto,
Ellys ther xall no man hym se.

            [*To the audience*]

Now gostly to owr purpos, worschypfull soverence,
460 We intende to gather mony, yf yt plesse yowr neclygence,
For a man wyth a hede that ys of grett omnipotens.
    Nowadays. Kepe yowr tayll, in goodnes I prey yow, goode brother!
He ys a worschyppull man, sers, savyng yowr reverens.
He lovyth no grotys, nor pens of to pens.
465 Gyf ws rede reyallys yf ye wyll se hys abhomynabull presens.
    New Guyse. Not so! Ye that mow not pay the ton, pay the tother.

At the goodeman of this house fyrst we wyll assay.
Gode blysse yow, master! Ye say as yll, yet ye wyll not sey nay.
Lett ws go by and by and do them pay.
470 Ye pay all alyke; well mut ye fare!
    Nought. I sey, New Gyse, Nowadays: 'Estis vos pecuniatus?'
I have cryed a fayer wyll, I beschrew yowr patus!
    Nowadays. Ita vere, magister. [*To Titivillus*] Cumme forth now yowr
        gatus!
He ys a goodly man, sers; make space and beware!

[*Enter Titivillus*]

Titivillus. Ego sum dominancium dominus and my name ys
Titivillus.   475
Ye that have goode hors, to yow I sey *caveatis*!
Here ys an abyll felyschyppe to tryse hem out at yowr gatys.
                    Loquitur ad New Gyse [*he speaks to New Gyse*]

Ego probo sic: ser New Gys, lende me a peny!
    New Gyse. I have a grett purse, ser, but I have no monay.
By the masse, I fayll .ii. farthyngys of an halpeny;   480
Yyt hade I .x. li. this nyght that was.
    Tityvillus loquitur ad Nowadays. What ys in thi purse? thou art a
    stout felon.
    Nowadays. The Deull have the qwytt! I am a clen jentyllman.
I prey God I be never wers storyde then I am.
Yt xall be otherwyse, I hope, or this nyght passe.   485
    Tytivillus loquitur ad Nought. Herke now! I say thou hast many
    a peny.
    Nought. Non nobis, domine, non nobis, by Sent Deny!
The Deull may daunce in my purse for ony peny;
Yt ys as clen as a byrdys ars.
    Titivillus. Now I say yet ageyn, *caveatis*!   490
Her ys an abyll felschyppe to tryse hem out of yowr gatys.

Now I sey, New Gyse, Nowadays, and Nought,
Go and serche the contré, anon yt be sowghte,
Summe here, summe ther; what yf ye may cache owghte?

Yf ye fayll of hors take what ye may ellys.   495
    New Gyse. Then speke to Mankynde for the recumbentibus of my
    jewellys.
    Nowadays. Remember my brokyn hede in the worschyppe of the
    .v. vowellys.
    Nought. Ye, goode ser, and the sytyca in my arme.
    Titivillus. I know full well what Mankynde dyde to yow.
Myschyff hat informyde of all the matere thorow.   500
I xall venge yowr quarell, I make Gode avow.
Forth, and espye were ye may do harme.
Take William Fyde, yf ye wyll have ony mo.
I sey, New Gyse, wethere art thou avysyde to go?

    New Gyse. Fyrst I xall begyn at Master Huntyngton of Sauston,   505
Fro thens I xall go to Wyllyam Thurlay of Hauston,

251

Ande so forth to Pycharde of Trumpyngton.
I wyll kepe me to thes .iii.
   Nowadays. I xall go to Wyllyham Baker of Waltom,
510   To Rycherde Bollman of Gayton;
I xall spare Master Woode of Fullburn,
He ys a noli me tangere.

   Nought. I xall goo to Wyllyam Patryke of Massyngham,
I xall spare Master Alyngton of Botysam
515   Ande Hamonde of Soffeham,
For drede of *in manus tuas* qweke.
Felous, cum forth, and go we hens togethyr.
   Neu Gyse. Syth we xall go, lett ws be well ware wethere.
If we may be take, we com no more hethyr.
520   Lett ws con well owr neke-verse, that we have not a cheke.

   Tityvillus. Goo yowr wey, a deull wey, go yowr wey all!
I blysse yow wyth my lyfte honde: foull yow befall!
Com agayn, I werne, as son as I yow call,
And brynge yowr avantage into this place.
                [Exeunt New Guise and his companions
525   To speke wyth Mankynde I wyll tary here this tyde
Ande assay hys goode purpose for to sett asyde.
The goode man Mercy xall no lenger be hys gyde.
I xall make hym to dawnce another trace!

Ever I go invysybull, yt ys my jett,
530   Ande befor hys ey thus I wyll hange my nett
To blench hys syght; I hope to have hys fote-mett.
To yrke hym of hys labur I xall make a frame.
Thys borde xall be hyde wnder the erth prevely;   *[He buries it*
535   Hys spade xall enter, I hope, onredyly;
Be then he hath assayde, he xall be very angry
Ande lose hys pacyens, peyn of schame.
I xall menge hys corne wyth drawke and wyth durnell;
Yt xall not be lyke to sow nor to sell.
Yondyr he commyth; I prey of cownsell.
540   He xall wene grace were wane.

          [Enter Mankind]

   Mankynd. Now Gode of hys mercy sende ws of hys sonde!
I have brought sede here to sow wyth my londe.
Qwyll I overdylew yt, here yt xall stonde.
In nomine Patris et Filii et Spiritus Sancti, now I wyll begyn.

Thys londe ys so harde yt makyth wnlusty and yrke.   545
I xall sow my corn at wynter and lett Gode werke.
Alasse, my corn ys lost! here ys a foull werke!
I se well by tyllynge lytyll xall I wyn.
Here I gyff wppe my spade for now and for ever.
> *Here Titivillus goth out wyth the spade*
To occupye my body I wyll not put me in dever.   550
I wyll here my ewynsonge here or I dyssever.
Thys place I assyng as for my kyrke.
Here in my kerke I knell on my kneys.
Peter noster qui es in celis.

[*Enter Titivillus*]

Tytyvillus. I promes yow I have no lede on my helys.   555
I am here ageyn to make this felow yrke.

Qwyst! pesse! I xall go to hys ere and tytyll therein.
> *[He approaches Mankind and whispers in his ear*
A schorte preyere thyrlyth hewyn—of thi preyere blyn!
Thou art holyer then ever was ony of thi kyn.
Aryse and avent the! nature compellys.   560
  Mankynde [to the audience]. I wyll into thi yerde, soverens, and cum
    ageyn son.
For drede of the colyke and eke of the ston
I wyll go do that nedys must be don.
My bedys xall be here for whosummever wyll ellys.   *Exiat*

Tityvillus. Mankynde was besy in hys prayere, yet I dyde hym
    aryse.   565
He ys conveyde, be Cryst, from hys dyvyn servyce.
Wethere ys he, trow ye? Iwysse I am wonder wyse;
I have sent hym forth to schyte lesynges.
Yff ye have ony sylver, in happe pure brasse,
Take a lytyll powder of Parysch and cast over hys face,   570
Ande ewyn in the howll-flyght let hym passe.
Titivillus kan lerne yow many praty thyngys.

I trow Mankynde wyll cum ageyn son,
Or ellys I fere me ewynsonge wyll be don.
Hys bedys xall be trysyde asyde, and that anon.   575
Ye xall a goode sport yf ye wyll abyde.
Mankynde cummyth ageyn, well fare he!
I xall answere hym *ad omnia quare.*

Ther xall be sett abroche a clerycall mater.
580   I hope of hys purpose to sett hym asyde.

[Enter Mankind]

   Mankynde. Ewynsong hath be in the saynge, I trow, a fayer wyll.
I am yrke of yt; yt ys to longe be on myle.
Do wey! I wyll no more so oft over the chyrche-style.
Be as be may, I xall do another.
585   Of labure and preyer, I am nere yrke of both—
I wyll no more of yt, thow Mercy be wroth.
My hede ys very hevy, I tell yow forsoth.
I xall slepe full my bely and he wore my brother.

[He goes to sleep and snores]

   Tityvillus. Ande ever ye dyde, for me kepe now yowr sylence.
590   Not a worde, I charge yow, peyn of .xl. pens.
A praty game xall be scheude yow or ye go hens.
Ye may here hym snore; he ys sade aslepe.
Qwyst! pesse! the deull ys dede! I xall goo ronde in hys ere.
                [He approaches Mankind and whispers in his ear
Alasse, Mankynde, alasse! Mercy stown a mere!
595   He ys runn away fro hys master, ther wot no man where;
Moreover, he stale both a hors and a nete.

But yet I herde sey he brake hys neke as he rode in Fraunce;
But I thynke he rydyth on the galouse, to lern for to daunce,
Bycause of hys theft, that ys hys governance.
600   Trust no more on hym, he ys a marryde man.
Mekyll sorow wyth thi spade beforn thou hast wrought.
Aryse and aske mercy of Neu Gyse, Nowadays, and Nought.
Thei cun avyse the for the best; lett ther goode wyll be sought,
Ande thi own wyff brethell, and take the a lemman.

[To the audience]

605   Farwell, everychon, for I have don my game,
For I have brought Mankynde to myscheff and to schame.   *[Exit*

   Mankynd [waking up]. Whope who! Mercy hath brokyn hys
      neke-kycher, avows,
Or he hangyth by the neke hye wppon the gallouse.
Adew, fayer masters! I wyll hast me to the ale-house
610   Ande speke wyth New Gyse, Nowadays and Nought
And geett me a lemman wyth a smattrynge face

[*Enter New Guise through the audience, with part of a rope round his neck*]

New Gyse. Make space, for cokkys body sakyrde,make space!
A ha! well overron! Gode gyff hym ewyll grace!
We were nere Sent Patrykes wey, by hym that me bought.

I was twychyde by the neke; the game was begunne.   615
A grace was, the halter brast asonder—*ecce signum*!
The halff ys abowte my neke—we hade a nere rune!
'Beware', quod the goodewyff when sche smot of here husbondys
    hede, 'beware!'
Myscheff ys a convicte, for he coude hys neke-verse.
My body gaff a swynge when I hynge wppon the casse.   620
Alasse, he wyll hange such a lyghly man, and a fers,
For stelynge of an horse, I prey Gode gyf hym care!

Do wey this halter! What deull doth Mankynde here, wyth sorow!
Alasse, how my neke ys sore, I make avowe!
    Mankynde. Ye be welcom, Neu Gyse! Ser, what chere wyth yow?   625

    New Gyse. Well ser, I have no cause to morn.
    Mankynd. What was that abowte yowr neke, so Gode yow
        amende?
    Neu Gyse. In feyth, Sent Audrys holy bende.
I have a lytyll dyshes, as yt plesse Gode to sende,
Wyth a runnynge ryngeworme.   630

                    [*Enter Now-a-days*]

Nowadays. Stonde a-rom, I prey the, brother myn!
I have laburryde all this nyght—wen xall we go dyn?
A chyrche her besyde xall pay for ale, brede, and wyn.
Lo, here ys stoff wyll serve.
    New Gyse. Now by the holy Mary, thou art better merchande
        then I!   635

                    [*Enter Nought*]

Nought. Avante, knawys, lett me go by!
I kan not geet and I xulde sterve.

                    [*Enter Mischief*]

Myscheff. Here cummyth a man of armys! Why stonde ye so styll?
Of murder and manslawter I have my bely-fyll.
    Nowadays. What, Myscheff, have ye ben in presun? And yt be
        yowr wyll,   640

                           255

Me semyth ye have scoryde a peyr of fetters.

Myscheff. I was chenyde by the armys: lo, I have them here!
The chenys I brast asundyr and kyllyde the jaylere,
Ye, ande hys fayer wyff halsyde in a cornere;

645 A, how swetly I kyssyde the swete mowth of hers!

When I hade do, I was myn own bottler;
I brought awey wyth me both dysch and dublere.
Here ys anow for me; be of goode chere!
Yet well fare the new chesance!

650   *Mankynde.* I aske mercy of New Gyse, Nowadays, and Nought.
Onys wyth my spade I remember that I faught.
I wyll make yow amendys yf I hurt yow ought
Or dyde ony grevaunce.

        New Gyse. What a deull lykyth the to be of this dysposycyon?

655   *Mankynde.* I drempt Mercy was hange—this was my vysyon—
Ande that to yow .iii. I xulde have recors and remocyon.
Now I prey yow hertyly of yowr goode wyll.
I crye yow mercy of all that I dyde amysse.
        Nowadays. I sey, New Gys, Nought, Tytivillus made all this:

660 As sekyr as Gode ys in hewyn, so yt ys.
        Nought. Stonde wppe on yowr feet! why stonde ye so styll?

        Neu Gyse. Master Myscheff, we wyll yow exort
Mankyndys name in yowr bok for to report.
        Myscheff. I wyll not so; I wyll sett a corte.

665 Nowadays, mak proclamacyon,
And do yt *sub forma jurys*, dasarde!
        Nowadays. Oyyt! Oyyyt! Oyet! All manere of men and comun
            women
To the cort of Myschyff othere cum or sen!
Mankynde xall retorn; he ys on of owr men.

670   *Myscheff.* Nought, cum forth, thou xall be stewerde.

        New Gyse. Master Myscheff, hys syde gown may be tolde.
He may have a jakett therof, and mony tolde.
                                            Nought scribit [*writes*]
        Mankynde. I wyll do for the best, so I have no colde.
Holde, I prey yow, and take yt wyth yow.

675 Ande let me have yt ageyn in ony wyse.
        New Gyse. I promytt yow a fresch jakett after the new gyse.
        Mankynde. Go and do that longyth to yowr offyce,
And spare that ye mow!   [*Exist New Guise with Mankind's coat*

Nought [*gives Mischief the document*]. Holde, master Myscheff, and
   rede this.
   Myscheff. Here ys *blottybus in blottis,*   680
Blottorum blottibus istis.
I beschrew yowr erys, a fayer hande!
   Nowadays. Ye, yt ys a goode rennynge fyst.
Such an hande may not be myst.
   Nought. I xulde have don better, hade I wyst.   685
   Myscheff. Take hede, sers, yt stonde you on hande.

                  [*He reads*]

Carici tenta generalis
In a place ther goode ale ys
Anno regni regitalis
Edwardi nullateni   690
On yestern day in Feverere—the yere passyth fully,
As Nought hath wrytyn; here ys owr Tulli,
Anno regni regis nulli!

   Nowadays. What how, Neu Gyse! thou makyst moche taryynge.
That jakett xall not be worth a ferthynge.   695

   [*Enter New Guise with Mankind's coat much shortened*]

   New Gyse. Out of my wey, sers, for drede of fyghtynge!
Lo, here ys a feet tayll, lyght to leppe abowte!
   Nought. Yt ys not schapyn worth a morsell of brede;
Ther ys to moche cloth, yt weys as ony lede.
I xall goo and mende yt, ellys I wyll lose my hede.   700
Make space, sers, lett me go owte.   [*Exit, with the coat*

   Myscheff. Mankynde, cum hethere! God sende yow the gowte!
Ye xall goo to all the goode felouse in the cuntré aboute;
Onto the goodewyff when the goodeman ys owte.
'I wyll,' say ye.
   Mankynde. I wyll, ser.   705
   New Gyse. There arn but sex dedly synnys, lechery ys non,
As yt may be verefyede by ws brethellys everychon.
Ye xall goo robbe, stell, and kyll, as fast as ye may gon.
'I wyll,' sey ye.
   Mankynde. I wyll, ser.
   Nowadays. On Sundays on the morow erly betyme   710
Ye xall wyth ws to the all-house erly to go dyn
And forbere masse and matens, owres and prime.
'I wyll,' sey ye.

Mankynde. I wyll, ser.

Myscheff. Ye must have be yowr syde a longe da pacem,

715 As trew men ryde be the wey for to onbrace them,
Take ther monay, kytt ther throtys, thus overface them.
'I wyll,' sey ye.
Mankynde. I wyll, ser.

[*Enter Nought, with the coat now even shorter*]

Nought. Here ys a joly jakett! How sey ye?
New Gyse. Yt ys a goode jake of fence for a mannys body.

720 Hay, doog, hay! whoppe whoo! Go yowr wey lyghtly!
Ye are well made for to ren.
Myscheff. Tydyngys, tydyngys! I have aspyede on!
Hens wyth yowr stuff, fast we were gon!
I beschrew the last xall com to hys hom.

725 *Dicant Omnes* [*let all say*]. Amen!

[*Enter Mercy*]

Mercy. What how, Mankynde! Fle that felyschyppe, I yow prey!
Mankynde. I xall speke wyth the another tyme, tomorn, or the next
day.
We xall goo forth to kepe my faders yer-day.
A tapster, a tapster! Stow, statt, stow!

730 *Myscheff.* A myscheff go wyth! here I have a foull fall.
Hens, awey fro me, or I xall beschyte yow all.
New Gyse. What how, ostlere, hostlere! Lende ws a football!
Whoppe whow! Anow, anow, anow, anow! [*Exeunt all except Mercy*

Mercy. My mynde ys dyspersyde, my body trymmelyth as the aspen
leffe.

735 The terys xuld trekyll down by my chekys, were not yowr reverrence.
Yt were to me solace, the cruell vysytacyon of deth.
Wythout rude behaver I kan not expresse this inconvenyens.
Wepynge, sythynge, and sobbynge were my suffycyens;
All naturall nutriment to me as caren ys odybull.

740 My inwarde afflixcyon yeldyth me tedyouse wnto yowr presens.
I kan not bere yt ewynly that Mankynde ys so flexybull.

Man onkynde wherever thou be, for all this world was not
aprehensyble
To dyscharge thin orygynall offence, thraldam and captyvyté,
Tyll Godys own welbelovyde son was obedient and passyble.

745 Every droppe of hys bloode was schede to purge thin iniquité!

I dyscomende and dysalow thin oftyn mutabylyté;
To every creature thou art dyspectuose and odyble.
Why art thou so oncurtess, so inconsyderatt? Alasse, who ys me!
As the fane that turnyth wyth the wynde, so thou art convertyble.

In trust ys treson; thi promes ys not credyble;   750
Thy perversyose ingratytyde I can not rehers.
To God and to all the holy corte of hewyn thou art despectyble,
As a nobyll versyfyer makyth mencyon in this verse:
Lex et natura, Cristus et omnia jura
Damnant ingratum, lugent eum fore natum.   755

O goode Lady and Mother of mercy, have pety and compassyon
Of the wrechydnes of Mankynde, that ys so wanton and so frayll!
Lett mercy excede justyce, dere Mother, amytt this supplycacyon,
Equyté to be leyde on-party and mercy to prevayll.

To sensuall lyvynge ys reprovable, that ys nowadays,   760
As be the comprehence of this mater yt may be specyfyede.
New Gyse, Nowadays, Nought wyth ther allectuose ways
They have pervertyde Mankynde, my swet sun, I have well espyede.

A, wyth thes cursyde caytyfs, and I may, he xall not long indure.
I, Mercy, hys father gostly, wyll procede forth and do my propyrté.   765
Lady, helpe! this maner of lyvynge ys a detestabull plesure.
Vanitas vanitatum, all ys but a vanyté.

Mercy xall never be convicte of hys oncurtes condycyon.
Wyth wepynge terys be nyghte and be day I wyll goo and never sesse.
Xall I not fynde hym? Yes, I hope. Now Gode be my proteccyon!   770
My predylecte son, where be ye? Mankynde, *ubi es?*

[Enter Mischief and his companions]

Myscheff. My prepotent fader, when ye sowpe, sowpe owt yowr
    messe.
Ye are all togloryede in yowr termys; ye make many a lesse.
Wyll ye here? He cryeth ever 'Mankynde, *ubi es?*'
   New Gyse. Hic hyc, hic hic, hic hic, hic hic!   775
That ys to sey, here, here, here! ny dede in the cryke.
Yf ye wyll have hym, goo and syke, syke, syke!
Syke not overlong, for losynge of yowr mynde!   *[Exit Mercy*

   Nowadays. Yf ye wyll have Mankynde, how *domine, domine,*
    dominus!

259

780 Ye must speke to the schryve for a *cepe coppus*,
Ellys ye must be fayn to retorn wyth *non est inventus*.
How sey ye ser? My bolte ys schett.
　　Nought. I am doynge of my nedyngys; be ware how ye schott!
Fy, fy, fy! I have fowll arayde my fote.
785 Be wyse for schotynge wyth yowr takyllys, for Gode wott
My fote ys fowly overschett.

　　Myscheff. A parlement, a parlement! Cum forth, Nought, behynde.
A cownsell belyve! I am aferde Mercy wyll hym fynde.
How sey ye, and what sey ye? How xall we do wyth Mankynde?
790 　　*Neu Gyse.* Tysche! a flyes weyng! Wyll ye do well?
He wenyth Mercy were honge for stelyng of a mere.
Myscheff, go sey to hym that Mercy sekyth everywere.
He wyll honge hymselff, I wndyrtake, for fere.
　　Myscheff. I assent therto; yt ys wyttyly seyde and well.

795 　　*Nowadays.* Qwyppe yt in thi cote; anon yt were don.
Now Sent Gabryellys modyr save the clothes of thi schon!
All the bokys in the worlde, yf thei hade be wndon,
Kowde not a cownselde ws bett.　　　　　　　　*Hic exit Myscheff*
　　Myscheff. How, Mankynde! Cumm and speke wyth Mercy, he is
　　here fast by.

[Enter Mankind and Michief]

800 　　*Mankynde.* A roppe, a rope, a rope! I am not worthy.
　　Myscheff. Anon, anon, anon! I have yt here redy,
Wyth a tre also that I have gett.

Holde the tre, Nowadays, Nought! Take hede and be wyse!
　　Neu Gyse. Lo, Mankynde! do as I do; this ys thi new gyse.
805 Gyff the roppe just to thye neke—this ys myn avyse.
　　Myscheff. Helpe thisylff, Nought! *[Enter Mercy]* Lo, Mercy ys here!
He skarith ws wyth a bales; we may no lengere tary.
　　Neu Gyse. Qweke, qweke, qweke! Alass, my thrott! I beschrew
　　yow, mary!
A, Mercy, Crystys coppyde curse go wyth yow, and Sent Davy!
Alasse, my wesant! Ye were sumwhat to nere.　　　　　*Exiant*

811 　　*Mercy.* Aryse, my precyose redempt son! Ye be to me full dere.
He ys so tymerouse, me semyth hys vytall spryt doth exspyre.
　　Mankynde. Alasse, I have be so bestyally dysposyde, I dare not
　　apere.
To se yowr solaycyose face I am not worthy to dysyere.

Mercy. Yowr crymynose compleynt wondyth my hert as a lance.   815
Dyspose yowrsylff mekly to aske mercy, and I wyll assent.
Yelde me nethyr golde nor tresure, but yowr humbyll obeysyance,
The voluntary subjeccyon of yowr hert, and I am content.

 Mankynde. What, aske mercy yet onys agayn? Alas, yt were a wyle
  petycyun.
Ewyr to offend and ever to aske mercy, yt ys a puerilité.   820
Yt ys so abhominabyll to rehers my iterat transgrescion,
I am not worthy to hawe mercy be no possibilité.

 Mercy. O Mankend, my singler solas, this is a lamentabyll excuse.
The dolorus terys of my hert, how thei begyn to amownt!
O pirssid Jesu, help thou this synfull synner to redouce!   825
Nam hec est mutacio dextre Excelsi; vertit impios et non sunt.

Aryse and aske mercy, Mankend, and be associat to me.
Thy deth schall be my hewynesse; alas, tys pety yt schwld be thus.
Thy obstinacy wyll exclude the fro the glorius perpetuité.
Yet for my lofe ope thy lyppys and sey '*Miserere mei, Deus!*'   830

 Mankend. The egall justyse of God wyll not permytte sych a
  synfull wrech
To be rewyvyd and restoryd ageyn; yt were impossibyll.
 Mercy. The justyce of God wyll as I wyll, as hymsylfe doth precyse:
Nolo mortem peccatoris, inquit, yff he wyll be redusyble.

 Mankend. Than mercy, good Mercy! What ys a man wythowte
  mercy?   835
Lytyll ys our parte of paradyse were mercy ne were.
Good Mercy, excuse the inevytabyll objeccion of my gostly enmy.
The prowerbe seyth 'the trewth tryith the sylfe.' Alas, I hawe mech
  care!

 Mercy. God wyll not make yow prevy onto hys last jugement.
Justyce and Equité xall be fortyfyid, I wyll not denye.   840
Trowthe may not so cruelly procede in hys streyt argument
But that Mercy schall rewle the mater wythowte contraversye.

Aryse now and go wyth me in thys deambulatorye.
Inclyne yowyr capacité; my doctrine ys convenient.
Synne not in hope of mercy; that ys a cryme notary.   845
To truste overmoche in a prince yt ys not expedient.

In hope when ye syn ye thynke to hawe mercy, be ware of that
    awenture.
The good Lord seyd to the lecherus woman of Chanane,
The holy gospell ys the awtorité, as we rede in scrypture,
850 *Vade et jam amplius noli peccare.*

Cryst preserwyd this synfull woman takeyn in awowtry;
He seyde to here theis wordys, 'Go and syn no more.'
So to yow, go and syn no more. Beware of weyn confidens of mercy;
Offend not a prince on trust of hys favour, as I seyd before.

855 Yf ye fele yoursylfe trappyd in the snare of your gostly enmy,
Aske mercy anon; beware of the contynuance.
Whyll a wond ys fresch yt ys prowyd curabyll be surgery,
That yf yt procede ovyrlong, yt ys cawse of gret grewans.

    Mankend. To aske mercy and to hawe, this ys a lyberall
        possescion.
860 Schall this expedycius petycion ever be alowyd, as ye hawe insyght?
    Mercy. In this present lyfe ys plenté, tyll deth makyth hys
        dywysion;
But whan ye be go, *usque ad minimum quadrantem* ye schall rekyn
    your ryght.
Aske mercy and hawe, whyll the body wyth the sowle hath hys
    annexion;
Yf ye tary tyll your dyscesse, ye may hap of your desyre to mysse.
865 Be repentant here, trust not the owr of deth; thynke on this lessun:
    Ecce nunc tempus acceptabile, ecce nunc dies salutis!

All the wertu in the word yf ye myght comprehend
Your merytys were not premyabyll to the blys abowe,
Not to the lest joy of hewyn, of your propyr efforte to ascend.
870 Wyth mercy ye may; I tell yow no fabyll, scrypture doth prowe.

    Mankend. O Mercy, my suavius solas and synguler recreatory,
My predilecte spesyall, ye are worthy to hawe my lowe;
For wythowte deserte and menys supplicatorie
Ye be compacient to my inexcusabyll reprowe.

875 A, yt swemyth my hert to thynk how onwysely I hawe wroght.
Tytivillus, that goth invisibele, hyng hys nett before my eye
And by hys fantasticall visionys sediciusly sowght,
To New Gyse, Nowadayis, Nowght causyd me to obey.

Mercy. Mankend, ye were oblivyows of my doctrine monytoryc.
I scyd before, Titivillus wold asay yow a bronte.   880
Beware fro hensforth of hys fablys delusory.
The prowerbe seyth, *Jacula prestita minus ledunt.*

Ye hawe .iii. adversaryis and he ys mayster of hem all:
That ys to sey, the dewell, the world, the flesch and the fell.
The New Gyse, Nowadayis, Nowgth, the world we may hem call;   885
And propyrly Titivillus syngnyfyth the fend of helle;

The flesch, that ys the unclene concupissens of your body.
These be your .iii. gostly enmyis, in whom ye hawe put your
     confidens.
Thei browt yow to Myscheffe to conclude your temporall glory,
As yt hath be schewyd before this worcheppyll audiens.   890

Remembyr how redy I was to help yow; fro swheche I was not
     dangerus;
Wherfore, goode sunne, absteyne fro syn evermore after this.
Ye may both save and spyll yowr sowle that ys so precyus.
Libere welle, libere nolle God may not deny iwys.

Beware of Titivillus wyth his net and of all enmys will,   895
Of your synfull delectacion that grewyth your gostly substans.
Your body ys your enmy; let hym not have hys wyll.
Take your lewe whan ye wyll. God send yow good perseverans!

Mankend. Syth I schall departe, blyse me, fader, her then I go.
God send ws all plenté of hys gret mercy!   900
   Mercy. Dominus custodit te ab omni malo
In nomine Patris et Filii et Spiritus Sancti. Amen!   *Hic exit Mankend*

Wyrschepyll sofereyns, I hawe do my propirté:
Mankynd ys deliveryd by my faverall patrocynyc.
God preserve hym fro all wyckyd captivité   905
And send hym grace hys sensuall condicions to mortifye!

Now for hys lowe that for us receywyd hys humanité,
Serge your condicyons wyth dew examinacion.
Thynke and remembyr the world ys but a wanité,
And yt ys prowyd daly by diverse transmutacyon.   910

Mankend ys wrechyd, he hath sufficyent prowe.
Therefore God grant yow all *per suam misericordiam*
That ye may be pleyferys wyth the angellys abowe
And hawe to your porcyon *vitam eternam*. Amen!

17

LEARNING AND EDUCATION

IN THE intellectual history of this period old interests and new exist side by side, and are often reflected in literary texts. Leaving aside works in Latin (and thus forgoing the *Itineraries* of William Worcester, that very traditional fifteenth-century scholar who is at the same time an important precursor of the great antiquarians of the following century) and vernacular encyclopaedic collections of popularized learning, we can still find a miscellany of interesting and not very well known texts. If Walton's verse translation of the favourite author Boethius—a translation which is not inspired, but on occasion does justice to the Platonic imagery of the lyrics—may be taken to represent a long-standing general interest in the literature of antiquity (as evidenced by Lydgate and others in this volume), perhaps the translation in unrhymed verse of Claudian's *De Consulatu Stilichonis* (extract D) looks ahead to the closer and more scholarly translations of Douglas (20 B) and Barclay (22 D). The writings of 'modern' classical scholars are also represented. Of Petrarch's Latin works, the *De Remediis Utriusque Fortunae* seems to have been especially popular; it fits fairly easily into a familiar pattern of moral works which deal with and offer consolation for the snares of Fortune and the instability of life, and it is not surprising to find a piece of it translated (extract B). The translation of part of the *Secretum* (C), a personal and intense dialogue between Petrarch and St Augustine, is much more unusual; it appears in a later anthology which contains much religious and moral matter but which shows a fairly wide range of interests. With Tiptoft's *Declamacion of Noblesse* (E), we are quite clearly dealing with a vernacular by-product of a newly developing humanism. John Tiptoft, Earl of Worcester (1427–70), who has been called 'the English nobleman of his age who came closest to the Italian prince of the Renaissance', was a great collector of books, who visited Italy and studied there. His *Declamation* is a free version of a Latin work on the nature of true nobility (which 'resteth neyther in rychesse ne in blood, but in a free and noble courage, which is neyther servaunt to vyce ne unclennesse, but is exercised in connyng and vertu'), which is humanistic in style, topic, and form. Tiptoft brings out the dramatic possibilities of the speeches of the two rival suitors, Gaius Flaminius and Publius Cornelius Scipio (and creates the model for the later play by Medwall, *Fulgens and Lucrece* (? c.1497)). The dialogue has some excellent prose, especially in passages of invective ('and thou hast forsaken the bryght path whiche ledeth to worship, and hast wilfully drowned thyself in the derke pytte of foryetefulness'); Gaius Flaminius' praise of his library 'wel stuffed with fayr bookes of Greke and Latyn' makes us think of the scholarly ideal embodied in Pico della Mirandola (see 26 A).

In the *Utopia* (1516), More refers to 'incompetent schoolmasters, who prefer caning their pupils to teaching them', but in spite of the gloomy view taken by the erring schoolboy of the lyric (11 Q), not all schoolmasters were brutal and incompetent. The fifteenth century shared with the sixteenth a faith in the value of education: new schools and new colleges were founded, and the class of educated, literate laymen seems to have expanded. The humbler forms of 'educational' literature have an interest of their own. The aims are often very practical and utilitarian, as in our 'treatise' (F) on elementary French. Some of the books intended for children still 'under the rod', like introductory Latin grammars, now begin to appear in the vernacular: 'What schalt thow doo whan thow hast an Englysch to make yn Latin?' 'I shall reherse myne englyshe onys ii or iii, and loke owt my principall verbe.' This is excellent advice, but this sort of material tends to lose its charm after a few pages. Fortunately, there is one attractive set of works which deal with 'making English in Latin'. These are the *vulgaria*, collections of English and Latin sentences for translations, one or two of which were written by masters who had some understanding of their pupils' attitudes and habits, and considerable literary flair (their vivid and colloquial phraseology, incidentally, gives the lie to the notion that there is something mystically superior about the colloquial language of the Elizabethans). There is no room, alas, for the excellent Eton master, Horman, whose collection (1519) has an enthusiasm sometimes reminiscent of Douglas ('*exiluit gaudio*: he hopped and daunsed for joye'), a liking for curious lore ('men have xxxii tethe: women nat past xxx', 'an oyster is thyn and lene in the wanyng of the mone') which sometimes has a strange imaginative quality ('some fisshe go in scollys: some wander about alone'), and a very wide range of reference. Learning Latin from translating sentences such as 'he studied at a glasse to make his countenaunce grymme and ferefull' cannot have been all 'monishing and stripes'. Our examples come from a collection from Magdalen College School, Oxford (*c.*1500), and they can speak for themselves. The *vulgaria* did not survive the more correct humanist grammar masters, and the New Learning made its influence felt on the curriculum in other ways. We end with the St Paul's statutes of that influential humanist Colet, which give an attractive picture of the austere life envisaged for the pupils who study not 'blotterature' but 'literature', the authors 'that hathe with wysdome joinyde the pure chaste eloquence'.

A

JOHN WALTON, *LIBER BOETII DE CONSOLATIONE PHILOSOPHIAE*

Heu quam precipiti (i, m. 2)

'Allas!' sche seide, 'how that this manis mynde
Is casten doun nowe into depe derknesse,
Forlet the clerenesse of his propur kynde,
Myntyng for to goo to strange derknesse,
Als oftetyme as noyous besynesse
Withouten mesure begynnyth to encresse,
When worldly wynd with mescheef and distresse
Hath hym beraft al oute of merthe and pesse.

'This is the man that whilom was so free
To whom be craft was gifen for to kunne,   10
Up into hevenes to behold and see,
And to mesure the mevyng of the sonne;
Bi wyt also that konnyng had he wonne
How that the mone chaungeth for to preve;
And what recourse the sterres havith ironne   15
And in thaire speres how dyversly thei meve,

'As victour hath he subtyly conquered,
And all this craft that noumber comprehendeth;
Fro whennes eke these wyndes ben arerid,
The smothe see that turneth so and wendith;   20
And why the sterre that is in the est ascendeth
Eft in the west adowne ayeyn to lowte;
And what spirit so besily entendeth
The rounde world to wenden all aboute;

'And what attempreth so the lusty oures   25
Of thilke faire first somer sesoun,
Arayeng it with rede rose floures
The whiche in wynter skarse ben and gesoun;
All these, lo, couthe he schewe be verray resoun,
In fulle yeres who is that us fedeth   30
With grete grapes that the peple plesoun
And other fruytes that us alle nedeth.

'Wont he was also to seke and knawe
The privé causes for to telle of kynde.
Allas, witles now lyth this man full lawe   35
Under full hevy bondes that hym bynde,
And now can he none othere comfort fynde,
But hevely his chere he hathe dounfolde;
So is he all desmayed in hys mynde
That nedes wrecchid erth he must beholde.'   40

Huc omnes pariter (iii, m. 10)

'Now cometh alle ye that ben ibroght
In bondes full of busy bitternesse
Of erthly lust abidyng in your thoght!
Here is the reste of all youre busynesse,

45 Here is the port of pees and restfulnesse
To theim that stonde in stormes and desese,
Refut overt to wrecches in distresse,
And all confort of myschief and mysese.

'For all that evire Tagus doth the bede
50 Of faire golden gravell stones bright;
Or that Erynus with his strondes rede
May yeven yow to plese with your sight;
Or that ryvere whiche that Indus hight
That is full nyhe the hote regioun,
55 Whiche that the grene stones with his myght
Wyth white perles turneth up-so-doun;

'They schynen wondir clere unto your eye
Bot your insight in sothe they maken blynde,
And with there derke clowdes perelously
60 In vanité your hertes done thei bynde,
For how that evire thei plesen to your mynde
As praysed worthy many a thowsand pound,
Yit ben they full unworthi in theire kynde
As norished in the caves of the ground.

65 'Bot lo, the schenyng of that sovereyn light,
Be whiche the hihe hevene governed is,
Chaseth awey that foule derke nyght
That hath youre soules drawen all amys.
This sovereyn light, if thou may see iwis,
70 Beholde it well and kepe it if thou kunne,
And thou schalt seen that in regarde of this,
There be no brighte bemes in the sonne.'

B

A TRANSLATION OF PETRARCH, *DE REMEDIIS UTRIUSQUE FORTUNAE*

Of Poor Birth

Adversité. The stok of my nativité is simple and pore.
Resoun. Mater of mekenesse is non odious condicioun. What meneth the but vanité that thou wolt that men talede of the that were come of

268

higghe blod? Fro depe rotes and derke proceden deleitable braunches. Yif
fortune of vertu profer the frenchip, thou may lefulli ascende, and yif hit   5
happe that thou sitte in a place of dignité, thi glorie schal not be denyed.
Among thi progenitoures thou schalt have alle the hole preisinge.
Whatsoever thou weel dost, thou schalt repe the thank thisilff. And yif
thou have lawful issu thou schalt be kald a foundere of a gentil lenage;
wich name thou mayst not kalenge be right yif thi auncceteres hadde ben   10
noble. Deme now wethur is fairere to yeve cleernesse with sunne, or light
to borwe with the mone.

Adversité. Homly folk and rude brought me into this worlde.

Resoun. Thou art the more excusable yif thou be rude thisilf. And yif
thou be man of sich honesté that thou be worthili magnified, the bright   15
bemes of thi fame schal worschipe alle thi kynne. Virgil was of low kynne,
yit the sors of his wisdom was of so swete an odour that it was deynté to
princes to have knowlech of him. That the sones of pore men governen
may riche remes, telle it for no tythingges, for it is no novelté. Ayenward,
the nobleye of many gentiimennes children suffren such a clips that wereof   20
thei profiten unnethe it is perceyved. Emperours and kynges, sitte thei
nevere so highe, here trone tremblith undur hem, but vertu holde hem up.
Fiche thi feet therfore in the path of vertu for be his grees maist thou most
sekirli ascende.

Adversité. I am komen of koterelles.   25

Resoun. Opene it is that Fortune schewith not chere ilik to alle men at
here first komynge into this world, for summe sche lullith in clothis of
gold, and on summe sche voucheth saf unnethes a fewe ragges. But Grace
is of a more gentil condicioun. What mannes childe that evere hit be that
kometh to the fonstone, sche welkometh hit worschipfulli, and clenly   30
araiyeth it, and alle tho childryn that dame Grace kissith ben so acceptable
to the kyng of kyngges that he maketh hem gentil folk, and wol be callid
here fader. Sik not thoow thou were born naked of sibreden of wordli
princes wilis thou art son to sich an emperour and coseyn unto seyntes.
Falle not fro that fairehed thou toke in thi baptim and thou maist lawfulli   35
cleyme hevene for heritage. Thou tellist that thin beginnynge was of pore
reputacion: studie to have a glorous ende. . . .

C

A TRANSLATION OF PETRARCH, *SECRETUM*

An Exchange between the Poet and St Augustine

Franciscus What therefore, what ys thyn entent?
Augustinus That conscyens hathe made the to wepe soore,

But thy purpose chaunged never the more.
Fran. How ofte have I seyde I myght noo ferre!
5 *Aug.* How ofte have I answerd thou woldyst noo nerre!
Nee I merveyle thoff thou be lapped in thies ambages,
As whilom I was in my wylde rages
Whyle I was abowte to chaunge myn olde lyff—
What sorowe I suffred, dyseese, angre and stryff,
10 Cracchynge myn here, my chekys all totare,
Wrythynge my fyngres for angwysshe and care,
Watrynge the erthe with my byttre salte teres
That the crye of my syghes ascended to Goddys eres,
My knees with myn handys grasped togedyre soore,
15 And yitt I stode the same man I was afore
Tyl a depe profounde remembraunce att the laste
Hadd all my wrecchednesse afore myn eyn caste
Soo that fully whan I woold and myght,
And hadde of perfeccyon a verrey clere syght,
20 Subdaynlye and with a wondyrfull swyftenesse,
As my booke of *Confessyons* wyll expresse,
I was transformate into a newe Augustyn,
The whiche hystory I trowe thou knoweste wele and fyn.
Fran. Hytt ys trewe, that fictree remembre I well
25 That lesson may never ought of my mynde.
Aug. Thou sayste well, for neythyr yvé nee wodebynde,
Myrre-tree, ne the fresshe laurer greene,
Lady to Phebus bryght and shene,
To whome thyes gaye poetys bene homagers—
30 Thou in especyall that oonly in thy yeres
Deservede of hyr braunches to bere a coroune—
Shulde nott be holden in gretter renoune
Than remembraunce of that blessede tre
Thorowe whom all heele ys promitted to the! . . .

D

OSBERN BOKENHAM (?), A TRANSLATION OF CLAUDIAN, *DE CONSULATU STILICHONIS*

Rome Araieth Stilico in Vesture of the Consul

With thise maner yiftes the goddesse Rome the princys herte moevid,
Yivyng a ceptre unto his right hande, that of ivore was white,

Tookenys of deeth which loong were feeryd in haste she turnyd awey
With divers signes of prosperous lyfe by wedris and foulys take.
Than she araied his able aarmys with armour defensable,   5
And clothid him in Romulys roobys, which was hir first patrone;
The panys of Italie before his brest expressid his nobil birthe;
His habergeoun was with gowne wele coverid, such as Gradivus usid
What tyme he came from Histirlonde or Scicia as conquerour,
And wolde not shew his shelde of stele, ne harneys that was bright.   10
In riche roobys, with mylkewhite hors, he entrith the citee—
Quirinus his bridels governyd him by; Bellona this fadris chare
With riche clothis that al rede was, an oke beryng in hande,
Yede beforne, and evir hir handis unto the sterris helde up.
Metus as jailer sewid aftir the chare, and Pavor his brother clepid   15
Boonde the barbarys handis behynde with cheynes that were not
    smothe.
Thise personys tweyn had lorer boughes upon her helmes shene;
Whos hors folowid nere Formido righte bleike, beryng the axe of
    dethe. . . .

E

JOHN TIPTOFT, EARL OF WORCESTER, *THE DECLAMACION OF NOBLESSE*

True Nobility: Gaius Flaminius refutes Publius Cornelius, his Rival for the Hand of Lucretia

. . . Faders conscript, ye have understanden the playsyr of noble Lucresse touchyng the choys of us tweyne, and how Cornelius hath be bolde to descryve noblesse, and sette it in blood and rychesse, and so to preve that he is more noble than I, and ferthermore tolde of the worshipful dedes of his auncestres, and how grete rychesse and havoyrs his fadre had lefte to   5
hym. Soth it is that the substaunce of his speche resteth in this, but he caude nothyng remembre of hymself, that *he* had doo ony thyng worthy or dygne of rehersayll or remembraunce. And therfore he uttred nothyng of his owne lyf and maners. And forsothe I trowe that noblesse resteth not in the glorye of another man, or in the flyttyng goodes of fortune, but in a   10
mannes owen vertue and glorye; for what is noblesse other than a certayn excellence in vertue and manhode, whiche proveth one man worthy to be preferred another. For semblably as man excelleth alle other beestys, and not for his force but for his reason, so by the vertu that one man hath whiche another hath not, he excellyth hym. For whan a man hath be   15

exercised in the craftes of grettest noblesse, that is to saye in justice, pyté, constaunce, magnanymyté, attemperaunce, and prudence, deservying a fame of excellence in theym, and hath quyte hym wel to the goddes inmortall, to his fader and moder, to his frendes, kynne, and his contreye, and hath be nourysshed and brought up in the doctryne of lectrure, thenne 20 me semeth forsothe he shold be called and reputed more noble, worshipful, and more famous than another, as Corneli hymself saide a lytil byfore, whan he spak of his owne maners. And on that other syde, he that is corrupt with cursed craftes, and betaketh hymself to cruelnesse, rechelesnesse, cowardyse, dystemperaunce and injustyce, and gyveth no 25 force of relygyon, ne of the good wille of his frendes, or not to use pyté to his fader and moder in tyme of theyr nede, forsoth me semeth he shold be judged of alle men a wretche, unnoble, shameful, and worthy to be sette asyde fro alle good companye. It is not habondaunce of rychesse ne the noblenes of byrthe that may gyve or take away noblesse fro ony persone, 30 for the courage of man is the veray restyng-place of noblesse, the whiche dame Nature th'emperesse of alle thynges here bynethe hath ordeyned and establysshed to have chief preemynence in the lyf of man, and hath ensude it evenly in alle men mortall fro the fyrst day of theyr byrthe. And she nevir joined it to the enherytaunce of possessions, for she wyll be at 35 her lyberté and fredam by th'advyse of vertue to gyve it to whom she lyketh beste. And lykewise as a glasse or a myrrour wel made sheweth the fygure sette byfore it—yf it be faire, fairer, and yf it be fowle, fowler—so the courage which is pure and free is disposed to take noblesse or innoblesse indiffrently. And ther shold no man accuse the largesse of nature in this 40 moost best and excellent gyfte of fredom, for she gyveth to every man a lyke courage, and taketh none heede of theyr kynne, powerer or richer, for ther is no man so nedy, so vyle, ne so lytil sette by, but whan he is brought into this world he is endowed with as good courage as the sone of an emperour or kynge, and as apt to vertue and manhode.... 45

Cornely, thenne thynke, what be thy condicions, or what is thy disposicions? Where dydest thou ony thyng in thy dayes that thou canste reherce whereby thou woldest clayme or chalenge worship or noblesse? Where evyr receyved oure cyté ony benefete by the, or ony thyng of lawde, whereby it myght understonde that thou were born in this world, for thou 50 lyvest emong us here more lyke a dede man than a quyck. Where is there evir ony man that hath be holpen or relevyd by the? Where has thou used the noblesse and lyberalyté that thou spekyst of? Peradventure thou hast be prodygal unto wantone and unshamefaste creatures, and thereby thou hast wasted thy hows, thyne apparaylle, and alle thy goodes. Thou trowest 55 thyself thou art passyng worshipful whan thou hast alle thy loves aboute the, japynge, ragynge, and wrastlynge with theym in thy dronkenhede. And thenne to preche of the noble dedes of thyn olders! I wil not saye naye, but confesse that thyne auncestres have be of soverayne auctorité and worship

in this cyté. And thou, unwyseman, to thy grete shame, whan thou 60
remembrest thyne owne slouthe and symplenesse, ther may be nothyng be
more detestable or unthryfty than this is; for where thou haddest thyne
auncestres shynyng in worship lyke bryght Phebus, shewyng to the by
theyr clerenesse the streyght hye waye to the same, to lede so derke and so
blynde a lyf as thou doost, for they gaf to the a ful worshipful example in 65
many and dyverse wyses, how thou sholdest mowe deserve the grete lawde
and thanke of th'estate publyque. And by theyr bryghtnesse they shewed to
the the veray path to noblesse, as yf they shold saye: this waye we have
holde, and it is easy ynough unto the for to folowe us. And thou hast
forsaken the bryght path whiche ledeth to worship, and hast wilfully 70
drowned thyself in the derke pytte of foryetefulnesse. Trowest thou to
flowre in oure cyté by theyr merytes, whan thyself has so defowled the
same wyth thy vyces? And trowest thou to atteyne worship by theyr
benefayttes whan thou doste nothyng wel to our cyté? Supposest thou with
thy sleep, reste, ydelnesse, wyne, mangerye, lustys, and unshamefastnes, to 75
gete that worshipful fame whiche they gate by theyr laborous watches,
contynencys, hunger, thurst, hete, colde, and so many dyverse happes?
Thou doste erre ful hugely, for it must nedes be, yf thou wylt have suche
title of fame as they had, that thou make thyself suche in condycions and
maners as they were. Vertue is not a thynge of enherytaunce; and therfor 80
essaye whether thou mayst fynde suche reason and wysedom as they used,
for in theyr bequeste thou shalt not fynde that they bequethed to the their
vertue. . . .

. . . We complayne ofte causelees upon fortune, and therefore, Cornely,
stynte of thy booste of rychesse, whiche sheweth moche rather thy 85
cowardyse than manhode, and seace to despyse my meane suffysaunce of
goodes and seace to sette noblesse in the goodes of fortune, whiche be but
lente to us, and yet they ben flyttyng and unstable. Noblesse shold be
knytte to vertue, and vertue with noblesse, and ye maye, lady Lucresse,
which excell all other of this age in wysedom and beauté, knowe wel what 90
veray noblesse is, and by your grete wysedom ye have atteyned to the same.
And I wote wel the vulgar playes, the wantone array of wymmen, the
ryche owches sette with precious stones, the clothes of gold, the dayly
dawnsyng and syngynge, be not the thynges that please you moost, for ye
knowe all thies thynges ben but subgettis and servauntes to vicious and 95
dishonest thynges; for ye have gyven youre lyf to phylosophye, lyberall
studyes, continence, laboure, shamefastnesse, watches, and vertuous
besynesse. And in thiese, ye excelle alle other of youre yeres in this cyté,
and these ben the thynges that I love you in especial fore, and for the
which I shal payne me to please you and serve you; and ther be no thynges 100
which maye better be coupled, than suche as ben lyke in the noble desyres
of vertue and good will, and lyke maners and disposicion of lyvyng. And
ther is nothyng more grevous and disacordyng to love, than whan one

desireth vertue, and another desyreth vyce. Therfore, whyle I have some
105 convenyence with youre maner of lyvyng in vertue, and Cornelius in all
wyse difference, it must nedes shewe that ye love not hym, but love me.
For what pleasyr shold ye have to lyve with hym, whan ye are disposed to
the vertuouse besynesse of studye, and he is the gretest enemye that
science hath? And whan ye wolde feyne attende therto, he in his
110 dronkenesse, with his stomblyng, yoxing and pratyng shold lette you; ye
wold be glad to see your hous floure in shamefastnes and honesté, he wold
be glad on that other syde to see it servaunt to flesshely luste and ryote. Ye
wold be glad to speke with sad and connyng persones, and demaunde
theym of the merveyllous causes of thynges, of the moevynge of the
115 planetes, and the discyplyne of maners, and he emonge his companye of
wymmen abjecte wolde booste of ryote, unclenesse, and folye. And howe
may ther be reste or acorde bytwene tho courages, whiche be so gretely
dyfferent? But, my lady Lucresse, yf it please you, I shal brynge you to my
poure lodgyng, where ye shal fynde quyete reste. And howbeit that yf it be
120 not so superfluously beseen as Cornelius is, yet I truste ye shal fynde it
bettir furnysshed of vertue, maner, and suche pleasyrs, as youre moost
womanly courage delyteth in. And fyrst I shal shewe you my lyberary, wel
stuffed with fayr bookes of Greke and Latyn, wherunto in every adversyté
is my chief resorte for counseyll and comforte. And ther shall we dyverse
125 tymes have commynycacyon and comforte of the connynge and doctryne
of my lady and maystresse phylosophye; and there I shal repete to you the
merveyllous doctryne of the philosophers of Athenes, whiche I have herd
and enjoye me gretly whan I remember it. No besynes of famylyar thynges
shal agayn your wyll departe you from suche plesaunt ydelnes, for I truste
130 to oure goddes that my lytil feelde, of the which I am enbrayded by
Corneli, shal suffise for our dayly lyvelode. Nevirtheles one thyng I have in
avauntage that he hath not, for though my lytil feeld were take away fro
me, my connynge and lectrure by whiche I shold mowe atteyne to gretter
possessions than that, duryng my lyf cannot be taken from me. As
135 touchyng to you, madame, it shal be in your free choyse, whether ye wil be
ydle or studye. And yf it please you to studye, ther shal be none so hardy to
breke your plesaunt thoughtes in that byhalve, ne ther shal no chaterynge
or janglynge of unchast wymmen lette your studye or cause you to fere of
the stable love of your true servaunt. And the cause of oure maryage shal
140 with joyous love right sone be had to your playsyr, I truste to our goddes no
doubte of. Th'ordre of matrymony is as it were a dyvyne relygion for the
conservacion of mankynde, to the whiche yf it shal please you t'entende in
suche wyse as I have said, I truste ye shal thynke yourself evir hereaftir
durynge youre lyf more and more fortunat, for what maye be more blessyd
145 in this temporal lyf for you, than to passe your age in tranquyll
joyousnesse, vertue, and noble fame. And what is more vertuous than to
occupye youre mynde in good and vertuous thoughtes, and what more

joyous than to take hym for your perpetuel servaunt and soveraynly delyteth ih that which ye chyefly desyre? Therfore, ye faders conscript, in whos grete wysedomes resteth the jugement and conclusion of this 150 contravercye, weye ye in your brestys what I have said, and publysshe ye rypely and soone youre sentence touchyng this contencion. We stryve for noblesse, and whiche of us two shold be reputed more noble; and in that byhalve our lyf, our fortune, our studye, and maners, howbeit they were wel knowen to youre noble advertences, yet now they be in bryef 155 remembred. Nevirtheles, th'yssue of this contravercye is this: this day honesté stryveth with unshamefastnes, contynence with luste, magnanymyté with cowardyse, lectrure with inscience, and vertue with neglygence. And whether of thise partyes is the better, I leve it to your dome and sentence.

F

A Lytell Treatyse for to Lerne Englysshe and Frensshe

For to aske the waye	*Pour demander le chemin*	
Frende, god save you	Amy, dieu vous sauve	
Whiche is the ryght waye	Quelle est la voye droite	
For to goo from hens to Parys?	Pour aller d'icy a Paris?	
Syr, ye muste holde the waye on the ryght hande.	Sire, il vous fault tenir le chemin a la droite main.	5
Now saye me, my frende,	Or me dites, mon amy,	
Yf that ony good lodgynge	Y'a il point de bon logis	
Be betwixt this and the next vyllage?	Entre cy et ce prochayn village?	
There is a ryght good one.	Il en y'a ung tresbon.	
Ye shall be there ryght well lodged	Vous serez tresbien logé.	10
Ye and also your horse.	Vous et aussi vostre chevaul.	
My frende, God yelde it you.	Mon ami, dieu vous le rende,	
And I shall doo an other tyme	Et je feraye ung aultre fois	
As moche for you, and I maye.	Autant pour vous se je puis.	
God be with you.	Dieu soit avecques vous.	15
Dame, shall I be here well lodged?	Dame, seroy je icy bien logé?	
Ye syr, ryght well.	Ouy sire, tresbien.	
Nowe doo me have a good chambre	Or me faites avoir ungne bonne chambre.	
And a good fyre	Et bon feu	20
And doo that my horse	Et faites que mon chevaul	
Maye be well governed	Puisse estre bien governé	

275

And gyve hym good hay and good otes.	Et lui donnes bon foin et bon avoine.
Dame, is all redy for to dyne?	Dame, est tout prest pour aller digner?
25 Ye syr, whan it please you.	Oui sire, quant il vous plaise.
Syr, moche good do it you.	Sire, bon preu vous face.
I praye you make good chere	Je vous prie faictes bonne chere.
And be mery—I drynke to you!	Et soiez joieux, je boy a vous!
Now hostes, saye me howe moche have we spende at this dyner?	Hostesse, or me dites combien nous avons despendu a ce digner?
30	
I shall tell you with a good wyll	Je le vous diray voulenticrs
Ye have in alle eyght shelynges. . . .	Vous avez en tout huyt sols. . . .

G

Sentences from a Tudor *Vulgaria*

Put off shortely that longe hevy gowne and have a lyghter, and lete us go to Hedynton grove and ther we shall have an hare stert. Why standist thou styll? Se how the wether lokyth up lustely agayne our jorneye.

'Gode spede, praty childe!' 'And youe also.' 'I know that ye have lurned
5 youre grammer, but wher, I pray youe?' 'By my faith, sum at Wynchester, sum in other places.' 'And I am an Oxforde man. Woll youe we shall assay how we can talke in Latyn?' 'Yee, for Gode, ryght fayne!'

Wolde it not angre a man to be lyde upon of this fascyon? Thei say that I kepe a dawe in my chambre, but iwys thei lye falsly upon me, for it is but a
10 pore conye.

All the yonge folkes almoste of this towne dyde rune yesterday to the castell to se a bere batyde with fers dogges within the wallys. It was greatly to be wondred for he dyde defend hymselfe so with hys craftynes and his wyllynes from the cruell doggys methought he sett not a whitt be their
15 woodenes nor by their fersnes.

Many scholars of this université wolde spende wastfully all their fathers goodes in japys and trifulles this faire yf they myght have it at their liberté, for thies Londyners be so craftye and so wyly in dressynge their gere so gloriusly that they may deceyve us scholars lyghtly.

20 Yesterdaye, I departyde asyde prively oute of the feldys from my felows

276

and went be myselfe into a manys orcherde wher I dyde not only ete rype apples my bely full, but I toke away as many as I coulde bere.

I was yesternyght late at Carfaxe with strangers. When we hade stonde styll a whyle, we perceyvede that ther were certeyne getters, and as sone as we saw them, I ranne away as faste as I coulde, that for overmych hast I fell in the myer. 25

It is a great pité (in my mynde) to see scholars so corruppede as nowadais, be reason of over great liberté, of the which sum ther be that sitt bousynge and drynkynge so late in the nyght that in the mornynge they be so slogguysh they cannot holde upe their hedys. And sum, contrary, use so 30 immesurable slepe that they seme to take hede of non other thynge except mete and drynke, the which they muste nedys have to suffice nature. Thies be suche as ye se swolne in the face and holow eyde, with pale colour and bent, fadyde, rather seme to be apte to ber a tankerd then a booke in their hondys. 35

It is a worlde to se the delectacioun and pleasur that a man shall have which riseth erly in thies summer mornynges, for the very dew shal be so confortable to hym that it shal cause hym inwardely to rejose; beside that, to here the birdes synge on every side, the larke, the jais, and the sparowe, with many other, a man wolde thynke he hade an hevenly lyff. Who wolde 40 than lye thus loterynge in his bedde, brother, as thou dost, and gyve hymself only to slepe, be the which thou shalt hurt greatly thyself and also short the tyme of thy lyff? It shall cause the, furthermore, to be dull and voide of connynge, withoute which lyff and deth be both on.

Upon a faire, clere nyght, the skye garnyshede with sterrys oute off 45 nombre shynnyth goodely, whych and ye take hede ye may see them twynkle as it were a candle or a tapre brennynge, and emonge them the moone with hire full light goith forth by litell and litell, glidynge softly. Be not thies pleasant thynges?

The worlde waxeth worse every day, and all is turnede upside down, 50 contrary to th'olde guyse; for all that was to me a pleasure when I was a childe, from .iii. yere olde to .x. (for now I go upon the .xii. yere) while I was undre my father and mothers kepyng, be tornyde now to tormentes and payne. For than I was wont to lye styll abedde tyll it was forth dais, delitynge myself in slepe and ease. The sone sent in his beamys at the 55 wyndowes, that gave me lyght in stede of a candle. O, what a sporte it was every mornynge when the son was upe to take my lusty pleasur betwixte the shetes, to beholde the rofe, the beamys, and the rafters of my chambre, and loke on the clothes that the chambre was hangede with. Ther durste

60 no man but he were made awake me oute of my slepe upon his owne hede
while me list to slepe. At my wyll I arose with intreatese, and whan
th'appetite of rest went his way by his owne accord, than I awoke and
callede whom me list to lay my gere redy to me. My brekefaste was brought
to my beddys side as ofte as me liste to call therfor, and so many tymes I
65 was first fedde or I were cledde. So I hade many pleasurs mo besides thes,
wherof sum be forgoten, sum I do remembre well, but I have no leysure to
reherce them nowe. But nowe the worlde rennyth upon another whele, for
nowe at fyve of the clocke by the monelyght I most go to my booke and lete
slepe and slouthe alon, and yff oure maister hape to awake us, he bryngeth
70 a rode stede of a candle. Now I leve pleasurs that I hade sumtyme. Here is
nought els preferryde but monyshynge and strypys; brekfastes that were
sumtyme brought at my biddynge is dryven oute of contrey and never shall
cum agayne. I wolde tell more of my mysfortunes, but thoughe I have
leysure to say, yet I have no pleasure, for the reherse of them makyth my
75 mynde more hevy. I sech all the ways I can to lyve ons at myn ease, that I
myght rise and go to the bede when me liste oute of the fere of betynge.

As I was chepynge of a booke, ther cam on that proferd mor than I, and
bought it oute of my handes.

As I walked be the woode side, I herde a thrushe synge merely, and the
80 blake osell and the nychtyngall.

H

Colet's Statutes for St Paul's School

... Theare shalbe taught in the scoole children of all naciouns and
countreys indifferently to the noumber of .cliii. acordynge to the noumber
of the setes in the scoole.

The High Maister shall admytt thes childre as they shalbe offeryde fro
5 tyme to tyme, but fyrste see theye can theyre catechison, and also that he
can rede and write competentlye, elles lett hym not be admyttyde in no
wyse. . . .

The children shall come unto the scoole in the mornynge at .vii. of the
cloke bothe winter and somer and tarye theare untyll a .xi. and retourne
10 agen at one of the cloke and departe at .v. and thrise in the day prostrate
they shall saye the prayers with due tracte and pawsinge, as theye be

278

conteynyde in a table in the scoole, that is to saye in the mornynge and at none and at evenynge. . . .

    Also I will thay bringe no mete or drynke nether botelles, nor use in the scole no brekefaste nor drynkynge in the time of lernynge in no wise; yf 15 they nede drynke let theme be provydyde in sum other place.

    . . . In generall processions whene they be warnyde theye shall go tweyne and tweyne togither soberly and not synge oute, but saye devoutly tweyne and tweyne .vii. psalmes with latany.

    . . . As touching in this scoole what shalbe taughte of the maisters and 20 lernyde of the scolers it passith my wyte to devyse and determyn in particler but in generall to speke and sumwhat to saye my mynde, I wolde there were taughte alway the good litterature bothe Laten and Greeke, and goode auctours suche as have the veray Romayne eloquence joynyde withe wisdome, specially Cristen auctours that wrote there wisdome with clene 25 and chast Latten, other in verse or in prose, for my entent is by this scoole specially to encrease knowlege and worshippinge of God and of oure lorde Crist Jesu and good Cristen life and maners in the children. And for that entente, I will the children lerne firste and above all the cathechizone in Inglyshe, and after the *Accydence* that I made, or sum other yf eny be better 30 to the purpose to induce children more spedely to Laten speche, and then *Institutum Christiani Hominis*, whiche that lernyde Erasmus made at my requeste, and the boke called *Copia* of the same Erasmus; and then other auctours Christians as Lactantius, Prudentius, and Proba, and Sedulius, and Juvencus, and Baptista Mantuanus, and suche other as shalbe 35 thoughte convenyent and moste to purpose unto true Laten spech. All barbarye and corrupcioun, all Laten adulterate, whiche ignorant blynde foles broughte into this worlde and with that same hathe distaynyde and poysonyde the olde Laten speche and the veray Romayne tonge, which in the tyme of Tully and Salust and Virgill and Terence was usid, which also 40 saynte Jerome, and saynte Ambrose, and saynte Augustyne and many holy doctors lernyd in there tymes, I say that fylthenes and all suche abusyon wich the latter blynde worlde broughte in, whiche more rather may be callyde blotterature thenne litterature, I utterly abbanyshe and exclude oute of this scoole, and charge the maisters that theye teche alway that is 45 the best, and instructe the children in Greke and Laten in redynge unto them suche auctours that hathe with wysdome joinyde the pure chaste eloquence.

18

ROBERT HENRYSON

THE death (? 1505) of 'Master Robert Henryson' is recorded in Dunbar's 'Lament for the Makers' (No. 19 F); of his life little is known. He was a graduate of some university; the tradition that he was a schoolmaster at Dunfermline seems well founded. If he is the 'venerabilis vir Magister Robertus Henrisone' admitted as a member of the University of Glasgow in 1462, the adjective *venerabilis* would suggest that he was not then a young man, and would support the view that he flourished in the mid-fifteenth century. Henryson stands out as one of the most impressive and original poets of the period; the full range and complexity of his art are only now being realized. Of a number of short poems attributed to him, *Robene and Makene* has long been a favourite. It is no lifeless imitation of classical pastoral or French *pastourelle*, but a merry tale of Scottish country life, wittily and ironically presenting the wayward paths of love and the consequences of missing an opportunity. Henryson's collection of thirteen fables (from the Latin 'Aesop' and the tales of Reynard the Fox) is a masterpiece. Indeed, apart from Chaucer's *Nun's Priest's Tale*, the animal fable has never been better handled in English. Our example (which should be compared with the rudimentary version translated by Caxton, No. 15 D) illustrates some of the skills he brought to this demanding 'miniature' form—the clever exploitation of the shifting relationship between animal and human in his speaking animals, the sudden revelation of a personality through gesture or remark (cf. the wether's 'It is not the lamb, bot the, that I desyre'), a delicate sense of narrative rhythm, a characteristic blending of 'earnest' and 'game', of sympathy and detached irony. The grim and sudden ending (for those who lack prudence or cunning or luck the little world of 'Aesop' is a perilous place) leads easily to the 'fructuous sentence' of the morality (a traditional and essential part of a fable), the need for self-knowledge and an awareness of one's limitations. *The Testament of Cresseid* is a powerful, disturbing poem, which has aroused considerable debate. It is a tragedy (line 4)—that is, a 'cairfull dyte'—which tells the fate of the heroine of Chaucer's *Troilus and Criseyde* after her shameful 'exclusion' by Diomede. Possibly Henryson invented the story, possibly the 'uther quair' of line 61 really did exist. It excites pity and horror; the pathos is emphasized by the eloquent laments and the intense and passionate outbursts that are part of the style of a medieval tragedy. The poet-narrator is both a dramaturge, presenting the action, and a choric voice, commenting upon it. The pity that he—like some of the human bystanders—expresses sets off the horror of the living death which is the nemesis that follows Cresseid's blasphemy against the gods. The ending of the poem after the strange meeting with Troilus is enigmatic: some critics see some kind of 'redemption' for Cresseid; others see only a degree of painful self-recognition and remorse, before death brings her to a 'short conclusion'.

A

Robene and Makyne

Robene sat on gud grene hill
Kepand a flok of fe;
Mirry Makyne said him till:
'Robene, thow rew on me!
I haif the luvit lowd and still   5
Thir yeiris two or thre;
My dule in dern bot gif thow dill,
Dowtles but dreid I de.'

Robene ansuerit: 'Be the rude!
Nathing of lufe I knaw,   10
Bot keipis my scheip under yone wude—
Lo, quhair thay raik on raw!
Quhat hes marrit the in thy mude,
Makyne, to me thow schaw:
Or quhat is lufe, or to be lude?   15
Fane wald I leir that law.'

'At luvis lair gife thow will leir,
Take thair ane ABC:
Be heynd, courtas, and fair of feir,
Wyse, hardy, and fre;   20
So that no denger do the deir,
Quhat dule in dern thow dre,
Preis the with pane at all poweir—
Be patient and previe.'

Robene ansuerit hir agane: 25
'I wait nocht quhat is luve,
Bot I haif mervell in certane
Quhat makis the this wanrufe;
The weddir is fair and I am fane,
My scheip gois haill aboif;   30
And we wald play ws in this plane
Thay wald ws bayth reproif.'

'Robene, tak tent unto my taill,
And wirk all as I reid,
And thow sall haif my hairt all haill,
Eik and my madinheid:
Sen God sendis bute for baill
And for murning remeid,
I dern with the bot gif I daill,
Dowtles I am bot deid.'

'Makyne, tomorne this ilka tyde,
And ye will meit me heir,
Perauenture my scheip ma gang besyd
Quhill we haif liggit full neir—
Bot mawgré haif I, and I byd,
Fra thay begin to steir;
Quhat lyis on hairt I will nocht hyd;
Makyn, than mak gud cheir.'

'Robene, thow reivis me roif and rest—
I luve bot the allone.'
'Makyne, adew; the sone gois west,
The day is neir-hand gone.'
'Robene, in dule I am so drest
That lufe wil be my bone.'
'Ga lufe, Makyne, quhairever thow list,
For lemman I bid none.'

'Robene, I stand in sic a styll;
I sicht—and that full sair.'
'Makyne, I haif bene heir this quhyle;
At hame God gif I wair!'
'My huny Robene, talk ane quhyll,
Gif thow will do na mair.'
'Makyne, sum uthir man begyle,
For hamewart I will fair.'

Robene on his wayis went
Als licht as leif of tre;
Mawkin murnit in hir intent
And trowd him neuir to se.
Robene brayd attour the bent;
Than Mawkyne cryit on hie:
'Now ma thow sing, for I am schent!
Quhat alis lufe at me?'

Mawkyne went hame withowttin faill;
Full wery eftir cowth weip:
Than Robene in a ful fair daill
Assemblit all his scheip.
Be that, sum pairte of Mawkynis aill
Outthrow his hairt cowd creip;
He fallowit fast thair till assaill,
And till hir tuke gude keip.

'Abyd, abyd, thow fair Makyne!
A word for ony thing!
For all my luve it sal be thyne,
Withowttin depairting.
All haill thy harte for till haif myne
Is all my cuvating;
My scheip tomorne quhill houris nyne
Will neid of no keiping.'

'Robene, thow hes hard soung and say
In gestis and storeis auld,
The man that will nocht quhen he may
Sall haif nocht quhen he wald.
I pray to Jesu every day
Mot eik thair cairis cauld
That first preisis with the to play
Be firth, forrest or fawld.'

'Makyne, the nicht is soft and dry,
The wedder is warme and fair,
And the grene woid rycht neir ws by
To walk attour allquhair;
Thair ma na janglour ws espy,
That is to lufe contrair;
Thairin, Makyne, bath ye and I
Unsene we ma repair.'

'Robene, that warld is all away
And quyt brocht till ane end,
And neuir agane thairto perfay,
Sall it be as thow wend:
For of my pane thow maid it play,
And all in vane I spend:
As thow hes done, sa sall I say:
Murne on! I think to mend.'

75

80

85

90

95

100

105

110

'Mawkyne, the howp of all my heill,
My hairt on the is sett,
115   And evirmair to the be leill,
Quhill I may leif but lett;
Nevir to faill as utheris feill,
Quhat grace that euir I gett.'
'Robene, with the I will nocht deill;
120   Adew! For thus we mett.'

Malkyne went hame blyth annewche
Attour the holttis hair:
Robene murnit, and Malkyne lewche,
Scho sang, he sichit sair—
125   And so left him bayth wo and wewche,
In dolour and in cair,
Kepand his hird under a huche,
Amang the holtis hair.

B

The Taill of the Wolf and the Wedder

Qwhylum thair wes, as Esope can report,
Ane scheipheird duelland be ane forrest neir,
Quhilk had ane hound that did him grit comfort;
Full war he wes to walk his fauld but weir,
5   That nouther wolff, nor wildcat durst appeir,
Nor foxe on feild nor yit no uther beist—
Bot he thame slew or chaissit at the leist.

Sa happinnit it—as euerilk beist man de—
This hound of suddand seiknes to be deid;
10   Bot than, God wait, the keipar off the fe
For verray wo woxe wanner nor the weid:
'Allace,' quod he, 'now se I na remeid
To saif the selie beistis that I keip,
For with the wolff weryit beis all my scheip!'

15   It wald have maid ane mannis hart sair to se
The selie scheiphirdis lamentatioun:
'Now is my darling deid, allace!' quod he;

'For now to beg my breid I may be boun,
With pyikstaff and with scrip to fair off toun;
For all the beistis befoir that bandonit bene
Will schute upon my beistis with ire and tene!'   20

With that ane wedder wichtlie wan on fute:
'Maister,' quod he, 'mak merie and be blyith:
To brek your hart for baill it is na bute;
For ane deid dogge ye na cair on yow kyith: 25
Ga fetche him hither and fla his skyn off swyth;
Syne sew it on me—and luke that it be meit,
Baith heid and crag, bodie, taill and feit.

'Than will the wolff trow that I am he,
For I sall follow him fast quhareuer he fair.   30
All haill the cure I tak it upon me
Your scheip to keip at midday, lait and air.
And he persew, be God, I sall not spair
To follow him as fast as did your doig,
Swa that I warrand ye sall not want ane hoig.'   35

Than said the scheipheird: 'This come of ane gude wit;
Thy counsall is baith sicker, leill and trew;
Quha sayis ane scheip is daft, thay lieit of it.'
With that in hy the doggis skyn off he flew
And on the scheip rycht softlie couth it sew.   40
Than worth the wedder wantoun off his weid:
'Now off the wolff', quod he, 'I have na dreid.'

In all thingis he counterfait the dog.
For all the nycht he stude and tuke na sleip—
Swa that weill lang thair wantit not ane hog: 45
Swa war he wes and walkryfe thame to keip,
That Lowrence durst not luke upon ane scheip—
For and he did, he followit him sa fast
That off his lyfe he maid him all agast.

Was nowther wolff, wildcat nor yit tod   50
Durst cum within thay boundis all about,
Bot he wald chase tham baith throw rouch and snod;
Thay bailfull beistis had of their lyvis sic dout,
For he wes mekill and semit to be stout,
That everilk beist thay dreid him as the deid   55
Within that woid, that nane durst hald thair heid.

Yit happinnit thair ane hungrie wolff to slyde
Outthrow his scheip quhair thay lay on ane le;
'I sall have ane,' quod he, 'quhateuer betyde—
60   Thocht I be werryit, for hunger or I de!'
With that ane lamb intill his cluke hint he.
The laif start up for thay wer all agast:
Bot God wait gif the wedder followit fast!

Went never hound mair haistelie fra the hand
65   Quhen he wes rynnand maist raklie at the ra
Nor went this wedder baith ouer mois and strand,
And stoppit nouther at bank, busk nor bra,
Bot followit ay sa ferslie on his fa,
With sic ane drift, quhill dust and dirt ouerdraif him,
70   And maid ane vow to God that he suld have him.

With that the wolff let out his taill on lenth,
For he wes hungrie and it drew neir the ene,
And schupe him for to ryn with all his strenth,
Fra he the wedder sa neir cummand had sene:
75   He dred his lyfe and he ouertane had bene;
Thairfoir he spairit nowther busk nor boig,
For weill he kennit the kenenes off the doig.

To mak him lycht he kest the lamb him fra,
Syne lap ouer leis and draif throw dub and myre.
80   'Na,' quod the wedder, 'in faith, we part not swa:
It is not the lamb bot the that I desyre!
I sall cum neir, for now I se the tyre.'
The wolff ran till ane rekill stude behind him—
Bot ay the neirar the wedder he couth bind him.

85   Sone efter that he followit him sa neir
Quhill that the wolff for fleidnes fylit the feild;
Syne left the gait and ran throw busk and breir,
And schupe him fra the schawis for to scheild.
He ran restles, for he wist off na beild;
90   The wedder followit him baith out and in,
Quhill that ane breir-busk raif rudelie off the skyn.

The wolff wes wer and blenkit him behind
And saw the wedder come thrawand throw the breir,
Syne saw the doggis skyn hingand on his lind:
95   'Na,' quod he, 'is this ye that is sa neir?

Richt now ane hound and now quhyte as ane freir;
I fled ouer-fer and I had kennit the cais:
To God I vow that ye sall rew this rais!

'Quhat wes the cause ye gaif me sic ane katche?'
With that in hy he hint him be the horne: 100
'For all your mowis ye met anis with your matche,
Suppois ye leuch me all this yeir to scorne.
For quhat enchessoun this doggis skyn have ye borne?'
'Maister,' quod he, 'bot to have playit with yow;
I yow requyre that ye nane uther trow.'   105

'Is this your bourding in ernist than?' quod he:
'For I am verray effeirit and on flocht;
Cum bak agane, and I sall let yow se.'
Than quhar the gait wes grimmit he him brocht:
'Quhether call ye this fair play or nocht—   110
To set your maister in sa fell effray
Quhill he for feiritnes hes fylit up the way?

'Thryis, be my saull, ye gart me schute behind—
Upon my hoichis the senyeis may be sene;
For feiritnes full oft I fylit the wind: 115
Now is this ye? Na, bot ane hound I wene!
Me think your teith ouer-schort to be sa kene.
Blissit be the busk that reft yow your array,
Ellis fleand, bursin had I bene this day!'

'Schir,' quod the wedder, 'suppois I ran in hy,   120
My mynd wes neuer to do your persoun ill;
Ane flear gettis ane follower commounly,
In play or ernist—preif quhassaeuer will:
Sen I bot playit, be gracious me till,
And I sall gar my freindis blis your banis: 125
Ane full gude servand will crab his maister anis.'

'I have bene oftymis set in grit effray;
Bot be the rude, sa rad yit wes I neuer
As thow hes maid me with thy prettie play.
I schot behind quhen thow ouertuke me euer;   130
Bot sikkerlie now sall we not disseuer!'
Than be the crag-bane smertlie he him tuke
Or euer he ceissit, and it in schunder schuke.

Moralitas

Esope that poete, first father of this fabill,
135 Wrait this parabole—quhilk is convenient
Because the sentence wes fructuous and agreabill,
In moralitie exemplative prudent—
Quhais problemes bene verray excellent;
Throw similitude of figuris, to this day,
140 Geuis doctrine to the redaris of it ay.

Heir may thow se that riches of array
Will cause pure men presumpteous for to be;
Thay think thay hald of nane, be thay als gay,
Bot counterfute ane lord in all degré.
145 Out of thair cais in pryde thay clym sa hie
That thay forbeir thair better in na steid,
Quhill sum man tit thair heillis ouer thair heid.

Richt swa in service uther sum exceidis,
And thay haif withgang, welth, and cherising,
150 That thay will lychtlie lordis in thair deidis,
And lukis not to thair blude nor thair offspring;
Bot yit nane wait how lang that reull will ring;
Bot he wes wyse that bad his sone considder:
'Bewar in welth, for hall-benkis ar rycht slidder!'

155 Thairfoir I counsell men of everilk stait
To knaw thameself and quhome thay suld forbeir,
And fall not with thair better in debait,
Suppois thay be als galland in thair geir:
It settis na servand for to uphald weir,
160 Nor clym sa hie quhill he fall of the ledder;
Bot think upon the wolf and on the wedder.

C

The Testament of Cresseid

Ane doolie sessoun to ane cairfull dyte
Suld correspond and be equivalent:
Richt sa it wes quhen I began to wryte

288

This tragedie, the wedder richt fervent,
Quhen Aries, in middis of the Lent,   5
Schouris of haill gart fra the north discend,
That scantlie fra the cauld I micht defend.

Yit neuertheles within myne oratur
I stude, quhen Titan had his bemis bricht
Withdrawin doun and sylit under cure,   10
And fair Venus, the bewtie of the nicht,
Uprais and set unto the west full richt
Hir goldin face, in oppositioun
Of God Phebus, direct discending doun.

Throwout the glas hir bemis brast sa fair   15
That I micht se on everie syde me by;
The northin wind had purifyit the air
And sched the mistie cloudis fra the sky;
The froist freisit, the blastis bitterly
Fra Pole Artick come quhisling loud and schill,   20
And causit me remufe aganis my will.

For I traistit that Venus, luifis quene,
To quhome sumtyme I hecht obedience,
My faidit hart of lufe scho wald mak grene,
And therupon with humbill reverence   25
I thocht to pray hir hie magnificence;
Bot for greit cald as than I lattit was
And in my chalmer to the fyre can pas.

Thocht lufe be hait, yit in ane man of age
It kendillis nocht sa sone as in youtheid,   30
Of quhome the blude is flowing in ane rage;
And in the auld the curage doif and deid
Of quhilk the fyre outward is best remeid:
To help be phisike quhair that nature faillit
I am expert, for baith I have assaillit.   35

I mend the fyre and beikit me about,
Than tuik ane drink, my spreitis to comfort,
And armit me weill fra tha cauld thairout.
To cut the winter nicht and mak it schort
I tuik ane quair—and left all uther sport—   40
Writtin be worthie Chaucer glorious
Of fair Creisseid and worthie Troylus.

And thair I fand, efter that Diomeid
Ressavit had that lady bricht of hew,
45   How Troilus neir out of wit abraid
And weipit soir with visage paill of hew;
For quhilk wanhope his teiris can renew,
Quhill esperans rejoisit him agane:
Thus quhyle in joy he levit, quhyle in pane.

50   Of hir behest he had greit comforting,
Traisting to Troy that scho suld mak retour,
Quhilk he desyrit maist of eirdly thing,
Forquhy scho was his only paramour.
Bot quhen he saw passit baith day and hour
55   Of hir ganecome, than sorrow can oppres
His wofull hart in cair and hevines.

Of his distres me neidis nocht reheirs,
For worthie Chauceir in the samin buik,
In gudelie termis and in joly veirs,
60   Compylit hes his cairis, quha will luik.
To brek my sleip ane uther quair I tuik,
In quhilk I fand the fatall destenie
Of fair Cresseid, that endit wretchitlie.

Quha wait gif all that Chauceir wrait was trew?
65   Nor I wait nocht gif this narratioun
Be authoreist, or fenyeit of the new
Be sum poeit, throw his inventioun
Maid to report the lamentatioun
And wofull end of this lustie Creisseid,
70   And quhat distres scho thoillit, and quhat deid.

Quhen Diomeid had all his appetyte,
And mair, fulfillit of this fair ladie,
Upon ane uther he set his haill delyte,
And send to hir ane lybell of repudie
75   And hir excludit fra his companie.
Than desolait scho walkit up and doun,
And sum men sayis, into the court, commoun.

O fair Cresseid, the flour and A per se
Of Troy and Grece, how was thow fortunait
80   To change in filth all thy feminitie,
And be with fleschelie lust sa maculait,

And go amang the Greikis air and lait,
Sa giglotlike takand thy foull plesance!
I have pietie thow suld fall sic mischance!

Yit neuertheles, quhateuer men deme or say   85
In scornefull langage of thy brukkilnes,
I sall excuse als far furth as I may
Thy womanheid, thy wisdome and fairnes,
The quhilk Fortoun hes put to sic distres
As hir pleisit, and nathing throw the gilt   90
Of the, throw wickit langage to be spilt!

This fair lady, in this wyse destitute
Of all comfort and consolatioun,
Richt privelie, but fellowschip or refute,
Disagysit passit far out of the toun   95
Ane myle or twa, unto ane mansioun
Beildit full gay, quhair hir father Calchas
Quhilk than amang the Greikis dwelland was.

Quhen he hir saw, the caus he can inquyre
Of hir cumming; scho said, siching full soir: 100
'Fra Diomeid had gottin his desyre
He wox werie and wald of me no moir.'
Quod Calchas: 'Douchter, weip thow not thairfoir;
Peraventure all cummis for the best.
Welcum to me; thow art ful deir ane gest!'   105

This auld Calchas, efter the law was tho,
Wes keiper of the tempill as ane preist
In quhilk Venus and hir sone Cupido
War honourit, and his chalmer was thame neist;
To quhilk Cresseid, with baill aneuch in breist,   110
Usit to pas, hir prayeris for to say,
Quhill at the last, upon ane solempne day,

As custome was, the pepill far and neir
Befoir the none unto the tempill went
With sacrifice, devoit in thair maneir;   115
Bot still Cresseid, hevie in hir intent,
Into the kirk wald not hirself present,
For giving of the pepill ony deming
Of hir expuls fra Diomeid the king;

120 Bot past into ane secreit orature,
    Quhair scho micht weip hir wofull desteny.
    Behind hir bak scho cloisit fast the dure,
    And on hir kneis bair fell doun in hy;
    Upon Venus and Cupide angerly
125 Scho cryit out, and said on this same wyse:
    'Allace, that euer I maid yow sacrifice!

    'Ye gave me anis ane devine responsaill
    That I suld be the flour of luif in Troy;
    Now am I maid ane unworthie outwaill,
130 And all in cair translatit is my joy.
    Quha sall me gyde? Quha sall me now convoy,
    Sen I fra Diomeid and nobill Troylus
    Am clene excludit, as abject odious?

    'O fals Cupide, is nane to wyte bot thow
135 And thy mother, of lufe the blind goddes!
    Ye causit me alwayis understand and trow
    The seid of lufe was sawin in my face,
    And ay grew grene throw your supplie and grace.
    But now, allace, that seid with froist is slane,
140 And I fra luifferis left and all forlane!'

    Quhen this was said, doun in ane extasie,
    Ravischit in spreit, intill ane dreame scho fell,
    And be apperance hard, quhair scho did ly,
    Cupide the king ringand ane silver bell,
145 Quhilk men micht heir fra hevin unto hell;
    At quhais sound befoir Cupide appeiris
    The sevin planetis, discending fra thair spheiris;

    Quhilk hes power of all thing generabill,
    To reull and steir be thair greit influence
150 Wedder and wind, and coursis variabill:
    And first of all Saturne gave his sentence,
    Quhilk gave to Cupide litill reverence,
    Bot as ane busteous churle on his maneir
    Come crabitlie with auster luik and cheir.

155 His face fronsit, his lyre was lyke the leid,
    His teith chatterit and cheverit with the chin,
    His ene drowpit, how sonkin in his heid,
    Out of his nois the meldrop fast can rin,

With lippis bla and cheikis leine and thin;
The ice-schoklis that fra his hair doun hang   160
Was wonder greit, and as ane speir als lang:

Atouir his belt his lyart lokkis lay
Felterit unfair, ouirfret with froistis hoir,
His garmound and his gyte full gay of gray,
His widderit weid fra him the wind out woir,   165
Ane busteous bow within his hand he boir
Under his girdill ane flasche of felloun flanis
Fedderit with ice and heidit with hailstanis.

Than Juppiter, richt fair and amiabill,
God of the starnis in the firmament   170
And nureis to all thing generabill;
Fra his father Saturne far different,
With burelie face and browis bricht and brent,
Upon his heid ane garland wonder gay
Of flouris fair, as it had bene in May.   175

His voice was cleir, as cristall wer his ene,
As goldin wyre sa glitterand was his hair,
His garmound and his gyte full gay of grene
With goldin listis gilt on everie gair;
Ane burelie brand about his middill bair,   180
In his richt hand he had ane groundin speir,
Of his father the wraith fra us to weir.

Nixt efter him come Mars the god of ire,
Of strife, debait, and all dissensioun,
To chide and fecht, als feirs as ony fyre,   185
In hard harnes, hewmound and habirgeoun,
And on his hanche ane roustie fell fachioun,
And in his hand he had ane roustie sword,
Wrything his face with mony angrie word.

Schaikand his sword, befoir Cupide he come,   190
With reid visage and grislie glowrand ene,
And at his mouth ane bullar stude of fome,
Lyke to ane bair quhetting his tuskis kene;
Richt tuilyeour-lyke but temperance in tene,
Ane horne he blew with mony bosteous brag,   195
Quhilk all this warld with weir hes maid to wag.

Than fair Phebus, lanterne and lamp of licht,
Of man and beist, baith frute and flourisching,
Tender nureis, and banischer of nicht;
200   And of the warld causing be his moving
And influence lyfe in all cirdlie thing,
Without comfort of quhome, of force to nocht
Must all ga die that in this warld is wrocht.

As king royall be raid upon his chair,
205   The quhilk Phaeton gydit sum tyme unricht
The brichtnes of his face quhen it was bair
Nane micht behald for peirsing of his sicht;
This goldin cart with fyrie bemis bricht
Four yokkit steidis full different of hew
210   But bait or tyring throw the spheiris drew.

The first was soyr, with mane als reid as rois,
Callit Eoye, into the orient;
The secund steid to name hecht Ethios,
Quhitlie and paill, and sum deill ascendent;
215   The thrid Peros, richt hait and richt fervent;
The feird was blak, and callit Philogie
Quhilk rollis Phebus doun into the sey.

Venus was thair present, that goddes gay,
Hir sonnis querrell for to defend, and mak
220   Hir awin complaint, cled in ane nyce array,
The ane half grene, the uther half sabill blak,
With hair as gold kemmit and sched abak;
Bot in hir face semit greit variance,
Quhyles perfyte treuth and quhyles inconstance.

225   Under smyling scho was dissimulait,
Provocative with blenkis amorous,
And suddanely changit and alterait,
Angrie as ony serpent vennemous,
Richt pungitive with wordis odious;
230   Thus variant scho was, quha list tak keip:
With ane eye lauch, and with the uther weip,

In taikning that all fleschelie paramour,
Quhilk Venus hes in reull and governance,
Is sum tyme sweit, sum tyme bitter and sour,
235   Richt unstabill and full of variance,

Mingit with cairfull joy and fals plesance,
Now hait, now cauld, now blyith, now full of wo,
Now grene as leif, now widderit and ago.

With buik in hand than come Mercurius,
Richt eloquent and full of rethorie,   240
With polite termis and delicious,
With pen and ink to report all reddie,
Setting sangis and singand merilie;
His hude was reid, heklit atouir his croun,
Lyke to ane poeit of the auld fassoun.   245

Boxis he bair with fyne electuairis,
And sugerit syropis for digestioun,
Spycis belangand to the pothecairis,
With mony hailsum sweit confectioun;
Doctour in phisick, cled in ane skarlot goun,   250
And furrit weill, as sic ane aucht to be;
Honest and gude, and not ane word culd lie.

Nixt efter him come Lady Cynthia,
The last of all and swiftest in hir spheir;
Of colour blak, buskit with hornis twa,   255
And in the nicht scho listis best appeir;
Haw as the leid, of colour nathing cleir,
For all hir licht scho borrowis at hir brother
Titan, for of hirself scho hes nane uther.

Hir gyte was gray and full of spottis blak,   260
And on hir breist ane churle paintit full euin
Beirand ane bunche of thornis on his bak,
Quhilk for his thift micht clim na nar the heuin.
Thus quhen thay gadderit war, thir goddes seuin,
Mercurius thay cheisit with ane assent   265
To be foirspeikar in the parliament.

Quha had bene thair and liken for to heir
His facound toung and termis exquisite,
Of rethorick the prettick he micht leir,
In breif sermone ane pregnant sentence wryte.   270
Befoir Cupide veiling his cap a-lyte,
Speiris the caus of that vocatioun,
And he anone schew his intentioun.

295

'Lo,' quod Cupide, 'quha will blaspheme the name
Of his awin god, outher in word or deid,
275 To all goddis he dois baith lak and schame,
And suld have bitter panis to his meid.
I say this by yon wretchit Cresseid,
The quhilk throw me was sum tyme flour of lufe,
280 Me and my mother starklie can reprufe,

'Saying of hir greit infelicitie
I was the caus, and my mother Venus,
Ane blind goddes hir cald that micht not se,
With sclander and defame injurious.
285 Thus hir leving unclene and lecherous
Scho wald retorte on me and my mother,
To quhome I schew my grace abone all uther.

'And sen ye ar all sevin deificait,
Participant of devyne sapience,
290 This greit injure done to our hie estait
Me think with pane we suld mak recompence;
Was never to goddes done sic violence:
As weill for yow as for myself I say,
Thairfoir ga help to revenge, I yow pray!'

295 Mercurius to Cupide gave answeir
And said: 'Schir King, my counsall is that ye
Refer yow to the hiest planeit heir
And tak to him the lawest of degré,
The pane of Cresseid for to modifie:
300 As God Saturne, with him tak Cynthia.'
'I am content', quod he, 'to tak thay twa.'

Than thus proceidit Saturne and the Mone
Quhen thay the mater rypelie had degest:
For the dispyte to Cupide scho had done
305 And to Venus, oppin and manifest,
In all hir lyfe with pane to be opprest,
And torment sair with seiknes incurabill,
And to all lovers be abhominabill.

This duleful sentence Saturne tuik on hand,
310 And passit doun quhair cairfull Cresseid lay,
And on hir heid he laid ane frostie wand;
Than lawfullie on this wyse can he say:

'Thy greit fairnes and all thy betwic gay,
Thy wantoun blude, and eik thy goldin hair,
Heir I exclude fra the for evermair.   315

'I change thy mirth into melancholy,
Quhilk is the mother of all pensivenes;
Thy moisture and thy heit in cald and dry;
Thyne insolence, thy play and wantones
To greit diseis; thy pomp and thy riches   320
In mortall neid; and greit penuritie
Thow suffer sall, and as ane beggar die.'

O cruell Saturne, fraward and angrie,
Hard is thy dome and to malitious!
On fair Cresseid quhy hes thow na mercie,   325
Quhilk was sa sweit, gentill and amorous?
Withdraw thy sentence and be gracious—
As thow was never; sa schawis throw thy deid,
Ane wraikfull sentence geuin on fair Cresseid.

Than Cynthia, quhen Saturne past away,   330
Out of hir sait discendit doun belyve,
And red ane bill on Cresseid quhair scho lay,
Contening this sentence diffinityve:
'Fra heit of bodie I the now depryve,
And to thy seiknes sall be na recure   335
Bot in dolour thy dayis to indure.

'Thy cristall ene mingit with blude I mak,
Thy voice sa cleir unplesand hoir and hace,
Thy lustie lyre ouirspred with spottis blak,
And lumpis haw appeirand in thy face: 340
Quhair thow cummis ilk man sall fle the place.
This sall thow go begging fra hous to hous
With cop and clapper lyke ane lazarous.'

This doolie dreame, this uglye visioun
Brocht to ane end, Cresseid fra it awoik,   345
And all that court and convocatioun
Vanischit away. Than rais scho up and tuik
Ane poleist glas, and hir schaddow culd luik;
And quhen scho saw hir face sa deformait,
Gif scho in hart was wa aneuch, God wait!   350

Weiping full sair, 'Lo, quhat it is', quod sche,
'With fraward langage for to mufe and steir
Our craibit goddis; and sa is sene on me!
My blaspheming now have I bocht full deir;
All eirdlie joy and mirth I set areir.
Allace, this day! allace, this wofull tyde
Quhen I began with my goddis for to chyde!'

355

Be this was said, ane chyld come fra the hall
To warne Cresseid the supper was reddy;
First knokkit at the dure, and syne culd call:
'Madame, your father biddis yow cum in hy:
He hes merwell sa lang on grouf ye ly,
And sayis your beedes bene to lang sum deill;
The goddis wait all your intent full weill.'

360

Quod scho: 'Fair chyld, ga to my father deir
And pray him cum to speik with me anone.'
And sa he did, and said, 'Douchter, quhat cheir?'
'Allace!' quod scho, 'Father, my mirth is gone!'
'How sa?' quod he; and scho can all expone,
As I have tauld, the vengeance and the wraik
For hir trespas Cupide on hir culd tak.

365

370

He luikit on hir uglye lipper face,
The quhylk befor was quhite as lillie flour;
Wringand his handis, oftymes he said, allace
That he had levit to se that wofull hour!
For he knew weill that thair was na succour
To hir seiknes, and that dowblit his pane;
Thus was thair cair aneuch betuix thame twane.

375

Quhen thay togidder murnit had full lang,
Quod Cresseid: 'Father, I wald not be kend;
Thairfoir in secreit wyse ye let me gang
Wnto yone spitall at the tounis end,
And thidder sum meit for cheritie me send
To leif upon, for all mirth in this eird
Is fra me gane; sic is my wickit weird!'

380

385

Than in ane mantill and ane bawer hat,
With cop and clapper, wonder prively,
He opnit ane secreit yet and out thairat
Convoyit hir, that na man suld espy,

Wnto ane village half ane myle thairby;   390
Delyverit hir in at the spittaill hous,
And daylie sent hir part of his almous.

Sum knew hir weill, and sum had na knawledge
Of hir becaus scho was sa deformait,
With bylis blak ouirspred in hir visage,   395
And hir fair colour faidit and alterait.
Yit thay presumit, for hir hie regrait
And still murning, scho was of nobill kin;
With better will thairfoir they tuik her in.

The day passit and Phebus went to rest,   400
The cloudis blak ouerheled all the sky.
God wait gif Cresseid was ane sorrowfull gest,
Seing that uncouth fair and harbery!
But meit or drink scho dressit hir to ly
In ane dark corner of the hous allone,   405
And on this wyse, weiping, scho maid hir mone:

'O sop of sorrow, sonkin into cair!
O cative Cresseid! For now and ever mair
Gane is thy joy and al thy mirth in eird;
Of all blyithnes now art thou blaiknit bair;   410
Thair is na salve may saif the of thy sair!
Fell is thy fortoun, wickit is thy weird,
Thy blys is baneist, and thy baill on breird!
Under the eirth God gif I gravin wer,
Quhair nane of Grece nor yit of Troy micht heird!   415

'Quhair is thy chalmer wantounlie besene,
With burely bed and bankouris browderit bene?
Spycis and wyne to thy collatioun,
The cowpis all of gold and silver schene,
The sweitmeitis servit in plaittis clene   420
With saipheron sals of ane gude sessoun?
Thy gay garmentis with mony gudely goun,
Thy plesand lawn pinnit with goldin prene?
All is areir, thy greit royall renoun!

'Quhair is thy garding with thir greissis gay   425
And fresche flowris, quhilk the quene Floray
Had paintit plesandly in everie pane,
Quhair thou was wont full merilye in May

299

To walk and tak the dew be it was day,
430 And heir the merle and mawis mony ane,
With ladyis fair in carrolling to gane
And se the royall rinkis in thair ray,
In garmentis gay garnischit on everie grane?

'Thy greit triumphand fame and hie honour,
435 Quhair thou was callit of eirdlye wichtis flour,
All is decayit, thy weird is welterit so;
Thy hie estait is turnit in darknes dour;
This lipper ludge tak for thy burelie bour,
And for thy bed tak now ane bunche of stro,
440 For waillit wyne and meitis thou had tho
Tak mowlit breid, peirrie and ceder sour;
Bot cop and clapper now is all ago.

'My cleir voice and courtlie carrolling,
Quhair I was wont with ladyis for to sing,
445 Is rawk as ruik full hiddeous, hoir and hace;
My plesand port, all utheris precelling,
Of lustines I was hald maist conding—
Now is deformit the figour of my face;
To luik on it na leid now lyking hes.
450 Sowpit in syte, I say with sair siching,
Ludgeit amang the lipper leid: "Allace!"

'O ladyis fair of Troy and Grece, attend
My miserie, quhilk nane may comprehend,
My frivoll fortoun, my infelicitie,
455 My greit mischief, quhilk na man can amend.
Be war in tyme, approchis neir the end,
And in your mynd ane mirrour make of me;
As I am now, peradventure that ye
For all your micht may cum to that same end,
460 Or ellis war, gif ony war may be.

'Nocht is your fairnes bot ane faiding flour,
Nocht is your famous laud and hie honour
Bot wind inflat in uther mennis eiris,
Your roising reid to rotting sall retour;
465 Exempill mak of me in your memour
Quhilk of sic thingis wofull witnes beiris.
All welth in eird away as wind it weiris;
Be war thairfoir, approchis neir the hour;
Fortoun is fikkill quhen scho beginnis and steiris.'

Thus chydand with hir drerie destenye,   470
Weiping scho woik the nicht fra end to end;
Bot all in vane—hir dule, hir cairfull cry,
Micht not remeid nor yit hir murning mend.
Ane lipper lady rais and till hir wend
And said: 'Quhy spurnis thow aganis the wall   475
To sla thyself and mend nathing at all?

'Sen thy weiping dowbillis bot thy wo,
I counsall the mak vertew of ane neid;
Go leir to clap thy clapper to and fro,
And leif efter the law of lipper leid.'   480
Thair was na buit, bot furth with thame scho yeid
Fra place to place, quhill cauld and hounger sair
Compellit hir to be ane rank beggair.

That samin tyme, of Troy the garnisoun,
Quhilk had to chiftane worthie Troylus,   485
Throw jeopardie of weir had strikken doun
Knichtis of Grece in number mervellous;
With greit tryumphe and laude victorious
Agane to Troy richt royallie thay raid
The way quhair Cresseid with the lipper baid.   490

Seing that companie, all with ane steuin;
Thay gaif ane cry and schuik coppis gude speid:
'Worthie lordis, for Goddis lufe of heuin,
To us lipper part of your almous-deid!'
Than to thair cry nobill Troylus tuik heid;   495
Having pietie, neir by the place can pas
Quhair Cresseid sat, not witting quhat scho was.

Than upon him scho kest up baith hir ene—
And with ane blenk it come into his thocht
That he sumtime hir face befoir had sene.   500
Bot scho was in sic plye he knew hir nocht;
Yit than hir luik into his mynd it brocht
The sweit visage and amorous blenking
Of fair Cresseid, sumtyme his awin darling.

Na wonder was, suppois in mynd that he   505
Tuik hir figure sa sone—and lo, now quhy:
The idole of ane thing in cace may be
Sa deip imprentit in the fantasy
That it deludis the wittis outwardly,

510 And sa appeiris in forme and lyke estait
Within the mynd as it was figurait.

Ane spark of lufe than till his hart culd spring
And kendlit all his bodie in ane fyre:
With hait fewir ane sweit and trimbling
515 Him tuik, quhill he was reddie to expyre;
To beir his scheild his breist began to tyre;
Within ane quhyle he changit mony hew,
And neuertheles not ane ane uther knew.

For knichtlie pietie and memoriall
520 Of fair Cresseid, ane gyrdill can he tak,
Ane purs of gold, and mony gay jowall,
And in the skirt of Cresseid doun can swak;
Than raid away and not ane word he spak,
Pensiwe in hart, quhill he come to the toun,
525 And for greit cair oftsyis almaist fell doun.

The lipper folk to Cresseid than can draw
To se the equall distributioun
Of the almous, bot quhen the gold thay saw,
Ilk ane to uther prevelie can roun,
530 And said: 'Yone lord hes mair affectioun,
Howeuer it be, unto yone lazarous
Than to us all; we know be his almous.'

'Quhat lord is yone,' quod scho, 'have ye na feill,
Hes done to us so greit humanitie?'
535 'Yes,' quod a lipper man, 'I knaw him weill;
Schir Troylus it is, gentill and fre.'
Quhen Cresseid understude that it was he,
Stiffer than steill thair stert ane bitter stound
Throwout hir hart, and fell doun to the ground,

540 Quhen scho ouircome, with siching sair and sad,
With mony cairfull cry and cald ochane:
'Now is my breist with stormie stoundis stad,
Wrappit in wo, ane wretch full will of wane!'
Than swounit scho oft or scho culd refrane,
545 And euir in hir swouning cryit scho thus:
'O fals Cresseid and trew knicht Troylus!

'Thy lufe, thy lawtie and thy gentilnes
I countit small in my prosperitie,
Sa efflated I was in wantones
And clam upon the fickill quheill sa hie.   550
All faith and lufe I promissit to the
Was in the self fickill and frivolous:
O fals Cresseid and trew knicht Troylus!

'For lufe of me thow keipit continence,
Honest and chaist in conversatioun.   555
Of all women protectour and defence
Thou was, and helpit thair opinioun;
My mynd in fleschelie foull affectioun
Was inclynit to lustis lecherous:
Fy, fals Cresseid! O trew knicht Troylus!   560

'Lovers be war and tak gude heid about
Quhome that ye lufe, for quhome ye suffer paine:
I lat yow wit thair is richt few thairout
Quhome ye may traist to have trew lufe agane—
Preif quhen ye will, your labour is in vaine.   565
Thairfoir I reid ye tak thame as ye find,
For thay ar sad as widdercock in wind.

'Becaus I knaw the greit unstabilnes,
Brukkill as glas, into myself, I say,
Traisting in uther als greit unfaithfulnes,   570
Als unconstant and als untrew of fay—
Thocht sum be trew, I wait richt few ar thay:
Quha findis treuth lat him his lady ruse!
Nane but myself as now I will accuse.'

Quhen this was said, with paper scho sat doun,   575
And on this maneir maid hir testament:
'Heir I beteiche my corps and carioun
With wormis and with taidis to be rent;
My cop and clapper and myne ornament,
And all my gold, the lipper folk sall have   580
Quhen I am deid, to burie me in grave.

'This royall ring set with this rubie reid
Quhilk Troylus in drowrie to me send,
To him agane I leif it quhen I am deid
To mak my cairfull deid unto him kend.   585

Thus I conclude schortlie, and mak ane end:
My spreit I leif to Diane quhair scho dwellis,
To walk with hir in waist woddis and wellis.

'O Diomeid, thou hes baith broche and belt
590 Quhilk Troylus gave me in takning
Of his trew lufe!' And with that word scho swelt.
And sone ane lipper man tuik of the ring,
Syne buryit hir withouttin tarying.
To Troylus furthwith the ring he bair
595 And of Cresseid the deith he can declair.

Quhen he had hard hir greit infirmitie,
Hir legacie and lamentatioun,
And how scho endit in sic povertie,
He swelt for wo and fell doun in ane swoun;
600 For greit sorrow his hart to brist was boun:
Siching full sadlie said: 'I can no moir—
Scho was untrew and wo is me thairfoir.'

Sum said he maid ane tomb of merbell gray,
And wrait hir name and superscriptioun,
605 And laid it on hir grave quhair that scho lay,
In golden letteris, conteining this ressoun:
'Lo, fair ladyis! Cresseid of Troyis toun,
Sumtyme countit the flour of womanheid,
Under this stane, lait lipper, lyis deid.'

610 Now, worthie wemen, in this ballet schort,
Maid for your worschip and instructioun,
Of cheritie, I monische and exhort,
Ming not your lufe with fals deceptioun.
Beir in your mynd this schort conclusioun
615 Of fair Cresseid, as I have said befoir;
Sen scho is deid, I speik of hir no moir.

19

WILLIAM DUNBAR

THE biographical record of Dunbar (b. ? c.1460) consists only of scraps. Perhaps he came from East Lothian; he was certainly a university graduate; perhaps he studied at St Andrews. By 1504 he had taken orders; he was regularly paid by King James IV from 1500 to 1513, after which date his name no longer appears. Two significant things at least are clear: that he was a cleric, and that he was a Court poet. Over eighty poems—none of them of great length—have survived. Dunbar is immediately attractive. He writes with compressed vigour and expressiveness ('lifly', 'schort', 'quyk', and 'of sentence hie'), and he is capable of virtuoso verbal display and of intricate and exhilarating sound effects. His imagination often has a fantastic or an apocalyptic quality. He makes many references to himself ('my heid did yak yester nicht', etc.), but any 'essential' poetic personality remains elusive. This is partly because he is *par excellence* the superb craftsman-poet, able to take up any one of a number of poetic kinds, submerge himself in them, discover their own essence, and transform them. He is hard to respresent fairly in a short selection, for he needs to be read extensively. We have the eloquent and moving melancholy poem 'Into thir dirk and drublie dayis' (the 'Meditatioun in Wyntir'), which ends with the shortening of the nights bringing him only a partial comfort, and the elaborately decorative opening of his allegorical dream-vision, *The Goldyn Targe*. He wrote a number of splendidly—and variously—comic poems. *The Tretis of the Tua Mariit Wemen and the Wedo* takes up the traditional theme of the 'gossips' meeting', and it owes a good deal to Chaucer's *Wife of Bath's Prologue*, but it goes its own way with a distinctive gusto. Our extract from the widow's speech (her 'preaching' as she playfully calls it) is a splendid piece of sustained hypocrisy. In *Ane Ballat of the Fenyeit Freir of Tungland* Dunbar's satirical imagination literally takes flight as he makes all the birds of the air unite against the grotesque and unnatural figure of the flying abbot. A wonderfully dramatic poem on the Resurrection represents a small but very distinguished group of religious lyrics (a genre to which Dunbar brings a new vitality and creativeness). Finally, the famous 'Lament for the Makaris' is another meditation, both personal and general, on death. It has the grim ironies of the macabre traditions ('thame helpis no conclusionis sle') and it ends with resignation to the inevitability of death's coming and with a fervent call to make ready for it. Yet the catalogue of the poets who have fallen to death is not only hauntingly moving, but in a way defiant: though the records have forgotten many of them, Dunbar's lines have rescued them—his 'brothers'—from total extinction.

A

In Winter

Into thir dirk and drublie dayis
Quhone sabill all the hevin arrayis
  With mystie vapouris, cluddis, and skyis,
  Nature all curage me denyis
Off sangis, ballattis, and of playis.   5

Quhone that the nycht dois lenthin houris
With wind, with haill, and havy schouris,
  My dulé spreit dois lurk for schoir;
  My hairt for languor dois forloir
For laik of Symmer with his flouris.   10

I walk, I turne, sleip may I nocht;
I vexit am with havie thocht,
  This warld all ovir I cast about,
  And ay the mair I am in dout
The mair that I remeid have socht.   15

I am assayit on everie syde:
Dispair sayis, 'Ay in tyme provyde
  And get sum thing quhairon to leif,
  Or with grit trouble and mischeif
Thow sall into this court abyd.'   20

Than Patience sayis, 'Be not agast:
Hald Hoip and Treuthe within the fast,
  And lat Fortoun wirk furthe hir rage,
  Quhome that no rasoun may assuage
Quhill that hir glas be run and past.'   25

And Prudence in my eir sayis ay,
'Quhy wald thow hald that will away?
  Or craif that thow may have mo space,
  Thow tending to ane uther place
A journay going everie day?'   30

And than sayis Age, 'My friend, cum neir,
And be not strange, I the requeir:

306

Cum, brodir, by the hand me tak,
Remember thow hes compt to mak
  Off all thi tyme thow spendit heir.'   35

Syne Deid castis upe his yettis wyd,
Saying, 'Thir oppin sall the abyd;
  Albeid that thow wer neuer sa stout,
  Undir this lyntall sall thow lowt:
Thair is nane uther way besyde.'   40

For feir of this all day I drowp;
No gold in kist, nor wyne in cowp,
  No ladeis bewtie, nor luiffis blys,
  May lat me to remember this,
How glaid that ever I dyne or sowp.   45

Yit, quhone the nycht begynnis to schort,
It dois my spreit sumpairt confort,
  Off thocht oppressit with the schowris.
  Cum, lustie Symmer, with thi flowris,
That I may leif in sum disport.   50

B

The Goldyn Targe

Ryght as the stern of day begouth to schyne,
Quhen gone to bed war Vesper and Lucyne,
  I raise, and by a rosere did me rest;
  Wp sprang the goldyn candill matutyne,
With clere depurit bemes cristallyne,   5
  Glading the mery foulis in thair nest;
  Or Phebus was in purpur cape revest
Wp raise the lark, the hevyns menstrale fyne
  In May, intill a morow myrthfullest.

Full angellike thir birdis sang thair houris   10
Within thair courtyns grene, into thair bouris
  Apparalit quhite and rede wyth blomes suete;
Anamalit was the felde wyth all colouris,
The perly droppis schake in silvir schouris,

15   Quhill all in balme did branch and levis flete;
        To part fra Phebus did Aurora grete;
        Hir cristall teris I saw hyng on the flouris,
          Quhilk he for lufe all drank up wyth his hete.

        For mirth of May, wyth skippis and wyth hoppis,
20   The birdis sang upon the tender croppis
          With curiouse note, as Venus chapell clerkis;
        The rosis yong, new spreding of thair knopis,
        War powdirit brycht with hevinly beriall droppis
          Throu bemes rede birnyng as ruby sperkis;
25   The skyes rang for schoutyng of the larkis,
        The purpur hevyn, ourscailit in silvir sloppis,
          Ourgilt the treis, branchis, lef, and barkis.

        Doun throu the ryce a ryvir ran wyth stremys,
        So lustily agayn thai lykand lemys
30   That all the lake as lamp did leme of licht,
        Quhilk schadowit all about wyth twynkling glemis
        That bewis bathit war in secund bemys
          Throu the reflex of Phebus visage brycht;
          On every syde the hegies raise on hicht,
35   The bank was grene, the bruke was full of bremys,
          The stanneris clere as stern in frosty nycht.

        The cristall air, the sapher firmament,
        The ruby skyes of the orient
          Kest beriall bemes on emerant bewis grene;
40   The rosy garth depaynt and redolent
        With purpur, azure, gold, and goulis gent
          Arayed was by dame Flora the quene
          So nobily that joy was for to sene;
        The roch agayn the rivir resplendent
45   As low enlumynit all the leves schene.

        Quhat throu the mery foulys armony
        And throu the ryveris soun quhilk ran me by
          On Florais mantill I slepit as I lay,
         Quhare sone into my dremes fantasy
50   I saw approch, agayn the orient sky
          A saill als quhite as blossum upon spray,
         Wyth merse of gold brycht as the stern of day,
         Quhilk tendit to the land full lustily
          As falcoun swift desyrouse of hir pray.

And hard on burd unto the blomyt medis   55
Amang the grene rispis and the redis
   Arrivit sche, quharfro anon thare landis
Ane hundreth ladyes, lusty into wedis,
Als fresch as flouris that in May upspredis
   In kirtillis grene, withoutyn kell or bandis;   60
    Thair brycht hairis hang gletering on the strandis
In tressis clere, wyppit wyth goldyn thredis;
   With pappis quhite, and mydlis small as wandis. . . .

C

THE TUA MARIIT WEMEN AND THE WEDO

The Widow has Buried her Second Husband

. . . 'Deid is now that dyvour and dollin in erd:
With him deit all my dule and my drery thoghtis;
Now done is my dolly nyght, my day is upsprungin;
Adew dolour, adew! my daynté now begynis!
Now am I a wedow iwise, and weill am at ese!   5
I weip as I wer woful, but wel is me for ever;
I busk as I wer bailfull, bot blith is my hert;
My mouth it makis murnyng, and my mynd lauchis;
My clokis thai ar caerfull in colour of sabill,
Bot courtly and ryght curyus my corse is therundir: 10
I drup with a ded luke in my dulé habit,
As with manis daill I had done for dayis of my lif.
   'Quhen that I go to the kirk, cled in cair-weid,
As foxe in a lambis fleise fenye I my cheir;
Than lay I furght my bright buke on breid on my kne,   15
With mony lusty lettir ellummynit with gold;
And drawis my clok forthwart our my face quhit,
That I may spy unaspyit a space me beside:
Full oft I blenk by my buke, and blynis of devotion,
To se quhat berne is best brand or bredest in schulderis,   20
Or forgeit is maist forcely to furnyse a bancat
In Venus chalmer valyeandly withoutin vane ruse.
And as the new mone all pale oppressit with change,
Kythis quhilis her cleir face through cluddis of sable,
So keik I through my clokis, and castis kynd lukis   25
To knychtis, and to cleirkis, and cortly personis.

'Quhen frendis of my husbandis behaldis me on fer,
I haif a wattir spunge for wa, within my wyde clokis,
Than wring I it full wylély and wetis my chekis;
With that wattiris myn ene and weltiris doune teris.
Than say thai all that sittis about, "Se ye nought, allace!
Yone lustlese led, so lelely scho luffit hir husband;
Yone is a peté to enprent in a princis hert,
That sic a perle of plesance suld yone pane dre!"
I sane me as I war ane sanct, and semys ane angell;
At langage of lichory I leit as I war crabit:
I sich, without sair hert or seiknes in body;
According to my sable weid I mon haif sad maneris,
Or thai will se all the suth; for certis we wemen
We set ws all fra the syght to syle men of treuth:
We dule for na evill deid, sa it be derne haldin.

'Wise wemen has wayis and wondirfull gydingis
With gret engyne to bejaip ther jolyus husbandis;
And quyetly with sic craft convoyis our materis
That undir Crist no creatur kennis of our doingis.
Bot folk a cury may miscuke that knawledge wantis,
And has na colouris for to cover thair awne kindly fautis;
As dois thir damysellis for derne dotit lufe
That dogonis haldis in dainté and delis with thaim so lang,
Quhill all the cuntré knaw ther kyndnes and faith:
Faith has a fair name, bot falsheid faris bettir:
Fy on hir that can nought feyne her fame for to saif!
Yit am I wise in sic werk and wes all my tyme;
Thoght I want wit in warldlynes I wylis haif in luf,
As ony happy woman has that is of hie blude:
Hutit be the halok lase a hundir yeir of eild!
I have ane secrete serwand, rycht sobir of his toung,
That me supportis of sic nedis quhen I a syne mak:
Thoght he be sympill to the sicht, he has a tong sickir;
Full mony semelyar sege wer service dois mak
Thoght I haif cair undir cloke the cleir day quhill nyght,
Yit haif I solace undir serk quhill the sone ryse.
Yit am I haldin a haly wif our all the haill schyre:
I am sa peteouse to the pur quhen ther is personis mony;
In passing of pilgrymage I pride me full mekle,
Mair for the prese of peple na ony perdoun wynyng.

'Bot yit me think the best bourd, quhen baronis and knychtis
And othir bachilleris, blith blwmyng in youth,
And all my luffaris lele my lugeng persewis
And fyllis me wyne wantonly with weilfair and joy:

310

Sum rownis, and sum ralyeis; and sum redis ballatis;
Sum raiffis furght rudly with riatus speche;
Sum plenis, and sum prayis; sum prasis mi bewté;
Sum kissis me; sum clappis me; sum kyndnes me proferis;
Sum kerffis to me curtasli; sum me the cop giffis;   75
Sum stalwardly steppis ben with a stout curage
And a stif standand thing staiffis in my neiff;
And mony blenkis ben our, that but full fer sittis,
That mai for the thik thrang nought thrif as thai wald.
Bot, with my fair calling I comfort thaim all: 80
For he that sittis me nixt, I nip on his finger;
I serf him on the tothir syde on the samin fasson;
And he that behind me sittis, I hard on him lene;
And him befor, with my fut fast on his I stramp;
And to the bernis far but sueit blenkis I cast;   85
To every man in speciall speke I sum wordis
So wisly and so womanly quhill warmys ther hertis.
Thar is no liffand leid so law of degré
That sall me luf unluffit, I am so loik-hertit;
And gif his lust so be lent into my lyre quhit   90
That he be lost or with me lig, his lif sall not danger.
I am so mercifull in mynd, and menys all wichtis,
My sely saull sal be saif, quhen Sabot all jugis.
Ladyis, leir thir lessonis and be no lassis fundin:
This is the legeand of my lif, thought Latyne it be nane.'   95
    Quhan endit had her ornat speche this eloquent wedow,
Lowd thai lewch all the laif, and loffit hir mekle,
And said thai suld exampill tak of her soverane teching
And wirk eftir hir wordis, that woman wes so prudent.
Than culit thai thair mouthis with confortable drinkis   100
And carpit full cummerlik with cop going round. . . .

D

The Fenyeit Freir of Tungland

As yung Awrora with cristall haile
In orient schew hir visage paile,
A swenyng swyth did me assaile
    Off sonis of Sathanis seid;

311

Me thocht a Turk of Tartary
Come throw the boundis of Barbary
And lay forloppin in Lumbardy
    Full lang in waithman weid.
Fra baptasing for to eschew,
Thair a religious man he slew,
And cled him in his abeit new,
    For he cowth wryte and reid.
Quhen kend was his dissimulance
And all his cursit govirnance,
For feir he fled and come in France
    With littill of Lumbard leid.
To be a leiche he fenyt him thair,
Quhilk mony a man micht rew euirmair,
For he left nowthir seik nor sair
    Unslane, or he hyne yeid.
Vane organis he full clenely carvit;
Quhen of his straik so mony starvit,
Dreid he had gottin that he desarvit
    He fled away gud speid.

In Scotland than the narrest way
He come his cunnyng till assay;
To sum man thair it was no play,
    The preving of his sciens.
In pottingry he wrocht grit pyne;
He murdreist mony in medecyne;
The jow was of a grit engyne
    And generit was of gyans.
In leichecraft he was homecyd;
He wald haif for a nicht to byd,
A haiknay and the hurt manis hyd,
    So meikle he was of myance.
His yrnis was rude as ony rawchtir,
Quhair he leit blude it was no lawchtir;
Full mony instrument for slawchtir
    Was in his gardevyance.

He cowth gif cure for laxatyve
To gar a wicht hors want his lyve,
Quha cuir assay wald, man or wyve,
    Thair hippis yeid hiddy giddy.
His practikis nevir war put to preif
But suddane deid or grit mischeif;

He had purgatioun to mak a theif
    To dee withowt a widdy.
Unto no mes pressit this prelat
For sound of sacring-bell nor skellat;   50
As blaksmyth bruikit was his pallatt
    For battering at the study.
Thocht he come hame a new maid channoun,
He had dispensit with matynnis channoun,
On him come nowther stole nor fannoun   55
    For smowking of the smydy.

Me thocht seir fassonis he assailyeit,
To mak the quintessance, and failyeit;
And quhen he saw that nocht availyeit,
    A fedrem on he tuke,   60
And schupe in Turky for to fle;
And quhen that he did mont on he,
All fowill ferleit quhat he sowld be
    That euir did on him luke.
Sum held he had bene Dedalus,   65
Sum the Menatair marvelus,
Sum Martis blaksmyth Vulcanus,
    And sum Saturnus kuke.
And euir the cuschettis at him tuggit,
The rukis him rent, the ravynis him druggit,   70
The hudit crawis his hair furth ruggit:
    The hevin he micht not bruke.

The myttane and Sanct Martynis fowle
Wend he had bene the hornit howle,
Thay set aupone him with a yowle   75
    And gaif him dynt for dynt.
The golk, the gormaw, and the gled,
Beft him with buffettis quhill he bled;
The sparhalk to the spring him sped
    Als fers as fyre of flynt.   80
The tarsall gaif him tug for tug,
A stanchell hang in ilka lug,
The pyot furth his pennis did rug,
    The stork straik ay but stynt;
The bissart, bissy but rebuik,   85
Scho was so cleverus of hir cluik
His bawis he micht not langer bruik—
    Scho held thame at ane hint.

Thik was the clud of kayis and crawis,
90 Of marleyonis, mittanis, and of mawis,
That bikkrit at his berd with blawis
    In battell him abowt.
Thay nybbillit him with noyis and cry,
The rerd of thame rais to the sky,
95 And euir he cryit on Fortoun, Fy!
    His lyfe was into dowt.
The ja him skrippit with a skryke
And skornit him as it was lyk;
The egill strong at him did stryke,
100   And rawcht him mony a rowt.
For feir uncunnandly he cawkit
Quhill all his pennis war drownd and drawkit;
He maid a hundreth nolt all hawkit
    Beneth him with a spowt.

105 He schewre his feddreme that was schene
And slippit owt of it full clene,
And in a myre up to the ene
    Amang the glar did glyd.
The fowlis all at the fedrem dang,
110 As at a monster thame amang
Quhill all the pennis of it owsprang
    Intill the air full wyde.
And he lay at the plunge euirmair
So lang as any ravin did rair;
115 The crawis him socht with cryis of cair
    In every schaw besyde;
Had he reveild bene to the ruikis,
Thay had him revin all with thair cluikis.
Thre dayis in dub amang the dukis
120   He did with dirt him hyde.
The air was dirkit with the fowlis,
That come with yawmeris and with yowlis,
With skryking, skrymming, and with scowlis
    To tak him in the tyde.
125 I walknit with the noyis and schowte,
So hiddowis beir was me abowte;
Sensyne I curs that cankerit rowte,
    Quhair euir I go or ryde.

E

The Resurrection of Christ

Done is a battell on the dragon blak;
Our campioun Chryst confoundit hes his force:
The yettis of hell ar brokin with a crak,
The signe triumphall rasit is of the croce,
The divillis trymmillis with hiddous voce, 5
The saulis ar borrowit and to the blis can go,
Chryst with his blud our ransonis dois indoce:
Surrexit Dominus de sepulchro.

Dungin is the deidly dragon Lucifer,
The crewall serpent with the mortall stang 10
The auld kene tegir with his teith on char,
Quhilk in a wait hes lyne for us so lang,
Thinking to grip us in his clowis strag;
The mercifull Lord wald nocht that it wer so,
He maid him for to felye of that fang: 15
Surrexit Dominus de sepulchro.

He for our saik that sufferit to be slane
And lyk a lamb in sacrifice wes dicht
Is lyk a lyone rissin up agane,
And as gyane raxit him on hicht; 20
Sprungin is Aurora radius and bricht,
On loft is gone the glorius Appollo,
The blisfull day depairtit fro the nycht:
Surrexit Dominus de sepulchro.

The grit victour agane is rissin on hicht 25
That for our querrell to the deth wes woundit;
The sone that wox all paill now schynis bricht
And dirknes clerit, our fayth is now refoundit;
The knell of mercy fra the hevin is soundit,
The Cristin ar deliverit of thair wo, 30
The Jowis and thair errour ar confoundit:
Surrexit Dominus de sepulchro.

The fo is chasit, the battell is done ceis,
The presone brokin, the jeuellouris fleit and flemit;
The weir is gon, confermit is the peis, 35
The fetteris lowsit and the dungeoun temit,

315

The ransoun maid, the presoneris redemit;
The feild is win, ourcumin is the fo,
Dispulit of the tresur that he yemit:
40   *Surrexit Dominus de sepulchro*!

F

Lament for the Makars

I that in heill wes and gladnes
Am trublit now with gret seiknes
And feblit with infermité:
Timor mortis conturbat me.

5   Our plesance heir is all vane glory,
This fals warld is bot transitory,
The flesch is brukle, the Fend is sle:
Timor mortis conturbat me.

The stait of man dois change and vary,
10   Now sound, now seik, now blith, now sary,
Now dansand mery, now like to dee:
Timor mortis conturbat me.

No stait in erd heir standis sickir;
As with the wynd wavis the wickir,
15   Wavis this warldis vanité:
Timor mortis conturbat me.

Onto the ded gois all estatis,
Princis, prelotis, and potestatis,
Baith riche and pur of al degré:
20   *Timor mortis conturbat me.*

He takis the knychtis into feild,
Anarmit undir helme and scheild;
Victour he is at all mellé:
Timor mortis conturbat me.

25   That strang unmercifull tyrand
Takis, on the moderis breist sowkand,
The bab full of benignité:
Timor mortis conturbat me.

He takis the campion in the stour,
The capitane closit in the tour, 30
The lady in bour full of bewté:
Timor mortis conturbat me.

He sparis no lord for his piscence,
Na clerk for his intelligence;
His awfull strak may no man fle: 35
Timor mortis conturbat me.

Art-magicianis, and astrologgis,
Rethoris, logicianis, and theologgis—
Thame helpis no conclusionis sle:
Timor mortis conturbat me. 40

In medicyne the most practicianis,
Lechis, surrigianis, and phisicianis,
Thameself fra ded may not supplé:
Timor mortis conturbat me.

I se that makaris amang the laif 45
Playis heir ther pageant, syne gois to graif;
Sparit is nocht ther faculté:
Timor mortis conturbat me.

He has done petuously devour,
The noble Chaucer, of makaris flour, 50
The Monk of Bery, and Gower, all thre:
Timor mortis conturbat me.

The gude Syr Hew of Eglintoun,
And eik Heryot, and Wyntoun,
He has tane out of this cuntré: 55
Timor mortis conturbat me.

That scorpion fell has done infek
Maister Johne Clerk, and James Afflek,
Fra balat making and tragidie:
Timor mortis conturbat me. 60

Holland and Barbour he has berevit;
Allace! that he nocht with ws lewit
Schir Mungo Lokert of the Le:
Timor mortis conturbat me.

65   Clerk of Tranent eik he has tane,
     That maid the anteris of Gawane;
     Schir Gilbert Hay endit has he:
     Timor mortis conturbat me.

     He has Blind Hary and Sandy Traill
70   Slane with his schour of mortall haill,
     Quhilk Patrik Johnestoun myght nought fle:
     Timor mortis conturbat me.

     He has reft Merseir his endite,
     That did in luf so lifly write,
75   So schort, so quyk, of sentence hie:
     Timor mortis conturbat me.

     He has tane Roull of Aberdene,
     And gentill Roull of Corstorphin—
     Two bettir fallowis did no man se:
80   *Timor mortis conturbat me.*

     In Dunfermelyne he has done roune
     With Maister Robert Henrisoun;
     Schir Johne the Ros enbrast has he:
     Timor mortis conturbat me.

85   And he has now tane, last of aw,
     Gud gentill Stobo and Quintyne Schaw,
     Of quham all wichtis has peté:
     Timor mortis conturbat me.

     Gud Maister Walter Kennedy
90   In poynt of ded lyis veraly—
     Gret reuth it wer that so suld be:
     Timor mortis conturbat me.

     Sen he has all my brether tane,
     He will nocht lat me lif alane,
95   On forse I man his nyxt pray be:
     Timor mortis conturbat me.

     Sen for the deid remeid is none,
     Best is that we for dede dispone,
     Eftir our deid that lif may we:
100   *Timor mortis conturbat me.*

318

20

GAVIN DOUGLAS

DOUGLAS (? 1475–1522), besides being an extremely fine poet, was a member of one of the most powerful families in Scotland. He was educated at St Andrews, and probably at Paris; he became a churchman, was Provost of St Giles' in Edinburgh by 1503, and in 1506 was made Bishop of Dunkeld. After Flodden (1513) and the accession of the child king James V, he became increasingly involved in the factions of political life, and died an exile in London. We can only regret that he abandoned poetry for politics, but the works that he left represent a very notable achievement. They are, however, sadly neglected except by a few enthusiasts. *The Palice of Honour* (1501) is a learned and original poem, encyclopaedic in scope, which shows a wide range of reading and considerable intellectual power. It discusses the nature of virtue and honour, distinguishing true nobility from worldly glory. Evidently a young man's work, much concerned with the education of a poet, it is sometimes over-lavish: as C. S. Lewis says, 'the poet is still too delighted with the whole world of poetry, as he understood it, to control his delight'. Yet it has some fine scenes, especially those which involve a conversation between the dreamer and the personages he meets. Douglas finished his translation of Virgil's *Aeneid* (together with the thirteenth book by the humanist Maffeo Vegio) in 1513. It is in every sense his *magnum opus*; it is hard to find any translation in English which can match its quality. Each book is preceded by a prologue which often contains an interesting discussion of the circumstances of composition or of the style or matter of the book he is translating. The prologues sometimes become poems in their own right, as in that of Book VII from which our extract comes, where the bleak wintry Northern landscape is brilliantly described. In the first prologue Douglas attacks Caxton's *Eneydos* (cf. No. 15 E), which is based on a French retelling of the story. He speaks with genuine scholarly horror ('I red his werk with harmes at my hert'): 'this Caxton' has made howlers, he has produced a book without 'sentence or engyne', he has perverted the story of Dido, the fifth book is 'ourhippit quyte'. The whole thing is 'na mair lyke Virgill . . . / Na the owle resemblis the papyngay'. Douglas's version is immensely readable. Unmarred by pedantry or stiff 'classicism', it moves with an enormous enthusiasm and verve, and does full justice to the excitement of the narrative. Much of Virgil's delicate melody and elegance of style is lost, and much of his concision, for Douglas regularly expands, either because of the exigencies of his couplet form, or because he wishes to work in an explanatory gloss, or simply because he is excited by the subject-matter. But the sheer energy of his translation is impressive: the famous example of his version of *laetitia exsultans* as 'he hoppit up for joy, he was so glaid' is only one of many. He is particularly successful with battles, storms, and (here) a volcano, but he can write simple and expressive lines ('the cald dreid ran in throw ther banis'). It is a triumphant display of the literary potential of his Scottish vernacular.

A

THE PALICE OF HONOUR

Calliope's Nymph Brings the Poet to the Palace of Honour

'. . . Come on,' sayd sche, 'this ordenance to vysyte!'
Than past we to that cristall palyce quhyte,
Quhare I abayd the entré til behald.
I bad na mare of plesance nor delyte,
5   Of lusty sycht, of joy and blys perfyte,
Nor mare weilfare til have abone the mold
Than for til se that yet of byrnyst gold,
Quhareon thair was maist curiusly ingrave,
All naturall thyng men may in erd consave.

10   Thare wes the erth enveronyt wyth the see,
Quhareon the schyppes saland myght I se,
The ayr, the fyre, all the four elymentis,
The speris sevyn, and Primum Mobile,
The sygnis twelf perfytly every gré,
15   The Zodiak hale as bukis representis,
The Poil Antertik that euer himselfe absentis,
The Poil Artik, and eik the Ursis twane,
The sevyn sterris, Pheton, and the Charlewane.

Thare wes ingraf quhow that Ganamedis
20   Wes reft till hevyn, as men in Ovyd redis,
And ontill Jupiter made his cheif butlare;
The douchters fare into thayr lusty wedis
Of Dorida amyd the see but dredis
Swymmand, and part wer figurit thare
25   Apon a crag dryand thair yalow hare,
With facis not onlyk, for quha thaym seyng
Mycht weil consyddir that thay al sisteris beyng.

Of the planetis all the conjunctionys,
Thare episciclis, and oppositionis
30   Wer porturyt thair, and quhow thair coursis swagis,
Thare naturale and dayly motionis,
Eclipsis, aspectis, and degressyonys.
Thare saw I mony gudly personagis,
Quhilkis semyt all lusty quyk ymagis,

The werkmanschip excedyng mony fold 35
The precyus mater, thocht it wes fynest gold.

Wondrand hereon, agane my wyll but lete
My nymphe in grif schot me in at the yet.
'Quhat Deuyl!' said scho, 'hes thou not ellis ado
Bot all thy wyt and fantasy to set 40
On sic dotyng?' And tho for fere I swet
Of her langage. Bot than anone said scho,
'List thou se farlyes, behald thaym yondir, lo!
Yit study not ouir mekil, a-dreid thow vary,
For I persave the halflyngis in a fary.' 45

Within that palyce sone I gat a sycht,
Quhare walkand went ful mony worthy wicht
Amyd the close, with all myrthys to wale.
For lyk Phebus with fyry bemys brycht
The wallys schane, castand sa gret a lycht, 50
It semyt lyk the heuin imperiall;
And as the cedir surmontyth the rammale
In perfyt hycht, sa of that court a glance
Excedis far all erdly vane plesance.

For lois of sycht considdir micht I nocht 55
Quhow perfytly the ryche wallys wer wrocht;
Swa the reflex of cristall stanys schone,
For brychtnes skarsly blenk thairon I mocht.
The purifyit silver soithly, as me thocht,
In steid of syment, wes ouir all that wone, 60
Yet round about ful mony a beriall stone,
And thaym conjunctly jonyt fast and quemyt;
The close wes paithit with silver as it semyt.

The durris and the wyndois all wer breddyt
With massy gold, quhareof the fynes scheddit. 65
With byrnyst evyr baith palyce and touris
Wer thekyt well, maist craftely that cled it,
For so the quhitly blanchit bone ouirspred it,
Mydlyt with gold, anamalyt all colouris,
Inporturat of byrdis and swete flouris, 70
Curius knottis and mony sle devyse,
Quhilkis to behald wes perfyt paradice.

And to proceid, my nymphe and I furth went
Straucht to the hall throwout the palyce jent,
75 And ten stagis of thopas did ascend.
Schit wes the dure; in at a boir I blent,
Quhare I beheld the gladdest represent
That euir in erth a wrachit catywe kend.
Breifly theis proces til conclude and end,
80 Me thocht the flure wes al of amatist,
Bot quhareof war the wallis I ne wist.

The multitud of prectius stonis sere
Thairon swa schane, my febill sycht but were
Mycht not behald thair vertuus gudlynes.
85 For all the ruf, as did to me appere,
Hang full of plesand lowpyt saphyrs clere;
Of dyamantis and rubys, as I ges,
Wer all the burdis maid of mast riches;
Of sardanus, of jaspe, and smaragdane
90 Trestis, formys, and benkis wer pollist plane.

Baith to and fro amyd the hall they went,
Rial princis in plate and armouris quent
Of byrnist gold, cuchit with precyus stonys.
Intronyt sat a god armypotent,
95 On quhais gloryus vissage as I blent
In extasy be his brychtnes atonys
He smate me doun and byrsyt all my bonys.
Thare lay I still in swoun with cullour blaucht
Quhil at the last my nymphe up hes me kaucht.

100 Syne wyth gret pane, with womentyng and care,
In hir armys scho bare me doun the stare,
And in the clois full softly laid me doun;
Held up my hede to tak the hailsum ayre,
For of my lyfe scho stude in gret dispare.
105 Me till awalk ay wes that lady boun,
Quhill finally out of my dedly swoun
I swyth ouircome, and up my eyne did cast.
'Be myrry, man!' quod scho, 'the werst is past.

'Get up,' scho said, 'for schame be na cowart.
110 My hede in wed, thow hes a wyfis hart,
That for a plesand sycht is so mysmaid!'
Than all in anger apon my fete I start,
And for hir wordis wer so apyrsmart

Onto the nymphe I maid a bustuus braid.
'Carlyng,' quod I, 'quhat wes yone at thow said?'   115
'Soft yow,' said sche 'thay ar not wyse that stryvys,
For kyrkmen wer ay jentill to ther wyvys.

'I am rycht glaid thou art wordyn so wycht;
Langere me thocht thow had nothir fors ne mycht,
Curage, nor wyll for till have grevyt a fla.   120
Quhat alyt the to fall?' Quod I, 'The sycht
Of yone goddes grym fyry vissage brycht
Ouirset my wyt and all my spretis swa,
I mycht not stand.' 'Bot wes that suyth?' 'Ya, ya!'
Than said the nymphe rycht merylie and leuch,   125
'Now I considdir thy mad hart weil eneuch.

'I wyl', quod scho, 'na mare the thus assay
With sic plesance quhilk may thy sprete effray.
Yit sall thow se suythly, sen thou art here,
My ladyis court in thair gudly array.   130
For till behald thair myrth cum on thy way!'
Than hand in hand suyth went we furth in fere
At a postrum towart the fair herbere,
In that passage full fast at hir I franyt
Quhat folk thay wer within the hall remanyt.   135

'Yon wer,' said sche, 'quhasa the richt discrivys,
Maist vailyeand folk, and vertuus in thair lyvys.
Now in the court of honour thay remane
Victoriusly, and in all plesance thryvys;
For thay with spere, with swerdys, and wyth knyvys   140
In just battell wer fundyn maist of mane.
In thair promyttis thay stude evir fyrm and plane;
In thaym aboundit worschyp and lawté
Illumynyt with liberalité.

'Honour', quod scho, 'to this hevinly ryng   145
Differris richt far from warldly honoring,
Quhilk is but pompe of erdly dignyté
Gyvyn for estate of blude, micht, or sic thyng.
And in this countré prynce, prelate, or kyng
Alanerly sall for vertue honoryt be.   150
For erdly glore is not bot vanyté
That as we se, sa suddandly will wend,
Bot vertuus honour nevir mare sall end.' . . .

323

B

THE *ENEADOS*

Aeneas sees Italy

Furth on, with this, throuowt the sey we slyde,
By the forland Cerawnya fast beside,
Quharfra, out our the fludis forto saill,
The schortast way and cours lyis to Itaill.

5   Down gois the son be than, and hillis hie
Wolx dyrknyt with schaddowis of the sky;
We sort our aris, and chesis rowaris ilke deill,
And at a sownd or cost we likit weill
We strike at nycht, and on the dry strandis

10   Dyd bawme and beyk our bodeys, feyt and handis.
Sone on our irkyt lymmys, lethis and banys
The naturale rest of sleip slaid al atanys,
And, or the speyre his howris rollit richt
Sa far about that it was scars mydnycht,

15   Not sweir, bot in hys dedis deligent,
Palynurus furth of his cowch upsprent,
Lysnyng about, and harknyng our-alquhar
With erys prest to kep the wynd or ayr.
Of every starn the twynklyng notis he

20   That in the still hevyn move cours we se,
Arthuris huyf, and Hyades betakynnand rayn,
Syne Watlyng Streit, the Horn and the Charle Wayne,
The fers Orion with hys goldyn glave,
And quhen he hes thame everyane persave

25   Into the cleir and serene firmament,
Furth of his eft-schip a bekyn gart he stent:
We rays and went on burd in our the waill,
Syne slakis down the schetis, and maid sayll.
    Be this the dawyng gan at morn walx red

30   And chasit away the starnys fra every sted;
The dym hillis on far we dyd aspy,
And saw the law landis of Italy.
'Italy! Italy!' fyrst cryis Achates,
Syne al our feris of clamour mycht nocht ces,

35   Bot with a voce atanys cryis, 'Itaill!'
And hailsyng gan the land with 'hey' and 'haill'.
Than my fader, ammyral of our flote,

324

A mekil tankart with wyne fild to the throte,
And tharon set a garland or a crown,
And to the goddis maid this orysoun, 40
Sittand in the hie eft-castell of our schip,
With ful devote reverens and wirschip:
'O ye', quod he, 'goddis haldis in pousté
Weddir and stormys, the land eik and the se,
Grant our vayage ane esy and reddy wynd, 45
Inspyre your favouris that prospir cours we fynd.'
    Scars this wes said quhen, evyn at our desyre,
The sessonabil ayr pipis up fair and schyre;
The havyn apperis, and thiddir nerrar we draw,
And of Mynerva the strang tempill saw 50
Set in the castell apon ane hillis hycht.
Our fallowis fangis in thar salys tyght,
And towart the cost thar stevynnys dyd addres.
A port thar is, quham the est fludis hes
In maner of a bow maid bowle or bay, 55
With rochys set forgane the streym ful stay,
To brek the salt fame of the seys stour.
On athir hand, als hie as ony towr,
The byg hewis strekis furth lyke a wall;
Within the hawyn goith lown, but wynd or wall, 60
And at the port the tempill may not be seyn.
Heir fyrst I saw apon the plesand greyn
A fatale takyn, fowr horssis quhite as snaw
Gnyppand gresys the large feildis on raw.
'Ha! lugyn land, batale thou us pretendis,' 65
Quod my fader Anchis, 'for as weil kend is,
Horssis ar dressit for the bargane feil sys;
Weir and debait thir stedis signyfis.
Bot, sen the sammyn four futtit bestis eik
Beyn oft usyt, ful towartly and meik, 70
To draw the cart and thoil brydill and renye,
It is gude hope pace follow sal,' says he.
Than wirschip we the godhead and gret mycht
Of Pallas, with clattering harnes fers in fyght,
Quhilk heth ws first ressavyt glaid and gay: 75
Our hedis befor the altar we array
With valys brown, eftir the Trojane gys,
And onto Juno of Arge our sacryfys
Maid reverently, as Helenus us bad,
Observyng weil, as he commandyt had, 80
The serymonys leill. Syne, but langar delay,

Fra that perfurnyst was our offerand day,
Onon the nokkis of our rays we writh;
Down fallys the schetis of the salys swith;
85 The Gregionys herbry and fronteris suspek
We left behynd, and efter, in effek,
Of Taurentum the fyrth we se, but les
(Biggit, as thai say, by worthy Hercules),
And, our forgane the tother syde alsso,
90 Rays up Lacynya the tempill of Juno,
Of Cawlon cité eik the wallys hie,
And Scyllacium quhar schipbrokyn mony be.
Syne, far of in the flude, we gan aspy
The byrnand Ethna into Sycilly,
95 And a fell rage rowting of the sey
A lang way thens, and on the rolkis hie
We hard the jawpys bete, and at the cost
A hydduus brayng of brokyn seys bost—
Apon schald bankis boldynnys hie the flude;
100 The stowr upbullyrris sand as it war wode.
My fader than cryis, 'Howe! feris, help away,
Streke aris atanys with all the fors ye may!
No wondir, this is the selkouth Caribdis;
Thir horribbill rolkis and craggis heir, iwys,
105 Helenus the prophete ful weil dyd ws declare.'
The sammyn wys as thai commandyt ware
Thai dyd onon, and Pallynurus fyrst
Hard halys the schete on syde, and fast gan thryst
The forschip to the wallis and the tyde,
110 Saland on bawburd towart the left syde;
Towart the left, with mony 'heys' and 'haill',
Socht all our flot fast baith with rowth and saill.
The swelland swyrl uphesyt us til hevyn;
Syne wald the waw swak us doun ful evyn,
115 As it apperit, under the sey to hell.
Thrys the holkyt craggis hard we yell,
Quharas the swelch had the rolkis thyrlyt;
And thrys the fame furth spowt, that so hie quhirlyt
It semyt watir the starnys, as we thocht.
120 Be this the son went to, and us forwrocht
Left dissolat; the wyndis calmyt eik.
We, not bekend quhat rycht cours mycht we seik,
War warp to seywart by the outwart tyde
Of Ciclopes onto the costis syde.
125 The port quhamto we cappit wes ful large,

And fra al wyndis blast for schip or barge
Sovir al tyme, but netheless fast by
The grisly Ethna dyd rummyll, schudder and cry,
Sum tyme thrawing owt heich in the skyis
The blak laithly smoke that oft dyd rys   130
As thunderis blast, and rekand as the pyk,
With gledis sparkand as the hail als thik.
Upspring the blesis and fyry lumpis we se,
Quhilk semyt forto lik the starnys hie;
Sum tyme it rasyt gret rochys, and oft will   135
Furth bok the bowellis or entralis of the hyll,
And lowsyt stanys upwarpys in the ayr
Rownd in a sop, with mony crak and rayr:
The stew of byrnand heyt law from the grond
Upstrikis thar, that doith to hevyn rebound.   140
The rumour is doun thrung undir this mont
Enchelades body with thundir lyis half bront,
And hydduus Ethna abufe his belly set.
Quhen he lyst gant or blaw the fyre is bet,
And from that furnys the flambe doith brist or glide: 145
Quhou oft he turnys our hys irkit syde
All Sycil trymlys, quaking with a rerd,
And ugly stew ourquhelmys hevyn and erd.
That nycht, lurkand in woddis we remane,
Of feirfull monstris sufferand mekil pane;   150
Bot quhat causyt syk noys na thing we saw,
For nowthir lycht of planetis mycht we knaw,
Nor the brycht Poyll, nor in the ayr a starn,
Bot in dyrk clowdis the hevynnys warpit darn;
The moyn was undir walk and gave na lycht,   155
Haldyn ful dym throu myrknes of the nycht.

Queen Dido Rides out Hunting

Furth of the sey, with this, the dawyng spryngis.
As Phebus rays, fast to the yettis thringis
The chos gallandis, and huntmen thame besyde,
With ralys and with nettys strang and wyde,   160
And huntyng sperys styf with hedis braid;
From Massilyne horsmen thik thiddir raid,
With rynnyng hundis, a full huge sort.
Nobillys of Cartage, hovand at the port,
The queyn awatys that lang in chawmyr dwellys;   165

327

Hyr fers steyd stude stampyng, reddy ellys,
Rungeand the fomy goldyn byt gynglyng;
Of gold and pal wrocht hys rych harnasyng.
And scho at last of palyce yschit owt,
170   With huge menye walking hir abowt,
Lappyt in a brusyt mantill of Sydony,
With gold and perle the bordour al bewry,
Hyngand by hir syde the cays with arowis grund;
Hir bricht tressis envolupyt war and wond
175   Intil a quayf of fyne gold wyrin threid;
The goldyn button claspyt hir purpour weid.
And furth scho passyt with all hir cumpany;
The Trojane pepill forgaderit by and by,
Joly and glaid the fresch Ascanyus yyng
180   Bot first of all, maist gudly, hymself thar kyng
Enee gan entir in falloschip, but dout,
And onto thame adjonyt hys large rowt.
Lyke quhen Apollo list depart or ga
Furth of hys wyntring realm of Lysya,
185   And leif the flude Exanthus for quhile,
To vissy Delos, his moderis land and ile,
Renewand ryngis and dansys, mony a rowt
Mixt togiddir, hys altaris standing about;
The pepil of Creit, and thame of Driopes,
190   And eik the payntit folkis Agathirces,
Schowtand on thar gys with clamour and vocis hie:
Apon thi top, mont Cynthus, walkis he,
Hys wavand haris, sum tyme, doyng doun thryng
With a soft garland of lawrer sweit smellyng,
195   And umquhile thame gan balmyng and enoynt
And into gold addres at full gude poynt,
Hys grundyn dartis clattering by hys syde—
Als fresch, als lusty, dyd Eneas ryde,
With als gret bewté in hys lordly face.
200   And eftyr thai ar cummyn to the chace,
Amang the montanys in the wild forest,
The rynnyng hundis of cuppillys sone thai kest,
And our the clewys and the holtis belyve
The wild beistis doun to the dail thai dryve.
205   Lo! thar the rays, rynnyng swyft as fyre,
Drevyn from the hyghtis, brekkis out at the swyre;
Ane othir part, syne yondyr mycht thou se
The herd of hartis with thar hedis hie,
Ourspynnerand with swyft cours the plane vaill,

The hepe of duste upstowryng at thar taill,   210
Fleand the hundis, levand the hie montanys.
And Ascanyus, the child, amyd the planys,
Joyus and blith hys startling steid to assay,
Now makis hys rynk yondir, and now this way,
Now prekis furth by thir and now by thame,   215
Langyng, amang faynt frayt beistis ontame,
The fomy bair, doun from the hyllis hycht,
Or the dun lyoun discend, recontyr he mycht.
   In the meyn quhile, the hevynnys al about
With fellon noys gan to rummyll and rowt.   220
A bub of weddir followyt in the tayll,
Thik schour of rayn myddillit ful of haill.
The Tyriane menye skalis wydequhar,
And al the gallandis of Troy fled heir and thar;
And eik with thame the yong Ascanyus,   225
Nevo to Kyng Dardan and to Venus.
For feir, to divers stedis throu the feildis,
Thai seik to haldis, howsis, hyrnys and beildis:
The ryveris rudly ruschit our hillis bedene.
Within a cave is entrit Dido queyn,   230
And eik the Trojane duke, al thame alane,
By aventur, as thai eschewyt the rane.
Erth, the first moder, maid a takyn of wo,
And eik of wedlok the pronuba Juno,
And of thar cuplyng wittering schew the ayr: 235
The flambe of fyreslaucht lychtnyt heir and thar
And on the hillys hie toppis but les
Sat murnand nymphis, hait Oreades.
This wes the formaste day of hir glaidnes
And first morrow of hir wofull distres.   240
For nother the fasson nor the maner sche
Attendis now, nor fame ne honesté,
Ne from thens furthwart Dido ony mor
Musis on lufe secrete, as of befor,
But clepis it spousage, and with that fayr name   245
Clokyt and hyd hir cryme of oppyn schame.

The Prologue of Book VII

As bryght Phebus, scheyn soverane hevynnys e,
The opposit held of hys chymmys hie,
Cleir schynand bemys, and goldyn symmyris hew,

In laton cullour alteryng haill of new,
Kythyng no syng of heyt be hys vissage,
So neir approchit he his wyntir stage;
Reddy he was to entyr the thrid morn
In clowdy skyis undre Capricorn;
All thocht he be the hart and lamp of hevyn,
Forfeblit wolx hys lemand gylty levyn,
Throu the declynyng of hys large round speir.
The frosty regioun ryngis of the yer,
The tyme and sesson bittir, cald and paill,
Tha schort days that clerkis clepe brumaill,
Quhen brym blastis of the northyn art
Ourquhelmyt had Neptunus in his cart,
And all to-schaik the levis of the treis,
The rageand storm ourweltrand wally seys.
Ryveris ran reid on spait with watir broune,
And burnys hurlys all thar bankis doune,
And landbrist rumland rudely with sik beir,
So lowd ne rumyst wild lyoun or ber.
Fludis monstreis, sik as meirswyne or quhalis,
Fro the tempest law in the deip devalis.
Mars occident retrograde in his speir,
Provocand stryfe, regnyt as lord that yer;
Rany Oryon with his stormy face
Bewavit oft the schipman by hys race;
Frawart Saturn, chill of complexioun,
Throu quhais aspect darth and infectioun
Beyn causyt oft, and mortal pestilens,
Went progressyve the greis of his ascens;
And lusty Hebe, Junoys douchtir gay,
Stude spulyeit of hir office and array.
The soyl ysowpit into watir wak,
The firmament ourcast with rokis blak,
The grond fadyt, and fawch wolx all the feildis,
Montane toppis slekit with snaw ourheild is;
On raggit rolkis of hard harsk quhynstane
With frosyn frontis cauld clynty clewis schane.
Bewté was lost, and barrand schew the landis,
With frostis hair ourfret the feldis standis.
Seir bittir bubbis and the schowris snell
Semyt on the sward a symylitude of hell,
Reducyng to our mynd in every sted
Gousty schaddois of eild and grisly ded.
Thik drumly skuggis dyrknyt so the hevyn,

Dym skyis oft furth warpit feirfull levyn,
Flaggis of fire, and mony felloun flaw,   295
Scharpe soppys of sleit and of the snypand snaw.
The dolly dichis war all donk and wait,
The law vallé flodderit all with spait,
The plane stretis and every hie way
Full of floschis, dubbis, myre and clay.   300
Laggerit leyis wallowit farnys schew,
Broune muris kythit thar wysnyt mossy hew,
Bank, bra and boddum blanchit wolx and bar;
For gurl weddir growit bestis hair.
The wynd maid waif the red wed on the dyke,   305
Bedowyn in donkis deip was every sike.
Our craggis and the front of rochis seir
Hang gret ische-schouchlis lang as ony speir.
The grond stud barrant, widderit, dosk or gray,
Herbis, flowris and gersis wallowyt away.   310
Woddis, forrestis, with nakyt bewis blowt,
Stude stripyt of thar weid in every howt.
So bustuusly Boreas his bugill blew,
The deyr full dern doun in the dalis drew;
Smale byrdis, flokkand throu thik ronys thrang,   315
In chyrmyng and with cheping changit thar sang,
Sekand hidlis and hyrnys thame to hyde
Fra feirfull thuddis of the tempestuus tyde.
The watir lynnys rowtis, and every lynd
Quhislit and brayt of the swouchand wynd.   320
Puyr lauboraris and bissy husbandmen
Went wait and wery draglit in the fen.
The silly scheip and thar litil hyrd-gromys
Lurkis undre le of bankis, woddis and bromys;
And other dantit grettar bestiall,   325
Within thar stabillis sesyt into stall,
Sik as mulis, horssis, oxin and ky,
Fed tuskyt barys and fat swyne in sty,
Sustenyt war by mannys governance
On hervist and on symmeris purvyance. . . .   330

331

21

EVERYMAN

THE austere morality play *The Somonynge of Everyman* appears in print in the early sixteenth century (? 1510–25). It seems to be based on the Dutch play *Elckerlijc*, which is even more austere in style (Knowledge's famous words in lines 522–3 correspond to a single remark of Kennisse: 'Elckerlijc, ic sal u bewaren') and stricter in its metrical form (*Everyman*'s author seems to be 'feeling his way towards a dramatic use of different verse-forms' (A. C. Cawley)). There is no room in this solemn piece for the comic vices of *Mankind*; with a remarkable fusion of theology and theatre it presents an intense, inward spiritual drama. It owes much to the late medieval moral writings which exploit the sudden confrontation of man by death—notably the 'Art of Dying', which instructed man on how to make preparation for his end—but the basic story is a parable which seems to be ultimately of Buddhist origin. As it develops, we become aware of other themes from parable and folk-tale—the necessity for a 'reckoning' (cf. lines 99, 101, 104, etc.), in the background of which lies the biblical parable of the talents, and the testing of friends, a simple morality pattern which is widespread (cf. the Western, *High Noon*), and which is not only essentially dramatic in itself, but (since in extreme crisis the difference between promises and deeds, between appearances and reality, becomes painfully apparent) also lends itself to moral satire. *Everyman* is very effective in performance, yet its dramatic subtlety is sometimes underestimated. For example, in the first meeting with Death (lines 85 ff.), Death has sometimes appeared on the modern stage as a skeleton (like the figure of death in the macabre tradition) or even 'as a marine commando with face blackened and armed literally to the teeth with knife, dynamite, napalm and lasso' (Glynne Wickham, *Shakespeare's Dramatic Heritage* [London, 1969], 33—of a Bristol performance in 1964). But the text indicates something less crude and more genuinely dramatic. It is clear that Everyman, who is going 'gayly' (and probably dressed as a gallant), does not at first recognize the stranger he meets. There is a long exchange before the sudden revelation is made by Death (line 115), and there is then a terrible poignancy in Everyman's remark, 'O Deth, thou comest whan I had the leest in mynde!' In the following conversation, too, which is well observed (note the rapidly changing attitudes of Everyman—offering money, pleading for time—confronted by the appalling thought of his unpreparedness), Death (God's trusted messenger in this play) does not speak with the scoffing, bitter tone he often has in the *Dance of Death*, but with an austere dignity, and even a sorrowful friendliness. By the time he has taken his leave (equally dramatically), not only has the playwright established the parable theme of 'reckoning', but one of the 'deep structures' of allegorical drama—the idea of a journey, or a pilgrimage (preparations for which were made as if for a journey to death)—has begun to emerge ('a longe journey', 'this pylgrymage'). As the play continues, this is treated with some sophistication in the handling of 'dramatic time'. Two contrary patterns are set up—on the one hand, suggestions that it will be a *long* journey (cf. lines 103, 242, 279, etc.), and, on the other, suggestions that the reckoning must be quickly made, and that time is slipping away (cf. lines 191, 193, etc.)—and their coexistence increases the dramatic tension. There follow many finely expressive scenes. Everyman is at his lowest point after the exit of Goodes (cf. his lament in lines 463 ff.), and here the second 'movement'—upwards—of the play begins with the dramatic discovery of Good Deed lying 'colde in the grounde', bound by Everyman's sins. It is emphasized by the heightened style of Everyman's prayer (580–607). The atmosphere is still sorrowful, but the pressures of the fear of sudden death and of despair are relaxed; thoughts of hope and comfort take their place as the careful preparation for a good death begins through visual and symbolic actions—the scourging, and the putting on of the garment of sorrow. Everyman can now say 'I wepe for very swetenesse of love', and there is a new sense of spiritual eagerness and excitement (cf. line 651 'without taryenge', and lines 665 ff.). After the last leave-taking, Everyman is left with only Good Deeds, his truest friend, and his 'vyage longe' (line 782) and 'pylgrymage' (line 818) consist only of a few final steps to the grave.

DRAMATIS PERSONAE

GOD	GOOD DEEDS
EVERYMAN	KNOWLEDGE
DEATH	CONFESSION
FELLOWSHIP	BEAUTY
KINDRED	STRENGTH
COUSIN	DISCRETION
GOODS	FIVE WITS

MESSENGER

ANGEL

DOCTOR

[*Enter Messenger*]

Messenger. I pray you all gyve your audyence,
And here this mater with reverence,
By fygure a morall playe:
The Somonynge of Everyman called it is,
That of our lyves and endynge shewes   5
How transytory we be all daye.

This mater is wonders precyous,
But the entent of it is more gracyous,
And swete to bere awaye.
10 The story sayth: Man, in the begynnynge
Loke well, and take good heed to the endynge,
Be you never so gay!
Ye thynke synne in the begynnynge full swete,
Whiche in the ende causeth the soule to wepe
15 Whan the body lyeth in claye.
Here shall you se how Felawshyp and Jolyté,
Bothe Strengthe, Pleasure, and Beauté
Wyll fade from the as floure in Maye;
For ye shall here how our Heven-Kynge
20 Calleth Everyman to a generall rekenynge.
Gyve audyence, and here what he doth saye. [*Exit*

God speketh [from above]

God. I perceyve, here in my majesté,
How that all creatures be to me unkynde,
Lyvynge without drede in worldly prosperyté.
25 Of ghostly syght the people be so blynde,
Drowned in synne, they know me not for theyr God.
In worldely ryches is all theyr mynde—
They fere not my ryghtwysnes, the sharpe rod.
My lawe that I shewed, whan I for them dyed,
30 They forgete clene, and shedynge of my blode rede.
I hanged bytwene two theves, it can not be denyed;
To gete them lyfe I suffred to be deed;
I heled theyr fete—with thornes hurt was my heed.
I coude do no more than I dyde, truely!
35 And nowe I se the people do clene forsake me.
They use the seven deedly synnes dampnable,
As pryde, coveytyse, wrath, and lechery
Now in the worlde be made commendable;
And thus they leve of aungelles the hevenly company.
40 Every man lyveth so after his owne pleasure,
And yet of theyr lyfe they be nothynge sure.
I se the more that I them forbere
The worse they be fro yere to yere.
All that lyveth appayreth faste.
45 Therfore I wyll, in all the haste,
Have a rekenynge of every mannes persone,
For and I leve the people thus alone
In theyr lyfe and wycked tempestes,

Veryly they will become moche worse than beestes,
For now one wolde by envy another up ete—   50
Charyté they do all clene forgete.
I hoped well that every man
In my glory sholde make his mansyon,
And therto I had them all electe;
But now I se, lyke traytours dejecte,   55
They thanke me not for the pleasure that I to them ment,
Nor yet for theyr beynge that I them have lent.
I profered the people grete multytude of mercy,
And fewe there be that asketh it hertly.
They be so combred with worldly ryches   60
That nedes on them I must do justyce,
On every man lyvynge without fere.
Where arte thou, Deth, thou myghty messengere?

                        [*Enter Death*]

  Dethe. Almyghty God, I am here at your wyll,
Your commaundement to fulfyll.   65
  God. Go thou to Everyman
And shewe hym, in my name,
A pylgrymage he must on hym take,
Whiche he in no wyse may escape;
And that he brynge with hym a sure rekenynge   70
Without delay or ony taryenge.   [*God withdraws*
  Dethe. Lorde, I wyll in the worlde go renne overall
And cruelly outserche bothe grete and small.
Every man wyll I beset that lyveth beestly
Out of Goddes lawes, and dredeth not foly.   75
He that loveth rychesse I wyll stryke with my darte,
His syght to blynde, and fro heven to departe—
Excepte that almes be his good frende—
In hell for to dwell, worlde without ende.
Loo, yonder I se Everyman walkynge.   80
Full lytell he thynketh on my comynge;
His mynde is on flesshely lustes and his treasure,
And grete payne it shall cause hym to endure
Before the Lorde, Heven-Kynge.

                     [*Enter Everyman*]

Everyman, stande styll! Whyder arte thou goynge   85
Thus gayly? Hast thou thy Maker forgete?
  Everyman. Why askest thou?
Woldest thou wete?

Dethe. Ye, syr. I wyll shewe you:

90 In grete hast I am sende to the
Fro God out of his magesté.
    Everyman. What, sente to me?
    Dethe. Ye, certaynly.
Thoughe thou have forgete hym here,

95 He thynketh on the in the hevenly spere,
As, or we departe, thou shalte knowe.
    Everyman. What desyreth God of me?
    Dethe. That shall I shewe the:
A rekenynge he wyll nedes have

100 Without ony lenger respyte.
    Everyman. To gyve a rekenynge longer layser I crave—
This blynde mater troubleth my wytte.
    Dethe. On the thou must take a longe journey;
Therfore thy boke of counte with the thou brynge,

105 For tourne agayne thou can not by no waye.
And loke thou be sure of thy rekenynge,
For before God thou shalte answere, and shewe
Thy many badde dedes, and good but a fewe,
How thou hast spente thy lyfe, and in what wyse,

110 Before the chefe Lorde of Paradyse.
Have ado that we were in that waye,
For wete thou well thou shalte make none attournay.
    Everyman. Full unredy I am suche rekenynge to gyve.
I knowe the not. What messenger arte thou?

115   *Dethe.* I am Dethe that no man dredeth—
For every man I reste—and no man spareth;
For it is Goddes commaundement
That all to me sholde be obedyent.
    Everyman. O Deth, thou comest whan I had the leest in mynde!

120 In thy power it lyeth me to save;
Yet of my good wyl I gyve the, yf thou wyl be kynde,
Ye, a thousande pounde shalte thou have,
And dyfferre this mater tyll another daye.
    Dethe. Everyman, it may not be by no waye.

125 I set not by golde, sylver, nor rychesse,
Ne by pope, emperour, kynge, duke, ne prynces;
For, I wolde receyve gyftes grete,
All the worlde I myght gete;
But my custome is clene contrary.

130 I gyve the no respyte. Come hens, and not tary!
    Everyman. Alas, shall I have no lenger respyte?
I may saye Deth gyveth no warnynge!

To thynke on the, it maketh my herte seke,
For all unredy is my boke of rekenynge.
But .xii. yere and I myght have abydynge,   135
My countynge-boke I wolde make so clere
That my rekenynge I sholde not nede to fere.
Wherfore, Deth, I praye the, for Goddes mercy,
Spare me tyll I be provyded of remedy!
   Dethe. The avayleth not to crye, wepe, and praye;   140
But hast the lyghtly that thou were gone that journaye,
And preve thy frendes yf thou can.
For wete thou well, the tyde abydeth no man,
And in the worlde eche lyvynge creature
For Adams synne must dye of nature.   145
   Everyman. Dethe, yf I sholde this pylgrymage take,
And my rekenynge suerly make,
Shewe me, for saynt charyté,
Sholde I not come agayne shortly?
   Dethe. No, Everyman; and thou be ones there,   150
Thou mayst never more come here,
Trust me veryly.
   Everyman. O gracyous God in the hye sete celestyall,
Have mercy on me in this moost nede!
Shall I have no company fro this vale terestryall   155
Of myne acqueyntaunce that way me to lede?
   Dethe. Ye, yf ony be so hardy
That wolde go with the and bere the company.
Hye the that thou were gone to Goddes magnyfycence,
Thy rekenynge to gyve before his presence.   160
What, wenest thou thy lyve is gyven the,
And thy worldely goddes also?
   Everyman. I had wende so, verylé.
   Dethe. Nay, nay, it was but lende the;
For as soone as thou arte go,   165
Another a whyle shall have it, and than go therfro
Even as thou hast done.
Everyman, thou arte made! Thou hast thy wyttes fyve,
And here on erthe wyll not amende thy lyve;
For sodeynly I do come.   170
   Everyman. O wretched caytyfe! Wheder shall I flee,
That I myght scape this endles sorowe?
Now, gentyll Deth, spare me tyll tomorowe,
That I may amende me
With good advysement.   175
   Dethe. Naye, therto I wyll not consent,

Nor no man wyll I respyte;
But to the herte sodeynly I shall smyte
Without ony advysement.
180 And now out of thy syght I wyll me hy—
Se thou make the redy shortely,
For thou mayst saye this is the daye
That no man lyvynge may scape awaye.   [*Exit Death*
    Everyman. Alas, I may well wepe with syghes depe!
185 Now have I no maner of company
To helpe me in my journey and me to kepe,
And also my wrytynge is full unredy.
How shall I do now for to exscuse me?
I wolde to God I had never be gete!
190 To my soule a full grete profyte it had be;
For now I fere paynes huge and grete.
The tyme passeth. Lorde, helpe, that all wrought!
For though I mourne, it avayleth nought.
The day passeth and is almoost ago;
195 I wote not well what for to do.
To whome were I best my complaynt to make?
What and I to Felawshyp therof spake,
And shewed hym of this sodeyne chaunce?
For in hym is all myne affyaunce;
200 We have in the worlde so many a daye
Be good frendes in sporte and playe.
I se hym yonder, certaynely.
I trust that he wyll bere me company;
Therfore to hym wyll I speke to ese my sorowe.
205 Well mette, good Felawshyp, and good morowe!

              Felawshyp speketh

    Felawship. Everyman, good morowe, by this daye!
Syr, why lokest thou so pyteously?
If ony thynge be amysse, I praye the me saye,
That I may helpe to remedy.
210   *Everyman.* Ye, good Felawshyp, ye,
I am in greate jeopardé.
    Felawship. My true frende, shewe to me your mynde.
I wyll not forsake the to my lyves ende,
In the waye of good company.
215   *Everyman.* That was well spoken and lovyngly.
    Felawshyp. Syr, I must nedes knowe your hevynesse;
I have pyté to se you in ony dystresse.
If ony have you wronged, ye shall revenged be,

Thoughe I on the grounde be slayne for the,
Though that I knowe before that I sholde dye. 220
    Everyman. Veryly, Felawshyp, gramercy!
    Felawship. Tusshe! by thy thankes I set not a strawe.
Shewe me your grefe, and saye no more.
Everyman. If I my herte sholde to you breke,
And than you to tourne your mynde fro me 225
And wolde not me comforte whan ye here me speke,
Than sholde I ten tymes soryer be.
    Felawship. Syr, I saye as I wyll do in dede.
    Everyman. Than be you a good frende at nede.
I have founde you true herebefore. 230
    Felawship. And so ye shall evermore;
For, in fayth, and thou go to hell,
I wyll not forsake the by the waye.
    Everyman. Ye speke lyke a good frende; I byleve you well.
I shall deserve it and I maye. 235
    Felawship. I speke of no deservynge, by this daye!
For he that wyll saye, and nothynge do,
Is not worthy with good company to go;
Therfore shewe me the grefe of your mynde,
As to your frende moost lovynge and kynde. 240
    Everyman. I shall shewe you how it is:
Commaunded I am to go a journaye,
A longe waye, harde and daungerous,
And gyve a strayte counte, without delaye,
Before the hye juge Adonay. 245
Wherfore, I pray you, bere me company,
As ye have promysed, in this journaye.
    Felawship. That is mater indede! Promyse is duty—
But, and I sholde take suche a vyage on me,
I knowe it well, it sholde be to my payne; 250
Also it maketh me aferde, certayne.
But let us take counsell here as well as we can,
For your wordes wolde fere a stronge man.
    Everyman. Why, ye sayd yf I had nede
Ye wolde me never forsake, quycke ne deed, 255
Thoughe it were to hell, truely.
    Felawship. So I sayd, certaynely,
But suche pleasures be set asyde, the sothe to saye;
And also, yf we toke suche a journaye,
Whan sholde we agayne come? 260
    Everyman. Naye, never agayne tyll the daye of dome.
    Felawship. In fayth, than wyll not I come there!

Who hath you these tydynges brought?
   Everyman. Indede, Deth was with me here.
265 *Felawshyp.* Now, by God that all hathe bought,
If Deth were the messenger,
For no man that is lyvynge todaye
I wyll not go that lothe journaye—
Not for the fader that bygate me!
270 *Everyman.* Ye promysed other wyse, pardé!
   Felawship. I wote well I sayd so, truely;
And yet, yf thou wylte ete and drynke and make good chere,
Or haunt to women the lusty company,
I wolde not forsake you whyle the daye is clere,
275 Trust me veryly!
   Everyman. Ye, therto ye wolde be redy!
To go to myrthe, solas, and playe
Your mynde wyll soner apply,
Than to bere me company in my longe journaye!
280 *Felawship.* Now, in good fayth, I wyll not that waye;
But and thou wyll murder, or ony man kyll,
In that I wyll helpe the with a good wyll.
   Everyman. O, that is a symple advyse indede.
Gentyll felawe, helpe me in my necessyté!
285 We have loved longe, and now I nede—
And now, gentyll Felawshyp, remembre me!
   Felawship. Wheder ye have loved me or no,
By Saynt John I wyll not with the go!
   Everyman. Yet, I pray the, take the labour and do so moche for me
290 To brynge me forwarde, for saynt charyté,
And comforte me tyll I come without the towne.
   Felawship. Nay, and thou wolde gyve me a newe gowne
I wyll not a fote with the go;
But, and thou had taryed, I wolde not have lefte the so.
295 And as now God spede the in thy journaye,
For from the I wyll departe as fast as I maye.
   Everyman. Wheder awaye, Felawshyp? Wyll thou forsake me?
   Felawship. Ye, by my faye! To God I betake the.
   Everyman. Farewell, good Felawshyp! For the my herte is sore.
300 Adewe for ever! I shall se the no more.
   Felawship. In fayth, Everyman, fare well now at the endynge!
For you I wyll remembre that partynge is mournynge.   [*Exit Fellowship*
   Everyman. Alacke, shall we thus departe indede—
A, Lady, helpe!—without ony more comforte?
305 Lo, Felawshyp forsaketh me in my moost nede.
For helpe in this worlde wheder shall I resorte?

Felawshyp herebefore with me wolde mery make,
And now lytell sorowe for me dooth he take.
It is sayd, 'In prosperyté men frendes may fynde,
Whiche in adversyté be full unkynde.'   310
Now wheder for socoure shall I flee,
Syth that Felawshyp hath forsaken me?
To my kynnesmen I wyll, truely,
Prayenge them to helpe me in my necessyté.
I byleve that they wyll do so,   315
For kynde wyll crepe where it may not go.
I wyll go saye, for yonder I se them.
Where be ye now, my frendes and kynnesmen?

[Enter Kindred and Cousin]

Kynrede. Here be we now at your commaundement.
Cosyn, I praye you shewe us your entent   320
In ony wyse, and not spare.
   Cosyn. Ye, Everyman, and to us declare
If ye be dysposed to go onywhyder;
For, wete you well, we wyll lyve and dye togyder.
   Kynrede. In welth and wo we wyll with you holde,   325
For over his kynne a man may be bolde.
   Everyman. Gramercy, my frendes and kynnesmen kynde!
Now shall I shewe you the grefe of my mynde:
I was commaunded by a messenger
That is a hye kynges chefe offycer.   330
He bad me go a pylgrymage, to my payne,
And I knowe well I shall never come agayne.
Also I must gyve a rekenynge strayte,
For I have a grete enemy that hath me in wayte,   335
Whiche entendeth me for to hynder.
   Kynrede. What acounte is that whiche ye must render?
That wolde I knowe.
   Everyman. Of all my workes I must shewe
How I have lyved and my dayes spent;
Also of yll dedes that I have used   340
In my tyme, syth lyfe was me lent;
And of all vertues that I have refused.
Therfore, I praye you, go thyder with me
To helpe to make myn accounte, for saynt charyté.
   Cosyn. What, to go thyder? Is that the mater?   345
Nay, Everyman, I had lever fast brede and water
All this fyve yere and more.
   Everyman. Alas, that ever I was bore!

For now shall I never be mery,
350   If that you forsake me.
            Kynrede. A, syr, what ye be a mery man!
        Take good herte to you, and make no mone.
        But one thynge I warne you, by Saynt Anne—
        As for me, ye shall go alone.
355   *Everyman.* My Cosyn, wyll you not with me go?
            Cosyn. No, by our Lady! I have the crampe in my to!
        Trust not to me; for, so God me spede,
        I wyll deceyve you in your moost nede.
            Kynrede. It avayleth not us to tyse.
360   Ye shall have my mayde with all my herte!
        She loveth to go to feestes, there to be nyse,
        And to daunce, and abrode to sterte.
        I wyll gyve her leve to helpe you in that journey,
        If that you and she may agree.
365   *Everyman.* Now shewe me the very effecte of your mynde:
        Wyll you go with me, or abyde behynde?
            Kynrede. Abyde behynde? Ye, that wyll I, and I maye!
        Therfore farewell tyll another daye!   [*Exit Kindred*
            Everyman. How sholde I be mery or gladde?
370   For fayre promyses men to me make,
        But whan I have moost nede they me forsake.
        I am deceyved; that maketh me sadde.
            Cosyn. Cosyn Everyman, farewell now,
        For veryly I wyll not go with you.
375   Also of myne owne an unredy rekenynge
        I have to accounte; therfore I make taryenge.
        Now God kepe the, for now I go.   [*Exit Cousin*
            Everyman. A, Jesus, is all come hereto?
        Lo, fayre wordes maketh fooles fayne;
380   They promyse, and nothynge wyll do, certayne.
        My kynnesmen promysed me faythfully
        For to abyde with me stedfastly,
        And now fast awaye do they flee.
        Even so Felawshyp promysed me.
385   What frende were best me of to provyde?
        I lose my tyme here longer to abyde.
        Yet in my mynde a thynge there is:
        All my lyfe I have loved ryches;
        If that my Good now helpe me myght,
390   He wolde make my herte full lyght.
        I wyll speke to hym in this dystresse.
        Where arte thou, my Gooddes and ryches?

[Goods speaks from a corner]

Goodes. Who calleth me? Everyman? What, hast thou haste?
I lye here in corners, trussed and pyled so hye,
And in chestes I am locked so fast,   395
Also sacked in bagges. Thou mayst se with thyn eye.
I can not styre; in packes lowe I lye.
What wolde ye have? Lyghtly me saye.
    Everyman. Come hyder, Good, in al the hast thou may,
For of counseyll I must desyre the.   400
    Goodes. Syr, and ye in the worlde have sorowe or adversyté,
That can I helpe you to remedy shortly.
    Everyman. It is another dysease that greveth me;
In this worlde it is not, I tell the so.
I am sent for, another way to go,   405
To gyve a strayte counte generall
Before the hyest Jupyter of all.
And all my lyfe I have had joye and pleasure in the,
Therfore, I pray the, go with me;
For, paraventure, thou mayst before God Almyghty   410
My rekenynge helpe to clene and puryfye,
For it is sayd ever amonge
That money maketh all ryght that is wronge.
    Goodes. Nay, Everyman, I synge another songe.
I folowe no man in suche vyages;   415
For, and I wente with the,
Thou sholdest fare moche the worse for me.
For bycause on me thou dyd set thy mynde,
Thy rekenynge I have made blotted and blynde,
That thyne accounte thou can not make truly;   420
And that hast thou for the love of me!
    Everyman. That wolde greve me full sore
Whan I sholde come to that ferefull answere.
Up, let us go thyder togyder.
    Goodes. Nay, not so! I am to brytell, I may not endure.   425
I wyll folowe no man one fote, be ye sure!
    Everyman. Alas, I have the loved, and had grete pleasure
All my lyfe-dayes on good and treasure.
    Goodes. That is to thy dampnacyon, without lesynge,
For my love is contrary to the love everlastynge.   430
But yf thou had me loved moderately durynge,
As to the poore gyve parte of me,
Than sholdest thou not in this dolour be,
Nor in this grete sorowe and care.

435   *Everyman.* Lo, now was I deceyved or I was ware,
And all I may wyte my spendynge of tyme.
    Goodes. What, wenest thou that I am thyne?
    Everyman. I had went so.
    Goodes. Naye, Everyman, I saye no.
440 As for a whyle I was lente the;
A season thou hast had me in prosperyté.
My condycyon is mannes soule to kyll;
If I save one, a thousande I do spyll.
Wenest thou that I wyll folowe the?
445 Nay, fro this worlde not, verylé.
    Everyman. I had wende otherwyse.
    Goodes. Therfore to thy soule Good is a thefe;
For whan thou arte deed, this is my gyse—
Another to deceyve in this same wyse
450 As I have done the, and all to his soules reprefe.
    Everyman. O false Good, cursed thou be,
Thou traytour to God, that hast deceyved me
And caught me in thy snare!
    Goodes. Mary, thou brought thyselfe in care,
455 Wherof I am gladde.
I must nedes laugh—I can not be sadde.
    Everyman. A, Good, thou has had longe my hertely love;
I gave the that whiche sholde be the Lordes above.
But wylte thou not go with me indede?
460 I praye the trouth to saye.
    Goodes. No, so God me spede!
Therfore fare well, and have good daye.   [*Exit Goods*
    Everyman. O, to whome shall I make my mone
For to go with me in that hevy journaye?
465 Fyrst Felawshyp sayd he wolde with me gone;
His wordes were very pleasaunt and gaye,
But afterwarde he lefte me alone.
Than spake I to my kynnesmen, all in dyspayre,
And also they gave me wordes fayre;
470 They lacked no fayre spekynge,
But all forsoke me in the endynge.
Than wente I to my Goodes that I loved best,
In hope to have comforte, but there had I leest;
For my Goodes sharpely dyd me tell
475 That he bryngeth many into hell.
Than of myselfe I was ashamed,
And so I am worthy to be blamed;
Thus may I well myselfe hate.

Of whome shall I now counseyll take?
I thynke that I shall never spede   480
Tyll that I go to my Good Dede.
But, alas, she is so weke
That she can nother go nor speke;
Yet wyll I venter on her now.
My Good Dedes, where be you?   485

[*Good Deeds speaks from the ground*]

   Good Dedes. Here I lye, colde in the grounde.
Thy synnes hath me sore bounde,
That I can not stere.
   Everyman. O Good Dedes, I stande in fere!
I must you pray of counseyll,   490
For helpe now sholde come ryght well.
   Good Dedes. Everyman, I have understandynge
That ye be somoned acounte to make
Before Myssyas, of Jerusalem kynge;
And you do by me, that journay with you wyll I take.   495
   Everyman. Therfore I come to you my moone to make.
I praye you that ye wyll go with me.
   Good Dedes. I wolde full fayne, but I can not stande, veryly.
   Everyman. Why, is there ony thynge on you fall?
   Good Dedes. Ye, syr, I may thanke you of all;   500
If ye had parfytely chered me,
Your boke of counte full redy had be.
Loke, the bokes of your workes and dedes eke;
A, se how they lye under the fete,
To your soules hevynes.   505
   Everyman. Our Lorde Jesus helpe me!
For one letter here I can not se.
   Good Dedes. There is a blynde rekenynge in tyme of dystres.
   Everyman. Good Dedes, I praye you helpe me in this nede,
Or elles I am for ever damned indede;   510
Therfore helpe me to make rekenynge
Before the Redemer of all thynge,
That kynge is, and was, and ever shall.
   Good Dedes. Everyman, I am sory of your fall,
And fayne wolde I helpe you, and I were able.   515
   Everyman. Good Dedes, your counseyll I pray you gyve me.
   Good Dedes. That shall I do veryly.
Thoughe that on my fete I may not go,
I have a syster that shall with you also,

520 Called Knowlege, whiche shall with you abyde,
To helpe you to make that dredefull rekenynge.

[Enter Knowledge]

   Knowlege. Everyman, I wyll go with the and be thy gyde,
In thy moost nede to go by thy syde.
   Everyman. In good condycyon I am now in every thynge,
525 And am holy content with this good thynge,
Thanked be God my Creature.
   Good Dedes. And whan she hath brought you there
Where thou shalte hele the of thy smarte,
Than go you with your rekenynge and your Good Dedes togyder,
530 For to make you joyfull at herte
Before the Blessyd Trynyté.
   Everyman. My Good Dedes, gramercy!
I am well content, certaynly,
With your wordes swete.
535   *Knowlege.* Now go we togyder lovyngly
To Confessyon, that clensynge ryvere.
   Everyman. For joy I wepe; I wolde we were there!
But, I pray you, gyve me cognycyon
Where dwelleth that holy man, Confessyon.
540   *Knowlege.* In the hous of salvacyon;
We shall fynde hym in that place,
That shall us comforte, by Goddes grace.
       [Knowledge leads Everyman to Confession
Lo, this is Confessyon. Knele downe and aske mercy,
For he is in good conceyte with God Almyghty.
545   *Everyman.* O gloryous fountayne, that all unclennes doth claryfy,
Wasshe fro me the spottes of vyce unclene,
That on me no synne may be sene,
I come with Knowlege for my redempcyon,
Redempte with herte and full contrycyon;
550 For I am commaunded a pylgrymage to take,
And grete accountes before God to make.
Now I praye you, Shryfte, moder of salvacyon,
Helpe my Good Dedes for my pyteous exclamacyon.
   Confessyon. I knowe your sorrowe well, Everyman.
555 Bycause with Knowlege ye come to me,
I wyll you comforte as well as I can.
And a precyous jewell I wyll gyve the,
Called Penaunce, voyder of adversyté;
Therwith shall your body chastysed be,
560 With abstynence and perseveraunce in Goddes servyture.

346

Here shall you receyve that scourge of me,
Whiche is penaunce stronge that ye muste endure,
To remembre thy Savyour was scourged for the
With sharpe scourges, and suffred it pacyently;
So must thou or thou passe that paynful pylgrymage.   565
Knowlege, kepe hym in this vyage,
And by that tyme Good Dedes wyll be with the.
But in ony wyse be seker of mercy,
For your tyme draweth fast; and ye wyll saved be,
Aske God mercy, and he wyll graunte truely.   570
Whan with the scourge of penaunce man doth hym bynde,
The oyle of forgyvenes than shall he fynde.
    Everyman. Thanked be God for his gracyous werke!
For now I wyll my penaunce begyn.
This hath rejoysed and lyghted my herte,   575
Though the knottes be paynful and harde, within.
    Knowlege. Everyman, loke your penaunce that ye fulfyll,
What payne that ever it to you be;
And Knowlege shall gyve you counseyll at wyll
How your accounte ye shall make clerely.   580
    Everyman. O eternall God! O hevenly fygure!
O way of ryghtwysnes! O goodly vysyon,
Whiche dyscended downe in a vyrgyn pure
Bycause he wolde every man redeme,
Whiche Adam forfayted by his dysobedyence!   585
O blessyd Godheed, electe and hye devyne,
Forgyve me my grevous offence!
Here I crye the mercy in this presence.
O ghostly treasure, O raunsomer and redemer,
Of all the worlde hope and conduyter,   590
Myrrour of joye, foundatour of mercy,
Whiche enlumyneth heven and erthe therby,
Here my clamorous complaynt, though it late be,
Receyve my prayers unworthy in this hevy lyfe!
Though I be a synner moost abhomynable,   595
Yet let my name be wryten in Moyses table.
O Mary, praye to the Maker of all thynge,
Me for to helpe at my endynge;
And save me fro the power of my enemy,
For Deth assayleth me strongly.   600
And, Lady, that I may by meane of thy prayer
Of your Sones glory to be partynere,
By the meanes of his passyon, I it crave;
I beseche you helpe my soule to save.

605 Knowlege, gyve me the scourge of penaunce;
     My flesshe therwith shall have acqueyntaunce.
     I wyll now begyn yf God gyve me grace.
         Knowlege. Everyman, God gyve you tyme and space!
     Thus I bequeth you in the handes of our Savyour;
610 Now may you make your rekenynge sure.
         Everyman. In the name of the Holy Trynyté,
     My body sore punysshed shall be:
     Take this, body, for the synne of the flesshe!   [*Scourges himself*
     Also thou delytest to go gay and fresshe,
615 And in the way of dampnacyon thou dyd me brynge,
     Therfore suffre now strokes of punysshynge.
     Now of penaunce I wyll wade the water clere,
     To save me from Purgatory, that sharpe fyre.   [*Good Deeds rises*
         Good Dedes. I thanke God, now I can walke and go,
620 And am delyvered of my sykenesse and wo.
     Therfore with Everyman I wyll go, and not spare;
     His good workes I wyll helpe hym to declare.
         Knowlege. Now, Everyman, be mery and glad!
     Your Good Dedes cometh now; ye may not be sad.
625 Now is your Good Dedes hole and sounde,
     Goynge upryght upon the grounde.
         Everyman. My herte is lyght, and shal be evermore;
     Now wyll I smyte faster than I dyde before.
         Good Dedes. Everyman, pylgryme, my specyall frende,
630 Blessyd be thou without ende!
     For the is preparate the eternall glory.
     Ye have me made hole and sounde,
     Therfore I wyll byde by the in every stounde.
         Everyman. Welcome, my Good Dedes! Now I here thy voyce,
635 I wepe for very swetenes of love.
         Knowlege. Be no more sad, but ever rejoyce;
     God seeth thy lyvynge in his trone above.
     Put on this garment to thy behove,
     Whiche is wette with your teres,
640 Or elles before God you may it mysse,
     Whan ye to your journeys ende come shall.
         Everyman. Gentyll Knowlege, what do ye it call?
         Knowlege. It is a garment of sorowe;
     Fro payne it wyll you borowe.
645 Contrycyon it is
     That getteth forgyvenes;
     He pleaseth God passynge well.
         Good Dedes. Everyman, wyll you were it for your hele?

Everyman. Now blessyd be Jesu, Maryes sone,   [*Puts on the robe*
For now have I on true contrycyon;   650
And lette us go now without taryenge.
Good Dedes, have we clere our rekenynge?
    Good Dedes. Ye, indede, I have it here.
    Everyman. Than I trust we nede not fere.
Now, frendes, let us not parte in twayne.   655
    Knowlege. Nay, Everyman, that wyll we not, certayne!
    Good Dedes. Yet must thou lede with the
Thre persones of grete myght.
    Everyman. Who sholde they be?
    Good Dedes. Dyscrecyon and Strenght they hyght,   660
And thy Beauté may not abyde behynde.
    Knowlege. Also ye must call to mynde
Your Fyve Wyttes as for your conseylours.
    Good Dedes. You must have them redy at all houres.
    Everyman. Howe shall I gette them hyder?   665
    Knowlege. You must call them all togyder,
And they wyll here you incontynent.
    Everyman. My frendes, come hyder and be present—
Dyscrecyon, Strengthe, my Fyve Wyttes, and Beauté!

    [*Enter Beauty, Strength, Discretion, and Five Wits*]

    Beauté. Here at your wyll we be all redy.   670
What wyll ye that we sholde do?
    Good Dedes. That ye wolde with Everyman go,
And helpe hym in his pylgrymage.
Advyse you, wyll ye with him or not in that vyage?
    Strength. We wyll brynge hym all thyder,   675
To his helpe and comforte, ye may byleve me.
    Dyscrecion. So wyll we go with hym all togyder.
    Everyman. Almyghty God, loued may thou be!
I gyve the laude that I have hyder brought
Strength, Dyscrecyon, Beauté, and .V. Wyttes—lacke I nought!   680
And my Good Dedes, with Knowlege clere,
All be in company at my wyll here.
I desyre no more to my besynes.
    Strengthe. And I, Strength, wyll by you stande in dystres,
Though thou wolde in batayle fyght on the grounde.   685
    V. Wyttes. And though it were thrugh the worlde rounde,
We wyll not departe for swete ne soure.
    Beauté. No more wyll I unto dethes houre,
Whatsoever therof befall!
    Dyscrecion. Everyman, advyse you fyrst of all;   690

349

Go with a good advysement and delyberacyon.
We all gyve you vertuous monycyon
That all shall be well.
  Everyman. My frendes, harken what I wyll tell:
695 I praye God rewarde you in his hevenly spere.
Now herken, all that be here,
For I wyll make my testament
Here before you all present:
In almes halfe my good I wyll gyve with my handes twayne
700 In the way of charyté with good entent,
And the other halfe styll shall remayne
In queth, to be retourned there it ought to be.
This I do in despyte of the fende of hell,
To go quyte out of his perell
705 Ever after and this daye.
  Knowlege. Everyman, herken what I saye:
Go to Presthode, I you advyse,
And receyve of hym in ony wyse
The holy sacrament and oyntement togyder.
710 Than shortly se ye tourne agayne hyder;
We wyll all abyde you here.
  V. Wyttes. Ye, Everyman, hye you that ye redy were.
There is no emperour, kynge, duke, ne baron,
That of God hath commycyon
715 As hath the leest preest in the worlde beynge;
For of the blessyd sacramentes pure and benygne
He bereth the keyes, and therof hath the cure
For mannes redempcyon—it is ever sure—
Whiche God for our soules medycyne
720 Gave us out of his herte with grete pyne.
Here in this transytory lyfe, for the and me,
The blessyd sacramentes .vii. there be:
Baptym, confyrmacyon, with preesthode good,
And the sacrament of Goddes precyous flesshe and blod,
725 Maryage, the holy extreme unccyon, and penaunce.
These seven be good to have in remembraunce,
Gracyous sacramentes of hye devynyté.
  Everyman. Fayne wolde I receyve that holy body,
And mekely to my ghostly fader I wyll go.
730 *V. Wyttes.* Everyman, that is the best that ye can do.
God wyll you to salvacyon brynge,
For preesthode excedeth all other thynge:
To us holy scrypture they do teche,
And converteth man fro synne, heven to reche;

God hath to them more power gyven   735
Than to ony aungell that is in heven.
With .v. wordes he may consecrate,
Goddes body in flesshe and blode to make,
And handeleth his Maker bytwene his handes.
The preest byndeth and unbyndeth all bandes,   740
Bothe in erthe and in heven.
Thou mynystres all the sacramentes seven;
Though we kyst thy fete, thou were worthy.
Thou arte surgyon that cureth synne deedly;
No remedy we fynde under God   745
But all onely preesthode.
Everyman, God gave preest that dygnyté,
And setteth them in his stede amonge us to be;
Thus be they above aungelles in degree.
                [*Everyman goes to the Priest for the Last Sacraments*
    Knowlege. If preestes be good, it is so, suerly.   750
But whan Jesu hanged on the crosse with grete smarte,
There he gave out of his blessyd herte
The seven sacramentes in grete tourment;
He solde them not to us, that Lorde omnypotent.
Therfore Saynt Peter the apostell dothe saye   755
That Jesus curse hath all they
Whiche God theyr Savyour do by or sell,
Or they for ony money do take or tell.
Synfull preestes gyveth the synners example bad:
Theyr chyldren sytteth by other mennes fyres, I have harde;   760
And some haunteth womens company
With unclene lyfe, as lustes of lechery.
These be with synne made blynde.
    V. Wyttes. I trust to God no suche may we fynde;
Therfore let us preesthode honour,   765
And folowe theyr doctryne for our soules socoure.
We be theyr shepe, and they shepeherdes be
By whome we all be kepte in suerté.
Peas! For yonder I se Everyman come,
Whiche hath made true satysfaccyon.   770
    Good Dedes. Me thynke it is he indede.

                    [*Enter Everyman*]

Everyman. Now Jesu be your alder spede!
I have receyved the sacrament for my redempycon,
And than myne extreme unccyon.
Blessyd be all they that counseyled me to take it!   775

And now, frendes, let us go without longer respyte.
I thanke God that ye have taryed so longe.
Now set eche of you on this rodde your honde,
And shortely folowe me.

780 I go before ther I wolde be. God be our gyde!
Strength. Everyman, we wyll not fro you go
Tyll ye have done this vyage longe.
Dyscrecion. I, Dyscrecyon, wyll byde by you also.
Knowlege. And though this pylgrymage be never so stronge,

785 I wyll never parte you fro.
Strength. Everyman, I wyll be as sure by the
As ever I dyde by Judas Machabee.

[*They go together to the grave*

Everyman. Alas, I am so faynt I may not stande;
My lymmes under me doth folde.

790 Frendes, let us not tourne agayne to this lande,
Not for all the worldes golde;
For into this cave must I crepe
And tourne to erth, and there to slepe.
Beauté. What, into this grave? Alas!

795 *Everyman.* Ye, there shall ye consume, more and lesse.
Beauté. And what, sholde I smoder here?
Everyman. Ye, by my fayth, and never more appere.
In this worlde lyve no more we shall,
But in heven before the hyest Lorde of all.

800 *Beauté.* I crosse out all this! Adewe, by Saynt Johan!
I take my tappe in my lappe and am gone.
Everyman. What, Beauté, whyder wyll ye?
Beauté. Peas! I am defe. I loke not behynde me,
Not and thou woldest gyve me all the golde in thy chest. [*Exit Beauty*

805 *Everyman.* Alas, wherto may I truste?
Beauté gothe fast awaye fro me.
She promysed with me to lyve and dye.
Strength. Everyman, I wyll the also forsake and denye;
Thy game lyketh me not at all.

810 *Everyman.* Why, than, ye wyll forsake me all?
Swete Strength, tary a lytell space.
Strength. Nay, syr, by the rode of grace!
I wyll hye me from the fast,
Though thou wepe to thy herte tobrast.

815 Everyman. Ye wolde ever byde by me, ye sayd.
Strength. Ye, I have you ferre ynoughe conveyde.
Ye be olde ynoughe, I understande,
Your pylgrymage to take on hande.

I repent me that I hyder came.
   Everyman. Strength, you to dysplease I am to blame.   820
Wyll ye breke promyse that is dette?
   Strength. In fayth, I care not.
Thou arte but a foole to complayne;
You spende your speche and wast your brayne.
Go thryst the into the grounde.   [*Exit Strength*
   Everyman. I had wende surer I sholde you have founde.   826
He that trusteth in his Strength,
She hym deceyveth at the length.
Bothe Strength and Beauté forsaketh me;
Yet they promysed me fayre and lovyngly.   830
   Dyscrecion. Everyman, I wyll after Strength be gone.
As for me, I wyll leve you alone.
   Everyman. Why, Dyscrecyon, wyll ye forsake me?
   Dyscrecion. Ye, in fayth, I wyll go fro the,
For whan Strength goth before   835
I folowe after ever more.
   Everyman. Yet, I pray the, for the love of the Trynyté,
Loke in my grave ones pyteously.
   Dyscrecion. Nay, so nye wyll I not come.
Fare well, everychone!   [*Exit Discretion*
   Everyman. O, all thynge fayleth, save God alone—   841
Beauté, Strength, and Dyscrecyon;
For whan Deth bloweth his blast,
They all renne fro me full fast.
   V. Wyttes. Everyman, my leve now of the I take.   845
I wyll folowe the other, for here I the forsake.
   Everyman. Alas, than may I wayle and wepe,
For I toke you for my best frende.
   V. Wyttes. I wyll no lenger the kepe.
Now fare well, and there an ende.   [*Exit Five Wits*
   Everyman. O Jesu, helpe! All hath forsaken me.   851
   Good Dedes. Nay, Everyman, I wyll byde with the.
I wyll not forsake the indede;
Thou shalte fynde me a good frende at nede.
   Everyman. Gramercy, Good Dedes! Now may I true frendes se.   855
They have forsaken me, everychone;
I loved them better than my Good Dedes alone.
Knowlege, wyll ye forsake me also?
   Knowlege. Ye, Everyman, whan ye to Deth shall go;
But not yet, for no maner of daunger.   860
   Everyman. Gramercy, Knowlege, with all my herte.
   Knowlege. Nay, yet I wyll not from hens departe

Tyll I se where ye shall become.

Everyman. Me thynke, alas, that I must be gone

865 To make my rekenynge and my dettes paye,

For I se my tyme is nye spent awaye.

Take example, all ye that this do here or se,

How they that I loved best do forsake me,

Excepte my Good Dedes that bydeth truely.

870   *Good Dedes.* All erthly thynges is but vanyté:

Beauté, Strength, and Dyscrecyon do man forsake,

Folysshe frendes and kynnesmen that fayre spake—

All fleeth save Good Dedes, and that am I.

    Everyman. Have mercy on me, God moost myghty,

875 And stande by me, thou moder and mayde, Mary!

    Good Dedes. Fere not; I wyll speke for the.

    Everyman. Here I crye God mercy.

    Good Dedes. Shorte our ende and mynysshe our payne;

Let us go and never come agayne.

880   *Everyman.* In to thy handes, Lorde, my soule I commende;

Receyve it, Lorde, that it be not lost.

As thou me boughtest, so me defende,

And save me from the fendes boost,

That I may appere with that blessyd hoost

That shall be saved at the day of dome.

885 *In manus tuas,* of myghtes moost

For ever, *Commendo spiritum meum.*

                           [*With Good Deeds he goes down into the grave*

    Knowlege. Now hath he suffred that we all shall endure;

The Good Dedes shall make all sure.

890 Now hath he made endynge;

Me thynketh that I here aungelles synge

And make grete joy and melody

Where Everymannes soule receyved shall be!

    The Aungell [*above*]. Come, excellente electe spouse, to Jesu!

895 Here above thou shalte go

Bycause of thy synguler vertue.

Now the soule is taken the body fro,

Thy rekenynge is crystall clere.

Now shalte thou into the hevenly spere,

900 Unto the whiche all ye shall come

That lyveth well before the daye of dome.

                 [*Enter Doctor*]

    Doctour. This memoryall men may have in mynde.

Ye herers, take it of worth, olde and yonge,

And forsake Pryde, for he deceyveth you in the ende;
And remembre Beauté, .V. Wyttes, Strength, and Dyscrecyon,   905
They all at the last do Everyman forsake,
Save his Good Dedes there dothe he take.
But beware, for and they be small,
Before God he hath no helpe at all:
None excuse may be there for Everyman.   910
Alas, how shall he do than?
For after dethe amendes may no man make,
For than mercy and pyté doth hym forsake.
If his rekenynge be not clere whan he doth come,
God wyll saye, *Ite, maledicti, in ignem eternum.*   915
And he that hath his accounte hole and sounde,
Hye in heven he shall be crounde.
Unto whiche place God brynge us all thyder,
That we may lyve body and soule togyder.
Therto helpe the Trynyté!   920
Amen, saye ye, for saynt charyté.

22

HAWES AND BARCLAY

THE poetry of Skelton's contemporaries in early Tudor England looks uninspired when set beside what was being written in Scotland, but it deserves some attention. Two poets especially show flashes of talent. Almost nothing is known of the life of Stephen Hawes (d. after 1521) except that he was educated at Oxford and that he was a groom of the chamber to Henry VII. As well as a number of minor poems, he left the ambitious *Passetyme of Pleasure* (printed in 1509). The hero, Graunde Amoure, determines to win the love of La Bell Pucell. After instruction in the Seven Arts and the accomplishments necessary for a perfect knight, and after adventures which test his courage and fidelity, he marries la Bell Pucell, and the poem ends with his death. It is at once a chivalric romance, an 'encyclopaedic' poem presenting traditional wisdom in an ordered, didactic manner, and an allegory of man's life. It is in some ways a precursor of *The Faerie Queene*, and may indeed have been read by Spenser, but Hawes did not have the imaginative power to make a success of this demanding and novel type of poem. The most pleasurable things in the *Passetyme* are small scenes like the meeting with Fame, or descriptive details such as the elaborate decorations on the Tower of Doctrine, or the glimpses of the mysterious world of romance, the 'jeoperdous waye' with its 'gyauntes grete' and 'many serpentes foule and odyous'. The attempts of Hawes to make his Chaucerian style more 'copious' and ample too often produce a windy verbosity, but in the epitaph for Graunde Amoure the power of that favourite theme of medieval poetry, the uncertainty of man's life and the certainty of death, takes hold of him, the wordiness falls away, and he writes with simplicity and a haunting beauty and solemnity.

Alexander Barclay (? 1475–1552), possibly of Scottish origin, was a priest of the college of Ottery St Mary in Devon, later a Benedictine monk at Ely, and remained a cleric after the Reformation, holding livings in Essex and London. A letter (1520) in which sir Nicholas Vaux asks Wolsey for help with the preparations for the Field of Cloth of Gold and requesting the sending of 'Maistre Barkleye, the blacke monke and poete, to devise histories and convenient raisons to florisshe the buildings and banquet house withal' suggests that he was a well-known literary figure. From his large output, we have brief examples from three works. In *The Shyp of Folys of the Worlde* he presents to English readers a contemporary best seller, the *Narren Schyff* (printed 1494) of Sebastian Brant, which in jaunty, proverbial, and colloquial German verse joyously enumerates the infinite types of folly (illustrated in a series of brilliant woodcuts, some of them by the young Dürer). Unfortunately, Brant's vigour, already dulled in the Latin translation by Locher which Barclay used, has almost totally disappeared. Although Barclay's poem is the first in English to use the word *satire* of itself, its satirical power is very limited; its words compare poorly with the woodcuts, and a slighting reference to Skelton makes us wish that he, instead of Barclay, had done the adaptation. Nevertheless, there are some lively passages—not least our list of the different kinds of drunkards. With the *Egloges*, written at Ely 1515–21, the influence of humanism is apparent. They are modelled on works by Aeneas Silvius Piccolomini (Pope Pius II) and Mantuan, and are the earliest English examples of the formal pastoral. Their historical importance is hardly matched by their literary quality, but again there are some entertaining and interesting moments, of which our glimpse of rural pastimes may serve as an example. Finally, an extract from his translation of Sallust's *Bellum Jugurthinum* (*c.*1520), which C. S. Lewis thought was 'incomparably his best work', shows that he could write vigorous and powerful prose, and gives us yet another example of the imaginative use of ancient literature.

A

HAWES, *THE PASSETYME OF PLEASURE*

Graunde Amour Meets Fame

Thus as I satte in a deedly slombre,
Of a grete horne I herde a ryall blast,
With whiche I awoke and hadde a grete wondre
From whens it came—it made me sore agast.
I loked aboute; the nyght was well nere paste   5
And fayre golden Phebus in the morowe graye
With cloude reed began to breke the daye.

I sawe come rydynge in a valaye ferre
A goodly lady envyronned aboute
With tongues of fyre as bryght as ony sterre,   10
That fyry flambes ensensed alwaye out
Whiche I behelde, and was in grete doubt;
Her palfraye swyfte, rennynge as the wynde,
With two whyte grehoundes, that were not behynde.

Whan that these grehoundes had me so espyed,   15
With faunynge chere of grete humylyté,
In goodly hast they fast unto me hyed.
I mused why and wherfore it shoulde be,
But I welcomed them in every degré.
They leped ofte, and were of me ryght fayne;   20
I suffred them and cherysshed them agayne.

357

Theyr colers were of golde and of tyssue fyne,
Wherin theyr names apered by scrypture;
Of dyamondes, that clerely do shyne
25 The lettres were graven fayre and pure.
To rede theyr names I dyde my besy cure:
The one was Governaunce, the other named Grace—
Than was I gladde of all this sodayne cace.

And than the lady with fyry flame
30 Of brennynge tongues was in my presence,
Upon her palfraye, whiche hadde unto name
Pegase the swyfte, so fayre in excellence,
Whiche somtyme longed with his premynence
To kynge Percyus the sone of Jubyter,
35 On whome he rode by the worlde so fer.

To me she sayde she mervayled moche why
That her grehoundes shewed me that favour;
What was my name she axed me treuly.
To whome I sayde it was la graunde Amour,
40 'Besechynge you to be to me socour
To the Toure of Doctryne, and also me tell
Your propre name, and where you do dwell.'

'My name', quod she, 'in all the worlde is knowen,
Yclypped Fame in every regyon,
45 For I my horne in sondry wyse have blowen
After the dethe of many a champyon,
And with my tonges have made aye mencyon
Of theyr grete actes, agayne to revyve
In flammynge tongues for to abyde on lyve.' . . .

Fame Tells Graunde Amour of la Bell Pucell

50 And after this Fame gan to expresse
Of jeoperdous waye to the toure peryllous,
And of the beauté and the semelynesse
Of la Bell Pucell, so gaye and gloryous,
That dwelled in the toure so mervaylous,
55 Unto which myght come no maner of creature
But by grete laboure and harde adventure.

358

For by the waye there ly in wayte
Gyauntes grete dysfygured of nature,
That all devoureth by theyr yll conceyte,
Ageynst whose strength there maye no man endure—   60
They are so huge and stronge out of mesure—
With many serpentes foule and odyous,
In sundry lykenesse, blacke and tydeus.

But behynde them a grate see there is,
Beyonde whiche see there is a goodly lande,   65
Moost full of fruyte, replete with joye and blysse;
Of ryght fyne golde appereth all the sande
In this fayre realme where the toure dothe stande,
Made all of golde, enameled aboute
With noble storyes which do appere without,   70

In whiche dwelleth, by grete auctoryté,
La bell Pucell, whiche is so fayre and bryght,
To whome in beauté no pere I can se,
For lyke as Phebus above all sterres in lyght
Whan that he is in his spere aryght   75
Dothe excede with his beames clere,
So dothe her beauté above other appeere.

She is bothe good, aye wyse, and vertuous,
And also dyscended of a noble lyne,
Ryche, comly, ryght meke and bounteous: 80
All maner vertues in her clerely shyne;
No vyce of her maye ryght longe domyne,
And I, Dame Fame, in every nacyon
Of her do make the same relacyon.

Her swete reporte so my herte set on fyre   85
With brennynge love, moost hote and fervent,
That her to se I hadde grete desyre,
Sayenge to Fame, 'O lady excellent,
I have determyned in my jugement
For la Bell Pucell the most fayre lady   90
To passe the waye of so grete jeopardy. . . .'

359

Graunde Amoure Comes to the Tower of Doctrine

Thus than I slepte tyll that Auroras beames
Gan for to sprede aboute the fyrmament,
And the clere sonne with his golden streames
Began for to ryse, fayre in the oryent,
95
Without Saturnus blacke encombrement,
And the lytell byrdes makynge melodye
Dyde me awake with theyr swete armonye

I loked aboute and sawe a craggy roche,
100
Ferre in the west nere to the element,
And as I dyde than unto it approche,
Upon the toppe I sawe refulgent
The ryall toure of morall document,
Made of fyne coper, with turrettes fayre and hye,
105
Whiche agaynst Phebus shone so mervaylously

That for the veray perfyte bryghtnes—
What of the toure and of the clere sonne—
I coude nothynge beholde the goodlynes
Of that palays where as doctryne dyde wonne,
110
Tyll at the last, with mysty wyndes donne,
The radyant bryghtnes of golden Phebus
Auster gan cover with cloudes tenebrus.

Than to the toure I drewe nere and nere,
And often mused of the grete hyghnes
115
Of the craggy rocke whiche quadrant dyde appere,
But the fayre toure so moche of rychesse
Was all about sexangled doubtles,
Gargeylde with grehoundes and with many lyons
Made of fyne golde, with dyvers sundry dragons.

120
The lytell turrets with ymages of golde
Aboute was set, wiche with the wynde aye moved
With propre vyces, that I dyde well beholde
Aboute the toures in sondry wyse they hoved
With goodly pypes in theyr mouthes ituned,
125
That with the wynde they pyped a daunce
Yclyped 'Amour de la hault pleasaunce'. . . .

The Epitaph of Graunde Amoure

O mortall folke, you may beholde and se
How I lye here somtyme a myghty knyght.
The ende of joye and all prosperyté
Is dethe at last, through his course and myght.　　130
After the day there cometh the derke nyght,
For though the day be never so longe
At last the belles ryngeth to evensonge.

And my selfe called la Graunde Amoure,
Sekynge adventure in the worldly glory　　135
For to attayne the ryches and honoure,
Dyde thynke full lytell that I sholde here ly
Tyll dethe dyde marke me full ryght pryvely.
Lo what I am, and where to you must:
Lyke as I am so shall you be all dust.　　140

B

BARCLAY, *THE SHIP OF FOOLS*

Of Glotons and Dronkardes

. . . Some sowe-dronke, swaloynge mete without mesure,
Some mawdelayne dronke, mournynge lowdly and hye,
Some beynge dronke no lenger can endure
Without they gyve them to bawdy rybawdry;
Some swereth armys, nayles, herte and body,　　5
Terynge our Lord worse than the Jowes hym arayed;
Some nought can speke, but harkenyth what is sayd.

Some spende all that they have and more at wast
With 'revell and revell, dasshe fyll the cup Joohn!'
Some their thryft lesyth with dyce at one cast;　　10
Some slepe as slogardes tyll their thryft be gone,
Some shewe theyr owne counsell for kepe can they none,
Some are ape-dronke, full of lawghter and of toyes,
Some mery dronke, syngynge with wynches and boyes.

15 Some spue, some stacker, some utterly ar lame,
    Lyeng on the grounde without power to ryse;
    Some bost them of bawdry, ferynge of no shame;
    Some dumme, and some speketh .ix. wordes at thryse;
    Some charge theyr bely with wyne in such wyse
20 That theyr legges skant can bere up the body—
    Here is a sort to drowne a hole navy!

C

BARCLAY, *EGLOGES*

Winter

Amintas first Speaketh:

The winter snowes, all covered is the grounde,
The north wind blowes sharpe and with ferefull sound,
The longe ise-sicles at the ewes hang.
The streame is frosen, the night is cold and long;
5   Where botes rowed, nowe cartes have passage.
From yoke the oxen be losed and bondage,
The ploweman resteth avoyde of businesse,
Save when he tendeth his harnes for to dresse;
Mably his wife sitteth before the fyre
10 All blacke and smoky, clothed in rude attire,
Sething some grewell, and sturring the pulment
Of pease or frument, a noble meat for Lent.
The summer season men counteth nowe laudable
Whose fervour before they thought intollerable;
15 The frosty winter and wether temperate
Which men then praysed, they nowe disprayse and hate—
Colde they desired, but nowe it is present,
They braule and grutche, their mindes not content.
Thus mutable men them pleased can not holde,
20 At great heat grutching, and grutching when it is cold.

Faustus:

All pleasour present of men is counted small,
Desire obtayned some counteth nought at all,
What men hope after that semeth great and deare,
As light by distaunce appeareth great and cleare.

362

Amintas:

Eche time and season hath his delite and joyes— 25
Loke in the stretes, beholde the little boyes,
Howe in fruite season for joy they sing and hop;
In Lent is eche one full busy with his top.
And nowe in winter for all the greevous colde,
All rent and ragged a man may them beholde; 30
They have great pleasour supposing well to dine,
When men be busied in killing of fat swine.
They get the bladder and blowe it great and thin,
With many beanes or peason put within;
It ratleth, soundeth, and shineth clere and fayre, 35
While it is throwen and caste up in the ayre;
Eche one contendeth and hath a great delite
With foote and with hande the bladder for to smite;
If it fall to grounde they lifte it up agayne,
This wise to labour they count it for no payne, 40
Renning and leaping they drive away the colde.
The sturdie plowmen lustie, strong, and bolde,
Overcommeth the winter with driving the foote ball,
Forgetting labour and many a grevous fall.

Faustus:

Men labour sorer in fruiteles vanitie 45
Then in fayre workes of great utilitie;
In suche trifles we labour for domage,
Worke we despise which bringeth advauntage.

Amintas:

Touching their labour it can not me displease,
While we be in rest and better here at ease 50
In the warme litter—small payne hath little hire—
Here may we walow while milke is on the fire,
If it be crudded of bread we nede no crome;
If thou bide, Faustus, thereof thou shalt have some.

D

BARCLAY, *THE FAMOUS CRONYCLE OF THE WARRE WHICH THE ROMAYNS HAD AGAYNST JUGURTH*

Marius Captures a Great Fortress on a Rock

But after that many dayes and great labours in this manere were overpassed and spent in vayne, Marius was sore angred and vexedde in his hert, revolvyng many thynges in mynde, but specially whyther he myght gyve over his purpose (seyng his labour frustrate) or els abyde the chaunce of fortune, whiche at many tymes before he hadde founde favorable and frendly to hym. Whyle Marius chafedde and, brennyng in desyre, tournede and revolved suche thynges in his mynde both day and night, it hapened by chaunce of fortune that a certayne Lumbard, a symple soudyour, one of the company which was last sende from Rome to Numidy to supply the army, strayedde abrode from his company a lytell way, whiche Lumbarde as he wandredde founde among the stones many small snayles crepyng on the grounde, nat farre from that syde of the castell which was over agaynst the syde which the Romayns besyged and assayled. Bycause this Lumbard in his countrey was acustomed lyke other of his countreymen to eate such snayles preparedde after their manere, therfore he gathered first one and than another, and after that many, assendyng up by lytell and lytell, somtyme crepyng, sometyme clymyng, for no nother intent or purpose save to gather such snayles, and so farre he proceded by lytell and lytell tyll at last he came almoost to the toppe of the mountayne. But whan he sawe all that syde of the castell desolat, and no person steryng, anone he beganne to have a pleasure and desyre in his mynde forto worke some maistry, as the propertie and condycion is of every man covetyng to wyn a name, laude and riches, and to be spoken of. By chance of fortune in the same place where the Lumbard stode in this advysement among the stones, grue a great and olde oke tre havyng the myddes a lytell bowyng downe towarde the grounde, and the remanent crokyng upwarde agayne with mighty armes and branches ascendyng to the hyest of the walles with the toppe erect and lyfted up as every herbe and tre of nature is wont to growe upwarde at the toppe. This Lumbard well advysed the same, and adventured to clyme upwarde takyng his holde somtyme by the branches and bowes of this oke, and somtyme takyng holde and leanynge by the stones which apperedde forth in the wall, tyll at the last he attaynedde unto the very toppe of the wall. And whan he sawe no man styring on that part, there stode he styll, espyed of no man, and notedde and consydred well at his pleasure all the inwarde part of the castell and the playne within the walles about the towre. This Lumbard had so moche

the more leasour to take so longe advysement unespyedde for all the
Numidyans, defenders of the castell, were on the other syde attendyng and
gyveng hede to the assaut, and defendyng themselfe and the castell agaynst
the Romayns. Whan the Lumbard had espyed and consydred everything 40
which he thought might be advantage to his after purpose, than he
descended agayne downewarde by the same way which he ascended, but
nat without hede nor with so lytell advysement as he ascended upwarde,
but provyng every way and lokyng about yf it were possyble to bringe into
the castell any company of men by that syde or nat. This well consydredde, 45
as sone as he descended, anone he went to Marius, and informyng of
everything as he had done, exhorting and requiryng hym to put in profe
whether the castell might be won on that syde where he had ben.
Farthermor he promysed himself to be gyde unto such as wold undertake
that enterprise, sayeng that in the mater was no danger. Marius hering 50
these wordes of the Lumbard sende forth with hym certayne of his men of
them which were there present to understande and knowe that trueth of
the mater. Whan they had ben there and retourned to Marius agayne,
some brought hym word that the mater was easy to do, and some other
sayd that it was very harde and perylous. The sentence of every man was 55
after as their mynde gave them. The cowardes thought it harde, but suche
as were of bolde hertes and desyrous of worshyppe thought it easy and
without moche peryll. Nevertheless the mynde of Marius was somewhat
exalted to comfort and good hope. Wherfore of all the company of
trumpettes and of other such mynstrelles as be wont to be in batayle to 60
gyve courage and signes to the fighters, he chose forth fyve which were
moost swyft and moost lyght and delyver, and .iiii. hundred men he
assigned to assyst and defende the sayd trumpettes. And all them he
commaunded to obey to the Lumbard and to be ruled and ordred by hym
in every thynge. The day next folowyng was assigned to them to procede 65
forth in their besynesse. Whan the tyme assigned and prefixed by Marius
was come, the Lumbard with his company had made redy and ordred
everythyng, and so went to the place where he had ben before. But whan
they were come thyder, the Lumbard their gyde caused them to change
their armour, and to make bare their heedes and their fete, to th'intent that 70
they so bareheded the better might se above them and on every syde of
them, and that they beyng barefote myght labour so moche the better and
take better holde in clymyng up by the stones. Their swerdes were fastned
behynde at their backes, and their buckelers withall, which were made
after the fassion of the Numidyans buckelers of lether, bycause of lyghter 75
weyght and burthen and also to th'intent that they shuld gyve lesse sound
or noyse if it hapned any stone to smyte agaynst them. This done, the
Lumbard went up before them, and bounde small cordes to the stones and
to the olde rotes which apered above the stones where he coude espy any
suche, wherby the soudyours sustaynyng themselfe and takyng holde might 80

more lightly and with more ease mount and clyme upwarde. And
sometyme he went before and helped them up with his handes, specially
such as for that uncustomed way were somwhat ferefull. Somtyme whan
th'assendyng or goyng up was overharde and sharpe, he put ech of them
85 up before hym without armour, and than he hymselfe folowed with the
armour and wepyn. Suche places where moost dout was in he specially
provede and assayd them moost of all, and in goyng and comyng
oftentymes up and downe by the same moost dangerous passages he
encreased audacyté and boldnesse to the remenaunt. Thus after they had
90 ben sore weryed, and with long and great labour endevored themselfe, at
last they came into the castell, which on that syde they founde desolate and
without defence. For (as sayd is before) all they which were within the
castell were occupyed in fightyng, or redy to fight agaynst the Romayns, as
they were on other dayes before. But whan Marius understode by
95 messangers how the Lumbard had done, howbeit that all the day before
his men had ben sore besied and occupyed in fightynge and assaylinge the
castell, nevertheles specially at this tyme he exhorted and enbolded them,
and he hymselfe departyng forth from under his pavases caused his
soudyours to adjoyne themselfe nere togyder, and to holde up their
100 sheldes above their heedes so that the conjoyning of them semed as it were
the frame of a volt. Marius kept hym under the same for his defence, and
so approched to the walles. And both he and his company which were nere
about hym valyantly assayled the castell, and also other of his company
which stode afarre of and coude nat come nere the walles for prease
105 assayledde the castell fiersly from afarre and sore vexed and put in feare
their ennemies within the castell throwyng agaynst them plumettes of leed
with slynges, arowes, dartes, and all other maner engyns of batell,
wherwith any thynge coude strongly be throwen into the castell. But the
Numidyans within the castell had often before this tyme overtourned and
110 brent the tentes and pavases of the Romayns, and toke therby so great
audacyté and boldnesse that they defended nat themselfe within the castell
walles, but walked up and downe without the castell walles bothe day and
nyght revilyng and reprovynge the Romayns and objectyng cowardyse
agaynst Marius, and thretnyng that his soudyours shulde be made
115 subgettes and bonde-men to Jugurth in tyme to come, whom they
purposed at that tyme to make bonde to them. Thus whyle they thought
themselfe sure and their mater in good case, they were harde and egar
ynough revyling and thretnyng the Romayns. In the mean space whyle the
Romayns and their ennemies were besyest fightyng with all their
120 might—the Romayns for laude, glorie, and lordshyp, and the Numidyans
for their helth and savyng of their lyves—anon sodenly the Lumbard with
his cumpany which were within the castell on the backsyde blewe their
trumpettes. First of all the women and chyldren which went to the walles
to se the bykering were all abasshed, and fledde inwarde to the castell, and

after them all the soudyours which were without and nerest to the walles 125
and coude escape in. And finally they all, both armed and unarmed, fledde
inwarde. Whan the Romayns sawe this, they assayled the castell more
fiersly: some they slewe and overthrue, some they wounded, overpassyng
or standyng upon the bodyes of them which were slayne. All their desyre
was with their handes to wynne glorie and worshyppe. They stryved to 130
ascende unto the walles, every man covetyng to be before other. None of
them all taryed, nor was let with spoylinges nor prayes. Their great
courage suffred them nat to loke thereafter tyll by manhode and strength
they had won the castell. Thus was fortune favorable to Marius, so that his
first neglygence and unwyse boldnesse to assayle a castell inexpugnable 135
was tourned by chance from rebuke to glorie and laude—such was his
fortune.

23

NIFLES, TRIFLES, AND
MERRY JESTS

A NUMBER of the literary forms represented here are of very great antiquity and are still with us. The Bible records (I Kgs. 10: 1) that the Queen of Sheba tested Solomon with 'hard questions', i.e. riddles, and yet the modern reader will have no difficulty in recognizing one or two of the 'hard questions' put in *The Demaundes Joyous* (and he will find a couple more noted in I. and P. Opie, *The Lore and Language of Schoolchildren* [Oxford, 1959], 73). Early riddles—as can be seen—do not evade the 'facts of life', and it is not surprising to find, in other collections, examples which, like some Anglo-Saxon riddles, playfully suggest an erotic answer, which turns out to be (formally, at least) incorrect: so H. A. Person, *Cambridge Middle English Lyrics* (Seattle, 1953), 54:

> I have a hole above my knee
> And pricked yt was and pricked shal be
> And yet yt is not sore
> And yet yt shal be pricked more—

to which the answer given is 'sheath'. In extract C, Solomon is involved in another literary form with a long history, a proverb contest. That there was evidently still a taste for this is shown also by an early sixteenth-century print, *The Wyse Chylde*, in which a three-year-old answers questions posed by 'Adryan Emperoure'. There is occasionally a pleasing riddling touch to his answers ('Sage enfant, howe is the skye made?'—'Yf it had ben made by the hande of man it hadde fallen forthwith, and yf it had be borne it hadde ben deed longe tyme syth ...'), but mostly they are predictably orthodox, and I have preferred the more earthy proverbs of Marcolphus, that misshapen fool, as ugly as Aesop, who is descended from the wise 'Chaldean earl' of the Old English *Solomon and Saturn*. The anti-feminist satire of *The Fyftene Joyes of Maryage* is perhaps to our taste less obviously 'merry'. This rather prosaic translation (showing, incidentally, that even in Tudor times verse was still commonly used as a 'staple' form for translations) cannot match the brilliant prose or the sly ironies of its French original, but it conveys something of its vivid and often abrasive satire and its disillusioned view of the miseries of marriage. *The Gospelles of Dystaves* is close both to Dunbar's *Twa Mariit Wemen and the Wedo* and to the folklore of old wives' tales. Finally, we have an example of the genuine 'merry tale' (of a kind which continued to flourish in the later sixteenth century in the merry tales of 'Skelton', 'Scoggin', and others). For our very engaging rogue probably the best epitaph is his own enthusiastic 'holde thyne owne, parson!'

A

The Demaundes Joyous

(i) Who was Adams moder?

(ii) What space is from the hyest space of the se to the depest?

(iii) How many calves tayles behoveth to reche from the erthe to the skye?

(iv) Which parte of a sergeaunte love ye best towarde you?

(v) Which is the moost profytable beest, and that men eteth leest of?

(vi) Which is the brodest water and leest jeopardye to passe over?

(vii) Why dryve men dogges out of the chyrche?

(viii) Why come dogges so often to the churche?

(ix) What beest is it that hath her tayle bytweene her eyen?

(x) Wherfore set they upon chyrche steples more a cocke than a henne?

(xi) Which was fyrst, the henne or the egge?

(xii) Why doth an ox or a cowe lye?

(xiii) What tyme in the yere bereth a gose moost feders?

[*For the answers, see the Commentary*]

B

(i) *A Question*

Ther was a man went into an orchard and toke sertayn apples; and he must pass .vii. gattes. And the porter of the first gate will not latt hym passe except he geve hym half his apples and on mo—and so he gave him. And than he commeth to the ii^de gate, and the porter toke from hym half his apples that he hade left and .i. mo. And so servid hym the iii^de portter and   5
the iiii^th portter, and v^th, and vi^th, and vii^th porter. So at the laste he bare but on apple away. How many apples had he at the first?

(ii)

Water frosen, Caynnes brother—
So hight my leman, and no other.

(iii)

Gardeyn ways, cumfort of flowres—
So hight my leman. What hight yowrs?

[*For the answers, see the Commentary*]

C

SALOMON AND MARCOLPHUS

The Arrival of Marcolphus

Upon a season hertofore as king Salomon, full of wisdome and richesse, sate upon the kinges sete or stole that was his fadres Davyd, sawe comyng a man out of th'Este that was named Marcolphus, of vysage greatly myshapen and fowle; nevyrethelesse he was right talkatyf, elloquend, and
5 wyse. His wif had he wyth hym, whiche was more ferefull and rude to beholde. And as they were bothe comen before king Salomon, he behelde thaym well. This Marcolf was of short stature and thykke. The hede had he great; a brode forhede rede and full of wrinkelys or frouncys; his erys hery and to the myddys of chekys hangyng; great yes and rennyng; his
10 nether lyppe hangyng lyke an horse; a berde harde and fowle lyke unto a gote; the handes short and blockyssh; his fyngres great and thycke; rounde feet and the nose thycke and croked; a face lyke an asse, and the here of hys heed lyke the heer of a gote. His shoes on his fete were ovyrmoche chorlysh and rude, and his clothys fowle and dyrty: a short kote to the
15 buttockys; his hosyn hynge full of wrynkelys, and alle his clothes were of the moost fowle coloure. . . .

. . . Salomon sayde, 'I have herd of the that thou kanst right wele clatre and speke, and that thou art subtyle of wyt, although that thou be mysshapyn and chorlyssh. Lete us have betwene us altercacion. I shal
20 make questyons to the, and thou shalt therto answere.' Marcolphus answeryd, 'He that singyth worste begynne furste.' Salomon: 'If thou kanst answere to alle my questyons I shall make the ryche, and be named above all othre withyn my reaume.' Marcolphus: 'The phisician promysyth the seeke folke helthe whan he hath no power.' Salomon: 'I have juged betwixt
25 two light women whiche dwellyd in oon house and forlaye a chylde.' Marcolphus: 'Were erys are, there are causes; where women be, there are wordys.' Salomon: 'God yave wysdam in my mouth; for me lyke is none in alle partys of the worlde.' Marcolphus: 'He that hath evyll neighborys praysyth hymself.' Salomon: 'The wykkyd man fleyth, no man folwyng.'
30 Marcolphus: 'Whan the kydde rennyth, men may se his ars.' Salomon: 'A

good wyf and a fayre is to hir husbonde a pleasure.' Marcolphus: 'A potfull
of mylke muste be kept wele from the katte.'. . .

His Departure

Marcolph, beryng in his mynde of the unkyndnesse that the king had
commanded hym that he shulde no more se hym betwixt the yes, thought
in hymself what was best to do. It happenyd that the next nyght folowyng 35
fyll a great snowe. Marcolphus toke a lytyll cyve or temse in his oon hande
and a foot of a bere in the othre hande, and he turnyd hys shoes that stode
forwardes upon his feet bakward. And upon the mornyng erly he began to
go lyke a beste upon alle foure feet through the strete. And whan he was
comen a lytyll wythouthe the towne, he founde an olde ovyn, and crept into 40
it. And as the lyght of the daye was on comen, oon of the kingys servauntys
founde the footstappys of Marcolph, and thought that it was the trace or
stappys of a merveylous beste, and in alle haste went and shewyd it to the
king. Thanne incontynent, wyth huntres and howndes, he wente to hunte
and seke the sayd wondrefull beeste, and folowed it unto they comen 45
before the oven, where they had loste and founde no more of the steppys.
The king Salomon discended from hys hors, and began to loke into the
oven. Marcolphus laye all crokyd, hys vysage from hymwardes; had put
downe hys breche into hys hammes that he myght se hys arshole and alle
hys othre fowle gere. As the kyng Salomon, that seyng, demawnded what 50
laye there, Marcolphus answeryd, 'I am here.' Salomon: 'Wherefore lyest
thou thus?' Marcolphus: 'For ye have commaunded me that ye shulde
nomore se me betwyxt myn yes. Now and ye woll not se me betwyxt myn
yes, ye may se me betwene my buttockys in the myddes of myn arsehole.'
Than was the king sore movyd; commaunded his servauntys to take hym 55
and hange hym upon a tre. Marcolphus so takyn sayde to the kyng, 'My
lord, well it please you to yeve me leve to chose the tre wherupon that I
shall hange.' Salomon sayde, 'Be it as thou haste desyred, for it forcyth not
on what tre that thou be hangyd.' Than the kynges servauntes token and
leddyn Marcolph wythoute the citie, and through the vale of Josaphath, 60
and ovyr the hyghte of the hylle of Olyvete from thens to Jericho, and
cowde fynde no tre that Marcolf wolde chese to be hanged on. From thens
went they ovyr the flome Jordane, and all Arabye through, and so forth all
the great wyldernesse unto the Rede See, and nevyrmore cowde Marcolph
fynde a tre that he wolde chese to hange on. And thus he askapyd out of 65
the dawnger and handes of King Salomon, and turnyd ayen unto hys
house and levyd in pease and joye.

D

THE FYFTENE JOYES OF MARYAGE

Disposing of a Pregnant Daughter

. . . This poore damoseyll with chylde is grete,
Whiche of conceyvynge hathe the tyme foryete,
For of herselfe knoweth she but lyte
How she was brought into suche case and plyte,
And she no thynges knoweth of that arte,   5
Ne what it is, she toke so lytell parte—
But, yf it please our Lorde God, she shall knowe
How sedes groweth after they be sowe.
The moder avyseth wele, and seeth her hewe,
Whiche knoweth the olde testament and newe,   10
And calleth her into a secrete place.
She sayth, 'Come hyder!' with an evyll grace,
'Have I not sayd to the afore this houre
That thou has lost thy worshyp and honoure
To do as thou hast done thus folyly?   15
But whan a thynge is done, what remedye?
That thou arte grete with chylde I knowe it wele—
Tell me the trouthe, and drede the neuer a dele.'
'Now, fayre moder, I wote not as ye saye
To tell you trouthe, wheder it be so or naye.'   20
Then sayth the moder, 'It semeth me alwaye
Whan that the morowe cometh every daye
I here the coughe, and pytously forbrake,
And dyvers other countenaunces make.'
'Now, truely, so it is,' she sayth, 'madame.'   25
'Ha!' sayth her moder, 'Holde thy pease, for shame!
Thou arte with chylde. Tell it not all aboute,
Ne to none erthely persone breke it out.
And alwaye take a good respecte and hede
To do as I the shall commaunde and bede.'   30
'Madame, so shall I do in every thynge,
And lowely you obeye and your byddynge.'
The moder then sayth to her doughter tho,
'Hast thou not sene so often come and go
Into our hous suche a yonge squyer ofte?'   35
And she sayth, 'Yes, madame' with wordes softe.
'Now then, advyse the wele, for in certayne

372

Tomorowe heder wyll he come agayne.
Then take good hede that thou make hym good chere
In godly wyse, and in thy best manere, 40
And whan that other gentylmen and me
Thou seest togyder talke, then cast an eye
On hym alwaye.' And this good moder so
Her doughter techeth wele how she shall do:
'Also I the commaunde and charge, yf he 45
Of ony maner thynges speke to the,
Herken hym wele, and answere curteysly,
And swetely rule thy speche and manerly.
And yf he speke of love or thynges lyke,
Thenne other whyles softely gyve a syke 50
And thanke hym hertyly, but say ywys
Thou knowest not yet what maner thynge love is,
Ne it to lerne thou wylte nat the apply.
Rule and demeane the well and womanly;
And golde or sylver yf he proffre the, 55
Thenne take it not in hast. But herken me—
Yf he the proffre juell, crosse, or rynge,
Gyrdell, bracelet, owche or other thynge,
Refuse it gracyousely, but at the last
Yf he it often offre the and fast, 60
Receyve it thenne in goodly wyse and take
For love of hym, saynge that for his sake
Thou wyll it kepe, thynkynge no vyllonye,
Shame ne deceyte that shall ensuye therby.
And whan he taketh leve of the to go, 65
Thenne hym demaunde or he departe the fro
Yf one shall see hym hastyly agayne,
Wherof say that thou wolde be glad and fayne.'
Here is this galaunt come whiche shall be cast
Ynto the lepe, and therin holden fast, 70
Forwhy the dame wyll cause hym forto wedde
Her doughter sone, and with her go to bedde,
Yf that she can by ony caste or wyle.
This galaunt she porposeth to begyle,
For he moche hathe of herytage and rent, 75
And is but symple, and an innocent.
Now cometh he this damoysell to see
In hast, for over wele at ease is he.
Ryght many galauntes bent have theyr engyne
To take this damoysell and undermyne. 80
The lady taketh a squyer by the hande,

373

Or elles a knyght; and other sytte or stande,
Whiche joyeously togyder talke and rayle.
This galaunt eke draweth to the damoysayle,
85 And by the hande he dothe her take and holde,
Sayenge, 'Fayre damoysell, good God it wolde
That ye my thought wele knewe and understode!'
'And how may I', she sayth, 'for any gode
Knowe it but yf ye wyll it to me saye?
90 What! Do ye thynke suche thynges as ye ne may
Telle me?' 'Nay, by my fayth, I wolde that ye
Knewe it so that it were not sayd by me!'
'Truely,' she sayth—and laugheth pratyly—
'Ye telle a thynge to me so mervaylousely
95 Whiche to be done it is as inpossyble
As for to cause an horse walke invysyble.'
'Yf it had lyked you,' this galaunt sayth,
'And no dyspleasyr taken in good fayth,
I wolde have playnely shewed you my thought.'
100 'Now, syr,' sayth she, 'Telle on, and spare it nought.
So moche of you knowe I that by the rode
Ye wyll not say ne shewe thynge but all gode.'
'Maystresse,' he sayth, 'Ye knowe ryght welle that I
Am but a poore gentylman, forwhy
105 I wote I am unworthy and unable
To be youre love, or with you compaygnable,
For ye be gentyll, fayre, and gracyouse,
And of all vertues full, and beauteuouse.
And yf it pleased you to do to me
110 Suche honour that your lover I myght be
I durst make myn avaunt that with good wylle
I sholde do all the pleasyrs you untylle
That any man by possybylyté
May to his lady do in soveraynté.
115 I shall you serve, and eke your honour kepe
More thenne myn owne, whether ye wake or slepe.'
'Graunt mercy, syr,' thenne sayth this damoysell,
'But for the love of God speke neuer a dell
Of suche thynges unto me after this,
120 For I knowe not what maner thynge love is,
Ne yet I wyll not lerne it ferthermore,
For it is not doctryne ne the lore
The whiche my moder hathe me taught alwaye.
Thenne sayth this squyer, 'Damoysell, in fay,
125 My fayre lady of whome ye speke is good,

374

But I wolde not yet that she understode
Suche thynges as be sayd betwexte us twaye.'
'A, syr,' she sayth, 'Of you I have herde saye
This other daye that ye sholde maryed be,
Wherof I marvayle and ye come to me   130
And speke suche ydell wordes.' And thenne he
Sayth, 'Damoysell, O *benedycyte!*
Now by my faythe, yf that it please yowe,
I shall never other wedde—I make avowe—
Whyle that I lyve, so that ye wyll me take   135
As for youre servaunt, and I undertake
That with my servyce ye shall be contente!'
'What! wolde ye have me deshonoured and shente?'
She sayth. 'Nay! yet me lever were to dye,'
Sayth he, 'thenne for to do you vyllonye!'   140
'For Goddes love be styll, and speke no more
Herof; and I shall tell you, syr, wherfore—
Yf that my moder it perceyve or wytte,
I shall destroyed be, I knowe wele it!'
And parauenture the moder maketh a sygne   145
That of her spekynge she shall cesse and fyne.
And thenne this galaunt gyveth her a rynge
Under her hande, or elles some other thynge,
Saynge to her, 'Fayre lady, I you pray,
Take this and kepe it for my love alway.'   150
'Certes,' sayth she, 'I wyll not take it, no!'
'Alas! my love,' he sayth, 'why saye ye so?
I pray you hertely!', and in her hande
He putteth it agayne so as they stande,
And she it taketh, and sayth, 'This I receyve   155
To have your love, as you may well perceyve,
Without thought of thynge but all honoure—
I take wytenesse unto my Savyoure!'
The lady of that house thus speketh then
In curteyse wyse unto the gentyll men,   160
'Tomoro we must igo with Goddes grace
Unto Our Blyssed Lady of suche a place,
On pylgrymage to suche a toune hereby.'
'Truely, madame,' they say, 'ryght vertuously
And well ye speke.' And forth withall they go   165
To souper, and this galaunt evermo
Anenst this damoysell is put or set,
That he to her may talke withouten let,
And she so well can make her personage

375

170   In suche a wyse that he, halfe in a rage,
With love is take of her that was so bryght
And beauteuous as semed to his syght.
The morowe cometh. This company must ryde
On pylgrymage, and lenger not abyde.
175   And all men say they cannot se ne fynde
An horse amonge them all that bereth behynde
Excepte this galauntes horse there, by Saynt Loy,
Whereof grete pleasure taketh he and joy,
For one the damoysell behynde his backe
180   Dooth sette uppon his horse—and he no lacke
Fyndeth therin—and she clyppeth hym fast
To holde her on the horse that he ne cast
Her doune, and, God wote, therwith he is eased,
As an hauke whiche hathe an heron seased.
185   Now draweth he nyghe the lepe withouten bote!
They do this foresayd vyage, God it wote,
With perfyte mynde and good entencyon,
And home retorne, as made is mencyon,
Where merély they set them doune to mete,
190   With suche vytayles as they can fynde and gete.
And after mete, the lady fayre and well
Gooth to her chambre and this damoysell,
To whome she sayth, 'Whan thou spekest with this man,
Say unto hym as sadly as thou can
195   That there is one whiche spoken hath to the
Of maryage, but thou ne wylte accorded be
As yet. And yf he offre the to take,
Thanke hym, and say that he must meanes make
To me, and put the mater to my wyll,
200   And that I do therin thou shalte fulfyll
On my behalfe, and say that there is none
Lyvynge in this worlde—I excepte not one—
That thou lovest halfe so wele in certaynté
As hym, so as may stande with honesté.'
205   And all they after walketh twayne and twayne
Togyder arme in arme to the gardeyne,
Whereas amonge the herbes and the floures
They smell and taste the holsom swete odoures,
And playenge take the floures by the stalke,
210   Whiche to theyr nose they put so as they walke—
One taketh a gelofer or vyolere,
Another pluketh of the englentere,
And every one of them as they espye

Take herbe or floure after theyr fantasye.
This galaunt squyre with the doughter gothe,   215
And telleth her every thynge, but she is wrothe.
'Alas!' she sayth, 'speke no more so, for I
Shall, yf ye do, forsake your company!
What wolde ye do? Me semeth ye suppose
To cause me myn honoure for to lose.   220
Have ye not herde of late dayes ysayde
That one to mary me hath spoke and prayde?'
'Now, by my soule!' he sayth, 'I can not blame
Hym though to mary you he wolde attame,
But I thynke that of myn habylyté   225
I am as good in value as is he,
Ane eke as able servyce you to do
As is the man of whome that ye speke so.'
'Now, by my fayth,' she sayth than with a syke,
'I wolde that he were to your persone lyke.'   230
'Graunt mercy, fayre damoysell,' he sayth,
'For of your grete curtesy, in fayth,
Well more than I am worthy ye me prayse.
But ye myn honoure gretely may up rayse
Yf ye wolde take me as your man to grace   235
To do you servyce all my lyves space.'
And she sayth, 'Syr, graunt mercy therwithall.
This must be spoken in especyall
Unto my fader sadly and my moder,
And to my kynne, and frendes dyvers oder.'   240
Than sayth he thus, 'Yf I myght knowe that they
Sholde be content, I wold bothe speke and prey.'
'A, syr,' she sayth, 'Be ware that ye ne saye
That ye to me have spoken by ony way,
For rather wolde I suffre dethe than ye   245
Sholde ony wordes shewe of prevyté
That hathe be sayd in ony maner wyse
Bytwene us twayne.' 'Nay! that is not my guyse!'
Sayth he, whiche to the moder speketh soone,
And, as God wolde, in suche poynte was the moone   250
Whan he unto the moder made request
That he all his desyre had at the leest,
For she and other have them trouthes plyght—
And peradventure caused them at nyght
Togyder for to lye in bedde and slepe.   255
Now is this poore squyre plonged depe
Within the lepe, and spedely they make

The weddynge for this gentyl womans sake,
And hastely they do this mater spede,
260 Bycause her frendes have grete doute and drede
Leste ony let may come in this matere,
For in the wynde the weder was clere.
The nyght is come after they be wedde:
This damoysell with man must go to bedde,
265 And—knowe ye wele—the olde wylé dame
Wyll teche her doughter somwhat of the game,
How she ryght maydenly shall her demeane,
As though she were an holy vyrgyn cleane.
Myn auctour sayth her moder dooth her teche
270 That whan her husbande wyll unto her reche
She shall for drede tremble, quake, and crye,
And hym withstande, and how that she shall lye
In many maner wyse as sholde a mayde
Upon the nyght whan she fyrst is assayde.
275 Also the moder dooth her well enfourme
How she shall her demeane and in what fourme:
Whan that this galaunt her wolde enforce or stryke,
Also sodaynly than shall she sterte and syke
As though she were cast in colde water depe
280 Up to the brestes—also she shall wepe.
But in conclusyon as to the dede,
She playeth metely wele whan she must nede.
And yet the fader and the moder bothe
For love and pyté angry be and wrothe
285 Whiche that they have upon theyr doughter yonge,
Supposynge that this man hath doone her wronge,
And causes them in presence to be brought.
Now hath this squyre founde that he hath sought!
Here may ye se one of the gretest payne,
290 For she, whiche with a ladde hath ben forlayne,
Or monethes thre may passe and come aboute,
Shall have a baby lapped in a cloute.
Oftymes ago then joyes and pleasaunce
To hevynes be tourned and penaunce.
295 And peradventure he shall her after bete,
And manace, curse, and chyde with wordes grete,
And never after shall good housholde kepe.
So in the lepe he put is for to stepe,
And out therof he never shall departe.
300 Of sorowe and hevynes he shall have parte,
And ever more abyde shall in dystres,
Endynge his dayes in care and wretchednes.

E

The Gospelles of Dystaves

The Mondaye at night bytwene seven and eyght of the clocke after souper
assembled the forsayd syxe ladyes togyder, and all the neyghbours that
were accustomed to come theder, and dyvers other that were somoned
theder for to here the mystery that sholde be done there. Dame Isengryne
of Glay came theder accompanyed with dyvers of her knowlege, the 5
whiche brought with them theyr dystaves and standardes, with theyr
spyndels and wherles and all that apperteyned to theyr arte. And, to make
it shorte, it semed a ryght market whereas is but solde wordes and reasons
and dyvers purposes of small effecte and lytell valour. The syege of dame
Isengryne was prepared at one syde, a lytell hyer than the other, and myn 10
was even besyde her, and afore me was a lampe full of oyle for to caste
lyght upon my werke, and all the assystentes had tourned theyr vysages
towarde dame Isengryne, the whiche after scylence obteyned spake in this
maner. But or that I begynne for to wryte her chapytres, I wyll reherse to
you the estate and genealogye of her. Dame Isengryne was of the aege of 15
.lxv. yere or thereaboute. She had ben a fayre wyfe in her tyme, but she was
becomen gretely wydred; her eyen were holowe, and her eyelyddes
somwhat reversed and reed, alwaye watrynge. She had had fyve husbandes
besyde her acquayntaunce aparte. She medled in her olde aege to receyve
yonge chyldren, but in her yonge aege she receyved grete chyldren. She 20
was moche experte in dyvers artes. Her husbande was yonge, of whome
she was ryght jalous, and made many complayntes of hym to her
neyghbours. Neverthelesse, scylence obtayned, she began her gospell, and
toke her substaunce of her husbande, and sayd: 'My good neyghbours,
there is none of you but ye knowe that I toke my husbande Josselyn more 25
for his beauté than for his rychesse, for a poore felowe he was. And loo, I
sawe hym not todaye nor yesterdaye, wherfore I have grete sorowe at my
herte. And certaynly he hath grete chepe of the goodes that my husbandes
his predecessours had assembled togyder with grete labour and payne,
wherfore I thynke it wyll be my deth. Now to this purpose, and for the fyrst 30
chapytre, I tell you for as true as the gospell that the man that spendeth the
goodes unduely that cometh to hym by his wyfe withouten leve shall gyve
accountes before God as of thynges stolen. . . .

. . . 'There is no thynge more certayne than the husbande that dooth
contrary to that whiche his wyfe counseyleth hym to do, and who that 35
gaynsayeth ony thynge that she sayth, he is false and dysloyall forsworne.'
Glose. 'Certaynly,' sayd Gonbarde of the Dytche, 'I have sene dyvers
myracles of them that have transgressed this chapytre for my stepfader
broke his legge bycause he wolde not byleve the counseyle of my
moder!. . . 40

... 'A mayden that wyll knowe the name of her to-comynge husbande ought to hange before her dore the fyrst threde that she spynneth that daye. And the fyrst man that passeth therby, aske his name, and knowe for certayne that the same name shall her husbande have.' *Glose.* At the same

45 wordes rose up one of the assystentes named Geffryne, Johan Blewes wyfe, and sayd that she had proved that thynge and that it had happened so to her; wherfore she cursed the houre that she had mette with suche a man, that had lost all colour and beauté, and yet he was so evyll a werkeman that he dyde nothynge but slepe....

50 ...'Ye sholde not gyve to yonge maydens to ete the heed of a hare to the ende that they sholde mary, and in especyall to them that be with chylde, for certaynly theyr chyldren might have cloven lyppes.' *Glose.* Then sayd anone Margaret of the Whete, 'Even so it happened to one of my cosyns, for bycause that she had eten of the heed of a hare her doughter

55 that was in her wombe brought forth foure lyppes....'

F

THE PARSON OF KALENBOROWE

The Parson and the Bishop's Lady Paramour

The parson of Kalenborowe perceyvynge that the bysshope wolde have hym with hym to every churche-holowynge, he sought a wyle to byde at home and kepe howse with his servant or wenche, for it was moste his ease. And incontynent he went to the bysshopes soverayne lady and prayed

5 her that she wolde help hym that he myght byde at home and nat go to no churche-halowynge, 'and I wyll gyve you a gode rewarde'. She answered agayne and sayd, 'That is nat in my power.' The parson sayd, 'Yes,' and sayd, 'Holde here a pursse with money for your labour, for I knowe well the bysshope wyll lay with you tonight; thus I pray you to shewe me the

10 hour of his commyng that I than may lay under the bed.' She answered and saide, 'Than come at seven of the clocke, for eight of the clocke is his houre.' And in the meane season she prepared the chamber lyke an erthely paradyse and sett rownde about the wallis of it candellis burnynge bright against the bisshopes commyng; and at the houre assigned the parson

15 come and crepte under the bedde in her chamber. Whan the bisshope com, he merveyled sore to se this sight and asked her what it ment. 'My lorde,' she saide, 'this is for the honoure of you, for this nyght I hope ye wyll halowe my lytell chapel standyng benethe my navyll in Venus valaye and that by and by, or ellys from hens forth I wyll shewe you no point of

20 love whylst I leve.'

The bysshope went to bedde with his soverayn lady and he fulfylled al her desyre and began to holowe her chapell to the best of his power. The parson laynge under the bedde herd this right well and began for to singe with a hye voyce lyke as they do at every church-holowynge in this maner, '*terribilis est locus iste*' etc., wherof the bisshop marvayled and was abasshed 25 and blessed hym with the signe of the holy crosse, and wenynge to hym that the devyll had bene in the chamber, and wolde have conjured hym. Than spake the parson laynge under the bedde with grete haste, saynge thus (and with that he crepte out), 'Reverende fader, I fere so sore to breke your commaundement that I had lever crepe on hande and fote to fulfyll 30 your mynde and wyll than to be absent at any of all your churche-holowinges, and for that cause I wolde be at this chapell also.' The bysshope sayde, 'I had nat called the to be at the holowynge herof! I trowe the devyll brought the hether! Get the hens out of my sight and come nomore to me!' 'My lorde, I thanke you and also your lady paramours.' 35 Thus went the preste on his way and thanked God that he was so rydde frome the bysshope, and so come home and kepte house with his fayr wenche as he was wont to do, the whiche was glad of his commynge home, for she had great disease of suche thynges as he was wonte to helpe her of. And some that envyed the preste shewed the bysshop that he had suche a 40 fayre wenche. And because he had layde under the bysshops bedde and playde hym that false touche, the bisshope sent a commyssion unto hym, that upon payne of curssinge he shold put awaye frome hym his yonge lusty wenche, and to kepe his house that he shold take an olde woman of .xl. yere of age, or ellys he sholde be put in pryson. The parson, hering 45 this, made a gret mournynge complaynt to his wenche and said, 'Now must I wasshe and plasshe, wringe and singe and do al my besines myselfe', wherof she gave hym gode comforte and said, 'The whele of fortune shall turne ones againe', and so departed for a seson. And than he toke gode hert a grece, and said to himselfe, 'No force, yet shall I begyle hym, for I 50 wyll kepe .ii. wentches of .xx. yere of age, and twise .xx. maketh .xl! Holde thyne owne, parson!'

24

JOHN SKELTON

THE poetic reputation of John Skelton (c.1460–21 June 1529) has been restored fully only in this century, when poets such as Graves and Auden found a new inspiration in the metrical and linguistic experiments of 'helter-skelter John'. Skelton was a learned man: he was educated at Cambridge, and was made 'poet laureate' (apparently a degree in rhetoric) by Oxford, Louvain, and Cambridge. He wrote poetry at the Court of Henry VII, and was appointed tutor to the King's younger son, later to become Henry VIII. He took orders in 1498, and after Prince Henry became heir to the throne in 1502 he became rector of Diss in Norfolk, a position he continued to hold although he lived in London for a number of years before his death. His learning was praised by Caxton (cf. No. 15 E) and later by Erasmus, but sixteenth-century tradition made him into a merry rogue like the parson of Kalenburg. He seems in fact to have been an orthodox cleric, and was a doughty defender of the Catholic faith. Our brief selection does not attempt to represent the full range of this important poet's writing: his famous later satires (*Colyn Cloute, Speke Parrot, Why Come Ye nat to Courte?*) on Cardinal Wolsey, who seems in the end to have proved too powerful an opponent, are therefore left aside in favour of a few extracts which show the younger Skelton, and how his work bridges old and new. His (rather awkward) prose translation of Diodorus Siculus (? finished c.1488) from Poggio's Latin is yet another example of the revival of interest in antiquity inspired by fifteenth-century humanism. *The Bowge of Court* (1498) takes its name from French *bouche de court* 'Court rations', i.e. the free food provided in a royal household—which, as satirists were fond of pointing out, was often of poor quality. Court fare in its larger sense is very unpalatable also, as the unfortunate central figure (aptly called Drede) in this dream vision soon learns, when he is confronted with sinister figures such as Harvey Hafter or (here) Riot. Skelton was to be the first English poet after Chaucer who could use his own language with bold originality and extraordinary flexibility; there are hints of this here in the dramatic way he uses snatches of popular songs and the rhythms of colloquial speech. In *Phyllyp Sparowe* (? 1505) Skelton leaves rhyme-royal stanzas for his favourite metre, 'Skeltonics'. This breathless, exhilarating doggerel, perhaps of demotic origin but transformed into an art form, is not simply a 'helter-skelter' flow of sound, which has in it (as Skelton says) 'some pith', and which is obviously appropriate for invectives. *Phyllyp Sparowe* shows how it can be used delicately and subtly, interweaving a variety of tones in a quite Chaucerian way. In the lament he gives to Jane Scrope for the death of her pet sparrow, killed by a cat 'of carlish kind', he contrives to blend parody (of the services for the dead), a touch of mock-heroic (in the gentle guying of her hyperbolic rhetoric), a remarkable imitation of the speaking voice, modes of thought, and literary judgements of the young girl, and the purest lyricism. The poet's gently mocking presence sets off this fresh and genuinely attractive poem.

A

A TRANSLATION OF DIODORUS SICULUS

Primitive Man

... And semblably, they saye, at the begynnyng men were engendryd; and that they sought their sustenaunce in the wylde felde, nakedly lyvyng in the busshy wyldernesse; unto whome herbes and fruytes of the tre of their owne natural growyng mynystred their dayly fode and repaste; and how wylde bestes and ravenous were toward this people, of cruelté moeved, 5 passyng noyous; whome to resiste and withstonde, they accompanyed theymself togydre for drede and wele encomyne; eche of theym dyde other assiste and supporte, ordeyned places for theymself to enhabyte; and whereas clateryng and noyse whiche they made in maner was but confuse, afterward it grewe unto a parfyght voys and language intelligyble, and so 10 they aptly applyed unto every thynge the very propre name. But forasmoche as they were situated in dyverce places of the world, men saye they spack not all after one language. Wherupon appiered varyaunce of speche, dyverse carrecters and figures of lettres. And how the first confluence of men togyder encompanyed, they saye, was the first orygynal 15 of their nacion and people.

Howbeit, peple at the begynnyng, so as they were by no subsidye relevyd, they lyvyd hardly. They were naked and destitute of habyllements, havyng noo habitacion of howsyng, not relevyd by the nutrytyf suffrage of fyre, dayly sekyng theyr bodyly sustenaunce, ignoraunt and havyng noo 20 provydence the fruytes of the wyldrenes for to reserve and kepe unto the tyme of nede, by occasion wherof many of theym perisshed in the frosty wynter and deyde eyther for honger or for colde. Thenne, afterward, whan they were taught by experyence, they gate them into dennys and caves themself to preserve from the forcyble storme of the sturdy colde. And so 25 they began to kepe fruytes as vytayll for theyr bodyly sustenaunce, apparayllyng the beneficyal knowlege of fyre and the commoditees of all other thingis whiche, in shorte processe, they fonde alle thynges necessarye unto the usual lyf of man.

B

THE BOWGE OF COURTE

The Dreamer meets Riot

. . . Wyth that came Ryotte, russhynge all at ones,
A rusty gallande, toragged and torente;
And on the borde he whyrled a payre of bones,
'*Quater treye dews!*' he clatered as he wente,
'Now have at all, by saynte Thomas of Kente!'
And ever he threwe and kyst I wote nere what:
His here was growen thoroweoute his hat.

Thenne I behelde how he dysgysed was:
His hede was hevy for watchynge over nyghte,
His eyen blereed, his face shone lyke a glas;
His gowne so shorte that it ne cover myghte
His rumpe, he wente so all for somer lyghte;
His hose was garded wyth a lyste of grene,
Yet at the knee they were broken, I wene.

His cote was checked with patches rede and blewe;
Of Kyrkeby Kendall was his shorte demye;
And ay he sange, 'In fayth, decon thou crewe';
His elbowe bare, he ware his gere so nye;
His nose a droppynge, his lyppes were full drye;
And by his syde his whynarde and his pouche,
The devyll myghte daunce therin for ony crowche.

Counter he coude *O lux* upon a potte;
An eestryche fedder of a capons tayle
He set up fresshely upon his hat alofte:
'What, revell-route!' quod he, and gan to rayle
How ofte he hadde hit Jenet on the tayle,
Of Felyce fetewse, and lytell prety Cate,
How ofte he knocked at her klycked gate.

What sholde I tell more of his rebaudrye?
I was ashamed so to here hym prate:
He had no pleasure but in harlotrye.
'Ay,' quod he, 'in the devylles date,
What arte thou? I sawe the nowe but late.'

'Forsothe,' quod I, 'in this courte I dwell nowe.'
'Welcome,' quod Ryote, 'I make God avowe.   35

'And, syr, in fayth why comste not us amonge,
To make the mery, as other felowes done?
Thou muste swere and stare, man, al daye longe,
And wake all nyghte, and slepe tyll it be none;
Thou mayste not studye, or muse on the mone;   40
This worlde is nothynge but ete, drynke, and slepe;
And thus with us good company to kepe,

'Pluck up thyne herte upon a mery pyne,
And lete us laugh a placke or tweyne at nale:
What the devyll, man, myrthe was never one!   45
What, loo, man, see here of dyce a bale!
A brydelynge caste for that is in thy male!
Now have at all that lyeth upon the burde!
Fye on this dyce, they be not worth a turde!

'Have at the hasarde, or at the dosen browne,   50
Or els I pas a peny to a pounde!
Now, wolde to God thou wolde leye money downe!
Lorde, how that I wolde caste it full rounde!
Ay, in my pouche a buckell I have founde;
The armes of Calyce, I have no coyne nor crosse!   55
I am not happy, I renne ay on the losse.

'Now renne muste I to the stewys syde,
To wete yf Malkyn, my lemman, have gete oughte:
I lete her to hyre, that men maye on her ryde,
Her harnes easy ferre and nere is soughte: 60
By Goddis sydes, syns I her thyder broughte,
She hath gote me more money with her tayle
Than hath some shyppe that into Bordews sayle.

'Had I as good an hors as she is a mare,
I durst aventure to journey thorugh Fraunce;   65
Who rydeth on her, he nedeth not to care,
For she is trussed for to breke a launce;
It is a curtel that wel can wynche and praunce:
To her wyll I nowe all my poverté lege;
And, tyll I come, have here is myne hat to plege.'   70

385

C

Phyllyp Sparowe

Pla ce bo,
Who is there, who?
Di le xi,
Dame Margery;
5   Fa, re, my, my,
Wherfore and why, why?
For the sowle of Philip Sparowe,
That was late slayn at Carowe,
Among the nones blake;
10   For that swete soules sake,
And for all sparowes soules,
Set in our bede-rolles,
Pater noster qui,
With an *Ave Mari*,
15   And with the corner of a Crede,
The more shal be your mede.
    Whan I remembre agayn
How mi Philyp was slayn,
Never halfe the payne
20   Was betwene you twayne,
Pyramus and Thesbe,
As than befell to me:
I wept and I wayled,
The tearys downe hayled;
25   But nothynge it avayled
To call Phylyp agayne,
Whom Gyb our cat hath slayne.
    Gib, I saye, our cat
Worrowyd her on that
30   Which I loved best:
It cannot be exprest
My sorowfull hevynesse,
But all without redresse;
For within that stounde,
35   Hafe slumbrynge in a sounde
I fell downe to the grounde.
    Unneth I kest myne eyes
Towarde the cloudy skyes;
But whan I dyd beholde

My sparow dead and colde, 40
No creatuer but that wolde
Have rewed upon me,
To behold and se
What hevynesse dyd me pange;
Wherewith my handes I wrange, 45
That my senaws cracked,
As though I had ben racked,
So payned and so strayned,
That no lyfe wellnye remayned.
    I syghed and I sobbed, 50
For that I was robbed
Of my sparowes lyfe.
O mayden, wydow, and wyfe,
Of what estate ye be,
Of hye or lowe degré, 55
Great sorowe than ye myght se,
And lerne to wepe at me!
Such paynes dyd me frete,
That myne hert dyd bete,
My vysage pale and dead, 60
Wanne, and blewe as lead;
The panges of hatefull death
Wellnye had stopped my breath.
    Heu, heu, me,
That I am wo for the! 65
Ad Dominum, cum tribularer, clamavi:
    Of God nothynge els crave I
But Phyllypes soule to kepe
From the marees deepe
Of Acherontes well, 70
That is a flode of hell;
And from the great Pluto,
The prynce of endles wo;
And from foule Alecto,
With vysage blacke and blo; 75
And from Medusa, that mare,
That lyke a fende doth stare;
And from Megeras edders,
For rufflynge of Phillips fethers,
And from her fyry sparklynges, 80
For burnynge of his wynges;
And from the smokes sowre
Of Proserpinas bowre;

And from the dennes darke,
85 Wher Cerberus doth barke,
Whom Theseus dyd afraye,
Whom Hercules dyd outraye,
As famous poetes say;
From that hell hounde,
90 That lyeth in cheynes bounde,
With gastly hedes thre,
To Jupyter pray we
That Phyllyp preserved may be!
Amen, say ye with me!
95   *Do mi nus*,
Helpe nowe, swete Jesus!
Levavi oculos meos in montes:
Wolde God I had Zenophontes,
Or Socrates the wyse,
100 To shew me their devyse
Moderatly to take
This sorow that I make
For Phyllip Sparowes sake!
So fervently I shake,
105 I fele my body quake;
So urgently I am brought
Into carefull thought.
      Like Andromach, Hectors wyfe,
Was wery of her lyfe,
110 Whan she had lost her joye,
Noble Hector of Troye;
In lyke maner also
Encreaseth my dedly wo,
For my sparowe is go.
115   It was so prety a fole,
It wold syt on a stole,
And lerned after my scole
For to kepe his cut,
With, 'Phyllyp, kepe your cut!'
120   It had a velvet cap,
And wold syt upon my lap,
And seke after small wormes,
And somtyme white bred crommes;
And many tymes and ofte
125 Betwene my brestes softe
It wolde lye and rest;
It was propre and prest.

388

Somtyme he wolde gaspe
Whan he sawe a waspe;
A fly or a gnat,   130
He wolde flye at that;
And prytely he wold pant
Whan he saw an ant;
Lord, how he wolde pry
After the butterfly!   135
Lorde, how he wolde hop
After the gressop!
And whan I sayd, 'Phyp, Phyp',
Than he wold lepe and skyp,
And take me by the lyp.   140
Alas, it wyll me slo,
That Phillyp is gone me fro!
   Si in i qui ta tes,
Alas, I was evyll at ease!
De pro fun dis cla ma vi,   145
Whan I sawe my sparowe dye!
   Nowe, after my dome,
Dame Sulpicia at Rome,
Whose name regystred was
For ever in tables of bras,   150
Because that she dyd pas
In poesy to endyte,
And eloquently to wryte,
Though she wolde pretende
My sparowe to commende,   155
I trowe she coude not amende
Reportynge the vertues all
Of my sparowe royall.
   For it wold come and go,
And fly so to and fro;   160
And on me it wolde lepe
Whan I was aslepe,
And his fether shake,
Wherewith he wolde make
Me often for to wake,   165
And for to take him in
Upon my naked skyn;
God wot, we thought no syn:
What though he crept so lowe?
It was no hurt, I trowe,   170
He dyd nothynge perdé

But syt upon my kne:
Phyllyp, though he were nyse,
In him it was no vyse,
175 Phyllyp had leve to go
To pyke my lytell too;
Phillip myght be bolde
And do what he wolde;
Phillip wolde seke and take
180 All the flees blake
That he coulde there espye
With his wanton eye. . . .

. . . O cat of carlyshe kynde,
The fynde was in thy mynde
185 Whan thou my byrde untwynde!
I wold thou haddest ben blynde!
The leopardes savage,
The lyons in theyr rage,
Myght catche the in theyr pawes,
190 And gnawe the in theyr jawes!
The serpentes of Lybany
Myght stynge the venymously!
The dragones with their tonges
Might poyson thy lyver and longes!
195 The mantycors of the montaynes
Myght fede them on thy braynes!
Melanchates, that hounde
That plucked Acteon to the grounde,
Gave hym his mortall wounde,
200 Chaunged to a dere,
The story doth appere,
Was chaunged to an harte;
So thou, foule cat that thou arte,
The selfe same hounde
205 Myght the confounde,
That his owne lord bote,
Myght byte asondre thy throte!
Of Inde the gredy grypes
Myght tere out all thy trypes!
210 Of Arcady the beares
Might plucke awaye thyne eares!
They wylde wolfe Lycaon
Byte asondre thy backe bone!
Of Ethna the brennynge hyll,

That day and night brenneth styl,   215
Set in thy tayle a blase,
That all the world may gase
And wonder upon the,
From Occyan the great se
Unto the Iles of Orchady,   220
From Tylbery fery
To the playne of Salysbery!
So trayterously my byrde to kyll
That never ought the evyll wyll!
   Was never byrde in cage   225
More gentle of corage
In doynge his homage
Unto his soverayne.
Alas, I say agayne,
Deth hath departed us twayne!   230
The false cat hath the slayne:
Farewell, Phyllyp, adew!
Our Lorde thy soule reskew!
Farewell without restore,
Farewell for evermore! . . .   235

25

LORD BERNERS

Sir John Bourchier, Lord Berners (c.1469–1533), is one of the unjustly neglected authors of this period. His Froissart is undoubtedly a 'classic'; as a translator, he stands beside Malory and Gavin Douglas, and is a worthy precursor of the great tradition of the later sixteenth century. His literary works (the order of composition of which is not certain) had to be fitted into a busy political and military life in the service of the Tudors, especially of Henry VIII, whom he accompanied to the Field of Cloth of Gold. Berners was Chancellor of the Exchequer from 1516, visited Spain in an embassy in 1518, and campaigned in France and Scotland. From 1520 to 1526 and from 1531 to 1533 he was Deputy of Calais, and it may well be that much of his translation was done in those periods. He was beset by serious financial problems, and on his death his effects were seized by the Crown (the inventory record that he owned eighty books is a testimony to the enthusiasm of his reading). The Froissart, printed during his lifetime (1523–5), does full justice to the excellence and the variety of its original, which is much more than a celebration of the chivalry of the Hundred Years War, 'the honorable and noble aventures of featis of armes done and achyved by the warres of France and Inglande'. Indeed, the anthologist confronted by the constant succession of vivid and famous scenes—the burghers of Calais, John Ball and the Peasants' Revolt, the madness of the French king, the fall of Richard II, to mention only a few—is likely to despair. I have chosen less well-known episodes: the death of Sir John Chandos, a great 'flower of chivalry', which gives some idea of how confidently Berners can reproduce Froissart's skilful dialogue and the precision of detail which gives the story a distinctly Malorian tone, and a couple of anecdotes of Court life, tragic and comic. Berners evidently approached his task with enthusiasm and imagination, and he had a very serious view of the duty of the chronicler: history, he says, is not only a mirror of moral behaviour, but in the completeness of its view 'may well be called a divyne provydence', for 'albeit that mortall folke are marveylously separated, both by lande and water ... yet are they and their actes (done peradventure by the space of a thousande yere) compact togyder by th'istographier, as it were the dedes of one selfe cyté, and in one mannes lyfe'. His translation is a remarkable literary example of what has been called 'the Indian summer of English chivalry'; it is directly in the tradition of Malory and of Caxton (who in his epilogue to *The Order of Chivalry* had encouraged the noblemen of England to read Froissart). Not surprisingly, he also had a taste for knightly romances. *The Boke of Duke Huon of Burdeux* (? after 1513) is translated from a long, rambling, but entertaining French romance. It is full of wonders; in this book Oberon, the fairy king, makes his first appearance in English literature. *Arthur of Lytell Brytayne* (? after 1514) is also a version of a French romance, and is also full of marvels (so much so that Berners in his prologue rather defensively remarks that in it there 'semeth to be so many unpossybylytees', but cites the histories of 'ancient conquerors', where there are adventures 'which by playne letter as to our understandynge sholde seme in a maner to be supernaturall'). Our example is an eerie and magical adventure in a fairy castle. Berners also translated (apparently from French) two contemporary Spanish best sellers. Of these *The Golden Boke of Marcus Aurelius* (completed in 1533) seems to have been by far the most popular of his works. He says that it was done at the request of his nephew Sir Francis Bryan (d. 1550), poet, courtier, admirer of Erasmus, and friend of Wyatt and Surrey. The original book of Antonio de Guevara (*c.*1480–1545), by modern standards a 'forgery', was immensely influential in the sixteenth century (North's *The Diall of Princes* [1557] is a later translation of an expanded version) even after the genuine *Meditations* of the real emperor had come to light. It is at once a book of consolation, of advice to princes, and a collection of golden 'sentences' in an elaborate, balanced style. Berners had to struggle with a French version that is sometimes desperately difficult, but his style is equal to subject-matter of a very different kind, and he manages to produce passages which have a genuine eloquence and nobility.

A

THE CRONYCLE OF SYR JOHN FROISSART

The Death of Sir John Chandos (1369–70)

And Sir John Chandos abode styll behynde, full of displeasure in that he had fayled of his purpose, and so stode in a kechyn, warmyng him by the fyre. And his servantes jangeled with hym to th'entent to bring him out of his melancholy. His servantes had prepared for hym a place to rest hym: than he demaunded if it were nere day. And therwith there came a man 5 into the house, and came before hym, and sayd, 'Sir, I have brought you tidynges.' 'What be they? Tell me.' 'Sir, surely the Frenchmen be ryding abrode.' 'How knowest thou that?' 'Sir,' sayd he, 'I departed fro Saynt Salvyn with them.' 'What waye be they ryden?' 'Sir, I can nat tell you the certentie, but surely they toke the high way to Poiters.' 'What Frenchmen 10 be they, canst thou tell me?' 'Sir, it is Sir Loys of Saynt Julyan, and Carlouet the Breton.' 'Well,' quod Sir Johan Chandos, 'I care nat. I have no lyst this night to ryde forthe. They may happe to be encountred thoughe I be nat there.' And so he taryed there styll a certayne space in a gret study, and at last, whan he had well advysed hymselfe, he sayde, 15 'Whatsoever I have sayd here before, I trowe it be good that I ryde forthe. I must retourne to Poicters, and anone it wyll be day.' 'That is true, sir,' quod the knightes about hym. Than he said, 'Make redy, for I wyll ryde forthe.' And so they dyd, and mounted on their horses, and departed and toke the right way to Poicters, costyng the ryver; and the Frenchmen the 20

same tyme were nat past a leag before hym in the same way, thinkyng to
passe the ryver at the bridge of Lusac. There the Englysshmen had
knowlege how they were in the trake of the Frenchmen, for the
Frenchmens horses cryed and brayed bycause of th'Englysshe horses that
25 were before them with Sir Thomas Percy. And anone it was fayre light
day, for in the begynnyng of January the mornynges be soone light. And
whan the Frenchmen and Bretons were within a leage of the bridge, they
perceyved on the other syde of the bridge Sir Thomas Percy and his
company; and he lykewise perceyved the Frenchmen, and rode as fast as
30 he might to get the advantage of the bridge, and sayd, 'Beholde yonder
Frenchmen be a great nombre agaynst us, therfore let us take the avantage
of the bridge.' And whan Sir Loys and Carlouet sawe th'Englysshmen
make suche hast to gette the bridge, they dyde in lyke wyse. Howbeit,
th'Englysshmen gate it first, and lighted all afote, and so raynged
35 themselfe in good order to defende the bridge. The Frenchmen likewyse
lighted afote and delyvered their horses to their pages, commaundynge
them to drawe abacke; and so dyde put themselfe in good order to go and
assayle th'Englysshmen, who kept themselfe close togider and were
nothyng afrayed though they were but a handfull of men as to the regard of
40 the Frenchmen. And thus as the Frenchmen and Bretons studyed and
ymagined howe and by what meanes to their advantage they might assayle
the Englisshmen, therwith there came behynd them Sir Johan Chandos,
his baner displayed, berynge therin sylver, a sharpe pyle goules; and Jakes
of Lery, a valyant man of armes, dyd bere it, and he had with hym a .xl.
45 speares. He aproched fiersly the Frenchmen; and whan he was a thre
forlonges fro the bridge, the Frenche pages who sawe them comynge were
afrayed, and so ran away with the horses and left their maisters there afote.
And whan Sir John Chandos was come nere to them, he sayd, 'Harke ye
Frenchmen, ye are but yvell men of warre. Ye ryde at youre pleasure and
50 ease day and night; ye take and wyn townes and forteresses in Poyctou,
wherof I am seneshall. Ye raunsome poore folke without my leave; ye ryde
all about clene armed. It shulde seme the countré is all yours. But I ensure
you it is nat so! Ye, Sir Loyes and Carlouet, ye ar to great maisters. It is
more than a yere and a half that I have sette all myne entent to fynde or
55 encountre with you, and nowe, I thanke God, I se you and speke to you,
nowe shall it be sene who is stronger, other you or I. It hath ben shewed
me often tymes that ye have greatly desyred to fynde me—nowe ye may se
me here! I am John Chandos, advyse me well. Your great feates of armes
wherwith ye be renowmed, by Goddes leave nowe shall we prove it!'
60 Whyle suche langage was spoken, Sir John Chandos company drewe
toguyder, and Sir Loyes and Carlouet kept themselfe close togyder,
makyng semblant to be glad to be fought withall. And of all this mater, Sir
Thomas Percy, who was on the other syde of the bridge, knewe nothynge,
for the bridge was hyghe in the myddes so that none coude se other.

Whyle Sir Johan Chandos reasoned thus with the Frenchmen, there 65
was a Breton toke his glayve and coude forbere no lenger, but came to an
Englysshe squyer called Simekyn Dodall and strake him so in the brest
that he cast hym downe fro his horse. Sir John Chandos, whan he herde
that noyse besyde him, he tourned that way and sawe his squyer lye on the
erthe and the Frenchmen layeng on him. Than he was more chafed than 70
he was before, and sayd to his company, 'Sirs, howe suffre you this squyer
thus to be slayne? Afote, afote!' And so he lepte afote and all his company,
and so Simekyn was rescued, and the batayle begone. Sir Johan Chandos,
who was a right hardy and a coragyous knight, with his baner before him
and his company about him, with his cote of armes on hym, great and 75
large, beten with his armes of whyte sarcenet with two pylles goules, one
before and another behynde, so that he semed to be a sufficyent knyght to
do a great feate of armes, and as one of the formast with his glayve in his
hande marched to his ennemyes. The same mornyng there had fallen a
great dewe, so that the grounde was somewhat moyst, and so in his goyng 80
forwarde he slode and fell downe at the joynyng with his enemyes, and as
he was arysing, there light a stroke on him, gyven by a squier called Jakes
of Saynt Martyn with his glayve, the whiche stroke entred into the flesshe
under his eye, bytwene the nose and the forheed. Sir John Chandos sawe
nat the stroke commyng on that syde, for he was blynde on the one eye. He 85
lost the sight therof a fyve yere before as he hunted after an hart in the
laundes of Burdeaux. And also he had on no vyser; the stroke was rude
and entred into his brayne, the whiche stroke greved him so sore that he
overthrue to the erthe, and tourned for payne two tymes upsodowne as he
that was wounded to dethe, for after the stroke he never spake worde. And 90
whan his men saw that mysfortune they were right dolorouse. Than his
uncle Edward Clifforde stepte and bestrode him, for the Frenchmen
wolde fayne have had him, and defended him so valyantly, and gave
rounde about him such strokes that none durst aproche nere to him. Also
Sir John Chambo and Sir Bertram of Case semed lyke men out of their 95
myndes whan they saw their maister lye on the erth. The Bretons and
Frenchmen were gretly conforted, whan they sawe the capitayne of their
enemyes on the erthe, thynking verily that he had his dethes wounde.
Than they avaunced themselfe, and sayd, 'Ye Englyshmen, yelde you, for
ye are all ours; ye canne nat scape us!' There the Englyshmen dyd 100
marveyls in armes, as well to defende themselfe as to reveng their maister
Sir John Chandos, whome they sawe lye in a harde case; and a squyer of
Sir John Chandos spyed Jaques of Saynt Martyn, who hadde gyven his
maister his mortall stroke, and ran to hym fiersly, and stroke hym wth
suche vyolence that his glayve pearsed through bothe his thyes; howebeit 105
for all that stroke he lefte nat styll to fight. If Sir Thomas Percy and his
company had knowen of this adventure, who were on the other syde of the
brige, they shulde well have socoured him. But bycause they knewe

nothyng therof nor herde no more of the Frenchmen, wenyng to them they
110 had ben gone backe, therfore he and his company departed and toke the
waye to Poycters, as they that knewe nothynge of that busynesse. Thus the
Englysshmen fought styll before the bridge of Lusac, and there was done
many a feat of armes: brevely, the Englysshmen coude endure no lenger
agaynst the Frenchmen, so that the moost parte of them were disconfyted
115 and taken. But alwayes Edwarde Clyfforde wolde nat departe fro his
nephue thereas he lay. So thus yf the Frenchmen hadde ben so happy as to
have had their horses there redy, as they had nat, for their pages were
ronne away fro them before, or els they might have departed with moche
honour and profite, and many a gode prisoner, and for lacke of them they
120 lost all: wherfore they were sore displeased, and sayd among themselfe, 'A!
This is an yvel order; for the journey is ours, and yet through faute of our
pages we can nat departe, seyng we be hevy armed and sore traveyled, so
that we can nat go afote through this countré, the whiche is full of our
enemyes, and contrary to us, and we are a sixe leages fro the next
125 forteresse that we have, and also dyvers of our company be sore hurt and
we may nat leave theym behynde us.' Thus as they were in this case, and
wyst nat what to do, and had sent two Bretons unarmed into the feldes to
se yf they might fynde any of their pages with their horses, there came on
them Sir Guyssharde Dangle, Sir Loyes Harcourt, the Lorde Parteney,
130 the lorde Tanyboton, the lorde Dargenton, the lorde of Pynan, Sir Jaques
of Surgyers, and dyvers other Englysshmen to the nombre of two hundred
speares, who rode about to seke for the Frenchmen, for it was shewed
them howe they were abrode. And so they fell in the trake of the horses,
and came in great hast with baners and penons wavyng in the wynde. And
135 as soone as the Bretons and Frenchmen sawe them comyng, they knewe
well they were their enemies; than they sayd to the Englysshmen whome
they had taken as prisoners before, 'Sirs, beholde, yonder cometh a bande
of your company to socour you, and we perceyve well that we can nat
endure agaynst them, and ye be our prisoners; we wyll quyte you, so that
140 ye wyll kepe us, and wyll become your prisoners, for we had rather yelde us
to you than to them that cometh yonder.' And they aunswered, 'As ye wyll,
so are we content.' Thus the Englysshmen were losed out of their prisons.
Than the Poictevyns, Gascoyns, and Englysshmen came on them, their
speares in their restes, cryeng their cryes; than the Frenchmen and
145 Bretons drewe asyde, and sayde to them, 'Sirs, leave! do us no hurt, we be
all prisoners aredy!' The Englysshmen affirmed the same, and said, 'They
be our prisoners.' Carlouet was prisoner with Sir Bertram of Case, and Sir
Loyes of Saynt Julyan with Sir Johan Cambo, so that there was none but
that he had a maister.
150   The barowns and knightes of Poictou were sore disconforted whan they
sawe their seneschall Sir Johan Chandos lye on the erthe and coude nat
speke. Than they lamentably complayned, and sayd, 'A, Sir Johan

Chandos, the floure of all chivalry, unhappely was that glayve forged that
thus hath wounded you, and brought you in parell of dethe!' They wept
piteously that were about hym, and he herde and understode theym well 155
but he coulde speke no worde. They wronge their handes and tare their
heeres and made many a pytefull complaynt, and specially suche as were of
his owne house. Than his servauntes unarmed him and layde him on
pavesses, and so bare him softely to Mortymer, the next forteresse to them;
and the other barons and knyghtes retourned to Poycters and ledde with 160
them their prisoners.

The Duke of Berry Thinks of Marriage (1389)

The Duke of Berrey, who had maryed the lady Jane of Armynake to his
first wyfe, after she was dysseased, he hadde great imagynacyon to be
maryed agayne; and that he well shewed, for whan he sawe howe he had
myssed of the Duke of Lancastres doughter, he than set clerkes to write, 165
and sent messangers to th'Erle Gascon of Foiz, who had the kepyng of the
Erle of Boulonges doughter more than the space of nyne yeres. And
bycause the Duke of Berrey coulde nat come to this maryage but by the
daunger of the Erle of Foize, for nother for Pope, father, mother, nor
frende that the damosell had, the erle wolde do nothynge without it were 170
his owne pleasure, than the Duke of Berrey desyred effectuously the
French kynge his nephue and the Duke of Burgoyne his brother to helpe
and assyst hym in this maryage. The Frenche kyng laught and had good
sporte at the Duke of Berrey his uncle bycause he was olde and so hote in
love, and said to him, 'Fayre uncle, what shall ye do with a yonge mayde? 175
She is nat twelve yere of age, and ye be .lx. By my faythe, it is great foly for
you to thynke therof! Speke for my cosyn Johan, your sonne. He is yonge;
the mater is more mete for hym than for you.' 'Syr,' quod the duke, 'I have
spoken allredy for my sonne, but the Erle of Foize wyll in no wyse agree
therto, bycause my sonne is of the blode of Armynake, who be at warre 180
togyder, and have ben longe. If the lady be yonge, I shall spare her a thre
or four yere tyll she be a parfyte woman.' 'Well, fayre uncle,' quod the
kyng, 'I feare me she wyll nat spare so longe, but seynge ye have so great
affection therto, I shall ayde you as moche as I may.' ...

Disaster at a Disguising (1393)

It fortuned that sone after the retayninge of this foresayd knyght a 185
maryage ,was made in the kynges house, bytwen a yonge knyght of
Vermandoys and one of the quenes gentylwomen; and bycause they were
bothe of the kynges house, the kinges uncles and other lordes, ladyes, and
damoselles made great tryumphe. There was the dukes of Orlyaunce,

190 Berrey, and Burgoyne, and their wyves, daunsynge and makynge great joye. The kynge made a great supper to the lordes and ladyes, and the quene kepte her estate, desirynge every man to be mery. And there was a squyer of Normandy, called Hogreymen of Gensay—he advysed to make some pastyme. The daye of the maryage, whiche was on a Tuesday before
195 Candelmas, he provyded for a mummery agaynst nyght. He devysed syxe cotes made of lynen clothe, covered with pytche, and theron flaxe lyke heare, and had them redy in a chambre. The kynge put on one of them, and th'erle of Jony, a yonge lusty knyght, another, and syr Charles of Poicters the thyrde, who was sonne to the erle of Valentenoys, and syr
200 Yvan of Foiz another, and the sonne of the lorde Nanthorillet had on the fyfte, and the squyer hymselfe had on the syxte. And whan they were thus arayed in these sayd cotes, and sowed fast in them, they semed lyke wylde wodehouses, full of heare fro the toppe of the heed to the sowle of the foote. This devyse pleased well the Frenche kynge, and was well content
205 with the squyer for it. They were aparelled in these cotes secretely in a chambre that no man knewe therof but such as holpe them. Whan syr Yvan of Foiz had well advysed these cotes, he sayd to the kynge, 'Syr, commaunde straytely that no man aproche nere us with any torches or fyre, for if the fyre fasten in any of these cotes we shall all be brent without
210 remedy.' The king aunswered and sayd, 'Yvan, ye speke well and wysely; it shall be doone as ye have devysed,' and incontynent sent for an ussher of his chambre, commaundyng him to go into the chambre where the ladyes daunsed, and to commaunde all the varlettes holdinge torches to stande up by the walles, and none of them to aproche nere to the wodehouses that
215 shulde come thyder to daunce. The ussher dyd the kynges commaunde-ment, whiche was fulfylled. Sone after, the duke of Orlyance entred into the hall, acompanyed with four knyghtes and syxe torches, and knewe nothynge of the kynges commaundement for the torches nor of the mummery that was commynge thyder, but thought to beholde the
220 daunsynge, and began hymselfe to daunce. Therwith the kynge with the fyve other came in; they were so dysguysed in flaxe that no man knewe them. Fyve of them were fastened one to another; the kynge was lose, and went before and led the devyse.

　　Whan they entred into the hall every man toke so great hede to them
225 that they forgate the torches. The kynge departed fro his company and went to the ladyes to sporte with them, as youth requyred, and so passed by the quene and came to the duchesse of Berrey, who toke and helde hym by the arme to knowe what he was, but the kynge wolde nat shewe his name. Than the duches sayd, 'Ye shall nat escape me tyll I knowe your name!' In
230 this meane season great myschyefe fell on the other, and by reason of the duke of Orlyance; howbeit it was by ignoraunce and agaynst his wyll, for if he had consydred before the mischefe that fell, he wolde nat have done as he dyd for all the good in the worlde. But he was so desyrous to knowe

what personages the fyve were that daunced, he put one of the torches that
his servauntes helde so nere that the heate of the fyre entred into the flaxe 235
(wherin if fyre take there is no remedy), and sodaynly was on a bright
flame, and so eche of them set fyre on other; the pytche was so fastened to
the lynen clothe, and their shyrtes so drye and fyne, and so joynynge to
their flesshe, that they began to brenne and to cry for helpe. None durste
come nere theym; they that dyd brente their handes by reason of the heate 240
of the pytche. One of them, called Nanthorillet advysed hym howe the
botry was therby; he fled thyder, and cast himselfe into a vessell full of
water wherin they rynsed pottes, whiche saved hym, or els he had ben
deed as the other were, yet he was sore hurt with the fyre. Whan the quene
herde the crye that they made, she douted her of the kynge, for she knewe 245
well that he shulde be one of the syxe, wherwith she fell in a sowne and
knightes and ladyes came and comforted her. A pyteous noyse there was in
the hall. The duchesse of Berrey delyvered the kynge fro that parell, for
she dyd caste over hym the trayne of her gowne, and covered him fro the
fyre. The kynge wolde have gone fro her. 'Whyder wyll ye go?' quod she, 250
'Ye se well howe your company brennes. What are ye?' 'I am the kyng,'
quod he. 'Haste you', quod she, 'and gette you into other apparell, that the
quene maye se you, for she is in great feare of you.' Therwith the kynge
departed out of the hall, and in all haste chaunged his apparell, and came
to the quene. And the duchesse of Berrey had somwhat comforted her, 255
and had shewed her howe she shulde se the kynge shortely. Therwith the
kynge came to the quene, and as soone as she sawe hym, for joy she
enbrased hym and fell in a sowne. Than she was borne into her chambre,
and the kynge wente with her. And the bastarde of Foiz, who was all on a
fyre, cryed ever with a loude voyce, 'Save the kynge! Save the kynge!' Thus 260
was the kynge saved. It was happy for hym that he went fro his company,
for els he had ben deed without remedy. . . .

B

HUON OF BURDEUX

Oberon

Whan Huon had harde Gerames, than he demaundyd forther of hym yf he
coude go to Babylon. 'Ye, syr,' quod Gerames, 'I can go thether by .ii.
wayes. The most surest way is hense a .xl. jurneys, and the other is but .xv.
jurneys. But I counsell you to take the long way, for yf ye take the shorter
way ye most passe throwout a wood a .xvi. leges of lenght; but the way is so 5
full of the fayrey and straunge thynges that suche as passe that way are lost,

for in that wood abydyth a kynge of the fayrey namyd Oberon. He is of
heyght but of .iii. fote and crokyd shulderyd, but yet he hathe an aungelyke
vysage so that there is no mortall man that seethe hym but that taketh grete
10 pleasure to beholde his fase. And ye shall no soner be enteryd in to that
wood, yf ye go that way he wyll fynde the maner to speke with you, and yf
ye speke to hym ye are lost for ever. And ye shall ever fynde hym before
you, so that it shal be in maner impossyble that ye can skape fro hym
without spekynge to hym, for his wordes be so pleasant to here that there is
15 no mortall man that can well skape without spekyng to hym; and yf he se
that ye wyll not speke a worde to hym, than he wyll be sore dyspleasyd with
you, and or ye can gete out of the wood he wyll cause reyne and wynde,
hayle and snowe, and wyll make mervelous tempestes with thonder and
lyghtenynges, so that it shall seme to you that all the worlde sholde
20 pereshe, and he shall make to seme before you a grete rynnynge river,
blacke and depe. But ye may passe it at your ease, and it shall not wete the
fete of your horse, for all is but fantesey and enchauntmentes that the
dwarfe shall make to th'entent to have you with hym. And yf ye can kepe
your selfe without spekynge to hym, ye maye than well skape. But, syr, to
25 eschew all perelles, I counsell you take the lenger way, for I thynke ye can
not skape fro hym, and than be ye lost for ever.' Whan Huon had well
harde Gerames he had grete mervayll, and he had grete desyre in hym
selfe to se that dwarfe kynge of the fayrey, and the straunge adventures
that were in that wood. . . .

C

ARTHUR OF LYTELL BRYTAYNE

How that Arthur Conquered the Castell of the Porte Noyre

Whan that Arthur was departed fro Governar, he toke the waye on the
ryghte hande, and so rode forth .iii. dayes without findinge of ony
adventure of ony maner of hous or place: howbeit, by the counseyle of his
hoost, he toke with hym sustenaunce for hymselfe and for his horse for the
5 space of thre or foure dayes; and thus he passed by many valeys and
mountaynes, so that he and his horse were right wery; and on the fourth
daye he founde an hydeous ryver, depe and perfound; the bankes were so
hye fro the water that he coude not se it ren, the whiche water rored and
brayed, and ran so swyftely that none myghte passe withoute drowning;
10 and in certayne places it was full of grete and myghty rockes, the whiche
were of suche heyght that fro the valey bynethe the toppe of them myght
unnethes be sene; the whiche rockes were soo full of vermyn that all the

ryver thereby stanke abhomynably. At the last, Arthur found a lytle way alonge by the ryvers syde on the lyfte hande, in the whyche he rode so long tyl it was hye none, and than he espyed a lytel streyght waye bytwene two 15 mountaynes, the whiche were of a mervaylous heyght. Than he founde a lytell narowe brydge over this ryver, the whiche with moche payne he passed over. Than he entred into a streyght causy made of stone, wherin he rode forth; and on every hande of hym all was but grete maresses and foule stynkynge waters, the whiche waye brought hym streyght unto the 20 Porte Noyre, the whiche was the strongest castell of all the worlde. And so whan he came to the brydge and gate therof, there he founde .xii. knyghtes all armed on horsbacke, .vi. at the one ende of the brydge, and .vi. at the other ende; and at the gate there were .xii. other knyghtes on fote, holdyng hatches and mases of stele in theyr handes, to the entent to kepe that none 25 sholde entre into the castell; and above, on the barbycans and bowlewerkes there stode men of warre with crosbowes and other wepens to defend the place. . . .

. . . Than Arthur mounted up certane greces to entre into the hall of the palays, the which was the way to the Mount Peryllous. And there he found 30 the moost fayre hous that ever was sene, sette all aboute with ymages of fyne golde, and the wyndowes were all of fyne ambre, wyth many hye clere wyndowes. And out of this hall he entred in to a chambre the moste rychest that ever was seen; for syth God first made mankynde there was no maner of hystorie nor bataile but in that chambre it was portrayed with 35 golde and asure and other fresshe coloures, so quyckely aourned that it was wonder to behold: there was portrayed how God dyde create the sonne and the mone, and in the rofe were all the .vii. planettes wrought with fyne golde and sylver, and all the sytuacyons of the hevens, wherin were pyght many carbuncles and other precyous stones, the whiche dyde 40 cast grete clerenes bothe by daye and by nyght. To saye the trouthe, it was the moost rychest chambre and the wonderfullest that ever was seen in all the worlde—Proserpyne, quene of the fayry, caused it thus to be made. Also there were dyverse beddes wonderfull ryche, but specyally one, the whiche stode in the myddes of the chambre, surmounted in beauté all 45 other, for the utterbrasses therof were of grene jasper wyth grete barres of golde set full of precyous stones, and the crampons were of fyne sylver enbordered wyth golde, the postes of yvery with pomelles of corall, and the staves closed in bokeram covered wyth crymesyn satyn, and shetes of sylke with a ryche coverynge of ermyns, and other clothes of cloth of golde, and 50 foure square pyllowes wrought amonge the Sarasyns. The curtaynes were of grene sendall vyroned wyth golde and asure, and rounde aboute this bedde there laye on the flour carpettes of sylke poynted and enbrowdred with ymages of golde. And at the foure corners of this bedde there were foure condytes mervaylously wrought by subtyll entayle, out of the whiche 55 there yssued so swet an odour and so delectable that al other swetenesse of the world were as nothynge to the regarde therof; and at the head of thys bedde there stode an ymage of golde, and had in hys lyfte hande a bowe of yvery, and in his right hande an arowe of fyne sylver; in the myddes of his brest there were lettres that sayd thus, 'Whan thys ymage shoteth, than all 60 this palais shall tourne like a whele, and whosoever lyeth in this bedde shall dye, without it be that knyghte to whome this bedde is destenyed unto.'

And whan Arthur saw the noblenesse of thys chambre, and specyally of this bedde, he had great plesure to behold it, and sayd to himselfe how that 65 at all adventures he wold lye downe on the bedde, and not to ferre for anye dred of death; and as he was lyeng downe on this bedde, he espyed in everye corner of the chambre a gret ymage of fine golde standynge, eche of theym holdynge in theyr handes a great horne of sylver, and, by theyr countenance, redy to blow. Than Arthur herde a great voyce, whyche was 70 so loude and horryble, that master Steven who was in the playes without the castell myght ryght wel here it; the which voyce sayd, 'Behold now the ende!' Than mayster Steven sayd to hys company, 'I am sure the knyght is entred into the palays within the castel; God defend hym from all yll encombraunce!' Than al the palays began to tremble and shake wondersly 75 so moche that at the last one of the .iiii. ymages began to blowe his horne so loud that it might wel be herde the space of a myle. Than the palays trembled so sore that all shold have fallen to peces; the dores and windowes often tymes dyd open and close agayne by theyre owne accord. Than Arthur hearde aboute him gret noyse of people, as though there had 80 bene a thousande men togyder, but he coulde se no creature: at the last he perceyved great lyghte of torches, and ever he herde styll the noyse of people comynge and goynge aboute the bedde, and also herde the brayenge of an hydeous ryver, so that it semed to hym that it had ben the roringe of the wylde see; therwith he felte suche a terryble wynde that he 85 had moche payne to sustayne hym on his fete. Than Arthur assayed agayne to have layne downe on the bedde. Than the voyce began to crye agayne, and sayd, 'Beholde now the ende!' Than the seconde ymage began to blowe; than came there in to the chambre suche noyse and tourment that Arthur was nye defe wyth the terryble dynne, and the palays than 90 began sorer to tremble than it dyde before so that Arthur thought surely that all the palays sholde have fallen. Than Arthur drewe hym towarde the bedde, and as he wold have layne hym downe, he sawe on hys ryght hande a grete lyon, fyers and fell, comynge to hymwarde, gapinge and rampynge to devour hym, and so assayled hym ryght rudely, and wyth hys pawes toke 95 Arthur so by the sholder that his harneys coulde not kepe him, but that his sharpe clawes entred into his fleshe. And as the lyon wolde have taken him by the heed, he cast his shelde before hym, and the lyon dasht it wyth his pawes all to peces, and nye had overthrowen hym to the erth. But than Arthur toke his strength to hym, and as the lyon was rampinge before hym, 100

he put his sworde clene thrugh his body, and so the lyon fell downe deed
to the erthe; and Arthur was ryght sore hurte in the sholder, and bledde
faste. Than he approched agayne to the bedde to have layde hym downe.
Than the thyrde ymage fyersly dyd blowe his horne, and out of the ende
therof by semynge to Arthur there yssued out an other lyon, greter and 105
stronger than the other was. Whan Arthur sawe hym, he cryed to God and
to our blessed Lady to helpe and socour hym from yll deth and foule
encombraunce. And so the lyon dressed hym towarde Arthur, and strake
at hym wyth hys brode pawes, and Arthur helde before hym the remenaunt
that was left of his shelde, but the lyon shortly brake it all to peces, as 110
though it had bene but glasse; and with one of his fete he toke Arthur by
the lyfte syde, and rased fro him a gret parte of his harneys, and his
doublet and shert, and a gret pece of his flessh to the bare rybbes; and if
God had not there helped him, he had rendred his mortall lyfe. Than
Arthur wyth his swerde strake of the lions fote that was under his syde, and 115
therwith the lyon fell to the erth, and, or he rose agayne, Arthur recovered
another stroke and strake of his heade by the shuldres. Than Arthur toke a
fayre cloth of sendall that laye on the bedde, and therwyth wrapped his
woundes and staunched them frome bledynge. Than he approched agayne
to the bedde to lye downe to rest hym; and than sodenly the fourth ymage 120
began terrybly to blow his horne. Therwith Arthur loked behind him, and
espyed a great giaunt comyng to himwarde, who was .xv. fote of length,
betynge togeder his tethe as though they had bene hamers strikinge on a
stythy, who had in his hand a great axe wherof the blade was wel thre fote
longe, the whiche was so longe and sharpe that it would cutte clene 125
asonder every thynge that it touched. And whan thys gyaunt sawe these
lyons dede, he was so sore dyspleased that he was all in a rage, and so
rowled up his eyen, and dashte togyder his tethe, and ran fyerselye at
Arthur, thynkynge to have stryken of his head. But Arthur feared moche
the stroke and lepte asyde, whereby the stroke wente besyde hym, and 130
dasht in to the pavement so rudely that the blade of the weapen entred
therin juste to the heade; and than Arthur strake him with his swerde, but
the stroke mounted up agayne and wold in no wyse enter, for he was
harneysed with the skynne of a serpent, the whiche was so hard that no
wepen coud empoyre it. And whan Arthur saw that, he was ryght sore 135
displeased, and lyfte up his swerde agayne and strake the giaunt on the
heade more rudely than he didde before; but all that avaled not, for it
semed to him that he strake on a stethy of stele. Than Arthur fered
himselfe gretely. Than the gyant strake many strokes at Arthur, but
alwayes he watched so the strokes that he dydde let theim passe by hym 140
without ony hurte or domage; for he perceyved ryght well that if the
gyaunte dyd light on him with a full stroke, there was none other way with
him but death. Thus this gyant ever pursued Arthur to have striken him,
but always Arthur watched the strokes and voyded them wysely, and

145 oftentymes strake the gyaunt agayne, but he coulde doo hym no hurte. Thus they fought a grete space, not ferre fro the ryche bedde in the myddes of the chambre. Than the giaunt with grete yre lyfte up his fauchon to have stryken Arthur upon the head, and the stroke came brayeng, and dasht into the erth lyke thonder, for Arthur avoyded craftely
150 the stroke, the which entred and cut asonder a greate brase of a benche that stode before the bedde, of white yvery; and so the stroke descended downe into the erth thrughout all the pavement, for the gyaunt was so sore dyspleased that his weapen entred thrugh bothe wode and stone, and into the erth to the hard head, and therwith the blade of his fauchon brast clene
155 asonder in the myddes. And whan the giaunt sawe that, he fared lyke a fende of hell, and so toke the handlynge therof and cast it at Arthur, but wysely he dyde avoyde it, and so it lyghted on the wall of the chambre, wherin the stroke entred well a fote and an halfe. Than the gyaunte lepte to the brase of the benche that he had cut asonder before, and wold have
160 rasshed it out of the benche, but it was so sore bounde with crampons of stele to the benche that he coude not remeve it; and as he stouped to pull therat, Arthur espyed hym, and how the serpentes skynne was but shorte behynde his backe, and so under the skynne he dasht his swerde into his bely to the crosse. Than the gyaunt fell downe and made a terryble
165 braynge, the whiche myght well be herde a grete waye of. Than Arthur recovered on hym an other stroke, and so dasht his swerde into his herte. Than he made a greter crye than he did before, and therwith his soule passed awaie to the devil of hell. Than the noyse was hearde agayne that sayde, 'Beholde th'ende!' Than was Arthur so very and so sore travayled
170 and his woundes bledde so fast that he had much payne to sustaine himselfe on his fete. Howbeit, as wel as he might, he repayred downe to the ryche bed, and alwayes his swerde in his hand, and therwith layd him down on the bed. Than the ymage of gold at the beddes head with his bow and arowe dyd shote, and hytte one of the wyndowes so sore that it flewe
175 wide open with the stroke; out of whiche window there yssued suche a smoke and fume so blacke that it made al the hous so darke that Arthur coude se nothing; the which fume stanke so abominably that Arthur therby was nye dead. Than there rose suche a wynde so grete and fervent that it brast the glasse windowes and latesses, so that the tyles and stones flew all
180 about the hous lyke hayle; and it thondred so terrybly that al the erth shoke and the paleys trembled like to have gone all to peces; and at the last he perceyved a brennynge spere all of fyre, the whiche was comynge to hymwarde. Therwith he lepte fro the bedde, and fledde fro the stroke, and sawe where yt wente in at an other lytell chambre by, and fell on a knyght
185 as he lay abedde, and so brente hym clene thrugh; and the fyre descended thrughout bedde and chambre and al, and sanke depe into the erth. Than sodeynly brast asonder two pyllers whiche susteyned the coverynge over the bedde, and than al the hole palays began to tourne about lyke a whele.

Than Arthur ranne to the ymage of golde that stode at the beddes heed
and enbraced it in his armes, for the ymage removed noo thinge; and this 190
tourneng of the palays endured a grete space. And Bawdewyn, Arthurs
squyer, who was wythout in the courte, pyteously wepte and demened
ryght grete sorow for the fere that he had of his mayster, for he thought
veryly how that he was but deed, and sayd, 'A! my lorde Arthur! the best
knight, the moost noble and hardy, the moost sage and curteyse creature 195
that ever was fourmed by Nature, alas! why dyde ye entre into this
unhappy castell, for I thynke surely ye are but deed!' And so than at the
last the tournynge of thys palays began to sece, and the derkenes began to
avoyde and to waxe fayre and clere, and the ayre peasyble. Than Arthur
sate hym downe upon the ryche beddes syde, ryght feble and faynt, 200
bycause of the grete troble that he had endured and for the ferefull
horryblenes that he had seen and herde. Than whan it was thus waxed
fayre and clere, than the voyce sayd agayne twyse, 'It ys ended! it ys
ended!'

D

THE GOLDEN BOKE OF MARCUS AURELIUS

The Emperor's Farewell

Nowe, my harty frendes, ye se that I am come to the ende of my last
journey, and to the begynnynge of my firste journey with the goddis. It is
reason that syth I have loved you in tyme past that ye beleve me nowe. For
the tyme is com that ye can demande nothyng of me, nor I have nothing to
offre you; nor myn eares as now can not here flateries, nor my herte suffre 5
importunities. Yf ye never knewe me, knowe me now. I have ben he that I
am, and am he that hath ben, in tymes paste lyke unto you somwhat. Nowe
ye se I am but lyttell, and within a lytell whyle I shal be nothynge. This
daye shall ende the lyfe of Marke your frende, this daye shall ende the lyfe
of Marc your parent, this day shal ende the fatall destenies of Marc your 10
lord, this day shall ende the signorie of Marke your emperour, and this day
shall ende his empire. I have vanquysshed many, and nowe I am overcome
with deth. I am he that hath caused many to dye, and I can not as now gyve
myselfe one day of lyfe. I am he that hath entred into chariottes of golde,
and this day I shall be layde on a biere of wodde. I am he for whome many 15
have songe merily, and this day they wepe. I am he that hath had company
in all exercitees, and this day I shall be gyven to hungry wormes. I am
Marcus greatly renoumed, that with famous triumph mounted into the
high Capitolle, and this daye with forgetfulnes I shall discende into the
sepulchre. I se nigh with myn eies that was farre hyd in my herte. And as 20

the goddis be favourable to you in this worlde, and equalle and favourable to me in another worlde, as my fleshe never toke pleasure to passe this lyfe, but my harte was sodaynely taken with the feare of deathe, than take no peyne for me, for eyther I muste see the ende of you, or you of me. I yelde

25 greatte thankes to the goddis that they take away this old person to rest with them, and leve you yonge for to serve in th'empire. And yet I wyl not deny but I do feare dethe, as a mortal man. For there is no comparison for to speake of deathe to the lyfe, nor to eschewe the dethe at the houre therof. Whan the lyfe passeth there is no prudence in a prudent, nor vertue

30 in a vertuous, nor lordshyp in a lorde that can take away the feare of the spirite nor peyne of the fleshe. At this tyme the sowle and the fleshe are so combyned and so conglutinate togyther, and the spirite with the bloude are so annexed, that the separation of the one from the other is the moste terrible, and the last terrible of all terriblenes. Certaynely it accordeth unto

35 good reasone that the sowle departe dolorously, leavynge the fleshe unto wormes, and the body as envious to se the soule go and sporte with the goddes. O what lyttell thoughte we take in this lyfe, untylle we falle grovelynge with our eyes uppon dethe! Beleve me, sythe I have passed from whens ye be, and have experimented that ye do see, that is the

40 vanities of us that are vayne, is so agreable to us, what whanne we begynne to lyve we ymagine that our lyfe wylle endure a holle worlde, and whanne it is ended, hit semeth us to be but a puffe or a blaste of wynde. And bycause than sensualitie peyneth for sensibylitie, and the fleshe for the fleshe, reason guyded with them that be mortall telleth me that it peyneth not with

45 the departynge. If I have lyved as a brute beaste, hit is reason that I dye as a discrete manne ought to do. I dyenge, this day shall dye al my syckenes; hungre shall dye, colde shall dye, all my peynes shall dye, my thought shall dye, my displeasure shall dye, and every thinge that gyveth peyne and sorowe. This daye the nyght shall be taken away, and the sonne shyne

50 bright in the skye. This daye the ruste shall be taken fro myn eies, and I shall see the sonne clerely. . . .

26

SIR THOMAS MORE

THE early works of Thomas More (1478–1535) may properly end this anthology, for they form both a natural conclusion to what has come before and look forward to a new period. As Alistair Fox says, they 'reveal that he experienced acutely the tensions arising from an age in transition. On the one hand he felt a calling towards the ascetic piety of medieval Catholicism, on the other he felt drawn towards the new learning and the possibilities it held out for the transformation of society.' In his youth (c.1491) More had a place in the household of Cardinal Morton (of whom he gives a memorable portrait in the first book of *Utopia*); he spent some time at Oxford, and returned to London to be trained as a lawyer. He thought of becoming a priest, but decided to remain in secular life, and married in 1504, in which year he also became an MP. He became undersheriff of the city of London in 1510, and eventually, in 1517, entered the King's service as a councillor. In 1529 he became Chancellor of England. His opposition to Henry VIII's divorce and remarriage and to any attack on the authority of the Pope caused him to be charged with misprision of treason in 1534. He was committed to the Tower, tried, and executed in 1535. More is a figure of fascinating brilliance and complexity, full of contradictions. He is both the humanist paragon admired by his friends Erasmus, Colet, and others, and the saintly figure revered by the Catholic exiles (he was finally canonized in 1935), but his writings show that he is many other persons as well (and it is not surprising to find him interested in plays, acting, and the playing of parts). He is equally capable of writing a scurrilous or cynical Latin epigram and an affectionate letter to his daughter Margaret. Significantly, he seems to have been very responsive both to the 'merry' aspects of Chaucer (he wrote a 'clean' fabliau, *A Merry Jest, How a Sergeant would learn to play the Friar*) and to that poet's sense of pathos and capacity for *pité* or compassion. As well as the 'merriness' that so delighted his friends, his own writings sometimes express a profound and intense melancholy, his personal dilemmas and soul-searchings. In his translation of the life of Pico della Mirandola (? written 1505), he shows an awareness of the tensions and paradoxes of the humanist's life, and seems clearly to be writing with himself in mind—in his admiration of the pattern of a scholarly and a holy life, and also in his recognition of Pico's pride before his conversion. In 1516 was printed his most famous work (in Latin), the *Utopia*, a dazzling creation of a wonderful land of nowhere (owing much to the quick-footed wit and sudden shifts of perspective he had learnt from Lucian, and something to the reports of the new-found lands), and an intellectual achievement of great imaginative richness. It shows 'that intensely serious play of mind which distinguished More from all his English predecessors' (Emrys Jones, in P. L. Heyworth [ed.], *Medieval Studies for J. A. W. Bennett* [Oxford, 1981], 272). His own doubts about becoming involved in the political life of England, which are so clearly expressed in Book I, are present also in his (unfinished) English *History of Richard III*, much of which may have been written *c.*1518. Here history is transformed by a poetic imagination into what is, decades before Shakespeare, a drama. The book is dramatic in structure, in the conduct of its scenes; and the grim story itself is like a play stage-managed by the villainous Richard, whose inner depravity is mirrored in his deformity. The brilliance of the 'portraits' (of Richard, Edward IV, Buckingham, and others) is a testimony to More's careful reading of the classical historians, notably Sallust, Suetonius, and Tacitus (to whose Tiberius his Richard is especially indebted). From *Richard III* there emerges a tragic sense of the extreme fragility of man's estate, and of the violence and misery of a period of civil dissension, together with a clear-sighted acknowledgement of the evil that wicked men are capable of, and of the ambivalence of their motives. Our extract is a brief portrait of a person of humble rank caught up in great events—the wife of the mercer Shore, mistress of the former King, Edward IV, and of the Lord Hastings, whom the Protector is intent on destroying—which shows both More's power of irony and sarcasm and a very human *pité*. It has been suggested that the judicial murder of the Duke of Buckingham in 1521 shocked More into the realization that the history of the tyrannical Richard was being re-enacted in his own day, and led to a retreat into an ascetic *contemptus mundi* in the *De Quatuor Novissimis* or *The Four Last Things* (? *c.*1522). The tone of this is unrelievedly sombre (cf. the way a hint of 'merriness' is severely rejected in line 22), and there is a powerful urgency in the treatment of two traditional images of the brief and doomed life of man—that he is like a poor player, and that he is like a poor prisoner. More went on to write a series of vehement refutations of Tyndale and other Protestants, and in his own final imprisonment a most humane and gentle book of consolation, *A Dialogue of Comfort*. But these belong to the new period; we leave him with examples of his very distinctive treatment of three themes which have been prominent in this anthology: the pursuit of learning, the 'untrouthe of Inglond', and the thought of death.

A

The Life of John Picus, Earl of Mirandula

. . . But bicause we will holde the reder no lenger in hand, we will speke of hys lerninge but a worde or twayne generally. Sume man hath shined in eloquence, but ignorans of naturall thinges hathe dishonested him. Some man hath flowred in the knowledge of divers straunge langages, but he 5 hath wanted all the cognition of philosophie. Sume man hath red the inventions of the olde philosophres, but he hath not ben excercised in the new scolis. Sume man hath sought connyng, as wel philosophi as divinité, for praise and vayneglory, and not for any profet or encrece of Christis chirch. But Picus all these thingis with equal study hath so 10 receyved, that thei might seme by hepis as a plentuouse streme to have flowen into him. For he was not of the condition of some folke (which to be excellent in one thinge set al othir aside) but he in all sciencis profited so excellently that which of them so ever ye had considered in hym, ye wolde have thought that he had taken that one for his onely studye. And al these thyngis were in him so muche the more mervelouse in that he cam 15 therto by himselfe, with the strength of his owne witte, for the love of God and profit of his chirch, withowt maisters, so that we maye sey of him that Epicure the philosophre said of himself, that he was his owne maister.

To the bryngyng foorth of so wondreful effectes in so small time I considre fyve causes to have come togedir: first, an incredible wit; 20 secondly, a mervelouse fast memory; thredly, grete substance, by the which to the bying of his bokes, as wel Latin as Greke and othir tongis, he was especially holpen—.vii.m. ducatis he had laide out in the gadering togither of volumes of all maner of litterature. The fourth cause was his besy and infatigable study; the fyft was the contempt or dispising of al 25 erthly thingis.

But nowe let us passe over those powars of his soule which appertaine to undrestonding and knowledge, and let us speke of them that belonge to the acheiving of noble actis. Let us, as we can, declare his excellent conditions, that his mynde enflamed to Godwarde may apere, and his 30 riches given owt to pore folke may be undrestonde, to th'entent that they which shall here his vertue may have occasion therbi to give especial laude and thanke therfor to Almighty God, of whose infinite godenesse al grace and vertue commith.

Thre yere before his deth, to th'ende that, all the charge and besines of 35 rule or lordship set aside, he might lede his life in rest and peace, wele considering to what ende this erthly honour and worldly dignité commith, all his patrimonye and dominions—that is to sey, the thred parte of th'erldome of Mirandula, and of Concordia—unto John Franscis his nevieu he solde, and that so good chepe that hyt semed rathir a gift then a 40 sale. All that ever he receyved of this bargaine, partly he gave owt to pore folke, partly he bestowed in the bieng of a litle londe to the finding of him and his howsolde. And over that, much silver vessel and plate, with othir preciouse and costly utensilis of howsold, he devided amonge pore peple. He was content with meane fare at his table, how be hyt somwhat yet reteyning of the olde plenty in deynty viande and silver vessell. Every day at certaine howris he gave himself to praier. To pore men alway, if eni cam, he plentuosly gave out his money, and, not content only to give that he had himself redy, he wrote over to one Hierom Benivenius, a Florentin, a wel letred man, whom for his great love toward him and the integrité of his 50 conditions he singularly favored, that he shold with his owen money ever helpe pore folk, and give maidens money to their mariage, and alway send him worde what he had laide out that he might paye hit him ageyn. This office he committed to hym, that he might the more easeli by him, as by a

55 faithfull messanger, releve the necessité and miseri of pore nedi peple, such as himself coude not cum by the knowledge of.

Over all this, many times (which ys not to be kept secret) he gave almes of hys own body. We knowe many men, which, as Seint Hierom saith, put forth their hande to pore folke but with the plesure of the flesh thei be
60 overcommen, but he mani daies (and namely those daies which represent unto us the passion and deth that Christ suffred for our sake) bet and scowrged hys own flesh in the remembraunce of that gret benefite, and for clensing of his olde offencis.

He was of chere alwaye mery, and of so benigne nature that he was
65 never trobled with angre. And he said onto his nevieu that what so evir sholde happen (fell there never so grete mysadventure) he coud never, as him thought, be moved to wrath, but if his chestis perished in which his bokes lay, that he had with grete travaile and watch compiled. But for as much as he considered that he laboured only for the love of God and profit
70 of his chirch, and that he had dedicate unto him all his warkis, his studies, and his doinges, and sith he sawe that, sith God is almighty, thei coulde not miscary, but if it were either by his commaundement or by his sufferaunce, he verily trusted, sith God is all good, that he wold not suffre him to have that occasion of hevines. O very happi mynde, which none
75 adversité might oppresse, which no prosperité might enhaunce! Not the conning of all philosophie was able to make hym prowde; not the knowledge of the Hebrew, Chaldey, and Arabie language, beside Greke and Laten, could make him vaingloriouse; not his grete substaunce, not hys noble blode coude blow up his hart; not the bewty of his body, not the
80 grete occasion of sin were able to pull him back into the voluptuouse brode way that ledith to helle. What thing was ther of so mervelouse strenght that might overtorne the minde of him, which now, as Seneke sayth, was gotin above fortune, as he which as well hir favoure as hir malice hath set at nought, that he might be cowpled with a spirituall knot unto Christ and his hevinly citeseynes?

B

THE HISTORY OF KING RICHARD III

Shore's Wife

Now then by and bi, as it wer for anger not for covetise, the Protector sent unto the house of Shores wife (for her husband dwelled not with her), and spoiled her of al that ever she had, above the value of .ii. or .iii.m. marks, and sent her body to prison. And when he had a while laide unto her for
5 the maner sake that she went about to bewitch him, and that she was of

counsel with the Lord Chamberlein to destroy him, in conclusion, when that no colour could fasten upon these matters, then he layd heinously to her charge the thing that herself could not deny, that al the world wist was true, and that natheles every man laughed at to here it then so sodainly so highly taken, that she was nought of her body. And for thys cause (as a goodly continent prince clene and fautles of himself, sent oute of heaven into this vicious world for the amendment of mens maners) he caused the Bishop of London to put her to open penance, going before the crosse in procession upon a Sonday with a taper in her hand. In which she went in countenance and pace demure so womanly; and albeit she were out of al array save her kyrtle only, yet went she so fair and lovely, namelye while the wondering of the people caste a comly rud in her chekes (of whiche she before had most misse) that her great shame wan her much praise, among those that were more amorous of her body then curious of her soule. And many good folke also that hated her living, and glad wer to se sin corrected, yet pitied thei more her penance then rejoyced therin when thei considred that the Protector procured it more of a corrupt intent then ani vertuous affeccion. This woman was born in London, worshipfully frended, honestly brought up, and very wel maryed (saving somewhat to sone), her husbande an honest citezen, yonge and goodly and of good substance. But forasmuche as they were coupled ere she wer wel ripe, she not very fervently loved for whom she never longed, which was happely the thinge that the more easily made her encline unto the kings appetite when he required her. Howbeit the respect of his royaltie, the hope of gay apparel, ease, plesure and other wanton welth, was hable soone to perse a softe tender hearte. But when the king had abused her, anon her husband (as he was an honest man, and one that could his good, not presuming to touch a kinges concubine) left her up to him al togither. When the king died, the Lord Chamberlen toke her; which in the kinges daies, albeit he was sore ennamored upon her, yet he forbare her, either for reverence, or for a certain frendly faithfulnes. Proper she was and faire; nothing in her body that you wold have changed, but if you would have wished her somewhat higher. Thus say thei that knew her in her youthe. Albeit some that now se her (for yet she liveth) deme her never to have ben wel visaged. Whose jugement semeth me somwhat like as though men should gesse the bewty of one longe before departed by her scalpe taken out of the charnel house; for now is she old, lene, withered, and dried up, nothing left but ryvilde skin and hard bone. And yet being even such, whoso wel advise her visage might gesse and devise which partes how filled wold make it a faire face. Yet delited not men so much in her bewty as in her plesant behaviour. For a proper wit had she, and could both rede wel and write, mery in company, redy and quick of aunswer, neither mute nor ful of bable, sometime taunting without displesure and not without disport. The king would say that he had .iii. concubines, which in three divers

50 properties diversly exceled: one the meriest, another the wiliest, the thirde
the holiest harlot in his realme, as one whom no man could get out of the
church lightly to any place but it wer to his bed. The other two were
somewhat greter parsonages, and natheles of their humilitie content to be
nameles, and to forbere the praise of those properties. But the meriest was
55 this Shoris wife, in whom the king therfore toke speciall pleasure. For
· many he had, but her he loved; whose favour to sai the trouth (for sinne it
wer to belie the devil) she never abused to any mans hurt, but to many a
mans comfort and relief. Where the king toke displeasure, she would
mitigate and appease his mind; where men were out of favour, she wold
60 bring them in his grace. For many that had highly offended, shee obtained
pardon. Of great forfetures she gate men remission. And, finally, in many
weighty sutes, she stode many men in gret stede, either for none or very
smal rewardes, and those rather gay then rich; either for that she was
content with the dede selfe well done, or for that she delited to be suid
65 unto, and to show what she was able to do wyth the king, or for that wanton
women and welthy be not alway covetouse. I doubt not some shal think this
women to sleight a thing to be written of and set amonge the
remembraunces of great matters—which thei shal specially think, that
happely shal esteme her only by that thei now see her. But me semeth the
70 chaunce so much the more worthy to be remembred in how much she is
now in the more beggerly condicion, unfrended and worne out of
acquaintance, after good substance, after as gret favour with the prince,
after as gret sute and seking to with al those that those days had busynes to
spede, as many other men were in their times, which be now famouse only
75 by the infamy of their il dedes. Her doinges were not much lesse, albeit
thei be muche less remembred, because thei were not so evil. For men
use, if they have an evil turne, to write it in marble, and whoso doth us a
good tourne, we write it in duste, which is not worst proved by her, for at
this daye shee beggeth of many at this daye living, that at this day had
80 begged if she had not bene.

C

THE FOUR LAST THINGS

Of Pride

Now the hye minde of proud fortune, rule, and authoritye, lord God, how
sleighe a thing it wolde seme to him that wolde often and depely
remember, that deth shal shortly take away al this ryalty, and his glorye
shal, as scripture saith, never walk with him into his grave. But he that
5 overloketh every man, and no man may be so homelye to come to nere

him, but thinketh that he dothe much for them whom he vouchsafeth to
take by the hand or beck upon, whom so many men drede and fere, so
many wait upon, he shal within a few yeres—and only God knoweth within
how few dayes—whan deth arresteth him, have his deinty body turned into
stinking carien, be born out of his princely paleys, layd in the ground and   10
there lefte alone, wher every leud lad wil be bolde to tread on his hed.
Wold not, wene ye, that depe consideracion of this sodein chaunge so
surely to come, and so shortly to come, withdraw that wind that puffeth us
up in pride upon the solemne sight of worldly worship. If thou sholdest
parceve that one wer ernestly proud of the wering of a gay golden gown   15
while the lorel playth the lord in a stage playe, woldest thou not laugh at his
foly, considering that thou art very sure that whan the play is done he shal
go walke a knave in his old cote? Now thou thinkest thyselfe wyse ynough
whyle thou art proude in thy players garment, and forgettest that whan thy
play is done thou shalt go forth as pore as he. Nor thou remembrest not   20
that thy pageant may happen to be done as sone as hys.

   We shal leve th'example of plaies and plaiers, which be to mery for this
matter. I shal put the a more ernest ymage of our condicion, and that not a
fained similtude, but a very true fassion and fygure of oure worshipful
estate. Mark this well, for of this thing we be very sure, that olde and yong,   25
man and woman, rich and pore, prince and page, al the while we live in
this world, we be but prisoners, and be within a sure prison, out of which
ther can no man escape. And in worse case be we than those that be taken
and imprisoned for theft. For thei, albeit their hert hevily harkeneth after
the sessions, yet have they some hope eyther to breke prison the while, or   30
to escape there by favor, or after condemnacion some hope of pardon. But
we stand al in other plight: we bee very sure that we be alredy condemned
to deth, som one, som other—none of us can tel what deth we be demed
to, but surely can we al tel that die we shal. And clerely know we that of
this deth we get no maner pardon, for the king by whose hyghe sentence   35
we be condemned to dye, wold not of this deth pardon his own sonne. As
for escaping, no man can looke for. The prison is large, and many
prisoners in it, but the gailor can lese none; he is so present in every place
that we can crepe into no corner out of his sight. For, as holy David saith
to this gailor, 'Whither shal I go fro thy spirit, and whither shal I fle fro thy   40
face?'—as who saith nowhither. There is no remedy therfore, but, as
condemned folk and remediles, in this prison of the yerth we drive forth a
while, some bounden to a poste, some wandring abrode, some in the
dungeon, some in the upper ward, some bylding them bowers and making
palaces in the prison, some weping, some laughing, some laboring, some   45
playing, some singing, some chidinge, some fighting, no man almoste
remembringe in what case he standeth, till that sodeynlye, nothyng lesse
loking for, yong, old, pore and rych, mery and sad, prince, page, pope and
pore soul-priest, now one, now other, some time a gret rable at once,

without order, without respect of age or of estate, all striped stark naked 50
and shifted out in a shete, bee put to deth in divers wise in some corner of
the same prison, and even ther throwen in an hole, and ether wormes eat
him under ground or crowes above. Nowe come foorth, ye proude
prisoner, for ywis ye be no better, loke ye never so hie; when ye build in the
prison a palais for your blode, is it not a gret rialty if it be wel considred? Ye 55
build the tower of Babilon in a corner of the prison, and be very proud
therof, and somtime the gailor beteth it down again with shame. Ye leve
your lodging for your owne blode, and the gailor, when ye be dede, setteth
a strange prisoner in your building, and thrusteth your blode into some
other caban. Ye be proud of the armes of your auncesters set up in the 60
prison—and al your pride is because ye forget that it is a prison. For if ye
toke the mater aright—the place a prison, yourself a prisoner condemned
to deth, fro which ye cannot escape—ye wold recken this gere as
worshipful as if a gentleman thefe, when he should goe to Tyburne, wold
leve for a memoriall th'armes of his auncesters painted on a post in 65
Newgate. Surely I suppose, that if we toke not true fygure for a fantasye,
but reckened it as it is in dede, the verye expresse fassion and maner of al
our estate, men wolde beare themself not much higher in theyr hertes for
any rule or authority that they bere in this world, which they may wel
parceyve to bee in deede no better, but one prisoner beryng a rule amonge 70
the remenaunte, as the tapster doth in the Marshalsye, or at the
uttermoste, one so put in trust with the gaylor that he is half an under-
gailor over his felowes till the shyryfe and the cart come for him.

COMMENTARY

The notes give brief references to textual sources, to some of the major editions and studies available, and in addition to various bibliographical guides (*STC*, *Index*, *MWME*) which contain further information. Other standard bibliographies are *The Cambridge Bibliography of English Literature*, the Modern Language Association of America's *International Bibliography*, and the Modern Humanities Research Association's *Annual Bibliography of English Language and Literature*. Besides the books and articles mentioned in the notes, the following general studies will be found useful:

Political, social, cultural history. M. Aston, *The Fifteenth Century: The Prospect of Europe* (London, 1968); J. M. Brown, *Scottish Society in the Fifteenth Century* (London, 1977); F. R. H. du Boulay, *An Age of Ambition* (London, 1970); M. H. Keen, *England in the Later Middle Ages* (London, 1973).

Literary history. H. S. Bennett, *Chaucer and the Fifteenth Century* (Oxford, 1947); E. K. Chambers, *English Literature at the Close of the Middle Ages* (Oxford, 1945); D. A. Pearsall, *Old English and Middle English Poetry* (London, 1977); V. J. Scattergood, *Politics and Poetry in the Fifteenth Century* (London, 1971); K. Wittig, *The Scottish Tradition in Literature* (Edinburgh, 1958).

1

A

MS BL Cleopatra C. iv, fo. 24ᵛ. *Index* 3213. *Ed.* C. L. Kingsford, *Chronicles of London* (Oxford, 1905), 119–21; *HP* No. 27.

These chronicles, an important source for fifteenth-century English history, seem to have begun to take shape about the beginning of the century; events, mainly in and around London, are recorded under the years of the mayoralty. They 'reflect in a measure the popular opinion of the capital on events of the time' (Kingsford, *English Historical Literature in the Fifteenth Century* [Oxford, 1913], 74). Henry V's victory is recorded in many chronicles (for eyewitness accounts, see Jean de Waurin, *Recueil des chroniques*, eds. W. and E. L. C. P. Hardy, RS 39 (1864–87), and the *Gesta Henrici Quinti*, eds. and trans. F. Taylor and J. S. Roskell [Oxford, 1975]). Of the poems inspired by the victory, the most famous is the 'Agincourt Carol' (*EEC* No. 426, *OBMEV* No. 151), but the best is this vigorous poem, with its emphatic alliteration and alliterative formulae, which gradually takes over from the chronicler's bald prose. In pursuit of his claim to France, Henry landed on 14 August 1415. After reducing Harfleur, he marched towards Calais with a force of about 6,000 men. His way was barred by a French army of about 40,000; battle was joined near Agincourt (Azincourt) on St Crispin's day (25 October). (The feast of St Simon and St Jude is on 28 October.)

Textual Notes. 18 thenke ye be] *MS* thenke be   64 frith] *MS* fright

3 ff. *the Frenssh kynge...*: King Charles VI; the Dauphin, John (d. 1417); John the Fearless, Duke of Burgundy. The Duke of 'Barre' is probably the Duke of Berry (the Duke of Bar was present at the battle). These remained behind in Rouen, and the French army was led by Marshal Boucicaut, the Constable D'Albret, and the Dukes of Bourbon and Orléans.

40 ff. *The Duke of Glowcestre...*: Humphrey, the king's brother; Edward, Duke of York (see No. 9U); John Holland, Earl of Huntingdon; Richard de Vere, Earl of Oxford, who commanded the rearguard; Michael Pole, Earl of Suffolk (whose father had died at the siege of Harfleur); Sir Richard Kighley; Sir William Boucer; Sir Thomas Erpingham, who commanded the archers.

69. *Thre dukes*: of Alençon, Bar, and Brabant, together with seven counts, and many other French nobles. The stanzas which follow in the chronicle list some of the French captives, and vehemently attack the 'fals Flemyngys' (the Burgundians).

B

MS Trin. Coll., Camb., O. 9. 1 (1413), fo. 210. *Ed.* F. W. D. Brie, *The* Brut *or the Chronicles of England*, EETS 131 (1906).

The *Brut*, 'the most popular and widely diffused history of the time' (Kingsford), is an account of British history from mythical times, written originally in French, translated into English towards the end of the fourteenth century, and extended by a series of continuations in the fifteenth. It appears in printed form in Caxton's *Chronicles of England* (1480). The French, inspired by Joan of Arc's victory at Patay, crowned Charles VII at Rheims on 18 July 1429. Bedford, the English regent, was determined to make it clear that Henry VI was the legitimate king of France, and had the boy brought to Paris in 1430. He was crowned there at the end of 1431, and returned in triumph to London on 21 February 1432. The pageants devised for his welcome (for a more detailed account by John Carpenter, the town clerk, and in verses by Lydgate, see McCracken, *Archiv*, 126 (1910–11), 75–102) resemble those for the triumphal return of Henry V after Agincourt. They emphasize the king's rightful claim to the dual monarchy, a common theme in English propaganda (cf. B. J. H. Rowe, *The Library*, 4th Ser., 13 (1933), 77–88, J. W. McKenna, *JWCI* 28 (1965), 145–62). Similar pageants for royal entries, coronations, weddings, etc. continue throughout the century to Tudor times (cf. S. Anglo, *Spectacle, Pageantry, and Early Tudor Policy* [Oxford, 1969], Glynne Wickham, *Early English Stages* i [London, 1959]) and beyond.

Textual Note. 32 .vii.] *MS* .vi.

23. *a gyaunt in a toure*: According to Carpenter, he was accompanied by two antelopes bearing the arms of France and England.

36. *the giftes of the Holy Gost*: cf. Isa. 11: 2. According to Carpenter the doves were released.

49. *Clennesse*: Clemency, according to Carpenter and Lydgate.

51. *the grete conduit*: an iron-bound lead cistern near the Hospital of St Thomas of Acon. The Earthly Paradise is presumably a 'figure' of a benevolent and blessed reign, bringing back the Golden Age. The 'wells', equivalent to the (four) rivers of Paradise, are associated (for Carpenter) with the wounds of the crucified Christ (cf. *NQ* 208 (1963), 166), and are probably also a punning allusion to the name of the Lord Mayor, John Welles.

58. *.ii. olde men*: 'lyke folkes off Feyry[e]' (Lydgate). Cf. Gen. 5: 21-4, 2 Kings 2:11. According to legend, Enoch and Elijah did not die, but continued to live in the Earthly Paradise, waiting to return when they were needed to challenge Antichrist and to help establish the Messianic kingdom. (Cf. *MÆ* 5 (1936), 32-3, and the Chester play of Antichrist, EETS, ss 3 [1974], 414 ff.)

C

MS BL Cotton Rolls ii. 23. *Index* 2338. *Ed. HP* No. 75.

William de la Pole, Duke of Suffolk (the 'fox of the South'), had become very unpopular with the commons, especially because of his support of the marriage of Margaret of Anjou to Henry VI, his part in the death of Duke Humphrey, and his supposed responsibility for recent defeats and losses in France. He was indicted on 7 February 1450 and held in the Tower. The king saved his life by banishing him for five years, but when he set out for France on 30 April he was intercepted and killed (cf. 2 F.). See also *HP* No. 76.

6. *Talbot*: John Talbot, Earl of Shrewsbury, a famous English general in the French wars (d. 1453): 'The inference is that Suffolk withheld funds or supplies from Talbot', (*HP*, p. 350). ('Oure dog' is a heraldic reference: 'talbot' is a kind of hound.)

12. *Salesbury*: William Ayscough, Bishop of Salisbury, the king's confessor, murdered in June 1450, partly because of a long-standing struggle between the citizens of Salisbury and their bishop.

17. *oure grete gandere*: Humphrey, Duke of Gloucester, Henry V's brother (whose badge was a swan). Suffolk brought charges against him and he died in captivity on 23 February 1447; there was widespread suspicion that he had been murdered.

18. *mony mon*: either 'many men wonder at him' (Robbins, *HP*)—a reference to the treatment of Humphrey's supporters, hanged but cut down alive on Suffolk's orders—or with *mon* as verb, 'must', i.e. a wish that Suffolk will be hanged.

19. *Jack Napys*: a tame ape, suggested by Suffolk's badge of clog and chain.

21. *Beaumownt*: John, Viscount Beaumont, Constable of England, who arrested Suffolk ('Rache' because 'Beaumont' was the name of a hound.)

D

Ed. J. S. Davies, *An English Chronicle 1377–1461*, Camden Soc. 64 (1856), 64.

The earlier part of the chronicle is apparently based on an original compiled *c.*1437 (Kingsford, *Eng. Hist. Lit.*, pp. 29, 122–3); the later part is probably 'the work of a single hand'. The last eleven years are very fully recorded. Cade's rebellion (cf. E. F. Jacob, *The Fifteenth Century* [Oxford, 1961], 496–7) seems to have been aimed at oppressive officials. There was a good deal of unrest in this year (cf. 1C): Gregory (see 1 F n.) records that 'many strange and woundyrfulle bylles were set in dyvers placys', and the soldiers returning from Normandy often behaved violently (cf. Flenley, *Six Town Chronicles* [Oxford, 1911], 134–5). See *HP* No. 24.

Textual Note. 40 comyng] *text* comyns.

34. *lord Say*: the Treasurer of England, James Fiennes, a rich and powerful magnate in the South-east, who, with his friends, was 'largely responsible for arousing the indignation against the corrupt deals, sharp practice and perversion of the sheriff's jurisdiction, which culminated in Cade's rebellion' (Jacob, *Fifteenth Century*, p. 333).

66. *the Standard in Chepe*: a pump, and also a favourite place of execution.

69. *Crowmer*: William Crowmer, sheriff in 1444–5, 1449 (his widow married Sir Alexander Iden, who caught and killed Cade).

82 ff. Thomas, Lord Scales (d. 1460), Matthew Gough, and John Sutton, Baron Dudley (d. 1487) were all distinguished veterans of the French wars.

86. *the brigge of tre*: the drawbridge on London Bridge.

E

MS BL Add. 27879, fo. 87 (fo. 43, new numbering). *Index* 1011.5. *Ed.* F. J. Furnivall and J. W. Hales, *Bishop Percy's Folio Manuscript* (London, 1867), i. 212–34 (MS of *c*.1650); J. Robson, *Publ. Chetham Soc.* 37 (1855–6) (from the earlier (sixteenth-century) incomplete Lyme MS); J. P. Oakden, ibid., NS 94 (1935) (from both MSS); I. F. Baird (New York, 1982).

On the versions, and on other poems on Flodden, see I. Baird, *NQ* 226 (1981), 15–19. The alliterative poem, written by a gentleman of Baguley in Cheshire, pays particular honour to the Stanleys (Sir Edward Stanley led the left wing; James Stanley, Bishop of Ely, and Sir John Stanley, his natural son, were also present); cf. D. A. Lawton, *LSE* 10 (1978), 42–57. *The trewe encountre or batayle lately done betwene Englande and Scotlande* (? 1513) gives an account in prose. James IV invaded England with a large army in August 1513, and was defeated near Flodden (see R. Nicholson, *Scotland: The Later Middle Ages* [Edinburgh, 1974], 600–6). Our extracts correspond to lines 301–29, 373–401 in the Oakden edition.

Textual Notes. 3 ryncke] *Lyme MS*: *MS* ring; him] *L. MS* he.   4 feteled] *L. MS* fettlen   15 soughe] *L. MS* faugh; there . . . enemies] *L. MS* there we seene our enemyes   16 macch] *MS* macth   18 and we egerlie] *L. MS* Soe eagerly   19 then] *L. MS* they   20 shawe] *L. MS* showe   24 egerlie they shotten] *L. MS om.*   26 the] *L.* MS they; harnes] *L. MS* harnish   42 care] *L. MS* race   43 For] *L. MS* But   45 flye] *L. MS* slye   56 their stode like stakes] *L. MS om.*   58 brynke] *L. MS* brinck: *MS* bryke   59 ghostes] *L. MS* guests

F

MS BL Egerton 1995, fo. 219. *Ed.* J. Gairdner, *The Historical Collections of a London Citizen*, Camden Soc. 123 (1876).

The chronicle covers the years 1440–70; the attribution to William Gregory (d. 1467), Mayor in 1451–2, is unlikely (cf. Kingsford, *Eng. Hist. Lit.*, pp. 96–8), although the author was certainly a London citizen. This extract is an example of the frequent accounts of the defiance and the deaths of Lollards, from the famous and notable cases at the beginning of the century, such as that of Sir John Oldcastle (in 1417), to more obscure but no less defiant men, like William Wakeham of Devizes, who is alleged to have held that it was no better for a layman to say the Lord's Prayer in Latin than it was for him to say 'bibull babull' (J. A. F. Thomson,

The Later Lollards, 1414–1520 [Oxford, 1965], 33). Dissent of a more disreputable kind is illustrated in the following story of sacrilege.

Textual Note. 1 herretyke] *MS* herryke

49. *Wylliam Ivé*: (d. 1485), a theologian from Magdalen Coll., Oxford, and headmaster of Winchester (1444–54).

G

MS Bodl., Rawl. c. 208, fos. 26ᵛ, 38ᵛ, 55.

Thorpe seems to have survived his ordeal (on him and his text, see A. Hudson, *Selections from English Wycliffite Writings* [Cambridge, 1978], 155–6). The work also exists in Latin, and was known in Hussite Bohemia (possibly Thorpe himself fled to Prague). It circulated in the early sixteenth century, appeared in print (*The Examinacion of Master William Thorpe* [Antwerp, 1530], *STC* 24045), and eventually found its way into Foxe's *Book of Martyrs* (cf. A. W. Pollard, *Fifteenth-Century Verse and Prose* [London, 1903], pp. 97–174); see A. Hudson, 'No Newe Thyng', in D. Gray and E. G. Stanley (eds.), *Middle English Studies Presented to Norman Davis* (Oxford, 1983), 162–4. Our extracts refer to a number of questions commonly raised by and against Lollards: the nature of the Church and the priesthood, transubstantiation, pilgrimages. Cf. J. A. F. Thomson, *Later Lollards*, and M. Aston, *History*, 49 (1964), 149–170. For Lollard texts, see A. Hudson, *Selections*; *Jack Upland, Friar Daw's Reply, and Upland's Rejoinder*, ed. P. L. Heyworth (Oxford, 1968); and *The Lanterne of Liȝt*, ed. L. M. Swinburn, EETS 151 (1917).

Textual Notes. 18 her] *MS* her her   86 trowe] *MS* trowide   123 mennis] *MS* men   130 borowen] *MS* borowynge   173 peples] *MS* peple

11. *Seynt Chaddis chirche*: old St Chad's in Shrewsbury.
136. *baggepipis*: cf. Chaucer's Miller, *CT Gen. Prol.* A 565–6.
152. Rom. 12: 15.
159. Ps. 150: 3–5.
166. 1 Cor. 10: 11.
167. Matt. 9: 23.

H

MS BL Harley 367, fo. 127. *Index* 3759. *Ed. HP* No. 50; (from a longer version in Harley 542) *EVCS*, p. 237.

For London in the later Middle Ages, see D. W. Robertson, *Chaucer's London* (New York, 1968), Stow's *Survey of London*, ed. C. L. Kingsford (Oxford, 1908, repr. 1971).

Textual Notes. 3 Westmynster] *MS* Westmyster   56 myght not speede] *MS* myght not (thus *or* ther? *deleted*) be (*inserted*) speede   60 strabery] *MS* stabery   98 wantyng] *MS* wantynyng

3. *To Westmynster-ward*: Westminster was outside the city walls (cf. line 57): 'the area between London Wall and Westminster was thickly populated by royal clerks, lawyers and apprentices at law' (Robertson, p. 13).
11. *the Kynges Bench*: This dealt originally with criminal trespasses against the

king's peace. The poet visits three courts of law: (1) this; (2) the 'common place' (22), i.e. of Common Pleas, dealing with civil disputes between private persons; and (3) that of the Lord Chancellor, the Master of the Rolls, and the masters of the Chancery (30), which dealt with cases concerning revenue. Cf. Stow, ed. Kingsford, ii. 117–18.

23. *a sylken hoode*: worn by sergeants. Cf. *PP.B Prol.* 210–15 (lines which are similar in sentiment, and may possibly have been in our poet's mind).

36. *Westmynster Hall*: the large hall, where Parliament held sessions.

46 ff. *Flemynges*: Flemish weavers and traders were prominent in London life from the time of Edward III. They were sometimes the object of riots: 'it is possible that discrimination was in part responsible for the fact that many of the ladies of Cock Lane and of the stews across the river in Southwark were Flemish' (Robertson, p. 22).

59 ff. Langland's Prol. also uses the cries of the sellers and of itinerant peddlars which could have been heard by city-dwellers up to (and beyond) the days of Sweet Molly Malone. They have attracted the attention of antiquarians, illustrators, and musicians. Cf. Karen F. Beall, *Kaufrufe und Strassenhandler. Cries and Itinerant Trades* (Hamburg, 1975), J. F. Bridge, *Old Cryes of London* (London, 1921). In France they were collected as early as the thirteenth-century *Crieries de Paris*, and in the early sixteenth-century *Les Cris de Paris*.

64. *the Chepe*: The ward contained one of the great markets, and numbered among its inhabitants mercers and cordwainers, as well as bakers, fishmongers, poulterers, and cheesemongers. Cf. H. Hobhouse *The Ward of Cheap in the City of London* (London, 1963).

71. *London stone*: a stone pillar near St Swithin's church. Cf. Stow, ed. Kingsford, i. 224–5.

72. *Canwyke streete*: Candlewick Street (now Cannon Street) runs into East Cheap, and was a centre for chandlers, weavers, and drapers.

85. *Cornhyll*: renowned for its haberdashers' shops (cf. Stow, ed. Kingsford, i. 199) and many small tenements where laces, points, caps, etc. were sold (cf. the lists in H. T. Riley, *Memorials of London* [London, 1868], 422–3). See Robertson, pp. 47–9.

99. *Belyngsgate*: Billingsgate, east of London bridge, long famous for its fishmarkets.

I

Ed. J. S. Davies (see 1 D n.), p. 72.

Textual Note. 16 reseved] *text* rescued

2. *seynt James in Spayne*: the shrine of St James at Compostela; cf. 1 N and note.

J

Text: *The copye of the letter how that the moste mervelous and wonderfull felde was foughten, whiche of late hathe bene sene in the londe of Bergame* (Antwerp, 1518). *STC* 5405.

The printer Jan van Doesborgh (cf. R. Proctor, *J. van Doesborgh*, Bibliographical Soc. Illustrated Monographs, 2 [London, 1894]) produced a number of books for the English market, including—besides those represented here in Nos. 1 R, 7 O, 12 B, and 23 F—*Frederick of Jennen*, *Tyll Howleglas*, and *The Lyfe of Virgilus*. This letter (supposedly by Bartholomeus de Clere Ville or de Cleremont) is an interesting early example of the taste for 'wonderful news' (of prodigies, marvellous fish, etc.) which later printers were to exploit. The story seems to be remotely related to those of fairy battles. Cf. Capgrave's *Chronicle*, RS 1, p. 281 (1402): 'In this somyr eke, fast by the tounes of Bedforth and Bikilhswade, appered certeyn men of dyvers colouris, renning oute of wodes, and fytyng horibly. This was seyne on morownygis and at mydday: and whan men folowid to loke what it was, thei coude se rite nawt.' Together with this letter Doesborgh prints a letter purporting to be from the Great Turk to the Pope. It may be that we are meant to take the strange event as a portent. A similar story of a wild hunt is so taken in Guicciardini's *History of Italy* ch. ix (trans. C. Grayson [1964], 145): besides other signs which heralded the French invasion of Italy, 'in the Arezzo district a vast number of armed men on enormous horses were seen passing through the air day after day with a hideous noise of drums and trumpets.' In popular belief, some battle sites (e.g. Nevilles Cross) are still haunted by the noise of fighting (see W. Henderson, *Notes on Folklore of the Northern Counties*, [London, 1879], 308–9).

Textual Note. 15 or] *text* of

K

MS Bodl., Ashmole 59, fo. 78. *Index* 3986. Cf. *HP* No. 47 and note.

A large number of these prophecies survive, of varying length (cf. *HP* Nos. 43–7), often 'skimble-skamble stuff' and full of enigmatic symbolism. This example is similar to the satirical poems on the 'evils of the age' (cf. *HP* Nos. 54 ff.). Prophecies are often indiscriminately attributed to Merlin (cf. L. Paton, *Les Prophécies de Merlin* [New York, 1926], M. E. Griffiths, *Early Vaticination in Welsh* [Cardiff, 1937], P. Zumthor, *Merlin le prophète* [Lausanne, 1943]), or to John of Bridlington, Thomas of Ercildoune, or John Ball. They remained popular in England until the seventeenth century (cf. R. Taylor, *The Political Prophecy in England* [New York, 1911, repr. 1967]). On the more intellectual prophetic tradition, reflected in the Joachimite dream of a *renovatio mundi*, cf. M. Reeves, *The Influence of Prophecy in the Later Middle Ages* (Oxford, 1969).

Textual Note. 7 Than is the] *MS* that is is

7–18. Cf. *King Lear*, III. ii. 80–95.

L

STC 20414 (Wynkyn de Worde, 1497). A number of such prognostications survive, often in very battered copies. The genre has maintained its popularity throughout the history of printing (cf. B. Capp, *Astrology and the Popular Press: English Almanacs 1500–1800* [London, 1979]). The rather general nature of the predictions has also remained constant. In this example, 'prynce Arthure' is Henry VII's eldest son (d. 1502), 'my lorde Herry' the future Henry VIII, and 'my lady Margarete' Margaret Tudor (b. 1489), who in 1503 married James IV of Scotland.

Textual Note. [Some letters lost when the first leaf was trimmed have been replaced.] 2 fortunate] *text* fornunate

M

Text: *The Delectable Newesse of the Glorious Victorye of the Rhodyans agaynest the Turkes* (? *c*.1482–4), fo. 11ʸ. *STC* 4594. Facs. edn.: *The Siege of Rhodes*, Scholars' Facsimiles and Reprints (Delmar, NY, 1975). Cf. Robbins, *Br. Mus. Qly.* 27 (1964), 13–14.

John Kaye, 'hys humble poete laureate and most lowley servant', dedicates to Edward IV this free version of the *Obsidionis Rhodie Urbis Descriptio*, an eyewitness account by Caoursin, vice-chancellor of the Knights of Rhodes, of the great siege in the summer of 1480. (A French version, closer to the Latin, also exists, e.g. in BL Add. 41062.) The repulse of the armies of Muhammed II, the conqueror of Constantinople, who had overrun Bosnia and Herzegovina, was 'delectable news' to the West, but for Rhodes it was only a respite; the island finally fell to Soliman the Magnificent in 1522. Cf. 12 C 201 ff. and 12 D.

Textual Notes. 6 quarter] *text* quater   17 cutted] *text has* cu *inverted*   39 nyght] *text* nyhgt

3. *the tour of Seynt Nycolas*: a fort on the promontary flanking the outer harbour, of vital strategic importance.

16. *wel experte in swymmyng*: L. (? 1480, BL 1 A 20502) 'quidam rerum maritimarum non ignarus' (F. 'moult expert es choses de la mer').

25. *.vii. or .viii. . . . careckes*: L. 'nonnulla navigia parandarias vulgo dictas' (F. 'navires appellees parendoures').

50. L. does not refer to Achilles or Hector.

57. *horryble crye*: L. remarks also on their drums (a well-known feature of Turkish attacks).

73. *ded men . . .*: Felix Faber, the German pilgrim (cf. 1 O 4 n.), visited Rhodes just after the siege was over: 'we rowed into the city . . . passing through the bodies of dead Turks cast up by the sea, wherewith the shore was covered. When we entered the city we found it terribly ruined, full of stone cannon-balls great and small, which the Turks had fired into it, of which there were said to be eight thousand and one scattered about the streets and lanes.'

N

MS Trin. Coll., Camb., R. 3. 19, fo. 208. *Index* 2148. *Ed. OBMEV* No. 236; F. J. Furnivall, EETS 25 (1867), p. 37.

The shrine of Santiago de Compostela in north-west Spain, where the body of the Apostle St James was reputed to lie, was a favourite place of pilgrimage. There were various overland routes, but English travellers often went by sea.

O

MS Bodl., Bodley 565, fo, 4ʸ. *Ed.* G. Williams, *The Itineraries of William Wey*, Roxburghe Club 75 (1857). Wey, a Fellow of Eton College (d. 1476), went on pilgrimage to Jerusalem in 1458 and 1462. The MS also contains notes on rates of exchange (e.g. 'take none Englysch golde with yow from Brugies, for ye schal lese in the chaunge; and also for the most part of the wey they wyl nat chaunge hyt'), a short Greek vocabulary (including some useful phrases such as 'I understond the not', 'Howe moche?', 'Wher ys the taverne?', and 'Bryng heder wyne!'), English verses on the way to Jerusalem and on the holy places, and Latin narratives of his two pilgrimages. In the second, he records the election of the Doge, and at Rhodes the news of the exploits of the cruel 'Flake' or 'Flak' against the Turks in the Balkans (this is none other than the historical exemplar of the celebrated Count Dracula, Wlad 'the Impaler', vaivode of Walachia). Wey's 'prevysyoun' appears in later travel books, such as *The Informacyon for Pylgrymes* (ed. E. G. Duff [London, 1893]).

Textual Note. 62 ye[1]| *MS. om.*

4 ff. The items are numbered in the MS. Cf. the similar contract recorded by the German fifteenth-century pilgrim, Felix Faber or Fabri (Felix Schmid) (trans. A. Stewart, *The Book of the Wanderings of Brother Felix Fabri*, Palestine Pilgrims' Text Soc., [1892–3] i. 86–91).

5–6. *overest stage . . .*: Fabri (i. 125 ff.) gives a vivid account of the discomforts of life on board, including smouldering heat and stuffiness. The pilgrims slept in a large cabin, unlit except for the hatchways, with their feet stretching out towards one another. Their chests and trunks stood in the middle. Under a deck was the belly of the galley, filled with sand, where the pilgrims buried their bottles of wine, eggs, and other things which had to be kept cool. Below was the well for bilge-water, from which arose 'a worse smell than that from any closet of human ordure'.

19–21. Fabri also mentions a traditional belief that 'the air of Cyprus is unwholesome for Germans'.

58–60. Fabri's contract specified that the captain should 'assign to the pilgrims some convenient place . . . for keeping chickens or fowls', and that his cooks should allow the pilgrims' cook to use their fire.

P

Text: *The Pylgrymage of Sir Richarde Guylforde knyght and controuler unto our late soveraygne lorde Kynge Henry the .vii.* (1511), fos. E ii, H v. *STC* 12549. *Ed.* H. Ellis, Camden Soc. 51 (1851).

An account by a chaplain of the ill-fated journey of Sir Richard and the Prior of Giseburn, who left Rye in April 1506 and reached the Holy Land only to die there in September. The author returned to England in March 1507.

Textual Notes. 39 maryners] *text* marynes   44 particuler] *text* particules 59 gretely] *text* gertely

1 ff. *Bethlem . . .*: All medieval pilgrims' books praise the beauty of Bethlehem. In his description this author (like others) seems to be following a guidebook account, adding remarks of his own. The standard early description is by Burchard of Mount Sion (tr. A. Stewart, Palestine Pilgrims' Text Soc. [1896]); cf. also Fabri [see note on 1 O 4 ff.], ii. 547 ff.

22 ff. Cf. Burchard: 'this chapel is all lined with mosaic work ("like the church of St. Mark at Venice", says Fabri), paved with marble, and most sumptuously built . . . I have never seen or heard anyone say that he had seen a holier church anywhere in the whole world . . . all the nave of the church above the pillars, even to the roof, is of most beauteous and noble mosaic work . . . the whole church is paved with marble of divers colours, adorned with paintings of all history from the creation of the world to the coming of the Lord to judgment . . .'

28–30. In spite of a widely reported miracle (mentioned earlier in the book) when a huge serpent appeared to deter a sultan from removing pillars and slabs, there had been much dilapidation. Fabri says that many slabs had been torn from the walls by Eastern Christians (although on his second visit (1483–4) he reports that the roof had been restored and that the pigeons and sparrows nesting in it and defiling the pavement were being kept under control by martens).

31 ff. Dangerous Mediterranean storms are frequently described in the pilgrims' books (cf. the vivid account in Fabri, pp. 36 ff., where the pilgrims call on saints, make great vows, etc., rather in the manner described in the famous dialogue of Erasmus). However, this author seems to have had a particularly hard winter voyage home. This incident is the culmination of a series of storms which had continually driven them back to Milos or to one of the neighbouring islands in the Cyclades far to the north of their route from Crete to Corfu.

41. *Salve Regina*: an antiphon to the Virgin Mary.

43. *our blessed Lady de Myraculis*: a miraculous image of the Virgin, enshrined in the church of Santa Maria dei Miracoli.

59. *oure Ladyes daye*: 8 December, the feast of the Conception of the Virgin.

Q

MS BL Add. 28561, fo. 18. *Ed.* W. J. Loftie, *Ye Oldest Diarie of Englysshe Travell* (London, 1884).

Richard Torkington, Rector of Mulberton (Norfolk) left Rye on 20 March 1517, and returned on 17 April 1518. He takes a great deal from Guylforde: of this description of Venice the first few sentences (with the exception of the 'Marchose of Mantua') are Guylforde's.

Textual Notes. 6 galye] *text* gayle   *dominii*] *text domini.*

1 ff. The splendours of Venice made a profound impression on early travellers. Important 'sights' which are often mentioned are the great Arsenal, the glass of Murano, and the many relics in the churches and monasteries.

5. *The Duke*: Leonardo Loredano (1438–1521).

6. *archa triumphali*: the Bucintoro, which, says Fabri, 'is a great ship fashioned like a tabernacle, painted, covered with gilding, and shrouded with silken hangings; and all this takes place with pompous ceremonial, with the ringing of all the bells in the city, the braying of trumpets, and the singing of various hymns by the clergy.'

7. *the Marchose*: Francesco Gonzaga (1484–1519).

9. *with a ryng*: Fabri, who also saw the Ascension Day ceremony of the espousal of the sea (i. 98 ff.), remarks that afterwards 'many strip and dive to the bottom to seek that ring. He who finds it keeps it for his own, and, moreover, dwells for that whole year in the city free from all the burdens to which the dwellers in that republic are subject.'

10. *In signum. . .*: 'in sign of true and perpetual lordship'.

12. *the Abbey . . .*: the monastery of St Nicholas on the Lido.

R

Text: *Of the newe landes* (? 1520), fo. 1. *STC* 7677. *Ed.* E. Arber, *The First Three English Books on America* (Birmingham, 1885).

Printed by Doesborgh (see 1 J n.), who was obviously interested in the market for books of exotic travel: he also produced *Van Pape Jans landendes* (? *c*.1506) and *Van der niewer Welt*, a version of Vespucci's *Mundus Novus* (? *c*.1507), and *Die Reyse van Lissebone*. *Of the newe landes* seems to be a slavish translation of a Dutch or Flemish original (but not *Van der niewer Welt*), which derives ultimately from one of Amerigo Vespucci's accounts of his voyages (the reference at the beginning seems to be to his voyage of 1501–2 for Don Manoel of Portugal). On Vespucci's reputation and on his immensely popular narratives ('now universally read', according to More's *Utopia* (1516)), see S. E. Morison, *The European Discovery of America. The Southern Voyages 1492–1616* (New York, 1974), 294–7, 306–311, and J. Hemming, *Red Gold* (London, 1978), 12–21, 532–5. *Of the newe landes* has (from Vespucci's vivid descriptions) most of the stereotypes of the early Western view of Indians: nakedness, feathers, communism (especially with regard to women), longevity, and cannibalism. The print has a woodcut depicting feathered Indians, with naked children and a head being dried over a fire.

Textual Note. 5 myles] *text* mylee

6–8. *selandes . . . Armenica*: The text is difficult to follow here. It may be that *selandes* is a garbled form of some place-name, or it may simply reproduce MDu. *seelant* 'land beside the sea'. In the *Mundus Novus*, Vespucci says he skirted the whole African coast as far as Cape Verde, and then sailed across the Atlantic for two months (about 700 leagues) to land on the coast of the new continent. He then followed the coast east for about 300 leagues. The name America (from Amerigo) was suggested by Waldseemüller in his *Cosmographiae Introductio* (1507).

2

A

MS BL Cotton Cleopatra F. iii, fo. 70^v^. *Ed.* F. C. Hingeston, *Royal and Historical Letters during the Reign of Henry IV*. RS 18 (1860), i. 35–8.

J. Beverley Smith (*Bull. of the Board of Celtic Studies*, 22 (1967), 250–6) assigns the letter to the later stages of the Glyndwr rebellion (1410–12). Lord Grey de Ruthin (d. 1440) was a notable opponent (and for a time the captive) of Owen Glyndwr; Mered ap Owyn was Maredudd, a son of Owen. The original letter of Gruffudd ('the strengest thiefe of Wales', according to Lord Grey) is printed in H. Ellis, *Original Letters Illustrative of English History*, 2nd Ser., vol. i (London, 1827), 5–7.

Textual Note. 2 Deykus] *or (?)* Deykns

B

Ed. J. Stevenson, *Letters and Papers of King Henry VI*, RS 22 (1861), i. 421–2.

4. *siege of Hareflewe*: Harfleur, taken by Henry V at the beginning of the Agincourt campaign.

C

Ed. G. Williams, *Official Correspondence of Thomas Bekynton*, RS 56 (1872), i. 109.

William Grey, Bishop of Lincoln, 1431–6; Thomas Bekynton, then Archdeacon of Buckinghamshire and Dean of the Arches, previously a Fellow of New College, later to become (1442) a munificent Bishop of Bath and Wells and Lord Privy Seal. Of the places mentioned, Colnbrook, Boveney, and Burnham are in Buckinghamshire, Eynsham is near Oxford.

Textual Note. 2, 14 ye] *text* þe

D

Ed. S. A. Moore, *Letters and Papers of John Shillingford, Mayor of Exeter 1447–50*, Camden Soc. 107 (1871), 16–17.

Shillingford was in London dealing with the people of Exeter's case against the bishop, Edmund Lacey. Cf. L. Lyell, *A Mediaeval Postbag* (London, 1934), 69–76.

12. *si recte . . .*: 'if thou shalt live righteously'; (*Distichs of Cato*, III, 2).

E

MS BL Add. 43488, fo. 13. *Ed.* N. Davis, *Paston Letters and Papers of the Fifteenth Century*, ii (Oxford, 1976), No. 450.

On the letters, see H. S. Bennett, *The Pastons and their England* (Cambridge, 1922, repr. 1968). William Lomnor, of Mannington near Gresham, was an adviser and agent of the Pastons. John Paston I, later JP and MP for Norfolk, b. 1421, d. 1466. On Suffolk, cf. 1 C.

Textual Notes. 31 gown] *MS* gowy   36 fer] *MS* for

24. *Stacy*: In 1451 the Commons petitioned that Thomas Stacy should be removed from the King's presence.

38. *the freere*: Friar John Hauteyn had claimed the manor of Oxnead (the main residence of the later Pastons, near Aylsham, Norfolk) since 1443.

F

MS BL Add. 43488, fo. 21. *Ed.* Davis, vol. ii, No. 512.

Henry VI became mad in August 1453, and did not recover until Christmas 1454. Edmund Clere, a trustee under William Paston I's testament, frequently mentioned in the correspondence.

Textual Note. 6 prynce] *MS* pryne

5. *Seint Edward*: the shrine of Edward the Confessor (Westminster Abbey).

11 ff. *the Cardinal . . .*: Cardinal Henry Beaufort, Bishop of Winchester, d. 1447; William Waynflete (d. 1486), the founder of Magdalen College, Oxford, succeeded Beaufort as Bishop of Winchester; Robert Botyll, the Prior of the Order of St John of Jerusalem.

G

MS BL Add. 43491, fo. 11. *Ed.* Davis, vol. i, No. 330.

John Paston III, younger brother of John Paston II, knighted by Henry VII, d. 1504; Margaret Paston (d. 1484), wife of John Paston I. The two elder Paston brothers accompanied Princess Margaret, sister of Edward IV, to Bruges in 1468 for her marriage to Charles the Bold, Duke of Burgundy.

Textual Notes. 32 lordys] *MS* lordy   43 that] *MS* tha

15. *my lord the Bastard*: the father of Charles the Bold, Anthony, Count de la Roche, natural son of Philip the Good.

24. *my Lord Scalys*: Anthony Woodville, Lord Scales, and later (1469) Earl Rivers, the brother of the queen, beheaded by Richard III in 1483; a literary man and translator of some note.

H

MS BL Add. 43489, fo. 44. *Ed.* Davis, vol. i, No. 261.

The two Paston brothers fought (probably as followers of the Earl of Oxford) with the Lancastrians under Warwick when they were defeated by Edward IV at Barnet on 14 April 1471. The persons mentioned in lines 6–18 are: (6–7) the Milsents, servants of the Pastons; (10) Archbishop George Neville, younger brother of Warwick; (14) Richard Neville, Earl of Warwick, the 'Kingmaker' (1449–71); (15) Montacu: John Neville, his younger brother; William Tyrell, JP and MP for Essex; John Lewis, sheriff, JP and MP; (16) William Godmanston of Frinton, Essex; Richard Bothe, sheriff, JP and MP; (17) Humphrey Cromwell, son of the Earl of Essex; William Fiennes, the son of the Lord Saye, who was killed by Cade's men (cf. 1 D); Sir Humphrey Bourchier, son of Lord Berners.

Textual Notes. 20 it] *MS om.*   34 I] *MS om.*

20 ff. Queen Margaret, wife of Henry VI, had landed at Weymouth on the day of the battle; she was defeated at Tewkesbury on 4 May, and captured soon afterwards.

24. *my cosyn Lomnore*: the writer of 2 E, mentioned again in 2 I 6.

I

MS BL Add. 27445, fo. 45. *Ed.* Davis, vol. i, No. 346.

Textual Note. 32 your] *MS* you

14. *the Holt*: Holt, Norfolk.

24. *Ser Jamys*: James Gloys, the Paston family chaplain.

35. *Gelston*: Geldeston, Norfolk. It is possible that John III had been born there and that he 'used this description as a kind of private code to his mother to conceal his identity from strangers who might read the letter (which significantly bears no address)' (Davis).

J

MS BL Add. 43490, fo. 23. *Ed*. Davis, vol. i, No. 415.

Written in the hand of Thomas Kela, a servant of the Brews family at Topcroft (10 m. south of Norwich). This is the first of two Valentines from Margery Brews to John Paston III (they were married later in 1477). An earlier letter in February from Dame Elizabeth Brews (Davis, vol. i, No. 791) to John III says that Margery has become 'suche advokett for yowe that I may never hafe rest nyght ner day, for callyng and cryeng uppon to brynge the saide mater to effecte', remarks that Friday is St Valentine's Day 'and every brydde chesyth hym a make', and invites him to come on Thursday and stay, so that he can speak to her husband.

K

MS PRO, SC 1 53/119. *Ed.* A. Hanham, *The Cely Letters*, EETS 273 (1975), 150–2.

Nothing came of this wooing, but Richard Cely the younger seems to have been a susceptible soul: Hanham (p. xv) remarks that 'he had previously favoured one of the Chester family, and nine days after his visit to Northleach his friend Harry Bryan urged on him another mercantile connection, with Anne, daughter of Richard Rawson ... a wealthy mercer from Yorkshire'. She had a dowry of 500 marks, and he had married her by February 1483. Matchmaking is frequently discussed in fifteenth-century letters. Edward Plumpton (*Plumpton Correspondence*, No. XCVI) writes to tell his father that friends 'hath brought me unto the sight of a gentlewoman, a wedow of the age of .xl. yeres and more, and of good substance; first she is goodly and beautyfull, womanly and wyse ... of a good stocke and worshipful. Hir name is Agnes' (whereupon he quickly turns to the financial details). The setting for Richard Cely's encounter is the rich wool-producing area of the Cotswolds—Burford, Chipping Camden, Northleach, and Winchcomb—and the men mentioned are great merchants—William Midwinter (d. 1501), a frequent correspondent of the Celys, whose memorial brass is still in Northleach church; William Bretlen, a member of the Staple; Thomas Limrick of Cirencester; and Stowell, JP and MP for Gloucestershire. Pettyt (line 21) is presumably the merchant John Petite, who with the woolman John Bolle was appointed in 1484 to make search throughout the realm for defective wool. ('Inwinding' was the illegal practice of winding inferior wool among the locks of good fleeces.)

Textual Notes. 13 and sche] *MS* and and sche   24 and] *MS* and and

L

Ed. T. Stapleton, *Plumpton Correspondence*, Camden Soc. 4 (1839), No. XXXIX.

Sir Robert Plumpton (1453–1523), the elder of two bastard sons of Sir William Plumpton (d. 1480), was declared his heir in 1472. Killinghall: in Yorkshire, just north of Harrogate.

M

Ed. Stapleton, No. LXII.

Edward Plumpton, a cousin of Sir Robert, had accompanied Lord Strange at the battle of Stoke in June 1487 (*the feild*, line 13). Latham Hall (Lancashire) was a seat of the Earls of Derby.

N

Ed. Stapleton, No. LXXVIII.

Henry Percy, either the fourth Earl of Northumberland (1446–89) or his son, the fifth (b. 1478); *Spetel of the street* is Spital in the Street, Lincolnshire.

O

Ed. Stapleton, No. CLXV.

Dorothy Plumpton obviously regarded her situation in the household of Lady Darcy, her stepmother's mother (at Temple Hirst, Birkin, Yorks.), as beneath her status.

3

Hoccleve: *The Minor Poems*, eds. F. J. Furnivall and I. Gollancz, EETS, ES 61, 73 (rev. edn. J. Mitchell and I. Doyle [1970]); *The Regement of Princes*, ed. F. J. Furnivall, EETS, ES 72 (1897); Selections, ed. M. C. Seymour (Oxford, 1981), and ed. B. O'Donoghue (Manchester, 1982).

Studies include: H. S. Bennett, *Six Medieval Men and Women* (Cambridge, 1955), ch. 3; J. A. Burrow, 'Autobiographical Poetry in the Middle Ages: The Case of Thomas Hoccleve', *PBA* 68 (1982), 389–412; G. Mathew, *The Court of Richard II* (London, 1968) 55–8; S. Medcalf, *The Later Middle Ages* (London, 1981), 124–40; J. Mitchell, *Thomas Hoccleve* (Urbana, 1968); I. Robinson, *Chaucer's Prosody* (Cambridge, 1971), 190–9, A. C. Reeves, *M & H*, NS 5 (1974), 201–14; H. Schulz, *Speculum*, 12 (1937), 71–81. See *MWME* iii. 746–56, 903–8.

A

MS Huntington Library, HM 744, fo. 46. *Index* 666. *Ed.* EETS, *Minor Poems*, pp. 72–91; Skeat, *COP*, pp. 217–232 (both from MS Fairfax 16). This extract represents lines 274–341 of the poem. (French text ed. M. Roy, SATF 2 (1891), pp. 1–27.)

On Christine de Pisan, see M.-J. Pinet, *Christine de Pisan, 1364–1430* (Paris, 1927, repr. Geneva, 1974); S. Solente in *Histoire littéraire de la France*, xl (Paris, 1969). She returns to the defence of women in *La Cité des dames* (tr. into English by B. Anslay, *c.*1520), where she answers the anti-feminist book of Matheolus. She appears to have had an early connection with England—her son Jean was with the

Earl of Salisbury in 1397—and a number of her works were turned into English in the fifteenth and early sixteenth centuries (cf. Campbell, *Revue de littérature comparée*, 5 (1925), 659–70; M. C. Curnow, *Les Bonnes Feuilles*, 3 (1971), 116–37). J. V. Fleming, *MÆ* 40 (1971), 21–40, argues that Hoccleve alters the French poem in such a way as to engage himself on the side of Christine's opponents in the controversy.

8. *John de Meun*: author of the second part of the *Roman de la rose*, notorious for his satirical and supposedly anti-feminist remarks.

29 ff. Hoccleve adds this reference to Chaucer's *LGW* (Cupid's 'our Legende of Martirs'), which tells the stories of Medea and Dido.

B

MS Huntington Library, HM 111, fo. 38ᵛ. *Index* 3480, 3224. *Ed.* EETS, *Minor Poems*, pp. 59–60; Hammond, *EVCS*, pp. 66–7.

Written (? December 1407 or 1408) when Sir Henry Somer was Sub-Treasurer (he later became Chancellor of the Exchequer).

1. *Sonne*: i.e. gold. Cf. Lydgate's *Letter to Gloucester*: 'Sol and luna were clypsyd of ther liht'.

13–15. I.e., the previous quarter's salary had not been paid.

21. *shippes*: a reference to the stamp of a ship on the gold noble. Cf. *Letter to Gloucester*: 'ship was ther noon nor seilis reed of hewe'.

25–6. These are Hoccleve's fellow clerks in the Privy Seal; see A. L. Brown, in D. A. Bullough and R. L. Storey (eds.), *The Study of Medieval Records* (Oxford, 1971), 260–81.

C

MS BL Arundel 38, fos. 2, 38 (the MS is a presentation copy made for Henry, Prince of Wales, later Henry V). *Index* 2229. *Ed.* EETS, *Regement* (from BL MS Harley 4866). These extracts represent lines 71–168 and 2073–107 of the poem.

Textual Notes. 23 wyht] *MS* wyth   30 though] *MS* thought (*faded or erased*)   41 despoylyd] *MS* d.spoylyd (*with worm-hole*)   47 dressed] *MS* dresse   65 the] *MS om.*   71 compaygnye] *MS* compaygne   90 of] *MS om.*   97 I] *MS om.*   99 is] *MS* as   101 in] *MS om.*   108 hath] *MS om.*   119 lyf] *MS* yf   126 iliche] *MS* ileche

99 ff. The question whether Hoccleve had ever met his admired Chaucer in person has been much debated (cf. Mitchell, pp. 115–18; Ingram, *NQ* 218 (1973), 42–3), without any conclusive result. He certainly knew Chaucer's works, and here gives his lament a Chaucerian ring—for example, the word *combre-world* (117) is used by Chaucer's Troilus of himself (*TC* 4. 279). Later in the poem, another passage praising Chaucer (lines 4977 ff.) is accompanied in some MSS by a 'portrait' of the poet.

D

MS Bodl., Selden supra 53, fos. 76, 78. *Index* 124. *Ed.* EETS, *Minor Poems*, pp. 95–110 (from Durham Cathedral MS Cosin V. iii. 9).

A. G. Rigg, *Speculum*, 45 (1970), 564–74, discusses the didactic and consolatory aspects of the poem. On traditional treatments of madness, see Penelope Doob, *Nebuchadnezzar's Children: Conventions of Madness in Middle English Literature* (New Haven, 1974). However, Hoccleve's account seems very detailed and vivid, and there is some documentary evidence (see *RES*, NS 20 (1969), 482) which could suggest that Hoccleve was ill in 1416. Cf. Chaucer's descriptions of melancholy and despair in *TC* 5. 617–30, 1212–25.

Textual Note. 36 my] *MS* me

4

Lydgate: Selections in Hammond, *EVCS*, and (with full commentary) in J. Norton-Smith, *John Lydgate: Poems* (Oxford, 1966). Complete texts (a select list): *The Fall of Princes*, ed. H. Bergen, EETS, ES 121–4 (1924–7); *Troy Book*, ed. H. Bergen, EETS, ES 97, 103, 106, 126 (1906–35); *The Siege of Thebes*, eds. A. Erdmann and E. Ekwall, EETS, ES 108, 125 (1911, 1920); *Reason and Sensuality*, ed. E. Sieper, EETS, ES 84, 89, (1901, 1903); *The Temple of Glass*, ed. J. Schick, EETS, ES 60 (1981), and Norton-Smith (ed. cit.); *The Life of Our Lady*, eds. J. A. Lauritis, R. A. Klinefelter, and V. F. Gallagher, Duquesne Studies, Philological Series, 2 (1961); *Minor Poems*, ed. H. N. MacCracken, EETS, ES 107, OS 192 (1910, 1934).

Studies include: W. F. Schirmer, *John Lydgate: A Study in the Culture of the Fifteenth Century* (Tübingen, 1952), trans. A. E. Keep (London, 1961); A. Renoir, *The Poetry of John Lydgate* (London, 1967); D. Pearsall, *John Lydgate* (London, 1970). See *MWME* vi. 1809–1920, 2071–175.

A

MS BL Add. 16165, fo. 248. *Index* 2571. *Ed.* Norton-Smith, No. 2.

Thomas Chaucer (1364–1434), the son of the poet, was MP for Oxfordshire and Speaker for Parliament on a number of occasions. He married Maud Burghersh, the daughter of Sir John Burghersh of Ewelme, Oxfordshire, where she lies with their daughter Alice, who married, as her third husband, the Duke of Suffolk (cf. 1 C, 2 E). Norton-Smith identifies the poem as a *propempticon* (a poem wishing a friend a safe voyage); possibly it relates to the events of 4 June 1414, when Thomas Chaucer was sent to treat with the ambassadors of the Duke of Burgundy.

Textual Notes. 6 herte] *MS* hert   10 eke now no] *MS* eke no   15 the] *N.-S.*: *MS om.*   17 in] *N.-S.*: *MS om*   29 Ceres] *MS* certes   34 Wher] *N.-S.*: *MS* with   54 have] *MS* hathe   65 have] *MS* hathe   72 think] *MS* thenk   76 herte] *MS* hert   77 To] *MS* And

43. *Molyns*: William de Moleyns, JP and Commissioner of Array in 1399 and 1403.

50. A gloss in the MS reads 'la femme Chaucer'.

51. St Helena visited the Holy Land, and, according to legend, discovered the true Cross; probably 'Ynde' = any distant region.

56. '*Goddes soule*': possibly the prayer *Anima Christi*.

68. *Saint Julyan*: patron saint of hospitality; a nice compliment by an allusion to Chaucer's father's description of the generous Franklin (*CT* A 339–56): 'Seint Julian he was in his contree.'

B

MS Fitzwilliam Museum, Cambr., McClean 182, fo. 4. *Ed.* H. N. MacCracken, *The Serpent of Division* (London and New Haven, 1911).

Lydgate relates the episode in Lucan's *Pharsalia*, i. 183 ff., but he seems also (thus MacCracken) to have used a version of the French *Li Fait des Romains* (eds. L.-F. Flutre and K. Sneyders de Vogel [Paris, 1937–8], i. 347–51).

Textual Notes. 7 there] *MS* thei   11 the] *MS* ther   15 ficche] *MS* fecche   23 assautes] *MS* assentes   25 no] *so other MSS*: *MS* a   28 deliberacion] *MS* deliberance   31 sewe] *so other MSS*: *MS* be sched   reised] *MS* resseyved   84 and] *MS* of

3–4. *Alpies . . . the colde frosty hillis*: Lucan's 'gelidas Alpes'.

5. *Assoine*: (?) Ausonia, i.e. Italy (suggested by a later line in Lucan: 'Limes ab Ausoniis disterminat arva colonis' (216)

7. *Rubicanis*: gen. sg. from Lucan ('Rubiconis ad undas').

an olde auncien lady: In Lucan she is a vision of his distressed country ('patriae trepidantis imago')

78. *Arymynum*: Ariminum, now Rimini.

C

MS Bodl., Bodley 263, p. 85. *Index* 1168. *Ed.* EETS, *Fall of Princes*; this passage (Book I, lines 6882–7035) is in *EVCS*, pp. 164–8.

Lydgate expands the briefest hint in Laurent ('Machareus le filz du roy Eolus aima Canace sa suer dont elle eut un enfant' (*Des cas des nobles hommes et femmes*, Book I, ed. P. M. Gathercole [Chapel Hill, 1968], 170)) into this pathetic lament in the manner of Ovid's *Heroides* (XI). The story is also told by Gower, *CA* 3. 143 ff.

Textual Notes. 7 enclosid] *MS* onclosid   44 gilt] *MS* gile   52 Nor] *MS* Nar   58 than] *MS* than any   65 comparable] *MS* incomparable   111 sharpe] *MS* sharp   120 swiftte] *MS* swifft   144 hir[1]] *MS* his   150 sharpe] *MS* sharp

105 ff. Cf. E. Panofsky, *Studies in Iconology* (Oxford, 1939, repr. New York, 1962), ch. IV, 'Blind Cupid'.

D

MS Bodl., Selden supra 53, fo. 148. *Index* 2591. *Ed.* F. Warren and B. White, EETS 181 (1930); *EVCS*, pp. 124–42.

The English translation exists in two recensions. Lydgate says that he found the French original 'on a wall' in Paris. It seems likely that he is translating the version of the French *Danse macabre* which was painted in the cemetery of the Innocents in 1424/5 (French texts in *EVCS*, pp. 426–35; E. F. Chaney, *La Danse macabre* [Manchester, 1945]). On the Dance of Death, see J. M. Clark, *The Dance of Death in the Middle Ages and the Renaissance* (Glasgow, 1950); W. Stammler *Der Totentanz: Entstehung und Deutung* (Munich, 1948).

3. *appil round*: F. 'la pomme d'or', i.e. orb.

12. *my grave to ateyne*: Lydgate loses the irony of F. '*armer* me fault de pic de pelle'.

25 ff. The words of the squire (a figure traditionally associated with youth and love) seem to echo the 'farewell' formulae found in some love lyrics. Cf. *SL*, Nos. 202–4.

41–2. F. 'De cecy neusse point envye | Mais il convient le pas passer | Las, or nay je pas en ma vie | Garde mon ordre sans casser.' 'Envye' = desire (for the summons); Lydgate 'seems to institute a contrast between the loss of power and the death as a cloisterer' (Hammond). He seems also to be changing the anti-monastic satire.

60. *at plow*: apparently an English adaptation of F. 'estre es vingnes'.

5

MS Bodl., Selden B. 24 fo. 194ᵛ. *Index* 1215; *MWME* iv. 961–5, 1124–35. *Ed.* J. Norton-Smith (Oxford, 1971, repr. Leiden, 1981), with full commentary; also by Skeat, (STS, 1884), W. M. Mackenzie (London, 1939), J. R. Simon (Paris, 1967), M. P. McDiarmid (London, 1973).

Numerous studies include Lewis, *AL*, pp. 235–7; J. Preston, 'Fortunys Exiltree', *RES*, NS 7 (1956), 339–47; J. MacQueen 'Tradition and the Interpretation of the *KQ*', *RES*, NS 12 (1961), 117–131; L. A. Ebin, 'Boethius, Chaucer and the *KQ*', *PQ* 53 (1974), 321–41; J. A. W. Bennett, 'A King's Quire', *Poetica*, 3 (1975), 1–16; A. C. Spearing, *Medieval Dream Poetry* (Cambridge, 1976), 181–7; G. Kratzmann, *Anglo-Scottish Literary Relations 1430–1550* (Cambridge, 1980), 33–62. This extract corresponds to lines 204–497 of the whole poem.

Textual Notes. 18 scharpe] *MS* scharp   22 smalle] *MS* small   27 of] *MS* on   74 yonge] *MS* yong   124 burnettis] *N.-S.*: *MS* jonettis   130 herte] *MS* hert   138 lo] *MS* to   158 suiche] *MS* such   218 sche] *MS* he   251 newe] *MS* new   275 calde] *MS* cald   276 hennesfurth] *MS* heñsfurth

1. An echo of Chaucer, *TC* 1.547. This passage (like the rest of the poem) is full of allusions to Chaucer. Phrases from *TC* come readily to the poet's mind when he is describing the situation of the lover, e.g. 'kalendis . . .' (30) ~ *TC* 2. 7, or the nature of love, e.g. 'Quhat lyf is this' (45) ~ *TC* 4. 1604, 47 ~ *TC* 1. 810, 54 ~ *TC* 1. 237, 3. 1767, 'lufis daunce' (109) ~ *TC* 2. 1106.

8 ff. The description of the garden recalls the scene in Chaucer's *Kn. T.* (*CT* A 1034 ff.), where Palamon and Arcite see Emelye (whose association with flowers probably suggests the word *floure* in line 74).

31 ff. Cf. the birds' song of welcome to summer in *PF* 687 ff. (and cf. *LGW* Prol. F 167–70).

76–7. Cf. *BD* 488 ff. C. S. Lewis (*AL*, p. 237) remarks that the lines record 'with singular fidelity that first sense of shock which is common to all vivid emotions as they arise and which transcends the common antithesis of pain and pleasure'.

90–1. Cf. *Kn. T.* A 1101 ff. This is an ancient topos; the first occurrence in Western literature is *Odyssey* VI, where Odysseus asks Nausicaa if she is a goddess or a mortal woman.

92. *god Cupidis owin princesse*: possibly Alceste (cf. *LGW* F 213 ff.).

94. *verray Nature the goddesse*: cf. *PF* 302 ff.

129 ff. The ruby recalls *TC* 3. 13707; lines 141 ff. are a reminiscence of the description of the virtuous Constance in *MLT*.

177. *Proigne*: Procne took vengeance on her husband Tereus for his brutal ravishing of her sister Philomena. She was transformed into a swallow, her sister into a nightingale (cf. *philomene* (225)). Cf. Ovid, *Met.* 6. 424–674; *LGW* 2228 ff.; Gower, *CA* 5. 5551 ff.

281. *Tantalus*: punished in Hades by being placed in a pool of water which always receded when he tried to drink from it. Cf. *BD* 704–9.

289 ff. Cf. *BD* 599–615.

6

A

MS Bodl., Fairfax 16, fo. 314; Facs. edn.: J. Norton-Smith (Scolar Press, London, 1979). *Index* 4186. *MWME* iv. 1074–5, 1294. *Ed.* Hammond, *EVCS*, pp. 207–13.

Textual Notes. 31 Loves] *MS* love   44 hyr] *MS* hys

1. *Introibo*: 'et introibo ad altare Dei' ('then will I go unto the altar of God'), words spoken by the priest at the beginning of Mass.

15. *Confiteor*: the Confession—'I confess to Almighty God, to Blessed Mary ever Virgin . . .'. Cf. *TC* 2. 522 ff.

41. *Misereatur*: 'May Almighty God have mercy upon thee, forgive thee thy sins, and bring thee to life everlasting.'

56. *Genius*: This figure appears in Alanus's *De Planctu Naturae*, the *Roman de la Rose*, the *Confessio Amantis* (as priest of Love). See Lewis, *AL*, App. I; Knowlton, *Class. Philology*, 15 (1920), 380–4, *MLN* 39 (1924), 89–95; J. C. Nitzsche, *The Genius Figure in Antiquity and the Middle Ages* (New York and London, 1975).

57. *Officium*: the Introit at the beginning of Mass.

74. *Kyrie . . .*: *Kyrie eleison . . . Christe eleison* ('Lord, have mercy upon us . . . Christ have mercy upon us').

98 ff. *Worshyppe . . .*: the equivalent of the Mass's *Gloria in excelsis Deo* ('Glory to God in the highest').

124. Proverbial; cf. Whiting, D 41.

B

MS CUL Ff. 1. 6, fo. 121. *Index* 1086. *MWME* iv. 1093–4, 1301–2. (The poem appears in Thynne's edition of Chaucer.) *Ed.* Skeat, *COP*, pp. 299–326.

See E. Seaton, *Sir Richard Roos . . . Lancastrian Poet* (London, 1961), a study of the supposed translator, and valuable on fifteenth-century poetic MSS; but Seaton makes unjustified additions to the canon of his work, which, as far as we know, consists only of this poem. On Chartier, see J. C. Laidlaw, *The Poetical Works of Alain Chartier* (Cambridge, 1974). He was born *c.*1380–90, became a royal notary and secretary, and died 1429/30; he wrote *La Belle Dame* in 1424. A number of his prose works were also translated into English (see 8 C; and there is a Caxton version of the *De Vita Curiali* (EETS, ES 54)). This extract corresponds to lines 197–348 of the poem. The poet comes upon a courtly company in a garden, and overhears a dialogue between a sorrowful lover and his mistress.

Textual Notes. 30 it nought] *MS Harley 372 (= H)*: *MS* it at nought   42 ay] *H*: *MS* alwey   45 yeve] *MS* ye: *H* gif   50 yaf answere] *H*: *MS* yaf hym answere 55 and] *MS* an   58 wer] *MS* war   62 thilke] *H*: *MS* the   63 forber] *MS* forbar   77 her] *Thynne*: *MS* his   114 grete desire] *H (F. 'grant desir')*: *MS* ryght gret love   136 eres] *MS* yeres   152 his] *MS* their *(F. 'sa')*

69. F. 'Se moy ou aultre vous regarde', i.e. 'if I or someone else look at you'.
92. *chayne*: F. 'laz'.
131–2. F. '. . . pour un peu de plaisans bourdes | Confites en belles parolles'.
144. F. '(pensee de douleur) . . . Preuve ses parolles par euvre'.

C

Text: *The Workes of our antient and lerned English poet, G. Chaucer newly printed* (T. Speght, 1598), fo. 367. *Index* 4026. *STC* 5077. *MWME* iv. 1095–6, 1303–4. *Ed.* D. Pearsall (London, 1962) (with full commentary); Skeat, *COP*, pp. 361–79. This extract corresponds to lines 295–378 of the poem.

Textual Notes. 2 worthy] *text* worldly   22 enclined] *text* enclining   40 knightes] *text* knights   44 heades] *text* heads. 60 how] *text om.*   66 knightes] *text* knights

1. *they*: knights who have been jousting. The poet is later given an explanation of the two groups: those in white are servants to the Leaf, and their queen is the chaste Diana; those in green are the servants of the Flower, and their goddess is Flora.

D

Text: *The Boke of Fame, made by G. Chaucer. With dyvers other of his workes* (R. Pynson, ? 1526), fo. v (the poem is headed by a small picture of Dido with a sword, beside a burning pyre). *Index* 811.5. *MWME* iv. 1097–8, 1305. *STC* 5088.
    Cf. Ovid, *Heroides* vii. 67 ff.

Textual Notes. 40 of] *text* on   49 his] *text* hir   62 your] *text* you

16. *Ascany*: Ascanius, son of Aeneas.
100. *Sechee*: Sychaeus, Dido's former husband.

7

A

MS Bodl., Bodley 505, fo. 126. *Ed.* M. Doiron (from St John's Coll., Cambridge, MS 71), *Archivio italiano per la storia della Pietà*, 5 (1968) (with Appendix by E. Colledge and R. Guarnieri); modernized edn. by C. Kirchberger (London, 1927).

A translation (late fourteenth- or early fifteenth-century) by an unknown 'M.N.' of *Le Mirouer des simples ames anienties* by the béguine Marguerite Porete, who was burnt at Paris in 1310 for her adherence to the doctrines of the Brethren of the Free Spirit. On these, see R. Guarnieri, *Dict. de spiritualité*, v. 1241–68; *Archivio italiano per la storia della Pietà*, 4 (1968) (with Chantilly MS of the *Mirouer*); G. Leff, *Heresy in the Later Middle Ages* (Manchester, 1967), i. 308–407. The Brethren were alleged to teach the annihilation of the soul in the deity, and its restoration to innocence in a state of 'freedom', so that it becomes indifferent to sin, and incapable of it, and that it 'taketh leave of virtues'. They were accused of spiritual and physical libertinism. Whether or not 'M.N.' knew of the book's history, he is convinced of its essential orthodoxy (much of it, indeed, is similar to the works of Flemish mysticism which were popular as devout reading in late medieval England). On points which 'M.N.' finds difficult or potentially misleading, he adds explanatory glosses (cf. the Appendix to Doiron's edition).

13. *stremynge . . . fluences*: F. (Chantilly) 'fluans et decourans de la Divinite'.

B

MS CUL Add. 6578, fo. 18. *Ed.* L. F. Powell (from Brasenose Coll. MS e 9) (Oxford, 1908).

Studies include: E. Salter, *Nicholas Love's 'Myrrour of the Blessyd Lyf of Jesu Christ'*, Analecta Cartusiana, 10 (Salzburg, 1974), and in *RES*, NS (6 (1955), 113–27, *MÆ* 26 (1957), 25–31. Nicholas Love was rector and prior of Mount Grace Charterhouse in 1409–10. His book (which survives in a large number of MSS) is a fairly free adaptation of the anonymous *Meditationes Vitae Christi* (late thirteenth- or early fourteenth-century). (Latin text in *Opera Omnia S. Bonaventurae*, ed. A. C. Peltier (Paris, 1868), vol. xii; trans. into English by I. Ragusa (Princeton, 1961). Love aims at a more general audience, and omits some of the more obviously homiletic matter.

Textual Note. 10 crache] *MS* craches

1 ff. Love omits some of L.'s detail: the Virgin stands leaning against a pillar; Joseph sits 'downcast', then takes hay from the manger and places it at her feet (hence Love's line 4).

10. *brething at hir neses*: L. 'flantes per nares'. This detail (derived from Hab. 3: 2, in the older Latin versions) is often illustrated by medieval artists.

16–17. In L., Joseph takes from the saddle a cushion, and it is the saddle which is the support.

26. *In Nat. Dom.*, sermo v, n. 5.

29–30. Ps. 10: 14; Luke 6: 24.

33. *jangelers and gret spekers*: L. 'garrulos'.
33–4. *Cristes . . . laghers*: L. 'non consolantur Christi lacryme cachinnantes'.
48. *seynt Bernarde*: *De Nat. Dom.*, sermo iii, n. 1.

C

MS University Coll., Oxford, 181, fo. 134. *Ed.* K. I. Cust (London, 1859) (from Caxton's 1483 print, with omissions).

An early fifteenth-century translation (1400 according to MS Univ. 181 and MS Bodl., Bodley 770; 1413 according to Caxton), with 'somewhat of addicions', of the *Pèlerinage de l'Âme*, the second of three allegorical poems by the Cistercian Guillaume de Deguilleville (ed. J. J. Stürzinger, Roxburghe Club [1895]), written 1355–8; cf. E. Faral in *Hist. litt. de la France*, xxxix (1962), 1–132; R. Tuve, *Allegorical Imagery* (Princeton, 1966), ch. 3. The English book contains some accomplished prose, which does justice to the vivid scenes in the rather discursive narrative. This extract renders lines 9630–90. The soul, whose pilgrimage began with the death of its body, has been taken out of Purgatory, and is led by its angel up through the heavenly spheres until it glimpses the heavenly Jerusalem.

Textual Notes. 4 grettnesse] *MS* gretteste   6 in^2] *MS om.*   15 receyved] *MS* rceyved   22 environyng] *MS* environed   26 as] *MS om.*   30 joynenge here] *MS* noyenge with here

6. *in manere of a reynebowe*: F. simply 'par dedens li son tour faisant | Et li aussi com trescoupant'. Possibly the translator has been influenced by one of the MS illustrations.
8. F. 'estoit mesureement | A ligne et ordeneement | Estele d'estoiles luisans'.
21. *assembled hem*: F. 's'assemblerent'.

D

MS BL Add. 61823, fos. 33, 87. *Ed.* S. B. Meech and H. E. Allen, EETS 212 (1940) (with full commentary); modernized edn. by W. Butler-Bowden (London, 1936).

Studies include: E. Colledge, in J. Walsh (ed.), *Pre-Reformation Spirituality* (London, 1965); D. Knowles, *The English Mystical Tradition* (London, 1961); M. Thornton, *Margery Kempe* (London, 1960); C. W. Atkinson, *Mystic and Pilgrim* (Ithaca, 1983). Margery Kempe was born in King's Lynn, probably *c.*1373. Her book records her conversion and her subsequent wanderings and visionary experiences. According to the proem, some twenty years after her first revelation she was charged by God to set down 'hyr felyngys and revelacyons and the forme of her lovyng'. This was done by an Englishman dwelling in 'Dewchland' (possibly her son). After his death, she showed it to a priest, who found it 'so evel wretyn that he cowd lytyl skyll theron, for it was neithyr good Englysch ne Dewch, ne the lettyr was not schapyn ne formyd as other letters ben'. Eventually, with her help, he produced a new version (cf. J. Hirsh, *MÆ* 44 (1975), 145–50). He began to write in 1436, and in 1438 he added a shorter second book ('aftyr hyr owyn tunge') describing her journey to the Baltic (1433–4).

Textual Note. 38 ellys] *MS* elly

1 ff. Book I, ch 28. Margery left for the Holy Land probably in autumn 1413.
34. *the fyrst cry*: Pilgrims to Jerusalem often wept (cf. EETS edn., p. 291), but Margery's crying was of a particularly intense kind, which often caused distress and hostility.
65 ff. Book I, ch. 76. She married John Kempe, burgess, and had fourteen children. He died probably in 1431.

E

MS Bodl., Bodley 220, fo. 57ᵛ. *Ed.* T. A. Halligan (Toronto, 1979).
A translation (called 'The Boke of Gostely Grace' or 'The Boke of Seynte Mawte') of the *Liber Specialis Gratiae* of St Mechtild of Hackeborn (*c.*1241–98/9), a Cistercian nun of Helfta. Mechtild's visions are notable for their strikingly visual quality and for a delight in colours and light.

1. *Asperges me Domine*: Ps. 50 (Vg.): 9 ('Thou shalt wash me, O Lord').
11. *Seynt Poule*: Gal. 5: 22–3.
25. *lykenes of a gardener*: cf. John 20: 15.

F

MS Lambeth Palace Library 72, fos. 203 and 184. *MWME* ii. 432–6, 559–60.
Cf. M. Görlach, *The South English Legendary, Gilte Legende and Golden Legend* (Braunschweig, 1972). The thirteenth-century *Legenda Aurea* of Jacobus de Voragine found its way into various vernaculars. Caxton in his *Golden Legend* (1493) drew attention to the existence of this earlier version, which he used. According to the rubric of MS Bodl., Douce 372, it was translated from the French in 1438 'bi a synfulle wrecche' (see Görlach, p. 9).

Textual Notes. 8 atte] *MS* alle   44 laborith] *MS* laborid   63 eche] *MS* and eche

1 ff. This life of the fifth-/sixth-century Irish saint is one of those added to *The Gilte Legende*; it is based on the earlier *South English Legendary* (Görlach, p. 62, points out some rhymes still embedded in the prose). The ultimate source is the *Navigatio Sancti Brendani*, probably written in Ireland, perhaps as early as 800 (ed. C. Selmer [Notre Dame, 1959]; tr. J. J. O'Meara [Dublin, 1976]). On voyages to the Other World, see H. R. Patch, *The Other World* (Cambridge, Mass., 1950).
75. *ther procuratour*: the 'ful good man' of line 25.
104 ff. The life of Saint Christopher comes from the *Golden Legend* proper. The episode with the Christ-child was a favourite subject in wall-painting (cf. H. C. Whaite, *St. Christopher in Medieval English Wall-Painting* [London, 1929]); the image was thought to give protection against a 'bad death' (cf. Gray, *TIMERL*, pp. 157–8, 279).

G

MS Trinity Coll., Dublin, F. 5. 8, I, ch. XXIII. *Ed.* J. K. Ingram, EETS 63 (1893).
A good, close translation of the Latin text. On the background of this famous devotional text, attributed to Thomas à Kempis (1380–1471), see S. Axters, *The*

Spirituality of the Old Low Countries, trans. D. Attwater (London, 1954), ch. IV. Three books of the *Imitation* were also translated by Dr William Atkynson at the request of Margaret, Countess of Richmond and Derby, the mother of Henry VII; she herself translated Book IV from French. With the subject-matter of this extract, cf. 26 A.

Textual Note. 19 behete] *MS* be here: *CUL MS* byhiete

H

Note. The items in this section are arranged according to topic rather than chronologically.

(i) *The Rosarye of Our Lady in Englysshe* (W. Vorsterman, Antwerp, *c.*1525), fo. A iii'. *STC*² 17544.

This is an illustrated book of devotion, in which each prayer appears at the foot of a picture—in this case of the Nativity, with the animals.

(ii) and (iii) *MS* CUL Add. 4120, fos. 3', 10. Cf. similar versions in *The Prymer*, ed. H. Littlehales, EETS 109 (1897), 6–7, 12–13.

(iv) *MS* Lambeth Palace Library 546, fo. 73. Modernized edn. by R. H. Benson, *The Book of the Love of Jesus* (London, 1904).

From 'a meditacioun with mentalle prayer and inwarde thankynges to God, prostrate on the grounde'. The other devotions in the MS are often in a similar ecstatic style. The phraseology of the last lines (and those which follow) seems to echo a prayer of St Catherine of Siena (Cf. *The Lyf of Saint Katherin of Senis* [*STC* 24766], fo. n. 5'): 'O depthe! O endeles godhede! O depe see! What myghtest thou more gyve me than thyself? Thou art fyre that ever brennyste, and thou wastest never . . .'

Textual Notes. 50 myght] *MS* myghty   52 0 my] *MS* O the my

(v) *MS* BL Add. 15216, fo. 10.

(vi) *MS* Bodl., Douce 322, fo. 38'. Modernized edn. by F. M. Comper, *A Book of the Craft of Dying* (London, 1917).

From the *Ars Moriendi*, the popular fifteenth-century treatise instructing the Christians how to die 'well and surely' (see M. C. O'Connor, *The Art of Dying Well* [New York, 1942]; N. L. Beaty, *The Craft of Dying* [New Haven and London, 1970]. This is the ancient prayer, *Profiscere anima christiana*, used later by Newman in *The Dream of Gerontius*.

Textual Note. 99 pryncehodes] *MS* pryncihodes

I

Text: In die Innocencium sermo pro episcopo puero (Wynkyn de Worde, n.d.), fo. a iii'. (Before 1496: it contains a reference to Thomas Kempe, 'late bishop' of London (d. 1489—his successor, Hill, d. 1495 or 1496).) *STC* 282, 283. *Ed.* J. G. Nichols, 'Two Sermons preached by the Boy Bishop', *Camden Miscellany*, 7 (Camden Soc., 1875) (on boy bishops, see E. K. Chambers, *The Medieval Stage* [Oxford, 1903], i. 336–71).

Neither edition bears Alcock's name, but the appearance of the books is very similar to the printed copies of his other sermons, and it is sometimes attributed to him (e.g. by E. G. Duff, *Fifteenth-Century English Books*); *STC*[1]; and *BRUC*). John Alcock (1430–1500) became successively Bishop of Rochester (1472), Worcester (1476), and Ely (1486). He was the founder of Jesus College, Cambridge, and enjoyed a high reputation for learning and piety (see *DNB*, *BRUC*).

3. *sermonem* . . .: 'righteous speech and the spirit of the gods'.

14. *Jeremie primo*: 'in the first chapter of Jeremiah'; Jer. 1: 11 ('What do you see . . . ?).

17. *lumbi mei* . . .: Ps. 37 (Vg.): 8 ('my loins are filled with (?) fevers, and there is no health in my flesh. I am afflicted and humiliated exceedingly').

19–20. *operuit* . . . *labia mea*: cf. Hab. 3: 16 ('confusion covered my face; my lips trembled at the voice').

20–1. *Nero* . . . *wolde*: i.e. 'that he should make away with himself' (Nichols).

25–6. *the Kynges Benche*: the Court of the King's Bench (so called because it was originally presided over by the sovereign); but here, presumably, a reference to the stocks.

31. *Via Tiburtina*: leading to Tibur, i.e. Tyburn.

J

Text: *The chirche of the evyll men and women* (Wynkyn de Worde, 1511), fo. A. iii. *STC* 1966, 5213; another edn. by Pynson (n.d.), *STC* 1967.

A close translation by Henry Watson (who also made versions of *Valentine and Orson* (cf. 14 D) and *The Ship of Fools*) of *La Petite Dyablerie dont Lucifer est le chef intitule Leglise des mauvais*, adapted by Thomas Varnet and Natalis Beda from St Bernardino of Siena (1380–1444). BL *Catalogue* suggests 'De Alearum Ludo' (Sermon 42, 'Quadragesimale de Cristiana religione', *Opera omnia* [Quaracchi, 1950], ii. 21–4) as the source. Cf. also *Le prediche volgari*, ed. C. Cannarozzi (Pistoia, 1934), i. 434 ff. However, the ending of our extract does not have a close equivalent in either of these. Possibly another sermon was also used; possibly the adapters simply extended Bernardino's conceit (Watson says they 'added and dymynysshed that the whiche they sawe serve unto the matter'). Something of the vividness of the style of the celebrated Franciscan wandering preacher survives in this version. His tirades against gambling (a common theme of medieval moralists) are said to have led to scenes of public repentance and the burning of boards and dice.

8 ff. *all the prelates* . . .: F. (BL, *Petite Dyablerie* [Paris, ? 1520]) et tous les prelats qui collerent les yeulx, dont procedent . . .' Either we have a careless translation (taking *yeulx* for *jeux*) or an error in Watson's F.

10–11. A rather awkward translation. F. 'tous ceulx qui les pourroient oster, combien que eulx mesmes ne jouent point'.

11. *Quia qui* . . .: 'for he who is silent seems to consent'.

17 ff. F. 'les jeux de paulme, de quille, de bille, de barlan, de franc de carreau et autres semblables la ou on tient lescolle a jouer'. 'Tenysplayes' were repeatedly forbidden (cf. J. Strutt, *The Sports and Pastimes of the People of England*, rev. J. C. Cox [London, 1903, repr. 1969], 82 ff.).

closshe: a game 'with a ball or bowl prohibited in many successive statutes in the 15th–16th centuries' (*OED*). It seems that the bowl was driven by 'a spade or chisel-shaped implement . . . through a hoop or ring as in croquet'.

berlan: not recorded in dictionaries, but cf. the name *berlondere* 'gambler', OF *berlandier* (*MED*).

fre square ('franc de carreau'): not recorded ('franc de carreau' appears in the huge list of games in ch. 22 of Rabelais's *Gargantua*, and is translated by Urquhart as 'at span-counter', a game involving the throwing of counters).

20–1. *hote houses dyssolute*: F. 'estuves dissolus'.

26. *butyn or wynnynge*: Pynson *boty*, but both words were in use (both first recorded in Caxton's *Chesse* [1474]). F. also has a doublet: 'butin ou gaing'.

30. *oratoryes . . . praye in*: F. 'des oratoires'.

35–6. *the abovesaid . . . wages*: F. 'les dessusdicts pour leurs services, distributions et gaiges'.

50. *the auncyent men*: F. 'les vieulx'.

K

Text: *A lyttell story of a mayde that was named Mary of Nemmegen* (J. van Doesborgh [see 1 J n.], *c*.1518–19), fos. A iii, B v, B v^v, *STC* 17557. Facsimile edn. with intro. by H. M. Ayres and A. J. Barnouw (Cambridge, Mass., 1932).

For studies see E. Krispyn, *JEGP* 75 (1976), 361–8; M. Schlauch, *Philologica Pragensia*, 6 (1963), 4–11. A version of the Dutch verse play *Mariken van Nieumeghen*, printed by Vorsterman at about the same time as the English (G. W. Wolthuis, *ES* 16 (1934), 183–9) (Dutch edn. by A. L. Verhofstede [Antwerp, 1951], trans. H. M. Ayres and A. J. Barnouw [The Hague, 1924]). The Dutch play contains passages of prose—possibly intended to be spoken by a 'stage manager', possibly added for the benefit of readers—and is remarkable for its use of a play within a play. The English translation is often clumsy and stilted, but keeps something of the dramatic quality of the dialogue. It has been transformed into an exemplary and melodramatic story (a type which remained popular in the broadsheets of the sixteenth and seventeenth centuries).

Textual Notes. 3 went] *text* wene   31 What] *text* whan   35 alone] *text* alons   61 chonge] *text* chonse   63 Gretenyn] *poss.* Grecenyn   92 didycacion] *text* dilycacion   117 grownde] *text* growne

1. Mary has been sent to Nijmegen by her uncle, a priest. When she asks her aunt for lodging for the night, she is turned away with taunts.

10. *the lekenes of a man*: Here the text has a woodcut (like the others, apparently taken or imitated from those in the Dutch print), showing Mary beside a hedge being greeted by the Devil in human shape, with rich robes and a hat, through which protrude two long horns.

11. *he had but one yee*: In the Dutch this information is given in his own monologue: 'My name is Moenen with the one eye.'

49. *geste*: Dutch 'gheest'.

63. In the Dutch the names are Lijsken, Grietken, and Lijnken.

84–5. *Shertegenbosshe . . . Anwarpe*: 's Hertogenbosch . . . Antwerp.

86. *the .vii. free scyences*: possibly a literal translation of the Dutch 'die zeven vrije consten', but cf. *OED*, s.v. 'free' (adjective), 4b. Similarly, *yender* (line 95) and *wordy*

(line 109) are possible fifteenth-century English forms, but may have been suggested by Dutch 'ghindere', 'weerdich'.

96. *a play*: The reference in the Dutch is more specifically to a 'waggon-play' (*waghenspel*) called *Masscharoen*, after the character in it who is Lucifer's advocate. It is also (rather more realistically) Emmeken who recalls that it is played every year on this day. In the Dutch, it is presented in full. Moenen watches with her, and her contrition begins to appear in a little exchange with him in the middle. In the play, the Virgin Mary opposes Masscharoen and intercedes with God for sinful man. God's final speech emphatically states that mercy is always present for those who are truly repentent.

122. *caryed hyr up*: A woodcut shows a black fiend carrying Mary into the air. However, she survives and is reunited with her uncle. The Pope imposes on her the penance of wearing three large iron rings on her arms and neck. She enters a nunnery of converted sinners, and finally, as a sign of God's forgiveness, an angel frees her from the rings. Two years later she dies; her grave and the rings hanging over it are still to be seen.

L

Text: *Treatise concernynge the fruytful saynges of Davyd* (Wynkyn de Worde, 1509 [1st edn. 1508]), fo. ee i. *STC* 10902–8. *Ed.* J. E. B. Mayor, *The English Works of John Fisher*, EETS, ES 27 (1876).

Studies include: E. E. Reynolds, *Saint John Fisher* (rev. edn., Wheathamstead, 1972); J. Rouschausse, *La Vie et l'œuvre de John Fisher* (Angers, 1972); E. Surtz, *The Works and Days of John Fisher* (Cambridge, Mass., 1967). Cf. also J. W. Blench, *Preaching in England in the late Fifteenth and Sixteenth Centuries* (Oxford, 1964). John Fisher (1459–1535) (born, like Alcock, in Beverley) became Vice-Chancellor, and later Chancellor, of the University of Cambridge, and Bishop of Rochester. He was devoted to learning and collected an impressive library; he helped to induce Erasmus to visit Cambridge. He preached vehemently against Luther and his ideas. Because of his opposition to the doctrine of royal supremacy and the king's divorce he was executed in 1535. Cf. *BRUC*. His sermons on the Penitential Psalms were preached in August and September 1505, and were published at the request of Lady Margaret Beaufort, the mother of Henry VII. Latin translation in his *Opera omnia* (Würzburg, 1597).

1. *Que est ista . . .*: S. of S. 6: 9 ('Who is she that cometh forth as the dawn rising?').

8. *Zacharie . . .*: Luke 1: 78–9 ('the Orient from on high hath visited us, to enlighten those that sit in darkness and in the shadow of death').

12. *gospel of Johan . . .*: cf. John 8: 56 ('Abraham saw my day and rejoiced').

23–4. *multi reges . . .*: Luke 10: 24 ('many kings and prophets have desired to see the things that you see, and have not seen them').

66. *unable to be shewed*: L. '[Prudentia divina] in quam error cadere non potest, idem praestiterit' perhaps suggests that something has dropped out of the English text.

67. *salutem . . .*: Ps. 73: 12 ('he hath wrought salvation in the midst of the earth').

69. *saynt Poule*: cf. Rom. 13: 1 ('and those which are ordained are ordained of God').

8

A

Pecock: *The Repressor of Overmuch Blaming of the Clergy*, ed. C. Babington, RS 129, 130 (1860); *The Donet*, ed. E. V. Hitchcock, EETS 156 (1921); *The Folewer to the Donet*, ed. E. V. Hitchcock, EETS 164 (1924); *The Reule of Crysten Religioun*, ed. W. C. Greet, EETS 171 (1927); *The Book of Faith*, ed. J. L. Morison (Glasgow, 1909).

Studies include V. H. H. Green, *Reginald Pecock* (Cambridge, 1945); E. F. Jacob, 'Reynold Pecock, Bishop of Chichester', *PBA* 37 (1951); S. I. Tucker, *NQ* 203 (1958), 477–9.

(i) *MS* CUL Kk. 4. 26, fo. 53. *Repressor* II, ch. 3.

On Lollard attacks on images, and answers to them, see A. Hudson, *Selections from English Wycliffite Writings* (Cambridge, 1978), 179–81; Joy Russell-Smith, *Dominican Studies*, 7 (1954), 180–214.

(ii) *MS* BL Royal 17. D. ix, fo. 68.

109–10. Cf. Aristotle, *Ethics* I. 6.

B

MS Bodl., Laud misc. 593, fo. 2. *Ed.* C. Plummer (Oxford, 1885); *Life and Works*, ed. T. Fortescue, Lord Clermont (1869); *De Laudibus Legum Anglie*, ed. and trans. S. B. Chrimes (Cambridge, 1942).

Studies include: C. A. J. Skeel, *Tr. RHS* 10 (1916), 77–114; S. B. Chrimes, ibid. 17 (1934), 117–47; A. E. Levett in F. J. C. Hearnshaw, *The Social and Political Ideas of Some Great Thinkers of the Renaissance and the Reformation* (London, 1925), 61–87; A. B. Ferguson, *The Articulate Citizen and the English Renaissance* (Durham, NC, 1965), 111–29; C. F. Arrowood, *Speculum*, 10 (1935), 404–10.

Textual Notes. 32 the[1]] *MS om.*   40 and therfore] *MS om.*

39. *jus regale* ('monarchical law'), in which the king 'mey rule his peple bi such lawes as he makyth hymself'; cf. *jus polliticum et regale* (61) ('political and monarchical law'), in which a king 'may not rule his peple bi other lawes than such as thai assenten unto'.

46. Cf. Geoffrey of Monmouth, *Hist. Regum Britanniae* VI, ch. 4.

56–7. Cf. Matt. 7: 16, 20 ('by their fruits shall ye know them').

C

MS Bodl., Rawlinson A 338, fos. 54[v], 9[v]. *Ed.* M. S. Blayney, EETS 270 (1974). Cf. Blayney, *SP* 55 (1958), 154–63; *RES* 9 (1958), 8–17. French edn. by A. Duchesne, *Les Œuvres de maistre Alain Chartier* (Paris, 1617).

Textual Notes. 20 Likewise the] *MS* like   36 the] *MS* their. *Omissions in R supplied by Blayney from other MSS at the following places*: 30 of; 39 his, redy; 41 defendid; 43 me; 65 me

1 ff. The author, tormented by Dame Melancholy, sees in a vision Deffyaunce, Indignation, and Despair. Understanding is awakened by their words: there follow two dialogues between Understanding and Faith, and Understanding and Hope. This extract comes from a speech by Faith.

27 ff. In the *Quadrilogue*, the author, torn between Hope and Despair, falls asleep, and in his dream sees France, a noble lady, but sorrowful of countenance and with her mantle torn and defaced, with her three sons—Nobility, Clergy, and People—and listens to her reproofs and their complaints.

D

MS BL Add. 32091, fo. 52. *Ed.* D. M. Brodie, (Cambridge, 1948); ed. anon (from Chetham MS 11376) (Manchester, 1859).

Textual Notes. 13 occasioner . . . helper] *so C: MS* occasion . . . help   30 man . . . man] *MS* men . . . men

9

On MSS containing scientific and practical information, see H. S. Bennett, 'Science and Information in English Writings of the Fifteenth Century', *MLR* 39 (1944), 1–8, and R. H. Robbins 'Mirth in MSS', *E&S* NS 21 (1968), 1–25.

A

MS BL Harley 2341, fo. 5. *Index* 3571. *Ed. SL* No. 68.

This mnemonic jingle becomes a modern nursery rhyme (I. and P. Opie, *The Oxford Dictionary of Nursery Rhymes* [Oxford, 1951], 380–1). Cf. R. H. Robbins, 'English Almanacks of the Fifteenth Century', *PQ* 18 (1939), 321–31.

B

MS Bodl., Bodley 591, fo. 38ᵛ.

The Conversion of St Paul falls on 25 January. This type of prognostication is common in MSS, and remained popular (cf., for example L. Digges, *A Prognostication* [London, 1555].)

C

MS Bodl., Digby 88, fo. 97ᵛ. *Index* 579. *Ed. SL* No. 67.

The verses are accompanied by crude emblematic illustrations above each line (representing a fire, a spade, a bird on a bough, etc.). On the theme of the Labours of the Months in art and literature, see R. Tuve, *Seasons and Months* (Bryn Mawr, 1933); J. F. Willard, *Bodleian Qly. Record*, 7, No. 74 (1932), 33–9; J. C. Webster, *The Labours of the Months* (Evanston, Ill., 1938).

D

MS University Coll., Oxford, 85, p. 109. *Ed.* M. Manzaloui, *Secretum Secretorum. Nine English Versions*, EETS 276 (1977), 348.

This popular encyclopedia (ultimately from an Arabic source) purports to be an epistle from Aristotle to Alexander; it contains information on kingship, moral philosophy, cosmology, medicine, etc. For other English versions, Cf. EETS, ES 66 (1894), 74 (1898).

Textual Notes. 1 Autumpne] *MS* lutumpne   2 viii dayes] *em. Manzaloui: MS* xviii dayes   3 Decembre] *em. Manzaloui: MS* Novembre.

1. *the Leon*: Dr J. D. North points out to me that Leo must be in error for Libra, the zodiacal sign which the sun enters in mid-September.

E

MS BL Sloane 686, fo. 7ᵛ.

Walter had been a bailiff; according to a rubric in one MS he was first a knight, then a preaching friar. His original thirteenth-century work in 'anglicized Norman French' (ed. D. Oschinsky, *Walter of Henley and other treatises on Estate Management* [Oxford, 1971]) appears in an English translation (cf. Oschinsky, pp. 129–30), which presents a revised version 'belonging to a later type of agricultural literature'. It exists in a number of MSS, and is printed by Wynkyn de Worde (? *c.*1508) (facsimile in F. H. Cripps-Day, *The Manor Farm* [London, 1931]). Fifteenth-century MSS often include instructions on planting and grafting; there exists also a translation of Palladius, *De Re Rustica* (ed. M. Liddell [Berlin, 1896]), made for Humfrey, Duke of Gloucester (see *EVCS*, pp. 202–6).

Textual Note. 3 be] *MS* þe

2. *medled*: F. 'medlez'.
5. *so sharpe . . . beryng*: F. 'sy poynantz'.
11 ff. The remark about the rain is not in F.

F

Text: *The Boke of Husbandry* (R. Pynson, 1523), fo. a vii. *STC* 10994.

Attributed (by *STC* etc.) to John Fitzherbert, brother of the noted judge Sir Anthony Fitzherbert.

Textual Notes. 16 tak] *Berthelet edn. text* caste   thonge] *B. text* shonge

G

MS BL Add. 8151, fo. 201ᵛ. *Index* 1920.

From *The Lytylle Childrenes Lytil Boke*, ed. (from BL Harley 541) F. J. Furnivall, *Manners and Meals in Olden Time*, EETS 32 (1868), a volume which contains a rich array of similar advice on carving, serving, and courteous behaviour. Cf. also Caxton's *Book of Curtesye*, ed. F. J. Furnivall, EETS, ES 3 (1868). Such 'courtesy books' continue into the Renaissance (cf., for example, Giovanni della Casa's *Galateo*) and beyond. Moral instruction of a more general sort for the young is given in *The Good Wife Taught her Daughter*, ed. T. F. Mustanoja (Helsinki, 1948), or Peter Idley's *Instructions to his Son*, ed. C. D'Evelyn (Boston and London, 1935).

Textual Notes. 10 thyne] *MS om.*   12 cherlis] *MS* chorlis   24 etist] *MS* etest

H

These recipes come from two MSS: (1) Magdalene Coll., Cambridge, Pepys 1047, probably compiled at the end of the fifteenth century (ed. G. A. J. Hodgett, *Stere hit well* [London, 1972], with note on recipes by Delia Smith) contains 'capons stewed' (fo. 7ᵛ; Hodgett, p. 14) and 'tartes owte of [i.e. not during] Lente' (fo. 14; Hodgett, p. 27) (described by Delia Smith as a 'forerunner of cheese-cake'); (2) Bodl., e Mus 52, contains 'sawmon irosted' (fo. 70; cf. Hodgett, p. 18), 'partryche stewyde' (fo. 68), and 'leche lumbarde' (fo. 68ᵛ). Similar recipes occur in other MSS. Printed editions include (besides Hodgett) T. Austin, *Two Fifteenth-Century Cookery Books*, EETS 91 (1888); R. Morris, *Liber Cure Cocorum* (Berlin, 1862); Mrs A. Napier, *A Noble Boke off Cookry* (London, 1882); C. B. Hieatt and S. Butler, *Pleyn Delit* (Toronto, 1976). Cf. M. S. Serjeantson, 'The Vocabulary of Cookery in the Fifteenth Century', *E&S* 23 (1937), 25–37; on descriptions of banquets etc., W. E. Mead, *The English Medieval Feast* (London, 1931), especially ch. 3.

Textual Notes. 19 bottom] *MS* bottomb   25 and] *MS* a

I

'Aqua aurea' ('golden water for writing is made thus'): *MS* Bodl., Rawlinson C 211, fo. 14.

'Shynyng water': *MS* Bodl., Ashmole 1416, fo. 124ᵛ.

8. *globeris*: above the line the word *glowormes* has been written, apparently to explain the older term. Cf. the similar recipe in MS Bodl., e Mus 52 (fo. 61ᵛ): 'For to make a lyghte that woll schewe be nyghte. Take a grete quantyté of wormes that schynen be nyghte, and put hem in a vessell of yren on the fyre with essye hete; and then wryng ought all the mater of hem; and then put yt in a vyale of glase; and then put therto as moche of mercurii; and then sette yt in a derke place or herne [corner], and yt woll schewen lyghte inowe and yt woll lasten as long as ye woll late yt lastyn.' In Hardy's *Return of the Native* (III, ch. viii) the gamblers use glowworms as lamps.

'To sle lyse': *MS* Magdelene Coll., Cambridge, Pepys 1047, fo. 18; Hodgett, p. 35.

'To make a wyld hors tame': *MS* Bodl., Wood D 8, fo. 117.

From a work entitled 'The crafte of horsys and medysyns for the same', ended (according to the colophon) in May 1485. (It includes one or two tricks of the trade, e.g. 'to mak an old horse seme yonge'.)

Textual Note. 15–17 fest them to] *MS* fest them to them to

J

MS Bodl., Rawlinson C 506, fo. 16ᵛ.

Charms for this and other ailments are commonly found; cf. Gray, 'Notes on Some Middle English Charms', in B. Rowland, *Chaucer and Middle English Studies in Honour of R. H. Robbins* (London, 1974), 56–71.

K

MS Bodl., Bodley 591, fo. 9ᵛ.

On medical works, see Robbins, 'Medical Manuscripts in Middle English', *Speculum*, 45 (1970), 393–415; cf. C. H. Talbot, *Medicine in Medieval England* (London, 1967). Surgical works in translation include Guy de Chauliac, *Cyrurgie*, ed. M. S. Ogden, EETS 265 (1971), and Lanfranc, *Cirurgie*, ed. R. van Fleischhacker, EETS 102 (1894). John Arderne's fourteenth-century treatise *Fistula in Ano*, translated in the fifteenth century (ed. D'A. Power, EETS 139 [1910]), contains not only technical information but also some early advice on the bedside manner (e.g. to make the patients laugh with good tales) and on other matters of concern to surgeons (e.g. to make sure that the patient knows the cost before the operation is done).

Textual Note. 1 sckoll] *MS* scloll

12–13. *rede poudyr . . . oynemente*: A recipe for the 'red powder' is given at fo. 106 of the MS; the 'ointment' is probably 'this oynement apostolicon' (so called because it was made of twelve ingredients), the making of which is also described (fo. 101).

L

MS Bodl., Douce 304, fo. 5.

The MS describes various diseases and remedies, arranged according to the parts of the body.

Textual Notes. 1 is] *MS* his   10 thilke] *MS* thikke

M

Printed editions of collections of similar recipes include G. Henslow, *Medical Works of the Fourteenth Century* (London, 1899), and W. R. Dawson, *A Leechbook of the Fifteenth Century* (London, 1934). These examples are taken from BL Add. 30338, fo. 180ᵛ (items 1–3), Bodl., Laud Misc. 685, fo. 74ᵛ (item 4), and Bodley 591, fos. 45, 49ᵛ, and 55ᵛ (items 5–7).

8 ff. Cf. the recipe to 'kepe here fro fallyng' in Bodl., Bodley 591, fo. 75ᵛ: 'make leye [lye] of dovys donge and therwith wasche thyn heed.'

22 ff. Another recipe 'to gete a chylde' in the same MS (fo. 94ᵛ) involves a powder made from 'the balloke of an olde cocke or else of a yong pygge that sockythe on the moder'. The 'balockis of boris' are prescribed elsewhere (H. Schöffler, *Beiträge zur mittelenglischen Medizinliteratur* [Halle, 1919], 252). It would seem likely, therefore, that the mysterious 'blake' of line 25 is an error for *baloke*, 'testicle'.

Textual Note. 17 gladly] *MS* galdly

N

MS BL Sloane 2276, fo. 191. D. W. Singer and A. Anderson, *Catalogue of Latin and Vernacular Plague Tracts in Great Britain and Eire in Manuscripts written before the Sixteenth Century* (London, 1950), No. 22.

An English translation of the *Regimen contra epidemium sive pestem*, attributed to Benedictus Canutius (Bishop Bengt Knutsson, according to Singer and Anderson), several times printed (see *STC* 4589–93). On plague tracts, see also Robbins, *Speculum*, 45 (1970), 407; Singer, *Proc. Roy. Soc. Medicine*, 9 (1916), Pt. II (History of Medicine), 159–212; K. Sudhoff, *Archiv f. Gesch. der Medizin*, 5 (1912), especially pp. 56–61; R. H. Bowers, *Southern Folklore*, 20 (1956), 118–25.

Textual Notes. 1 whan] *MS* wh . . (*edge trimmed*) 3 wyndy] *MS* wy . . . 10 sygne] *MS* synge 12 lyghtnyng] *MS* lyghtyng

2. *appereth to reyn*: L. 'apparet pluviosa'.
7. *venemous and infecte*: L. 'aer venenosus sit et infectus'.
10. *blasyng sterre*: L. 'cometa'.

O

MS Bodl., Bodley 591, fo. 40ʳ.

Cf. the meteorological lore in Higden's translation of Bartholomaeus Anglicus, *On the Properties of Things*, eds. M. C. Seymour *et al.* (Oxford, 1975), 587 ff.

Textual Notes. 12 whight] *MS* whght 25 includit] *MS* includithe 27 cloude this] *MS* cloude & this 29, 31 brekyng] *MS* breyng

P–R

On alchemical MSS see D. W. Singer, *Catalogue of Latin and Vernacular Alchemical Manuscripts . . . dating from before the Sixteenth Century* (Brussels, 1928–31); R. H. Robbins, 'Alchemical Texts in Middle English Verse: Corrigenda and Addenda', *Ambix*, 13 (1966), 62–73. Many texts are collected in E. Ashmole, *Theatrum Chemicum* (London, 1652); modern editions include *The Book of Quinte Essence*, EETS 16 (1866), and Norton's *Ordinal of Alchemy*, ed. J. Reidy, EETS 272 (1975). Books on alchemy include: E. J. Holmyard, *Alchemy* (Harmondsworth, 1957); T. Burckhardt, *Alchemy*, trans. W. Stoddart (London, 1967); J. Read, *Through Alchemy to Chemistry* (London, 1957); C. G. Jung, *Psychology and Alchemy* (London, 1953), and *Mysterium Conjunctionis* (London, 1963), in *Collected Works*, trans. R. F. C. Hull, vols. xi–xii, xiv.

P

MS BL Harley 2407, fo. 17. *Index* 1364. Singer, *Cat. Alchem. Manuscripts*, No. 854. *Ed.* Ashmole, *Th. Chem.*, p. 350.

It is accompanied in the MS by an illustration, reprinted in *Th. Chem.* This poem on the Magi turns on the symbolic parallel (cf. Read, *Through Alchemy*, p. 60) between Christ and the Stone or *Lapis* of the alchemists, that substance variously reputed to be able to transmute base metals into precious ones, to prolong life, and to work a spiritual transformation of man. The three kings come to look upon the Christ-child (traditionally associated with the corner-stone of the building rejected by the builders), who 'figures' the Stone of Wisdom sent to Solomon. Their three gifts are equivalent to the elements of the alchemists, and to body, soul, and spirit, united like the Trinity (in the alchemical process, body, soul, and spirit are said to combine to form a permanent and indissoluble essence).

Textual Notes. 1 and] *MS om.*   4 syght] *MS* swyght   5 owr] *MS* howr   9 present] *MS* persent   10 *Aurum*] *MS* aurem   10, 16 *Myram*] *MS* meram   24 an angele] *MS* a nagels   30 cheryté] *MS* cheyte

5. *I figure*: It is tempting to suppose an error for *in figure*, but it may be possible to take it as 'I [the speaker of line 1] represent allegorically'.

10. *Aurum . . .*: 'Gold, frankincense, and myrrh'.

12. *oure luneyré*: Lunary, or moonwort, has an important role in alchemical literature (cf. the poem in *Th. Chem.*, pp. 348–9). It is, according to CCC, Oxford, MS 185, fo. 185, the 'perfection of this science': its name can be interpreted etymologically as Sun/Gold, Moon/Silver, and Mercury/Quicksilver. Perhaps the word 'oure' suggests that we are to interpret it here as the 'mystical' moonwort of the alchemists, of which the terrestrial plant is the 'shadow'.

Q

MS CUL Kk. 6. 30, fo. 14^v.

For the process of producing the Stone, see Holmyard, *Alchemy*, pp. 15–16. The insistence on its simplicity and naturalness, and the comparison to the union of bridegroom and bride, are commonly found.

Textual Notes. 14 we] *MS* whe   25, 27 oute] *MS* ou3te

22. *rede man . . . whyet woman*: These figures often appear. Thomas Norton (ed. Reidy, lines 2661–4) quotes 'Hermes':

> *Candida tunc rubeo iacet uxor nupta marito;*
> That is to say, if ye take hede therto,
> Then is the faire white woman
> Mariede to the rodie mane.

The 'red man' is 'the masculine principle in the alchemical marriage, sophic sulphur' (Reidy); the 'white woman' is the feminine principle, mercury or the alchemists' 'magnesia' (silver mixed with mercury).

R

MS Bodl., Ashmole 1492, p. 126. Singer *Cat. Alchem. Manuscripts*, No. 282.

A fragment of a fifteenth-century translation of the early fourteenth-century alchemist John Dastin (see L. Thorndike, *A History of Magic and Experimental Science* [New York, 1923–58], vol. iii, ch. V; Holmyard, *Alchemy*, pp. 145–8). There are later versions, including a verse rendering in *Th. Chem.*

Textual Notes. 5 infeccions] *MS* infeccons   27 mylke] *MS* myke

6. *leperus scab*: Base metals were commonly compared to lepers (cf. Holmyard, *Alchemy*, pp. 151, 158).

34. Here the fragment breaks off. The *Visio* continues (Thorndike's summary):

He enjoined upon nine virgins to protect his coming infancy from the poisonous

COMMENTARY ON PP. 143-5

serpent. He then entered his chamber, was absorbed by his spouse who hid him in her vitals from the serpent. She with her maidens ascended into an upper chamber. A son was born who devoured three of the virgins and turned from black to white. The serpent renewed his attacks, but the son ate the other six virgins and was turned to earth. After 40 days more he donned whitest raiment, but the colour of his countenance kept altering. We are told that that whose head is red, feet white, and eyes black is the whole mastery. Finally we reach complete triumph over the poisonous serpent and the last stage of projection in the alchemical process.

S

MS Bodl., Laud Misc. 733, fo. 6ᵛ.

An illustrated treatise on heraldry, an early fifteenth-century translation of Johannes de Bado Aureo, *De Arte Heraldica* (O. Pächt and J. J. G. Alexander, *Illuminated Manuscripts in the Bodleian Library*, iii [Oxford, 1973], No. 905). The English follows the Latin (ed. Bysshe, *Tractatus de Armis* [London, 1654]) in saying that it was compiled at the instance of Anne, sometime Queen of England (Anne of Bohemia, d. 1394). Other heraldic works include Nicholas Upton's *De Studio Militari* (ed. Bysshe), dedicated to Humfrey, Duke of Gloucester (an early sixteenth-century English translation by John Blount exists in Bodl., Eng. misc. d. 227—select edn. by F. P. Barnard [Oxford 1931]); material in *The Boke of St Albans* (see T n.); a short manual in Bodl., Bodley 487. Cf. A. R. Wagner, *Heralds and Heraldry in the Middle Ages* (Oxford, 1956).

1 ff. The information on the habits of animals is common encyclopaedic material (cf., for example, Higden's Bartholomaeus, ed. Seymour, pp. 1175-8 (the hart), 614 (the owl)). The references to authorities are rather vague: Aristotle's remark on the absence of gall is in *Hist. Animalium* II. 15; Isidore, *Etymologiae* XII, ch. 1 (*PL* 82. 427), speaks of their hostility to serpents and their curious ways of dealing with them.

T

Text: The Boke of St Albans (printed in 1486 by the 'schoolmaster printer' of St Albans), fos. f vi–f vii. *STC* 3308. Printed again by Wynkyn de Worde in 1496. Facs. edn. by W. Blades (London, 1881), and in part, with intro. and notes, by R. Hands, *English Hawking and Hunting in the Boke of St Albans* (Oxford, 1975).

The book is a 'manual of instruction in hawking, hunting, coat-armour and blazing' with other miscellaneous information. See E. F. Jacob, 'The Book of St Albans', *BJRL* 28 (1944), 99–118, reprinted in his *Essays in Late Medieval History* (Manchester, 1968). This selection comes from a list of 'terms of association' (see R. Corner, *RES*, NS 13 (1962), 229–44.

U

MS BL Cotton Vespasian B. XII, fos. 15ᵛ, 36, 95ᵛ. *Ed.* W. A. and F. Baillie-Grohman (London, 1904) (nineteen manuscripts listed). A translation by Edward, Duke of York (Master of Game in 1406), of the *Livre de Chasse* of Gaston

'Phoebus', Count of Foix and Bearn (d. 1391). (French text ed. G. Tilander [Karlshamn, 1971]; facs. edn. of BN fr. 616, with commentary, by M. Thomas and F. Avril, *Codices Selecti*, liii [Graz, 1976]).

Textual Notes. 2 seeth] *MS* sawe 5 lereth] *MS* bereth 8 shyne] *MS* sheyne 17 meve] *MS* mewe 18 what] *MS* whan 21 leire] *MS* leiþe 28 myghtily] *MS* myghtly 30 shul] *MS* shuld 32 likynge] *MS* likynge and likyng 34 gret] *MS om.* 40 and²] *MS* and his and 43 and wel] *MS* and wel and wel 44 evenyng] *MS* evenyngis 54 he] *MS om.* 61 men] *MS* man 74 hounde] *MS* houndes 75 is] *MS om.* 78 the³] *MS om.* 79 Devour] *em. B.-G.*: *MS* dedow 87 shulde] *MS om.* 91 strake] *MS* shuld strake 94 the hert] *MS om.* 95 shulde] *MS om.* 99 non] *MS* not the 106 third] *MS* first 107 than] *MS* that 111 first] *MS* frist 112 sergeaunt] *MS* shergeaunt 114 speke] *MS* spekis.

12. *semblé or gaderyng*: F. 'a lassemblee'.

21. *to the leire . . . the fewes*: F. 'au lit'.

64 ff. This extract comes from a section at the end of the book which has been added by the English translator.

67. *hertis hede*: presumably by the right side (B.-G.).

V

MS Bodl., e Mus 52, fos. 59, 59ᵛ.

Textual Notes. 9 take] *MS* take take 16 outher] *MS* ouȝt

3. MS Magdalene Coll., Cambridge, Pepys 1047 (Hodgett, p. 13) has a less sporting bait for the pike: 'Take a raw chekyn and clense hit and fyll [hit with] blacke sope and knytt both the endys and pryck hit full of holys and ley hit in the ryver and as sone as he hath etyn hit he wyll comme to land.'

W

Text: (lines 1–56) T. Satchell, *An Older Form of the Treatyse of Fysshynge with an Angle* (London, 1883) (from a MS then in private possession); (lines 56 to end) *Treatyse*, in *Boke of St Albans* (Wynkyn de Worde, 1496) (*STC* 3309), fo. i i (facs. edn. by M. G. Watkins [London, 1880]).

The work is certainly prior to the Book of St Albans; Satchell's MS (which went only as far as the instructions on trout fishing) came from the first half of the fifteenth century and was probably copied from an earlier, complete text (see Jacob, 'Book of St Albans'). The author in his defence of fishing against hunting refers to the Duke of York (d. 1415), '*late* callid mayster of game'. Izaak Walton, whose Piscator also defends fishing against a hunter and a hawker, made extensive use of this earlier treatise.

Textual Notes. 6 laburus] *S.* labure 15 folowyng] *S.* folowys 18 hym] *S.* hyt 20 brydes] *S.* bryde 30 rewares] *S.* rewarde 38 ye] *S.* he 41 cumburus] *S.* cumburs 52 deynty] *W.* deyty

3. *the seyd parabul*: recalling the opening words of the *Treatyse*, 'Salomon in hys paraboles seith that a glad spirit maket a flowryng age.'

41. *for commynly*: cf. Walton (I, 4th day, ch. 7): '[he] swims in the deep and broad

parts of the water, and usually in the middle, and near the ground, and . . . there you are to fish for him, and . . . he is to be caught, as the Trout is, with a worm, a minnow . . . or with a fly.'

52. On the chavender or chub, see Walton, I, 3rd day, ch. 3 (the old name 'cheven' was still in use in his time).

54. *he hathe the more baytes*: Cf. A. N. Marston, *Encyclopaedia of Angling* (London, 1963, 1969), s.v. 'chub': 'Chub feed on almost anything in the water, on the bottom, in weed or near the surface.' Walton recommends grasshoppers, worms, almost any kind of live fly, including 'the dor or beetle, which you may find under cow-dung; or a bob, which you will find in the same place', snails, the humble-bee, and cherries (cf. line 73), which are still listed as bait for bottom-feeding fish in Marston (p. 22).

10

A

MS NLS Asloan, fo. 291ᵛ (lines 443–546 of the poem). *Index* 1554. *Ed.* Ritchie, STS, NS 26 (1930); F. J. Amours, STS 27, 38 (1897).

Studies include: M. P. McDiarmid, *MÆ* 38 (1969), 277–90; M. M. Stewart, *Innes Rev.* 23 (1972), 3–15. On Holland's elaboration of the legend of the Bruce's heart, see Amours, pp. 297–300.

Textual Notes. 6 thay] *Bannatyne MS*: *MS* thow   40 to] *Bann.*: *MS om.*   99 flang] *Bann.*: *MS* slang.

B

MS NLS Adv. 19. 2. 2, fo. 48. *Index* 2701. *Ed.* M. P. McDiarmid, STS, 4th Ser., 4 (1968–9) (with full commentary; for this extract see VII. 407–70).

The story of Wallace's revenge for the cruel hanging of Sir Reginald Crawford and Sir Bryce Blair (who were actually executed in 1307) and other Scottish nobles is based on a similar episode in Barbour's *Bruce* (McDiarmid, ii. 138–40).

Textual Notes. 14 the] *MS om.*   34 walkning] *MS* walkand   48 thar] *MS* thai   62 thaim *MS om.*

11. *Boid*: Sir Robert Boyd, in Barbour's poem one of Bruce's earliest followers, here a steadfast companion of Wallace.

C

MS NLS Asloan, fo. 231 (lines 136–281 of the *Talis*). *Index* *303.3. *Ed.* W. Craigie, STS, NS 16 (1925).

See I. W. A. Jamieson, *Parergon*, 2 (1972), 26–36. The story is found in the twelfth-century *Speculum Stultorum* of Nigel Wireker (T. Wright, *The Anglo-Latin Satirical Poets*, RS 59 [London, 1872], i. 54–62, trans. J. H. Mozley, *A Mirror for Fools* [Oxford, 1961]). This story is that referred to in Chaucer's *NPT* (3312–16).

Textual Note. 25 this, this yong] *MS* this

1. *Kentschire*: in Nigel's version it is Apulia, and Gundulfus's father is a priest (and he does not go to Oxford to study).

29. *Coping*: cf. *Copok* in line 34, a form which occurs in Henryson's *Fables* 983. *Coppa* appears as the name of a hen in Nigel, but he has no description of the cock's marriage.

43. There is no gap in the MS, but something has been lost here. Nigel has 'Creverat et multum jam jam Gundulfus in altum, | Jamque suo patri substituendus erat' ('And Gundulf too grown tall claimed as his own | His father's living'—Mozley).

11

Edd.: A number of anthologies include these and other fifteenth-century or early sixteenth-century lyrics, e.g. those of Carleton Brown, *CB XV*; Chambers and Sidgwick, *EEL*; Davies, *MEL*; Gray, *SRL*; Greene, *EEC*; Robbins, *SL*; Sisam, *OBMEV*; Stevens, *MC* and *M&P*.

Studies include Gray, *TIMERL*; A. K. Moore, *The Secular Lyric in Middle English* (Lexington, 1951); J. Stevens, *M&P*; R. Woolf, *The English Religious Lyric in the Middle Ages* (Oxford, 1968). Performances of some of these lyrics are available on records: Argo (2) RG (5) 433 A (*Medieval English Lyrics*) (E and H), and Argo ZRG 566 (*To Entertain a King. Music for Henry VIII*) (T and U).

A

MS BL Sloane 2593, fo. 11. *Index* 117. *Ed. MEL* No. 71; *SRL* No. 2.

2. *Fowre thowsand wynter*: a traditional estimate; cf. Dante, *Paradiso* xxvi.
8. *Deo gracias!*: 'Thanks be to God'.

B

MS BL Sloane 2593, fo. 10ᵛ. *Index* 1367. *Ed. MEL* No. 66; *SRL* No. 6.

Textual Notes. 1 I syng of] *MS* I syng A of   mayden] *MS* myden.

C

MS BL Sloane 2593, fo. 34. *Index* 377. *Ed. EEC* No. 457; *MEL* No. 73; *SL* No. 27.

22. *Benedicamus Domino*: 'Let us bless the Lord'.
23. *Deo gracias*: 'Thanks be to God'.

D

MS Trinity Coll., Cambridge, O. 3. 58 (1230). *Index* 3536. *Ed. EEC* No. 173; *SRL* No. 12.

COMMENTARY ON PP. 163-6

For the music, see *MC*, p. 10. Latin words and phrases = 'Alleluia'; 'a thing to be marvelled at'; 'in one substance'; 'glory to God in the highest'; 'let us rejoice'; 'let us go on'.

E

MS Bodl., Arch. Selden B. 26, fo. 14ᵛ. *Index* 2733. See *MC*, pp. 18, 114. *Ed. EEC* No. 30; *MEL* No. 100; *SRL* No. 9.
Inspired by an Advent Epistle (Rom. 13: 11–12).

F

MS BL Add. 5666, fo. 4ᵛ. *Index* 1352. See *MC*, p. 1. *Ed. EEC* No. 144.

G

MS BL Royal 19 B. IV, fo. 97ᵛ. *Index* 1622. *Ed. EEC* No. 418.3; *SL* No. 48.
A similar folk-song has been recorded in both England and America in modern times (see G. Perkins, *Jnl. of Amer. Folklore*, 74 (1961), 235–44; ibid. 77 (1964), 263–65).

Textual Notes. 7 yerde] *MS* yarde   9 yow] *MS* yowre

1. *Pax vobis*: 'Peace be unto you'.
15. *heye*: *OBMEV* suggests '(?) eye'; 'hedge' (*OED*, s.v. 'hay' *sb.* 2) gives better sense (cf. *Owl and Nightingale* 819: 'the vox can crope bi the heie'), but a less accurate rhyme (? unless *creye* derives from MDu. *craeyen*).

H

MS Bodl., Ashmole 191, fo. 192ᵛ. *Index* 925. *Ed. MEL* No. 141; *SL* No. 155.

I–N

These are from the collection of English poems associated with the name of Charles of Orléans. *Ed.* R. Steele and M. Day, EETS 215, 220 (1941, 1946; repr. 1970). (French texts in Charles d'Orléans, *Poésies*, vol. i, ed. P. Champion [Paris, 1956]).
Studies include: D. Poirion, *Le Poète et le prince* (Paris, 1965); J. Fox, *The Lyric Poetry of Charles d'Orléans* (Oxford, 1969); N. L. Goodrich, *Charles of Orléans* (Geneva, 1967).

I

MS BL Harley 682, fo. 38ᵛ. *Index* 144. F. (Champion, p. 81) 'Las! Mort qui t'a fait si hardie'.

Textual Note. The scribal erasures and insertions (see EETS 215, p. 68) which improve the metre have been adopted.

8. *in this karfull tragedy*: F. 'en tourment'.

454

J

MS BL Harley 682, fo. 44ᵛ. *Index* 1313, F. (Champion, p. 95) 'J'ay fait l'obseque de ma dame'.

4. *In thought maylyng*: In F. 'thought' is personified, and the subject: 'le service . . . | A chanté Penser Doloreux'.

8. *karfull cry*: F. 'Regrez'.

12. *an ymage*: F. 'une lame' ('sheet').

14–15. For the qualities of the sapphire, cf. J. Evans and M. S. Serjeantson, *English Medieval Lapidaries*, EETS 190 (1937), pp. 100–3.

17. *enrous trewe*: differs from F. ('Car Eur et Loyauté pourtraire | Voulu'.

K

MS BL Harley 682, fo. 46ᵛ. *Index* 1549. F. (Champion, p. 88) 'En la forest d'Ennuyeuse Tristesse'.

3. *of Love the . . . goddes*: F. 'l'Amoureuse Deesse'.

5–8. In F. these lines are in indirect speech.

8. *forlost*: F. 'esgaré'.

14. *made thee wroth*: F. 'l'en osta'.

22. *passyng frendship . . .*: F. 'qui me guidoit, si bien m'accompaigne'.

26. F. 'affin que ne forvoye, | Je vois tastant mon chemin, ça et la'.

L

MS BL Harley 682, fo 84. *Index* 4284. F. (Champion, p. 232) 'Vostre bouche dit: Baisiez moy'.

11–12. F. 'Je prie a Dieu que mal feu l'arde! | Il fust temps qui'il se tenist coy.'

M

MS BL Harley 682, fo. 88ᵛ. *Index* 2243. No F. equivalent. *Ed. SL* No. 185; *MEL* No. 90.

N

MS BL Harley 682, fo. 98. *Index* 3890. No F. equivalent.

O

MS Trinity Coll., Cambridge, O. 2. 53 (1157), fo. 67. *Index* 769. *Ed. MEL* No. 109; *SRL* No. 89.

Textual Notes. 7, 19, 25 trowth . . . gile, 29–35 *supplied from Balliol Coll., MS 354.*

8. *a cheyré feyre*: a fair held in cherry orchards (during the brief season); a frequent symbol of the shortness of human life.

29. *the tide abidith no man*: proverbial (Whiting, T 318); cf. 21, line 143.

32. *Requiem eternam*: 'eternal rest [give unto them, O Lord]'.

P

MS CUL Add. 7350, Box 2 (a bifolium, possibly once in a King's College MS in the fifteenth century; see P. J. Croft, *RES* 32 (1981), 1–15). *Index* 3443.5. *Ed. EEC* No. 461.1 (cf. 461) (but see Croft for corrections in the text).

The topic became a popular one in later ballads (see Croft, and C. M. Simpson, *The British Broadside Ballad* [New Brunswick, 1966], 238–40).

Textual Note. 27 taught] *MS* tauȝght

1. *Inducas* . . .: Cf. the Pater Noster: 'et ne nos inducas in tentationem' ('lead us not into temptation') (Luke 11: 4).

11. *Othe*: Croft suggests that this is a variant form of *Ut*, the first syllable of the medieval scale.

15. *Bequory*: Croft identifies this as *bequarre* (ult. ⟨L. *B quadratum*⟩), the name for the note B.

19. *Veni ad me*: 'come to me'; cf. Matt. 11: 28, 12: 18.

21. Greene suggests that *tollum* may be intended for *telum* 'weapon'; Croft thinks it more likely to be a Latinization of *thole*, a vertical peg, or a peg used for fastening. ? 'And I shall set my peg to you'.

23. *bemoll*: B flat; possibly with a pun on 'be soft' (Greene).

27–9. 'Often . . . the stones have overcome me' (with an obvious sexual pun). Croft, who pointed out the correct reading *Sepe* ('often'), remarks that it is an echo of the beginning of Ps. 128 (Vg.), which was recited at compline in the Office of the Blessed Virgin.

Q

MS Balliol Coll., Oxford, 354, fo. 252. *Index* 1399. *Ed. EEC* No. 413; *MEL* No. 178.

Textual Note. 15 Milke] *em. OBMEV*: *MS* milked

15. *Milke dukkes*: 'my mother told me to milk ducks', a saucy answer to an inquisitive question (see *EEC* ad loc.).

R

MS Balliol Coll., Oxford, 354, fo. 165ᵛ. *Index* 1132.

Often reprinted, but *EEC* No. 322 offers the fullest annotation, and the complete texts of the later traditional versions (sometimes called 'The Bells of Paradise'). The interpretation of this lyric has caused considerable disagreement (see *EEC*). R. L. Greene argues (there, and in *MÆ* 29 (1960), 10–21, ibid. 33 (1964), 53–60) that it is political and topical, referring to Henry VIII's desertion of Catherine of Aragon for Anne Boleyn (one of whose badges was a white falcon). Others are unconvinced by this, and regard the poem as primarily concerned with the suffering Christ-Knight (cf. Gray, *TIMERL*, pp. 164–7). A connection with the Holy Grail has also been suggested, but can hardly be regarded as proven. It is perhaps worth remarking that Richard Hill seems to have had a taste for puzzles (see 23 B) and for riddling or enigmatic poems (e.g. *SL* No. 114, *EEC* No. 321).

S

Text: *Christmas carolles newely Inprynted* (Richard Kele, *c.*1550). *Index* 2250.8. *Ed.* *EEC* No. 473.

6. *The Saynt*: St Thomas à Becket (but 'Saynt Katheryn of Kent' (29) is unknown).
9. Apparently a line from a popular song (Greene).

T

MS BL Add. 31922 ('Henry VIII's manuscript'), fo. 37ᵛ. *Index* 409.5. *Ed. M&P*, pp. 398–9; *EEC* No. 448.
   See Stevens, *M&P*, pp. 4 ff., 386–7, and *Musica Britannica*, xviii (London, 1958).
Textual Note. 5 As] *MS* A

U

MS BL Add. 31922, fo. 39ᵛ. *Index* 3199.8. *Ed.* M&P, pp. 400–1; *EEC* No. 466.1.
   The *double entendre* is common in lyrics of this type.
Textual Note. 19 more] *MS* mere

V

MS BL Add. 31922, fo. 45ᵛ. *Index* 3405.5. *Ed. M&P*, p. 402. EEC No. 463; *EEL* No. 25.
   Possibly the name Amyas had a topical interest at court (see *EEL*, p. 337). It is also possible that this carol may have been used in a court disguising (see *EEC* ad loc. and *M&P*, ch. 11).

W

MS BL Royal App. 58, fo. 5. *Index* 3899.3. *Ed. EEL* No. 31.
   See *M&P*, p. 130.

12

A

Text: *A Gest of Robyn Hode* (Lettersnijder edn., possibly printed by Jan van Doesborch, ? *c.*1510–15). Facs. edn. by W. Beattie, *The Chapman and Myllar Prints* (Edinburgh, 1950); also printed by Wynkyn de Worde (*STC* 13689). *Index* 1915. *Ed.* F. J. Child, *The English and Scottish Popular Ballads* (Boston, 1882–98), No. 117; R. B. Dobson and J. Taylor, *Rymes of Robyn Hood* (London, 1976). No. 1.
   Numerous studies of this and other Robin Hood ballads include: W. H. Clawson, *The Gest of Robin Hood* (Toronto, 1909); Dobson and Taylor; J. C. Holt, *Robin Hood* (London, 1982), D. Gray, *Poetica*, 18 (1984), 1–39; cf. also M. Keen,

The Outlaws of Medieval Legend (London, 1961); D. C. Fowler, *A Literary History of the Popular Ballad* (Durham, NC, 1968). See *MWME* vi. 1753–808, 2019–70.

Textual Notes. 10 *de Worde print has better metre*: Fastynge so longe to be   12 thou]
W.: text om.   23 Though] *text* thougt   27 there] *W.: text* therfore 28 and wyne]
W.: text and of wyne   34 wolde] *text* wol be   43 avowe] *text* anowe   60 me]
W.: text om.   75 wolde] *text* wode   83 masars] *text* wasars   85 they] *W.:*
text om.   87 streyte] *text* steyte   101 avowe] *text* abowe   129 shyref] *text*
shyrel   144 hame] *W.: text* home   159 toke] *W.: text* to   166 schert] *W.*
sherte: *text* chert   168 gan] *W.* do: *text* gan to

9. *Grenelefe* Reynolde Grenelef is the alias given by Little John at the beginning of the fytte. An actual Tudor highwayman adopted the name 'Greneleff' (1502), 'the which . . . had many thevis at his retynew . . . of the which was reported dedes and doynges after Robyn Hode' (*Chronicles of London*, ed. C. L. Kingsford [Oxford, 1905], 257).

21. *tap*: cf. *Sir Gawain*, lines 406, 2357.

B

Text: *A litell treatise of the knight of Curtesy and the lady of Faguell* (W. Copland, ? 1556). *Index* 1486. *STC* 24223. *MWME* i. 166–7, 324–5. *Ed.* E. McCausland, *The Knight of Curtesy* (Northampton, Mass., 1922).

For the background of the story, see refs. in *MWME*, and especially McCausland Introduction and J. E. Matzke, 'The Roman du Chatelain de Couci and Fauchet's Chronique', in *Studies in Honor of A. Marshall Elliott* (Baltimore, 1910). The romance belongs to a large group of stories with the theme of 'The Eaten Heart' and to that subgroup in which the hero dies away from his lady and commands his servant to carry his heart back to her. It is similar to the *Roman du Chatelain de Couci* (eds. Matzke and Delbouille, SATF 90 [Paris, 1936]), where the hero is Renaut, Chatelain de Couci (possibly the remote progenitor of our 'Curtesy'), who dies on crusade, and the heroine la dame de Faiel (cf. our 'Faguell'). But their love is consummated secretly, and the squire is the husband's spy. A shorter and possibly older version in Fauchet's Chronicle has some close links with the English poem (e.g. the fatal wound is received 'a ung siege que les chrestiens tenoyent devant sarrazins oultre mer', and the husband has to threaten the squire with death). The date of the English romance is certainly earlier than that of Copland's print. *MWME* places it in the late fourteenth century, but the reference to the siege of Rhodes by 'Saracens' (lines 281 ff.) suggests that in its present form at least it is later: a Turkish fleet was driven off in 1320, and in 1444 the city was bombarded by the Egyptians, but the most likely reference is to the great siege of 1480 (cf. 1 M).

Textual Notes. 17 curteys] *text* curtesy   37 townes] *text* towenes   76 swoune]
text swonue   87 knyght] *text* kynght   92 Fro] *text* for   121 suffre] *text*
suffce   122 joye] *text* love   123 She] *text* he   127 lande] *text om.*   128
Were] *text* where   145 Me] *text* my   160 my] *text* me   163 herte] *text*
hirte   180 curteyse knight] *text* cutuyse knighe   191 depaynt] *text* detaynt
192 wofully] *text* wofull   211 thought] *text* tohught   244 sterte] *text* sterted
260 *text has prob. om. a word: edd. sugg.* quyckely, *but* fyersly, lyghtly, *etc. would be*
possible   264 bodi] *text* bodt   265 scarcely] *text* scartely   282 armed] *text*
armen   291 she] *text om.*   304 chast] *text* cast   306 Without] *text*

458

wichout   333 semely] *text* femely   378 withouten] *text* without   408
here] *text* herte   427 thought] *text* though   500 her] *text* us

C

Text: *Capystranus* (Wynkyn de Worde, *c*.1515) fo. B iv^v. *STC* 14649 (an incomplete text, with woodcuts. There are two later fragments of *c*.1527 and *c*.1530, possibly reflecting an interest in the continuing Turkish threat—Belgrade fell to Soliman the Magnificent in 1521, and the Hungarians were defeated by him at Mohács in 1526).

See E. Rona, in *Studies in Honor of Margaret Schlauch* (Warsaw, 1966). After the fall of Constantinople, Pope Calixtus III preached a crusade in 1455, and legates were sent to various European Courts. The Franciscan friar John (later St John) Capistrano (1386–1456) preached to great effect in Buda and elsewhere. In the spring of 1456, Muhammed advanced to Belgrade with a large army. The raising of the siege by John Hunyady, the veteran defender of Christian Hungary, accompanied by the friar and his enthusiastic followers, caused great excitement in Western Europe. On the historical events, see R. Nisbet Bain, *EHR* 7 (1892) 235–52; and J. Hofer, *Johannes Kapistran* (Heidelberg, 1964); cf. R. Schwoebel, *The Shadow of the Crescent* (Nieuwkoop, 1967), 41–8. This was an area where romantic fictions could flourish; cf. the development of the story which is the plot of Johnson's *Irene* (see S. C. Chew, *The Crescent and the Rose* [New York, 1937], 480–2). The English romance puts the friar directly in the centre of the story—it is he who after the fall of 'Constantyne' warns the Pope, and goes to Hungary to raise the standard of the crusade. It must derive from sources which are very sympathetic to the saint and which intensify the miraculous elements (there are hints of this in versions of the letters of Capistrano's companion, John of Tagliacozzo (cf. *Analecta Bollandiana*, 39 (1921), 144–7)). The popular Charlemagne romances seem to have been in the author's mind. In the printed text, the lines run continuously, but the poem seems to be in irregular tail-rhyme stanzas.

Textual Notes. 15 fereful] *text* freful   20 daye] *Bodl. frag., fo. 5: text om.*   24 go] *text* gone   39 sare] *text* sore   42 mare] *text* more   53 The] *text* they   66 laye] *text* lawe   77 agayne] *text* anone   101 crucyfyxe] *text* curcyfyxe   106 hyght] *text* hye   117 dysprave] *text* dyspray   146 stode] *text* shone   151 men] *text* mon   159 agayne they rose] *text* they rose agayne

2. *Obedyanus*: Hunyady. Possibly this form may owe something to oral transmission (Rona), but he appears as 'Onidianus' in the French chronicle of Mathieu d'Escouchy, ed. G. du Fresne de Beaucourt (Paris, 1863), ii. 325.

4. *Grecuswyssynburgh*: Belgrade (cf. German *Kriechisch Weissenburg*).

10 ff. The chroniclers were impressed by the size and number of the Turkish guns. (Tagliacozzo, ed. Wadding, p. 344). The noise (line 15) is said to have been heard nearly 100 miles away (Bain, p. 244).

20. *The Maudeleyne daye*: 22 July. Two battles have been telescoped. Hunyady entered the town by water on 14 July, at night. From the date of this naval engagement until 21 July there was an incessant bombardment (Bain, p. 246). The huge assault that followed lasted through the night. The chronicles quite commonly treat the raising of the siege as a single great battle, associated with St Mary Magdalene's day.

46. *Morpath and blacke Johan*: 'Rycharde of Morpathe a knyghte of Englonde' is not known, nor is 'blacke Johan', said to have been formerly a Turk but now 'a curteys knyght' (the text gives his name as 'Syr John Elacke'—perhaps a misprint for Blacke, or else a 'Saracen' name). Some of the crusaders certainly came from far afield—Tagliacozzo mentions Germans, Poles, and Slavs, and the Speyer chronicle (F. J. Mone, *Quellensammlung der badischen Landesgeschichte* [Karlsruhe, 1848], i. 409) adds that they came from 'England, France . . . and all lands and kingdoms in Christendom'. All agree that the majority were humble and poor.

73. *dromydaryes*: animals (cf. line 81), not 'dromonds' or vessels (Rona, pp. 349–50). They often feature in romance descriptions of battles with Saracens.

94. This was in fact a ruse of Hunyady's; the Turks were allowed to enter the outer walls unopposed.

106 ff. The basis of this incident (Capistranus's prayer) is found in the chronicles, and it is easy to see how the encouragement of the weary crusaders could develop into the miracle of our romance. Mathieu d'Escouchy (p. 327) says that through his prayer the divine power restored them so that they were fresher and of greater courage than they had been in the previous assaults. There are also hints of the reproachful, almost querulous, tone of his address to the Virgin Mary—in d'Escouchy he ends his prayer by saying to God, 'Come, lest the Turks and unbelievers say, Where is God?' Cf. also the fierce reproaches addressed by Bishop Turpin to the Virgin for allowing the Saracens to slay the French (*Sege of Melayne*, ed. S. J. Herrtage, EETS, ES 35 (1880), lines 547–8).

143–7. Cf. *Chanson de Roland*, ed. F. Whitehead (Oxford, 1947), line 2459, Caxton's *Charles the Grete*, ed. S. J. Herrtage, EETS ES 36 (1881), p. 242 etc.

148–50. Cf. Exod. 14. When he sacks Constantinople at the beginning of the romance, Muhammed is compared to Pharaoh.

13

Malory: *Ed.* E. Vinaver (Oxford, 1947, etc.) (with full commentary). Facs. edn. of Winchester MS (now BL Add. 59678), intro. N. R. Ker, EETS, SS 4 (1976); of Caxton's *Le Morte Darthur reduced in to englysshe by syr Thomas Malory* (1485), (*STC* 801), intro. P. Needham (London, 1976).

For a possible connection of the Winchester MS with Caxton in the 1480s, see L. Hellinga and H. Kelliher, *Br. Lib. Jnl.* 3 (1977), 91–113. On Malory's life, see especially P. J. C. Field, *BJRL* 64 (1982), 433–56. Numerous literary studies include: J. A. W. Bennett (ed.), *Essays on Malory* (Oxford, 1963); L. D. Benson, *Malory's* Morte Darthur (Cambridge, Mass., 1977); P. J. C. Field, *Romance and Chronicle: A Study of Malory's Prose Style* (London, 1970); M. Lambert, *Malory: Style and Vision in* Le Morte Darthur (New Haven and London, 1975).

A

MS BL Add. 59678, fos. 283, 285 (Caxton Bk. x. 55).

Malory's story of Tristan is based on a thirteenth-century French prose romance, and is worked into the framework of the Arthurian cycle.

Textual Notes. 10 seyde²] *MS om.*　　　20 hoved] *MS* heved　　　82 and what cometh thereof] *Caxton: MS om.*　　　84. .iii.] *MS* .iiii.

48. *Joyus Garde*: Sir Lancelot's castle ('Somme men say it was Anwyk, and somme men say it was Bamborow'—Alnwick and Bamburgh in Northumberland).

51. *Marke*: King of Cornwall, husband of Iseult, and uncle of Tristan. Dinadan had made a lay 'whyche spake the most vylany by kynge Marke and of his treson that ever man herde', and which makes the king 'wondirly wrothe' (Vinaver, pp. 626–7).

80–2. Malory has reduced a long speech by Dinadan on his attitude to love (F. in Vinaver, pp. 1499–1500).

83. *Bleoberys de Galys*: usually *de Ganys* (F. *Gaunes, Gannes*). At the end of Malory's book, he goes to the Holy Land with Sir Bors and Sir Ector.

B

MS BL Add. 59678, fo. 478 (Caxton Bk xxi. 3).

In this section, Malory took the outline of the story from the French prose *Mort Artu* (ed. J. Frappier [Paris, 1936], trans. J. Cable [Harmondsworth, 1971]) and an English stanzaic poem, *Le Morte Arthur* (ed. J. D. Bruce, EETS, ES 88 [London, 1903]), but added much new material. Mordred, Arthur's son by his sister Morgawse, has treacherously crowned himself king in his father's absence.

Textual Notes. (MS damaged in parts: restored readings from Vinaver.) 13–14 in the rychest] *Caxton: MS om.*　　　31 for¹] *C.: MS* wyth　　　37 slayne] *MS* slayne for　　　55 that all] *MS* all that all　　　60 hoost] *C.: MS om.*　　　62 I] *C.: MS om.*　　　68 they] *C.: MS om.*　　　101–2 good lord . . . dreme and] *C.: MS om.*　　　130 of¹] *MS* of of　　　152 hyeth] *C. (cf.* Le MA *'hye the faste'): MS* passyth on　　　204 wyl] *C.: MS* muste *(cf.* Le MA *'I will wende')*

6–8. Possibly the geographical details suggest that Malory was thinking of a similar distribution of supporters of Yorkists and Lancastrians at the time of the Wars of the Roses (Vinaver).

11–42. The description of the dream is based on the English poem.

23–4. Gawain, the king's nephew, died in an earlier battle with Mordred (Vinaver, pp. 1230–2).

115–16. This detail has been added by Malory.

128–31. This incident is found in the English poem; it is close to the realities of warfare.

166. *wawis and wyndys*: cf. 'watirs wap and wawys wanne' (173–4). Malory seems to have generated these evocative phrases from the poem's 'nothynge | But watres depe and wawes wanne'. He was not afraid of alliterative patterns in his prose (as can be seen in his version of the story of Arthur and Lucius, based on an actual alliterative poem).

14

A

MS Lincoln Cath. 91, fo. 38ᵛ. *MWME* i. 109–10, 272. *Ed.* J. S. Westlake, EETS 143 (1913); facs. edn., *The Thornton MS*, intro. D. S. Brewer and A. E. B. Owen (London, 1977).

The romance is a version of one of the recensions of the tenth-century Latin *Historia de Preliis*. On the Alexander story, see G. Cary, *The Medieval Alexander* (Cambridge, 1956); cf. M. Lascelles, *MÆ* 5 (1936), 173–88.

Textual Notes. 77 dominator| *MS* dominatorum   78 patrium| *MS* patrum

B

MS BL Royal 18 B ii, fo. 187. *MWME* i. 165, 321–3. *Ed.* A. K. Donald, EETS, ES 68 (1895). Translated from a printed version (? Geneva, 1478) of the late fourteenth-century French prose romance *Melusine* of Jean d'Arras (ed. L. Stouff [Dijon and Paris, 1932]; 1478 edn. repr. C. Brunet [Paris, 1854]). It is both a fairy-tale and a history, based on the 'vraie cronique' of the fortress of Lusignan (supposedly built by Melusine) and of the rise and fall of the family. Numerous studies include: L. Stouff, *Essai sur* Melusine (Dijon and Paris, 1930); K. Heissig, *Fabula*, 3 (1960), 170–81; J. le Goff, *Annales*, 26 (1971), 587–603 (trans. in Le Goff, *Time, Work, and Culture in the Middle Ages* [Chicago and London, 1980]).

The English is by no means a slavish translation. Some words are taken over directly from the French (e.g. *sage* (6), *doubte* (20), etc.), but there are cases where a slightly stiff diction is clearly the work of the English writer (e.g. *assistaunce* (13), *lyf naturel* (F. *vivant*) (16), *respection* (59), *revertid* (68), *serpentous* (85), etc.). Occasionally F. is expanded by means of doublets (e.g. lines 10, 16, 17–18). On the whole the translator tries to increase the pathos of the episode.

21. *Geffray*: called 'with the great tooth' (like others of Melusine's offspring he has a physical oddity—in this case a tooth that protrudes an inch or more). He is 'hardy and cruel', and has just burnt down an abbey, thus provoking his father's denunciation of Melusine. In the end, he repents.

23. *Raymond and Theoderyk*: F. 'Raimonnet', 'Thierry'. Melusine later returns in human form to nurse her children.

27. All these places are in Poitou and not far from Lusignan: Parthenay, Vouvant, La Rochelle.

28. *Forestz*: an area, F. 'Forez' (the count of Forez was Raymondin's father).

30. *Horryble*: F. 'Horrible'. Besides his terrible appearance he was so evil that when he was four years old he killed two of his nurses. He is taken to a cave and suffocated.

35–6. F. has been shortened, and possibly misunderstood here: 'mais pour Dieu et pitié ne me veuillez pas tant deshonnourer, mais veuillez demourer . . .' Eng. *wyl* probably means 'be willing to'.

43. *feed myn eyen . . .*: F. 'auray je recreation en toy'.

57. *they syghyng*: F. 'encores en souspirant' refers to Melusine.

69–70. *Adieu . . . damoyselles*: F. 'adieu tous et toutes'.

74-6. *ye reproche . . . Elynas*: F. has been redrafted—or misunderstood—here: 'affin que vous ne reprochés pas à mes enfans qu'ilz soient enfans de malvaise femme, ne de serpente, ne de faée, car je suys fille du roy Elinas . . .'

91. *an horryble cry and pyteous*: F. 'ung cri si merveilleux'.

101-2. *lyke the voyce of a mermayde*: F. 'de voix seraine'.

C

Text: *The hystory of the two valyaunte brethren Valentyne and Orson* (W. Copland, *c.*1555), fo. D iii' (there is a fragment of an earlier edn. by Wynkyn de Worde, *c.*1510). *STC* 24571.7 etc. *MWME* i. 155–6, 312–14. *Ed.* A. Dickson, EETS 204 (1937).

Studies include A. Dickson, *Valentine and Orson: A Study in Late Medieval Romance* (New York, 1929). Translated by Henry Watson (see 7 J) from a late fifteenth-century French romance (perhaps the Maillet print of 1489), which is possibly based on a lost fourteenth-century story. It is a close translation. Watson quite often uses the French word (e.g. *martyre* 115, *doubted* 128, *redoubted* 161), and sometimes there is an awkward over-literalness, e.g. in lines 56 (F. (Maillet, 1489) 'tira son chemin'), 60 (F. 'apres le salut fait'), 113 (F. 'vos propres enfans legitimes du sang royall issus'), 119 (F. 'en bon point'), 135 (F. 'la mort'), 136 (F. 'suis delibre de'), 157–8 (F. 'chargez dangoisses'), etc. But he is quite prepared to shorten the French, e.g. in lines 80 (F. 'au rebours et contraire'), 106 (F. 'plus dolente ne plus desconforte femme'), 123 (F. 'ire et courouce'), 159 (F. 'nourist e alaitta'); and on the whole his version has confidence and some style.

Textual Notes. 32 wyth] *text* wys   134 eschewe] *text* sechewe   140 their] *text* theie   141 speake] *text* seakpe   166 leding] *text* ledang

18. *a beer*: It is female in F. ('une grande ourse').

63-5. F. 'quant au respect et regard des nouvelles a peine vous en scauroye dire de bonnes car trop a de mal vostre seur'.

104. *discharged*: F. 'getta'.

109. F. 'entre toutes les desolees la plus desolee'.

109-10. F. 'vous estes cause de ma mort avancer a tort'.

151. F. 'pour cause de la nutrition de l'ourse'.

151-66. On medieval stories of 'wild men', see R. Bernheimer, *Wild Men in the Middle Ages* (Cambridge, Mass., 1952). They also appear in courtly disguisings (cf. 25 A). The son taken by King Pepin, baptized Valentine, becomes a paragon of chivalry. Orson is later conquered and tamed by his brother, and they fight as companions.

15

Caxton: Selections, ed. N. F. Blake, Clarendon Medieval and Tudor Series, (Oxford, 1973); *Prologues and Epilogues*, ed. W. J. B. Crotch, EETS 176 (1928). The following select list (in addition to the books represented in the extracts) will give some idea of Caxton's output: Chaucer's *Canterbury Tales* and *The Temple of*

Bras (*The Parliament of Fowls*); Gower's *Confessio Amantis*; various works by Lydgate, Malory, Earl Rivers (*The Dictes or sayengis of the philosophres*), and Tiptoft (see 17 E). Romances include: *Charles the Grete*, (ed. S. J. Herrtage, EETS 36, 37 [1880–1]); *The Foure Sonnes of Aymon* (ed. O. Richardson, EETS, ES 44, 45 [1884–5]); *The Recuyell of the historyes of Troye* (ed. O. Sommer [London, 1894]); *Paris and Vienne* (ed. M. Leach, EETS 234 [1957]). Religious works include: *The Craft for to Deye* (ed. F. M. Comper [London, 1917]); Mirk's *Festial*; *The Legende of Sayntes* (*The Golden Legend*; cf. 7 F n.); *The Pilgremage of the Sowle* (cf. 7 C). Moral-didactic, historical works include: *The Mirrour of the World* (ed. O. H. Prior, EETS 110 [1913]); *The Ordre of Chyvalry* (ed. A. T. P. Byles, EETS 168 [1926]); *The Chronicles of England* (cf. 1 B n.).

Numerous studies of Caxton include: N. S. Aurner, *Caxton: Mirror of Fifteenth-Century Letters* (London, 1926); W. Blades, *The Life and Typography of William Caxton* (London and Strasburg, 1861–3); N. F. Blake, *Caxton and his World* (London, 1969); C. F. Bühler, *William Caxton and his Critics* (Syracuse, NY, 1960); G. D. Painter, *William Caxton* (London, 1977); Lotte Hellinga, *Caxton in Focus* (London, 1982); and the essays in *Jnl. of the Printing Historical Society*, 11 (1975–6). Cf. also H. S. Bennett, *English Books and Readers 1475 to 1557* (Cambridge, 1922; 2nd edn. 1970); C. F. Bühler, *The Fifteenth-Century Book* (Philadelphia, 1960); K. L. Scott, *The Caxton Master and his Patrons* (Cambridge Bibl. Soc., 1976). See also *MWME* iii. 771–807, 924–51.

A

MS Magdalene Coll., Cambridge, Pepys 2124, fos. 21, 30ᵛ. *Ed.* S. Gaselee and H. F. B. Brett-Smith, *Ovyde hys booke of Methamorphose* (Oxford, 1924); facs. edn., *The Metamorphoses of Ovid translated by William Caxton 1480* (New York, 1968).

This work, a translation (1480) of a French *Ovide moralisé*, was not printed by Caxton. The first nine books were discovered only in 1966 (cf. J. A. W. Bennett, *TLS*, 14 Nov. 1966) and have been reunited with the rest of the MS.

Textual Notes. 47 servyse] *MS* sevyse   63 she²] *MS* he

2. *The eage and worlde of golde*: cf. 24 A. Ovid's original description is in *Metamorphoses* 1. 89–112.

22. *Daphne*: cf. *Met.* 1. 452–567.

24. *Phiton the grete serpente*: The story of Apollo's slaying of Python comes immediately before (*Met.* 1. 416–51).

76. The story concludes with the 'sens allegorique': the sun causes laurel trees to grow in profusion on the banks of the river Peneus (the father of Daphne), or, in another allegorical interpretation, the story illustrates the virtue of chastity.

B

Text: *The Historye of Reynart the Foxe* (1481), fo. b 1ᵛ. STC 20919. *Ed.* N. F. Blake, EETS 263 (1970) (with full commentary). Facs. edn. Paradine Reprints (London, 1976).

Studies of the Reynard stories include: R. Bossuat, *Le Roman de Renard* (Paris, 1957); J. Flinn, *Le Roman de Renart* (Toronto, 1963); H. R. Jauss, *Untersuchungen zur mittelalterlichen Tierdichtung* (Tübingen, 1959). Caxton made his translation from a Dutch version, probably that printed by Gerard Leeu at Gouda in 1479.

Textual Notes. 10 he] *text* be   31 can] *text* cam   35 ye] *text* yt   were] *text* woere   46 cratched] *text* crutched   48 the[1]] *text* de   72 his[2]] *text* this   74 his] *text* is   136 be] *text om.*

92. *Chafporte*: Blake points out that Caxton has taken a low nickname (MDu. *cafpoerte* 'chaff-gate', i.e. 'exit for waste') as a place-name.

136. *Chiere priestre . . .*: 'dear priest, may God protect you'.

C

Text: *The book callid Caton* (1483), fo. b vii. *STC* 4853.

Caxton says that he translated the book from French (probably from one of the versions of *Le Cathon en françoys*), and it is clear even from this extract that he has often taken over French words and forms. The book consists of a series of (more or less) moral tales. This story is a version of the extremely popular tale 'the weeping bitch' or 'the weeping puppy' (see *The* Disciplina Clericalis *of Petrus Alfonsi*, ed. and trans. E. Hermes, trans. P. R. Quarrie [London, 1977], 9 ff.); its numerous appearances include the ME *Dame Sirith* (*EMEVP* No. VI).

1. *Peter Alphons*: Petrus Alfonsi, in his twelfth-century collection, the *Disciplina Clericalis* (eds. A. Hilka and W. Söderhjelm, Acta Soc. Scient. Fennicae 38. 4 [Helsingfors, 1911]), tells the story (No. XIII; Quarrie, pp. 124–5), but with a dog not a cat. Caxton seems to have been attached to the cat; when he translates the same story again from Macho's Aesop (in the 'Fables of Alfonce', No. XI) he transforms F. *chienne* into *catte*.

D

Text: *The Book of the subtyl historyes and Fables of Esope* (1484), fos. m 5', r 6. *STC* 175. *Ed.* R. T. Lenaghan (Cambridge, Mass., 1967); facs. edn., Scholars' Facsimiles and Reprints (Delmar, NY, 1975).

Caxton's 'Aesop', a fine book with many woodcuts, is translated from Julien Macho's version of the fable collection of Steinhöwel. The book consists of a 'Life' of Aesop, the main medieval collections of Aesopic fables, fables of Avianus (*c.*AD 400), and stories from the *Disciplina Clericalis* and from Poggio's *Facetiae*. Our first fable (Book V, No. XV) is from a group of fables called by Steinhöwel *extravagantes antique* (ancient, but not in the accepted canon of the 'Romulus' collection of Aesopic fables). It is very similar to that told by Henryson (18 B). The second is from the collection of *facetiae* of the Italian humanist Poggio Bracciolini (1380–1459) (cf. 24 A n.).

Textual Notes. 2 rercerceth] *text* rerherceth   27 dyde] *text* dyte   47 so] *text* so so   50 as] *text om.*

3. *herd or flock*: F. 'tropeau'.

48. *of hit*: F. 'qui nous a donne tant de biens'.

E

Text: *The boke of Eneydos* (1490), fo. A i. *STC* 24796. *Ed.* W. T. Culley and F. J. Furnivall, EETS 57 (1890).

Translated from a French retelling, the *Livre des Eneydes*.

Textual Note. 66 and] *text* dna

28–9. On Caxton's connection with the abbey, see Blake, *Caxton and his World*, pp. 80–2.

70–1. See W. Nelson, *John Skelton, Laureate* (New York, 1939), 40 ff. Skelton was very fond of this title.

75. *epystlys of Tulle*: This work has not survived. For Skelton's Diodorus, see 24 A.

87. Arthur: the eldest son of Henry VII (d. 1502, aged fifteen).

16

MS Folger Libr., Washington, V. a. 354, fo. 122. *Index* 3495. *MWME* v. 1371–4, 1611–13. *Ed.* M. Eccles, in *The Macro Plays*, EETS 262 (1969) (with commentary); cf. facs. edn. of Macro Plays (so named after an early owner, The Revd Cox Macro), ed. D. Bevington (New York, 1972).

Studies of the play include: M. P. Coogan, *An Interpretation of the Moral Play, Mankind* (Washington, 1947); W. K. Smart, *MP* 14 (1916), 45–58, 293–313, *MLN* 32 (1917), 21–5; P. Neuss, in *Stratford-upon-Avon Stud.* 16 (1973). On morality plays in general, see D. M. Bevington, *From Mankind to Marlowe* (Cambridge, Mass., 1962); T. W. Craik, *The Tudor Interlude* (Leicester, 1958); R. Potter, *The English Morality Play* (London, 1975); B. Spivack, *Shakespeare and the Allegory of Evil* (New York, 1958); R. Weimann, *Shakespeare und die Tradition des Volkstheaters* (Berlin, 1967) (= *Shakespeare and the Popular Tradition in the Theater*, ed. R. Schwartz [Baltimore, 1978]); G. Wickham, *Early English Stages 1300 to 1600*, vol. i (London, 1959); A. Williams, *Annuale Medievale*, 4 (1963), 5–22; F. P. Wilson, *The English Drama 1485–1585*, ed. G. K. Hunter (Oxford, 1969).

Textual Notes. 7 have hade] *MS* hade   27 avaunte] *MS* avaunce   33 certyfye] *MS* crertyfye   40 venymousse] *MS* vemynousse   42 ther] *MS* the   streyt] *MS* strerat   49 *MS* dryff draff mysse masche   88 play] *MS* pray   216 synfull] *MS* sympull   228 *milicia*] *MS* nnilicia   252 gesonne] *MS* gesumme   275 And] *MS* A   wery] *MS* wery wery   276 tomorn] *MS* tomorow   286 in] *MS* and   296 yowr] *MS* ther   298 this] *MS* thi   301 for] *MS* fo   303 ey] *MS* eyn   307 schelde] *MS* schede   346 this] *MS* ?ths   385 xuld] *MS* xull   397 *hasta*] *MS* hastu   442 Cristys] *MS* crastys   443 wer] *MS* wher   453 flowte] *MS* flewte   457 Ye] *MS* yo   461 ys] *MS om.*   477 hem] *MS* hym   482 felon] *MS* felow   483 the qwytt] *MS* qwyll   487 *non*] *MS* no   516–17 *These lines transposed in MS*   518 wethere] *MS* & wethere   520 con] *MS* com   524 And] *MS* A   597 as] *MS* ab   605 Farwell] *MS* For well   611 And] *MS* A   646 own] *MS* ow3n   666, 678 And] *MS* A   683 rennynge] *MS* rennyge   694 taryynge] *edd.: MS om.*   712 And] *MS* A   727 the¹] *MS om.*   736 solace] *MS* solalace   737 not] *edd.: MS om.*   752 to God and to] *Eccles: MS* go on to   754 *et²*] *MS* sit   764 caytyfs] *MS* cayftys   776 ny] *MS* my   805 thye] *MS* pye   812 ys] *MS* ys ys   825 pirssid] *Eccles: MS* pirssie   829 the] *MS om.*   834

be redusyble] *MS* reducylle, *corr. to* redusyble   844 *MS* My doctrine ys convenient
Inclyne yowr capacite   854 I] *MS* he   862 shall] *MS* scha   863 sowle]
MS sowe   hys] *MS* yys   870 prowe] *MS* prewe 879 monytorye] *MS* manyterge
894 *libere*] *MS* liebere 906 condicions] *MS* condocions   910 diverse] *MS*
duerse   912 grant] *Eccles: MS om.* 913 angellys] *MS* angell

1. Mercy is a man in this play (cf. 'ser', line 48).
32. Cf. Col. 1: 18, 1 Cor. 12: 27.
43. Cf. Matt. 3: 12, Luke 3: 17.
57. 'Corn serves for bread', etc.
72. A leaf is missing from the MS. More vices have arrived to mock Mercy; Nought is dancing.
126. *Pravo te*: 'I curse thee'.
142. *Osculare . . .*: 'kiss the anus'.
154–5. Proverbial; cf. Whiting, W 300.
180. Gal. 6: 7, but proverbial (Whiting, S 542).
228. 'The life of man is a warfare on the earth'; cf. Job 7: 1 (Vg.).
234. Cf. 11 O, line 8 n.
237. *Mesure ys tresure*: Proverbial; cf. Whiting, M 461.
287. Cf. Job 23: 10.
292. Cf. Job 1: 21; 'The Lord gave, and the Lord hath taken away, as was pleasing to him; blessed be the name of the Lord.'
301. *Tytivillus*: This devil is often referred to (his function is often to collect the words of chatterers in church), but it is only in this play that he has a major role. See M. D. Anderson, *Drama and Imagery in English Medieval Churches* (Cambridge, 1963), 173–7; Gray, *SRL* No. 78; M. Jennings, 'Tutivillus', *SP* 74 (1977) (Texts and Studies).
321. 'Remember, O man, that thou art ashes, and to ashes thou shalt return'; cf. Job 34: 15 (the phrase is frequently used in devotional works).
322. *the bagge*: Possibly the badge is the sign of the cross written on the paper, which Mankind is wearing (Smart; Eccles compares *Mary Magdalene*, where the three Maries enter 'with sygnis of the passion pryntyde upon ther breste'). Possibly it is simply the verse from Job, which is to remind him of his mortal nature.
324–6. Cf. Ps. 17: 26 (AV), 'With the pure thou wilt show thyself pure; and with the froward thou wilt shew thyself froward'; Ps. 132: 1 (AV), 'Behold how good and how pleasant it is for brethren to dwell together in unity'.
343. *Hoylyke*: meaningless? Perhaps 'a pun on *holy*, with possible meanings "hole-like", "hole-lick", or a leek called *holleke*' (Eccles).
397. 'Neither with the spear nor with the sword does the Lord save'; cf. 1 Sam. 17: 47 (the reference is to David's words as he approaches the heavily armed Goliath).
435. Smart (pp. 21–5) points out a similarity to the 'resurrection' scenes in mumming plays. Cf. A. Brown, *Folklore* 63 (1952), 65–8.
440. *in nomine patris*: 'in the name of the Father'.
456. *si dedero*: 'If I shall give [sc. I shall expect money in return]'.
461. This seems to be a reference to some large and grotesque devil mask which Titivillus is wearing.
471. *Estis . . .*: 'Are you monied?
473. *Ita . . .*: 'Yes, truly, master.'

475. 'I am the lord of lords'; cf. Deut. 10: 17, Rev. 19: 16. The phrase is used by the tyrannical Pilate in one of the Towneley plays (XXIV), as is the word *caveatis* 'beware'.

478. *Ego probo sic*: 'I will test him thus'.

487. 'Not unto us, O Lord, not unto us'; Ps. 113: 9.

488–9. Proverbial; cf. Whiting, D 191, B 317.

497. *.v. vowellys*: Perhaps an allusion to the '.v. wellys', i.e. the Five Wounds of Christ (Smart, pp. 297–8). Eccles suggests that Nowadays may be 'varying this formula to refer to his cries of pain: "A! e! i! o! u!"'.

505–15. The villages named are all in East Anglia: Sawston, Hauxton, and Trumpington just south of Cambridge; Fulbourn, Bottisham, and Swaffham to the east of Cambridge; East Walton, Gayton, Massingham, and another Swaffham are in Norfolk, near Lynn. The named people (or at least their families) have been identified in records. It is probably significant that two of the three avoided by the vices (Alexander Wood of Fulbourn and William Allington of Bottisham) are known to have been justices.

512. *a noli me tangere*: 'a touch-me-not' (cf. John 20: 17, but probably proverbial (Whiting, N 121)), i.e. an irritable fellow, not be to interfered with.

516. *For drede . . .tuas*: 'for fear of hanging'. *In manus tuas . . .* 'into thy hands, O Lord, I commend my spirit' (Ps. 30: 6, Luke 23: 46) was used in prayers to be said before going to sleep and by the dying; *qweke* is used jocularly for the sound of choking.

520. *neke-verse*: a Latin verse (usually Ps. 50: 3) which if read might save a first offender from hanging.

522. the left hand is the Devil's.

544. 'In the name of the Father, and of the Son, and of the Holy Spirit'.

554. 'Our Father, which art in heaven'.

555. *lede on my helys*: cf. Whiting, L 132.

576. *xall*: 'shall (have)'.

578. *ad omnia quare*: ? 'with a reason for everything'.

593. *the deull ys dede*: cf. Whiting, D 187.

614. *Sent Patrykes wey*: i.e. to death, for in legend St Patrick was taken in a vision down to hell and purgatory.

616. *ecce signum*: 'behold, a sign'.

628. *Sent Audrys holy bende*: i.e. silk bands (for the neck). Eccles notes that such 'tawdrey laces' were hallowed at the shrine of St Audrey in Ely Cathedral.

660. Cf. Whiting, G 194.

665. *sub forma jurys*: 'in legal form'.

685. *hade I wyst*: cf. Whiting, H 9.

687–93. *Carici tenta*: Nought's attempt at *Curia tenta*, 'the usual heading for a manor roll' (Eccles). Similarly, he has *regitalis* for *regis* and *nullateni* for *nullatenus*.

692. *Tulli*: Cicero, i.e. 'our rhetorician'.

693. *Anno regni regis nulli*: 'in the regnal year of King Nobody'. This, with the earlier reference to Edward, has been taken as an indication that the play was written when Edward IV was 'no king' (i.e. between October 1470 and April 1471), but it may simply be a joke at the expense of Nought. After 693 a line has apparently been omitted.

750. *In trust ys treson*: cf. Whiting, T 492.

754–5. 'Law and nature, Christ and all justice condemn the ungrateful one, and lament that he was ever born.'

767. Eccles. 1: 2.

771. *ubi es?*: 'where are you?'

779. *domine . . .*: 'O lord, lord, lord'.

780. *cepe coppus*: i.e. *cape corpus* ('take the body'), 'a capias or writ of arrest and the sheriff's answer in his return that the defendant has not been found in his jurisdiction' (Eccles).

781. *non est inventus*: 'he is not found'.

826. 'For this is the change of the right hand of the Most High: he overthrows the wicked, and they are not'; Ps. 76: 11, Prov. 12: 7.

830. *Miserere . . .*: 'Have mercy on me, O God.'

834. *Nolo . . . inquit*: 'I do not wish the death of a sinner, he said'; cf. Ezek. 33: 11.

838. *The proverbe*: cf. Whiting, T 514.

850. 'Go, and now sin no more'; John 8: 11.

857–8. Cf. Whiting, W 693.

862. *usque . . . quadrantem*: 'up to the last farthing'. Cf. Matt. 5: 26.

866. 'Behold, now is the accepted time! behold, now is the day of salvation'; 2 Cor. 6: 2 (used as a Lenten epistle).

882. *Jacula . . . ledunt*: 'Darts fore-announced wound less'. Proverbial, apparently.

894. *Libere . . . nolle*: 'Freely to will, freely not to will'.

901–2. 'The Lord preserves thee from all evil. In the name of the Father, the Son, and the Holy Spirit'; cf. Ps. 120: 7.

912. *per suam misericordiam*: 'through his mercy'.

914. *vitam eternam*: 'eternal life'.

17

On scholarship and learning, see R. Weiss, *Humanism in England during the Fifteenth Century* (Oxford, 1957); W. F. Schirmer, *Der englische Frühhumanismus* (Leipzig, 1931); E. Sammut, *Unfredo duca di Gloucester e gli umanisti italiani* (Padua, 1980); E. F. Jacob, *Florida Verborum Venustas* (Manchester, 1973); K. B. McFarlane, 'William Worcester: A Preliminary Survey' in J. Conway Davies (ed.), *Studies presented to Sir Hilary Jenkinson* (Oxford, 1957), 196–221; S. Moore, *PMLA* 27 (1912), 188–207, ibid., 28 (1913), 79–105. Worcestre's *Itineraries* are edited by J. H. Harvey (Oxford, 1969).

A

MS BL Royal 18 A. xxiii, fos. 7ᵛ, 61. *Index* 1597. *Ed.* (from Lincoln Cath. MS) M. Science, EETS 170 (1925).

A number of MSS date the translation to 1410; one describes the author as 'John Walton, formerly canon of Osney'. See Hammond, *EVCS*, pp. 39–41. Cf. P. P. Courcelle, *La Consolation de philosophie dans la tradition littéraire* (Paris, 1967); M. Gibson, *Boethius* (Oxford, 1981).

Textual Notes. 16 in] *Linc. Cath. MS: MS om.* 24 wenden] *L.: MS* wende 30 fulle] *L.: MS* full 40 he] *MS* hem 41 alle] *L.: MS* all 52 yow] *MS* yov 56 perles] *MS* pereles 57 eye] *so two other MSS: MS* sight 66 governed] *so four other MSS: MS* grounded 67 derke] *MS* derk 72 in] *L.: MS* of

1. *sche*: Lady Philosophy, who has approached the bed of the sorrowful Boethius.

41. At the end of the preceding prose, Boethius and Philosophy have concluded that God and true happiness are one and the same thing. The first stanza of this *metrum* of Walton's is written out, apparently as a devotional lyric, in the margin of an early sixteenth-century book; see *SRL* No. 91.

49. *Tagus*: a river (Tajo) in Spain famous for its gold-bearing sand.

51. *Erynus*: Hermus, a river in Turkey, also famed for its gold.

53. *Indus*: the great river which flows from Kashmir through Pakistan.

55. *grene stones*: L. 'virides lapillos', i.e. emeralds, which the Indus mixes (L. 'miscens') with pearls.

B

MS CUL Ii. 6. 39, fo. 180ᵛ. *Ed.* F. N. M. Diekstra, *A Dialogue Between Reason and Adversity* (Assen, 1968).

The MS (probably early fifteenth-century) contains contemplative and theological works as well as this paraphrase of the first ten dialogues of Book II of *De Remediis Utriusque Fortunae* (1358–66). On Petrarch and his influence in England, see N. Mann, *Petrarch Manuscripts in the British Isles* (Padua, 1975), and in *Apollo*, 94 (Sept. 1971), 176–83; and *Il Petrarca ad Arquà*, eds. G. Billanovich and G. Frasso (Padua, 1975), 279–89; cf. also C. Trinkaus, *The Poet as Philosopher* (New Haven and London, 1979). For the topic of 'true nobility' cf. E below.

Textual Notes. 2 odious] *MS* odiouȝs 6 not be] *MS* not be not 25 am] *MS* ham 27 sche] *MS* sch

C

MS BL Add. 60577, fo. 14. Facs. edn. by E. Wilson, *The Winchester Anthology* (Cambridge, 1981).

The anthology (last quarter of the fifteenth century) contains many religious, moral, and miscellaneous pieces, as well as this verse translation of the proem and Book I of Petrarch's *Secretum* (Latin text in *Opere latine di Francesco Petrarca*, eds. A. Bufano *et al.* [Turin, 1975], 43–259; trans. W. H. Draper [London, 1911]).

21 ff. Cf. Augustine, *Confessions* viii–ix.

24. *fictree*: 'I cast myself down . . . under a certain fig-tree, giving full vent to my tears; and the floods of mine eyes gushed out . . .' (*Conf.* viii).

D

MS BL Add. 11814, fo. 22. *Index* 1526. *Ed.* E. Flügel, *Anglia*, 28 (1905), 255–99, 421–38.

The English translation of part of Claudian's *De Consulatu Stilichonis* (done in 1445 at Clare, Suffolk, according to the MS) may well be the work of Osbern

Bokenham (see N. Toner in *Sanctus Augustinus*, ii (Rome, 1956), 493–523).
Bokenham (b. 1393, d. after 1464), was an Augustinian Friar of Stoke Clare, and
visited Italy at least twice; he was also the author of *The Legendys of Hooly Wummen*
(ed. M. S. Serjeantson, EETS 206 [1938]) and of the *Mappula Angliae*, a
translation of that part of Higden's *Polychronicon* which deals with England, as well
as of other works. (For a possible political (Yorkist) significance in the translation,
see Flügel.) The metre of the main part of the translation—long unrhymed lines,
with a caesura in the middle (marked in the MS) and occasional alliteration—is
very unusual. In the MS the translation faces a copy of the Latin text. Claudian (b.
c.AD 370) was a popular poet in the Middle Ages, especially for his *De Raptu
Proserpinae*; see O. A. W. Dilke, *Claudian—Poet of Declining Empire* (Leeds, 1969);
A. Cameron, *Claudian—Poetry and Propaganda at the Court of Honorius* (Oxford,
1970). *De Consulatu* celebrates the consulship (AD 400) of the Vandal commander-
in-chief of the armies of Rome, Stilicho. He is unwilling to accept the office: the
regions of the empire all lament, and eventually appeal to Rome, who finally
succeeds in persuading him. (Our extract corresponds to Claudian II. 362–85.)

6. *which was ... patrone*: not in L. (Romulus was the legendary founder of
Rome).
8. *Gradivus*: Mars, the god of war.
9. *Histirlonde*: the land of the Danube (L. *Hister*).
Scicia: Scythia (the translation has used the spelling of the Latin in the MS).
12. *Quirinus*: originally a local god of Rome, later identified with Romulus (MS
notes 'Romulus idem').
Bellona: Roman goddess of war (MS notes 'dea belli').
13. *an oke*: associated with fortitude in MS note ('quercus. fortitudo').
14. *hir handis ... helde up*: in devotion according to MS note ('elevacio manuum.
devocio').
15–18. *Metus ... Pavor ... Formido*: explained in a note at the foot of the MS:

metus. is		of consideracion of perell
pavor. is	dreed	sodeyn. withouwte consideracion
formido. is		taking awey mannis wittis.

(In L. Metus is called a lictor.)
17. *lorer boughes*: associated with wisdom in MS note ('laurus arbor sapientiae').
18. *righte bleike*: not in L. (unless it is an attempt at L. 'succincta', 'girt up').

E

Text: *The declamacyon which laboureth to shewe wherin honoure sholde reste* (Caxton,
following the *Boke of Tulle of Old Age* [1481], probably translated by the antiquarian
William Worcester, and *de Amicicia*), fos. c 4ᵛ, f 4ᵛ, f 6. *STC* 5293. *Ed.* R. J.
Mitchell, *John Tiptoft* (London, 1938), App. I.
Studies include: R. J. Mitchell; Weiss, *Humanism*, especially pp. 112–22;
Schirmer, *Frühhumanismus*, pp. 107–16. Tiptoft probably became interested in
humanistic studies while he was at University College, Oxford. He was in Italy in
1458–61, studied under Guarino, and collected books—he possessed copies of
Sallust, Lucretius, and other classical and humanistic writers (see Weiss, *Bodleian
Qly. Record*, 8 (1935–8), 157–64; Mitchell, *The Library*, 18 (1937), 67–83). He

became deeply involved in English politics and highly unpopular, and was executed in 1470. Caxton also attributes to him the translation of Cicero's *De Amicitia* and there seems no reason to doubt this (see the discussion by N. Davis in D. A. Pearsall and R. A. Waldron (eds.), *Medieval Literature and Civilization. Studies in Memory of G. N. Garmonsway* [London, 1969], 251–3). The *Declamation* is a fairly free version of the *De Nobilitate*, probably by Buonaccorso da Montemagno (d. 1429). (A French translation by Miélot also exists.) The topic of the nature of true nobility was much discussed in antiquity, the Middle Ages, and especially fifteenth-century Italy: see C. Trinkaus, *Adversity's Noblemen* (New York, 1940); M. Greaves, *The Blazon of Honour* (London, 1964); Mitchell, *Engl. Miscellany*, 9 (1958), 23–37.

Textual Notes. 25 rechelesnesse) *text* rechelenesse   46 thynke] *text* thyn   72 theyr] *text* the

1. *Faders conscript*: the equivalent of L. *patres conscripti* ('elected fathers'), the collective title of the Roman senators.

71. *drowned . . . foryetefulnesse*: cf. L. 'medias in tenebras demersus es' (BL Harley 3332).

123–4. *wherunto . . . comforte*: L. 'in qua semper omnem spem detuli meam'.

133. *connynge and lectrure*: L. 'virtutem'.

F

Text: A Lytell Treatyse . . . (Wynkyn de Worde, 1497), fo. A iv. *STC* 24866.

Other sections include 'other maner speche to bye and selle'. The conversation manual is followed by a courtesy book with an interlinear French translation, a specimen business letter ('A prentyse wryteth to his mayster fyrste in Englysshe and after in Frensshe'), and another letter to a 'ryght dere and wellbeloved gossep'. Another French vocabulary by Caxton is edited by H. Bradley, EETS, ES 79 (1900).

G

MS BL Arundel 249, fos. 9, 11, 14ᵛ, 15, 16, 17, 17, 21ᵛ, 21ᵛ, 28, 46, 60, 60ᵛ. *Ed.* W. Nelson, *A Fifteenth-Century School Book* (Oxford, 1956).

Probably composed about 1500. For another (probably early sixteenth-century) *Vulgaria* from Magdalen College School, see N. Orme, *Renaissance Qly.* 34 (1981), 11–39. Other examples in printed books include the *Vulgaria quedam abs Terencio* of Anwykyll (the first Magdalen College School grammar master), that of his successor Stanbridge (ed. White, EETS 187 [1932]), and the collection of Horman (1519) (ed. M. R. James, Roxburghe Club 169 [1926]). The Winchester anthology (see 17 C) has one which includes some verses.

Textual Note. 20 oute of the] *MS* oute the of

2. *Hedynton*: Headington, now a suburb of Oxford.

9. *a dawe*: Nelson notes that the rules of most schools forbade the keeping of pets.

12. *the castell*: Oxford Castle, now a prison.

17. *this faire*: Possibly the annual fair of St Giles (early September).

23. *Carfaxe*: the central cross-roads of Oxford. The great fourteenth-century riot on St Scholastica's Day began in the Swyndlestock Tavern here. Oxford life was still violent: another sentence (Nelson, No. 221) says that many scholars keep in their chambers all day 'forto be seen vertuouse felows' but at night they rush out armed into the streets 'like as foxis doth oute of their holys' to rob men of their money.

H

MS BL Add. 6274, fo. 6 (a late sixteenth-century transcript). Reprinted in J. H. Lupton, *The Life of John Colet* (London, 1909), 277 ff.

On Colet, see Lupton; J. B. Trapp, in R. R. Bolgar (ed.), *Classical Influences in European Culture 1500–1700* (Cambridge, 1976), 205–21, and in *Studies in Church History*, 17 (1981), 127–48; Sears Jayne, *John Colet and Marsilio Ficino* (Oxford, 1963); Emden, *BRUO*, pp. 462–3. Colet spent his early academic life in Oxford (with a visit to Italy in 1492–3); from 1505 he was in London, as Dean of St Paul's. The Statutes were handed over to the first High Master of his school, William Lily, in 1518.

Textual Notes. 30 other] *MS* oder   31 induce] *MS* indure   34–5 Sedulius . . . Juvencus] *MS* Sedulus . . . Juvencius

30. *the Accydence*: his *Aeditio*, which became part of 'Lily's Grammar'; see Lupton, App. B.

32. *Institutum . . .*: *Christiani hominis Institutum*, written for the school, and printed first in a miscellaneous volume, *Lucubrationes* (1514); see S. Knight, *The Life of Dr. John Colet* (Oxford, 1823), 384–7.

33. *Copia*: Erasmus's book on rhetoric, *De Copia Verborum*.

34–5. The 'Christian authors' mentioned are all early—Lactantius (third century; probably author of a poem on the phoenix), Prudentius (fourth century; writer of hymns and lyrics, and didactic poems like the *Psychomachia*), Proba (fourth century; daughter of a Consul, and author of a Christian Virgilian cento), Sedulius (fifth century; author of the *Carmen Paschale*), Juvencus (fourth century; author of a poem on the Gospels)—except for the contemporary humanist Mantuan (= Giovan Battista Spagnoli) (1448–1516). They were, of course, read in the Middle Ages, but their Latin is clearly thought by Colet to be 'literature' rather than 'blotterature'.

18

Henryson: *The Poems of Robert Henryson*, ed. Denton Fox (Oxford, 1981) (with full commentary); Selections: *Robert Henryson. Poems*, ed. C. Elliott (2nd edn., Oxford, 1974).

Studies include M. W. Stearns, *Robert Henryson* (New York, 1949); J. MacQueen, *Robert Henryson* (Oxford, 1967); D. Gray, *Robert Henryson* (Leiden, 1979).

A

MS NLS Adv. 1. 1. 6, fo. 365 (this is the 'Bannatyne' MS, an extensive collection of early Scottish poetry made by George Bannatyne of Edinburgh in the 1560s; facs. edn., intro. D. Fox and W. A. Ringler [London, 1980]). *Index* 2831.

Textual Notes. 11 wude] *MS* wid   125 wewche] *MS* wrewche

91–2. For the proverb, see Whiting, W 275.

B

Text: *The Morall Fabillis of Esope The Phrygian* (T. Bassandyne, Edinburgh, 1571). *Index* 3703.

Henryson's collection of thirteen fables derives from two medieval traditions—the Latin Aesopic fable (represented by a twelfth-century collection) and the stories of Reynard the Fox. The nearest equivalent to 'The Wolf and the Wedder' is in one of Steinhöwel's *fabulae extravagantes* (see 15 D n.). It is a widespread folktale.

Textual Notes. 14 with] *text* wit   20 that] *Hart print*: *text om.*   22 wichtlie] *Craik* (NQ *204 (1959), 88–9)*: *text* wretchitlie   62 thay] *text* lhay   83 till ane rekill] *Charteris print*: *text* still quhill ane strand   94 Syne] *text* Tyne

96. *quhyte as ane freir*: i.e. a Carmelite, or White Friar, who would wear a white mantle.

122, 126. Proverbial.

153. Proverbial; cf. Whiting, H 47.

161. Proverbial; cf. Whiting, C 296.

C

Text: *The Testament of Cresseid* (H. Charteris, Edinburgh, 1593). *Index* 285.

This poem is much discussed; see the studies listed above, the references given by them, and Fox's notes.

Textual Notes. 6 gart] *Ruthven MS*: *text* can   48 esperans] *Anderson print* esperance: *text* Esperus   89 quhilk] *text* quhik   94 or refute] *Thynne 1532 edn. of Chaucer*: *text* on fute   155 fronsit] *text* frosnit   164 *gyte*] *edd. (Th.* gate)   *text* gyis   178 gyte] *Th.* gyte: *text* gyis   gay] *Th.*: *text om.*   205 unricht] *Th.* unright: *text* upricht   216 and] *An.*: *text om.*   216 Philogie] *An.*: *text* Philogie   222 With] *An.*: *text* Quhyte   238 widderit] *text* widderit   260 gyte] *Th.*: *text* gyse   275 or] *Th.*: *text* in   286 retorte] *Th.*: *text* returne   328 throw] *text* thow   337 mingit] *Th.* menged: *text* minglit   363 beedes] *Th.*: *text* prayers   382 spitall] *text* hospitall   432 ray] *Th.*: *text* array   442 clapper] *text* clappper   479 Go] *Th.*: *text* To   480 leif] *text* leir   487 mervellous] *text* mervellons   489 richt] *text* richt richt   491 companie] *text* companie thai come   493 Worthie] *Th.*: *text* Said worthie   523 he] *text om.*   549 efflated *An.*: *text* elevait   554 keipit] *Th., An.* keipt: *text* keipt gude

5. *in middis of the Lent*: i.e. it is the first month of spring (the sun enters Aries on the vernal equinox).

43. *Diomeid*: the Greek prince who had become Cresseid's lover after she was sent from Troy to the Greek camp.

62. *the fatall destenie*: cf. Chaucer, *TC* 5. 1.

151–263. For full discussion of Henryson's descriptions of the planetary gods, see the studies listed above and Fox's notes. He uses traditional details with great freedom and imagination—e.g. the association of Saturn with melancholy, leprosy, coldness, age, and beggars, or of Jupiter, his traditional enemy, with brightness and youth, etc.

261–3. There was a legend that the man in the moon was banished there for stealing thorns; see O. F. Emerson, *PMLA* 21 (1906), 831–929.

343. *cop and clapper*: the traditional equipment of the leper. On leprosy in medieval literature and life, see R. M. Clay, *The Medieval Hospitals of England* (London, 1909); S. N. Brady, *The Disease of the Soul* (Ithaca, NY, 1974); P. Richards, *The Medieval Leper and his Northern Heirs* (Cambridge, 1977).

407–69. This formal lament of Cresseid (in nine-line stanzas) uses topics from 'mortality' literature (e.g. the *ubi sunt*) and from the complaints of fallen princes (cf. the refrain 'all women may be ware by me' in the 'Lament of the Duchess of Gloucester' (1441), in Robbins, *HP* No. 72).

19

Dunbar: *Ed.* J. Kinsley, *The Poems of William Dunbar* (Oxford, 1979).

Studies include: J. W. Baxter, *William Dunbar: A Biographical Study* (Edinburgh, 1952); I. S. Ross, *William Dunbar* (Leiden, 1981).

A

MS Magdalene College, Camb., Pepys 2553 (Maitland Folio MS), p. 318. *Index* 1599.5.

Textual Note. 24 Quhome] *MS* Quhone

B

Text: Ane litil tretie intitulit The Goldyn Targe (Chepman and Myllar, Edinburgh, n.d.) (Walter Chepman and Androw Myllar, the first printers in Scotland, were granted a patent by James IV in September 1507; facs. edn. of their prints with notes by W. Beattie [Edinburgh, 1950]). *STC* 7349. *Index* 2820.5.

On *The Goldyn Targe* see D. Fox, *ELH* 26 (1959), 311–34. This extract is the beginning of the poem.

Textual Notes. 19 hoppis] *text* happis   47 quhilk] *text* rycht

7. *in purpur cape revest*: cf. Virgil, *Aen.* vi. 1640–1.

14. Cf. Chaucer *Kn. T., CT* A 1496.

63. The 'hundred ladies' include Nature, Venus, and other goddesses. When the poet creeps closer, he is arrested by the archers of the Queen of Love.

C

Text: 'Rouen' print of *The Tretis of the Tua Mariit Wemen and the Wedo* (either printed in Rouen, or by foreign workmen in Scotland; see Beattie, pp. xiv–xv), fo. b i. *STC* 7350. *Index* 3845.5.

This extract corresponds to lines 410–510 of the poem. On Midsummer Eve, the poet sees three 'ladies' in green, who speak at some length about their husbands. The discussion ends with a satiric question: 'Quhilk wald ye waill to your wif gif ye suld wed one?'

Textual Notes (the many minor printing errors in this text (see Beattie facs.) have been silently emended). 40 fra] *Maitland Folio MS: text* for   wemen] *MF: text* men   83 sittis] *MF: text om.*   91 lig] *MF: text* lak

6 ff. Cf. Chaucer, *WB Prol.*, *CT* D 587–92.

14. Proverbial (Matt. 7: 15); cf. Whiting, W 474.

95. *legeand*: a word associated with saints' lives (the Wedo earlier has described her 'taill' as a 'preching' and a 'lesson' to her 'sisters in schrift').

D

MS NLS Adv. 1. 1. 6 (Bannatyne), fo. 117. *Index* 417.5.

John Damian was made Abbot of Tungland in 1504; he was an alchemist as well as a 'medicinar'.

Textual Note. 67 blaksmyth] *Asloan MS: MS* myth

16. Probably a reference to the medical learning for which Bologna was famous.

65 ff. Daedalus made wings for himself and Icarus in order to escape from the Labyrinth, which contained the Minotaur, half-bull, half-man; Vulcan was a fire-god and smith who made thunderbolts, thrown down—according to one story—from heaven by Jupiter.

73. *Sanct Martynis fowle*: perhaps the martin (which migrates at Martinmas) or (Kinsley) the hen-harrier (F. *oiseau de Saint-Martin*), a bird of prey.

E

MS NLS, Adv. 1. 1. 6, fo. 35. *Index* 688.3.

Textual Note. 13 clowis] *MS* clowss

8. *Surrexit dominus* . . .: 'The Lord has risen from the tomb', a versicle from the Mass for Easter Day.

9–10. Cf. Rev. 12: 9.

29. Probably an allusion to the ringing of bells on Easter Day (Kinsley; cf. Langland's 'men rongen to the ressurexion', *PP1.* B. xviii. 425).

F

Text: 'Rouen' print, fo. b 3. *Index* 1370.5.

Textual Notes (as in C, minor printing errors are silently corrected). 15 vanité] *text* vainte   26 Takis] *Bannatyne MS: text* tak   59 tragidie] *text* trigide

4. *Timor mortis conturbat me*: 'The fear of death disturbs me'. The phrase comes from the Office of the Dead; it is used elsewhere (see *EEC* No. 370).

17 ff. That all estates 'go to' death, and that death 'takes' irresistibly young and old, rich and poor, are ideas prominent in the Dance of Death (cf. 4 D), but found also in other kinds of medieval 'mortality' literature (e.g. the 'Vado Mori'; see *CB XV* No. 158). Dunbar does not allude to the distinctive 'dance' of the victims with Death.

46. *Playis heir ther pageant*: cf. 26 C 17 (an almost identical phrase is used in a 'Lament of Edward IV', perhaps by Skelton (*CB XV* No. 159)).

51. *The Monk of Bery*: Lydgate.

53 ff. Not all the names in this list of Scottish poets can be identified. Of the following something is known: *the gude Syr Hew* (53) is probably Sir Hugh Eglinton, brother-in-law of Robert II, not otherwise known as a poet; Andrew of Wyntoun (54), prior of Lochleven in the early fifteenth century, author of a verse chronicle; Johne Clerk (58) may be the 'Clerk' to whom some poems in the Bannatyne MS are attributed; for Holland (61) see 10 A; John Barbour (61), author of the *Bruce*; Sir Mungo Lockhart (63) of Lanarkshire, not otherwise known as a poet; Sir Gilbert Hay (*fl.* 1450) (67), translator of *The Buke of the Law of Armys* and author of an Alexander poem; for Blind Hary (69), see 10 B; Patrick Johnestoun (71) is known as a producer of interludes at Court in the late fifteenth century, and the 'Thre Deid Pollis' usually attributed to Henryson is attributed to him in the Bannatyne MS; Merseir (73) is presumably the 'Mersar' to whom a number of poems are attributed in the Bannatyne MS; possibly one of the two Roulls (77–8) is the author of 'the cursing of Sr Johine Rowlis upoun the steilaris of his fowlis' in the Bannatyne MS; on Henryson (82) see 18; Johne the Ros (83) is mentioned in Dunbar's *Flyting with Kennedy* (Kinsley, No. 23); Stobo (86) is John Reid, priest, secretary to successive kings; Quintyne Shaw (86) has a poem in the Maitland Folio MS attributed to him; Walter Kennedy (89) is Dunbar's adversary in the *Flyting* and the author of some surviving poems (see Kinsley, No. 23).

20

Douglas: *Edd.* Priscilla J. Bawcutt, *The Shorter Poems of Gavin Douglas*, STS 4th Ser., 3 (1967) D. F. C. Coldwell, *Virgil's* Aeneid *translated into Scottish Verse by Gavin Douglas*, STS 3rd Ser., 25, 27, 28, 30 (1950–7).
  Studies include Priscilla Bawcutt, *Gavin Douglas* (Edinburgh, 1976).

A

Text: *The Palis of Honoure* (W. Copland, London, *c.*1553), fo. I ii. *STC* 7073. *Index* 4002.5.
  This extract corresponds to lines 1828–1980 of the poem. In a dream, Douglas is taken before Venus, and 'tried' for blasphemy against her. Calliope intercedes for him, and entrusts him to a nymph, who accompanies him to the Palace of Honour.

Textual Notes. 8 was] *Charteris edn. (Edinburgh, 1579): text* of   19 ingraf] *text*

ingarf   29 oppositionis] *text* opposionis   32 Eclipsis] *Ch.: text* eclipse   57 Swa]
Ch.: text Fra   59 soithly] *text* soithla   me] *text* my   126 mad] *Ch.: text*
malt   130 ladyis] *text* lydyis   134 passage] *Ch.: text* passagis   141 mane]
Ch.: text name

17. *the Ursis twane*: the constellations of the Great and the Little Bear.

18. *the sevyn sterris*: the Pleiades.

Pheton: Phaethon, son of Helios, the Sun, who attempted to drive the chariot of his father.

The Charlewane: Charles's (i.e. Charlemagne's) Wain, the Plough.

19-21. Cf. Ovid, *Met.* 10. 155-61. Ganymede was carried off by the eagle of Zeus, and became his cupbearer.

23. *Dorida*: cf. Ovid, *Met.* 2. 11-14. Doris, wife of Nereus, mother of the sea-maidens, the Nereids.

B

MS Trinity Coll., Cambr. O. 3. 12 (1184), fos. 53ᵛ, 65, 130. *Index* 1842.5; cf. *STC* 24797.

Textual Note. 10 bawme] *text* bawne

1 ff. This extract (iii, ch. 8) corresponds to lines 506-87 of *Aeneid* iii.

2. *the forland Cerawnya*: the Ceraunian mountains in Epirus.

7. L. 'sortiti remos' ('after we had allotted the order of rowing').

11-12. L. 'fessos sopor inrigat artus' ('slumber flows through our tired limbs').

16. *Palynurus*: Palinurus, the pilot of Aeneas' ship.

21. *Arthuris huyf*: Arcturus.

The Hyades (L. 'pluviasque Hyadas') were the daughters of Atlas, nymphs who gave moisture to the earth, and were placed in the sky as stars.

22. *Watlyng Streit*: the Milky Way.

the Horn: Ursa Minor.

Charle Wayne: see 20 A 17-18.

These correspond to L. 'geminosque Triones' ('the twin Bears, i.e. Ursa Major and Ursa Minor).

23. *fers Orion*: a giant and hunter, turned into a constellation; lines of stars form his belt and sword.

26. *a bekyn*: L. 'clarum . . . signum', probably 'a loud signal'.

50-1. Castrum Minervae in Calabria, south of Brindisi (the harbour is the Portus Veneris).

65. *lugyn land*: L. 'terra hospita' ('land of our sojourn').

79. *Helenus*: a son of Priam.

90-2. These places—Lacinium, Caulon, Scylaceum (mod. Squillace)—are on or close to the south coast of Calabria.

103. *Caribdis*: Charybdis, a whirlpool in the straits of Messina.

124. The Cyclopes were one-eyed giants; their 'coast' is in the area of Mt. Etna.

127-40. Much expanded from *Aeneid* iii. 571-7.

142. *Enchelades*: Enceladus, a giant killed by Jupiter and buried under Mt. Etna.

157 ff. This extract (iv, ch. 4) corresponds to lines 129-72 of *Aeneid* iv.

162. *From Massilyne horsmen*: L. 'Massylique . . . equites'. The Massyli were a people of North Africa.

163. *a full huge sort*: L. 'odora canum vis' ('keen-scented, powerful hounds').

179. *Ascanyus*: Ascanius, the son of Aeneas.

189–90. L. 'Cretesque Dryopesque fremunt pictique Agathyrsi'. The Dryopes were supposed to live near Mt. Parnassus, the Agathyrsi perhaps in Thrace.

223. *Tyriane*: of Tyre; i.e. of Carthage, colonized from Tyre.

226. *Dardan*: Dardanius, a son of Jupiter and Electra, founder of the Trojan race.

238. *nymphis, hait Oreades*: L. 'Nymphae'. The Oreades were mountain nymphs.

245–6. L. 'coniugium vocat, hoc praetexit nomine culpam'.

247 ff. On this prologue, see Bawcutt, especially pp. 180–6.

254–5. It is the morning of 15 December, the winter solstice.

273. The setting and rising of Orion (see line 23 n.) were associated with storms and rain. In *Aeneid* i. 535 he is called 'nimbosus' (Douglas: 'stormy Orion'), and the constellation itself thought to be hostile to sailors.

275–6. Cf. Henryson at 18 C 151–68.

279–80. Hebe is the daughter of Zeus (Jupiter) and Hera (Juno), the handmaiden of the gods, who poured out nectar for them. She is associated with youth and the renewal of life, but 'her nakedness and loss of "array" is linked with the fall of leaves in autumn. Ganymede, who took over her "office", is identified with the sign Aquarius into which the sun moves on leaving Capricorn' (Bawcutt, p. 185).

21

Text: A Treatyse how ye hye fader of heven sendeth Dethe to somon every creature (J. Skot, n.d.). *STC* 10606 (cf. 10603–5). *Index* 1341.8. *MWME* v. 1374–7, 1613–18. *Ed.* A. C. Cawley (Manchester, 1961) (with commentary). (*Elckerlijk*, ed. H. Logeman [Ghent, 1892], trans. A. J. Barnouw, *The Mirror of Salvation* [The Hague, 1971].)

Studies include (in addition to the books listed in 16 n.): C. Brooks and R. B. Heilman, *Understanding Drama* (New York, 1945), 100–10; V. A. Kolve in S. Sticca (ed.), *The Medieval Drama* (Albany, 1972); L. V. Ryan, *Speculum*, 32 (1957), 722–35.

Textual Notes (see Cawley for more extensive refs.). 28 rod] *text* rood   31 theves] *text om.*   111 ado that] *text* I do   156 acqueyntaunce] *text* acqueynce   251 maketh] *text* make   260 agayne come] *text* come agayne   271 sayd] *text* say   286 remembre] *text* remenbre   301 endynge] *text* ende   303 thus] *text* this   317 them] *text* them go   324 we] *text om.*   325 holde] *text* bolde   326 bolde] *text* holde   417 sholdest] *text* sholdes   426 no] *text om.*   453 caught] *text* caugh   469 And] *text* An   471 forsoke] *Pynson frag.*: *text* forsake   526 be] *text* by   527 she] *text* he   558 voyder] *text* voyce voyder   560 servyture] *text* servyce   565 passe] *P.*: *text* scape 587 me] *text om.*   606 have] *P.*: *text* gyve   653 have it] *text* have 656 *Knowlege*] *text* Kynrede   657 lede] *text* led   666 *Knowlege*] *text* Kynrede   678 may] *text* myght   682 in] *text* in my   695 hevenly] *text* heven   720 pyne] *text* payne   727 devynyté] *text* devyuyte   739 handes] *text* hande   743 kyst] *P.*: *text* kysse   753 seven sacramentes] *text* same sacrament   780 our] *text*

your   786 *Strength*| *P.: text om.*   868 loved| *text* love   875 Mary| *P.: text*
Holy Mary   902 memoryall| *text* morall   905 Dyscrecyon| *text* dycrecyon
908 for and| *text* and

10–11. Proverbial: Ecclus. 7: 36; cf. Whiting, E 84.

33. *I heled theyr fete*: Christ washed the disciples' feet (John 13: 5 ff.); here used as an image of his healing of suffering mankind.

36–7. *the seven deedly synnes . . .*: of which four are mentioned. The others are Envy, Gluttony, and Sloth.

50. Cf. Gal. 5: 15.

116. Cf. 11 O 2. In the *Dance of Death*, the Constable is arrested by Death (cf. *Hamlet* V. ii. 328–9: 'this fell sergeant Death | Is strict in his arrest').

117–18. Cf. Gen. 3: 19.

119. Cf. Matt. 24: 50–1. The suddenness of Death's coming is emphasized in 'mortality' literature; cf. 11 O 11–12.

143. Proverbial (cf. 11 O 29).

144–5. Cf. Rom. 5: 12.

168. *wyttes fyve*: the five senses: sight, smell, hearing, taste, touch.

248. *Promyse is duty*: cf. line 821. (Proverbial; cf. Whiting, W 609).

302. Proverbial; Whiting, D 162.

309–10. Proverbial; Whiting, P 418.

379. Probably proverbial (Cawley compares 'fayre promese ofte makyth foollis fayne').

413. Proverbial; Whiting, M 630.

457–8. Cf. Chaucer, *Pars. T.* (*CT* I 358): 'Soothly, whan man loveth any creature moore than Jesu Crist oure Creatour, thanne is it deadly synne.'

536. *Confessyon*: the second part of penance, the first being contrition (549), and the others absolution (568 ff.) and satisfaction (707).

545. Cf. Zech. 13: 1.

552. *moder of salvacyon*: probably referring to confession in general (cf. 536, 545) rather than to the character on the stage.

572. *oyle of forgyvenes*: probably a general reference to the healing quality of oil, rather than a specific reference to the oil of the sacrament of extreme unction (the 'oyntement' of line 709).

581 ff. This prayer is similar to the prayers to be said by a dying person in the *Book of the Craft of Dying* (ed. C. Horstman, *Yorkshire Writers*, ii. 414–15) (Cawley).

596. *Moyses table*: The two tables of the law given to Moses on Mt. Sinai were sometimes taken as 'figures' of the sacrament of baptism and penance.

618. *Purgatory*: the place where those who die in God's grace must be purified from their venial sins and suffer the punishment still due for mortal sins that have been forgiven.

638. The garment of contrition, perhaps the white sheet worn by public penitents, is put on (possibly over Everyman's original fine clothes, or more probably over his partially naked body, which has been bared for the scourging).

697–8. The making of a testament was an essential and solemn step in the preparation for a good death.

707. *Presthode*: Priesthood, who gives Everyman, now in a state of grace, communion and extreme unction (709), could well have been played by the actor who took the part of Confession.

714–18. The authority of a priest, because it is spiritual, is superior to all civil and temporal authority (which is itself derived from God).

737. *.v. wordes*: the words of consecration used by the priest at Mass, 'hoc est enim corpus meum' ('for this is my body').

740. Cf. Matt. 16: 19, 18: 18.

755 ff. Cf. Acts 8: 18–20. The reference is to the sin of simony, the buying and selling of spiritual things.

769. Presumably Everyman has gone off, or to another part of the stage, to receive the last sacrament (749), and the preceding attack on bad priests is addressed to the audience (Cawley).

787. *Judas Machabee*: Judas Maccabeus, the leader of the Jews in their revolt against Syria.

801. Probably a proverbial expression meaning 'I'm off!' Perhaps 'tappe' is 'top, the tow on a distaff' (said by women taking their distaff to a neighbour's house), or 'tape', i.e. 'I tuck up my skirts and fasten them'.

870. Cf. Eccles. 12: 8.

885. I.e. at the Last Judgement, the general judgement of all men at the end of the world.

886–7. *in manus tuas . . .*: see 16, line 516 n.

891. It is likely (though not absolutely necessary) that this remark refers to actual singing of a liturgical or ecclesiastical kind, with its strong associations of the heavenly choirs of angels. The angel must appear on some raised structure (cf. 'Here above', 895).

915. *Ite, maledicti . . .*: 'Go, ye accursed ones, into eternal fire' (Matt. 25: 41).

22

A

Text: *The Passetyme of Pleasure* (Wynkyn de Worde, 1517). *STC* 12949 (cf. 12948, 12950–2). *Index* 4004. *Ed.* W. E. Mead, EETS 173 (1928) (with notes).

On Hawes, see also Hammond, *EVCS*, pp. 268–71; *Minor Poems*, ed. F. Gluck and A. B. Morgan, EETS 271 (1974). These extracts correspond to lines 148–96, 253–94, 337–71, 5474–87 of the poem.

Textual Notes. 26 theyr] *text* rheyr   37 grehoundes] *text* grehounde   53 gloryous] *text* glorions   64 behynde] *text* behonde   72 La] *text* Of la   76 with] *text* wich

32. *Pegase*: Pegasus, the winged horse which sprang from the blood of Medusa when Perseus slew her.

97. Cf. Chaucer, *Gen. Prol.*, *CT* A 9.

120 ff. There seems to have been in the Middle Ages, as well as later, a fascination with automata and exotic mechanical toys (see Mead's note, H. R. Patch, *The Other World* (Cambridge, Mass., 1950) 267 and n.; cf. Mandeville's description (ch. 23) of the golden peacocks that are made to dance and sing at the feasts of the Great Khan).

126. *Amour*: 'Love of exquisite delight'.
132–4. Cf. Whiting, D 40.

B

Text: *The Shyp of Folys of the Worlde* (R. Pynson, 1509), fo. h ii. *STC* 3545. *Ed.* T. H. Jamieson (Edinburgh, 1874; repr. New York, 1966).

Studies include: A. Pompen, *The English Versions of the Ship of Fools* (London, 1925; repr. New York, 1965). Brant's German text is edited by F. Zarncke (Leipzig, 1854), M. Lemmer (Tübingen, 1962); trans. E. H. Zeydel (New York, 1944). Barclay used Jacob Locher's Latin adaptation, the *Stultifera Navis* (printed 1497) and a French version by Rivière (printed 1497). There is another English (prose) version by H. Watson (see 7 J) (Wynkyn de Worde, 1509).

12–13. A common idea; cf. Chaucer, *Pard. T.*, *CT* C 473–4 (which Barclay may well be echoing), *Pars. T.*, *CT* I 591.

C

Text: *Certayne Egloges of Alexander Barclay Priest*, appended to *Stultifera Navis* (J. Cawood, 1570). *STC* 3546 (cf. 1384–5). *Ed.* B. White, EETS 175 (1928) (with long introduction).

Cf. H. Cooper, *Pastoral* (Cambridge, 1977). Eclogues i–iii are based on the *Miseriae Curialium* of Aeneas Silvius, iv–v on the Eclogues (printed 1498) of Mantuan (Giovan Battista Spagnoli (1448–1516)). This extract is from Eclogue v (lines 62–116); Latin text in White.

Textual Note. 24 As] *text* At

43. *driving the foote ball*: a very popular and very violent sport, often leading to 'great effusion of blood', repeatedly condemned and forbidden (see White's note; J. Strutt, *The Sports and Pastimes of the People of England* [1801], ed. J. C. Cox [London, 1903; repr. Bath, 1969], 93–7; J. Robertson, *Uppies and Doonies* [Aberdeen, 1967]).

D

Text: *The famous Cronycle of the warre which the Romayns had agaynst Jugurth* (R. Pynson, ? 1525) fo. N iv^v (1st edn. ? 1520). *STC* 21626–7.

On Sallust in the Middle Ages, see B. Smalley in R. R. Bolgar (ed.), *Classical Influences on European Culture A.D. 500–1500* (Cambridge, 1971), 165–75. The Latin text is *Bellum Jugurthinum*, xciii. This episode from the account of the campaign of the consul Marius (157–86 BC) against Jugurtha, the ruler of Numidia in North Africa, concerns the taking of a fortress set in a great rock in the middle of a plain.

Textual Notes. 23 By] *text* But   25 lytell] *text* tytell   41 thought] *text* though   83 as] *1557 edn.*: *text* and

4. *seyng . . . frustrate*: L. 'quoniam frustra erat'.
8. *a certayne Lumbard*: L. 'Ligus' ('Ligurian').
14–16. *Bycause . . . manere*: apparently Barclay's expansion. There are in this

extract a number of other expansions or explanations, e.g. line 17 'somtyme crepyng, somtyme clymyng', 44–6 (L. 'temptans omnia et circumspiciens'), 56–8 (L. 'uti cuiusque ingenium erat'), 99–101 (the explanation of the military testudo), 134–7 (the rather generalized version of L. 'sic forte correcta Mari temeritas gloriam ex culpa invenit').

62. *.iiii. hundred men*: L. 'quattuor centuriones' ('four centurions').

89. *audacyté and boldnesse*: L. 'audaciam'.

113–14. *objectyng cowardyse agaynst Marius*: L. 'Mario vecordiam objectare'.

23

Other examples of this miscellaneous 'merry matter' include the burlesque *Turnament of Tottenham* (in *Middle English Metrical Romances*, eds. W. H. French and C. B. Hale [New York, 1930]) and comic tales like those of 'Howleglass' or Till Eulenspiegel (see. C. H. Herford, *Studies in the Literary Relations of England and Germany in the Sixteenth Century* [Cambridge, 1886], F. W. D. Brie, *Eulenspiegel in England* [Berlin, 1903]) or *The Friar and the Boy*, *The Boke of Mayd Emlyn that had .v. Husbondes and all Kockoldes*, etc. See the collection in W. C. Hazlitt, *Remains of the Early Popular Poetry of England* (London, 1864–6). For a selection from jestbooks and merry tales see J. Wardroper, *Jest upon Jest* (London, 1970). On jestbooks, cf. S. J. Kahrl, *SR* 13 (1966); on fabliaux in this period, see R. H. Robbins, *Moderna Språk*, 142 (1970), 237–44.

A

Text: *The demaundes joyous* (Wynkyn de Worde, 1511). *STC* 6573. *Ed.*: facs. edn., intro. J. Wardroper, (London, 1971).

This little collection of about fifty riddles is based partly on an early sixteenth-century French collection, *Demandes joyeuses en manière de quolibets*. Riddles are found scattered in MSS of the fifteenth and sixteenth centuries (see H. A. Person, *Cambridge Middle English Lyrics* (Seattle, 1953), Nos. 61–6, for some examples in verse). On riddles in general, see Archer Taylor, *The Literary Riddle before 1600* (Berkeley, 1951). The answers are: (i) The erthe; (ii) But a stones cast; (iii) No more but one if it be long ynough; (iv) His heles; (v) That is bees; (vi) The dewe; (vii) Bycause they come not up and offre; (viii) Bycause when they se the aulters covered they wene theyr maysters goo thyder to dyner; (ix) It is a catte when she lycketh her arse; (x) Yf men sholde sette there a henne, she wolde laye egges, and they wolde fall upon mennes hedes; (xi) The henne, whan God made her; (xii) Bycause she can not sytte; (xiii) Whan the gander is upon her back.

B

MS Balliol Coll., Oxford, 354, fos. 214, 219. Puzzles from Richard Hill's commonplace book (cf. 11 R); it also contains recipes and conjuring tricks.

Textual Note. 11 hight] *MS* high

The answers are: (i) 382 apples—and in this reconyng ther may remayn non odd apple in his hond tyll he cum to the last apple that he had with hym whan he went his way [a table setting out the various stages is given in MS]; (ii) That is to say, Yssabell; (iii) That is Alisson.

C

Text: *Here begynneth the dyalogus or commynicacion betwixt Salomon the King of Jherusalem and Marcolphus* . . . (G. Leeu, Antwerp, 1492), fos. a ii, a iii, d iv. *STC* 22905. *MWME* iii. 737–8, 895–7. *Ed.* E. G. Duff (London, 1892).

The OE dialogues between Solomon and Saturn present a debate between rival sages, and a wide range of learning. In the later Middle Ages Solomon's rival, under the name of Marcolphus, becomes his parodist, and a maker of proverbs or a fool. Leeu's version is probably based on one of the many Latin texts of the dialogue.

Textual Notes. 7 This] *text* Thls   11 gote] *text* goet   13 of] *text* ef   14 gote] *text* goet   15 hosyn] *text* hasyn   19 altercacion] *text* altercacon   22 answere] *text* vnswere   27 yave] *text* yawe   37 that] *text* tyat   42 thought] *text* thougt   43 a] *text* &   49 he] *text* be   52 commaunded] *text* commannded   55 movyd] *text* meovyd   61 thens] *text* theus   Jericho] *text* jerirho

D

Text: *The fyftene joyes of maryage* (Wynkyn de Worde, 1509), fo. k ii˅. *STC* 15258 (cf. 15257.5, a fragment of 1507 edn.). Utley, *CR* No. 274. (French *Les XV. Joies de Mariage* (? late fourteenth/early fifteenth century), ed. J. Rychner [Geneva, 1963], J. Crow [Oxford 1969].)

The English version is probably based on a Lyons edn. *c.*1480–90, repr. F. Heuckenkamp (Halle, 1901) (Crow). A much more polished later version is *The Batchelars Banquet* (1603) (ed. F. P. Wilson [Oxford, 1929]).

Textual Notes. 59 gracyousely] *text* gracyouesely   63 thynkynge] *text* thykynge   69 Here] *text* htre   72 go] *text* do   97 galaunt] *text* glaunt   111 make] *text* maste   128 Of] *text* yf   141 Goddes] *text* goodes   151 it] *text om.*   162 Our] *text* a   163 suche] *text* snche   279 were] *text* wrre   282 playeth] *text* playneth

24. *dyvers other countenaunces make*: F. (Heuckenkamp) 'faire telle contenance et telle' perhaps suggests that she imitates the various 'faces' made.

69–70. *cast | Ynto the lepe*: F. 'mis en la nasse'. This image, which is frequent in the work (cf. lines 185, 257, 303), is introduced at the beginning of the author's prologue.

79–80. In F. it is the ladies who have 'bent . . . theyr engyne' ('toutes ont tendu leur engin pour le prendre').

82. *other*: 'the others' (F. 'et autres aussi').

97 ff. Crow notes that the author of the *Quinze Joies* 'hits off exactly the formal courtesies of this amorous exchange', but that there is 'the underlying irony of a game played according to rules, but whose outcome is already determined'.

145–6. F. 'Et a ladvanture la dame lui a fait signe quelle se tayse'.

151. F. 'je ne le prendrai point'.

162 ff. F. 'a Nostre Dame de tel lieu'. The reference to a pilgrimage is removed in *The Batchelars Banquet*, where the mother 'makes motion of a journey . . . to visit or feast with some friend, or to some faire, or whatsoever other occasion presents its selfe'. The bad reputation which pilgrimages—at least in the eyes of some moralists—could have appears prominently in the 'second joy'.

177. *Saynt Loy*: St Eligius, b. *c*.590 in Limoges. He is appropriate because he is French and especially because (as patron of smiths and carriers) he is associated with horses; see N. Davis, *LSE* 1 (1967), 13–14, and H. Bächtold-Stäubli, *Handwörterbuch des Deutschen Aberglaubens*, ii (Berlin, 1929–30), 785–9.

205–13. Much expanded from F. 'Puys sen vont tous au jardin, et vont jouant par les violiers . . .'.

E

Text: *The Gospelles of Dystaves* (Wynkyn de Worde, *c*.1507–9) fo. a vᵛ. *STC* 12091. Translated by 'H.W.' (? Henry Watson: see 7 J n.) from *Les Evangiles des Quenouilles* (printed 1475 and later). French quoted below from 1493 Lyons edn., repr. in *Collection de facéties, raretés et curiosités littéraires* [Paris, 1829]). See Utley, *CR* No. 79. The book is an example of the very popular theme of the 'Gossips' Meeting' (cf. Dunbar's *Twa Mariit Women and the Wedow*, Skelton's *The Tunning of Eleanor Rummyng*, *EEC* No. 419 (and the references given there)) in the form of a parody of an ecclesiastical book of Gospels, with chapter divisions and commentary (*glose*).

Textual Notes. 21 dyvers] *text* dyves   37 Gonbarde] *text* Gonbande   44 husbande] *text* husbaude

5. *dyvers of her knowlege*: F. 'plusieurs de sa cognoissance'. Similarly, 'syege' (9), 'assystentes' (12, 45), 'vysages' (12), 'obteyned' (13) (= 'obtenue', *p.p.*), 'chapytres' (14), 'reversed' (18) (= 'renversees'), 'medled . . . to receyve' (19) (= 'se mesloyt . . . de recevoir') more or less exactly reproduce the words in F.

8. *a ryght market*: F. 'ung droyt marche'.

41. *her to-comynge husbande*: F. 'de son mary advenir'.

52. *cloven lyppes*: i.e. harelips (similar to the cleft lip of a hare). On the folklore of hares, see G. E. Evans and D. Thomson, *The Leaping Hare* (Newton Abbott, 1974), esp. pp. 127–41, 220–1.

53. *Margaret of the Whete*: F. 'Margot des Bles'.

F

Text: *The parson of Kalenborowe* (J. van Doesborch, Antwerp, *c*.1520), fo. C i. *STC* 14894.5. *Ed.* E. Schröder, *Jahrbuch des Vereins für Niederdeutsche Sprachforschung*, 13 (1887).

Calenburg is in Lower Saxony. The book contains a series of merry tales of this sort (e.g. of how the parson gets rid of some bad wine by inviting his parishioners to come and see him fly from the church steeple). See C. H. Herford, *Studies in the Literary Relations of England and Germany in the Sixteenth Century* (Cambridge, 1886), 272–82. There is a German poem on his doings; according to K. Schorbach, *Seltene Drucke*, v (Halle, 1905), the Low German text of the stories was turned into Dutch prose, and this was the source of the English translation.

21. In the text this new section is headed 'Howe the bisshope holowed the chapell whereas the parson lay under the bedde'.

25. *terribilis est locus iste*: 'terrible is this place' (Gen. 28: 17); used in the consecration of churches.

24

Skelton: Poems, ed. A. Dyce (London, 1843); V. J. Scattergood (Harmondsworth, 1983); Selections, ed. R. S. Kinsman (Oxford, 1969). The morality play *Magnyfycence* is edited by R. L. Ramsay, EETS, ES 98 (1908), and P. Neuss (Manchester, 1980).

Studies include: W. Nelson, *John Skelton, Laureate* (New York, 1939); H. L. R. Edwards, *Skelton: The Life and Times of an Early Tudor Poet* (London, 1949); A. R. Heiserman, *Skelton and Satire* (Chicago, 1961); M. Pollet, *John Skelton: Contribution à l'histoire de la prérenaissance anglaise* (Paris, 1962), English trans., *John Skelton, Poet of Tudor England* (London, 1971); S. E. Fish, *John Skelton's Poetry* (New Haven, 1965).

A

MS CCC, Cambridge, 357, fo. 9. *Ed.* F. M. Salter and H. L. R. Edwards, EETS 233, 239 (1956-7).

The *Bibliotheca Historica* of Diodorus Siculus (*c*.40 BC) is a universal history, and a compilation of legends. The first five books were translated from Greek into Latin by the humanist Poggio Bracciolini (completed by 1449) and it is from this that Skelton's version is derived (? written *c*.1485-8; cf. 15 E). With this extract cf. 15 A. Diodorus is an interesting early example of 'anti-primitivism': see A. O. Lovejoy and G. Boas, *Primitivism and Related Ideas in Antiquity* (Baltimore, 1935), 220-1.

Textual Note. 23 or] *MS* of

B

Text: *A lytell treatyse named the bowge of courte* (Wynkyn de Worde, ? 1499). *STC* 22597. *Index* 1470.5.

Perhaps written in late 1498. This extract corresponds to lines 344-413 of the poem.

Textual Notes. 35 avowe] *text* avwe   60 harnes] *Kinsman: text* harmes   68 curtel] *text* curtet

7. A proverb used of spendthrifts; cf. Whiting, H 22.

16. *Kyrkeby Kendall*: in Westmorland, renowned for its green woollen cloth ('Kendal green').

17. A snatch of a popular song that has not survived.

21. *The devyll myghte daunce therin*: proverbial; Whiting, D 191 (cf. 16, line 488).

22. *O lux*: a hymn, 'O lux beata Trinitas' (Dreves, ii. 34).

32. *in the devylles date*: proverbial: cf. Whiting, D 200.

43. proverbial: cf. Whiting, P 215.

45. *one*: perh. 'solitary' (Kinsman). But the rhyme fails, unusually. Both editions printed during Skelton's lifetime have this reading; the 1568 edition's reading 'is here within' sounds like an attempt to improve it. Possibly 'one' represents a misreading of 'sine' ('sin'); the expression would be similar, then, to such proverbs as 'lechery is no sin' (Whiting, L 167) or 'Alas, that ever love is sin' (L 478).

55. *The armes of Calyce*: presumably an oath (cf. 'Cockes armes'); perhaps referring to the coins that were minted at Calais in the first half of the fifteenth century, some of which bore the royal arms (Kinsman).

C

Text: *The boke of Phyllyp Sparowe* (R. Kele, ? 1545). *STC* 22594. *Index* 2756.5.

Probably written *c*.1505-7, when Skelton was rector of Diss. These extracts correspond to lines 1-182, 282-334 of the poem.

Textual Note. 153 eloquently] *text* eloquenly

1. *Pla ce bo*: 'I shall please [the Lord]'; Ps. 114: 9 (Vg.), the opening antiphon of Vespers of the Office for the Dead. The spacing of the syllables is probably to suggest the singing of plainchant.

3. *Di le xi*: 'I have loved'; Ps. 114: 1 (Vg.), the opening psalm of Vespers of the Office for the Dead.

4. *Dame Margery*: There was a senior nun at Carrow called Margery. Carrow, near Norwich, was a nunnery of 'nones blake' (9) or Benedictines; Jane Scrope lived there with her sisters and her widowed mother.

21. The tragic story of the young lovers Pyramus and Thisbe (Ovid, *Met.* 4. 55-166) was well known in the Middle Ages (cf. Chaucer, *LGW* 706-923).

53 ff. Probably a parody of the laments of the Virgin Mary over the dead Christ, a favourite subject of religious lyrics (*CB XV* No. 8 contains the phrase 'lerne to wepe wyth me', and *CB XV* No. 9 has for its refrain 'Who cannot wepe come lerne at me').

64, 66. The Latin phrases ('Woe is me'; 'In my distress I cried unto the Lord') are, or echo, phrases from Ps. 119: 5, 1, used in the Vespers of the Office for the Dead.

71 ff. *Acherontes well*: Acheron was one of the rivers of Hades. The denizens of the infernal regions mentioned in the following lines are: Pluto (72), god of the underworld; Allecto (74), one of the Furies; Medusa (76), one of the Gorgons (whose heads turned to stone anything that met their eyes); Megaera (78), another Fury; Proserpina (83) the queen of Pluto, carried off by him to the lower world; Cerberus (85), the monstrous dog who guarded the entry to the underworld; Theseus (86) son of Aegeus, a great hero-king, one of whose adventures was a descent to Hades; Hercules (87), the famous hero of immense strength and courage, who succeeded in carrying up Cerberus from Hades.

95, 97. The Latin phrases ('the Lord [is thy keeper]'; 'I have lifted up my eyes to the hills') are from Ps. 120: 5, 1, used in the Vespers.

98. *Zenophontes*: Xenophon (b. *c*.430 BC), a follower of Socrates and author of works on a variety of topics (in his *Memorabilia* he frequently praises Socrates for his temperance and moderation).

108. *Andromach*: the sorrow and laments of Andromache for Hector were known through the various stories of the siege of Troy (Chaucer refers to the prophetic dream of 'Andromacha, Ectores wyf' (*NPT*, *CT* B 3141)).

125–6. Cf. Catullus ii. 1–2, 'Passer, deliciae meae puellae, | Quicum ludere, quem in sinu tenere . . .' ('Sparrow, my lady's pet, with whom she often plays whilst she holds you in her lap . . .') (trans. Cornish).

143, 145. The Latin phrases ('If [thou, Lord, shouldest mark] iniquities'; 'Out of the depths have I cried') are from Ps. 129: 3, 1, used in the Vespers.

148. *Sulpicia*: There are two poetesses of this name, who may have been (deliberately?) confused by Skelton: Sulpicia, a niece of Messalla, the patron of Tibullus, who wrote some passionate love elegies, and a later Sulpicia, wife of Calenus, praised by Martial (*Epigrams* x. 35) for the propriety of her life and verses.

195. *mantycors*: manticores, bloodthirsty legendary monsters (deriving ultimately from Pliny's *Natural History*) shaped like a lion but with the face of a man and three rows of teeth (see the illustration from Topsell's *Historie of Four-Footed Beastes*, reproduced in T. H. White, *The Book of Beasts* [London, 1954], 247).

197. *Melanchates*: one of Actaeon's hounds, who took the lead in falling upon his master when he was changed into a stag (see Ovid, *Met.* 3. 232).

212. *Lycaon*: a legendary king of Arcadia, transformed into a wolf (see Ovid, *Met.* 1. 163 ff.).

25

Berners: studies include: C. S. Lewis, *English Literature in the Sixteenth Century* (Oxford, 1954), 149–56; N. Blake, 'Lord Berners. A Survey', *M&H* 2 (1971), 119–32.

A

Text: *Sir Johan Froissart: of the cronycles of England Fraunce Spayne Portyngale Scotlande Bretayne Flaunders and other places adjoyning* (R. Pynson, 1523, 1525), vol. i, fo. hh ii, vol. ii, fos. kk ii^v, BBB iii. STC 11396, 11397. Ed. W. P. Ker, *The Chronicle of Froissart*, 6 vols. (London, 1901–3). (French text in *Œuvres*, ed. Kervyn de Lettenhove, [Paris, 1867–77].)

Froissart began to write his *Chronicles* in 1369 or shortly after. For the period up to 1360–1 he used the chronicle of Jean Le Bel; he continues his narrative up to the fall of Richard II. On the cultural and political background of the *Chronicles*, see K. Fowler, *The Age of Plantagenet and Valois* (London, 1967) (with illustrations of several of the men mentioned in this extract).

Textual Notes. 12 *etc.* Carlouet] *text* Carlonet   32 bridge] *text* bride   40 studyed] *text* stuyed   50 forteresses] *text* foteresses   67, 73 Simekyn] *text* Sunekyn   101 armes] *text* armers   143 Poictevyns] *text* poictenyns   176 .lx.] *text* xl.   198 Jony] *text* Jouy   200 and] *text om.*   206 chambre] *text* chamre

1. *Sir John Chandos*: One of the great English generals of the Hundred Years War, and a veteran of the battles of Crécy and Poitiers, he had become Seneschal of Poitiers in 1369. At the end of that year he and Sir Thomas Percy, the Seneschal of La Rochelle, had failed to recapture the abbey of St Savin, near Poitiers. The engagement at the bridge of Lussac described here took place on 31 December, and Chandos died on 1 January.

3. In F. (for comparison, I quote the Le Noir edn., 1505) it is Chandos who 'jangloit a ses gens & ses gens a luy'.

11 ff. The English, and sometimes the French, names in Froissart (already not always easily recognizable), coming to Berners from a much later French version, have suffered some wonderful transformations. Thus Carlouet (12), Froissart's Caruels or Charuels, is probably Jean de Keranlouet or Karalouet; Jakes of Lery (43–4), Froissart's Jakes Aleri, is probably [William] Dalby; Chambo (95), Froissart's Clambo or Clanbo, is Clanvowe; Bertram of Case (95) is Bertran de Casalis or Casalitz. In lines 129–31 appear the lords of Tannay-Bouton, Partenay, Poyanne, and Argenton, together with Louis d'Harcourt and Jacques de Surgères.

15. *had well advysed hymselfe*: F. 'se advisa'. But Berners is rarely over-literal; cf. other close but perfectly acceptable translations, e.g. 'toke the right way' (20) (F. 'le droit chemin') or 'costyng the ryver' (20) (F. 'en costoyant la riviere').

17. In F. this remark is in indirect speech.

40–1. F. 'estuioient et ymaginoyent' (similarly 'fynde or encountre' (56) represents a doublet in F.).

131. *Englysshmen*: often used by Froissart to refer to allegiance rather than nationality.

159. *Mortymer*: Mortemer, north-west of Lussac.

162 ff. The persons involved in this episode are all from the higher nobility: Jean, Duke of Berry (d. 1416), uncle of the French king Charles VI and a famous patron of the arts; John of Gaunt, Duke of Lancaster (d. 1399) (whose daughter Catherine had been married, after much negotiation, to the King of Castile); Gaston de Foix (see 9 U), a rival of the powerful counts of Armagnac; the Duke of Burgundy, Philip the Bold (d. 1404).

182. *parfyte woman* F. 'femme parfaicte et formee'.

184. The King was as good as his word and sent ambassadors. At first Gaston was cold (because Gaunt had been making overtures on behalf of his son, the future Henry IV), but the Duke of Berry kept up the pressure and Gaston, being 'sage and subtyle' and seeing the 'ardent desyre that the duke of Berrey had', contrived to extract 30,000 francs 'for the charges of the ladyes expenses for suche yeres as she had been with hym' (and, says Froissart, 'if he had more demaunded, more he shulde have had, but he dyd it so to have thanke of the Duke of Berrey, and that he shulde perceyve that he had done somewhat for hym').

185. Jean de Foix, known as Yvain de Béarn, bastard son of Gaston de Foix, was a favourite of the King (they were 'moche of one age'), and was retained as one of the knights of his chamber.

193. *Hogreymen*: Hugonin de Guisay.

200. *Nanthorillet*: Nantoullet.

202–3. *wylde wodehouses*: F. 'hommes sauvaiges'. Cf. 14 C 151–66 n.

227. *the duchesse*: the young wife of the preceding episode (F. 'la duchesse de Berry qui estoit sa tante & la plus jeune').

B

Text: *The Boke of Duke Huon of Burdeux* (? Wynkyn de Worde, *c*.1534), fo. xvi. *STC* 13998.1. *MWME* i. 98–100, 266. *Ed.* S. L. Lee, EETS, ES 40, 41, 43, 50 (1882–7). It is a translation of a fifteenth-century French prose romance of composite origins (the first section deriving from an earlier *chanson de geste*), probably made from the printed edition of Le Noir (1513). Because of a feud, Huon is deprived of his lands by Charlemagne, and has to bring from Babylon the beard and the black teeth of the 'Admiral' Gaudyse. He meets Gerames, an old man, formerly a captive of the Saracens, who has lived for thirty years in the forest. Eventually, Huon gains the favour of Oberon, who helps him to success and to the winning of the Admiral's daughter, Esclaramonde. The romance (especially the second half) is full of exotic oriental episodes, dazzling successions of wonders, and strange meetings with figures like Judas and Cain.

5–6. F. 'mais tant est plain de faerye et choses estranges'.

8. *crokyd shulderyd*: F. 'tout bossu'.

8–9. *an aungelyke vysage*: F. 'ung visaige angelicque'.

C

Text: *The hystory of the moost noble and valyaunt knyght Arthur of Lytell Brytayne* (W. Copland for R. Redborne, ? 1555) fos. xlv[v], xlvi[v]. *STC* 807. *MWME* i. 79, 256. *Ed.* E. V. Utterson (London, 1814).

Studies include K. J. Oberent, *M&H* 5 (1974), 191–9. A translation of a French romance of the fourteenth century (the French quoted below for comparison is from the early sixteenth-century printed edition of Le Noir). It tells the story of Arthur, the son of Duke John (from the lineage of Lancelot), so named in memory of the king, and of his love for Jehannet.

Textual Notes. 6 mountaynes] *text* monntaynes   and] *text* hod   53 flour] *text* four   54 at] *text* all   131 the[1]] *text om.*   151 longe[1]] *text* lone   155 giaunt] *text* giannt   159 the[1]] *text* thee

1. *Governar*: Arthur's tutor.

32. F. distinguishes between 'fenestres dambre' and 'haultes verrieres claires'.

43. *Proserpyne, quene of the fayry*: cf. Chaucer, *Merch. T.*, *CT* E 2227–9.

71. *master Steven*: the clerk ('a soverayne clerke, specially in astronomy and nigromancy') of Florence, daughter of Emendus, King of Soroloys.

96. *gapinge . . . assayled*: F. 'A gueulle bee et lassaillit' (if this edn. is Berners's source, this would suggest that he is imagining the scene in a strongly visual way).

D

Text: *The Golden Boke of Marcus Aurelius Emperour and eloquent oratour* (T. Berthelet, 1535), fo. 81. *STC* 12436. *Ed.* J. M. G. Olivares in *Guevara in England* (Berlin, 1916).

Translated from the French translation of R. Berthault (Paris, 1531) of Guevara's Spanish *Libro áureo de Marco Aurelio* (Seville, 1528). The French is often obscure; Berners treats it freely, creating new syntactic and rhetorical patterns.

Textual Note. 26–9 And yet . . . man. For . . . therof.] *Text reverses these two sentences (this emendation, which restores F. order, is suggested by Mrs K. Ward-Perkins)*

17. *exercitees*: F. 'ay este a compaigne dexercites', i.e. 'by armies' [L. *exercitus*]. Berners's word may mean this, or perhaps 'occupations' (*OED*, s.v. 'Exercite' *sb.*²).

32. F. 'conjoincte & conglutinee'.

26

More: *The Yale Edition of the Complete Works of St Thomas More* (New Haven, 1963–).

Studies include: R. W. Chambers, *Thomas More* (London, 1935); R. J. Schoeck, *The Achievement of Thomas More*, Eng. Lit. Studies, Monograph No. 7 (Univ. of Victoria, 1976); A. L. Fox, *Thomas More: History and Providence* (Oxford, 1983). There is a wealth of material and illustration in J. B. Trapp and Hubertus Schulte Herbrüggen, *'The King's Good Servant': Sir Thomas More 1477/8–1535* (London, National Portrait Gallery, 1977; repr. 1978).

A

Text: *The Lyfe of Johan Picus erle of Mirandula* (J. Rastell, ? 1510), fo. b ii^v. *STC* 19897.7. *Ed.* J. M. Rigg (London, 1890), M. Kullnick, *Archiv*, 121 (1908), 47–75, 316–40, ibid. 122 (1909), 27–50.

Dedicated to Joyeuce Lee, a poor Clare and the sister of a friend. More gives the gist of the life of Pico della Mirandola (1463–94), written by his nephew Gianfrancesco and prefixed to his *Opera*, summarizes Pico's theses, and offers his own version of the Twelve Rules for Spiritual Warfare. Cf. G. B. Parks, in E. P. Mahony (ed.), *Philosophy and Humanism in Honor of P. O. Kristeller* (Leiden, 1976).

Textual Notes. 13 considered] *text* cousidered   14 thought] *text* though   25 or] *Workes 1557: text om.*   40, 65 nevieu] *text* nevien   47 himself] *text* hemself   64 benigne] *text* beninge   78 vaingloriouse] *text* waingloriouse

3. *hathe dishonested*: L. 'dehonestatus est'.

10–11. *might seme by hepis . . . to him*: L. 'ut turmatim et coacervatim in eum confluxisse videretur'.

18. *Epicure*: Epicurus (341–270 BC) stressed the importance of the evidence of the senses and of a self-reliant wisdom in the conduct of life; cf. Diogenes Laertius, *Vitae Philosophorum*, x. 13 (where it is recorded that he claimed to be self-taught).

49. *Benivenius*: Girolamo Benivieni, author of the *Canzone dell'Amore Celeste e Divino*, on which Pico wrote a commentary.

58. *Seint Heirom*: cf. St Jerome's *Epistola ad Eustochium Virginem* (*PL* 22. 892).

82. *Seneke*: Rigg compares the *De Sapientis Constantia* (see, e.g., section 8).

B

Text: *The Workes of Sir Thomas More Knyght* (London, 1557), fo. d iiii^v. *STC* 18076. *Ed.* R. S. Sylvester (New Haven, 1963) (with full commentary).

Probably written 1514–18. Studies include: A. F. Pollard, in J. G. Edwards, V. H. Galbraith, and E. F. Jacob (eds.), *Historical Essays in Honour of James Tait* (Manchester, 1933), 223–38; A. Hanham, *Richard III and his Early Historians 1483–1535* (Oxford, 1975).

Textual Note. 58 would] *text* wolud

2. *Shores wife*: She became later the legendary Jane Shore (cf. Rowe's play, 1714). More is the principal source of information about the historical woman, who seems in fact to have been called Elizabeth (see *TLS*, 7 July 1972, p. 777). She was the daughter of John Lambert, mercer; her marriage to William Shore was annulled *c.*1476 because of his impotence. She was accused of sorcery by Richard on 13 June 1483, when Hastings was condemned.

C

Text: Workes (1557), fo. g ii.
An unfinished treatise, probably written *c.*1522.

4. *as scripture saith*: cf. Ps. 4: 8.
16. *in a stage playe*: For the image, cf. 19 F 46. Its extended development here perhaps reflects More's own interest in drama; his biographer Roper records that in his youth, in Cardinal Morton's house, he would 'at Christmas tide suddenly sometimes step in among the players, and never studying for the matter, make a part of his own there presently among them, which made the lookers on more sport than all the players beside' (Chambers, p. 54).
39. *holy David*: Ps. 138 (Vg): 7.

NOTES ON GRAMMAR AND SPELLING IN THE FIFTEENTH CENTURY

Norman Davis

By the latter part of the fourteenth century, though Latin and French were still commonly written in England—Latin especially in ecclesiastical and French in legal use—English had come to be extensively used in writing of many kinds, both verse and prose. Much of the material may broadly be called literary, such as lyric and narrative poetry, romances, chronicles, verse drama, political propaganda and polemic, devotional treatises, and sermons; but English had made some advance also in administrative and commercial documents—petitions to Parliament, records of the proceedings of guilds and local inquiries, inventories, and wills. The spelling and grammatical forms of the language written in different parts of the country, and even by different writers in the same area, were far from uniform, and it is impossible to present a comprehensive grammar of 'Late Middle English' which would be valid for every text. It now appears that the type of English written in approximately the London region, but deriving important elements from the Midlands, had before the end of the fourteenth century acquired a position of major influence in the gradual trend towards a generally accepted written language. Though it is not in every particular the forerunner of later English, and indeed is not in every way internally consistent, the language of good manuscripts of the works of Chaucer is not far from it. Of the extracts in this book the poems of Thomas Hoccleve (No. 3), who spent his working life at Westminster and proclaimed his devotion to the example of Chaucer, sufficiently exemplify the kind of English composed and written by a minor official of some education about the turn of the century. Hoccleve is especially important for historical study because a number of his surviving works are written in his own hand, so that the language is free from the scribal interference that often disguises an author's usage. Long before the latest of our selections, from the works of Sir Thomas More (No. 26), the boundary between 'Middle' and 'Modern' English had been decisively crossed. Exact dates in such matters are clearly unattainable. The simplest mark of the development is the reduction in the use of grammatical inflexions embodied in the final syllables of many words; but of course this is a relative, not an absolute, criterion—a number of inflexions have never been lost at all. The *Middle English Dictionary* terminates its collections at about 1475, just before the introduction of printing to England; and for the practical purposes of most readers this suffices well enough.

Hoccleve is often blamed for his metrical irregularity, but in fact a high proportion of his lines move naturally in a five-stress pattern with alternating stresses; for example

And wél they cán a mánnës íre asswáge
With sóftë wórdës díscreet ánd benigne (3 A 68–9),

in which *mannes*, *softe*, and *wordes* each form two syllables, as they historically had done, and the -*e* of *ire* is elided before the initial vowel of the following word. This pattern is frequent enough to justify the belief that Hoccleve in general intended his verses to be read as five-stress lines. The unstressed vowels of inflexional syllables are normally written *e*, as in this quotation, but sometimes, especially later in the fifteenth century, *i* or *y* is used when a consonant follows, as in *lykith* 3 A 6, *fulfillid* 28, *crabbid* 51, *fadir* 3 C 104, *commyn* 13 A 2, *ellys* 12, *lovyth* 27.

The usual inflexions early in the fifteenth century appear as follows (most of the examples given are from Hoccleve, but a few from other authors are used to illustrate particular points).

Nouns. The only regular inflexions are those of the plural and of the genitive or possessive of both numbers. A relic of the old dative or prepositional singular appears in a few phrases, even at the end of the century, as in *on lyve* 'alive' 22 A 49, when the common form is *lif/lyf*. Most nouns form the plural by the addition of -*es* (often -*is* or -*ys*), which with monosyllabic nouns makes a second syllable; but with a disyllable, especially one of French origin or sometimes a native word ending in -*r*, the consonant -*s* only is added: *wordes* 3 A 69, *clerkis* 4 B 77, but *perils* 3 A 12, *martirs* 43, *waters* 4 A 2. A small number of nouns form their plural by change of vowel as they still do—*wommen* 3 A 1, *feet* 3 D 40—and some keep the old 'weak' ending -*en* (OE -*an*) instead of -*es*: most frequently *eyen/iyen/yen* 'eyes', e.g. 3 D 42, 1 G 97, and *bretheren* 7 F 12, *childeryn* 4 B 83, occasionally *sistren* 2 O 3, *foon* 'foes' 4 B 23, *shoon* 9 U 39, *hosen* 12 A 156; *eyren* 'eggs' appears beside *egges* in 9 H 41, 45. Exceptional -*en* plurals are *horsen*, *housen* 2 A 17, 35 (in a letter). The possessive is also normally formed with -*es*, as *mannes* 3 A 68, *sonnes* 3 B 34. A few nouns denoting relation, ending in -*r*, leave the possessive unchanged, as *moder* 7 B 3; and other relics of a type of declension without -*es* are *soule* 7 G 56, *hevene* 11 A 6.

Adjectives. The ending -*e*, which descends from the 'weak' inflexion of the adjective, earlier normal in definite use, is sometimes preserved after a defining word; e.g. *the dirkë shour* 3 D 25, but the forms are inconsistent in *thys oldë greye* 3 C 64 beside *thys old man* 56. The plural has -*e*, in predicative position, in *wysë* 3 C 77, but not regularly.

Pronouns. (i) *Personal.* The second person singular distinguishes *thow/thou* nominative and *thee* objective, the plural *ye(e)* nominative (e.g. 3 B 11) and *yow/you* objective (e.g. 3 B 22). In the third person singular neuter *hit/hyt* survives beside *it*, as at 2 D 3, 4 B 22, 4 C 23. The third person plural has *they* nominative and, early in the century, *hire* and *her(e)* possessive (3 A 7, 3 D 3), *hem* objective (3 A 4), but forms with initial *th-* gradually appear, as *ther* 6 A 25, *their* 6 C 15, *them* 83.

(ii) *Demonstrative*. The plural 'those' is *tho*, as at 3 A 26. *Thilke* is an occasional demonstrative, both singular and plural. From its derivation it should mean 'the same' (*ilke*) but it combines illogically with *same* 4 B 65. The definite article sometimes retains its old neuter form *that* in the phrase *that oon, that other* 1 B 58–9.

(iii) *Relative*. Pronouns used with both personal and inanimate antecedents are *that* (much the commonest, e.g. 3 A 4, 3 B 33, 3 C 49, 4 A 33, etc.), *which(e)* 4 B 3, 4 C 12, *wiche* 3 D 15, often after prepositions, e.g. *of which* 3 A 20, 3 B 16, 3 C 56, also *whyche that* 3 C 83, 4 B 60, *the whiche* 4 B 24, 15 C 15, and adjectivally *whiche booke* 15 E 6. Of persons the possessive *whos* may be used, as at 4 C 125, and objective *whom*, e.g. *by whom* 3 A 32, *to whom* 3 B 11 (not yet the nominative *who*). Relative *where* is combined with *as* in *whereas* 'where' 3 C 24. *Where* also stands for the general relative as the object of a preposition, as *wherethorowe* 'through which' 4 B 68, *whereby* 90, etc.

(iv) *Reflexive*. When *self*, whether reflexive or emphatic, is added to a plural pronoun it remains uninflected: *hemsilfe* 1 A 7, *thaymself* 1 D 52, *yowreselfe* 4 B 21. Generally the ordinary personal pronouns in objective form function also as reflexives: *hem* 3 A 5, *me* 3 C 47.

Verbs. The infinitive often keeps the ending *-en* (*-in/-yn*); e.g. *rollen* 3 A 12, *stonden* 21, *holdyn* 4 B 58, or is syncopated in verbs with stems ending in vowels, e.g. *seen* 3 A 15; but the *-n* is very often dropped: *faille* 3 A 16, *make* 17, etc. The resulting final *-e* may be syllabic: *make* 3 A 20, 3 B 30. The present plural also often ends in *-(e)n*: *been* 3 A 3, *arn* 47, *seyn* 50, *oppressen* 59; and again *-n* is often lost: *feyne* 3 A 26, *clappe* 55. But the ending is *-yth* in the Exeter letter: *menyth* 2 D 9. The second person singular ends in *-(e)st*, e.g. *tremblest, gost* 3 C 93, except for special cases such as *art* 3 C 92. The third person singular mostly has *-eth/-ith*: *lykith* 3 A 6, *askith* 23, *yeveth* 3 B 4. Verbs with stems ending in a dental consonant sometimes syncopate the ending and assimilate the consonant: *sit* (for *sitteth*) 3 A 66, *list/lyst* 3 B 22, 3 C 71, *stant* 4 C 98. Northerly and north Midland texts have *-(e)s*, e.g. *dos* 11 C 8. The imperative plural sometimes has the full ending *-eth*, e.g. *haastith* 3 B 27, *advertith*, *considerith* 4 B 23, but often dispenses with it, e.g. *yeve* 3 B 19. The present participle usually ends in *-ing/-yng(e)*: *norisshynge* 3 B 2, *lakkyng* 3. Strong verbs form the past tense by change of stem vowel, and many of the forms are directly descended from recorded earlier types, e.g. *faught* 1 A 1 from *feaht/fæht, fowghten* (pl.) 1 A 52 from *fuhton, sungen* 7 C 11 from *sungon.* Some, however, have developed from alternative variants, or applied forms historically singular to the plural, or made other formal changes under particular influences. For instance, *sey* 1 A 9 develops from the plural *sēgon,* and the alternative *saw* 1 A 8 arises from the substitution in that form of the descendant of the vowel *æ* proper to the singular *sæh.* Forms appropriate to the singular are often used in plural function, e.g. *roode* 1 B 3, *sat* 1 D 64; *spake* 3 D 59 has the *a* of the old singular, but *beer* 3 D 31, a singular, has the long *ē* formerly proper to the plural. The final *-en* characteristic of the plural is often dropped, e.g. *withdrow* 1 D 88. Modal auxiliaries similarly treat *-(e)n* as optional, and use singular forms in plural function: *shuln* 3 A 56, *wole* 3 B 8, *shall(e)* (pl.) 1 L 6, 15 D 11. In *if thou kunne* 17 A 70, *kunne* has kept its historical form, with the stem vowel and the ending proper to the second person subjunctive. Past participles of strong verbs, and of monosyllabic verbs, end in their full form in *-(e)n,* but the *-n* is often lost, especially in southerly texts and in verbs having a nasal consonant or group at the end of the stem. Some varied examples are *wonne* 3 A 3, *forswore* 37, *unknowe* 49, *dolve* 4 D 62, *holden* 3 B 35, *gon* 3 C 43, *seen* 76, *don* 109, *slayn* 118, *be* 128, *ben* 3 D 4, *holde* 52, *borne* 87, *fallen* 91.

Weak verbs form the past tense by the addition of a suffix containing a dental consonant, primarily *-de* or *-ed(e),* and the past participle by the suffix *-ed (-id): fulfillid* 3 A 28, *releeved* 39, *inned* 3 B 29, *thankid* 36. The suffix normally makes a separate syllable, but the vowel may be lost after some verb stems and the consonant assimilated to a voiceless stop. Some irregularities go back to ancient processes: *quitte* 3 A 31, *thoughte* 3 C 21, *broughte* 3 D 8, *wente* 43. This sometimes leads to the shortening of the stem vowel: *felte* 3 C 8, *drempt* 39, *kepte* 3 D 54. The plural of the past tense may end in *-en: seiden* 3 D 29, *labouriden* 57, *quykneden, scharpiden* 1 G 175. The second person singular ends in *-est/-ist,* like the present, e.g. *filwedist* 3 C 116.

The past tense of verbs other than auxiliaries may also be expressed in verse texts by a periphrasis using the verb *gan* (pl. *gunne(n))* and the infinitive, in the same way as *did* functions (mostly somewhat later): *gan assaylle* 1 A 56, *gan wade* 3 C 48, *gan walk* 5, line 4.

The past participle of both strong and weak verbs mainly in southerly texts often takes the prefix *i-/y-: yslayne* 1 D 46, *ydo* 7 A 8, *ymeved* 18, *ibowndyn* 11 A 1.

To illustrate the language as it was written approximately a century later than Hoccleve the works of Hawes and Barclay may serve as specimens. The surviving printed texts probably do not represent in all particulars what the authors wrote, but most of them at least date from their lifetimes and may be taken to show accepted usage of the time. There are forms in other early printed works, such as *Everyman* (No. 21), which are characteristic of a state of the language later than these authors; but the text of *Everyman* comes from a late print and cannot be trusted to preserve the details of the original language.

Noun plurals continue to be written *-es/-ys*. This sometimes appears to be intended as a separate syllable, but scansion in these authors is not so regular that confidence is possible: *beames* 22 A 76, *nayles, armys* 22 B 5. In other places the lines move better if such words are pronounced as single syllables: *tongues* 22 A 10, *names* 23, 26, *sterres* 74. Spellings and rhymes occasionally show that after a vowel or diphthong the vowel of the ending was lost; *lyse* rhyming *wyse* at 16, lines 139–40, *days* 362. Relics of the weak plural in *-en* survive in *fone* (rhyming *echeone*) 12 B 332, *peason* 22 C 34, but in general the number of such plurals is reduced; instead of *eyen*, earlier common, *eyes* (rhyming *skyes*) appears at 24 C 37.

Plural adjectives no longer pronounced a final *-e*, e.g. *grete* 22 A 58; *all* is uninflected in 22 A 74. Nor is it pronounced in an adjective following a defining word: *this fayre realme* 22 A 68. It is uncertain whether *derke* in *the derke nyght* 22 A 131 is to be read as two syllables. Occasionally an adjective of French origin following a plural noun takes the inflexion *-s*: *ymages humaines* 15 A 2. A relic of the old genitive plural in *-ra* is *alder* as late as 21, line 772, conventionalized as an intensive in *althergrettyst* 'greatest of all' 6 B 102.

Pronouns of the second person plural sometimes have *you(e)* as nominative, e.g. 22 A 127, 139, 25 A 71, 12 B 440, 17 G 6, as well as objective, e.g. 22 A 40. (The use of *ye/you* in addressing a single person instead of *thou/thee* goes back to the fourteenth century. It is a social rather than a grammatical matter.) The third person plural by the end of the century generally has possessive *theyr* (e.g. 22 A 59), objective *them*, sometimes *theym* (25 C 69). Some texts still show a mixture of old and new forms: 6 A has *hyr* 44, *her* 135, but *ther* 25, 50, 103. *Those* appears as the demonstrative plural in the late 7 K 14. Relatives remain essentially as they had been: *as he which* 26 A 83; *they the whiche beholdeth* 7 J 41; *by occasion wherof* 24 A 22.

Verbs usually have the infinitive written with *-e*, but this is not pronounced: *breke* 22 A 7, *come* 8, *rede* 26. The second and third persons singular of the present indicative usually end in *-(e)st*, *-(e)th*: *askest* 21, line 87, *mayst* 151, *seest* 23 D 42, *appereth* 22 A 67, *resteth* 22 C 7, *sayth* 23 D 97; but the northerly *-s* in the third person appears in *blowes* 22 C 2, and somewhat earlier in East Anglia: *spekys* 16, line 253, *compellys* 560. The present plural usually has *-e* or no ending: *ly* 22 A 57, *disprayse, hate* 22 C 16, *hop* 27; but Hawes and Barclay both use *-eth* as well: *devoureth* 22 A 59, *swereth* 22 B 5, *lesyth* 10, *counteth* 22 C 13, *overcommeth* 43. So does the Winchester Malory: *lovyth* 13 A 54, *doth* 90. The plural of 'be' is *ar(e)* (22 A 61, 22 B 13), as well as *be* (22 C 6, 32). Cf. *ye ar* 13 A 5 but *ye* *bene* 13 A 90, *ben* 8 B 53. *Beth* 8 B 13, *bith* 4, etc. are exceptional southerly forms. The present participle ends in *-yng(e)*: *besechynge* 22 A 40, *renning* 22 C 41. Past participles of strong and anomalous verbs are *graven* 22 A 25, *knowen* 43, *blowen* 45, *frosen* 22 C 4, *throwen* 36, 22 D 108, *spoken* 23, *won* 48, 134, *come* 69, *slayne* 129, *ben* 48, 53, *gone* 22 B 11. There has apparently been some generalizing of the *-(e)n* ending, except in verbs with a nasal consonant at the end of the stem, e.g. *won* and *come*.

Some constructions involving verbs appear or increase during the fifteenth century. The most far-reaching is 'auxiliary *do*', which is found occasionally in the fourteenth century (including a few examples in Chaucer), but greatly increases in the fifteenth. In the past tense *dyd* functions as *gan* had done for a long time (see p. 496 above), but in the present *do*, in the appropriate person, becomes frequent in a way that *gin* did not. Thus, *doth menace* 1 B 24, *doth disdeyne* 4 C 82, *doth devyse* 6 A 8, and in the past *dyd wryte* 1 H 16, *duddest gete* 2 A 16, *dyd dwell* 12 B 2. Most of the occurrences are in positive sentences, but a few are in questions, including negatives: *Why dyd we not perysche? Why dyd we syt...?* 9 R 26; *Do ye thynke...?* 23 D 90. A verb is still commonly negated by a following *not*, but exceptionally it may precede, e.g. *y so not presuppose* 8 A 94. The causative use of *do*, which had been one of its main functions, survives for a time beside the periphrastic use; e.g. *do say a masse* 1 I 35, *doo me have* 17 F 18, and itself may take a periphrastic past; e.g. *ded do shewe* 15 E 29. The 'expanded form' of verbs—a part of 'be' with a present participle—is used sparingly in most of these texts, e.g. *was walkynge* 12 B 117, *was chepynge* 17 G 77, *Whyder arte thou goynge?* 21, line 85.

When an infinitive of purpose is accompanied by a preposition defining the relation of the verb to the object, the preposition is usually placed immediately after the infinitive: *to maynteyne with hise errours* 'to maintain his errors' 1 G 60, *for to praise with God* 160, *to dight with her mete* 7 F 37, *to plese with your sight* 17 A 52. But an infinitive phrase embodying a preposition as a descriptive adjunct to a noun usually has the preposition at the end: *to be spoken of* 22 D 23, *to sleight a thing to be written of* 26 B 67, *a qwischyn Our Lady to sitte on* 7 B 17 (where modern use would require *for* before *Our Lady*), *clothes to wrappe him inne* 52. In a relative clause using the pronoun *that* a preposition comes at the end: *the cuntré that he was born yn* 9 S 26, *the man that ye bowt hit of* 1 O 55.

Spelling and Sounds

At the date of the earliest texts in this book the spelling of English was in some respects still very unstable. Irregularities were reduced but not eliminated during the period from which the selection is drawn. The tradition of writing English, which had never been entirely uniform but had achieved a measure of homogeneity in the Late Old English period, was severely disturbed by the adoption of many French conventions after the Norman Conquest. In general, writers seem to have attempted to match their spelling to their pronunciation, but there was often more than one way of representing the same sound. (For the most part the number of homophones was not yet large enough to call for much use of etymological distinctions in spelling.) Until the end of the fourteenth century most of the letters of the Roman alphabet had similar values in indicating pronunciation in the different countries in which they were used, though there were a number of individual peculiarities. (Some special letters were used in English—ȝ and þ—but in this book they have been replaced by their modern equivalents.) By about 1400 it appears that speakers of English in the region of London and the South-East used the following sounds in stressed syllables, the letters having the values usual in Continental languages such as German or Italian, not modern English. Vowels might be short, long, or diphthongal. The short were *a, e, i, o, u*, using mostly these letters, in closed syllables (that is, when followed by a consonant final in a word, or more than one consonant), but also having *y* as an alternative to *i* and *o* as an alternative to *u* in some positions. Typical examples are *man*, its plural *men*, *lim* or *lym* 'limb', *god* 'god', *luue* or *loue* 'love'. (The letter *u* was used also to represent the consonantal sound later written *v*: in this function *v* is substituted in this book.) The long vowels were *ā, ẹ̄, ɛ̄, ī, ọ̄, ǭ, ū*, and probably, at least in important areas, *ǖ*, which was not distinguished in the South by a diacritic. Examples are *nāme, mẹ̄ten* 'meet', *mẹ̄te* 'food', *mīn* or *mȳn* 'mine', *gọ̄d* 'good', *brǭd* 'broad', *hous* or *hows* 'house', *mūwe* 'mew' (of a hawk); *ou/ow* is a French spelling for *ū* which was generally adopted in English by the fourteenth century. Long vowels were sometimes, but quite unsystematically, written with a double letter, as in *meete, mood*, especially when no other vowel came after the following consonant. A single vowel symbol followed by a single consonant and another vowel, e.g. *same, grete, nyce*, normally represents a long vowel. Before some consonant groups, especially *ld, mb, nd*, vowels were generally long, but were evidently often shortened again before *nd*, as in *hond, stonden*.

Of the long vowels, *ā* must have been articulated further to the front than the vowel of modern *father*; *ẹ̄* was 'close' like the *e* of French *été* but longer; *ɛ̄* was 'open' like the *e* of French *fête*: *ī* like the *i* of *machine*; *ọ̄* close like that of French *rôle*; *ǭ* open like that of French *fort* or approximately like *oa* of English *broad*; *ū* like the vowel of *rule*; *ǖ* like that of French *pur*. The difference between close and open *o* was not shown in the spelling of most scribes. The pronunciation can usually be understood from the modern forms of the words concerned, for the sounds have remained distinct and the descendant of close *ǭ* later came to be written *oo*, that of open *ǭ* often *oa*. Close *ọ̄* has mostly been raised to *ū* ([u:]) while retaining the spelling *oo*, as in *food*, but the vowel has sometimes been shortened before a consonant, as in *good*, or unrounded as well, as in *blood*. Open *ō* mainly developed to the diphthong now used in *road*, but in *broad* and before *r*, as in *roar*, it has retained its older quality. The vowels which in the fourteenth century were close and open *ē*, *ę̄* and *ē̦*, are for the most part no longer distinguished in modern English and their early pronunciation has to be deduced from etymology. Somewhat later, from the fifteenth century onwards, writers and then printers began to mark the difference by the spelling. The close sound was commonly represented by *ee*, the open sound by *ea*, and the modern spellings are generally a good indication of the pronunciation in late Middle English, as in the pair *meet* and *meat*. (*Break* and *great* exceptionally preserve a different sound relation which has been lost in most other words; cf. the rhyme *great* ~ *bete* 6 D 13–14, but the spelling *great heat* 22 C 20.) The spelling *ea*, adopted from Anglo-Norman, which in turn had taken it over from earlier English, became fairly common in the latter half of the fifteenth century, especially in words from French such as *ease* and *please*, beside the alternative *ese*, *plese*. There is a varied group of examples of both French and native origin in extract 22 C—*pease*, *meat*, *season*, *pleased*, *great*, and others. It seems that a pronunciation with close *ę̄* of words historically having the open sound developed at first regionally in the East and North, and was generally adopted about the end of the seventeenth century. Well before that, rhymes between historically close and open vowels are fairly numerous in some areas. For instance, though *drede* rhymes with the traditionally open vowel in *dede* 'dead' at 3 A 46–7, it is linked with the close vowel in *bleede* 4 C 141–3. The spelling *meate* for the verb 'meet' in 12 B 241 shows that this scribe at any rate did not make the distinction. The existence, for a time, of the high front rounded vowel *ü* ([y:]), as in French *pur*, is inferred from rhymes of words adopted from French which contained this sound and were not normally linked with native English words having the diphthong [iu], such as *newe*, which might have been regarded as a sufficient rhyme and indeed was later so used. The diphthongs were *ai/ei*, *au*, *iu*, *eu*, *ou*, *oi*, as in *dai/wey*, *cause*, *newe*, *fewe*, *soule*, *joye*. These were apparently pronounced with the stress on the first element ('falling'). In the fourteenth century the diphthongs *ai* and *ei*, earlier distinct, had come to rhyme together and evidently merged in a sound close to *ai*. But the *ęu* descended from earlier *īw/ēow* had become [iu], and was separate from *ɛu* derived from *ēaw/ǣw*, so that *newe* did not rhyme with *fewe*. No such distinction of close and open first element can be discerned in the diphthongs containing *o*: for instance *growe*, which historically had close *ǭ*, rhymes at 3 A 48 with *unknowe*, which had the open vowel from earlier *ā*. The spelling *ou/ow* is therefore ambiguous: it may represent the simple long vowel *ū*, as noted above, or it may mean the diphthong just mentioned.

This account of late fourteenth-century vowel sounds applies to the vowels of stressed syllables. Those of unstressed syllables may differ substantially, ranging from slightly modified varieties of the full vowel to the neutral vowel [ə] with loss of distinctive quality. Words of more than one syllable often distributed the stress in a way different from that of the later language. This mostly affects words of French origin, which frequently stress a syllable other than the first: *baréyne* 3 A 25, *malíce* 50, *servýse* 3 C 6, *preyére* 68, *favóur* 3 D 23, *spiríte* 27 (rhyming with *delíte*). The frequent suffix *-cio(u)n* formed two syllables, so that *discrecion* 3 C 85 can rhyme with *resón* 87 and *conclucioun* 3 D 14 with *adoun*. On the other hand the stress sometimes falls on a prefix that is unstressed today, e.g. *répreef* 3 A 46, and words of more than two syllables have a secondary stress on a prefix as well as a stronger one on the final syllable; e.g. *rèsisténce* (rhyming *deffense*) 3 A 20, *rèmembráunce* 3 B 41. Most prefixes, however, are unstressed and come before the main stress of the word, whether of romance origin, such as *assaille* 3 A 18, or native, as in *ageyn* 3 B 19. Such syllables contain the neutral vowel; but other prefixes have the higher *i*, whether reduced from *ge-*, as in *iliche* 3 C 126, *ynow* 3 D 62, or in such forms as *byheeste* 3 A 45, or in romance words like *disese* 3 A 4. In informal writing weak stress of a word within a sentence may sometimes be expressed in the spelling: *thow sche xuld* a *be ded* 7 D 32, *a pottful* a *wortys* 16, line 272. Many unstressed syllables are inflexional endings, some of which took the form of *-e*. A major event in the history of weak syllables in the fifteenth century was the complete loss of this final vowel. (It still survived in some positions at the beginning of the century, as is shown by the rhyme *tyme* ~ *by me* at 3 C 50–2.) One consequence of the loss was that words historically ending in *-ie*, which in careful fourteenth-century writers had rhymed only with others of similar pattern, could now normally rhyme with final *-i/-y*; so *dye* ~ *mercye* 6 A 95 (*-e* in *mercye* is etymologically unwarranted), *foly* ~ *y* 6 B 53. More generally, the fact that final *-e* was no longer pronounced meant that it could be written indiscriminately by scribes, to occupy a space or merely wilfully. Unconnected with this development was a raising of [e:] in a final syllable so that it rhymed with [i]: *truly* ~ *me* 21, lines 420–1, *be* ~ *clerely* 578–80.

The consonants at the end of the fourteenth century were for the most part the same as in the later language and were written with the same letters, except for ʒ and þ noted above. Some consonants which have since become silent in certain positions were still sounded—initial *g* and *k* before *n* in words like *gnaw*, *know*, *w* before consonants, as in *wlatsom*, *writen*, *l* before consonants, as in *calm*, *folk*, *half* and weakly stressed words like *should* and *would*, *r* when final or before a consonant. The letter *c* by the late fourteenth century was distributed much as it still is, representing *s* before a front vowel, as in *citee*, but *k* before a back vowel or *l*, as *can*, *clene*: but some scribes used *k* sporadically in the latter position as well, as *konne*

3 C 86. The combination *ch* represented the sound that it still has in *church*, and the originally long form of the same affricate was written *cch*, e.g. *picche* 4 B 35. The sound now spelt *sh* was already mostly so written in initial position, but an important alternative throughout the century was *sch*, e.g. *shee* 3 A 24, *sche* 3 C 127; in other positions it was usually *ssh*, e.g. *fressh* 3 B 37, *wasshe* 4 C 92. Until the sixteenth century English used—though not everywhere—a group of consonantal sounds that have since been lost except in dialects, namely the front and back fricatives most commonly spelt *gh* (*h* alone in the practice of some scribes, e.g. *siht* 4 C 78), the place of articulation depending on neighbouring sounds in the same way as the consonants of *ich* and *ach* in German. These sounds could occur medially between vowels, e.g. *sighynge* 3 D 18, finally in a word, e.g. *sygh* 3 C 63, and most frequently preceding the consonant *t*, e.g. *bright* 3 D 24, *myght* 15, *broughte* 8. The fricative consonants represented by *f*, *s*, and *th* were apparently voiceless except between vowels and in unstressed position, so that *was* rhymes with *glass* at 3 D 64. Between vowels and after a stressed syllable they were voiced, so that nouns ending in the nominative singular in *f* are written with *v*, and so pronounced, before a vocalic ending: *greeves* (pl. of *greef*) 3 A 39, *livis ende* 4 B 62, *on lyve* 'alive' 15 C 7, 22 A 49. The same no doubt held for the other fricatives, but the spelling could not show it: *howses* 3 A 62 would contain the same consonants as it does now.

Words which historically contained medial *d* before a final unstressed *-er*, such as *fader, moder, gader, togider*, in the course of the fifteenth century changed the plosive *d* to a voiced fricative *th*. This is irregularly shown in the spelling; e.g. *mother, godfather* 2 K 2. Even in the late No. 21 *d* is the usual spelling, e.g. *togyder* 324, *moder* 552, *fader* 729; *father* and *mother* appear in 25 A 169, but *togyder* at 181. Cf. Skelton's spelling *fethers* rhyming with *edders* at 24 C 79.

The pronunciations in stressed syllables so far noticed are those in which the vowels were free from the influence of neighbouring sounds. During the Middle English period some of the vowels changed their quality in particular environments. The changes were often shown by spelling adjustments made by scribes, but not invariably, and sometimes old and new spellings occur in the same piece of writing. For example, the short back vowels *a* and *o* acquired a transitional glide before a velar fricative, and this combined with the vowel to form a diphthong, *au* and *ou*. Thus, *faught(e)* 1 A 1, 1 D 82 developed from an earlier *faght* (Old Anglian *fæht*). On the other hand *foght* 1 A 36 has taken the vowel proper to the past participle (OE *fohten*) and the diphthong is not shown in the spelling; *fowghten* (OE pl. *fuhton*) 1 A 52 presents the normal development. Both spellings are seen side by side in 3 C 3 *nought* but *Thoght*. *Doughtir* 1 D 70 preserves the historical vowel *o*, which exceptionally in this word was lowered to *a* and early gave the modern *au*. Diphthongization of a similar kind is seen substantially later when *a* before *l* plus another consonant, or double *l*, appears as *au/aw*—usually in unskilled writing, e.g. *schawll* 2 K 13, *aull* 19. In contrast to these exceptional forms, *au* before a nasal consonant mainly in words of French origin is extremely frequent from the fourteenth century onwards: *obeysaunce* 1 B 18, *gyaunt* 23, *sergeauntes* 49, *braunches* 65. Before the consonant group *ng* the short vowel *e* was raised to *i*, notably in *England*, which is often written *Inglond(e)* in the fifteenth century, as in 1 A 14. A similar raising between the consonants *g* and *d* took place in *togider(e)*, as in 8 A 16, and before *l* in *fille* 'fell' 1 D 55, *hylde* 'held' 1 F 36. On the other hand, when short *e* was followed by *r*, whether final in a word or before another consonant, it was often lowered to *a*, so that *herte*, for example, came to be pronounced *harte*, as it is spelt at 8 C 19, and rhymes with *departe* at 16, line 259, even with unchanged spelling. This change was not carried out regularly in every word apparently providing the conditions: *afer* and other words in 6 B 60–2 rhyme with the infinitive *forber*, which is unlikely to have been subject to the lowering. In *person* 1 F 9, which is another spelling of *parson*, the two pronunciations have not yet split into distinct words.

Outside such particular environments the Middle English short vowels maintained their quality into the early modern period, except that in eastern dialects, often spreading to London, short *i* was often lowered to *e*. This affected both native words, such as *chekyns* 1 F 26, *kenge* 2 E 35, *hedyr* 'hither' 2 I 22, *whech* 7 D 10, *mech* 36, *smetton* 15 A 37, and adoptions from French such as *peté* 'pity' 1 A 46, *preson* 1 F 4, *dener* 2 G 11, *rever* 16, line 36. The long vowels, however, behaved differently, so that phonetic relations of the sounds were drastically altered. The process cannot easily be followed from spellings except in particular words or groups, because naturally the spelling would convey to a reader whatever sound a vowel had acquired at the time of its use. The changes are known mainly from descriptions given by writers on pronunciation in the sixteenth century and later, partly from comparisons with foreign sounds made by writers on Continental languages, and partly from a peculiar text, apparently of the late fifteenth century, in which a hymn composed in English is written down in the spelling used in Welsh. Occasional spellings which have been supposed to show the use of English letters as if they expressed the values of the 'Continental' system can usually be explained by various special developments. Some eccentricities, however, appear to be significant because they use letters in a way that deviates from the normal system. For example, in the late fifteenth century the Court of Common Pleas is sometimes called 'Common Place', as at 1 H 22, which implies that those who used this spelling (which never became general) had raised and fronted the [a:] of *place* to the [ɛ:] of *plea*. Another problem is presented by the spelling *oblegyd* at 7 F 130. Here *e* represents the French vowel [i:], and might be taken to imply that the Middle English [e:] had been raised to [i:] so that the letter *e* could have that value. But the spelling *oblege* is cited by *OED* from the fourteenth century, well before there are general signs of such raising. It may be an isolated form with altered stress and shortened vowel. Again, the spellings *spyede* 13 B 109 and *fyete* 145 might well, in view of the date, be meant to show the raising of [e:] by using the spelling known from words like *thief*; but since as early as Gower close *ę* was sometimes so spelt, this is uncertain. Such examples illustrate something of the difficulty of judging the meaning of some spelling innovations. From evidence of many kinds, however, it is clear that in the course of the fifteenth century the high vowels [i:] and [u:] were diphthongized, the first element being some kind of central vowel, so that [i:] had become [ɔi] and [u:] had become [ɔu] or [ʌu]; and the tongue position of the other long vowels was raised. Thus [a:] became [æ:], close [e:] became [i:], open [ɛ:] except before *r* moved towards [e:], though in its early stages this development was regional and was not generally carried out until the seventeenth century. Of the back vowels, [o:] was raised to [u:] and [ɔ:] to [o:]. So by the end of the fifteenth century the pattern of vowel sounds was markedly different from what it had been in Chaucer's day.

Beside these general developments there were some movements of limited range. One of these involved a number of words in which [e:] came before *r*, such as *brere*, *frere*, *quere*. These have developed in modern English to *brier*, *friar*, *choir*, which shows that the vowel must have been raised to [i:] in time to undergo the diphthongization described above. This is in part indicated by spellings such as *fryre*, which are widely but irregularly recorded. A small number of other words having historical [e:] are also sometimes written with *i* or *y*, but have not acquired the diphthong in the modern language; for example *hyre* is the spelling of 'hear' at 1 F 31 and 13 A 63, and of 'here' at 13 A 83. It is not certain whether such words had in special circumstances developed the high vowel [i:] like *friar*, which has not survived, or whether the vowel had been shortened so that *hyre* would have been pronounced in the same way as the pronoun 'her', spelt identically. Similar cases are *whyle* 'wheel' 13 B 17, and the rhyme *clere ~ fyre* 21, lines 617–18. An originally regional development affected the diphthong written *ai*, which in the South was maintained until the sixteenth or even seventeenth century, but in the North was monophthong-ized as early as the late fourteenth and came to be written *a*, e.g. *daly* 'daily' 16, line 910, *pane* 'pain' 18 C 49, and to rhyme with the sound descended from Middle English *ā*, e.g. *fayre ~ ware* 12 B 469–71.

Variation may appear in consonants also. Notably *y*, or its frequent earlier equivalent ʒ, may vary with *g* in words descended alternatively from Old English or Old Norse. The OE derivative has *y*, the ON *g*, as in the frequent variants *ayein/again*, *yeve/give*. The Norse form appears earliest in the North, but spread widely and of course eventually became general. Many texts in the fifteenth century have both types.

Marked regional characteristics are sometimes shown by East Anglian scribes. The most conspicuous features are: 'shall' and 'should' written *xall, xuld(e)* 16, lines 33, 55; *wh-* replaced by *qw-*, e.g. *qweche* 'which' 2 E 6, *qwyll* 'while' 16, line 543; *-ght* replaced by *t* or *th* in words like *knyt* 2 G 31, *ryth* 1 (and *gh* unhistorically inserted in *smyght* 16, line 442), after *o* by *wt*, e.g. *browt* 2 G 27, *wrowt* 7 D 9 (and with unhistorical *gh* in *owght* 'out' 2 I 16). The frequency of such spellings shows that the fricative in this position must have ceased to be pronounced in that area. The loss is occasionally shown also in other texts, e.g. *knyt* 8 A 55.

Though most of such forms are typical of particular regions, some of them early became known beyond the areas where they were at home, and a large number of documents contain a mixture of spelling conventions. The particular combination of possibly variant forms that a scribe uses can sometimes be highly characteristic of his work. It also sometimes happens that a scribe will introduce hitherto unfamiliar forms into his repertoire, and discard those formerly normal; and predominant forms may ultimately spread over a wide area so as to obliterate many of the features formerly typical of regional usage. As the years passed there was an ever stronger trend in English towards uniformity, and before the middle of the sixteenth century a written language that was generally accepted in most of its features had been adopted for literary and formal works. The drift towards it was very uneven. Caxton, who in the famous preface to his edition of *Eneydos* in 1490 (15 E) shows himself fully aware of the inconvenience for a publisher of linguistic variation, admits more than one form of many common words. Even in these brief extracts (No. 15) numerous alternatives occur: *ayenst* B 8 ~ *agayn* E 21; *gyve* A 27 ~ *yeve* B 55; *it* C 3 ~ *hit* 5; *hyther* D 29 ~ *thyder* C 59; *hem* B 94 ~ *them* A 10; *her* B 66 ~ *their* A 14 ~ *theyr* B 103; *mykle* D 40 ~ *moche* 58; *please* C 59 ~ *playse* E 48; *wryton* E 29 ~ *wreton* 31.

Regional usage at its most distinctive is to be found in Scotland, naturally enough since the language was developed by a cultivated and highly self-conscious society. Scots itself was by no means homogeneous, but the varieties within it have not yet been fully worked out in relation to the date and origin of documents; see especially A. J. Aitken, 'Variation and Variety in written Middle Scots', in A. J. Aitken, A. McIntosh, and H. Pálsson (eds.), *Edinburgh Studies in English and Scots* (London, 1971), 177–209. The following brief account, selecting the most striking features of spelling and inflexions, follows the order of items set out above (pp. 493 ff.)

Nouns. The plural ending is mostly *-is/-ys*, e.g. *lordis* 10 A 4, *mornys*

10 C 5, *dayis* 19 A 1. Monosyllabic nouns often make their ending an additional syllable: *cairis* 18 A 94, *foulis* 19 B 6. A few words form the plural by change of vowel, not necessarily in the same way as southerly dialects: *brether* 19 F 93, *ky* 'cows' 20 B 327. A few have the plural in *-n*: *ene* 'eyes' 18 C 176 (rhyming with *grene*), 19 C 30, *eyne* 20 A 107, *oxin* 20 B 327. The possessive ending is also *-is*: *doggis* 18 B 94, *wyfis* 20 A 110.

Adjectives. There is no inflexion after a defining word, e.g. *the gud king* 10 A 21, *this fair ladie* 18 C 72, or in the plural, e.g. *hir kneis bair* 18 C 123, *all women* 556, *thair brycht hairis* 19 B 61. But *The Kingis Quair* in some passages follows Chaucerian practice, e.g. *the smallë grenë twistis* 5, line 22.

Pronouns. (i) *Personal.* The third person has the characteristic feminine nominative *scho*, e.g. 10 C 31, 18 A 124, 20 B 169; *sche* also occurs, e.g. 20 A 1. The second person plural normally distinguishes *ye* nominative, *yow* objective, e.g. 10 A 14, 18 B 25. The third person plural nominative is usually *thai/thay*, e.g. 10 B 46, 18 B 55. The possessive is *thair/thayr*, e.g. 10 A 88, 18 C 432, 20 A 22, or *thar(e)*, e.g. 10 B 5, 10 C 82; objective *thaim/thaym*, e.g. 10 A 56, 10 B 5, 20 A 43, or *tham*, e.g. 10 A 18.

(ii) *Demonstratives.* The plural of *that* is *thay*, e.g. 18 B 53, and the plural of *this* is *thir*, e.g. 10 A 102, 18 A 6. As an indefinite article *ane* is frequent before a consonant as well as a vowel: *ane wy* 10 A 71, *ane quhyll* 18 A 61, *ane uther* 19 A 29.

(iii) *Relative.* The commonest relative referring to both persons and things is *that*, e.g. 10 A 2, 18 B 3, 19 B 59; *at* is occasional, e.g. 10 B 29 (of persons), 20 A 115 (inanimate). Also very frequent for both persons and things is *quhilk*, e.g. 18 C 33, 19 B 18, and *the quhilk*, e.g. 18 C 89. With a plural antecedent *quhilkis* appears at 20 A 34. The possessive for both persons and things is *quhais*, e.g. 18 C 146 (of a bell), 20 A 95 (of a god), or *quhois* at 5, line 187. The personal objective may be *quhome*, e.g. 18 C 23, 31, *quham*, e.g. 20 B 54, *quhome that*, e.g. 19 A 24. The relative as object of a preposition is often represented by *quhair/quhar*, to which the preposition is appended: *quhairon* 19 A 18, *quhareon* 20 A 8, *quharfra* 20 B 3, *quhareby* 5, line 129; but *quhamto* (of a port) at 20 B 125.

Verbs. The infinitive may be written with *-e*, but this is not pronounced: *rayke* 10 A 1, *wirk* 16, *leir* 18 A 17, *ryde* 20 B 198. The first person singular of the present indicative ends in *-is* provided that the personal pronoun does not stand next—if it does there is no ending: *I knaw* but *keipis* 18 A 11–12, *wring I* but *wetis* 19 C 29. The second and third person singular both have *-is*: *thou gynnis* 5, line 196, *thow reivis* 18 A 49, also *thow hes* 89; *it movis* 10 A 19, *God sendis* 18 A 37, *quhasa discrivys* 20 A 136. Douglas occasionally has *-th*: *doith* 20 B 145. The plural also ends in *-is*, e.g. *slepis* 10 C 80, *lukis* 18 B 15, *behaldis* 19 C 27, *thay . . . that stryvys* 20 A 116, except when a pronoun subject stands next, e.g. *ye hald* 10 C 99, *thai cry* 109, *thay dreid* 18 B 55, *we part* 80. At 18 B 14 *beis* functions as a future. In *The Kingis Quair* some infinitives and plurals have the 'Chaucerian' ending *-en*: *counterfeten* 5, line 49, *setten* 54.

The present participle usually ends in *-and*: *slepand* 10 B 34, *kepand* 18 A 2, *duelland* 18 B 2, *standand* 19 C 77. But Henryson and Dunbar sometimes use the southern *-ing/-yng*, e.g. *quhisling* 18 C 20, *flowing* 31, *birnyng* 19 B 24. The past tense of some strong verbs has a characteristic form different from the southerly type. In particular, instead of *-ough/-ow* in the past of verbs like 'laugh' the Scots form often has *-euch*, e.g. *lewche* 18 A 123, *leuch* 18 B 102 (also *lauch* 18 C 231); and the past forms of 'slay' and 'draw' are *slew* (18 B 7) and *drew* (20 B 314). 'Stand' has *stude* at 10 A 19. Past participles of strong verbs normally keep *-in*: *drewyn* 10 B 59, *brokin* 10 C 13, *ouertane* 18 B 75, *writtin* 18 C 41, *sawin* 'sown' 137, *sonkin* 157, *groundin* 181, *gravin* 414, *fundin* 19 C 94, *sprungin* 19 E 21; but *soung* 18 A 89, *ingrave* 20 A 8.

Weak verbs usually have the past tense and past participle ending in *-it*: *awowit* 10 A 1, *marrit* 18 A 13, *vexit* 19 A 12, *figurit* 20 A 24. Some uses of auxiliary verbs may be noted. *Can* may have the same function as southerly *gan* (see p. 496) in acting as a periphrastic formative of the past tense: *can renew* 18 C 47, *can oppres* 55, *can rin* 158; the use is not exclusively Scots: *can rayne* 11 W 2. The past *couth* often has the same function, e.g. *he couth wend* 10 A 26, *cowth weip* 18 A 74, *couth it sew* 18 B 40; also *culd* in *culd spring* 18 C 512. The normal Scots causative is *gar*, past *gart*: *I sall gar* 18 B 125, *he gart hallowe* 10 A 34, 18 B 113. *Do* is also used in its common causative sense, e.g. *is done ceis* 19 E 33, and in the perfective idiom *he has done roune* 19 F 81. *Mon/man* is frequent as a synonym of 'must', e.g. in 10 C 62, 18 B 8, 19 C 38, 19 F 95. Some Scots poets favour the adoption of past participles of Latin verbs, especially of the first conjugation, without inflexional ending: *maculait* 18 C 81, *dissimulait* 225, *deificait* 288, *inporturat* 20 A 70.

Spelling and sounds. The most familiar and conspicuous feature of Scots pronunciation (which it shares with northern dialects of English) is the general use of *ā* where Midland and southern dialects have open *ǫ*: *ga* 10 B 11 (rhyming with *ma*, which, being a contraction of *make*, must have had *ā*), 20 B 183 (rhyming with *Lysya*), *twa* 18 C 255 (rhyming with *Cynthia*), *alane* 19 F 94 (rhyming with *tane*). The vowel had evidently been raised and fronted so that it merged with the descendant of the earlier diphthong *ai*, and could be spelt accordingly: *gayne* 'gone' 10 B 54, *saik* 10 C 90, *fane* 'fain' 18 A 29, *rayr* 'roar' 20 B 138 (rhyming with *ayr*). Before *ld*, which in the South caused lengthening of short *a* to *ā*, which was then rounded to *ǫ*, *a* is usually retained, e.g. *behald* 10 A 101, *cald* 20 B 259, but spelling sometimes shows a rounded vowel written *au/aw*, e.g. *auld* 18 A 90, *fawld* 96. The Scots forms are not invariably used.

Southerly variants with *o* are occasionally adopted, and rhymes prove that they are the poet's own forms, not merely scribal. Thus, *sore* 10 A 82 rhymes with *before*, *soir* 18 C 100 with *thairfoir*, *tho* 106 with *Cupido*, *go* 19 E 6, *so* 14, *wo* 30, and *fo* 38 with *sepulchro*. The spelling *oi* or *oy* (as in *Poyll* 'Pole' 20 B 153) in such cases is a device to indicate a long *o*, apparently based on the frequent *ai* as the equivalent of long *ā*. Similarly, the spelling *ei* is often used for long *ē* (which by this date represented [i:]), e.g. *deid* 18 C 32, *sleip* 19 A 11. Corresponding to the close *ǭ* of southerly dialects Scots usually has a fronted vowel written *u* or *ui*: *pure* 'poor' 10 C 137 (rhyming with *assure*), *rude* 'rood' 18 A 9, *buik* 18 C 58, *flude* 20 B 99. When followed by a fricative this becomes *eu*, e.g. *beugh* 5, line 39. Corresponding to the diphthong which in the South was written *ei/ey* in words like *eye*, Scots, and in part northern dialects of English, had the simple vowel *ē* ([i:]), e.g. *de* 'die' 18 B 60, (rhyming with *he*), *dee* 19 F 11 (rhyming with *me*), *ene* 'eyes' 19 D 107 (rhyming with *clene*). The spelling does not always fit the sound: cf. *see* rhyming with *eye* at 12 C 158. Of consonants, the most general Scots feature is the plosive instead of the southerly affricate in *kirk* 'church' 10 C 112, *sic* 'such' 141, *quhilk* 'which' 18 B 135. Against this general relation the word 'gate' has initial *y*- in *yett* 10 B 14. The spelling *quh*- is usual for the initial sound now written *wh* (OE *hw*): *quhen* 'when' 10 A 3, *quhat* 'what' 26. This is distinguished from *qu* in such words as *quair* 18 C 40. The fricative consonant palatal or velar is usually spelt *ch*, e.g. *aneuch* 18 C 110, *nocht* 10 A 7, *hecht* 28, *mycht* 42; but the southerly *gh* appears occasionally, e.g. *tyght* 20 B 52. The initial sound of 'shall' and 'should' is *s*, e.g. *sall* 10 A 16, *suld* 18 B 70, but that of 'sir' is *sch* in *schir* 10 C 90, 18 B 120. Before final -*er* medial *d* is often so spelt, e.g. *moderis* 19 F 26, *fader* 20 B 101, but sometimes also *th*, e.g. *mother* 18 C 135, *father* 97.

Certain prepositions and conjunctions have characteristic Scots forms: *gif* 'if' 10 A 17, 18 A 7, *til(l)* 'to' 18 A 79, 80, 19 D 26, 20 A 6, *quhill* 'until' 10 B 64, 20 A 106.

GLOSSARY

THE Glossary contains only words, forms, or senses which may cause difficulty to a modern reader. Some entries therefore record only 'contextual' senses. Words explained in the Commentary are not included, nor usually are common variant forms such as the plural of nouns in *-es/-is*, present-tense third-person singular forms ending in *-eth/-ith* and plurals in *-en*, or past tenses in *-ed/-id*.

The letter *y* when it represents a vowel is treated as the equivalent of *i*; the letter *i* when it represents an initial consonant is listed under initial consonantal *y-*.

The following abbreviations are used:

adj.	adjective	n.	noun
adv.	adverb(ial)	num.	numeral
alchem.	alchemical	occas.	occasionally
art.	article	orig.	originally
astron.	astronomical	pa.	past tense
auxil.	auxiliary	person.	personified
coll.	collective	phr.	phrase
comp.	comparative	pl.	plural
conj.	conjunction	poss.	possessive
dat.	dative	p.p.	past participle
def.	definite	pr.	present tense
demons.	demonstrative	prep.	preposition
F	French	prob.	probably
gen.	genitive	pron.	pronoun
her.	heraldic	pr.p.	present participle
imper.	imperative	refl.	reflexive
impers.	impersonal	rel.	relative
indef.	indefinite	sg.	singular
interj.	interjection	subj.	subjunctive
interrog.	interrogative	sup.	superlative
It	Italian	v.	verb
L	Latin	W	Welsh

a *see* **hawe**
a, ane *adj., indef. art.* one; a, an; (with numeral adjectives) some, about: ~ *fyve yere before*, etc.
a *adv.* ever, always
a *pron.* he
a *prep.* on, in; of
abay *n.* barking of hounds at the death of the prey; *(be) at* ~, *(turne) to* ~ be in extremities, turn in desperation
abayd *see* **abyd(e)**
abaien *pr. 3 pl.* bark at
abaisit, aba(i)s(s)hed *p.p.* abashed, dismayed, humbled

abak(e) *adv.* back(wards) *putte* ~ reject, repel
abate *n.* faintness
abated *pa. 3 sg.* grew dim
abey *v.* pay for
abeit *see* **habit**
abyd(e) *v.* wait, remain, stay, wait for; **abayd, abode, abood** *pa.,* **abiden, abydyn** *p.p.*
abydynge *n.* pause, delay
abyll *adj.* seemly, proper
abject(e) *adj., n.* degraded, despicable; outcast
abode, abood *n.* staying, delay, pause

aboif, above, abo(u)n(e), abovyn, abufe *adv., prep.* above, on the surface, upon

abo(u)t, aboughte *adv., prep.* about, around, on every side

abraide *v.* break out; take leave of; **abraid, abreide** *pa. 3 sg.*

abroche *adv.: sett* ~ broached, opened up

abrode *adv.* abroad, around, at large, wide

accompanyed *pa. 3 pl., refl.* congregated (24 A 6)

accompted *p.p.* accounted

accordynge *adj.* fitting

acombred *p.p.* oppressed

acomplyshe *v.:* ~ *up his armys* complete his jousts

acountin *pr. 3 pl.* reckon, count

adamande *n.* adamant (a hard mineral)

adauntid *p.p.* subdued

adawe *v.* dawn, arise

addres(se) *v.* prepare, put on, order; redress; introduce; direct

adewe *adv.* gone, departed

adjoyne *v.* join, unite; **adjonyt** *pa. 3 sg.*

adjutory *adj.* helping

ado: *in phr. have* ~ have to do; make ready (21. 111)

adoghtyd *p.p.* afraid

adrad, adredde *p.p.* afraid, frightened

a-dreid *adv. phr.* for fear that, lest

adventure *see* **aventur(e)**

advertences *n. pl.* observations

advertith *imper. pl.* take heed

advyse *see* **avyse**

advysement *n.* consideration; deliberation; warning

afe(e)rd(e) *p.p., adj.* afraid

afer *adv.* afar

affeccio(u)n, affectioun *n.* affection, fondness, love, desire

affectuously *adv.* earnestly, with emotion

affya(u)nce *n.* faith, trust

afor(e) *adv., prep., conj.* before, formerly, beforehand, ahead; ~ *that* before

afote *adv. phr.* on foot

afray(e), affray *n.* affray, battle, attack; tumult, storm; terror, fear

afraye *v.* frighten, terrify

afronte *adv.* abreast

after *adj.* later

after, af(f)tir, aftur, *adv., prep., conj.* afterwards, following: *withynne ii daies* ~, *on the morwe* ~; after, according to, for, along ~ *that* after; ~ *as* according as

aga(y)n(e), ageyn(e), aye(y)n(e) *adv., prep.* back, again; in reply, in return; against, contrary to, for

agaynes, agaynst(e), aye(i)ns(t)(e) *prep.* towards, facing, against, on, to

agast(e) *p.p., adj.* frightened, afraid

Agnus Dei (L. 'Lamb of God') a prayer said or sung as the consecrated host is broken at mass

ago(ne), agoo(n) *p.p., adv.* gone; ago, in times past

agrise *v.* quake, feel terror

ay(e) *adv.* always, ever

ayle *v.* (occas. impers.) ail, be the matter with; *alis ... at* hold against; **alit, eyled** *pa. sg.*

aill *n.* ailment

ayr *n.* justice ayre (a circuit court)

air *adv.* early; ~ *and late* at all times, continuously

aythir *see* **eithyr**

akehornes *n. pl.* acorns

aknowe *p.p.:* **am/be** ~ confess, avow, acknowledge

al, all(e), aull, aw *n., adj., adv.* everything; all; completely, entirely, only; ~ *be me loth* although it is hateful to me

a-land(e), a-londe *adv. phr.* on land, ashore

alanerly *adv.* solely, only

a-lawe *adv. phr.* downwards

a-lawyng laughing

alday *adv.* always, all the time

ald(e) *see* **oolde**

alder *adj., gen. pl.: your* ~ *spede* the helper of you all

algate *adv.* at any rate, nevertheless, in every way

Alhalwyn *n. gen. pl.:* ~ *yeven* All-Hallows Eve (the eve of All Saints' Day, 31 October)

alis, alit *see* **ayle**

a-lyte *adv. phr.* a little

alla(y)ne *adj., adv.* alone (sometimes with prefixed pron.: *hym/the* ~)

all(e) *see* **al**

alle *n.* ale

allectuose *adj.* alluring

all(e)so(o) *see* **als**

all-house *n.* ale-house

al(l)owid, allowit *p.p.* allowed, granted; commended, honoured

allquhair *adv.* everywhere

GLOSSARY

al(l)ther *adj. gen. pl.*: ~ *maist*, ~ *grettist* most/greatest of all

almes(se), almous *n.* alms, charity: ~ dede/ deid

a-londe *see* a-land(e)

alonge *adv.*: *all* ~ fully, at full length

alowyd *see* al(l)owid

als, also, all(e)so(o) *adv., conj.* also, as, just as

alterith(e) *pr. 3 sg.* corrupts; changes; alterait *p.p.*

althergrettyst *see* al(l)ther

amaille *n.* enamel

amang *see* among(e)

amased *p.p.* bewildered, astounded

amatist *n.* amethyst

ambages *n. pl.* equivocations, ambiguities

ambiguité *n.* perplexity, hesitation

ambre *n.* amber

amende *v.* improve (upon), grow better; (refl.) reform one's ways

(a)mis *adv.* wrongly, wrongfully; amiss

amyté *n.* friendship, love

amytt *v.* grant

ammyral *n.* admiral

among(e), amang, emange, emonge *prep., adv.* among(st): *tham* ~; continually: *ever* ~; always, perpetually; at times, from time to time, in a group, to be found

amonycioun *n.* admonition, reproof

amorettis *n. pl.* (?) love-knots; (?) wild flowers of some kind

amount *v.* mount up, ascent

an *see* hawe; on

anamalyt *p.p.* enamelled

anarmit *p.p.* armed, in armour

ancer, ancre *n.* anchor; ancures *pl.*

and, and if *conj.* if

ane *see* a

anenst, anentis *prep.* beside, concerning

aneuch *see* inogh(e)

angerly *adv.* angrily, resentfully

angyll-pertes *n. pl.* (?) earthworms of some kind used in fishing

Angnus *see* Agnus Dei

angry *adj.* vexed, troubled, sorrowing

angur *n.* vexation, affliction, sorrow

a-nyght by night

anis *see* ones

anything, onything(e) *adv.* at all, to any extent, in any way

ankir *n.* hermit, anchorite

annewche *see* inogh(e)

annexed *p.p.* united, conjoined

annexion *n.* union

an(n)oye *n.* displeasure, trouble

anoder *adj.* another

anoye *v.* trouble

anon(e), anoon, onon *adv.* at once, immediately, quickly; ~ *as* as soon as; ~ryght *adv.* immediately

anow *n., adj.* enough

anteris *see* aventur(e)

antymes *n. pl.* anthems

aourned *p.p., adj.* adorned

apaid *p.p.* pleased

apeertly *adv.* openly, publicly

apeyre *v.* damage, injure; degenerate, decay; appayreth *pr. 3 sg.*; aperyd *p.p.*

apere; apese *see* ap(p)ere; ap(p)ese

A per se *n.* paragon

apyrsmart *adj.* sharp, severe

aplye, aplyde; apoynt(ed) *see* apply; ap(p)oynted

aport *n.* bearing

appayreth *see* apeyre

apparaile *n.* equipment, attire, array

apparayllyng *pr. p.* preparing, making use of

apparence *n.* apparition

appechementes *n. pl.* criminal charges

apperance *n.* appearance; *be* ~ seemingly

ap(p)ere, appeir *v.* appear, be plain; ~ *forth* become visible; appiereth, appeiris *p.p. 3 sg., pl.*; ap(p)e(e)rid, appiered *pa.*

ap(p)ese *v.* appease, lessen, relieve; subside, grow calm; ap(p)e(a)sed *p.p.*

apply, aplye *v.* (refl.) apply oneself; be attached to, rely on, have recourse to; aplyede *p.p.* devoted

ap(p)oynted, apoynt *p.p.* made an appointment, made arrangements for; (?) ordained, i.e. it is because of (12 C 136); *well* ~ well equipped, well fitted out; appoyntynge *pr. p.* making ready

appose *v.* interrogate

appreveth *pr. 3 sg.* proves, supports

appropred *p.p., adj.* set, fixed, appropriate

aprehensyble *adj.* able to understand

apt(e) *adj.* fitted, suited

aray(e), array *n.* array, garb; *out of al* ~ without any attire; manner, state

araye *v.* array, equip; beat; ar(r)aid, arayde *p.p.*: *fowll* ~ soiled

arraysed *pa. 3 sg.* levied, raised

511

are *adv.* previously, before
aredy *adj., adv.* ready; already
are(e)st *n.* stop, cessation, interruption
areir *adv.* behind
arerid *p.p.* raised
aryght, ariht *adv.* aright, properly, correctly, exactly
aris *n. pl.* oars
arke *n.* arc (circle through which a planet or star passes)
armypotent *adj.* mighty in arms
arn(e) *pr. 3 pl.* are
a-rom(e) *adv.* at a distance
a-rowe *adv.* in succession, one after another
array *see* **aray(e)**
arraunte *adj.* errant, wandering
arreyned *p.p.* arraigned
arrette *v.* impute
Arrogoners *n. pl.* men of Aragon
art *n.* direction, area (20 B 261)
arted *p.p.* constrained
art-magicianis *n. pl.* practitioners of the magical art
arwes *n. pl.* arrows
as, asse *adv., conj.* as, as far as, according as, as if, when; (emphatic) ~ *for me, ~had thou not . . .* then you had not . . .; (with imper.) ~ *go, etc.;* ~ *at/for this/ the tyme;* ~ *now/than* just now/then; ~ *they myght heye* as fast as they could go; as it were; ~ *he/they that* as one/ people who
asay(e); aschyn *see* **assay; axe**
ascrive *v.* ascribe
ascwysyd *pa. 1 sg., refl.* excused (myself)
asell, eysel *n.* vinegar
asythe *n.* reparation
askith *see* **axe**
asondre *adv.* asunder, in two
asoted *p.p.* infatuated
aspectis *n. pl.* (astron.) aspects (the relative positions of the planets as seen from Earth)
aspye, aspyin *v.* espy, peer, spy out, discern, notice
assay, asay(e) *v.* try, test, attempt, appeal to; **assayit** *p.p.* assailed (19 A 16)
assail(l)(e) *v.* attack; try, make trial of; **assailyeit** *pa. 3 sg.;* **assaillit** *p.p.*
assays *n. pl.,: at all* ~ in all circumstances, always
assaut *n.* assault, attack
asse *see* **as**

assent *n.* agreement, compliance; *by one* ~ with one accord
assewred *see* **assure**
assyng *v.* designate, assign, indicate, arrange, fix; **assigneth** *pr. 3 sg.;* **assygned** *p.p.*
assistaunce, assistens *n.* presence, attendance; bystanders
assyste *pr. 3 pl.* are present
assystentes *n. pl.* bystanders, those present
assoille *v.* shrive, give absolution to, have mercy on; **assoyled** *pa. 3 sg.*
assure *n.* azure, blue
assure *v.* find security, be confident, trust; **assewred** *pa. 3 pl., p.p.;* **assured** *p.p.*
astat(e) *see* **estate**
astert(e) *v.* escape; start, rush; **astert** *pa. 3 sg.*
astoneth *pr. 3 sg.* is amazed; **astoynd** *pp.* astonished
astrologgis *n. pl.* astrologers
at *prep.* at, to, in
at *rel. pron., conj.* that
ateyne; athir *see* **at(t)eyne; eithyr**
atyre *n.* head-dress (5. 114)
atonys, atanys *adv.* at once
a-too *adv. phr.* in two
atouir, attour *prep.* over
attame *v.* venture
atte at the
at(t)eyne *v.* come to, attain, reach, obtain
attemperaunce *n.* temperance
attempred *p.p., adj.* equable, mild; **attempreth** *pr. 3 sg.* tempers, controls
attilld *pa. pl. refl.* made ready
attis at this
attour *see* **atouir**
attournay *n.* advocate; *make . . .* ~ appoint an advocate
atwen *prep.* between
atwite *v.* blame (for)
aucht *pa. sg.* ought
aughte eight
auld; aull *see* **oolde; al**
auncien, auncyent *adj.* ancient, old; **auncyentes** *n. pl.* old ones
aupone *prep.* upon
auster *adj.* austere, stern
auter, autir *n.* altar; *sacrament of the* ~ the Mass, the consecrated host
authoreist *p.p.* having authority
autours *n. pl.* authors

avayle *n.* advantage, prowess

avance; avantage *see* **ava(u)nce; ava(u)ntage**

avant(e) *adv., interj.* forward, away; ~ *baner* advance the banners!

avastithe *pr. 3 sg.* wastes away

ava(u)nce *v.* advance, come forward; help, better; bring more quickly; **avaunced** *pa. pl. refl.*

ava(u)ntage *n.* advantage, profit, benefit, winnings, opportunity, place of vantage

avaunt(e) *n.* vow, boast

avent *imper., refl.* relieve (yourself)

aventur(e), adventure, awentour/ -ture, awnter *n.* fortune, chance, risk: *at* ~ at random, anyhow; *at all* ~ *s* at all costs, at any risk; *at our* ~ no matter what befalls us; *be/by/of(f)* ~ by chance, perchance; plight, misfortune, peril: *(putte)* . . . *in* ~ risk; **anteris** *pl.*

aventure *v.* venture

avyse, advyse *n.* counsel, advice; *with- owt* ~ without question

avyse, advyse, awyse *v.* observe, note; counsel; (refl.) consider, take heed; **avysed/-yde** *p.p.*: *ewyll* ~ unwise; *I woll be* ~ I will consider

avisynes *n.* deliberation

avision *n.* vision, dream

avoyde *v.* depart, go away; **avoyde (of)** *p.p., adj.* free (of)

avow(e) *n.* vow, promise

avows (?) *interj.* assuredly, certainly (16. 607)

aw *see* **al**

awayt *n.* watchfulness

awalk *v.* awake

awansing *n.* advancement

awappid *p.p.* confounded, stupefied by fear

awentour, awenture; awin; awyse *see* **aventur(e); owyn(e); avyse**

awmener *n.* almoner

awnter; awne *see* **aventur(e); owyn(e)**

awowit *pa. 3 sg.* vowed

awowtry *n.* adultery

awrokyn *p.p.* revenged

axe *v.* ask, demand, require; **askith** *pr. 3 sg.* **axen, aschyn** *pr. 3 pl.*

axynge *n.* request

axis *n.* fever

ayeen, ayeyn, ayen(e); ayeinst, ayens(te) *see* **aga(y)n(e); agaynes**

ayen-callyng *n.* calling back

ayenward *adv.* conversely, on the contrary

ba *imper. sg.* kiss

bab *n.* baby

bable *n.* bauble, plaything

bachelere, bachillare *n.* (young) knight; bachelor (one who has taken his first degree); **bachilleris** *pl.*

bad(d)(e) *see* **bede**

bagge *n.* badge

baid *see* **byd(e)**

bailfull *adj.* harmful, destructive; miserable, wretched

baill *n.* misery, sorrow

bail(l)yes *n. pl.* bailiffs

bayne *n.* bone; **banys, boonys** *pl.*

bayned *p.p.* bathed

bair; baysnet *see* **bar, ber(e), boor; basonet**

bayt *n.* halt

baith *see* **bothe**

balas *n. pl.* balas rubies

bale *n.* set (of dice)

bales, ballys *n.* rod, scourge, switch

balestres *n. pl.* crossbows

balk *n.* beam

ballet *n.* poem, song; **balyttys, ballat(t)is** *pl.*

ballys; balme, balmyng *see* **bales; bawme**

bancat *n.* banquet

band *n.* bond(s), bondage

bandonit *p.p.* subdued

baneist *p.p.* banished

banys *see* **bayne**

bank(e) *n.* hillside, bank, slope

bankouris *n. pl.* coverings for seats or benches

banned, bannyd *pa. 3 sg.* cursed, swore at

bar, bair *adj.* bare, destitute (of)

barbaris *gen. pl.* barbarians'

barbycans *n. pl.* barbicans (outer fortifications, towers over gates and bridges)

bar(e) *see* **ber(e)**

bareyn(e), barrayne, barrand, barrant *adj.* barren, devoid; (of deer) barren (without fawn, hence fair game)

bargane *n.* fight

bargaret *n.* pastoral song

bargen *n.* purchase, bargain

bargyes *n. pl.* barges, boats

barys *see* **boor**

barm(e) *n.* bosom

barne *n.* child

baronnye *n.* barons

barrayne, barrand, barrant *see* **bareyn(e)**

bas *imper. sg.* kiss

basonet, baysnet *n.* basnet (a small light steel helmet)

basse *adj.* low, bottom

bastard *n.* bastard, a sweet Spanish wine

bata(y)l(l)e, bate(y)ll(e) *n.* battle; battle array, division, army, host; **bat(t)allis** *pl.*

bathe *see* **bothe**

batur(e) *n.* batter

bawburd *n.* larboard

bawdrik *n.* belt, girdle

bawer *(n. as) adj.* beaver

bawis *n. pl.* balls, testicles

bawme, balme *n.* balm, fragrance

bawme *v.* anoint with balm; anoint, smear; **balmyng** *n.* anointing with balm

be *see* **bi**

be, ben(e), byn *v.* be; **be** *pr. subj.*; **by** (8 C 19), **bith, beth(e), ben(e), beyn(g)** *pr. pl.*; **beis** *pr. 3 pl. as future* (18 B 14) **was(e), wes, whos, vhos, wer(e)(n), wair, war(e), wher** *pa.* was, were; **by, be(e)th** *imper. sg., pl.*; **beynge** *pr. p., adj.* living; **beyn, be(n)(e), ybe** *p.p.*

beamys *n. pl.* trumpets

bearnes *see* **berne**

bebled *p.p., adj.* covered with blood

beck *v.* nod

bede *n.* prayer, prayer-bead; **beedes, bedys** *pl.*; ~**-rolles** *n. pl.* prayer-rolls, lists of people to be prayed for; ~**-woman** *n.* woman who prays for a benefactor

bede, byd(e) *v.* bid, command, order; offer; pray, ask; desire, seek; **byddys** *pr. 3 sg.*; **bad(d)(e)** *pa.*

bedene, bydene *adv.* quickly; together

bedowyn *p.p.* immersed

beedes; beer *see* **bede; bere, ber(e)**

beerners, beorno(u)rs *n. pl.* attendants in charge of hownds

bees *n. pl.* rings, bracelets

be(e)stly; beete(n); beeth *see* **best(e); bete; be**

bef(f)e *n.* beef

befoir, befor(n)e, byfor(n)e *adv., prep.* in front, beforehand; before, in front of

beft *pa. pl.* struck

begon(n)e, begoon *p.p.* begun, befallen; *wel* ~ fortunate, happy; **begouth** *pa. 3 sg.* began

behest(e), byheeste *n.* promise

behete, bihet, behight *v.* promise; encourage; **beheght, behyght** *pa. 3 sg., p.p.*

behove *n.* use, benefit, advantage

beyk *v.* warm; **beikit** *pa. sg.*

be(i)ld *n.* refuge, sheltering-place; relief, succour

beildit *p.p.* constructed

beyn(g)(e) *see* **be**

beir *n.* noise, clamour, din

beyren *see* **ber(e)**

bekend *p.p.* instructed

bekyn *n.* beacon, signal

belaft *p.p.* left

belangand *pr. p.* pertaining

belches *pr. 3 pl.* blaze, burn

beld *see* **be(i)ld**

beleve, bile(i)ve *n.* belief

beleve, belevyn, bileeven *v.* believe; **bileeveden** *pa. 3 pl.* **bilyvyng** *pr. p.*

bely *n.* belly: *my* ~ *full* as much as I can eat; ~**-fyll** *n.* bellyful; ~**-mett** *adj.* amply satisfying

belyve *adv.* quickly, at once

beme *n.* beam of light, light

ben *adv.* within, to an inner room

bene *adv.* handsomely

ben(e) *see* **be**

benedycyte *interj.* bless you/us

benygne *adj.* gracious, gentle, kind, merciful; **beny(g)ngly** *adv.* graciously

benignyté *n.* graciousness, kindness, goodness

benkis *n. pl.* benches

bent *n.* field

bent *pa. sg.* turned, directed; **bent** *p.p.* struck, driven; turned, strained

beorno(u)rs *see* **beerners**

berd(e) *n.* beard

bere, beer *n.*[1] bear

bere *n.*[2] beer

ber(e), berre, beryn *v.* bear, carry; (her.) display on a shield; ~ *the belle* be pre-eminent; ~ *behynde* be able to carry (a second person) behind; ~ *a rule* wield power, authority; ~ *upon*, ~ *(an/on/ upon) ho(o)nd(e)* maintain, assert against; **beryt** *pr. sg.*, **be(y)ren** *pr. pl.*; **bar(e), bair, beer, boir, bur** *pa.*; **berande** *pr. p.*; **bar(e), bore** *p.p.* carried, born

berevit *see* **bireve**

beriall *n.* beryl

beryn, beryt *see* **ber(e)**
beryt *pa. sg.* bellowed, roared
berne *n.* young fellow, man, warrior; **bernis, bearnes** *pl.*
bernys *n. pl.* barns
berre(st) *see* **ber(e)**
bertnyt *p.p.* hewed
beschadit *pa. pl.* cast a shadow over
beschrew *v.* curse
bese(e)n(e), beseyn *p.p., adj.* furnished, equipped, -looking (with adv.): *wele/richely* ~
besily, bisily *adv.* diligently, busily, eagerly, zealously
besynes(se), bisynesse *n.* business, work, activity, task, occupation, concern: *to my* ~ for my purpose; trouble, solicitude, anxiety
best(e) *n.* beast, animal; **be(e)stly** *adj., adv.* bestial, like a beast
bestiall *n.* animals
bestly *see* **be(e)stly**
bestow(e) *v.* stow (things) into; (refl.) find shelter
bet *see* **bete; bet(t)**
betake *v.* commit; (refl.) give (oneself) to
betakynnand *pr. p.* betokening
bete, beete(n) *v.* beat, strike, lay on; overcome, defeat; inlay, embroider; **bet(e), bett(e), beeten** *pa.*; **bet(en), betyn** *p.p.*
beteiche *v.* commit, yield
betels; beth(e) *see* **betle; be**
bethoght, bethowt *pa. sg. (refl.)* thought on, considered
betyde *v.* befall, happen; **betyde** *pr. subj.* may (it) befall; **betid(de)** *pa., pp.*
betyme *adv.* in good time, on time
betle *n.* wedge; **betels** *pl.*
bet(t) *adj. comp.* better
bet(t)(e), betyn *see* **bete**
beugh, bewis *see* **bowe**
bewavit *pa. 3 sg.* blew about
bewry *p.p.* overlaid
bewtynes *n.* beauty
by *see* **be**
by, bie *v.* buy, pay for, redeem; ~ *yow* buy for yourself; **boght, bowt(e)** *pa., p.p.*, **bocht, (y)bought** *p.p.*
bi, bye *adv., prep.* beside: ~ *and* ~ presently, at once; by, about, concerning: *the/me* ~ according to; from; when: ~ *that* by the time that; ~ *derke/the morwe* in, on; ~ *tyme* in

good time, early
byclipped *pa. 3 sg.* enclosed, embraced
bycome *pa. 3 sg.*: ~ *well in our waye* turned to our favour
bid, byddys *see* **bede**
byd(e) *v.* stay, stay with, dwell; **bydis** *pr. 3 sg.*; **baid** *pa. 3 sg.*
byd(e); bydene; byforne *see* **bede; bedene; befoir**
byg(ge) *adj.* big, powerful, (of ground) (?) solid, heavy
byggyns *n. pl.* buildings
biggit *p.p.* built, made
bihalfe, byhalve *n.* (in/on) behalf, respect (of); *in that* ~ in respect of that
byheeste; bihet *see* **behest(e); behete**
bykering *n.* skirmish
bikkrit *pa. 3 pl.* attacked with repeated blows
bileeven, bileeveden, bile(i)ve *see* **beleve**
bylis *n. pl.* boils
bilyvyng *see* **beleve**
bill(e) *n.* writing, formal document, letter
bills *n. pl.* halberds (long weapons with both axehead and spearhead)
byn *see* **be**
bind(e) *v.* bind, punish; (refl.) *couth* ~ *him* attached himself; **boonde** *pa.*; **bounde, boundin** *p.p.* bound, under legal obligation (to), captivated
by-path *n.* side-path
birde *n.* maiden
bireve *v.* deprive of, despoil, rob, take by force; **berevit, biraft** *p.p.*
byrnyst *p.p., adj.* burnished
byrsyt *pa. 3 sg.* bruised
byscocte, byscokte *n.* biscuit
byse *n.* bice, azure
bisettith *pr. 3 sg.* suits, becomes, befits
bisily; bisynesse *see* **besily; besynes(se)**
bissart *n.* buzzard
bissy *adj.* active, busy, diligent
bith *see* **be**
bityt *pr. 3 sg.* bites; **bote** *pa.* bit
bittyng *n.* biting
bla *adj.* livid, bluish
blac, blak(e) *adj.* black; ~ *monkys* *n. pl.* Benedictine monks
blaiknit *p.p.* made pale
blanchit *p.p.* bleached, whitened
blanked *pa. 1 pl.* disconcerted, brought to nought
blasyng sterre *n.* comet
blasmed *p.p.* blamed, reproached

blaucht *p.p., adj.* (turned) pale
blawis *n. pl.* blows, strokes
bleef *pa. 3 sg.* remained
ble(y)ke *n.* bleak, a small river-fish
bleike *adj.* pale
blench *v.* deceive
blenk *n.* glance, look
blenk *v.* glance, look; **blent** *pa. 1 sg.*;
  ~**ing** *n.* glancing
blereed *p.p., adj.* bleared, watery
blesis *n. pl.* fires, flames, torches
bl(y)ith(e) *adj.* merry, joyful, glad, delighted, gracious; **blyithnes** *n.* happiness
blyn *v.* wait, cease
blo, bloo *adj.* blackish-blue, leaden-
  coloured
blockyssh *adj.* gross
blomes *n. pl.* flowers
blomyt; bloo *see* **blwmyng; blo**
blowt *adj.* barren, bare
blwmyng *pr.p., adj.* flourishing; **blomyt**
  p.p., adj. blossomed
bobbe *n.* grub or larva of a fly or beetle
  (used for bait)
bocht, boght *see* **by**
boddum *n.* low-lying land
body *n.* body; nave (of church); person:
  her ~ her, *of his own* ~ personally
boig *n.* bog, mire
boir *n.* hole, chink
boir; boyt; bok *see* **ber(e); bo(o)te; bolke**
bokeram *b.* buckram (linen used for
  lining)
boldynnys *pr. 3 sg.* swells
boles *n. pl.* trunks (of trees)
bolke, bok *v.* belch; **bok** *pa.*
bollewerkes, bowlewerkes *n. pl.* bul-
  warks, ramparts
bombardes *n. pl.* cannon
bonde *n.* bondman, peasant
bondis *see* **bo(u)ndis**
bone *n.* slayer
bone *n.* request, prayer
book-othe *n.* oath sworn on the Bible
boonys; boord(e) *see* **bayne; borde**
boor, bair *n.* boar; **barys** *pl.*
bo(o)st *n.* boasting, threatening, menace,
  arrogance
bo(o)te, boyt *n.*[1] boat
bo(o)te, bothe, bu(i)t(e) *n.*[2] remedy,
  help, helper
borde, boord(e), burd(e) *n.* table; food;
  plank, board, side of ship: *hygh* ~ top

deck, *on* ~ on board; *hard on* ~ close
  at hand; **burdis** *pl.*
bordelles *n. pl.* brothels
bordour, bordure *n.* border, edge
bore *see* **ber(e)**
borh *n.* town
borow *n.* surety
bor(o)we(n) *v.* borrow; save, protect;
  redeem; **borowit** *p.p.*
bost; bosteous; bot(e); bote; boteler *see*
  **bo(o)st; busteous; but; bo(o)te, bityt;
  butlare**
bot(e)ry *n.* buttery
bothe *see* **bo(o)te**
bothe, bothyn, baith, bathe *adj., adv.*
  both, as well; **her bothins** of both of
  them
bottler *see* **butlare**
boun *adj.* ready, attentive
bounde, boundin *see* **bind(e)**
bo(u)ndis, bowndis *n. pl.* bounds, bound-
  aries, frontiers
bountee *n.* goodness
bountevous *adj.* generous
bour *see* **bowr(e)**
bourd *n.* jest; ~**er** *n.* jester; ~**ing** *n.*
  jesting
bourgeys(e) *see* **burges**
bousynge *n.* boozing, guzzling
bout *see* **but**
bowe, beugh *n.* bough, branch; **bewis** *pl.*
bowlewerkes; bowdes/-is *see* **bollewerkes; bo(u)ndis**
bownyt *pa. 3 sg.* went
bowr(e), bour *n.* bower, bed-chamber
bowt(e) *see* **by**
bra *n.* bank, hillside
brace *v.* fasten, tie up
bradden *see* **braid**
brag *n.* blast, bray
braid *see* **brode**
braid *n.* sudden movement
braid *pa. 3 sg.* rushed, burst, sprang;
  bradden *pa. 3 pl.*
bray(e) *v.* cry, roar, neigh, resound; **brayt**
  pa.; **brayeng** *pr. p.* crashing
brayeng(e), brayng(e) *n.* roaring
brayles *n. pl.* ropes used for furling sails
braithly *adv.* violently, strongly
brak(e) *see* **brek(e)**
brand *n.* burning brand; sword; **brundis**
  pl.
brand *adj.* muscled, brawny
brast(e) *see* **brest(e)**

brathly *adj.* violent, strong, impetuous

breddyt *p.p.* boarded

brede, breid *n.* breadth; *on* ~ open(ly)

bredest *see* **brode**

bredynge *n.* reproach, upbraiding

bredyt(h) *pr. 3 sg.* breeds

breeke *see* **brek(e)**

breffe *v.*: ~ *a byll* draw up a petition

breid *see* **brede**

breir *n.* briar

breird *n.* shoot, sprout; *on* ~ spread

brek(e) *v.* break; break into, interrupt; break out, escape from; ~ *out* knock out, escape; ~ *it out* reveal, ~ . . . *to* make known; **brekkis** *pr. 3 pl.*; **brak(e)**, **breeke** *pa.*; **broke, brokyn** *p.p.*

bremys *n. pl.* breams (fish, a variety of carp)

brended *p.p., adj.* brindled, streaked; *a grete* ~ *flye* (?) the brandling or dew-worm (used in angling)

brenge *v.* bring; ~ *forth* banish; **browt(e)**, **brwght** *pa., p.p.*; (i) **bro(u)ght** *p.p.*

bren(ne) *v.* burn; **brende, brynt** *pa.*; **brent(e), ibrende, bront** *p.p.*; **brennynge** *pr.p., adj., n.* burning

brent *adj.* lofty, smooth

bresyd *see* **bruse**

brest(e), brast, brist *v.* break, burst; **braste** *pa.*; **brostyn, bursin** *p.p.*

brethell *v.* (?) make into a worthless person

brethellys, brothelys *n. pl.* rascals, scoundrels

brether *n. pl.* brothers

Bretouns *n. pl.* Britons

brevit *pa. 3 sg.* related, told

briddes, brydes, bridis *n. pl.* (small) birds

brydelynge *pr.p., adj.*: *a* ~ *caste* (?) a final throw

brigaundynes *n. pl.*: *a peire of* ~ body armour in two halves

brygge *n.* bridge

brym *n.* edge, brim

brym(e) *adj.* fierce, strong, furious

brynke *n.* edge, bank

brynt; bryst *see* **bren(ne); brest(e)**

bryst *n.* breast

brytell *adj.* frail, weak

brochys *n. pl.* brooches

brode, brood, braid *adj.* broad, wide; coarse, unrefined; **bredest** *sup.* widest

broder, brodyr *n.* brother

brodys *n. pl.* broods

broke *see* **brek(e)**

brome *n.* broom, broom-plant; **bromys** *pl.*

bront *see* **bren(ne)**

bront(e) *n.* attack, onset

brood; brostyn; brothelys; bro(u)ght *see* **brode; brest(e); brethellys; brenge**

browderit *p.p.* embroidered

browesses *n. pl.* broths

browis *n. pl.* eyebrows, forehead

browt(e) *see* **brenge**

bruikit *p.p., adj.* blackened, streaked with smoke (from an alchemical furnace)

bruke *n.* brook

bruke, bruik *v.* have the use of, reach

brukkill, brukle *adj.* brittle, frail, fragile; **brukilnes** *n.* frailty

brumaill *adj.* wintry

brundis *see* **brand**

bruse *v.* bruise, crush, break; **bresyd** *p.p.*

brusyt *p.p.* embroidered

brwght *see* **brenge**

bub *n.* storm, squall, blast; **bubbis** *pl.*

buckelers *n. pl.* bucklers, shields

bugill *n.* bugle

buik *n.* book, **bukis** *pl.*

buit *see* **bo(o)te**

bukkissh *adj.* wild, frenzied, violent

bullar *n.* bubble

bur; burd(e) *see* **ber(e); borde**

burely, burelie *adj.* handsome, imposing, strong

burges, bourgeys *n.* burgess, citizen, merchant; **bourgeyse** *n.* merchant's wife; **burgesyse, burgeyses** *pl.*

burned *p.p.* burnished, brilliant

burneseth *imper. pl.* burnish

burnettis *n. pl.* dark-blue flowers (? burnels or pimpernels)

burnys *n. pl.* brooks

burre *n.* broad iron ring on a spear (behind the place for the hand)

bursin *see* **brest(e)**

busk *n.* bush, thicket

busk(e) *v.* dress, adorn, array, make ready, make haste; **buskit** *p.p.*

busteous, bustuus, bosteous *adj.* rough, rude, cruel, violent, wild; **bustuusly** *adv.* rudely

but, bot(e), bout *prep., conj., adv.* without, lacking; but, except (for), unless: ~ *if* unless, *no creatuer* ~ *that* (there was)

but, bot(e), bout (*cont.*):
no creature who (would not have . . .),
he was ~ deed he was as good as dead;
only, simply, outside: *far ~* far out (19
C 85)
bute *see* **bo(o)te**
butyn *n.* booty, winnings
butlare, bottler, boteler *n.* cup-bearer,
butler, officer in charge of wine-cellar
butles *adj.* without remedy

caban *n.* hut, cabin
cac(c)he *v.* catch, get, receive
cace *see* **cas(e)**
cace, cays *n.* casket; quiver
cache, katche *n.* pursuit, hunt, chase (in
1 C 22 perh. with pun on **cas** 'plight')
cair *n.* sorrow, distress, anxiety; *~*full,
caer-/karfull *adj.* sorrowful, melancholy; *~*weid *n.* mourning garments
cais *see* **cace, cas(e)**
caytyf(e), catywe *n.* wretch, worthless
person; villain; **caitives** *pl.*
calcacyon *n.* trampling
cald(e) *see* **cauld**
calling *n.* address, welcome
campio(u)n *n.* champion
can, canst *see* **con(ne)**
canell, cannel *n.* cinnamon
canker *n.* canker-worm
cankerit *p.p., adj.* evil, depraved
Cantirbirie bellis *n. pl.* small bells on
pilgrims' horses
capacité *n.* understanding, comprehen-
sion (16. 844)
cape *n.* cap
cappit *pa. 1 pl.* headed, sailed
careckes, carrakes *n. pl.* carracks (large
ships)
car(i)en, carioun(e) *n.* carrion, dead
body; (coll.) dead flesh, corpses
carlyng *n.* old woman
carlyshe *adj.* churlish
carped, carpit *pa.* spoke, talked
carrolling *n.* singing and dancing of
carols or ring-dances
cart(e) *n.* chariot; cart: *at the ~ goone* go
with the farm-cart
cas(e), cace, cais *n.* case, circumstance(s);
I putt ~ suppose; state, condition,
plight: *in good ~*; event, happening,
chance: *in ~* by chance
casse *n.* (?) case = frame of gallows (16.
620)

cast(e) *n.* throw; volley; stratagem, contrivance, device
cast(e), kest *v.* throw, throw a stone (5.
212), cast loose (20 B 202), put,
commit; deliberate, ponder, consider,
search; resolve, decide; purpose, intend; *~ up* throw open (gates), (of
clouds) (?) rise up, (?) gather; **kyst** *pa.*;
casted *pa., p.p.*, **cast(e)(n), kest** *p.p.*
catalle, catell *n.* livestock, cattle
catechison, cathechizone *n.* catechism
cative *adj.* wretched, miserable
catywe *see* **caytyf(e)**
caudel *n.* caudle, 'a warm drink consisting of thin gruel, mixed with wine or
ale, sweetened and spiced, given chiefly
to sick people' (*OED*)
caudron, cawdren *n.* cauldron, pot
cauld, cald(e) *n., adj.* cold, sorrowful
caunvas *n.* canvas, coarse cloth
cause *n.* cause, reason: *for ~ that* because;
in ~ to blame
causy *n.* causeway
cautele *n.* deceit, trick
caw *v.* call; **cauld** *p.p.*
cawk *n.* chalk; **cawkit** *v., pa. 3 sg.* chalked
cawkit *pa. 3 sg.* shat, voided excrement
ceder *n.* cider
ceyntis *n. pl.* girdles
cely *see* **sely**
ces(se), ceis, se(a)ce, ses(s)e, sees *v.*
cease, stop; **ceissit** *pa. 3 sg.*; **cessyng**
n. ceasing
chaare, chace *see* **chare; chase**
chacechiens *n. pl.* grooms for hounds
chafed(de) *p.p., pa. 3 sg.* vexed, fretted,
(became) irritated
chafflet *n.* scaffold, platform
chair *see* **chare**
chayre, cheyere *n.* throne
Chaldey *adj.* Chaldean, Aramaic
chalenge *n.* claim
chalenge, chalange, kalenge *v.* claim,
lay claim to
chalmer, chambyr/-b(o)ur /-bre *see*
cha(u)mbre
chamlett *n.* camlet, a kind of fine cloth
chance *see* **cha(u)nce**
channoun *n.* canon (cleric living according to canonical rule); **chanons** *pl.*;
adj. canonical
chapyt *pa. 3 pl.* escaped
char *n.* turn; *on ~* ajar
chare, chaare, chair *n.* chariot

charge *n.* burden, difficulty; responsibility: *gyve yow in* ~ commend, charge yow

charge *v.* care for, attach weight to; load; weigh down, burden; **charched** *p.p.*

chase, chace *n.* hunt, pursuit, chase, (?) a hunting note (1 C 15)

cha(u)nce *n.* chance, fortune, luck; case, event, adventure, deed

chavefith *pr. 3 sg.* inflames

cha(w)mbre, chawmyr, chalmer, chamb(o)ur/-bre/-byr *n.* chamber, bedroom, private room

che *pron.* she

cheere, cheir(e); cheerid; cheyere; cheisit *see* **cher(e); chere; chayre; chese**

cheke *n.* disaster

chekyn(s) *n. pl.* chickens

chep(e) *n.* bargain: *have goyd/grete* ~ have a good bargain

chepynge *pr. p.* buying

cher(e), cheir(e), cheere *n.* countenance, bearing, demeanour, manner, spirit(s); favour, grace; *quhat/what* ~ *?* how are things/you?, etc.; *mak(e) (a) gud/doolful* ~ behave pleasantly/sadly, put on a (pleasant/sad) appearance; *mak . . .* ~ make glad

chere *v.* comfort, encourage; **cheerid** *p.p.*: *glad* ~ of cheerful/benevolent disposition; **cherfull** *adj.* gladsome, lively, joyous

cheryschet *p.p.* well cared for, well looked after; **cherysshed** *pa. 1 sg.* caressed, made much of

cherising *n.* encouragement

cherle, churle *n.* churl, rustic, peasant, low-born fellow; **cherlis** *pl.*; **chorlysh** *adj.* mean, vulgar, rustic

cherme *n.* singing

chesance *n.* way of getting money

ches(e) *n.* cheese

chese *v.* choose; **ches(e), cheisit** *pa.*; **chos** *p.p., adj.* chosen, excellent

cheverit *pa. 3 pl.* shivered

chevice *v., refl.* take care of oneself, fend for oneself

chevyn *n.* chub (a fish)

chevit *pa. 3 sg.* achieved, won

chyde *v.* dispute, quarrel; complain against

chierté *n.* regard, devotion

chiftane *n.* commander

chymmis *n. pl.* mansions, dwellings

chynes *n. pl.* chains

chyrmyng *n.* chirping

chorlysh; chos *see* **cherle; chese**

chough *n.* (Cornish) chough (red-legged crow)

churche-holowynge *n.* hallowing of a church

circulit *p.p.* surrounded

circumstaunce, sircumstance *n.* ado; ceremony; adjuncts, details

cyve *n.* sieve

clay *n.* mud (20 B 300)

clam *pa. 3 sg.* climbed

clappe *v.* clap, pat; chatter, say loudly; flap (wings); **clappis** *pr. pl.*; **clapit** *pa. 3 sg., p.p.*

clarett *n.* a wine of yellowish or light red colour

clarioneris *n. pl.* trumpeters

clarke; clathe *see* **clerk(e); clooth**

clatre *v.* clatter; chatter, gabble; **clat(t)ered** *pa.*; **clateryng** *n.* babbling, chattering

cled *pa. 3 sg.* covered

cleyght *pa. 3 sg.* clasped

clene *adj.* clean, pure, exquisite; complete: ~ *remyssyon*; **cle(a)ne** *adv.* completely, absolutely, fully: ~ *armed*; **~ly** *adv.* completely; elegantly; chastely, in purity; **clennes(se)** *n.* purity

clepe, clepyn *v.* call; **clepid(en)** *pa.*; **clepid, yclyp(p)ed** *p.p.*

cler(e), cleer, cleir *adj., adv.* clear, transparent, bright, fair, beautiful; *adv.* clearly, brightly; **clerast** *adj. sup.* clear est; **~ly** *adv.* clearly, brightly, **clerenes(se)** *n.* clarity, brightness, luminousness

clerycall *adj.* clerkly, learned

clerit *p.p.* cleared away

clerk(e), clarke *n.* cleric, (parish) clerk; learned man, scholar

clerons *n. pl.* clarions (shrill trumpets with narrow tube)

cleve *v.*[1] split

cleve *v.*[2] stick (to), cling (to); **clivid** *pa. 3 sg.*

cleverus *adj.* skilful

clewys *see* **clowes**

clyft(e) *n.* cleft

clynty *adj.* stony

clyppeth *pr. 3 sg.* clasps, embraces; **clipping** *pr.p.*

clips *n.* eclipse, deprivation

clivid *see* **cleve**

clogge *n.* block

GLOSSARY

clois; cloisit *see* **close; clos**
cloistrer *n.* monk
clok *n.* cloak; **clokis** *pl.*; **clokit** *pa. 3 sg.* cloaked, concealed
clo(o)s, close *adj.* closed, enclosed, tightly closed, restrictive, quiet, secret, hidden; *kepte . . . me ~ held him ~*
clooth, clathe *n.* cloth, tapestry; **clothys** *pl.*
clos *v.* close, enclose, entrust; **cloisit** *pa. 3 sg.*; **closit** *p.p.*
close, clois *n.* courtyard
cloth *v.* cover
clothes *n. pl.* (?) cloths wrapped around shoes, (?) cleats (16. 796)
cloute *n.* swaddling-clothes
clowes, clewys *n. pl.* gorges, valleys
clowys *n. pl.* cloves
clud *n.* cloud; **cluddis** *pl.*
cluik, cluke *n.* claw
cock (alteration of *God*): *by ~*; *by cokkys body sakyrde* by God's consecrated body, by the sacrament
cocoldis *n. pl.* cuckolds
cod-worme *n.* caddis worm
coffyn *n.* mould of dough for a pie case
cognycyon *n.* knowledge
coke, kuke *n.* cook
cold, coolde *see* **con(ne)**
cole, coll *n.* coal; **colys** *pl.*
collasyun, collatioun *n.* light meal
collegeners *n. pl.* members of a college
collettis *n. pl.* collects
collour *imper. sg.* colour
colour(e), cullour *n.* colour, complexion; show of reason, pretext, disguise
combred *p.p.* encumbered
combre-world *n.* burden to the world
com(e)(n), cum, cwm *v.* come; *~ at* approach, come near; *~ thertoo* manage to get it; **comyt** *pr. 3 sg.*; **cam, come, comyn** *pa.*; **(y)come, com(m)yn, cummyn** *p.p.*
comers-bye *n. pl.* passers-by
comynalté *n.* commons
comynecacyon, com(m)ynycacyon *n.* conversation, communication, instruction
comin(liche) *see* **com(m)oun**
commanded *pa. 3 sg., refl.* commended (herself)
commycyyon, commyssion *n.* charge, command; authority
com(m)oun, comune, comyn *adj.* com-

mon, usual, well-known; promiscuous; *~ profit* public good; **comouns** *n. pl.* commons, common people; **cominliche** *adv.* commonly
comounté *n.* community
compacient *adj.* compassionate
compaynable *adj.* friendly
compas *n.* circuit: *in ~* all around; space
compasse *n.* compost
compylit *p.p.* described, written
complexioun *n.* temperament, combination of humours
complyn *n.* compline (the last service of the day)
comprehence *n.* significance
comprehend *v.* attain
compromyse *n.: putte in ~* put to arbitration
compt(e) *n.* account, reckoning; *made no ~* took no account
comune; con *see* **com(m)oun; con(ne)**
conceyte *n.* thought, mind; esteem; idea, opinion
conceyve, conseyve, consave *v.* understand, comprehend, observe, perceive
concell *see* **counseyl(l)**
condescende *p.p.* agreed
condicio(u)n, condition *n.* condition; behaviour, disposition, nature, quality, state, habit; **condyscyons** *pl.*
conding *adv.* worthy
condyt; condyte *see* **conduyted; conduyt**
conduce *v.* bring, conduct
conduyt, condyte *n.* conduit, fountain
conduyted *pa. 3 sg.* led; **conduted, condyt** *p.p.* brought, conducted
conduyter *n.* guide
confectioun *n.* medicinal preparation; **confectyunnys** *pl.*
confluence *n.* concourse, assemblage
confortatyvys *n. pl.* cordials, reviving medicines
congelid(e) *p.p., adj.* congealed, frozen
conglutinate *p.p., adj.* cemented together
congruence *n.* propriety; *of ~* appropriately, properly
conye, conynge *n.* rabbit
conjunctionys *n. pl.* (astron.) conjunctions (the proximity of two planets as seen from Earth)
conjunctly *adv.* together, in conjunction
conjured *see* **counger**
con(n)e, can, kunne *v.* know, understand; learn, know how to, be capable of, be

able to, can; (auxil.) do, did; **co(o)ld(e), culd(e), coude/koude, cowd(e)/ kowd, cuth, couth(e)(n), cowth(e), could** *pa.* ~ *his good* knew what was good for him

con(n)yng *adj.* skilful, intelligent, learned

connyng(e), konnyng(e), cunnyng(e)/ kunnynge *n.* knowledge, skill, ability, understanding, wisdom

conqueryng *n.* winning

consayll; consave, conseyve; conseitis *see* **counse(y)l(l), counseylle; conceyve; conceyte**

consideracions *n. pl.* agreements, contracts

consyence *n.* scruple (1 F 7)

constaunce *n.* constancy

constrayn, constreine *v.* compel, constrain; afflict, distress

constre *v.* construe, interpret

constreynte *n.* affliction, distress, agony

construccyon *n.* explanation, second meaning

consume *v.* decay

contenance *see* **co(u)ntenaunce**

contynencys *n. pl.* continent behaviour

contré, contrey(e) *see* **co(u)ntré**

contune *v.* continue

convay, convey *v.* accompany, guide, convey; (refl.) take one's way

convenable *adj.* becoming, fitting

convenyence *n.* congruity, similarity

convenient *adj.* fitting, appropriate, becoming

conversacyon, conversatioun *n.* conduct; sexual intercourse (1 R 14)

convertyble *adj.* changeable

convicte *v.* overcome, vanquish

convoy(e) *v.* guide, protect, escort, conduct

coolde; coort; cooste *see* **con(ne); co(u)-rt(e); cost**

cope *n.* robe

copen *v.* buy

copill, copple *n.* couplet, pair (of harmonies); couple; **couples, cuppillys** *pl.* leashes

coppyde *p.p., adj.:* ~ *curs* (?) heaped up curse

corage *see* **co(u)rage**

corante: *raysens of* ~ currants

cory *imper. sg.* curry, rub down, dress

cornarde *p.p., adj.* cornered

coroned *p.p.* crowned

corruppede *p.p.* corrupted

corse *n.* body

corte *see* **co(u)rte**

cosse *n.* kiss

cost, cooste *n.* coast; **costes** *pl.*

cost *n.* cost, expenses, upkeep; **costes** *pl.*; *at my* ~ (?) at my expense, (?) in spite of my efforts

costage *n.* expense, outlay

costyng *pr.p.* riding along the side of

costlye *adv.* richly, splendidly

cot-armers *n. pl.* men who bear coat-armour

cote *n.* cottage

cote of armes *n.* tunic embroidered with heraldic arms

cote-of-pie *n.* short jacket

cotes *gen. sg.* quoit's

cotidianly *adv.* daily

couchit, cuchit *p.p.* adorned, embroidered, inlaid, set

coude, could *see* **con(ne)**

coumfytes *n. pl.* comfits (sweets made of fruits preserved in sugar)

counfort *v.* comfort

counfort(e), cumforde *n.* comfort; ~**les** *adj.* without comfort

counger *v.* conjure, work magic, exorcize; **conjured** *p.p.*

counse(y)l(l), co(u)nce(y)l(l)e/-cell, consayll, cownsell *n.* advice, counsel; purpose, thoughts, opinion; secret purpose, secrecy; *was of* ~ had plotted; council, advisers, conference

counseylle, co(u)nsayll, counceyl *v.* counsel, advise; **counseled** *pa.*

counte *n.* account: *boke of* ~ account book

co(u)ntena(u)nce, countenans/ti-naunce *n.* appearance, face, bearing, demeanour, behaviour; *shewed with* ~ (?) (who) showed by (his) demeanour (that), (?) (which) was displayed elaborately (1 B 24)

counter *v.* sing a part (over plainsong or melody)

counterfeten, counterfute *v.* imitate, counterfeit

countynge-boke *n.* book of account

countre *adv.* in the opposite direction (to that which the hunted animal has gone) (1 C 4)

co(u)ntré, co(u)ntrey(e), cuntré, cuntree *n.* land, country, region, area

couple *v.* fasten hounds together in pairs,

couple (*cont.*):
leash together; unite, marry
couples/-lys *see* **copill**
co(u)rage, curage *n.* heart, spirit, mind, thought, desire
cours *n.* course, pattern of events; flow
coursoures *n. pl.* chargers
courtas *see* **curteys(e)**
courtaus *n. pl.* curtals (a kind of cannon)
co(u)rte, coort *n.* court; ~ *of the parlement*; *sett a* ~ fix a session of the court
couth(e)(n) *see* **con(ne)**
cove(y)tyse *n.* covetousness
covente *n.* convent
coverte *n.* shelter
cowd(e) *see* **con(ne)**
cowerit *pa. 3 sg.* made his way, advanced
cowle *n.* tub
cownsell; cowthe *see* **counse(y)l(l); con(ne)**
crab *v.* annoy; **cra(i)bit, crabbid** *p.p., adj.* vexed, ill-natured, perverse, ~**lie** *adv.* ill-naturedly, bad-temperedly
crac(c)h(e) *n.* crib, manger
cracchynge *pr. p.* scratching
craftely *adv.* skilfully
crag *n.* neck; ~**-bane** *n.* neck-bone
craibit *see* **crab**
craif *v.* crave, beg
crake *v.* talk scornfully; shout; **crakit** *pr. 3 sg.* sings in very short notes
crampons *n. pl.* grips, braces
cratched *pa. 3 sg.* scratched
cra(uf)ft(e) *n.* skill, craft, art, occupation
crawis *n. pl.* crows
creatour, creature *n.* creator
cred(e) *n.* creed
creye *v.* cry, make a loud noise
cryke *n.* brook
cryme *n.* cream
crym(e)syn *adj.* crimson
crymynose *adj.* acknowledging guilt
croce *see* **crosse**
croked, crokyd *adj.* crooked, bent; ~ **shulderyd** hunchbacked; (as adv.) *gon* ~
crokyng *pr.p.* curving, bending
crome *n.* crumb; **crommes** *pl.*
cropen *p.p.* crept
croppis *n. pl.* growing tips of plants, shoots
crosse, croce *n.* cross; hilt (of sword); coin marked with a cross
crosse *v.* cross out, cancel

crounde *p.p.* crowned
croun(e) *n.* crown, crown of head, tonsure
crowche *n.* coin marked ,with a cross
crudded *p.p.* curded, coagulated
cruellest *adj. sup.* most fierce, most savage
cubytes *n. pl.* cubits (a measure of *c.*18–22 inches)
cuchit; culd(e); cullour *see* **couchit; con(ne); colour(e)**
culit *pa. 3 pl.* cooled
cultre *n.* coulter
cum, cummand, cummyn, cummis *see* **com(e)**
cumburus *adj.* troublesome
cumforde *see* **counfort**
cummerlik *adv.* like gossips
cunnyng(e); cuntré, cuntree, cuntreis *see* **connyng(e); co(u)ntré**
cupbord *n.* sideboard
cuplyng *n.* union
cuppillys; curage *see* **copill; co(u)rage**
cure *n.*[1] cure; charge, attention: *dyde my besy* ~ did my very best; trouble, care
cure *n.*[2] cover
cury *n.* (cooked) dish
cury(o)us *adj.* concerned (for); intricate, elaborate, abstruse; exquisite, beautiful
curssinge *n.* cursing, excommunication
curteys(e), curtese, courtas *adj.* courteous, gracious; ~**ly, curtasli** *adv.* courteously
curtel *n.* curtal (a small horse)
curtesye *n.* courtesy, grace
curtly *adv.* briefly
cuschettis *n. pl.* wood-pigeons
custumable *adj.* customary
cut *n.*: *kepe his/your* ~ behave demurely
cuth *see* **con(ne)**
cuvating *n.* desire
cwm *see* **com(e)**

da pacem dagger (L 'give peace')
day *see* **dy**
daill *n.* dealing, sexual intercourse
dail(l), dale *n.* valley; **dalis** *pl.*
daill; daynté; daysshed *see* **dele; deynté; dasch**
daysprynge *n.* daybreak, early dawn
dait; dalfe *see* **date; delf(f)e**
dalyacyon *n.* chattering
dalyaunce, dalyawnce *n.* conversation; loving intimacy
daly(e) *adj., adv.* daily
dam(m)age *n.* harm, injury

damoisele, damo(y)se(y)l(l) *n.* maiden, girl

dampned, dampnyd *p.p., adj.* damned, condemned

dang *see* **dynge**

danger *v.* be in danger

dangere; dangerus *see* **daunger; daungerouse**

dantit *p.p., adj.* tamed, brought under control

dare *n.* dace (a small freshwater fish)

darn *adj.* dark

darth *n.* dearth

dasarde *n.* dullard, blockhead

dasch, dasshe *v.* strike, dash; (in interj.) . . . *revell ~ fylle the cup;* **daysshed** *pa. 3 sg.* fell

date, dait *n.* time; *in the devylles ~* in the Devil's name

daunceth *imper. pl.* dance

daunger, dangere, denger *n.* peril, danger; power; disdain; reserve (occas. person.)

dangerouse, dangerus *adj.* dangerous, perilous; disdainful, reluctant

dawe *n.* jackdaw

dawyng *n.* dawn

de; deade *see* **dy; dede**

deambulatorye *n.* cloister

debait *n.* contention, strife

debonayre *adj.* humble, meek

debrused *p.p.* broken, crushed

deceyte, disceit *n.* deceit

deceyve *v.* deceive

decertys *n. pl.* deserts

decrees *n. pl. bukis of ~* decretals

decresid *p.p.* lessened, diminished

ded(d)(e); ded(e), dedyst/-yn *see* **deeth; do**

dede, deid, deade *n.* deed, action; *in ~; as to the ~* as events turned out

ded(e), deed, deid *adj.* dead, deathly; **de(e)dly, deidly** *adj.* deadly, mortal; (of sleep) death-like, profound

dee; deel; deemyd; deered *see* **dy; del(e); deme; dere**

deeth, de(d)d(e), deid, deythe *n.* death; *(blow) the ~* (blow) the hunting-note to signal the death of the game; **deidis** *pl.*

defau(l)t(e), defawte *n.* lack, want, lack of food; fault, defect: *in his ~* through his fault; offence, sin

deferent *adj.: cercle ~ n.* the circular orbit of the epicycle in which a planet moves

deffense, defence *n.: stonden at ~* defend itself; *of grete ~* strongly defended, heavily armed

defied *p.p.* set at nought, disdained

degest *p.p.* digested, considered

degré, degree *n.* rank, station; status, condition; way: *in eche/every ~, in all ~* in all respects; astronomical degree

degressyonys *n. pl.* astronomical devitions

dey(e), deyde/-ist/-id; deid(is), deidly *see* **dy; ded(e), dede, deeth**

deificait *p.p.* deified

deill *see* **del(e), dele**

deynté, daynté *n.* honour, esteem; pleasure, delight

deyntous *adj.* delicious, choice

deynty *adj.* fine, exquisite, delicious, handsome

deyr; deis, deit; deythe *see* **dere; dy; deeth**

dejecte *adj.* abject, cast down

dekenes *n. pl.* deacons

del(e), deel, de(i)ll *n.* part, extent, number; *sum ~* somewhat, to some extent; *neuer a ~* not at all, nothing

dele, daill, deill *v.* deal, have to do with; make love; divide, distribute; **delis** *pr. 3 pl.*

delectabyl, deleit-/delictable *adj.* pleasing, delightful

delf(f)e *v.* dig; **dalfe** *pa. 3 sg.;* **dolve** *p.p.;* **dolvyng** *adj., n.* digging

delibered *pa., p.p.* deliberated, resolved

delices *n. pl.* delights, pleasures

delyng *n.* dealing, conduct

delis *see* **dele**

delyte *n.* pleasure, delight, joy

delyte *v.* delight, rejoice

delyver *adj.* nimble, quick

dell *see* **del(e)**

deme, demyn *v.* judge, think, decree; **demyd, demtyn** *pa.;* **deemyd** *p.p.*

demeane *v.* express; (refl.) behave, conduct oneself; **demened** *pa. 3 sg.*

demeyne *n.* dominion, power

demye *n.* short gown

deming *n.* suspicion

demonycall *adj.* of devils; *~ frayry* (prob. with punning ref. to Dominican friars)

demtyn *see* **deme**

dene *n.* noise

dener; denger *see* dyner; da(u)nger

dennes, dennys *n. pl.* caves

denomynacyon *n.* designation

dent *see* dynt

depaynt *v.* depict, describe, paint, colour, decorate; depaynt/-peynt *p.p.*

depairting *n.* dividing, division

depart(e), depert *v.* part, separate, divide; distribute, dispense; depairtit *p.p.*

depe *imper. sg.* dip

deppest *adj. sup.* deepest

depurit *p.p., adj.* purified

dere, deyr, diere *n.* deer; animal

der(e), dyre *adj., adv.* dear, precious, expensive; dearly; derrest *adj. sup.* dearest

dere, deir *v.* injure, harm; deered *pa. 3 pl.*

derfe *adj.* bold, sturdy; derfly *adv.* sternly

deryvatt *p.p., adj.* derived

derke, dirk(e) *adj.* dark; (as n.) *by* ~ in darkness; ~nes(se) *n.* darkness

dern(e) *adj., adv.* secret, concealed; secretly; *n.* secret place, secrecy: *i(n)* ~ in secret

derrest *see* der(e)

derworth *adj.* precious

descryve *v.* describe; discrivys *pr. 3 sg.*

dese(a)se; deseyved *see* dysease; deceyve

deserte *adj.* uncultivated

desola(i)t, dissolat *p.p., adj.* desolate, abandoned, solitary, deserted

despectyble *adj.* despicable

despeired; despyte *see* dispeyre; dispyte

desporte *v. refl.* disport oneself

determined *p.p.* concluded, completed

det(te) *n.* debt, duty, obligation

deuke; deull(ys) *see* duke; devil

devalis *pr. 3 pl.* descend

dever, devoure *n.* duty; *put me in* ~ endeavour, do what I can

devil, devell(e), deu(y)l(l), dyvell, dyvyll *n.* devil; *a* ~ *way, in the xx*[u] ~ *way* in the Devil's name; *what (a)* ~ why/what the devil; deullys *gen. sg.*; divillis *pl.*

devine *adj.* divine; *n.* divinity

devyse *n.* device, opinion; a masked procession

devyse *v.* describe, imagine; arrange, ordain, require

devoid *v.* relieve

devoit *adj.* pious, devout

devors *n.* separation

devou(i)r *v.* devour

devoure *see* dever

dy, day, de(e), dey(e) *v.* die; deis *pr. 3 sg.*; deit, deyed, deyde, deydyst, dyde *pa.*; deyid *p.p.*

dyche *n.* ditch, moat; ~ canker *n.* a kind of caterpillar or canker worm used as bait

diched *p.p.* dug ditches

dicht; dyd(e); diere *see* dight; do; dere

diffame *n.* dishonour, shame

diffame *v.* accuse, defame; diffamed *p.p.* shamed

diffamyng *n.* dishonour, shame, disgrace

diffautis *see* defau(l)t(e)

dyffere *v.* defer, postpone; dyfferred *p.p.*

diffiaunce *n.* hostility, defiance

dight *v.* prepare, make ready; *to deth/deid* ~ consign to death, be overcome by death; dyght *pa., p.p.*, dicht *p.p.*

dygne *adj.* worthy, deserving

dilacion *n.* delay

dill *v.* assuage

dym *adj.* dark, obscure; ~lie *adv.* with a dim light

dyner, dener *n.* dinner (a mid-day meal, cf. 1 O 22)

dynge *v.* hit, beat, overcome; dang, donge *pa. 3 pl.*; dungin *p.p.*

dynt, dent *n.* blow

Dyocesan *n.* the bishop of a diocese

dyre; dirk(e), dirknes(se) *see* der(e); derke

dirkit *p.p.* darkened

dyrknyt *pa. 3 pl., p.p.* darkened

disagysit, dysgysed *p.p.* disguised, clothed

dysalow *v.* blame

disceit; disceyved; discever *see* deceyte; deceyve; disseuer

discharge *v.* disburden, make void; dispossess; send forth, utter

disconfyted *p.p.* overcome

dyscordeth *pr. 3 pl.* differ from; discordinge *pr.p., adj.* disagreeing

dyscreaseth, discreecyn *pr. 3 sg., pl.* decrease(s)

discrete *adj.* judicious, rational

discrivys *see* descryve

dyscure *v.* reveal

disdeyne *v.:* ~ *at* be indignant against, take offence at

dysease, dyse(e)se, dese(a)se, diseis, dyshes *n.* trouble, torment, distress, misery, discomfort, lack of pleasure; dyssesys *pl.*

disese *imper. sg.* disturb
dysfygured *p.p., adj.* deformed
dysgysed; dyshes *see* **disagysit; dysease**
dishonested *p.p.* dishonoured, shamed
dysyere *n.* desire
dysyere *v.* desire, ask; **dysyryde** *p.p.*
disjoynt *n.* perplexity, misery
disparblid *see* **disperpulid**
dyspectuose *adj.* contemptible
dispeyr, dyspayer, dyspa(y)re *n.* despair
dispeyre *v.* despair; **despeired** *p.p., adj.* in despair of, having abandoned
dyspend *v.* have as income
disperpulid, disparblid *p.p., adj.* scattered, dispersed, divided, thrown into confusion
dyspersyde *p.p., adj.* distracted
dispyte, despyte *n.* resentment, hatred; defiance; injury
dispone *v.* make ready, dispose of; **disponit** *p.p.*
disport(e) *n.* pastime, amusement, merriment, sport
dyspose *v. refl.* make arrangements, prepare (oneself); **disposud, dysposyd(e)** *p.p.* inclined, disposed
disposicions *n. pl.* natural inclinations
disprave *v.* harm
dispulit *p.p.* stripped
dispurveid *p.p.* destitute
dysseased *p.p.* deceased
dysseyved; dyssesys *see* **deceyve; dysease**
disseuer, dissever/-cever *v.* separate, part, depart
dissimulait *adj.* deceitful
dissolat *see* **desola(i)t**
distaynyde *p.p.* stained, defiled
dystemperaunce *n.* excess, intemperance
dystempure *v.* disorder, disturb
distressid *p.p.* crushed
dyte *n.* writing, poem
dyte *v.* compose
ditee *n.* poem; meaning (of a song)
dyvell, dyvyll, divillis *see* **devil**
dyverte *imper. sg., refl.* go astray
dyvour *n.* debtor, bankrupt
do *n.* doe
do, doo, don(e) *v.* do, act, perform, make; cause (something to be done); (as auxil.); cause, inflict; put, add, place; *~ foorth interj.* come on! *~ of* take off; *~ wey* take away, stop; **dois** *pr. 3 sg.*, **doon, done** *pr. pl.*; **dyd(e),**

ded(e)/-yst/-yn, dudde(st) *pa., did right well* looked splendid (6 C 38); **ydo, do(o)(n)** *p.p.*
dobelette, doblettys *see* **do(w)blet**
docke-canker *n.* a grub or the larva of a beetle of some kind, used for bait
document *n.* doctrine
dogonis *n. pl.* rascals
doif *adj.* dull, spiritless
doig *n.* dog
doyll, dule, dool *n.* sorrow, grief, pity; *~ful adj.* mournful, sad
doyng, dois *see* **do**
doket *n.* ducat, gold or silver coin; Venetian coin worth *c.9s.*; **doket(t)is, ducatis** *pl.*
dolent *adj.* sorrowful
dolly, doolie, dulé *adj.* dismal
dollin *p.p.* buried
dolve, dolvyng *see* **delf(f)e**
dome, doom *n.* judgment, sentence; opinion
dom(m)age *n.* hurt, trouble
domyne *v.* rule, control
don(e); donge *see* **do; dynge**
donk *adj.* damp
donkis *n. pl.* wet places
donne; doo, doon; dool; doolie; doom; *see* **dun, do; doyll; dolly; dome**
dorre *n.* a flying beetle (? the cockchafer, ? the dung-beetle) used for bait
dose(y)n *n.* dozen; *the ~ browne* ? a full dozen (poss. a game of chance)
dosk *adj.* dark, dusky
dote *v.* think, act foolishly; **doted, dotit** *p.p., adj.* foolish, mad, stupid
dotyng *n.* folly, foolish thinking
double *adj.* deceitful, guilty of duplicity; *~nesse,* **doubilnesse** *n.* duplicity, deceitfulness
doubt(e); doubted *see* **dout(e); doute**
doubtous *adj.* fearful
douchter, douchtir, dowtyr *n.* daughter
douleur *n.* sorrow
dounfolde *p.p.* cast down
dour *adj.* stern, harsh
dout(e), doubt(e), dowt(e) *n.* fear, apprehension, doubt; *but ~* indeed; *~les(se) adv.* indeed, certainly
doute *v.* fear (occas. refl.); **dou(b)ted** *pa.*
do(w)blet, dubelet, dobelette *n.* doublet
dowe *n.* dough
dowit *pa. 3 sg.* weakened, enfeebled

dowté *n.* duty

dowt(e); dowtyr *see* dout(e); douchter

dowves *n. pl.* doves

draglit *p.p., adj.* bedraggled

draif *see* drive

draw(e), drawne *v.* (occas. refl.) draw, make one's way, approach, draw to an end; drew, drough *pa.*; drawe *p.p.*

drawke *n.* drawk (a weed)

drawkit *p.p.* drenched

dre, drye *v.* endure, suffer

drede *v.* fear (occas. refl.); dre(i)d *pa.*; dredyng *pr. p.*; dreid *p.p., adj.* afraid, fearing

dre(e)d(e), dreid *n.* fear; for fear that (19 D 23); *but* ~ without doubt; dredis *pl.*; dred(e)ful *adj.* fearful; fearsome

drey *adj.* dry

dreid *see* drede, dre(e)d(e)

dreye *v.* dry

drenchith *pr. 3 sg.* drowns

dreré, drery, drerie *adj.* dreary, sorrowful, sad, miserable

dresse *v.* prepare, put in order; (refl.) go, make one's way, advance, position oneself; dressit *pa., p.p.*; drest *p.p.*

drevin, drewyn; drye *see* drive; dre

dryff-draff *n.* refuse, dregs

drift *n.* impetus, rush

dryt *n.* dirt, droppings

drive *v.* drive; ~ *forth* endure; *forth . . .* ~ press on; rush; draif, droof *pa.*; drevin, drewyn *p.p.*

dronke, dronkyn *p.p.* drunk

dronkenhede *n.* drunkenness

dropping *pr.p., adj.* soaked

drough *see* draw(e)

drowp, drup *v.* droop, be dispirited, drowpit *pa.*

drowrie *n.* love-token, love

drublie *adj.* clouded, turbid

druggit *pa. 3 pl.* dragged

drumly *adj.* cloudy, gloomy

drup *see* drowp

dub *n.*[1] pool, puddle; dubbis *pl.*

dub *n.*[2] dub, angler's artificial fly

dublere *n.* platter, dish

ducatis; dudde(st) *see* doket; do

duke, dwk(e), deuke *n.* duke, leader, chief; Doge; powder dwke a powder made of spices and sugar

dukis *n. pl.* ducks

dule; dulé *see* doyll; dolly

dule *v.* lament, sorrow

duleful *adj.* sorrowful

dun, donne *adj.* dark, brown

dunned *pa. 3 sg.* resounded

dungin *see* dynge

duras *n.* affliction

dure *n.* door; dur(r)(i)s *pl.*

dure *v.* last

duresse *n.* harshness

durynge *pr.p.* lasting; *moderately* ~ with moderate persistence; duryngly *adv.* continuously

durnell *n.* darnel (a weed)

dur(r)is, durs; dwk(e) *see* dure; duke

e *see* eie

eage *n.* age

eayr *see* eyer

eary *v.* plough

ease; eased *see* ese; esed

ech(e), ich *adj., pron.* every; each (one)

echone *pron.* each one

edders *n. pl.* adders, snakes

eer *see* er

eerynge *n.* ploughing

(e)erys; eese *see* ere; ese

eestryche *n.* ostrich

eete *see* ete

effecte, effek *n.* purpose, effect; *in* ~ verily

effectuously *adv.* urgently, importunately

effeirit *p.p.* frightened

efflated *p.p.* puffed out

effray *n.* fear

effray *v.* frighten

effte, eft *adv.* again

eft-castell *n.* structure at rear of ship, poop

efter, eftir *prep., adv.* after, according as, ~ *that*; afterwards

eft-schip *n.* rear of ship

eftsones *adv.* afterwards

egal(l) *adj.* equal, equitable

egar *adj.* ardent, fierce, angry; egerlie *adv.* eagerly, keenly

egill *n.* eagle

eie, e(y), ye(e) *n.* eye; ey(e)n(e), e(gh)ne, (i)yen, yes *pl.*

eyer, eyre, eayr *n.* air

eik *v.* increase

eik, eke, ~ *and adv.* also

eild *n.* age

eyled; eyn(e); eir *see* ayle; eie; hier, ere

e(i)rd *n.* earth; ~ly/lie *adv.* earthly

eyre; eiris *see* eyer; ere

eyren, eyrine *n. pl.* eggs

eyrours *n. pl.* female swans, brood swans

eis; eischewyt; eysel; eite(n) *see* ese; eschew(e); asell; ete

eithyr, a(y)thir, ether *adj., pron., conj.* either, every; each: *of her* ~ of each of them

eke *see* eik

electe *adj.* chosen, exalted

electuaris *n. pl.* electuaries (medicines compounded with syrup into a paste)

element *n.* sky

elles, el(l)is, els *adv.* otherwise, else

ellum(m)ynit *p.p.* illuminated, made bright

elne *n.* ell (a measure of *c.*45 inches)

emange *see* among(e)

embatayle *v.* join in battle; embateylyd *p.p.* drawn up in battle array

embrouded, enbrouded, enbrowdred *p.p.* embroidered

eme *n.* uncle

emerant, emeraut *n.* emerald

emysperye *n.* hemisphere

emonge *see* among(e)

emongist *prep.* amongst

empocesse *v.* endow, invest with possessions

empoyre *v.* harm, damage; empeireth *pr. 3 pl.*

emprise *n.* undertaking

enarmyd, enermede *p.p.* armed

enbrayded *p.p.* taunted, mocked, upbraided

enbrast *p.p.* embraced

enbrouded, enbrowdred *see* embrouded

enchace *v.* hunt, pursue

enchesso(u)n *n.* reason, cause

enchewyn *v.* avoid

enclinant *adj.* (favourably) inclined (to)

enclyne *v.* incline, be disposed towards, favour; bow; enclinande *pr.p.*

encludet *p.p.* enclosed

encomb(e)raunce *n.* trouble, tribulation, temptation

encombrement *n.* molestation

encomyne *see* wele ~

encompanyed *p.p.* associated in comanies

encreace, encres(e) *n.* increase, profit

encreace, encres(s)e *v.* increase, grow; encrescit *pr. 3 sg.*

ende *conj.* and

endelonge *prep.* along

endetted *p.p., adj.* in debt

endevoyre *v. refl.* endeavour, exert oneself; endevored *pa. 3 pl.*

endewed *pa. 3 pl.* invested

endite *n.* writing

endyte *v.* compose, write; indyte *p.p.*

enduce *v.* lead, bring

endure *v.* remain, stay; endure, last; harden

ene; enermede; eneuch *see* eie, eve; enarmyd; inogh(e)

enforce *v.* force, press hard upon; enforsist *pr. 2 sg.* strive, labour

engyn(e) *n.* intelligence, cunning, ingenuity, contrivance; engyns *pl.* siege engines

englentere *n.* eglantine, sweet-briar

enhaunce *v.* exalt with pride

enprent *v.* imprint, print; enprynted *p.p.*

enpryse *v.* undertake

enquyre *v.* seek; enquirreth *pr. 3 sg.*/enquyrreide *p.p.* rewards/rewarded (hounds)

ensaumple *n.* example

ensensed *pa. 3 pl.* burned

ensude *p.p.* (?) sown in, implanted (17 E 34)

ensuye *v.* ensue, follow

entayle *n.* carving

entalentid *p.p., adj.* stimulated, inspired, excited

ente(e)r(e) *adj.* complete, entire, total; enteirly, entyerly int(i)erly *adv.* entirely, completely, heartily, sincerely

entende *v.* purpose, incline

entent(e) *n.* purpose, intention: *to th'* ~ *(to be)/of* ~ with the intention that/of; mind, attention: *tooke* ~ paid attention; meaning; ententis *pl.*

entermete *v.* concern oneself, busy oneself

entretyd *pa. 3 pl.* negotiated with

entrikid *p.p.* deceitfully involved

enveronyt, envyronned *p.p.* surrounded

envie *n.* resentment

environing *pr.p.* surrounding, circling

envyroun *adv.* around

envolupyt *p.p.* enwrapped, enclosed

episciclis *n. pl.* epicycles (technical term for the circle in which a planet rotates on its axis)

equalle *adj.* equitable, just

equypolent *adj.* equal in power

er, eer *conj., prep.* before

erbe *n.* herb, grass
erd; erdly *see* **e(i)rd; e(i)rdly**
er(e) *conj.* or
ere, eere; eir *n.* ear; **(e)erys, eiris** *pl.*
ermony *n.* harmony, harmonious consort
ern *see* **yren(e)**
erste *adv. sup.* before, earlier, rather; *non* ~ not till then
eschew(e) *v.* escape, avoid; **e(i)schewyt** *pr. 3 sg., pa. 3 pl.*; **eschuying** *pr.p.*; **eschewyng** *n.* avoiding
ese, ease, eese, eis *n.* ease, comfort, pleasure, safety, betterment, cure; *(wel) at his (own)* ~ happy, without anxiety, *all at* ~ comfortably; *do (the/ yow)* ~/ *have yowre* ~ bring/have ... relief, comfort; **easis** *pl.* luxuries, prosperity
esed, eased, esyd *p.p.* relieved, comforted, delighted
esely, esily *adv.* gently, easily
esement *n.* evacuation of excrement: *don his* ~
especyall *adj.*: *in* ~ chiefly, in particular
esperans *n.* hope
esprysed *p.p.* inflamed
esquierys *n. pl.* squires
estate, astat(e) *n.* rank, estate; condition, state; ~ *publyque* commonwealth
Ester, Estyr, Estern(e) *n.* Easter
ete, eite *v.* eat; **etith** *imper. pl.*; **eete** *pa. 3 pl.*; **ete, etun** *p.p.*
ether *see* **eithyr**
euirilk *adj.* every
eve, ene, evyn, yeven *n.* evening; *Saint Thomas* ~ *of Caunterbury* the vigil of the feast of St Thomas of Canterbury
evel *see* **evyl(l)**
even, evyn, euin, ewyn *adv.* even, evenly; just, exactly, strictly, utterly; *ful* ~ in exactly the same way, ~ *forthwith* immediately; **ewynly** *adv.* calmly
ever amange *adv.* now and then; always
everych(e) *pron.* each, each one, every one; **everychon(e)** *pron.* every one; **everydele** *adv.* every part
evesong *n.* evensong, vespers
evdences *n. pl.* legal documents, charters, deeds
evyl(l), evel *adj.* evil, bad; **evel** *n.* wickedness; **evyl(l), yvell, ewyll, yevell** *adv.* badly
evyn; evyr *see* **even, eve; yvery**
ewes *n. pl.* eaves
ewyll; ewyn(ly) *see* **evyl(l); even**

ewyr *adv.* ever
ewrous *adj.* fortunate
exaltacioun *n.* state of being lifted up, material which has been lifted up
exalted *p.p.* honoured, uplifted
exclude *v.* banish; **excludit** *p.p.*
exe *n.* axe
expedycius *adj.* quickly made
expedient *adj.* fitting
experimented *p.p.* experienced
expert *adj.* experienced
expleyten *v.* prosper
exployt *n.* achievement
expo(w)ne *v.* expound, explain
expresse *adv.* expressly, fully
extasy/-ie *n.* ecstasy, trance, frenzy

fa; fachioun; facio(u)n; facoun *see* **foo; fauc(h)on; fassion; fawcon**
facound *adj.* eloquent
facture *n.* form, lineaments
faculté *n.* skill
fade *adj.* wan
fader, fadir, fadure *n.* father, ancestor, protector; **fad(e)res** *gen. sg. his* ~ *Davyd* his father David's; **fadirli** *adj.* fatherly
fadom *n.* fathom, cubit (the length of the forearm)
fay(e) *n.* faith, truth
faill, felye *v.* fail; become weary; slack; be lacking in; **falye** *pr. 3 sg. subj.*: ~ *this* if this fails (to happen); **fayles** *pr. 2 sg.*; **faillit, faileyeit** *pa.*
fayn(e), fane *adj.* glad, well-pleased; **fayn(e), fawyn** *adv.* fain, gladly
fained *see* **fenye**
faynte *n.* faintness, exhaustion
fair *see* **fare**
fair *n.* fare
fair(e), fayer, fare, feyr(e) *adj.* fair, fine, good; (as n.) beautiful creature, lady; **feyriste** *sup.*; **fayre** *adv.* fairly, courteously, neatly
fair(h)ed *n.* beauty
fayr(e)y *n.* the fairies, fairyland
fayrse; fays *see* **fyers; foo**
fayte, feat *n.* act, deed; doings, situation; **faytes** *pl.*
faytour *n.* deceiver
fall *n.* accident
fall(e) *v.* fall; come to, befall; get, obtain; ~ *to/inne (to)* begin (to), take to; **fyl(l)(e)** *pa.*; **falle/-yn** *p.p.*

falloschip; fallowis; fallowit; falye *see* **fela(u)shyp(e); felouse; folowe; faill**

falsen *v.* betray

fame *n.* foam

famose *adj.* commonly known, usual, ordinary

fane *see* **fayn(e)**

fane *n.* weather-vane

fang *n.* prey

fangis *pr. 3 pl.* pull

fannoun *n.* maniple (embroidered band worn by priest when celebrating mass)

fantasy(e), fantesey *n.* imagination, memory; fancy, imagining, fantasy

fare *see* **fair(e)**

fare, fair *v.* fare, go, get on, behave; ~ *as* act as if; **fure** *pa. 3 sg.*; **ferd** *p.p.*: ~ *with* treated

farest *adj. sup.* (?) longest, (?) fairest, easiest (10 C 75)

fary *n.* confused state of mind, turmoil

farlyes *n. pl.* wonders

farnys *n. pl.* ferns

fass(i)o(u)n, facio(u)n *n.* fashion, kind, way, means

fast(e), fest *adv.* firmly, strongly, hard; quickly, persistently, pressingly, sharply; ~ *by* close by; *al to* ~ wholly; **fastly** *adv.* speedily, quickly

fasted *see* **fest**

fauc(h)on, fachioun *n.* falchion, sword with a curved blade

faught(ed) *see* **fecht**

fauld *n.* fold

faute, fawt(e) *n.* fault, defect, wrong, sin, default; **fautles** *adj.* faultless

faverall *adj.* benevolent

fawch *adj.* brown, yellow, withered

fawcon, facoun *n.* falcon

fawkners *n. pl.* falconers

fawyn *see* **fayn(e)**

fawld *n.* fold, enclosed field

fawt(e); fe; feare; feat *see* **faute; fe(e); fere; fayte**

febyll(e), feble *adj.* weak, wretched, of poor quality; ~**nys, febilnesse** *n.* weakness

febled, feblit *p.p., adj.* weakened, enfeebled

feche *v.* fetch

fecht *n.* fight

fecht, feyght *v.* fight; **faught(ed)** *pa.*; **fowghten, fo(u)ghten** *pa. p.p.*; ~ *felde* battlefield

fedder, fedyr *n.* feather

fedderit, federid *p.p.* feathered; feathered with arrows, pierced

fed(d)rem(e) *n.* coat of feathers

fe(e) *n.* reward, payment; livestock

feele; feende; feere; feeryd *see* **fele; fend(e); fyer; fere**

feet *adj.* handsome

feye *adj.* doomed to die

feyght; feild *see* **fecht; feld(e)**

feile, feil(l) *adj.* many

feill *n.* knowledge, idea

feynit; feir *see* **fenye; fer(e)**

feir *n.* bearing, demeanour; **feris** *pl.* looks

feird *adj.* fourth

feyr(e) *see* **fayr(e)**

feiritnes *n.* fear

feirs; fel *see* **fyers; fel(e)**

fela(u)ship(e), fele-/felaws(c)hip(pe), felys(s)(c)hip(pe), falloschip *n.* company, fellowship

feld(e), feild, fylde *n.* field, battlefield

fel(e), feele *v.* feel, comprehend, experience; **feeliden** *pa. 3 pl.*

felest *pr. 2 sg.* fill

felye *see* **faill**

fell *n.* skin

fell(e) *adj., adv.* fierce, ferocious, cruel, strong, wicked; violently; **felli** *adv.* fiercely

fello(u)n *adj.* fierce, savage, cruel, deadly

felouse, fallowis *n. pl.* companions, fellows, friends

felterit *p.p.* tangled, matted

fence *n.* defence

fend(e), feende, fynde *n.* devil, fiend, monster

fenye *v.* feign, dissimulate; **fenyt** *pa.*; **fained, feynit, fenyeit** *p.p., adj.* invented, imagined, feigned

fenix *n.* phoenix

ferd *see* **fare**

ferder *adv. comp.* further

fer(e) *see* **ferr(e)**

fer(e), feir *n.[1]* fear, terror, doubt

fere *n.[2]* consort, wife, companion

fere, feare *n.[3]* company; *in* ~ together

fere, ferre *v.* fear; frighten; ~*d himselfe* *pa., refl.* was afraid; **feeryd** *p.p.*

ferforth *adv.* far, much; *so* ~ *that* to such an extent that, so much that

feryde *p.p.* set on fire

feris; ferys *see* **feir; fere**

ferleit *pa.* marvelled, wondered

GLOSSARY

ferly *adv.* wondrously
fermes *pr. 3 pl.* affirm
ferre *see* fere
ferr(e), fer(e) *adj., adv.* far, afar; ferre(re) *comp.* further; ferreste furthest; furthest point
fers(e), ferslie, fersnesse *see* fyers
fervence *n.* intense desire, passion
fervent *adj.* fervent, hot, stormy, intense
fesyk; fest *see* phisike; fast(e)
fest *n.* feast, festivity; feestes *pl.*
fest *imper. sg.* fasten, make fast; fested, fasted *pa.*
fete *adv.* becomingly, nobly
feteled, fettled *pa. 3 pl.* made ready
fetewse *adj.* well-formed, comely
fett *v.* fetch, bring; fet *pa. 3 sg.*; fette *p.p.*
fette *see* fote
Feverere, Feveryer *n.* February
fewes *n.* track
fewir *n.* fever
fewle *see* fo(u)le
fic(c)he *v.* fix, set
fych(e) *n.* fish
fyer, feere *n.* fire; fyrs *pl.* fires, burning passions
fyers, fe(i)rs(e), fayrse *adj.* bold, fierce; fyers(e)ly(e), ferslie *adv.* fiercely; impetuously; fersnesse *n.* eagerness
fyete *see* fote
figure, figour *n.* appearance, form, shape, image, symbol
figure(n) *v.* figure, express metaphorically; form, shape; ifiguriet, figurait *p.p.*
fylde *see* feld(e)
filith *pr. 3 sg.* infects; fylit *pa. 3 sg.* defiled, polluted
fyl(l)e; filwedist; fyn; fynde *see* fall(e); folowe; fyn(n)(e); fend(e)
fynde *v.* find; invent, devise; fand *pa.*; found *p.p.* discovered game (1 C 3); fo(u)nde(n), fowndyn, fundin *p.p.*
fynders *n. pl.* dogs which discover or start the deer
finding *n.* support, provision, resources; fyndingis *pl.*
fyne *v.* end, cease
fyn(e), fynes *see* fyn(n)(e)
fynkyll *n.* fennel
fyn(n)(e) *adj.* fine, excellent, of good quality, exquisite, thin; fyn *adv.* completely; fynes *n.* purity, fineness
fyré, fyry *adj.* fiery, gleaming like fire
fyreslaucht *n.* lightning-flash

fyryng *n.* fuel
fyrs *see* fyer
first *adj.*: ~ age youth, earliest period
firth *n.*[1] wood
fyrth *n.*[2] estuary, inlet
firtherne *v.* further
fla *n.* fly; fleys *pl.*
fla *v.* flay; flew *pa. 3 sg.*
flaggis *n. pl.* flashes
flambes *see* flawme
flanis *n. pl.* arrows
flasche *n.* sheaf
flaw *n.* squall, blast
flawe, flawgh *see* fle(e)
flawme *n.* flame; flambes, flammes *pl.*
flawmyng *pr.p.* flaming, gleaming
flear *n.* fugitive
fle(e) *v.* flee; fleand *pr.p.*; fleit *p.p.* escaped, frightened away
fle(e) *v.* fly; flawe, flaugh *pa.*; floughe *p.p.* flown
fleesshe *see* flesch(e)
fleidnes *n.* fright
fleys; fleischli; fleit *see* fla; fleschelie; fle(e)
flemit *p.p.* put to flight, banished
flemne *n.* phlegm (one of the humours of the body: cold and moist, apt to cause indolence or apathy)
flesch(e), fle(e)sshe *n.* flesh, meat
fleschelie, fleischli, flescly *adj.* fleshly, carnal, mortal
flete *v.* flow with moisture
flew *see* fla
flikerynge *n.* fluttering
flixe *see* flux(e)
flyttyng *adj.* transitory
flocht *n.* flutter, excitement
flodderit *p.p.* flooded
flode, flude *n.* sea, flood, water, river
flome, flum *n.* river
floot *n.* float (for angling)
floschis *n. pl.* pools, marshes
flot(e) *n.* fleet
floughe *see* flawe
flour, flure *n.* floor
flour(e) *n.* flower; ~-de-lice *n.* fleur-de-lis
flourisching *n.* blossom
flourished *pa.* threw out, displayed; flourished, grew luxuriantly
flowte *n.* pipe, flute
flude *see* flode
fluences *n. pl.* flowings, streams

530

flum; flure *see* flome; flour

flux(e), flixe *n.* flux, discharge of blood

foght(en) *see* fecht

foyne *v.* thrust; foynynge *n.* thrusting

foirspeikar *n.* chairman, speaker

fole, foll *n.* fool

fole; folewe *see* fo(u)le; folowe

foly, folie *n.* madness, folly

folyly *adv.* foolishly

folisch, folys(s)he *adj.* foolish; folysher *adj. comp. more* ~ more foolish

foll *see* fole

folowe, folewe, folwe(n) *v.* follow; folweth, fol(e)with *pr. 3 sg.*; filwedist *pa. 2 sg.*, fallowit *pa. 3 sg.*; foloyng *pr.p.*

fonde; fon(e) *see* fynde; foo

fonnedli *adv.* foolishly

fonstone *n.* fontstone

foo, fa *n.* foe, enemy; fo(o)n(e), foos, fays *pl.*

foorce; foorthe *see* forc(e); forth(e)

foppe *n.* fool

for, fore *prep., conj.* for; in respect of: ~ *me* as far as I am concerned; for fear of; against, to prevent; because (of); so that

forber(e), forbeir *v.* forbear, tolerate, refrain from injuring; give up, do without, keep away from; forbare *pa. 3 sg.*

forby *adv.* past

forbode *p.p.* forbidden

forbrake *v.* have a violent fit of vomiting

forbrent *p.p.* burnt up, completely burnt

force, foorce, forse *n.* strength, power; *it is* ~ it is necessary, *of/on* ~ of necessity, inevitably; matter, value; *gyff/gyveth no* ~ *(of)* set no store by, care nothing for

forcely *adv.* strongly

forcyble *adj.* severe

forcyth *pr. 3 sg. impers.: it* ~ *not* it matters not

forcolde *adj.* very cold, chilled

forcorven *p.p.* cut through

forfayted *pa. 3 sg.* lost by sin

forfeblit *p.p.* rendered feeble

forfetures *n. pl.* fines, penalties

forgaderit *pa.* assembled

forgane *prep.* over against, opposed to

forg(e)it *p.p., adj.* formed, fashioned

forgo(o)n(e) *v.* forgo, go without, be deprived of, lose

forlaye *pa. 3 pl.* lay with, smothered;

forla(y)ne *p.p.* lain with; laid aside, abandoned (18 C 140)

forland, forlond *n.* cape, headland

forlet *pr. 3 sg.* abandons

forloir *v.* become desolate

forlond *see* forland

forloppin *p.p.* renegade, runaway

forlost *p.p., adj.* completely lost

forquhy *conj.* because, since

forschip *n.* prow

forse *see* force

forshronke *p.p.* shrivelled up

forside *p.p., adj.* aforesaid

forslettes *n. pl.* little forts, fortifications

forslyngred *pa. 3 pl.* belaboured

forsoth(e), forsuth *adv.* truly, in truth

forth(e), foorthe, fourthe, furght, furth(e) *adv., prep.* forth, on, out, away; *als far* ~ as far; ~ *dais* late in the day; over, through; *fro this* ~ from this time on

forthwart *adv.* forward

fortyfyied *p.p.* strengthened, confirmed

fortirit *p.p.* tired out

forto *prep.* to, in order to

fortune *v.* bring fortune to; fortunait *p.p.* destined by fortune

forwhy *adv., conj.* for which reason, wherefore, therefore; because

forwrocht *p.p., adj.* exhausted

foryefnes *n.* forgiveness

foryete *v.* forget; foriete, forgete *p.p.*

foryetefulnesse *n.* oblivion

fote, fotte, fut(e) *n.* foot, foot's length; fette, f(y)ete *pl*; fote-mett *n.* measure

foughten, fowghten *see* fecht

fo(u)le, fewle, fowill *n.* bird, (coll.) birds; foul(l)ys *pl.*

foule *adj.: bothe in* ~ *and fayre* always

foundatour *n.* founder

found(en) *see* fynde

fourche *n.* fork (consisting of two branches) on a deer's horn

fourtened *adj.* fourteenth

fourthe; fowill; fra *see* forth(e); fo(u)le; fro

frayed, frayt *p.p.* frightened; frayis *pr. 3 sg.* frightens

frayry *n.* brotherhood (*see* demonycall)

frame *n.* device

franit *pa. 1 sg.* asked

fraunchise *n.* freedom; territory, domain

fraward, frawart *adj.* perverse, ill-humoured

frawde *n.* deception, trick

fre *adj.* free; generous, noble

fredam, fredom *n.* liberty; sanctuary; nobility, generosity

freel *adj.* frail

fre(e)re, freir, fryer *n.* friar

freisit *pa. 3 sg.* froze, became icy cold

frekes *n. pl.* men, warriors

frely *adv.* nobly

frended *p.p., adj.* provided with friends

frere, frerys *see* **fre(e)re**

fresch(e), fressh(e) *adj.* fresh, bright, gay, finely-dressed; ~**ly, freisshly** *adv.* freshly, intensely, clearly

fret *pa. 3 pl.* preened

frete *v.* consume, devour, wear down; **fretyth** *pr. 3 sg.* **fretynge** *pr. p., adj.*

fret-wise *adv.: in* ~ interlaced

fryer *see* **fre(e)re**

frith *n.* wood

frivoll *adj.* fickle

fro, fra *conj., prep.* from the time that, as soon as; ~ *that* when, after; from

froist *n.* frost, freezing, cold

fro(m)ward(e), frowardis *prep.* away from; (divided) ~ *hym* ~*es* away from him

fronsit *p.p., adj.* wrinkled

fronteris *n. pl.* borders, frontiers

frontis *n. pl.* faces (of cliffs)

frosshys *n. pl.* frogs

frouncys *n. pl.* creases, wrinkles

froward *adj.* evil

frowarde, frowardis *see* **fro(m)ward(e)**

fructuous *adj.* fruitful

frument *n.* corn, wheat

frust *see* **furste**

fulfillid/-it *p.p.* filled, filled completely

full *adj.* ~ *my bely* all I want

fulsum/-some *adj.* plentiful; **fulsom-nesse** *n.* abundance

fumes *n. pl.* droppings

fundin; fure; furght *see* **fynde; fare; forth(e)**

furyousness *n.* madness, torment

furnyse *v.* furnish, provide

furour(e) *n.* fury, wrath

furste, fruste *adv.* first

furth(e) *see* **forth(e)**

fusyon *n.* plenty

fut(e) *see* **fote**

ga *see* **go**

gabbyng *n.* lying, mocking

gables *n. pl.* cables

gadde *n.* spike, spear

gadre, gedyr *v.* gather; **gad(e)rid** *p.p.*

gagle *n.* gabbling

ga(i)f; gayne *see* **geve; go**

gair *n.* triangular piece of cloth forming part of a garment

gaist *see* **gost(e)**

gait *n.* road, way; **gatus** *pl.*

galaunt *n.* **galland(e)** *n., adj.* gallant, fine gentleman; splendid

galiard *adj.* brave

galymen *n. pl.* sailors in the galleys

galynnys *n. pl.* gallons

galland(e) *see* **galaunt**

galouse *n. pl.* gallows

game *n.* game, sport, pleasure, merriment, object of merriment: *make(a)* ~; hunting; a hunted animal

gan; gane *see* **gynnest; go**

ganecome *n.* return

gang *v.* go

gant *v.* yawn, gaped

gapyd *p.p.* yearned (for)

gar *v.* make, cause; **gart, gert** *pa.*

garded *p.p.* ornamented, trimmed

gardevyance *n.* trunk, chest

garding *n.* garden

gargeylde *p.p.* adorned with gargoyles

garmound, garnement *n.* garment

garnisoun *n.* garrison

gart *see* **gar**

garth *n.* enclosed garden

garth-webbe *n.* woven material for girths

gaspe *v.* open (his) beak

gat *n.* gate; **gatys, gattes** *pl.*

gat(e); gatus; gedyr; geet(t) *see* **gete; gait; gadre; gete**

gein *n.* help, remedy

geir, geyre; geys; geyte *see* **ger(e); gose; get(e)**

gelofer *n.* gillyflower

gender *v.* engender, beget; **generit** *p.p.*

generabill *adj.* capable of being generated

gent, jent *adj.* fine, excellent, noble

gentyl(l), gentell, jantyll, jentill *adj.* noble, fine, gracious

gentil(l)esse *n.* nobility, graciousness; noble deed

gentilnes *n.* nobility, graciousness

ger; gerd *see* **ger(e); girt**

gerdon *n.* reward

ger(e), geir(e) *n.* gear, equipment, property, belongings, wares, array, apparel

gersis *n. pl.* grasses
gert *see* **gar**
gesonne, gesoun *adj.* scarce, rare
ges(se) *v.* think, imagine
geste *see* **gost(e)**
gest(e) *n.* guest
gestyd *pa. 3 sg.* jested
gestis *n. pl.* tales, chonicles
get(e), geet(t), geyte *v.* get, obtain, receive; beget, earn money, win, produce; (refl.) betake oneself, go; **gat(e)** *pa.*; **got(t)in(e), goten(ne), gete** *p.p.*: ~ *forth* raised above
getters *n. pl.* swaggerers, roisterers
geve, gefe, gyf(f)(e) *v.* give, grant; **geuis, giffis** *pr. sg./pl.*; **ga(i)f** *pa.*; **geven, geuin, gevyne** *p.p.*
ghostes *see* **gost(e)**
gyane, gyaunt *n.* giant; **gyans** *pl.*
gyde, gyed *v.* guide, direct
gydyng(e) *n.* conduct, way of behaving, management; **gydingis** *pl.*
gye, guye *v.* guide; (refl.) conduct oneself
gyf(f)(e), giffis *see* **geve**
gyf(f)(e) *conj.* if
giglotlike *adv.* wantonly
gilt *p.p.* done amiss
gilt *p.p., adj.* gilded
gilt(e) *n.* guilt, fault, responsibility; ~**les** *adj.* guiltless
gylty *adj.* golden
gyngever *n.* ginger
gynnes *n. pl.* traps
gynnest, gynnis *pr. 2, 3 sg.* begin; (auxil.) do; **gan, gone** *pa.* began; did
girt, gerd *p.p.* girdled, girt
gys(e), guyse *n.* manner, fashion, mode, custom, practice, way of behaving
gyte *n.* mantle, cloak
gla(y)ve *n.* spear; sword; halberd
glar *n.* slime, mud
glas *n.: poleist* ~ mirror
gled *n.* kite
gledis *n. pl.* burning coals
gleyre *n.* glair, white of an egg
glore *n.* glory
glose *n.* gloss, explanatory comment
glosyng *n.* flattery
glowrand *pr.p., adj.* staring with wide-open eyes
gnyppand *pr.p.* nibbling
go, ga(ne), gon(e), goo(n), goen, igo *v.* go, move, walk, swim; *to* ~ by going; (imper.) ~ *to the helm* (?) put the helm over; (pr. 1 pl. subj.) ~ *we* let us go; **gois** *pr. 3 sg.*, **gone** *pr. pl.*; **ga(y)ne, go(o)(n)** *p.p.*: *(shuld he) be* ~ (?) be placed, be circumstanced
god(e), goyd, good, goud, gud(e) *adj.* good; *were as* ~ *to be dede* might as well be dead
gode, good, gude *n.* goods, property, money; good thing, benefit; *for any* ~ in any way; **goodes** *n. pl.* goodnesses
godly, gud(e)ly/-lie *adj.* goodly; **gudeliar** *comp.*
goen, gois; goyd *see* **go; god(e)**
goldin *adj.* golden, ~ *hour* dawn, most propitious moment
golk *n.* cuckoo
gome *n.* man
gon(e); gone; gonnes; goo; good, goodys/-es *see* **go; gynnest; gownes; go; god(e); gode**
goodeman *n.* husband, head of household; host (of inn)
goodewyff *n.* wife
goodlyhede, gudelihed *n.* excellence, bounty; beauty
goon, gooth; goost *see* **go; gost(e)**
gordys *n. pl.* gourds
gormaw *n.* cormorant
gose *n.* goose; **geys** *pl.*
gost(e), goost, gaist, geste *n.* spirit, ghost; **ghostes** *pl.*
gostly, goostly, ghostly *adj., adv.* spiritual, devout; devoutly, in a spiritual sense
goten(ne), gotyn(e), gottin *see* **get(e)**
gottes *gen. sg.* goat's
goud *see* **god(e)**
goules, goulis *n.* (her. term) red
gousty *adj.* vast, hollow
governaille *n.* control, guiding
governa(u)nce, govirnance *n.* government, rule, dominion, power, authority, control; conduct, behaviour
gownes, gonnes *n. pl.* guns
gracieux, gracyous *adj.* gracious; full of grace
gray *see* **greye**
gra(i)f *n.* grave; *haly* ~ Holy Sepulchre
grayne *n.* groan
gralynge *n.* grayling (a freshwater fish)
gramercy, graunt mercy *interj.* thank you
gramys *pr. 3 sg.* distresses
grane *n.* (?) point, particular
grange *n.* barn

grant *n.* granting, generous favour, generosity

grapsyng *pr.p.* groping

grauntfadir *n.* grandfather

graunt mercy *see* **gramercy**

grave *v.* dig; engrave, curve letters; **gravin** *p.p.* buried; **ygrave** *p.p.* graven, written

gré, gree *n.*[1] step; (astron.) degree; preeminence, mastery; **wyn** ~ be victorious; **grees, greis, greces, gresys** *pl.*

gré *n.*[2] goodwill, favour, pleasure; **greis, grece** *pl.*: *a* ~ with goodwill, in good part

gredeyrne *n.* gridiron

greet; greete, greetnes *see* **gret(e); grete**

gref(e), grif *n.* grief, sorrow, trouble, distress, anger; **greeves, grevous** *pl.*

Gregionys, Greikis *n. pl.* Greeks

greye, gray *adj. as n.* grey-haired man; grey cloth

greyn; greis; greissis; greit *see* **grene; gré; gresse; grete**

Grekys *adj.* Greek

grene *adj.* green; immature, youthful; ~, **greyn** *n.* green cloth; green, grassy ground

greshop, gressop *n.* grasshopper

gresys *see* **gré, gresse**

gresse *n.* grass; **gresys, greissis** *pl.* herbs, plants, grass

grete, greete *v.* weep, cry, cry out; **gret** *pa.*

grete, grate, great, gret(t)(e), gr(e)it *adj.* great, large, big; coarse; **gretter** *comp.*; **grettyste** *sup.*; **gret(t)nesse, greetnes** *n.* largeness, great size

greva(u)nce, grewans *n.* harm, distress, pain, injury, ailment, grievance

greve *v.* grieve; hurt, harm, trouble, distress; **grewyth** *pr. 3 sg.*; **grevyt** *p.p.*

greves *n. pl.* thickets, bushes

grevous, gryevous *adj.* troublesome, sorrowful

grevous; grewans *see* **gref; greva(u)nce**

grewell *n.* gruel

grewyth; grif *see* **greve; gref(e)**

grimmit *p.p.* befouled

grypes *n. pl.* griffins

grit *see* **grete**

gromes, gromys *n. pl.* grooms

grond *see* **gro(u)nd(e)**

grose *adj.* gross

grossynes *n. pl.* small coins

grotys *n. pl.* groats (coins, each worth *c*.4*d*.)

grouf *in adv. phr.*: *on* ~ prone, face down

gro(u)nd(e) *n.* earth, ground; battlefield; bottom, foundation, basis, cause; *atte* ~ on shore, on land

grounde, gr(o)und(yn) *p.p., adj.* sharpened, ground sharp

growit *pa. 3 sg.* shrank

grutche *v.* grumble, complain; **grucchith** *pr. 3 sg.*; **grucchid/-ed** *pa., p.p.*

guaryson *n.* cure

gud(e); gud(e)ly/-lie/-liar; gudelihed *see* **god(e); godly; goodlyhede**

gudlynes *n.* goodliness

guydit; guye; guyse *see* **gyde; gye; gys(e)**

gurding *pr. p. n.*: ~ *forth* (?) firing, (?) moving forward

gurl *adj.* stormy, rough, boisterous

ha; haastith *see* **hawe; hast**

habylyté *n.* suitableness, fitness; wealth

habyllements *n. pl.* clothes

habirgeoun *n.* habergeon (a sleeveless jacket of mail or armour)

habit, abeit *n.* dress, garb; habit (dress of a religious order)

habytacle *n.* dwelling-place, habitation

hable *v.* give strength, enable, make worthy

hable *adj.* able

habonda(u)nce, habunda(u)nce *n.* abundance, riches, plenty

habounde *adj.* overflowing

habowndawnt, habundaunt *adj.* abundant, abounding; generous; **habundantly** *adv.* abundantly

habunde *v.* abound, prevail

hace *adj.* hoarse

hade, haddyn; haert; ha(i)f(e) *see* **hawe; hert(e); hawe**

haiknay *n.* hackney, riding horse

haile; hayled, hailith; haill *see* **hole; hale; hole**

hailsyng *v.* greet, hail

hailsum; hair; hairt; hait *see* **holsom(e); hore; hert(e); hot, hote**

hakkyt *pr. 3 sg.* hacks

hald, haldyn, haldis; hale *see* **holde; hole**

hale *v.* pull, haul, draw; flow; **halys(t), hailith** *pr. sg.*; **hayled** *pr. 3 pl.*

halflyng(is) *adv.* half, partly

haly *adj.* holy

halke *n.* corner

hall-benkis *n. pl.* benches in hall

halok *adj.* giddy, thoughtless

halowe, hallowe, holowe *v.*[1] bless, hallow, sanctify

halow(e), *v.*[2] shout; ~ *every wight* (*pr. 3 sg. subj.*) let every man shout

halpe *see* helpe

hals *n.* neck

halsyde *pr. 1 sg.* embraced

halson *pr. 1 sg.* adjure

halte *see* holde

hamber *n.* amber (a measure: a pitcher or cask of liquid)

hame *n.* home

hamewart, hamward *adv.* homewards

hammes *n. pl.* hams, backs of the knees

hampryt *p.p., adj.* confined

han *see* hawe

hanch(e) *n.* haunch

hand(e), hond(e) *n.* hand; *in* ~ by the hand; *take (tuik) on* ~ undertake, take (took) charge of; *bere, stonde (on/an)* ~: *see* bere, stande; hands, hondis *pl.*: *(man) of . . . (his)* ~ (man) of skill, ability, strength, courage

handlynge *n.* handle

hang(yn) *see* hong

hap *v.* happen; happe *pr. 3 sg. subj.*; happyd/-ed *pa. sg.*: (with dat.) *hym* ~

happ(e) *n.* chance, event, deed; *upon* ~ by chance, *in* ~ perhaps; happes *pl.*; happ(e)ly *adv.* by chance, perchance, perhaps

harbery, herbry *n.* shelter, lodging-place, dwelling-place

harbour *v.* trace (a stag) to (his) lair

hard(e) *see* her(e), borde

hardy/ie *adj.* hardy, bold; ~ly, hard(e)ly *adv.* boldly, assuredly, indeed; ~nesse, hardenis *n.* boldness, courage

hardid *p.p.* hardened, made obdurate

hare *n.* hare; *rennyth* ~ (?) run with the hare, play a double game

haris *see* here

harkeneth *pr. 3 sg.* ~ *after* seeks to hear tidings of, inquires after

harnasyng *n.* trappings

harn(e)ys(e), harnes(se) *n.* armour, equipment, gear, harness; privy members; harneysed *v., p.p.* armoured, covered as with armour

harnes *n. pl.* brains

harnes(se) *see* harn(e)ys(e)

harowed *p.p.* harrowed, broken up with a harrow

harsk *adj.* harsh, rough

hart(e), harty, hartely *see* hert(e)

hasarde *n.* hazard, a game of dice; hasardours *n. pl.* gamblers

hast, ha(a)stith *imper. sg., pl.* hurry, make haste; speed, send quickly

hastyf *adj.* hasty, quick

hat *see* hawe

hatches *n. pl.* axes, hatchets

hatful *adj.* hateful

hatte *p.p., adj.* heated, warmed

hauberke *n.* hauberk, coat of mail

hauffte *n.* handle

hauke *v.* hunt with a hawk

hauld *see* holde

haunt *v.* frequent

hausyn; havy/-ie *see* hosen; hevy

havyn, haven, hawyn *n.* harbour, port; havenys *pl.*; havyn townys *n. pl.* seaport towns

havoyrs *n. pl.* possessions

haw *adj.* pale, livid

hawe, hawhe, ha(n), ha(i)f(e), a(n) *v.* have, hold; hes(t) *pr. sg.*, hat *pr. 3 sg.*; had(e), haddyn *pa.*

hawyn *see* havyn

hawkit *p.p., adj.* spotted, streaked

he; heare; hecht *see* hy(e); here; hot

hede, heid *n.* heed

hed(e), hedde, heed(e), heid, heved/-yd *n.* head; antlers; ruler; *hald thair* ~ show their faces; heydes *pl.*

heder, hedyr; heele *see* hethyr; hele

heep *n.* crowd, group, troop; hepis/-es *pl.*: *by* ~ in large quantities

he(e)r, heer(e) *see* here, her(e)

heeryd *p.p., adj.* having hair

heeste *n.* bidding; promise; vow; hestys, heestis *pl.*

hefe *conj.* if

hegg(h)e *n.* hedge; hegges, hegi(e)s *pl.*

heghe, hey, hey(e), heich; heid, heydes *see* hy(e); hed(e)

heidit *p.p.* headed

heye, heigh; heyer; heill *see* hy(e); hier; hele

heynd; heir; heyer *see* hende; her(e); hier

heynd *n.* end

heir *adv.* here

heird *v.* (*with pron.*) hear it

heyt *n.* heat

heklit *p.p., adj.* fringed
helas *interj.* alas
hele, helle, heele, heill *n.* health, well-being, salvation
hele, hell *v.*: ~ *up* heal; **helyde** *p.p.*
helpe, helpyn *v.* help; **helpyd, halpe, holp(e)/-yn** *pa.*: ~ ... *to masse* was/were present at mass, assisted at mass; **holpen/-yn** *p.p.*
helth(e) *n.* health, well-being, healing, cure, safety, salvation
hem *pron.* them; ~**selfe(n)**, ~**silfe** themselves
hende, heynd *adj., adv.* pleasant, gracious, courteous; graciously
hender; henge *see* **hynder; hong**
henge *n.* pluck (the heart, liver, etc., of an animal)
hensmen *n. pl.* squires, pages
hent(e) *pa. 3 sg.* seized; received
hepes, hepis; her *see* **heep; her(e)**
her *conj.* ere, before
heraud *n.* herald, precursor
herber(e) *n.* arbour, garden
herbes; herbry; herd(e) *see* **erbe; harbery; her(e)**
herd *adj.* hard
herdys *n. pl.* shepherds, herdsmen
here, heer(e), heare *n.* hair; **haris** *pl.*
her(e), heere, heir, heryn, hyre *v.* hear; **herit** *pr. 3 sg.*; **hard(e), herd(e)** *pa., p.p.*
her(e), hir *pron., adj. poss.* their, of them
hery *adj.* hairy
herien *v.* praise, worship
heryn, herit *see* **her(e)**
herytage *n.* inheritance, inherited wealth
heronsew *n.* young heron
hert(e), haert *n.* hart
hert(e), ha(i)rt(e) *n.* heart; innermost thoughts; *lyis on* ~ presses on (my) heart; *take/toke gode* ~ *(to)* be/was of good heart; ~**-depe** *adj., adv.* profoundly deep, in deep sorrow; **harty** *adj.* devoted, cordial; **hertely, hert(a)li, hert(y)ly, hartely** *adj., adv.* heartfelt, sincere; heartily, sincerely, earnestly
herte-roote *n.* depths of the heart
herto *adv.* to/for this
hervist, herwest *n.* harvest, autumn
hes, hest *see* **hawe**
hesp *n.* hasp
hestys; het *see* **heste; hot**
hethe-buysshe *n.* heath-bush

hethyr, heder/-yr, hyd(d)er/-ir *adv.* hither
heved, hevyd *see* **hed(e)**
heven(e), heuin, hevin *n.* heaven; the beloved; ~**nis** *pl.* blisful mates; **hevene** *gen. sg.*: ~ *qwen* queen of heaven
hevy, hevie, havy/ie *adj.* grievous, sorrowful, miserable, sad, dejected; **hevyly, hevely** *adv.* heavily, sorrowfully, grievously; **hevines(se), hewynesse** *n.* sorrow, grief, sadness
hewyr *conj.* before
hewis *n. pl.* cliffs, crags
hewmound *n.* helmet
hycht *see* **hight**
hyd *n.* hide, skin
hyd(d)er/-ir *see* **hethyr**
hiddy giddy *adv.* topsy-turvy, in a giddy whirl
hiddous, hiddowis, hydduus *adj.* hideous
hidlis *n. pl.* hiding-places
hy(e) *n.* haste; *an/in* ~ quickly
hy(e), hey(e) *v. (often refl.)* make haste, hurry; **highed** *pa.*
hy(e), hihe, hygh(e), he, he(i)gh(e), hey(e), heich *adj., adv.* high, lofty, sublime, proud; loud; complete, full; ~ *way* direct, main road; *an/on* ~ aloft, in heaven; ~ *pryme: see* **pryme**; proudly, strongly, loudly, lavishly; **highly** *adv.* greatly, seriously, solemnly
hier, eir, heyer *n.* heir; **heyres** *pl.*
highly; hight; hihe; hild, hylde *see* **hye; hot; hy(e); holde**
hight, hyght(e), hycht *n.* height, top; *on* ~ aloft, up, on high, loudly
hilded *pa. 3 sg.* poured
hiled *p.p.* covered, protected
hym *pron.* them
hynde *n.* servant
hynder, hyndre *v.* harm, injure; hinder; vilify, slander; **hyndred** *p.p.*
hynder, hender *adj.* last (as n.) rear
hyne *adv.* hence, thence
hyng, hyngand *see* **hong**
hint *n.* grip, clutch, grasp
hint *pa. 3 sg.* seized
hippis *n. pl.* hips, i.e. buttocks
hippit *pa. 3 pl.* hopped
hir *see* **her(e)**
hyrd-gromys *n. pl.* shepherd lads
hyre *see* **her(e)**
hyre *adv.* here

hyrnys *n. pl.* corners, nooks, hiding-places
hit *pron.* it
ho(c)ke *n.* hook
hoichis *n. pl.* hocks
ho(i)g *n.* young sheep
hoyll *n.* hole, anus; **holys** *pl.*
hoip; hoir *see* **hoope; hore**
holde, hauld *n.* possession, grasp; refuge, abode
holde, hald *v.* hold, have, contain, maintain: *gif I ~ me pes* if I keep silent; keep, hold to, consider: *~ of nane* have no superior; (*refl.*) consider oneself; *~ with* support, remain loyal to; **halte, holdet** *pr. 3 sg.*; **hild(e)** *pa.*; **hald(yn), holde(n)** *p.p.*
hole, holl(e), hool(e), haill, ha(i)le *adj., adv.* whole, complete, healthy, restored to health; wholly, altogether, utterly: *all ~* completely, *~ of new* completely afresh; *n.* whole; **hol(l)y** *adv.* wholly, completely
holyng *n.* healing
holkyt *p.p.* hollowed
holl(e), holly; holowe *see* **hole; hal(l)owe**
holowyng *n.* shouting
holowynge *n.* hallowing, consecration
holp(e)(n), holpyn *see* **helpe**
holsom(e), holsum, hailsum *adj.* healthy, wholesome, health-giving; **~ly** *adv.*
holt(t)is *see* **howt**
homagers *n. pl.* men who pay homage
homecyd *n.* man-slayer
hom(e)ly(e) *adj.* familiar, homely, domestic
hond(e) *see* **hand(e)**
honest(e) *adj.* noble, honourable, goodly, pleasant; **~ly** *adv.* honourably; nobly
honesté *n.* honour, good repute, decency, moral excellence
hong, henge, hyng *v.* hang; **hingand** *pr.p.*; **hang, hyng(e), honge(d)** *pa.*; **honge, hangyn** *p.p.* hung, hanged
hongre *n.* hunger
hool(e); hoond *see* **hole; hand(e)**
hoope, hoip, howp *n.* hope
hoope *v.* hope
hooste; hoot(e) *see* **oste; hote**
hopper *n.* basket
horatour *n.* petitioner, suppliant
hore, hair, hoir *adj.* hoary, grey, grey-haired, white; hoarse, grating, rough
hors *n.* horse; **hors** *gen. sg.*; **horsen** *pl.*; **hores-donge** *n.* horse-dung; **hors-grece** *n.* fat of a horse

hos *rel. pron.* whose
hosen/-yn, ha(u)sen *n. pl.* hose, breeches
hosteleris *n. pl.* innkeepers
hot *pr. 1 sg.* command; **he(ch)t, hight** *pa.* promised, vowed; is/are called; commanded; **hait, hecht** *p.p.* named, called
hote, hoot(e), hait, whote *adj.* hot, passionate
hote houses *n. pl.* bathhouses, stews
hough; houris *see* **how(e); oure**
house-combe *n.* the comb (a flat cake of wax) of a vespiary (used for bait)
houselyd *p.p.* given communion
housen *n. pl.* houses
houshold(e), howsold(e) *n.* household, household goods; *(good) ~ kepe* maintain a (good) house
hovable *adj.* suitable, fitting
hovand *see* **hoved**
hove *pa. 3 pl.* lifted
hoved *pa.* waited, lingered, remained; floated, moved; **howvyng, hovand** *pr.p.* pausing, lingering, stopping
how *adj.* hollow, sunken
how(e), hough, quhow *adv.* how, however, *~ that* ever/evire how-/whatever; *~ well that* although, even though; *~ beit, ~ be hyt* however; **quhou oft** whenever
howe *pron. indef.* whoever (1 R 26)
howede *p.p.* (?) hewed, cut
howle *n.* owl
howll-flyght *n.* twilight
howp *see* **hoope**
howr *pron., poss. adj.* our
howris; howsold(e) *see* **oure; houshold(e)**
howt *n.* wood, copse; **holt(t)is** *pl.*
howvyng *see* **hoved**
huche *n.* crag, steep, hill
hude *n.* hood
hudit crawis *n. pl.* hooded crows
huyf *n.* haunt
huke *n.* cape
humayne *adj.* human; **humaines** *pl.*
humanyté, humanitie *n.* benevolence, kindness, learning
humbylbee *n.* bumble-bee
humblesse *n.* humbleness, graciousness
humeres, humores *n. pl.* humours (the four chief fluids which determined a person's physical and mental qualities)
hunderde, hundir *n.* hundred
hunte *n.* huntsman
husbandes *n. pl.* husbandmen, peasants
husbondrie *n.* tilling the soil

hutit *p.p.*, *adj.* hooted at, mocked

i-/y- *(consonantal) see* **y-**
i *prep.* in
ybe; ybought; ybowndyn; ibrende; ibroght *see* **be; by; bind(e); bren(ne); brenge**
ice-schoklis, ische-schouchlis, ise-sicles *n. pl.* icicles
ich; yclyp(p)ed; ycome *see* **ech(e); clepe; come**
ydell, idill *adj.* idle, vain; **ydelnes** *n.* leisure (17 E 129)
idole *n.* image
ydo(on); ye(e), yen, iyen, yes *see* **do; eie**
yfere *adv.* together, in company
ifiguriet *see* **figure(n)**
yfollid *p.p.* baptized
igo; ygrave; iyen; ilaft *see* **go; grave; eie; leve**
yle *n.* aisle (1 P 7)
ilechede *p.p.* cut, sliced
i(le)lond(e) *n.* island; **ylandes** *pl.*
iliche, ilik(e) *adv.* alike
ilka, ilk(e) *adj.* each, every; same, very; ~ *deill* altogether, every part
ilokin *p.p.* locked
ymened *p.p.* mingled
ymeved *see* **meve**
imperiall *adj.* empyreal
ympnis *n. pl.* hymns
importable *adj.* unbearable
impreygnest *pr. 2 sg.* impregnate
incontynent(e) *adv.* straightway, immediately
inconvenyens *n.* trouble, misfortune
indignacyon *n.* disdain
indyte *see* **endyte**
indoce *v.* endorse
ynewe *see* **inogh(e)**
inexpugnable *adj.* impregnable
infek *v.* infect, poison
inflat *p.p.* puffed, inflated
influence *n.* (planetary) influence (streams of ethereal fluid which affected earthly things and persons)
infoundyd *p.p.* poured in, infused
ingraf, ingrave *p.p.* engraved, inscribed
inhibicyon *n.* prohibition
inhibited *pa. 3 sg.* prohibited
injure *n.* injury, insult
in mid *prep.* within
inned *p.p.* gathered in, harvested; **ynnynge** *n.* harvesting

in(n)ly *adj.*, *adv.* intimate, heartfelt; inwardly
innoblesse *n.* lack of nobility
innumerable *adj.* inexpressible (7 L 75)
inogh(e), ynou(g)h, inow(e), an(n)-ewch(e) *n.* enough; *adj.* sufficient, enough; **ynewe** *pl.* many; *adv.* enough, sufficiently, very, fully, exceedingly
inparfitnes *n.* imperfection
inporturat *p.p.* decorated with depictions
inrichely *adv.* splendidly
inscience *n.* lack of learning
insight *n.* vision, understanding
insolence *n.* pride
inspyre *v.* breathe, infuse
instytucyon *n.* ordained form
insufferit *p.p.* suffered
intent *n.* mind
interleccyon *n.* (?) something read by way of an interlude, (?) consultation
inthorowly *adv.* very thoroughly, intimately
int(i)erly *see* **enteirly**
intill *prep.* in, on, into
into *prep.* into, in, on, to
intreatese *n. pl.* entreaties
intromet, intromytt *imper.*, *refl.* introduce (yourself); concern (yourself)
intronyt *p.p.* enthroned
inventio(u)n *n.* (poetic) invention; finding
inward *adj.*, *adv.* interior, inner; inward, internally; ~**ly** *adv.* within the heart, in spirit
yren(e), ern *n.* iron; **yrnis** *pl.* surgical instruments
yrful *adj.* wrathful
yrke *v.* make weary; grow weary of; **irkyt** *p.p.*, *adj.* wearied, pained
yrke *adj.* weary, tired
yrnis; ironne; irosted *see* **yren(e); renne; roste**
is *pron.*, *poss. adj.* his
ysayde; ische-schouchlis, ise-sicles *see* **sey(e); ice-schoklis**
ischet, yschit *pa.* came out, issued
ysett; yshave; yslayne *see* **set(t); schaf; sle(e)(n)**
isope *n.* hyssop
ysowpit *p.p.* soaked
ytake *see* **take**
item *adv.* likewise
iterat *p.p.* repeated
ituned *p.p.* tuned
yvé *n.* ivy
yvell *see* **evyl(l)**

yvery, ivore, evyr *n.* ivory
ywhreton *see* writt
ywys, iwis(e) *adv.* certainly, to be sure, indeed

ja *n.* jay
jake *n.* jacket
jangill *v.* chatter, prattle; dispute; jangeled *pa. 3 pl.*; janglynge *n.* chattering
janglour *n.* gossip, backbiter; jangelers *pl.* chatterers, idle talkers
jantyll *see* gentyl(l)
jaspe *n.* jasper
jawpys *n. pl.* splashing waves
jenepere *n.* juniper
jent; jentil(l) *see* gent; gentyl(l)
jeopardé/-die, jeperté, joparté, jouperté *n.* jeopardy, danger, dangerous attack; chance
jest *n.* tale
jett *n.* fashion, custom
jeuellouris *n. pl.* jailors
jewellys *see* jowall
jewise *n.* penalty
joy(e)(n) *v.* feel joy; gladden
joynynge *adj.* close to
joly *adj.* pleasant, gay, splendid
jolyus *adj.* jealous
jonettis *n. pl.* (?) yellow marsh lilies, (?) flowers of the jonette pear (i.e. an early pear) (5. 123)
jonit *pa.* joined
joparté; jorney(e) *see* jeopardé; jo(u)rney(e)
jorneying *n.* journeying
jostyd *see* juste
jostys *n. pl.* jousts; ~ *of pese* jousts in which the weapons were blunted
jouperté *see* jeopardé
jo(u)rney(e), journaye/-é/-ee *n.* day, day's journey, journey; jurneys *pl.*
Jow *n.* Jew, infidel; Jowis/-es, Jues *pl.*
jowall, juell *n.* jewel; jewellys *pl.* testicles
juge *n.* judge
jugeler *n.* juggler, jongleur
jug(e)ment *n.* judgment, trial; opinion
Juyll July
junctly *adv.* jointly
jurneys *see* jo(u)rney(e)
just *adv.* closely; *by* ~ *be* very close to
juste *v.* joust; jostyd *p.p.*; justyng *n.* jousting
justyces *n. pl.* courts of justice

kayis *n. pl.* jackdaws
kalendis *n. pl.* first days, first indication
kalenge; kan; karfull; katche *see* chalenge; con(ne); cair; cache
kechyn *n.* kitchen
kedlokes *n. pl.* field mustard
keie *n.* key
keik *pr. 1 sg.* peep, glance
keyne; keip, keipis/-it *see* kene; kepe
keipar, keiper *n.* custodian, warden
keyshate *n.* sergeant of the peace [W *ceisiad*]
kell *n.* caul, woman's netted cap
kemmit *p.p.* combed
ken *v.* know, become acquainted with; kennis/-it *pr. 3 sg.*; kend *pa., p.p.*
kende *see* kynd(e)
kendill *v.* kindle, be aroused; kendillis *pr. 3 sg.*; kendlit *pa.*
kene, keyne *adj.* sharp, bitter, grievous, savage, fierce; kenenes *n.* fierceness
kenge *n.* king
kennis, kennit *see* ken
kepe, keip *n.* heed, attention: *take* ~ pay attention to
kep(e), keepe, kepyn *v.* keep, preserve; (refl.) refrain; protect, guard, hold, maintain; look after, care for, mark, observe; keipis/-it *pr. sg.*; keipit, kepte *pa.*; kepand *pr.p.*; kept *p.p.*
kerchif *n.* kerchief (a woman's head-dress); kevercheffes *pl.*
kerke *see* kyrk(e)
kerve *imper. sg.* cut; kerffis *pr. sg.* carves
kest; kevercheffes *see* cast(e); kerchif
ky *n. pl.* cows
kid(de), kyith *see* kythe
kynd(e), kende *n.* nature, kind, kinship; natural form, natural disposition, manner
kynde *adj.* kind, naturally loving; kindly *adv.* natural; kindly
kyn(n)e *n.* kin, people; kyns *gen. sg.*: *in no* ~ *wyse* in no manner
kynrede *n.* kindred
kyrk(e), kerke *n.* church, temple; kyrkmen *n. pl.* churchmen
kyrré *n.* quarry (in hunting, a heap of parts of the slain deer given to the hounds as a reward)
kirtell *n.* kirtle, tunic, gown; kirtillis *pl.*
kyst *see* cast(e)
kist *n.* chest
kythe, kyith *v.* show, display, make known;

kythe, kyith (*cont.*):
   kythit *pa. p.p.*, kidde *pa.*; kid *p.p.*
kytt(e), kute *v.* cut; kyt(te), kut(e) *p.p.*
klycked *n.* latch; ~ gate gate with a latch
knaiff, knave *n.* boy, serving-man; low-
   born menial, rascal; knawys *pl.*
knawe *see* know(e)
knet; knewe, knewyn *see* knyt(t)e;
   know(e)
knyllide *pa. 3 sg.* rang
knyt *n.* knight; knytys *pl.*
knyt(t)e, knet, knytted *p.p.* knit,
   fastened, intertwined, knitted
knopis, knoppes *n. pl.* buds
knot *n.* knot, cluster; knottis *pl.* interlaced figures
know(e), knawe *v.* know, experience,
   recognize, identify, find out, acknowledge; knewe/-yn *pa.*; knowe(n),
   knouwe *p.p.*
knowlach, kno(w)l(e)age, knowlech(e)/-
   lich *n.* knowledge; acquaintance,
   friends; information
knowleage, knowleche *v.* acknowledge;
   knowelechest *pr. 2 sg.*; knowlechyng
   n. acknowledgement
konne; konnyng(e) *see* con(ne); con-
   nyng(e)
koterelles *n. pl.* peasants
koude, kowd, kunne(n); kuke; kunnynge *see* con(ne); coke; connyng(e)
kussyd *pa. 3 sg.* kissed
kute *see* kytt(e)

laborer *n.* labourer, tiller; laboureurs,
   lauboris *pl.*
laborous, laburus *adj.* toilsome, difficult
labour, labowr, labur(e) *n.* toil, trouble,
   effort; *take the* ~ make the effort
labo(u)rith, labowrith *pr. 3 sg.* works
   (for), strives; labored/-yd, labour-
   id(en) *pa.*; labored *p.p.* worked (for),
   tried to persuade, urged
lace *n.* net
lacke; lackyd; lad(de) *see* lak(e); lake;
   lede
lade *p.p.* laden, covered
ladyship *n.* kindness, benevolence (as a
   lady)
laft *see* leve
laggerit *p.p.* covered with mire
lagh(e) *see* lawe
laghers *n. pl.* laughers

laid, layde, layeng *see* ley
laye *n.* law
laif(f) *n.* rest, remainder
laik *see* lak(e)
layke *n.* sport, contest
lair *n.* doctrine, teaching
layser, leasour *n.* leisure
laithly *adj.* loathsome
lak(e), lacke, laik *n.* fault, defect; lack,
   want; reproach, insult
lake *v.* want, be lacking; hem lakketh *pr.
   3 sg., impers.* they lack
landbrist *n.* surf
langage *n.* language, words, speech, discourse
langere *adv.* a while ago
langyng *pr. p.* longing
lanssyt *pa. 3 sg.* leapt
lap *see* lepe
lappe *n.* fold of a garment, lap
lap(pe) *v.* wrap, clothe, envelop; lappyt
   p.p.
larde *n.* bacon, pork fat
large *adj.* large, wide, expansive, prodigal;
   largely *adv.* generously
larges(se) *n.* generosity; large number
lase *n.* lass, girl; lassis *pl.* little girls
lassith *pr. 3 sg.* lessens, is less (than)
latany *n.* litany
lat(e); lat *see* let(e); let
latesses *n. pl.* lattices
latyn(g) *see* let(e)
laton *n.* latten, brass
latte, latting; lattit *see* let(e); let
latward *adv.* recently
lauboraris; lauch(is) *see* laborer; lawhe
laufullie *adv.* according to the procedure
   of the law
laundes *n. pl.* glades
laurer, lawrer, lorer *n.* laurel, laurel-tree
lavatorye *n.* cleansing
laverocke *n.* lark
lawchtir *n.* laughter, laughing matter
lawe, lagh(e) *n.* law; *olde* ~ Old Testament; *hafe done (me)* ~ treated me
   according to the law
lawhe *v.* laugh; lawgth, lauchis *pr. 3 sg.*;
   lauch, laugh, leuch, loughe, lowghe
   pa.
lawyst *adj. sup.* lowest
lawn(e) *n.* fine linen
lawrer; lawté/-tie *see* laurer; lewté
lazarous *n.* leper
le *n.*[1] lee, the sheltered side

le *n.*[2] lea, pasture (land), grassland; **le(y)is** *pl.*

leames; leasour *see* **lemys; layser**

leche *n.*[1]: ~ *lumbarde* Lombard leach (the name of a dish)

leche, leiche *n.*[2] physician; **le(i)checraft** *n.* medicine; *at* ~ receiving treatment

lecherdnes *n.* lechery

lectrure *see* **lett(e)rure**

led, leid *n.* man, person; people, folk; **leeds** *pl.*

ledded *see* **lede**

ledder *n.*[1] leather

ledder *n.*[2] ladder

lede, leede, leid *n.* lead

lede, leid *v.* lead, conduct, bring, preserve; **leddyn** *pa. pl.*; **lad(de), ledded, lede** *p.p.*

leded *p.p., adj.* covered with lead

leeds; leefe; leeful(l) *see* **led; leve; leful(l)**

leered *see* **lerde**

leest, lest(e) *adj. sup.*[1]: *at (the)* ~ *(wey)* at least

leest *adj. sup.*[2]: *at the* ~ last

lefe, leffe, left, lefte *see* **leve**

lefe *n.* leaf (of paper) (9 H 23)

lefte *imper. sg.* lift; **left** *pa.* lifted

leful(l), leeful(l), levefull *adj.* permissible, lawful; **lefulli** *adv.* permissibly, lawfully

lege *v.* plead, declare on oath; **legged** *p.p.* cited

ley *v.* lay, place, put; wager; ~ *adowne* lie down; **layeng** *pr.p.*: ~ *on* smiting; **laid, layde, leide** *pa., p.p.*: ~ *forth* laid out; ~ *on* imposed on; ~ *out* expended; ~ *them about* laid about them; ~ *unto her* charged/accused her; ~ *downe* ceased, ended

leiche, leichecraft; leid; leif; leyffand; leyis; leile, leill *see* **leche; led, lede; leve; lyf; le; lele**

leyn *v.* lean; **lened/-yd, lent** *pa.*; **lent** *p.p.* turned

leine; leir *see* **lene; lere**

leire *n.* lair

leis; leit *see* **le; let(e)**

leke *n.* leek (as an object of little value)

lekenes *n.* likeness

lekerous *adj.* lecherous, wanton

lele, leile, leill *adj.* loyal, faithful, true, lawful; **lelely** *adv.* loyally, faithfully

leman *see* **lem(m)an**

leme *v.* shine; **lemand, lemyng** *pr. p.* gleaming, shining; **lemed** *pa. 3 sg.* flamed

lemys, leames *n. pl.* rays, beams

lem(m)an *n.* mistress

lenage; lende *see* **ly(g)nage; lenne**

lene, leine *adj.* lean

lened *see* **leyn**

lenger(e) *adj. comp.* longer

lenght *n.* length

lenyd *see* **leyn**

lenne *v.* lend, give; **lent** *pa.*; **lent, lende** *p.p.*

lent *see* **leyn**

lent *n.* spring, lent

leo(u)n *n.* lion; *the* ~ the zodiacal sign of Leo

lepe *n.* basket for catching fish, fish-trap

lepe *v.* jump; **leppeth** *pr. 3 sg.*; **lap, lepe** *pa. 3 sg.* leapt, poured

lere, leir *v.* learn; **lerde, leered, lerit** *p.p., adj.* learned; *macke* . . . ~ teach a lesson

les, lesse *n.* lie; *but* ~ in truth, indeed

lese *v.*[1] release, set free

lese *v.*[2] lose; **lesyth** *pr. pl.*

lesynge *n.* lie; *without* ~ in truth; **lesingis** *pl.*

lesse; lest; lest(e) *see* **les; lyst; leest**

leste *v.* last

let, lett(e), lat *v.* hinder, prevent, stop; **let, lattit, lettyd** *p.p.*

let(e), lett(e) *n.* hindrance, delay; *but* ~ without delay, at once

let(e), leit, lat(e), latte *v.* let, allow; leave; let (for hire); let (blood); get something done, cause (to): ~ . . . *wit* make known, ~ *say (a masse)/*~ *do crye (a feest)* caused a mass/feast to be said/announced; ~ *as* act as if; **lett** *pr. 3 sg.*; **leit** *pa.*; **latyn, late** *p.p.*

leter, litter *n.* bedding (of straw, rushes, etc.)

lethis *n. pl.* joints

letter *n.*: *after the* ~ according to the literal sense

lett(e)rure, lectrure *n.* learning, book-learning, study of humane letters

lettyd; leuch; leud(e) *see* **let; lawhe; lewed**

levacyon *n.* elevation

leve *see* **lyf**

leve, lewe *n.* leave

leve, leefe, leffe, leif *v.* leave, be left, abandon, give up, grant; **levand** *pr.p.*; **levit, lewit, lefte, laft** *pa.*; **left, ilaft** *p.p.*

leve, lefe, lyff *adj.* dear, beloved; *had as* ~ would as soon; lever(e), levyr *comp.* rather: *the* ~ the better: *I had/me were* ~ I would rather

levefull; levene *see* leful(l); levyn

levetenauntes *n. pl.* lieutenants

levyd *see* lyf

levyn, levene *n.* lightning, flame, bright light, ray

levyn, levit; leving(e); levyr; lewch(e); lewe, lewit *see* lyf; lyvyng(e); leve; lawhe; leve

lewed, lewid, lewde, leud(e) *adj.* ignorant, common; lewdeste *sup.*

lewté, lawté/-tie *n.* loyalty, fidelity

li. *abbrev.* pound(s)

ly, lyg *v.* lie, remain, lie down; (refl.) ~ *theym;* ~ *on (me)* importune; lyth *pr. 3 sg.,* lyen, liggen *pr. 3 pl.;* liggand *pr. p.;* liggit, lyne *p.p.*

lyart *adj.* grey, streaked with grey

libardes *n. pl.* leopards

lybell *n.* bill, formal document

lych(e) *see* lyk(e)

lichory *n.* lechery

licht *see* lyght(e)

lychtlie *v.* make light of, disparage

licke *see* lyk(e)

licour *n.* liquid, liquor

lyde (upon) *p.p.* lied (against); lieit *pa.* told falsehoods

lyek; lyen *see* lyk(e); ly

lyeris *n. pl.* liars

lyessh *n.* leash, strap

lyf, lyve, leve/-yn, leif *v.* live; liffand, leyffand *pr.p.;* levit, levyd *p.p.*

lyf(e), lyff(e), lyve, liif *n.* life, livelihood, manner of living; *on* ~ alive; *my* ~ my beloved; living person; livis *gen. sg. pl.*

lyf(e)lode, lyvelode *n.* livelihood; property, estate

lyff; lyffand *see* leve; lyf

lifly *adv.* vigorously, vividly

lyft(e) *adj.* left

lyg, lyggand, liggen, liggit; lyghly *see* ly; likely

light *v.* lighten; alight, fall, land; light *pa. 3 sg.;* lighted *p.p.*

lyght *p.p., adj.* lighted, kindled

lyght(e), licht *adj., adv.* light, quick, eager, joyful, easy bright; brightly, light; *all for somer* ~ lightly dressed as if for summer; light(e)ly *adv.* easily, quickly, nimbly

lyghten *v.* shed light

ly(g)nage, lenage *n.* lineage, kin

lyke *v.*[1] (*often impers.*) please; lykand *pr.p.,* liken *pr.p. being pleased* (18 C 267); likid, lykit *pa.*

lyke *v.*[2] taste

lyk(e), lych(e), lyek, licke *adj., adv.* likely, fit, like, similar; in like manner; ~ *as* just as; ~ *to* likely to

lykely, lyghly *adj.* likely, able, promising

lykeng, likyng(e) *n.* pleasure, affection; *my* ~ my dearest one

lyklihood, lyklyod *n.* likelihood; *by all* ~ (as is) most likely

likned *p.p.* made like to

lymners *n. pl.* men who lead hounds on leash while tracking game

lyn; lynage *see* lyn(e); ly(g)nage

lyncloth *n.* linen cloth

lind *n.* loins, buttocks

lynd *n.* lime-tree

lyne *see* ly

lyn(e) *n.* line; *be* ~ by lineal descent; lyne-right *adv.* straight, in a straight line

lynnys *n. pl.* (water)falls

lynt *n.* flax

lyntall *n.* lintel

lipper *adj.* leprous; *n.* (*collect.*) lepers, leper folk

lippyn *v.* entrust

lyr(e) *n.* flesh, skin; face, complexion

lyst, lest *n.* desire

lyst *v.* listen, hear

lyst *conj.* lest

lyste *n.* strip of cloth, selvage, edging; listis *pl.*

lyst(e) *v.* desire, wish; please; ~ *better* prefer; (impers.) *if me* ~ if it pleases me

lite *n., adv.* little

lyte(y)ll, lyttel, litil(l)(e) *adj., adv.* small, little; (*by*) ~ *and* ~ gradually

lyth; lyve; lyvelode *see* ly; lyf, lyf(e); lyf(e)lode

lyveray *n. made large* ~ took a good allowance

lyvyng(e), lywynge, levyng(e) *n.* manner of living, way of life; livelihood; produce, crop

livis *see* lyf(e)

lodesterre *n.* guiding star

lofe; loffe, loffit *see* lufe; luf, loif

loft *n.* sky; *apon/on* ~ on high

loggid, loged; logyng *see* **luged; lugeing**
loif *v.* praise; **loved, loffit** *pa., p.p.*
loik-hertit *adj.* warm-hearted
lois *see* **los**
lois *n.* loss
loke, luik, luke *v.* look, see, consider, watch; (imper.) ~ *that* see that; **lukis** *pr. 3 pl.*; **lukand, lok(e)ing** *pr.p.*
lokyer *n.* locksmith
longanymyté *n.* long-suffering, forbearance
longe *adj.*: *a* ~ *myle* i.e. more than a mile; *no* ~ no long time, not long
longes *n. pl.* lungs
longyth *pr. 3 sg/pl.* pertain, belong (to), have to do (with)
lordshyp(e) *n.* dominion; country, district
lorel *n.* rogue, rascal
lorer(s) *see* **laurer**
los, lois *n.* praise, fame, honour
lose; losed *see* **lo(u)se; lowsyt**
losel *n.* rascal; **loselles** *pl.*
loste *n.* loss
loterynge *pr.p.* loitering, idling
loth(e) *adj.* hateful, loathsome; reluctant; **lothlyer** *comp.*
loued; lough *see* **loif; lawhe**
louyng *n.* praise
lo(u)se *adj.* loose, loosely clad, ungirt, not fastened
lowd *adv.*: ~ *and still* in every way
low(e) *n.* flame, fire, blaze
lowe; lowghe *see* **luf; lawhe**
lown *adj.* calm
lowpyt *p.p.* looped, coiled in loops
lowsyt, losed *p.p.* unbound, loosed, loosened
lowt(e) *v.* bow, bend, submit, descend; **lowtit** *pa. 3 sg.*
luce *n.* pike (fish)
lude *see* **luf**
ludge *n.* small dwelling, hut
ludgeit *see* **luged**
luf, loffe *v.* love; **lufis** *pr. 3 sg.*; **loffit, luffit** *pa.*; **lufing** *pr.p.*; **lude, luvit** *p.p.*; **lufingly** *adv.* lovingly; **luffaris, luifferis** *n. pl.* lovers
lufe, luif, lowe, lofe *n.* love; **lu(i)f(f)is** *gen. sg.*
luffaris, lufingly *see* **luf**
lug *n.* ear
luged *pa. 3 pl.* (*refl.*) made camp; **ludgeit, loggid, loged** *p.p.* lodged
lugeng, logyng *n.* residence; **lugyn land**

(?) land in which one can reside
luif(fis); luifferis *see* **lufe; luf**
luik *n.* look, appearance
luik, lukand, luke *see* **lukis, loke**
Lumbard(e) *n., adj.* Lombard
lurk *v.* shrink, cower; lurk, lie hidden; **lurkis** *pr. 3 pl.*
luschyng *n.* crashing down
lust(e) *n.* pleasure, delight, desire, lust; **lustlesse** *adj.* joyless
lusted *pa. 3 sg., impers.* pleased
lusty, lustie *adj.* joyful, pleasant, fine, beautiful, vigorous, passionate; **lustynes(se)** *n.* joy, happiness, vigour

ma; ma, maad *see* **ma(y); mak(e)**
macch *v.* be/prove a match for; **mached** *pa. pl.*
maces, masys *n.* mace (a spice)
macke *see* **mak(e)**
maculait *p.p.* defiled
mad *see* **mak(e)**
mafay *interj.* indeed
magnyfycence *n.* glory, greatness
magré *see* **ma(w)gré**
may *n.* maid
ma(y), mey *v.* may, can (with omitted verb of motion, 9 Q 27)
maid, maik *see* **mak(e)**
may-fley *n.* may-fly
mayled *p.p.* mailed, covered with rings or plates of metal
ma(y)n(e) *n.* strength, might
mayné *see* **meyné**
maynte(y)ne *v.* maintain, uphold, keep, control
mair *see* **mor(e)**
maire *n.* mayor; **mayres** *pl.*
maist *see* **mo(o)st**
ma(y)ster *n.* master, teacher; lord, captain; graduate; ~-**herte** *n.* hart which is leader; ~-**losel** *n.* leading villain, absolute rascal; ~-**veayne** *n.* chief vein, artery
maystry(e) *n.* mastery, power, skill; great exploit, feat
maystried *p.p.* conquered, overcome
makaris *n. pl.* poets
mak(e), maik *n.* mate; **makis** *pl.*; **makeles** *adj.* peerless, without a mate
mak(e), ma, macke, makyn *v.* make, create; make preparations for: *theyr takelyng to* ~ (?) make ready, (?) handle; **maid** *pa.*; **maid, ma(a)d** *p.p.*: ~ *in*

mak(e), ma, macke, makyn (*cont.*):
turned into; **makyng** *n.* performance
(9 U 118)

makeles; makyng *see* mak(e)

male *n.* wallet, bag, travelling-bag

malencolye, malancolye *n.* melancholy

malle *n.* club

malvesy, malvysy *n.* malvoisie (a strong
wine, orig. from Greece and Crete)

man *see* mon

manas(s)yng(e) *n.* menacing

mane *see* ma(y)ne, mone

man(e) *n.* man, vassal

maner *n.* manor

maner(e), maneir, maneer *n.* manner,
way; *in* ~ as it were; kind (of); manners,
behaviour, conduct, custom; *for the* ~
sake for the sake of appearances

manerly *adv.* in a well-mannered way

manesseth *pr. 3 sg.* menaces, threatens

mangerye *n.* feasting, gluttony

manhode *n.* valour, manliness

maquerel *n.* bawd, procurer

marchande, marcha(u)nt *n.* merchant;
marcha(u)ndise *n.* trade, merchandise

marchepanys *n. pl.* confections of marzi-
pan, sweets made of a paste of almonds,
sugar, etc.

marchose *n.* marquis [It *marchese*]

marcy(e) *n.* mercy

marcis; mare *see* merke; mor(e)

mare, mere *n.* mare; hag, monster; **marres** *gen. sg.*

marees *n.* marsh; **maresses** *pl.*

mary *n.* marrow

marke *v.* aim at, strike; indicate; give
heed to, take notice

market *n.* transaction, bargain

markyng *n.* (?) marking with a merchant's
mark

marle *n.* marl (a mixture of soil, clay, and
carbonate of lime)

marleyonis *n. pl.* merlins (a kind of
falcon)

marres *see* mare

marryde, marrit *p.p.* ruined, afflicted,
grieved, confused

marteloge *n.* martyrology

Martynesmasse *n.* feast of St Martin (11
November)

martyre *n.* torment, affliction

marvayled, marveyls *see* mervayle

masars *pl.* mazers, drinking-cups

masys; mast(e); master-veayne; mastry

see maces; mo(o)st; ma(y)ster;
maystry(e)

mate(e)r, matier *n.* matter, ground, subject, material, information, affair,
purpose

matynnis, mat(t)ens *n.* matins (an early-
morning liturgical office)

matutyne *adj.* morning

maudelayne *adj.* maudlin

maw *see* mow(e)n

ma(w)gré *n.* blame, displeasure, ill will

mawis *n.* song-thrush

mawis *n. pl.* mews, gulls

mazyd *p.p., adj.* confused

me *pron.* me; (as expletive or ethical
dative) *sawe I* ~ I saw, *then comes* ~ *one*
then one comes

meane *adj.* humble, low

meane; mech(e) *see* mene; moche

med(d)le, medele *v.* mix, mingle; concern
oneself, busy oneself, take part in; talk;
medlyst *pr. 2 sg.*; **medled** *pa.*;
med(e)led, myddillit, mydlyt *p.p.*

mede *n.* meadow

mede, meed(e), meid *n.* reward, hire

meene; meené *see* mene; meyné

mees *n.* dwelling, dwelling-place

mey; meid; meik *see* ma(y); mede; mek

meyné, mayné, meené, meynee, menye
n. company, train; a hunting note (to
signal that the deer was in full flight;
used also at the return of the hunts-
men)

meirswyne *n.* dolphin, porpoise

meit, meyter, meytes *see* met(e)

mek, meik *adj.* meek, gentle

mekil(l), me(i)kle, mykle, mykyll *adj.,
adv.* great, large, big, much

melancolius *adj.* melancholy

meldrop *n.* drop of mucus from the nose

melys *n. pl.* meals

mell *v.* associate; join battle; mix; **mellit**
pa. sg., p.p.

mellé *n.* combat, skirmish

memorye, memour *n.* memory,
memorial

menable *adj.* amenable, pleasant

mend *v.* recover; mend, improve, add
(fuel) to

mende *see* mynd(e)

mene, meane, meene *n.* means, way;
middle way, medial state; mediation,
mediator; **myance** *pl.*

mene *v.* mean, impute, intend for, design

for; **menyth(e)** *pr. 3 sg./pl.*; **ment** *pa., p.p.*

mene, meane *adj.* intermediate, intervening; (of time) mean; humble

meneth *see* **menys**

menge, ming *v.* mingle, mix; **mingit** *p.p.*

menye *v.* commemorate, mention

menye; menys *see* **meyné; mene**

menys *pr. 1 sg.* take pity on; **meneth (the)** *pr. 3 sg., impers.* complain

menowe *n.* minnow

ment; mere *see* **mene; mare**

meritorie *adj.* merited

merke *n. (coll. sg.)* marks (coins worth 13*s.* 4*d.*); **marcis** *pl.*

merle *n.* blackbird

merse *n.* ship's topcastle

merthe *n.* joy; **myrthis** *gen. sg.*

mervayle, mervayll, merve(y)l(e) *n.* wonder, marvel, miracle; **marveyls** *pl.*

mervayle, merv(e)yl(e), merwell *v.* (occas. refl.) wonder; **marvayled** *pa. pl.*

mervaylous, merveillous, mervelous(e) *adj.* marvellous, wondrous; **mervaylously** *adv.* wondrously

mescheef; meseur, messur *see* **myscheeff; mesure**

mess *n.* mass

messe *n.* portion

mes(s)uage *n.* message

mesurable *adj.* moderate; **mesurab(e)ly** *adv.* moderately

mesure, meseur, messur *n.* moderation, measure, *by/out of ~*; melody

mesure *v.* moderate, exercise moderation

met(e), meit, mette *n.* food, dish, piece of food; **meytes** pl.

met(e), meit *adj.* meet, fit, fitting, suitable; **meyter** *comp.*; **metely** *adv.* meetly, properly

metyng *n.* feeding, pasturing (9 U 17)

meve, mufe *v.* move, stir, provoke; broach (a subject), start (a deer); **moveth, movis** *pr. 3 sg.*; **moevid** *pa.*; **moeved, ymeved** *p.p.*; **mevyng(e)** *n.* moving, stirring

mewe *n.* pen, cage (for hawks); (fig.) *in ~ myance*; **mych(e)** *see* **mene; moche**

Mychelmas, Mygelmas, Mi(g)hel(l)-mas/-messe *n.* Michaelmas (feast of St Michael, 29 September)

micht *see* **myght, mow(e)n**

mid *adv. (in) ~ (of(f))* in the midst of

myddes, middis *n., prep.* middle part, midst; in the midst of

myddillit, mydlyt *see* **med(d)le**

mydell, mydul *n.* waist, middle; **mydlis** *pl.*

mydyll *adj.* middle-sized; (of wool) secondgrade

mydsyde *n.* middle of the side

mydway *n.* middle of the way

Mygelmas, Mighelmas, Mighelmesse *see* **Mychelmas**

myght, micht *n.* strength, might, power; **mytis** *pl.*

myght(en), migt, mygth, myht; Myhellmas, Myhelmesse; mykle, mykyll *see* **mow(e)n; Mychelmas; mekil(l)**

myle *n.* millet

mylle-pittes *n. pl.* mill-ponds

mynd(e), mende *n.* mind, thought, desire, memory, recollection; *~ of* thought for

ming, mingit *see* **meng**

mynysshe, mynusshe *v.* lessen, reduce, diminish

minster *v.* minister, give

myntyng *pr.p.* purposing, intending

myrknes *n.* darkness

myrre *n.* myrrh; *~-tree* myrrh-tree

mirthis; mys *see* **merthe; amis**

mischance *n.* bad fortune, disaster, ill luck

myscheef, myschief, mescheef *n.* misfortune, trouble, disaster, ruin, wickedness; **myschevys** *pl.*

myschevous *adj.* harmful

myserycorde *n.* mercy; a prayer for mercy said at mass

mysese *n.* distress

mysmaid(e) *p.p.* put out, disturbed, disfigured

misse *n.* loss, lack

mysse *v.* fail to achieve, miss

mysselyvynge *n.* sinful living

mysse-masche *n.* mish-mash

mysserved *p.p.* poorly served

mystery *n.* ministry, office, craft

myswent *p.p.* gone astray

myt(h); mytis *see* **mow(e)n; myght**

myttane *n.* a bird of prey

mo *adj., pron.* more (in number), more, others

moche, meche, mych(e) *adj., adv.* great, much, many; greatly, much, a long way

mocht *see* mow(e)n

mochulnes *n.* size, greatness

mode, mude *n.* mind, feeling, heart

moder, mooder, modir, moter *n.* mother; womb (9 M 23)

modifie *v.* assess, determine

moeved, moevid; moy; moyn; moyr *see* meve; mow(e)n; mone; mor(e)

mois *n.* bog, moorland

mold *n.* earth, ground

mon, man *v.* must (occas. with omitted v. of motion)

mone, moon(e), mane *n.* complaint, lament, grief

mone, moyn *n.* moan

moneth(e), monythe *n.* month; ~-day *n.* the corresponding day of the next month

monycyon *n.* admonition, warning, intimation

monische *v.* admonish; monyshynge *n.* admonishing

monythe *see* moneth(e)

monytorye *adj.* warning

mooder; moon(e) *see* moder; mone

moonyd *p.p., adj.* lamented

mo(o)st, ma(i)st(e) *adj. sup., adv.* greatest; most, mostly; (followed by another sup.) ~ *mysest/rychest,* etc.

moot *see* mote

moot, mot(e), mut *v.* must; may; most(e) *pa.*

more *n.* moor; muris *pl.*

mor(e), moir, ma(i)r(e) *adj. comp., adv.* greater, more, further; more, rather

morey *n.* murrey, mulberry-coloured cloth

mornyng(e) *see* murnyng

morun *n.* morn, morning

morwe *n.* morning

mosselle *n.* morsel; mossellys, mosseylys *pl.*

most; mot(e) *see* moot, mo(o)st; moot

mote, moot *n.* note (of hunting-horn)

moter *see* moder

mot(o)un *n.* mutton

moun; moveth, movis, movynge; mow(e) *see* mow(e)n; meve; mow(e)n

mountnance *n.* amount, space

mow *n.* grimace; jest; trick; mowis *pl.*

mow(e)n, mow(e) *v.* can, be able (to), may; may, maw, moy, mow, moun *pr.*; micht, my(g)ht(en), migt(h), myt(h), mocht, mowt *pa.*

mowlit *p.p., adj.* mouldy

mowrne, murn *v.* mourn, grieve, lament; murnand, murnynge *pr.p.*; moornyd, murnit *p.p.*

mude; mufe *see* mode; meve

muller *n.* muller (a stone used for grinding painters' colours)

mum *n.* sound, word

muris; murn(and), murnynge *see* more; mowrne

murnyng, mornyng(e) *n.* mourning, lament, lamentation

musicalle *adj.* pertaining to the Muses (15 E 80)

musyn *n.*: ~ *worke* mosaic

muskeadell *n.* muscatel (wine)

mustre *n.* display

mut *see* moot

na *see* no

na *conj.* than

nad(e) *pa.* did not have

naght *see* nought

nay(e) *adv.* not; *this is no* ~ there is no denying this; *without a* ~ without denial, for certain

nayne *see* non(e)

nale *n. at* ~ at the ale, as we drink

nam(e)ly(e), namelich *adv.* especially

namore; nane *see* nomor; non(e)

nappyll *n.* apple

nar *see* ner(e)

nard *pr. 2 sg.* are not

narrest *adj. sup.* shortest

natheles *adv.* nevertheless

nathing *see* nothyng(e)

nature *n.* nature, natural physical powers, vital functions; *of* ~ in the course of nature; *sustenance of* ~ natural sustenance

ne, nee *adv.* nor, not; ~ *hadde the appil take ben* if the apple had not been taken

ned(e), neid *n.* need, necessity, want, poverty; *hade* ~ would have to

nede *v.* need, be in need, be necessary; (occas. impers.) me neidis *pr. 3 sg.* I need; nedet *p.p.* obliged

nedes, nedys *adv.* necessarily, of necessity

nedyngys *n. pl.* bodily needs

neybowrys *n. pl.* neighbours

neid; neidis *see* ned(e); nede

neiff *n.* fist

neir; neir-hand; neist *see* ner(e); nerhand; nexst

neke-kycher *n.* neckerchief
nell *pr. 3 sg.* does not wish
nende *n.* end
nephue *see* neve(u)
nere *adv.* never, not
ner(e), nerre, neir, nar, nerrar *adv. comp.* near, nearer, nearer the wind (1 N 29), almost; *well(l)* ~ almost; ~ *of* close to
ner(e) *conj.* nor
ner(e) *pa. subj.* were not, would be nothing but
ner-hand, neir-hand *prep.* near
nesche, nesshe *adj.* soft
neses *see* nois
nessaryes *n. pl.* necessaries
nete *n.* ox, cow
netes *n. pl.* nits
nether *see* nother
nether *adj.* lower, bottom; netherest *sup.* lowest
neutrifaction *n.* nourishment
neve(u), nevew(e), nevieu, nephue, nevo *n.* nephew; grandson
new(e) *adj., adv.* new, *of (the)* ~ newly, anew, afresh; newly
nexst, nixt, neist *adj. sup., adv., conj.* nearest, most nigh; next; nearest to
ny, nye *adv.* near(ly), nigh, almost; closely, close to (the skin)
nybbillit *pa. 3 pl.* nipped
nyce, nyse *adj.* foolish, stupid, extravagant, flaunting, wanton
nygramansy, nygromancy *n.* necromancy
nyhe *adj.* near
nyped *pa., p.p.* nipped
nys *pr. 3 sg.* is not
nyse; nixt *see* nyce; nexst
no, noo, na *adj., adv.* no, not
nobleye *n.* nobility
nobles, noblys *n. pl.* gold coins (each worth 6*s.* 8*d.*)
nobut *adv.* only, merely
nocht, noght(e); noydyr *see* nought; nother
noye *v.* harm
noyng *n.* distressing, disturbing
noy(o)us *adj.* troublesome, grievous, injurious
nois *n.* nose; neses *pl.*
nokkis *n. pl.* tips of a yard-arm
nolt *n.* cattle
nomor, namore *adj.* no more

non(e), noon, nooun, na(y)ne *adj., adv., pron.* no, none; not, *or* ~ or not; no one
none *n.* noon, midday
noo *see* no
nor *conj.* than
not *n.* nothing
notary *adj.* notorious
note *n.* music, note
not(e) *pr. 1, 3 sg.* do/does not know
nother, nouther, noydyr, nothir, nether *pron., adv., conj.* neither, nor; *no* ~ none other
nothyng(e), nathing *adv.* not at all
nought, nowght, nocht, nowt, noght(e), naght *n., adj., adv.* nothing, wickedness; of no value, useless, arid, wicked, immoral; not, not at all
noumbreth *pr. 3 sg.* enumerates
nouryce, nureis *n.* nurse
nouther *see* nother
nowght, nowt *see* nought
nowhedyr, nowhither *adv.* to no place, (to) nowhere
nowmbles *n. pl.* numbles (inner parts of a deer used for food)
nuk *n.* corner, nook
nureis *see* nouryce

o *see* o(o)n
ob. *abbrev.* obolus, halfpenny; halfpenny's worth
obeyed *pa. pl.* bowed, saluted respectfully
obeysans, obeysaunce *n.* respectful greeting, deference; authority, command
obit *n.* obsequies, funeral rites
objeccion *n.* assault, attack
objectyng *pr.p.* imputing, reproaching
oblegyd *pa. 3 sg. refl.* bound (himself)
obsequyouse *adj.* obedient
occident *adj.* situated in the West
occupy(e) *v.* busy oneself with, employ, use; occupyede *p.p.*
ochane *interj., n.* alas
oder, odir *see* other
odyble, odybull *adj.* hateful
of, off(e) *prep., adv.* of, from, out of, by, for, over, because of, in respect of, as to; ~ *herselfe* as far as she is concerned; ~ newe *see* new(e); off
offensioune *n.* offensiveness
of-mange *adv. phr.* meanwhile, the while
oftesythe *adv.* often
oftsyis *adv.* often

GLOSSARY

oyle *n.*: ~ *benedictum* oil benedict (a kind of medicinal oil); ~ *olyfe* olive oil
oynement(e), oyntement *n.* ointment; oil (of Extreme Unction)
olders *n. pl.* ancestors
omage *n.* homage
on *see* o(o)n
on, one, an *prep.* on, in, in the case of, against
onavysed *see* unavised
onbrace *v.* (?) remove clothes, (?) carve up (16. 715)
onclene *adj.* unclean, foul
oncurtes(s); ondon; one *see* uncurteis; undo(o); on, o(o)n
onely, oonly, *adv.* only, alone; *but all* ~ except only; *lent not* ~ (?) gave nothing but only (15 A 63)
ones, on(y)s, anis *adv.* once
onethes *adv.* scarcely
oneto *see* unto
ony, oony *adj.* any
onything(e) *see* anything
onywhyder *adv.* anywhere
only; onkynde *see* on(e)ly; unkynde
onmerciable *adj.* merciless
onn; onon *see* o(o)n; anon(e)
on-party *adv.* apart
onpurveyed *p.p.* not provided with
onrecuperable *adj.* unrecoverable, beyond recovery
onredyly *adv.* with difficulty
ons *see* ones
onschett *imper. sg.* unlock
onthryfty; ontill; onto *see* unthrifty; untyll(e); unto
ontretable *adj.* intractable
oo *see* o(o)n
oolde, a(u)ld(e) *adj.* old
o(o)n, o(o), o(o)ne, onn, w(h)on(e) *num., adj., pron. indef.* one, a single; ~ *and* ~ one after the other; (intensifying sup.) ~ *the most* the most; same: *al* ~ same, *that is al* ~ *who I be* it is all the same whoever I be
oony; oonly; oost; ooth; oowte *see* only; on(e)ly; oste; othe; out(e)
ope *imper. sg.* open
opene, opyn, oppin *adj.* open; plain, evident; frank, full; (?) kept open (of surgical needle); *in* ~ openly; **openly** *adv.* publicly
opinioun *n.* reputation
oppositio(u)n *n.* (astron.) opposition (the relation of two planets when they are opposite each other as seen from Earth); *in* ~ *of* in (planetary) opposition (to)
oppres(se) *v.* oppress, burden, afflict; overwhelm, conquer
or *conj.* before; ~ *that/then* before
oratur(e) *n.* oratory, room for private study and devotion
ordayne, ordeyn(e) *v.* ordain, order, establish, prepare, arrange, make; **ordand** *pa. 3 sg.*
ordenance, ordyna(u)nce, ordonnaunce *n.* ordinance, command; appointed place; system of government; supply of military equipment
ordour, ordre *n.* ecclesiastical orders; order, practice, *by* ~ in an orderly way
ordred *p.p.* placed, set in order
orfeverye *n.* goldsmith's work
orgeynes, orgones *n. pl.* organs
oryble *adj.* horrible
originall *adj.* (?) fundamental (4 B 30)
orisoun *n.* prayer; **urisonnis** *pl.*
orlage *n.* clock
osell *n.* blackbird
osyer *n.* willow
oste *n.*[1] host, the bread consecrated at the Eucharist
oste, hoost *n.*[2] host, army
oste, oost *n.*[3] host, landlord
othe, ooth *n.* oath
other, othir, oder, outher, owther *adv., conj.* either, or; ~ ... ~ either ... or; ~ *ellys* or else; *noon* ~ not otherwise
other, oth(e)re, othir(e), oder/-ir, uther/-ir *adj., pron.* other, next, another, different; *pl.* others, other persons/things
otherwhile(s) *adv.* at other times
otys *n. pl.* oats
ouerdraif *pa. 3 sg.* covered over
ouer-fer *adv.* too far
ouerheled *pa. 3 pl.* covered over; **ourheild** *p.p.*
ouertane *p.p.* overtaken
ought, out, ow(gh)t(e) *n., adv.* anything: *of* ~ from anything, at all; at all, in any way
ought(e); ouir *see* out(e); over(e)
ouircome *pa. 1, 3 sg.* came to, recovered
ou(i)rfret *p.p.* covered as with embroidery or ornaments

ou(i)rset *pa. 3 sg.* overthrew, upset, destroyed

ouirspred *pa. 3 sg., p.p.* covered

oun; our *see* owyn(e); over(e)

our-alquhar *adv.* everywhere

ourcast *p.p.* overcast

ourcumin *p.p.* overcome

oure, ow(e)r(e), owyr *n.* hour; howris, hourys, oures *pl.* hours, canonical hours

oure; ourfret *see* over(e); ou(i)rfret

ourgayne *p.p.* overwhelmed

ourgilt *pa. 3 sg.* gilded over

ourheild *see* overheled

ourquhelmys *pr. 3 sg.* overwhelms; ourquhelmyt *p.p.*

ourscailit *p.p.* scattered, sprinkled

ourset *see* ou(i)rset

ourspynnerand *pr. p.* skimming over

ourweltrand *pr.p.* tossing over

out *see* ought

out, owt *prep.* without, out of

out(e), ought(e), owght, o(o)wt(e) *adv.* out, abroad, away from home; *gave ~* gave away; *~ of* out of, without, deprived of; *all ~* completely

outher *see* other

outrage *n.* (violent) injury, violent deed

outrageous, outragyous *adj.* violent

outraye *v.* vanquish, expel

outserche *v.* search out

outthrow *prep.* throughout, right through

outwaill *n.* outcast

outward *adj.* outside, external, foreign

overal(l) *adv.* everywhere

overblysse *v.* say a blessing over

overdylew *v.* dig over

over(e), ou(i)r, oure *prep., adv.* over, beyond, in addition to, *~ thus* besides; in addition, further, too

overest *adj. sup.* uppermost, highest

overface *v.* overcome

overlede *v.* tyrannize over

overloketh *pr. 3 sg.* looks down on

overrenne *v.* overrun, conquer; outrun, escape; overron/-run *p.p.*

overschett *p.p.* covered with dung

oversprad *p.p.* spread over, covered

overt *adj.* open

overthrue *pa. 3 sg.* fell down

overthwart, overthwert *prep., adv.* across; crosswise

ovyrgylt *p.p., adj.* gilded over

ovyrmoche *adv.* excessively, too

owche *n.* brooch, buckle

ower *see* oure

oweth, owith *pr. 3 sg.* ought: (impers.) *hym/hir ~* he/she ought; owen *pr. pl.*

owght; owgly *see* out(e), ought; ugly

owyn(e), oun, aw(i)n(e) *adj.* own

owyr *see* oure

owyr, owyrs *pron. gen.* our(s)

owith *see* oweth

ownded *p.p., adj.* waved, wavy

ownestabell *adj.* unstable

owr(e) *see* oure

owsprang *pa. 3 sg.* sprang forth

owt; owt(e); owther *see* out, out(e); ought; other

oyet, oy(y)yt *interj.* hear ye

paas; pace *see* pas; pese, pas(e)

pacokke *n.* peacock

paddoke *n.* frog

pageant *n.* pageant, scene, play; pagentys *pl.*

pagelles *n. pl.* (?) paigles, cowslips

paye *n.* pleasure; *to thy ~* to please you

paill *adj.* pale

pa(y)ne, peyn(e) *n.* pain, suffering, torment, distress, trouble; *by ~* with difficulty; penalty, punishment: *~ of* on pain of; effort

payne *v. refl.* take pains, exert oneself, make an effort; suffer, suffer pain (for)

paynted *see* peinte

paithit *p.p.* paved

palays, paleys *n.* palace

palen *pr. 3 pl.* make pale

palfreyman *n.* horse-keeper

pal(l) *n.* pall (a rich cloth)

pallatt *n.* pate, head

pament *n.* pavement, paved street

pane *see* pa(y)ne

pane *n.* (?) part, (?) side (of wall) (18 C 427)

pange *v.* pierce with pain

panys *n. pl.* garments

pap *n.* breast; pappis *pl.*

parabole, parabul *n.* parable, allegory

paramour(e) *n.* passion, love; loved one

paraventur(e); parceyvyd *see* peraventure; perseyve

pardé, perdé *interj.* indeed, certainly, to be sure

pardurably *adv.* everlastingly

parell(e) *n.* peril, danger

parent *n.* guardian, protector, kinsman

GLOSSARY

parfyght, parfit(e), perfi(gh)t(e) *adj., adv.* perfect, perfectly accomplished; perfectly

parfytely, parfitli, perfyghtli *adv.* perfectly, fully, completely

parfitours *n. pl.* finishers (the last hounds to be uncoupled during the chase)

parsonages; parsone *see* **personage; persone**

part (?) *imper. sg.* give a share (18 C 494); **partid/-it** *p.p.* separated, divided

parte *n.* concern, interest

party, partie *n.* part; party, side; respect; region; individual; match

partycypable *adj.* able to participate

participant *adj.* partaking

partycypatt *p.p., adj.* made to share

partid; partie *see* **part; party**

partynere *n.* sharer, partner; **partiners** *pl.*

partryche *n.* partridge

pas, paas *n.* pace, step, manner of walking: *a good* ~ quickly; **pases** *pl.*

pas(e), passe *v.* pass, pass through, spend time (during); go, reach; get across; surpass, excell; (? as a gambling term) (?) leave the game, (?) play a game of 'passage' (24 B 51); ~ *over whanne* pass over until; **passyn** *pr. 3 pl.*; **passiden** *pa. 3 pl.*; **passit** *pa., p.p.*

passyble *adj.* ready to suffer

passyng(e) *pr.p., adj., adv.* surpassing, exceeding, great; exceedingly, very; **passingly** *adv.* surpassingly

pasturyng *n.* feeding, grazing

patrocynye *n.* protection

patron(e) *n.* patron, defender; founder; captain; pattern, model

patus *n. pl.* pates, heads

paunflettis *n. pl.* pamphlets

pavases, pavesses *n. pl.* large shields, shelters for fighting

pax *n.* [L] peace, (in 12 C 63 with punning ref. to the pax, a tablet with a representation of the crucifixion which was kissed by the celebrating priest and the congregation at Mass); **paxbrede** *n.* pax, osculatory

pe(a)son *n. pl.* peas

pece *n.* piece; piece of artillery/armour: *armoure for all* ~*s* a complete set of armour; **pe(e)ces/-is** *pl.*

pees; peyn(e); peyneth *see* **pese; pa(y)ne; payne**

peinte *v.* paint, depict, adorn; feign; **paynted, peynted/-id** *p.p., adj.*

peireth *pr. 3 sg.* harms

peirrie *n.* perry

peirsing *n.* piercing, wounding

peis; peke *see* **pese; pyke**

pennis *n. pl.* feathers

pens *n. pl.*: ~ *of to* ~ coins worth twopence

pensyf(e) *adj.* brooding, melancholy, pensive

Pensyffhede *n.* Pensiveness, Melancholy

peraventure, paraventure, perawenture *adv.* perhaps, by chance

percelly *n.* parsley

perche *n.*[1] pole, stake

perche *n.*[2] perch (a freshwater fish)

perdé *see* **pardé**

perdiction *n.* loss

perdon *v.* pardon

perdo(u)n *n.* pardon

pere *n.*[1] pear; (something of little value): *nat a* ~

pere *n.*[2] peer, equal

perfay *interj.* by my faith, truly

perfight(e), perfite; perfyghtly *see* **parfyt; parfytely**

performe *v.* bring about, manage

perfound(e) *adj.* deep

perfurnyst *p.p.* completed, ended

pery *n.* squall

perke *n.* perch

perse *v.* pierce; **pearsed** *pa. 3 sg.*; **pirssid** *p.p.* (?) pierced (on the cross) (16. 825)

perseyve, persave *v.* perceive, see, become aware of; **parceyvyd** *pa.*; **persave** *p.p.*

persew *v.* follow, hunt, attack; proceed, go, come to

person *n.* parson

personage *n.* personage; *make her* ~ (?) present herself, (?) play her part; **parsonages** *pl.*

persone, parsone *n.* person, self; *what mans* ~ who this individual (was)

pertinente *adj.* belonging

pervercyonatt *adj.* perverted

perversyose *adj.* perverse

pescodes *n. pl.* pea-pods

pese, pe(e)s, pace, pe(i)s(se) *n.* peace

peson *see* **pe(a)son**

pesse *imper.* be silent

peté, pety; peteouse, petuously *see* **pité; pitous**

philesofris *n. pl.* philosophers; **phelisopheris** *gen. pl.*

philomene *n.* nightingale

phisike, phesik, fesik *n.* physic, natural science, medical science

picche *v.* pitch; fix, set up; thrust in; **pycche** *imper. sg.*; **pyght** *p.p.*

pietie; pyght *see* pité; picche

pyikstaff *n.* pikestaff, stick

pyk *n.* pitch

pyke, peke *n.* pike (a freshwater fish)

pyke *v.* pick

pykes *n. pl.* picks

pikois *n.* pickaxe

pyle *n.* (her.) pile (two lines meeting in the shape of an arrow-head); **pylles** *pl.*

pylle *v.* plunder, pillage; **pilyng** *pr.p.*

pyllours *n. pl.* plunderers

pylwys *n. pl.* pillows

pyment *n.* spiced wine

pyne *n.*[1] pin; *upon a mery* ~ in a merry humour

pyne *n.*[2] suffering, torment

pyot *n.* magpie

pipes *n. pl.* piping sounds

pipis *pr. 3 sg.* whistles

pirssid; piscence *see* perse; puissa(u)nce

pysmeers *gen. pl.* ants'

pistell, pistil(l) *n.* epistle; **pystles** *pl.*

pité, peté/-y, pietie, pitee *n.* pity, compassion, mercy; sorrowful event

pitous, peteouse, pytuose *adj.* piteous, full of pity, merciful; **pitously(e), petuously** *adv.* piteously, grievously

placke *n.*: *laugh a* ~ *or tweyne at nale* (?) let us laugh a bit over a drink (? plack, a coin of proverbially small value), (?) let us laugh while we drink a draught or two (i.e. plucke, a draught) (24 B 43)

play(e) *see* pley, pley(e)

playes *n.* place

playn, pleyne *v.* complain, lament; **plenis** *pr. 3 pl.*

playnt *n.* complaint, accusation

playsaunt; playse *see* plesa(u)nt; pleys

playsyr(e), plesere/-yer *n.* pleasure, happiness, delight

playster *n.* plaster

plane *adj.* clear; honest, without deceit; flat, level, smooth

plasshe *v.* splash

plat *adv.* directly, exactly, due

plate *n.* plate-armour; **plates** *pl.* pieces of armour, armour

plater(ry)s *n. pl.* platters, plates

platly *adv.* plainly, bluntly

plee *n.* lawsuit

pley, play(e) *n.* play, game, pleasure, proceeding

pley(e), playe *v.* play, rejoice, make sport; (refl.) enjoy oneself, disport oneself

pleyferys *n. pl.* playfellows, companions

pleying-feere *n.* companion

pleyne *see* playn

pleyn(e)ly *adv.* plainly, openly

pleys, playse *v.* please; **plesoun/-en** *pr. 3 pl.*; **ples** *pr. 3 sg. subj.* may it please; **plessyde, plesetheyde** *pa. sg.*; **pleisit** *pa. 3 sg. impers.*: *hir* ~ it seemed good to/pleased her

plenis *see* playn

plentevous *adj.* plenteous; **plentyvowsly** *adv.* abundantly

ples *see* pleys

plesand(ly) *see* plesa(u)nt

plesa(u)nce, plesawns *n.* pleasure, delight, joy

plesa(u)nt, playsaunt, plesand *adj.* pleasing, pleasant; **plesandly** *adv.* pleasantly

plesawns; plesere, plesyer; plesen, plesetheyde, plesoun, plessyde *see* plesa(u)nce; playsir(e); pleys

plicht *pa. sg.* plighted

plye *n.* plight, condition

plyte *n.* situation

plonkett *adj.* greyish blue

plucke *up imper. sg.* rouse, tune up; **plucked** *pa. 3 sg.* pulled

plumys *n. pl.* feathers

plunge *n.* pool

Poil(l) *see* Pole

poynt(e) *n.* purpose; *in* ~ *to, upon the* ~ *to* on the point of; spot, moment; detail, token; situation, condition; *at full gude* ~ in excellent condition, splendidly; tagged lace

poynted *p.p.* pointed, adorned

poynt(e)ment(e) *n.* appointment, arrangement

poke *n.* sack (a measure of wool, smaller than a sarpler; *see* **sarpellys**)

pokes *n. pl.* pox

Pole, Poil(l) *n.* pole, pole-star; ~ *Artick* the North Pole

pole *n.* pool

polecie *n.* constitution

poleist, pollist *p.p.* polished

polite *adj.* polished, elegant
polytyke *adj.* sagacious, prudent
pollist *see* **poleist**
pomell *n.* pommel; boss, knob
pore *see* **pouere**
porpos *v.* intend, purpose
port *n.* port, gate, harbour; ~ *salut* haven of safety, safe harbour
porturyt *p.p.* portrayed
postrum *n.* postern gate
postum *n.* abscess
potage *n.* broth, soup
potel, pottell *n.* pottle, half a gallon (a liquid measure)
potestatis *n. pl.* rulers, lords
pothecairis *n. pl.* apothecaries
pottell *see* **potel**
pottingry *n.* apothecary's art
pouer, powe(i)r *n.* power; *at all* ~ with all one's might; troop of soldiers
pouere, powr, po(ve)re, pu(y)r(e) *adj.* poor; **powerer** *comp.*
pousté *n.* power, authority
powder dwke; powe(i)r; powerer, powr; **practicianis, practikis** *see* **duke; pouer; pouere; pratik**
prayes *n. pl.* spoils, booty
praysed *p.p.* valued (17 A 62); **praysyng** *n.* value, praise
praty *adj.* pretty, fine, clever; **pratyly, prytely** *adv.* prettily
pratik, prettick *n.* practice; **practikis** *pl.* practices (of medicine); **practicianis** *n. pl.* practitioners
pratyng *n.* chattering, boasting
praunce, prawnce *v.* prance, caper
prease *see* **prees**
prebendaries *n. pl.* cathedral canons
precelling *pr.p.* surpassing
predycacyon *n.* preaching
predylecte *adj.* dearly beloved
prees, pre(a)se *n.* crowd, throng
preest(e), pryste, pre(y)st *n.* priest; **pre(e)sthode** *n.* priestly office, holy orders
prefixed *p.p.* fixed beforehand
preif *see* **profe, preve**
preis *imper. refl.* press, urge (one's cause); **preisis** *pr. 3 pl.* press on, urge (a case)
preyst; preived *see* **preest(e); preve**
prekis *pr. 3 sg.* spurs
premyabyll *adj.* deserving of reward
premynence *n.* pre-eminence
prene *n.* pin, brooch

prentis *n.* apprentice
prepotent *adj.* of great power
prese *see* **prees**
presently *adv.* without delay
presessyon *n.* procession
prest(e) *adj.* ready
preste, presthode *see* **preest(e)**
pretendis *pr. 2 sg.* portend, presage
prettick; prevatee *see* **pratik; privyté**
preve, preif, prove, prowe *v.* prove, test, make trial, learn, experience; **pre(i)vid, prowyd** *p.p., adj.*
prevely, prevelie, prevy, previe *see* **pryvé**
preving *n.* testing, trying out
prevysyoun *n.* advice before a journey, advance warning
prevy; prevyté; pryce *see* **pryvé; privyté; prys(e)**
pryke *v.* fasten
pryme *n.* prime (the canonical service for the first hour of the day); the beginning of the day: *hyghe* ~ (about 9 a.m.); a beginning
prymetemps *n.* springtime
Primum Mobile *n.* the First Mover (the outermost sphere in the heavens which revolved around the Earth in 24 hours carrying the other planetary spheres within it)
prynces *n.* princess
prys *adj.* excellent
prys(e), pryce *n.* worth, excellence, renown; prize, pre-eminence; *bereth the* ~ is pre-eminent
pryste; prytely *see* **preest(e); praty**
pryvé, prevy *adj.* secret, hidden, private; ~ *to* sharing a secret; **pryvely/-lie, prevelie, privyli** *adv.* secretly, privately, in private, stealthily
privyté, prevatee, prevyté *n.* private nature: *of* ~ secret; secret thought/ question, secret; private parts; **privitees** *pl.*
probacion *n.* test, proof
problemes *n. pl.* riddles, enigmas
proce(e)de *v.* proceed; go to law
procees, proces(se), prosses *n.* course, (course of an) argument; discourse, narrative, tale; passing of time; legal action
proched *pa. 3 pl.* pierced
procuratour *n.* procurator, steward
profe, preif *n.* test, trial; *put in* ~ test
profris *n. pl.* offers

proyne *v.* preen

promycyon *n.* promise

promytt *v.* promise; **promitted** *p.p.*; **promyttid** (?) given the promise of becoming, (?) *error for* promotid (7 I 24)

promyttis *n. pl.* promises

pronuba *n.* woman who presided over marriage ceremonies in ancient Rome

proper, proper-chaunt *see* **propre**

propertie, propyrté, propreté *n.* nature, quality, attribute, property; special function; **properties** *pl.*

propre, proper/-yr/-ur *adj.* own, one's own, proper, appropriate, individual: ~ *love* love of oneself; excellent, commendable; comely, pretty, handsome; **propyrly** *adv.* particularly; **proper-chaunt** *n.* proper chant (a set of hexachords beginning on C)

prospir *adj.* prosperous

prosses; prove *see* **procees; preve**

provente *n.* provender

provycyon *n.* providence

provyde *v.* provide: *me of to* ~ to provide myself with; **provyd** *p.p.*

provydence *n.* foresight, timely care

provyng *see* **preve**

provocand *pr.p.* calling forth, provoking

prow *n.* advantage, benefit

prowe, prowyd *see* **preve**

prowt *adj.* proud

publischid *p.p.* disseminated

puyr *see* **pouere**

puissa(u)nce, piscence *n.* power, strength

puyssaunt *adj.* powerful

pulment *n.* pottage

pungitive *adj.* stinging, biting

purchace *n.* (lawful) acquisition; takings; shifting for oneself; contrivance

purchace *v.* obtain, gain, win

pur(e) *see* **pouere**

pure *adv.* entirely

purfiled *p.p.* ornamented

purge *n.* purging

purpensed *pa. 1 sg.* resolved, planned

purp(o)ur, purpre *adj., n.* purple, crimson; purple cloth

purveye *v.* provide, prepare, destine

purvya(u)nce *n.* providence, providential guidance; provisions

putte *v.* put; make (a distinction); ~ *in (ruyne)* reduce to (ruins); ~ *on* urge, incite; ~ *over* knock over, fell; **putis** *pr. 3 sg.*; **put, putted** *pa.*

quadrant *adj.* square

quayf *n.* coif, head-dress

quair *n.* (small) book

quarell *see* **querele**

quart *n.* health

quater treye dews [F] four, three, two (throws of the dice)

queemyd *p.p.* appeased, calmed; **quemit** *pa.* fitted closely

quench *v.* destroy

quent *adj.* skilfully made, handsome

quere *n.* choir

querele, quer(r)ell, quarell *n.* quarrel, cause, cause for complaint

querester *n.* chorister

querulose *adj.* quarrelsome

quest *n.* quest, the hounds' search for game

queth *n.* bequest, legacy

quha; quhair; quhais *see* who; wher(e); who

quhalis *n. pl.* whales

quham; quhar(e), quhair, quhareuer *see* who; wher(e)

quhasaeuer *pron.* whosoever

quhat, quhateuer *see* what

quheill *n.* wheel

quhen *adv., conj.* when

quhereas; quhether *see* wher(e); whether

quhetting *pr.p.* whetting

quhy *adv.* why

quhich; quhil; quhyle, quhyll *see* which(e); quhil(l); while

quhyle *adv.* while; ~ ... ~ sometimes ... sometimes

quhylis, quhyles *adv.* at times; ~ ... ~ sometimes ... sometimes

quhilk, quhilkis *see* which(e)

quhil(l), qwyll *conj.* until, as long as: ~ *that*; while

quhilom *see* whilom

quhynstane *n.* whinstone (hard, dark-coloured stone)

quhirlyt *pa. 3 sg.* whirled

quhisling *pr.p.* whistling; **quhislit** *pa. 3 sg.* whistled

quhit(e) *see* whit

quhitly, quhitlie *adj.* whitish, pale

quho, quhom(e), quhois *see* who

quhone *conj.* when: ~ *that*

quhou, quhow *see* how(e)

quy(c)k(e), qwyk *adj.* living, alive, lifelike, lively; **quyckely** *adv.* in a lifelike way, in a lively manner

quyken *v.* bring to life, enliven; **quykneden** *pa. pl.*

quintessance *n.* quintessence, the 'fifth essence' (the substance of the heavenly bodies, latent in all things)

quyt(e) *adj.* free

quyte *v.* requite, reward; make recompense; (refl.) acquit oneself; **quitte** *pa. 3 sg.*; **quyte** *p.p.*

quytter *n.* pus, suppurating matter

quod *pa. 3 sg.* said

quoniam *n.* pudendum

quook, qwook *pa. 1, 3 sg.* trembled, quaked

qweche *see* **which(e)**

qwesye *adj.* unsettled

qwhylum *see* **whilom**

qw(y)en *n.* queen

qwyk; qwyll *see* **quyck(e); quhil(l)**

qwyppe *v.* whip, hide quickly

qwischyn *n.* cushion

qwyst *interj.* hush

qwytt; qwook *see* **whytt; quook**

ra *see* **roo**

race, rais *n.* course, path, running; rush, tumult

rache *n.* hunting dog

rad *adj.* frightened

rad(de) *pa., p.p.* read

radius *adj.* radiant, bright

radlye *adv.* quickly

rage *n.* frenzy, passion, violent feeling, sexual desire; storm, tempest, blast, tumult

rage *adj.* raging

raggit *p.p., adj.* ragged

raid *pa. 3 sg.* rode

ray(e) *n.*[1] array, ranks, garments

raye *n.*[2] striped cloth

raif; raiffis *see* **rofe; rave**

raik, rayke *v.* go, journey

rayle *v.* jest; **ralyeis** *pr. 3 pl.*

railit *p.p.* provided with rails

rair *v.* roar; (of a raven) caw, croak

rayr *n.* roar

rays *n. pl.* (?) yard-arms

rays; rais; rais(e) *see* **roo; race; rys**

rayse *v.* raise, lift, *up* ~ elevate, increase; **rasit, reysid** *pa., p.p.*

raith *adv.* quickly

rakynge *n.* moving, going forward

raklie *adv.* hastily, impetuously

ralyeis *see* **rayle**

ralys *n. pl.* enclosures, snares

rammale *n.* brushwood

rampand, rampinge *pr.p.* rearing, raging

ranke *adj.* rank, heavy, fertile, gross; absolute; (?) *n.:* ~ *beryng* having a sharp smell

ransaking *n.* searching

ransonis, ransoun *see* **rawnsome**

rased *pa. 3 sg.* tore

rasyd *p.p.* pulled

rasyns, reysenes/-sons *n. pl.* raisins; ~ *of corante see* **corante**

rasit; rasoun *see* **rayse; reso(u)n**

rasshed *p.p.* pulled, jerked

rather *adv.* rather, sooner, earlier; *the* ~ the more quickly

rave *v.* talk wildly/loudly; **raiffis** *pr. 3 pl.*

raw; rawcht *see* **rowe; reche**

rawchtir *n.* rafter, roof-beam

rawe *adj.* damp and cold

rawk *adj.* hoarse, raucous

rawnsome, ransoun *n.* ransom; **ransonis** *pl.*

raxit *pa. refl.* stretched (himself), started up

reaume; reasons; rebaudrye *see* **reme; reso(u)n; ribawdry**

rebound(e) *v.* leap up, arise

rebuik *n.* check, reproach

recched *see* **reche**

rece(y)ve *v.* receive, take in; **resseyved** *pa.*; **res(c)e(i)ved, ressavit, receywyd** *p.p.*

receyvour, recettour *n.* receiver; (official) collector

rechace *n.* return

reche *v.*[1] care for; **recketh** (impers. with dat.) concern **recched** *pa.*

reche *v.*[2] reach, give; **recched, rawcht** *pa.*

rechelesnesse *n.* reckless/thoughtless behaviour

recomand(e) *v.* commend

recomfort *n.* comfort, consolation

recomfort *v.* comfort, encourage, console

reconsyle *v.* reconcile, restore

recontyr *v.* meet; **recountred** *pa. 3 sg.*

recopes *n. pl.* recoupling (a note on a hunting-horn)

recorde *v.* call to mind

recors, recourse *n.* course, *have* ~ apply for help

recountred *see* recontyr

recovered *pa.* succeeded in giving a blow

recreacion *n.* comfort, consolation

recreatory *n.* source of comfort

recumbentibus *n.* a knock-down blow

recure *n.* cure, remedy

recure *v.* recover

rede, reed *n.* counsel, advice

rede, reed, reid *adj.* red; golden

redily *adv.* eagerly, truly

redis *n. pl.* reeds

redoubted *p.p.* feared

redouce, reduce *v.* turn, translate, bring back

reed *see* rede

reflex *n.* reflection

refoundit *p.p.* established again

refra(y)n(e) *v.* restrain, curb; forbear, cease

reft *see* reve

refus *adj.* rejected, outcast

refut(e) *n.* refuge, place of safety, protector

regioun *n.* season (20 B 258)

regystred *p.p.* recorded

regne, ryng *v.* reign, prevail; regnyt *pa.*

regrait *n.* lamentation, distress

rehe(i)rs(e), reherce *v.* repeat, recount, list, state, record

rehersaile *n.* recounting, mention

reherse *n.* recital

reyallys *n. pl.* royals (gold coins each worth 10s.)

reid *see* rede

reid *v.* counsel, help, succour

reid (?) *adv.* quickly, furiously (20 B 265)

reik *n.* smoke

reysenes, reysons; reivis *see* rasyns; reve

rekand *pr.p.* stinking, reeking

rekill *n.* (?) clamour, (?) heap

rekyn *v.* reckon, count on; rekne *imper. sg.*; rekenyd *pa.*

relece *v.* grant remission of

reles *n.* release

releve *v.* relieve, bring relief; rally, return to the attack; relevit, releeved *pa.*

reme, reaume, rewme *n.* realm; remes *pl.*

remede, remeid *n.* remedy

remeid *v.* provide a remedy

remeve, remufe *v.* remove; depart, escape; move away, withdraw; removed *pa.*

remissioun *n.* forgiveness, pardon for sins

remocyon *n.* inclination

remord *v.* recall with sorrow

remos *n.* remorse

removed, remufe; ren *see* remeve; ren(ne)

rendred *pa., p.p.* poured out; given up

renew(e) *v.* renew; recommence; be renewed, renew itself

renye *n.* rein

ren(ne), ryn, ronne(n) *v.* run; ~ *on* attack, rush at; *I ~ ay on the losse* I am always losing; renn(e)yth *pr. 3 sg.*; rennynge, rynnand, rynnyng *pr.p.*; ronne *pa.*; ironne *p.p.*

renners *n. pl.* ~ *aboute* gadabouts, vagabonds

renom(m)ed, renoumed *p.p., adj.* renowned

rent *n.* income

repayre, repeire *n.* return; resorting, haunt, dwelling-place

repayre *v.* return, go; repeyreth *pr. 3 sg.*

repe *v.* reap, gain

report(e) *v.* report, relate, record, set down; (refl.) *I ~ me* I appeal/refer to

repreef, reprefe, reprowe *n.* ignominy, shame; censure, reproof, reproving

represent *n.* sight

reprevable, reprovable *adj.* reprehensible, blameworthy

reproif, reprove, reprufe *v.* reprove, censure, accuse, reject; repreveth *pr. 3 sg.*

reprowe *see* repreef

repudie *n.* divorce

repugnaunce *n.* contradiction, inconsistency

requeir, requere, requyre *v.* request, ask, require

rerd *n.* din, uproar

rere *imper. sg.* raise

resceived, resceyveth, reseved *see* rece(y)ve

rescow *v.* rescue; reskewis *pr. 3 sg.* (with om. preceding rel. pron., 10 B 21)

residensaries *n. pl.* resident canons of a cathedral

resolved *p.p.* melted

reso(u)n, ressoun, rasoun *n.* reason, rational order; explanation, speech, statement; *of ~* rightfully; reasons, ressonis *pl.*; ~les *adj.* without reason

respection *n. havyng* ~ looking

respyte *v.* grant respite to; *for our excus reportis to* ~ to mitigate these slanders to excuse ourselves

responsaill *n.* response, reply (by an oracle)

ressavit, resseyved; ressonis, ressoun *see* **rece(y)ve; reso(u)n**

reste *v.* arrest

restles *adj.* without stopping

restoratyvys *n. pl.* cordials, medicines

restore *n.* restoration

rethorie, rethorik *n.* rhetoric, eloquence

rethoris *n. pl.* rhetoricians

retorte *n.* throw back

retour *n.* return

retour *v.* return

retribucyon *n.* recompense

retrograde *adj.* (of planet) moving in a direction contrary to the order of the signs of the zodiac, from east to west

reulen, reuling *see* **rewle**

reull *n.* revelry

reull; reuth *see* **rewle; routh(e)**

reve *v.* take from, snatch; **reivis** *pr. 2 sg.*; **reft** *p.p.*

revell-route *n.* great revelry; (as interj.) (?) let revelry run wild

rever *n.* river; **rewares** *pl.*

reversed *p.p.* turned up

reverte *v.* return, turn back

revest *p.p.* apparelled

revin *p.p.* torn apart

revolved *pa. 3 sg.* turned over (in the mind); **revolvyng** *pr.p.*

reward *n.* reward (in hunting, the giving of some parts of the killed game to the hounds)

rewares *see* **rever**

rew(e) *v.* have pity, show mercy; repent

rewelynge *n.* revelling, revelry

rewyvyd *p.p.* revived

rewlar(e) *n.* ruler, man of authority

rewle, reull *n.* rule, governing, control, conduct

rewle, reull, rule *v.* rule, control, govern; (refl.) conduct oneself; **reulen** *pr. 3 pl.*; **rewlid** *p.p.*; **reuling** *n.* usage

rewme *see* **reme**

rewmyd *pa. 3 sg.* lamented

rewmour *see* **rumour**

Rhodyans *n. pl.* men of Rhodes

ryal(l) *adj.* royal; **ryalty** *n.* sovereignty, magnificence, pomp

rybaud(e) *n.* scurrilous jester, villain; **rybawdry, rebaudrye** *n.* ribaldry

ryce *see* **ryse**

riches(se) *n.* wealth, riches, rich material/gems, splendour

richt *see* **ryght**

richtuis *adj.* righteous

rydde *v.* remove, exile

ryght, riht *n.* right, justice, due reward; *have* ~ be justified, be right

ryght, ri(c)ht, ryth, ryught *adj., adv.* direct, straight, correct, proper, veritable, right; directly, straight, exactly, just: ~ *now*, precisely, altogether; (intensive) very, extremely, indeed, assuredly

ryghtynge *pr.p.* setting in order

ryghtuysnes, ryghtwysnes *n.* righteousness

rigure *n.* (act of) severity

riht *see* **ryght**

rykyles *n.* incense

ryn *see* **ren(ne)**

ryncke *n.* warrior, knight, man; **rinkis** *pl.*

rynde *n.* bark

ryng *n.*[1] (?) neck-ring (2 A 52)

ryng *n.*[2] realm

ryng, ryngis *see* **regne**

ryngis *n. pl.* ring-dances

rynk *n.* course, gallop

rinkis; rynnand, rynnyng *see* **ryncke; ren(ne)**

rypely, rypelie *adv.* wisely, with deliberation

rys *v.* rise; **rais(e), roos** *pa.*; **rissin** *p.p.*

ryse *n.*[1] rice

ryse *n.*[2] spray, branch, twig

ryshes *n. pl.* rushes

rispis *n. pl.* sedge

rissin; ryth, ryught *see* **rys; ryght**

ryvage *n.* coast, shore

ryvilde *p.p., adj.* shrivelled, wrinkled

roch(e) *n.* rock, cliff; **rochys** *pl.*

roche *n.* roach (a small freshwater fish)

rodde *n.* rod, staff

rode, rude *n.* cross

rofe, rooff, raif *pa.* clove, pierced, tore

roy(e) *n.* king

roif *n.* peace

rois *n.* rose

roising *adj.* rosy

rokis *n. pl.* clouds, fogs (20 B 282)

rolkis *n. pl.* rocks

rollen *v.* roll, revolve, turn over in the

mind, meditate on; **rollit** *pa. 3 sg.*

rom, roume *n.* room, place

Romayns, Romeyns *n. pl.* Romans

roming *pr. p.* walking, wandering

romnay, romney *n.* rumney (a sweet white wine)

ronde *see* **roun(e)**

ronys *n. pl.* brambles

ronne(n) *see* **ren(ne)**

roo, ra *n.* roe (deer); **rays** *pl.*

rooff; roos *see* **rofe; rys**

rosere *n.* rose-bush

rote *n.*[1] root; **rottes** *pl.*

rote *n.*[2] rot (a disease of sheep)

rote *v.* rot; **rotyn** *p.p.*

rottes *see* **rote**

rouch *n.* rough ground

rought; roume *see* **rout(e); rom**

roun(e), ronde *v.* whisper, speak; **rownis** *pr. pl.*

roustie *see* **rusty**

rout(e), rought, rowt(e) *n.* host, company, crowd

rout(e), rowt *v.* shout; roar, resound; **rowtis** *pr. 3 pl.*; **rowting** *n.* roaring; **rowtinge** *pr. p., adj.* riotous

routh(e), reuth *n.* pity: *in ~* piteously

rowe, raw *n.* row, company; *by ~* in order; *on ~* together, in a line

rowyd *adj.* streaked

rownis; rowt(e) *see* **roun(e); rout(e)**

rowt *n.* heavy blow

rowth *n.* rowing

rowting, rowtinge, rowtis *see* **rout(e)**

rud *n.* redness

rude *see* **rode**

rude *adj.* rough, severe, uncouth, unrefined, of low birth; **rud(e)ly/-lie** *adv.* roughly, violently; **rudenes** *n.* harshness; boorishness, discourtesy; **rudesse** *n.* harshness, severity

ruf *n.* roof; **~-treis** *n. pl.* roof-beams

rug *v.* tug, pull roughly; **ruggit** *pa. 3 pl.*

ruik *n.* rook; **ru(i)kis** *pl.*

rule *see* **rewle**

rumyst *pa. 3 sg.* roared

rummyll *v.* roar, rumble; **rumland** *pr.p.*

rumour, rewmour *n.* uproar, clamour, alarm

rune *n.* run, escape

rungeand *pr.p.* gnawing, champing

runyng hounds *n. pl.* hunting dogs

ruse *n.* bragging

ruse *v.* praise, extol

russette *n.* russet (a coarse woollen cloth)

rusty, roustie *adj.* rusty; unkempt, of neglected appearance

.s. *abbrev.* scilicet, that is to say

sa, swa *adv.* so; *~ it be* so long as it is

Sabot *n.* God

sacyatt *adj.* satisfied

sacring(e)-bell(e) *n.* small bell rung at the elevation of the host

sad(e) *adj.* steadfast, firm, constant; strong, valiant; *~ aslepe* sound asleep; serious, thoughtful, sorrowful; grievous, calamitous; **sadly** *adv.* seriously, soberly, sadly, firmly; **sadnesse** *n.* stability

saf; saffe *see* **sauff; saufe**

saffegarde *n.* safe conduct

saf(f)eron, saferyn, safforne, saipheron *n.* saffron

safyr, safere, sapher *n.* sapphire; **sapheres, saphyrs** *pl.*; (as adj.) sapphire-coloured; **saphiryn** *adj.*

sage *adj.* wise

saghe, say *see* **se**

saye *v.* try, essay

saif *v.* save

saif; saipheron; sayr, sair; sait *see* **saufe; saf(f)eron; sare, sor(e); set(t)e**

sakyrde *adj.* consecrated

saland *pr.p.* sailing

salat *n.* sallet (a light helmet)

salere *n.* salt-cellar

sal(e)wed, saluste *pa.* saluted, greeted; **salewyng** *pr.p.*

sall *see* **schal(le)**

sals *n.* sauce

saluste, salwed; salut; samond(e) *see* **sal(e)wed; port salut; sawmon**

salvatouris *gen. sg.* saviour's

sam(m)yn *adj.* same

sanct *n.* saint

Sanctus *n.* Sanctus (a hymn, beginning 'Holy, holy, holy', sung during mass)

sane *v.* cross oneself

sangwyn *adj.* blood-red

sapher, sapheres, saphiryn, saphyrs *see* **safyr**

Sarazyns, Sarsenes, Sarazenis *n. pl.* Saracens

sarcenet *n.* sarsenet (a fine soft silk material)

sardanus *n.* sardonyx (a precious stone)

sare, sayr *n.* pain, wound

sare; sary *see* **sor(e); sory**

sarpellys *n. pl.* sarplers (large bales of wool, containing two English 'sacks' or 728 lb.)

Sarsenes; sate *see* **Sarazyns; site**

saufe, saffe, saif, save *adj.* safe, saved; ~ *and holl* cured

sauff, saf, save *prep.* save, except

saule, saull *see* **sawle**

saute *n.* rush, leap

sauter *n.* psalter

sautry *n.* psaltery, dulcimer (a stringed instrument)

savacioun *n.* salvation

save; sawcers *see* **saufe, sauff; sawserys**

sawe *n.* saying, statement, doctrine

sawe *v.* sow; **sowe, sawin** *p.p.*

sawle, saule, saull, sowle *n.* soul

sawmon, samond(e) *n.* salmon

sawserys, sawcers *n. pl.* sauce-dishes

Saxonis *n. pl.* Saxons, Englishmen

scalyt *pa. 3 sg.* rose, mounted

scantiloun *n.* measure, size

scantlie *adv.* scarcely

scape *v.* escape, avoid; recover; *and ~ hit but he dye thereof* (?) if he escapes dying from it; **skapyd** *p.p.*: ~ *over* got safely across

scarlet *n.* scarlet cloth

scars *adj.* scant

scathe *n.* injury

scaturyd *p.p.* scattered

schaddow *n.* shadow, image, reflected image; **schaddois** *pl.*

schadowit *pa.* reflected (19 B 31)

schaf *imper. sg.* shave; **schoef** *pa. 3 sg.* shaved; **yshave** *p.p.* shaven

schaikand *pr.p.* shaking; **schuik, schake** *pa.* shook, shook down

schal *see* **shal(le)**

schald *adj.* shallow

schamfaste *adj.* modest

schane *see* **schynand(e)**

schap *n.* appearance, form

s(c)hape *v.* devise, bring about; shape; (refl.) set oneself, intend, prepare, endeavour, bring about; **schupe** *pa. 3 sg.*; **schapin** *p.p.*

schare *n.* ploughshare

scharpe *adj.* keen, violent, grim, cruel; **scharpliche, scherpli, sharply** *adv.* sharply, severely; attentively, closely

scharpiden *pa. 3 pl.* sharpened

scharpliche *see* **scharpe**

schaw, shawe *n.* small wood, copse, thicket

schaw; schawll *see* **shewe; shal(le)**

sched *pa., p.p.*, **scheddit** *pa.*, **shadde** *p.p.* parted, (was) scattered, (was) dispersed, separated

scheyn, schene; scheiphird *see* **shene; scheperde**

schenyng *n.* shining

schent, shent(e) *p.p.* destroyed, harmed, disgraced, reviled, exhausted

scheperde, scheiphird *n.* shepherd

scherpli *see* **scharpe**

schetis *n. pl.* sheets (of cloth, etc.)

schetis; schett *see* **shete; schute**

schette *imper. sg.* shut; **shit** *pa.*; **schit, shet(te)** *p.p.*

schetun *p.p.* shitten

scheude, schew(e), schew(y)th; schewre *see* **shewe; shere**

schylde *pr. 3 sg. subj.* (may . . .) shield

schill *adv.* shrilly

schynand(e) *pr.p.* shining; **schyned, schane, shoon** *pa.* shone

schipbrokyn *p.p.* shipwrecked

schir sir

schyre *adj.* clear, bright

schit *see* **schette**

scho *pron.* she

schoir *n.* menace, threatening

schold; schon(e) *see* **shal(le); shon(e)**

s(c)hrewde, schrewed, schreude, schroude *adj.* wicked, evil, unlucky; severe; cunning; **schrewitly** *adv.* maliciously

schrewys; schryffe; schryve; schuik; schul(d)(en); schunder; schupe *see* **shrewe; shryve; shireve; schaikand; shal(le); sondre; schape**

schute, shote, schott *v.* shoot; defecate: ~ *behind*; ~ *under* drop quickly below; ~ *upon* rush upon, attack; **schot, shote, shott(en)** *pa.*; **schett** *p.p.*

schwld *see* **shal(le)**

science, sciens *n.* learning; science, art, branch of learning; **scyances** *pl.*

sckoll, sckull, skolle *n.* skull

sclaundre, sklaundir, slawndyr *n.* slander, disgrace, shame

sclaundrid, slawndryd *p.p.* slandered, reviled

scole *n.* school, teaching, method of teaching; **scolys** *pl.*

scoryde *p.p.* scoured, rubbed clean

scottlynge *n.* scuttling, scampering

scowlis *n. pl.* scowls, louring looks

scrip *n.* small bag, wallet

scripture *n.* written inscription; *by* ~ in writing

scute *n.* crown (*écu*, a French coin)

se, se(e)n(e) *v.* see, look, look up; **seis(t)(e), se(i)th** *pr.*; **saghe, say, sey(e), se(e), sy(e)** *pa.*; **seand** *pr. p.*; **seye, se(y)n(e)** *p.p.*

se(a)ce; season; seche *see* **ces(se); seso(u)n; suche**

sech(e)(n), se(i)k(e), syke *v.* seek; look for, seek out, go to, ~ *to*; afflict; **sought, sowght, socht** *pa.*; **sekand** *pr.p.*; **socht, sowte** *p.p.*

see, sey *n.* sea; *the gret(e)/great* ~ the ocean; **sees, seys** *gen. sg.*

se(e)ge *n.* man

seeke; seek(e)nesse *see* **syke; syk(e)nes(se)**

seekly *adj.* sick, miserable

seelde *adv.* seldom

seelis *n. pl.* seals

seen; sees; sege; sey *see* **se; ces(se); s(y)ege, se(e)ge; see, se**

sey(e), seyn(e) *v.* say, speak; **sei(e)n, seyng** *pr. pl.*; **seie** *pr. 3 subj.* let (him/her) say; **seyd(e)(n)/-yn** *pa.*; **se(i)ing(e)** *pr.p.*; **ysayde** *p.p.*

seye; seik; seik(e); seiknes; seyn(e); seir; seis(t)(e), seith *see* **se; sech(e)(n); syke; syk(e)nes(se); se, sey(e); sere; se**

seywart *adv.: to* ~; *see* **toward**

seke; seke, sekand; sekenes(se) *see* **syke; sech(e)(n); syk(e)nes(se)**

seker, sekyr, sicker/-ir *adj., adv.* secure, safe, trusty, reliable, firm, sure, certain; certainly; **sekyrly, sekirli, sikkerlie** *adv.* certainly, securely; **sekirnesse** *n.* security

sel(e), sell *n.* good fortune, happiness; time, season, moment

self(e), sylfe, silff *adj.* same: *same and* ~; (following noun) itself; *that/the* ~ itself

sely, selie, silly, cely *adj.* innocent, pitiable, poor, miserable, wretched, helpless

selkouth *adj.* marvellous, strange

semblable *adj.* similar; **semblably** *adv.* similarly, in like manner

semblance *n.* looks, appearance

semblaunt, senblant *n.* demeanour;

making ~ *to* having the appearance (of), looking as if; *shewed the* ~ *that* behaved as if, looked as if

semblé *n.* assembly; conflict, battle

semble *v.* meet, meet in battle

seme *v.* seem, appear; think; **semyt, semen** *pr. 3 sg./pl.*; **semyd, semyt** *pa.*; (impers.) *hym* ~*d lyke* he seemed to be, *the kyng(e)* ~*d* the king thought

semely *adj.* seemly, comely, fine; **semelyar** *comp.*

semyng(e) *n.: by* ~ *to* it seemed to; *to this maydenes* ~ it seemed to this maiden

semynge *adj.* seemly, fitting

Sen, Sin Saint

sen, *see* **sendyn, se, sithen**

senaws *n. pl.* sinews

senblant *see* **semblaunt**

sendall *n.* thin rich silk

sendyn, sen *v.* send; **send(e)** *pa., p.p.*

sene; senyeis *see* **se; syng**

senyorye *n.* body of lords (the Venetian Signoria)

sensibylitie *n.* sensation, feeling

sensyne *adv.* since then

sentence *n.* meaning, sense, signification; opinion; doctrine, statement; sentence, judgment

sepu(l)kyr, sepulcour *n.* sepulchre; **sepulcris** *n. pl.*

sepulture *n.* tomb, grave

seraphyn *n. pl.* Seraphim (the highest order of angels)

serch(e), serge *v.* search (out), examine; **sercheth** *pr. 3 sg.*

sere, seir *adj.* various, diverse, several, separate

serf *v.* serve

sergea(u)nt(e) *n.* sergeant, officer

serymonys *n. pl.* ceremonies, rituals

seryppe *n.* syrup

serys *n. pl.* sirs

serk *n.* shift

sermant, sermone, sermoun *n.* sermon; discourse, speech

serpentous *adj.* serpentine

servage *n.* servitude

serviture *n.* servant

servyture *n.* service

serwand *n.* servant

sesyt *p.p.* set, placed

sesonynge *n.* ripening

seso(u)n, sesso(u)n, season *n.* season, time: *in this meane* ~ in the meantime;

seso(u)n, sesso(u)n, season (*cont.*): seasoning, flavour

ses(s)e *see* **ces(se)**

sessonabil *adj.* fitting, suitable

seth *imper. sg.* boil; **sething** *pr.p.*; **sode(n), sodyn** *p.p., adj.* boiled (food)

seth; sethe(n) *see* **se; sithen**

set(t)e, sait *n.* seat, throne; **setes** *pl.*

set(te), setten *v.* set place, put; estimate; ~ *it (nought)*; fix, set (intention, purpose) on: ~ *by* set (any) store by, think highly of; bind; **(y)sett, set(te)** *p.p.* placed, set, adorned, inlaid

sevennyght *n.* week

sew *n.* juice, sauce

sew(e), sowe *imper. sg.* sew; **sowed/-yd** *p.p.*

sewe, sue *v.* follow, ensue; sue, petition; **sewid** *pa.*; **sued, suid** *p.p.*

sexangled *adj.* hexagonal

shadde *see* **sched**

shal(le) *v.* will, shall, is/are to, must; **sall, schal, schawll, shoule, shul(le), shuln, schulen, xalt** (*2 sg.*), **xal(l)** *pr.*; **suld, s(c)huld(e)(n), schold(e), schwld, sowld, xuld(e)** *pa.*; **xuldist** *pa. 2 sg.* should, would, were to

shamefastnes(se) *n.* modesty

shames *n. pl.* shawms (reed instruments like oboes)

shames *gen. sg.* (as adj.): *a ~ deth* a shameful death

shape; sharply; shawe *see* **schape; scharpe; schaw**

shene, sche(y)n(e) *adj.* bright, shining, fair, beautiful

shent(e) *see* **schent**

sheppe *n.* ship; **shepes, shepis** *pl.*; **shepmen** *n. pl.* mariners, sailors

shere *v.* shear, cut, tear; **schewre** *pa. 3 sg.*

sheres *n. pl.* scissors

shete *n.* sheet (rope fastened to the lower corners of a sail); **schetis** *pl.*

shet(te) *see* **schette**

shewe, schew, schaw *v.* show, make known (to), make manifest, reveal, tell, appear; **schawis, schew(y)th** *pr.*; **s(c)hew(de)** *pa.*; **scheude, s(c)hewyd** *p.p.*

shyfte *v.* move; ~ *for* make provision (for), manage (to); ~*d* **out/in** changed (into), dressed in

shireve, shyryfe, shreve, schryve, shryef *n.* sheriff

shit; shoef *see* **schette; schaf**

shoffe *pa. 3 sg.* made her way, went

shold(e) *see* **shal(le)**

shone, shoon, schon(e) *n. pl.* shoes

shoon; shote, shott(en); shoule *see* **schynand(e); schute; shal(le)**

shoules *n. pl.* shovels

shour, schour *n.* shower; **schowris** *pl.*

showte *n.* clamour, loud noise

shreve; shrewde *see* **shireve; s(c)hrewde**

shrewe *n.* villain, rascal, scoundrel; **schrewys** *pl.*

shryfte *n.* confession

shryve *v.* shrive, confess; **shryffe, shryve(nne)** *p.p.*

shuld(e), shuldest, shul(le), shuln; sy *see* **shal(le); se**

sibreden *n.* kinship

sic, sych(e); sich; siching; sycht; sicht, sichit; sicker, sickir *see* **suche; syk(e); sythynge; sight; syk(e); seker**

syde *adj.* long; haughty, proud

sy(e), syeste *see* **se**

s(y)ege *n.* seat, privy

sight, sycht, sygth, siht, syte *n.* sight, vision, appearance; *in ~* to see; *taken in ~* (?) taken to be

sy(g)ne, syng *n.* sign, signal; augury; **senyeis** *pl.*

signetes *n. pl.* cygnets

signorie *n.* rule, lordship

sik; syke *see* **syk(e), suche; sech(e)(n)**

sike *n.* brook, stream

syke *n.* sigh; **sihhes** *pl.*

syke, se(e)ke, seik(e) *adj.* sick

syk(e), sich(t), syth *v.* sigh; **siching** *pr.p.*; **sichit** *pa. 3 sg.*

syk(e)nes(se), se(e)k(e)nesse, seiknes *n.* sickness

sikkerlie *see* **seker**

syle *v.* cover, conceal; deceive, beguile; **sylit** *p.p.*

sylfe, silff; silly *see* **self(e); sely**

syment *n.* cement

symmer *see* **somer**

symplenesse *n.* ignorance, foolishness

symplesse *n.* simplicity

syn; syne; syng, syne *see* **sithen, sen; sithen; sy(g)ne**

sing(u)ler(e) *adj.* singular, special, particular; individual; unique, unequalled

syones, syonys *pl.* shoots, branches

sircumstance *see* **circumstaunce**

sys *n. pl.* times

site *v.* sit; befit, be proper; **sit** *pr. 3 sg.*; **sate** *pa. sg.*; **syttinge** *pr.p., adj.* fitting; **syttyn** *p.p.* waited

syte *n.* sorrow

syte; syth *see* **sight; syk(e)**

sithen, sith(e), sithyn, sethe(n), syn(e), sen *adv., prep., conj.* afterwards, then, thereupon; after, since; considering that, from the time that; ~ *that*

sithenesse *adv.* afterwards, later

sythynge, siching *n.* sighing

sytyca *n.* sciatica

syttyn, syttinge *see* **site**

skalis *pr. 3 sg.* scatters

skant *adv.* scarcely

skapyd *see* **scape**

skarsly *adv.* scarcely

skellat *n.* hand-bell

skyis *n. pl.* skies, clouds

sklaundir *see* **sclaundre**

skryke *n.* screech

skryking *n.* screeching, shrieking

skrymming *n.* skirmishing, darting

skrippit *pa. 3 sg.* mocked

skuggis *n. pl.* shadows

sla(a); slaid *see* **sie(e)(n); slode**

slakis *pr. 1 pl.* slacken, loosen

slawchtir *n.* slaughter

slawndyr; slawndryd; sle; slederyd *see* **sclaundre; sclaundrid; sle(ighe); slyther**

sle(e)(n), sley *v.* slay, kill, destroy; strike blows; **slow(e)** *pa. 3 sg.*; **yslayne, slane, sloo** *p.p.*

sle(ighe), sly *adj.* deceitful, crafty, cunning, cunningly made

sleight *adj.* slight, humble

slekit *p.p., adj.* smooth

slete, slyte *imper. sg.* slit

slidder *adj.* slippery

sliper *adj.* slippery, unsteady

slyther *v.* slip; **slederyd** *pa. 3 sg.*

slo *see* **sle(e)(n)**

slode, slaid *pa. 3 sg.* slipped, slid

slogardye *n.* sluggishness

slokin *v.* slake

sloo *see* **sle(e)(n)**

sloppis *n. pl.* (?) small trailing clouds

slow(e) *see* **sle(e)(n)**

smale, small(e) *adj.* small, slender, delicate

smaragdane *n.* emerald

smattrynge *adj.* (?) pretty, amorous, ready for kissing

smert, smarte *n.* pain

smerte *adj., adv.* brisk, quick; vigorously, sharply

smert(e) *v.* hurt; feel pain, suffer

smet, smotte *pa. sg.* smote; **smeten, smyt(e)(n), smetten** *p.p.* smitten, hammered, driven

smydy *n.* smithy

smoder *v.* suffocate, be smothered

smorit *pa. 3 pl.* (were) suffocated

smotte *see* **smet**

snaw(e) *n.* snow

snell *adj.* bitter, severe

snew *pa. 3 sg.* snowed

snypand *pr.p., adj.* biting, cutting

snod *adj.* smooth (ground)

socht; sode(n), sodyn; sofereyns *see* **sech(e)(n); seth; soverence**

soget *n.* subject

soyche; soir *see* **suche; sor(e)**

soyr *adj.* sorrel, reddish-brown

soyte; soithly *see* **sute; soth**

sojowryd *p.p.* stayed, sojourned

sokett *n.* socket, hole

sol *n.* (alchem.) sun, i.e. gold

solace, solas *n.* pleasure, delight, joy, bliss, comfort

solaycyose *adj.* consoling

solempne *adj.* solemn, sacred; ~**ly** *adv.* solemnly; **solempnité** *n.* solemn observance

somdell *adv.* somewhat

som(e), somme, sum(m)(e) *adj., pron. indef.* a certain, some; one, some

somer, symmer *n.* summer; **symmeris/-yris, sommers** *gen. sg.*

som(m)e *n.* sum, amount; whole, totality

somtyme, sumtym(e) *adv.* once, formerly; sometimes

sonde *n.* message, gift

sondes *n. pl.* sands

sondre, sounder, schunder *adv.* apart, asunder; *in* ~

son(e) *see* **sonn(e)**

son(e), sonne *n.* son

son(e), soone *adv.* straightway, quickly, soon; **son(n)er** *comp.* sooner, rather; **sonnest, sunnest** *sup.* soonest

sonk(in) *p.p., adj.* submerged, sunk; sunken, hollow

sonn(e), son(e) *n.* sun; (alchem.) gold; **sonnes/-ys** *pl.*

sonne, sonner, sonnest; soore *see* **son(e); sor(e)**

soot *adj.* sweet

sooth *see* **sothe**

sop *n.*[1] sop, piece of bread steeped in liquid

sop *n.*[2] mass, cloud; **soppys** *pl.*

soper, sopyr *n.* supper

sor(e), soore, sa(i)r(e), soir *adj., adv.* grievous, sorrowful, suffering; sorely, grievously, bitterly, gloomily, painfully, very, intensely, strongly, quickly

sory, sary *adj.* sorrowful, wretched

sorjon; sors *see* **surgeand; so(u)rs**

sort *pr. 1 pl.* allot

sort(e) *n.* kind, variety, set of people, company; *a good* ~ a great many

sorw(e) *n.* sorrow; **~ful, sorouful(l)** *adj.* sorrowful

sorwe *v.* sorrow

sotell *see* **subtyle**

soth *adj.* true; **sothely, soithly, suithly** *adv.* truly

sothe, sooth, su(y)th *n.* truth; **suthfast** *adj.* true; **sothefastnesse** *n.* truth

sotheroun *n. pl.* southerners, Englishmen

sotyd *p.p., adj.* besotted

sotil(l)(e) *see* **subtyle**

sotilté *n.* subtlety, cunning

soucor *n.* succour, assistance

soudyour *n.* soldier

souffisaunce *n.* sufficiency

soughe *n.* boggy place

sought(en); souketh *see* **sech(e)(n); sowkand**

soule *adj.* alone

soul-priest *n.* priest whose special function is to pray for the souls of the dead

sounde *n.* swoon

sounder *see* **sondre**

soundery *adj.* sundry, different

soun(e) *n.* sound, music; **sownes** *pl.*

so(u)rs *n.* source

soveraynté *n.* sovereignty; *in* ~ supremely

sovereyn(e) *adj.* supreme, sovereign; **soveraynly/-eynly** *adv.* supremely

soverence, sofereyns *n. pl.* lords, masters, gentlemen

soverent *adj.* most excellent

sovir *adj.* safe, secure

sowde *v.* close, unite

sowe; sowed/-yd; sowght; *see* sew(e), sawe; sew(e); sech(e)(n)

sowkand *pr.p.* sucking; **souketh** *pr. 3 sg.* sucks; **sowkynge** *n.* sucking

sowld; sowle *see* **shal(le); sawle**

sownd *n.* narrow channel

sowne *n.* swoon

sowned *pa. 3 sg.* swooned

sownes *see* **soun(e)**

sowp(e) *v.* eat supper, sup; ~ *out* drink up

sowpit *p.p.* wearied, sunk

sowrely; sowte *see* **surely; sech(e)(n)**

space *n.* time, opportunity, respite; place

spack(e) *see* **speke**

spaied *p.p.* killed by a sword or knife

Spaynardes *n. pl.* Spaniards

spait *n.* spate, flood

spak(ke) *see* **speke**

spangis *n. pl.* spangles

spare, sparyn *v.* spare, hold back, desist, refrain, leave unused

sparhalk *n.* sparrow-hawk

sparkand *pr.p.* throwing out like sparks

sparklynges *n. pl.* showers of sparks

speche *n.* speech, language; **spechis** *pl.* expressions, remarks; **~les** *adj.* speechless

sped(e), speid *n.* success, help, helper; **gud(e)** ~ quickly

spede, speede, spyede *v.* fare, succeed, prosper; assist, help, serve, provide for; press, speed, hasten; **sped(de)** *pa., p.p.*

spedely *adv.* speedily

speir; speir, speyre *see* **spere; spheir**

speiris *pr. 3 sg.* asks

speke, spekyn *v.* speak; **spak(ke), spack(e)** *pa.*

spende *v.* spend, use (up), wear out, waste; **spend, spent** *pa.*; **spendynge** *n.* spending, expending, wasting

spenne *v.* spend

spere, speir *n.* spear

sperk *n.* spark; **sperkis** *pl.*: *ruby* ~ small rubies

spesyall *n.* favourite, intimate friend

spheir, spere, speir(e) *n.* sphere

spyede *see* **spede**

spyll *v.* destroy, injure; be destroyed; **spilt(e)** *p.p.*

spyn(n)er *n.* pinnace

spyryte, spre(i)t(e), spry(gh)t *n.* spirit, vital spirit, mind, faculty; spiritual being; **spreitis, sprites** *pl.*

spirred *pa. 3 sg.* asked

spita(i)ll *n.* hospital; ~ *hous* leper-house

spytfull *adj.* hostile, malevolent

splene *n.* spleen, heart

splentys *n. pl.* splints

spoylid, spulyeit *p.p.* despoiled,

plundered; **spoylinges** *n. pl.* acts of pillaging

spon *n.* spoon

spores, sporis *n. pl.* spurs

sporned *pa. 3 sg.* kicked at, thrust at; **spurnis** *pr. 2 sg.* kick, beat

sporte *v. refl.* disport/entertain oneself

spreit, spre(i)tis, sprete, spryght *see* **spyryte**

spring(e) *n.* source, dawn; spring, attack

sprynge *v.* grow, spring up, shoot up, rise; **sprungin** *p.p.*; **spryngynge** *n.* rising

springolt *n.* missile fired by a catapult

spryt; sprungin; spulyeit; spurnis *see* **spyryte; sprynge; spoylid; sporned**

sqweymes *adj.* disdainful, offended

sq(u)yer *n.* squire; **sqwirs** *pl.*

sta(a)te, stait *n.* estate, rank, class; normal condition; **statis** *pl.*

stabelyssyng *n.* ordering, establishment

stacke *pa. 3 pl.* thrust at

stacker *v.* totter, stagger

stad *p.p.* beset

stage *n.* position; deck (of galley); **stagis** *pl.* steps

stay *adj.* steep, upright

staiffis *pr. 3 pl.* thrust

stait *see* **sta(a)te**

stak *n.* haystack

stale *see* **stele**

stall *n.* seat, place

stampe *v.* stamp; pound in a mortar

stanch *see* **sta(u)nch(e)**

stanchell *n.* kestrel

standardes *n. pl.* (?) rods (23 E 6)

stande, stond(e)(n)/-yn *v.* stand; *so as may ~ with* as far as is consistent with; *~ on hande* concern, be the duty of; **stant** *pr. 3 sg.*; **stode(n), stoude, stude** *pa.*; **standand** *pr.p.* standing, erect

stane *see* **ston(e)**

stang *n.* sting

stanneris *n. pl.* small stones, gravel

stapill *n.* staple, clasp

stappys *n. pl.* steps

stares *n. pl.* starlings

starke *adj.* sturdy; stiff, rigid; **starklie** *adv.* strongly

starn, stern *n.* star; **stern, starnys** *pl.*

start *n.* moment, short time

startling *pr. p., adj.* prancing

starvit; state *see* **sterve; sta(a)te**

statt *n.* stot (term of abuse for a woman)

sta(u)nch(e) *v.* stanch; cease flowing

sted(e), steid *n.* place, stead: *~ of* instead of; **stedis** *pl.*

stefyn *see* **steuin**

steir *v.* govern, guide

steir, stere, styr(r)(e) *v.* stir, move, disturb, bestir oneself, urge; **steryng, styring** *pr.p.*

stele, stell *v.* steal; **stale** *pa.*; **stalle, stown** *p.p.*

stellifyit *p.p.* made into a star

stent *see* **stynte**

stent *v.* set up

stepe *v.* soak

stepyll *n.* steeple

steppis *pr. 3 pl.* step, come

stere *adj.* strong, stout

stere; stern *see* **steir; starn**

sterre *n.* star; *~lyght* light of the stars

stert(e) *v.* leap, spring, rush, go: *abrode to ~* gad about; plunge; startle, start (an animal); **stert(e), stirte** *pa.*

sterve *v.* die, perish; **starvit** *pa. 3 pl.*

stethy *see* **stythy**

steuin, stefyn *n.* voice

stevynnys *n. pl.* prows

stew *n.* vapour, smoke

stewerde *n.* steward, recorder at a manor court

stewys *gen. pl.* of the brothels

styen *pr. 3 pl.* climb, ascend

styf(f)(e) *adj.* strong, stalwart; stiff; **stifly** *adv.* without yielding

styll *n.* condition

styl(l)(e) *adj., adv.* silent, quiet, still, untouched; motionless, silently, quietly, continually, always, still, yet

stillid *p.p.* distilled

stynt *n.* ceasing

stynt(t)e *imper. sg.*: *~ of* cease from; **stent, stynt(it)-ed** *pa.* stopped, ceased, was brought to a stop

styre, stirr; stirte *see* **steir; stert(e)**

stythy, stethy *n.* anvil

stode(n) *see* **stande**

stoff *n.* stuff, material

stoke *n.* stock

stole *n.*[1] throne, seat

stole *n.*[2] stole (a liturgical vestment)

stolle; stond(e)(n), stondyn *see* **stele; stande**

ston(e), stoon(e), stane *n.* stone; gem; the philosophers' stone; missile

stone-flye *n.* stone-fly (an insect whose larvae are found under stones, used for bait)

stonge *p.p.* stung, bitten

stoppe *imper. sg.* stuff, fill (9 H 16)

stoppelmaker *n.* reaper of stubble

store *n.*: *(kepe) in* ~ (keep) in reserve, (keep) restrained, keep back

storyde *p.p.* provided

stoud(e) *see* stande

stound(e), stownde *n.* time, while, moment; time of trial, pain, pang

stour, stowr *n.* combat, fight, storm, tumult

stout(e), stowt(e) *adj.* bold, fierce, strong, brave

stow *interj.* down, come

stown *see* stele

strabery *n. (collect. sg.)* strawberries

strah, stro *n.* straw; (as interj. of contempt)

stra(i)k *n.* stroke

straik *see* stryke

strayte, strey(gh)t(e), straucht *adj., adv.* strict, narrow; straight, directly; straytely, streihtli *adv.* strictly; tightly

strake *v.* blow (a horn), sound a call

stramp *v.* tread on

strand, stronde *n.* stream, brook, water; bank, shore

strang(e), stranger; straucht *see* stronge; strayte

stra(u)nge *adj.* foreign, strange, new; distant, aloof

straw *imper. sg.* strew

streyght, streyt(e), streihtli *see* strayte

streym *n.* stream

streyn *imper. sg.* bind tightly; streyned *p.p.* afflicted

streynour *n.* strainer

streyt(e) *see* strayte

streke *imper. sg.* extend, put out; strekis *pr. 3 pl.* stretch

strene *imper. sg.* strain

strenght *p.p.* strengthened

strenght(e). strength *n.* strength; force, violence; armed force, company of soldiers

strye *v.* destroy

stryke *v.* make one's way, come to; strike; pierce, enter; straik, strake *pa. sg.*

stryve *n.* strife

stro; stronde(s) *see* strah; strand

stronge, strang(e) *adj.* strong, painful, harsh, severe; stronger *adv. comp.*

more strongly

strowit *p.p.* strewed

stude; study *see* stande; stythy

study *n.* state of reverie, state of abstraction

studye *v.* brood, ponder, take thought; studyed *pa. 3 pl.*

stuffed *p.p.* padded

stulpes *n. pl.* pillars, posts

sturdy *adj.* strong, fierce, grim, harsh; sturdily *adv.* strongly, sharply

sture *adj.* strong

suavius *adj.* sweet

subdaynlye *adv.* suddenly

subsyde, subsidye *n.* assistance

substa(u)nce *n.* substance; wealth, possessions; matter (of speech)

subtyle, subtyll, sotell, sotil(l)(e) *adj.* subtle, cunning, crafty, clever, delicate; subtyly, sutelly *adv.* cleverly

suche, suich(e), swyche, swheche, soyche, seche, sic(he), sik *adj.* such: ~ *a place/squyer* (etc.) such and such a place/squire (etc.); *pron. pl.* such people, such things/matters

sue(d); suerd(e); suere, suerly, suerté *see* sewe; swerd; sure

sue(i)t(e), swe(y)t(e), swoot *adj., adv.* sweet; *for* ~ *ne soure* under any circumstances; sweetly; swetly *adv.* sweetly

suffycyens *n.* sustenance

sufficyent *adj.* capable, able

suffysaunce *n.* sufficiency

suffrage *n.* help

suger *v.* sugar, sweeten

suich(e); suid; suyth, suythly; suld *see* suche; sewe; swith, sothe; shal(le)

sulphir *n.* sulphur; (alchem.) one of the ultimate elements of all material substance

sum(e), summe *see* som(e)

sumpa(i)rt *adv.* somewhat, to some extent

sumtyme; sunnest *see* somtyme; son(e)

superatt *p.p.* conquered

supplé *v.* deliver

supplie *n.* assistance, support

suppoaille, suppoyle *n.* support

suppois *(imper. as) conj.* although, if, even if

supportacyo(u)n *n.* assistance, support

suppostes *n. pl.* subordinates, followers

suppowaylen *v.* be of service to, support; suppowailled *p.p.*

surcotes *n. pl.* surcoats, outer coats

sure, suere *adj.* certain, trusty, steadfast:

~ *by* faithful to; **suerly, surely, sowrely** *adv.* surely, securely; **suerté** *n.* security, safety

surgeand, surgyon, sorjon *n.* surgeon, physician; **surrigianis** *pl.*

surmontyth, surmownteth *pr. 3 sg.* surpasses, excels

surprysed *p.p.* passionately seized

suspect(e), suspek *adj.* suspect(ed); suspicious

susreal *n.* the uppermost branch of a stag's antler

sute, soyte *n.* kind, manner; *in* ~ *of* in accord with, to match; *in a* ~ of the same kind; suit, livery; law-suit

suth, suthfast; suttelly; swa *see* **sothe; subtyle; sa**

swagis *pr. 3 pl.* become calm, abate

swak *v.* hurl, fling, dash

swapping *n.* striking, smiting

swat, swet(te) *pa. sg.* sweated

sweir *adj.* sluggish, slow

sweit; sweyt *see* **swete; sue(i)t(e)**

sweitmeitis *n. pl.* dainties

swelch *n.* whirlpool, abyss

swelt *pa.* died; swooned, fainted, sweltered

swemyth *pr. 3 sg.* grieves

swenyng *n.* dream

swerd, suerd(e) *n.* sword

swete, sweit, swoot *n.* sweat

swet(e), swetly; swet(te); swheche, swyche *see* **sue(i)t(e); swat; suche**

swinging *n.* drawing

swyre *n.* hollow, valley

swith, suyth *adv.* quickly, swiftly, forthwith, at once

swoot *see* **swete, sue(i)t(e)**

swouchand *pr.p.* rushing

swoughe, swouh *n.* swoon

tabernacle *n.* tabernacle, dwelling-place; (as term of association) (?) referring to the elaborate structures made by pastry-cooks for feasts (9 T 5)

tabyll, table *n.* table; tablet, slab; table of the law given to Moses (of salvation); **tables** *pl.* backgammon

tackithe; taght *see* **tak(e); teche**

tay *n.* outer membrane

taidis *n. pl.* toads

taikning *see* **takning**

tayll(e) *n.* shape, cut; tax, payment, due; tally, reckoning; **tayles** *pl.*

tak(e) *v.* take, seize, capture, imprison;

~ . . . *by* take notice, set store by; ~ *on hand* take charge of; ~ *to* add, bring to; make: *covenant* ~ undertake; entrust to, give, deliver; ~ *the wynde* sniff/breathe the wind; take to: ~ *up* begin; come to: ~ *an ende*; **tackithe** *pr. 3 sg.*; **tu(i)k(e), to(o)k(e)(n)** *pa.*; **take(n), tane, ytake** *p.p.*

takelyng *n.* tackle, ropes

takyllys *n. pl.* implements; excretory organs

takyn *see* **token**

takning, taikning *n.* token, sign

tale *n.* account, reckoning

talede *pa. 3 pl.* spoke, said

tallages *n. pl.* taxes, levies

tame *v.* broach

tane *see* **tak(e)**

tary *v.* tarry, delay, linger, wait for

tarsall *n.* male falcon

teche *v.* teach, instruct; **ta(u)ght(e)** *pa., p.p.*

tegir *n.* tiger

teyntys *n. pl.* tents (rolls of soft material used in treating wounds)

tell *v.* declare; ~ *out*, count out, pay out, enumerate, relate; **teld(e), towlde** *pa.*; **told(e)** *p.p.*

temit *p.p.* emptied

tempestes *n. pl.* tumults, commotions

temse *n.* sieve

tendyn *v.* attend (to)

tending *pr.p.* going; **tendit** *pa. 3 sg.* moved

tene *n.* anger, affliction, trouble

tenebrus *adj.* dark, gloomy

tenement *n.* dwelling-place

tent *n.* heed, attention: *tak* ~ pay attention

tercyans *adj. pl.* tertian; *fevers* ~ fevers in which paroxysms recur every third day

tha *see* **tha(y)**

thay, thé *pron.* they; (?) people, anyone (5. 269)

tha(y) *demons adj. pl.* those

tha(y)m(e), theym(e) *pron.* them

thair, ~foir, ~out *see* **ther(e)**

thank(e) *n.* thanks, gratitude; *in* ~ gratefully

thar *pron. gen.* their

that *conj., pron. rel.* that, so that; that, which, who(m), that which, what; ~ *that*

the *pron.* thee, you

thé; the; theder(e), thedyr; thegh; theym(e) *see* **thay; the(n); thiddir;**

though; tha(y)m(e)

theine *adv.* thence; **thenforth** *adv.* thenceforth

theis, theyes *n. pl.* thighs; thees, theis *gen. sg.* thigh's

thekyt *p.p.* covered, roofed

the(n) *v.* prosper, thrive

thenforth; thenge, thenke *see* theine; thynk(e), thing

thennes, thennys *adv.* thence; elsewhere

theologgis *n. pl.* theologians

ther(e), thair, their, thore *adv.* there, where; ~*abowte* around there; ~*aftir* according to it; ~ *as* where, wherever; ~ *awaye* in that direction; ~ *bi* by this/it, beside, nearby; ~*foir* therefore; ~*of* thereof, for this; ~*out* outside, in the world, in existence; ~*to* to it; ~*upon* with reference to that; ~*whothe* with it/that; ~*mythall* thereupon

theves, thevys *n. pl.* thieves

thewes *n. pl.* virtues

thycke *adv.* quickly; indistinctly

thiddir, thider, theder(e)/-yr *adv.* thither; ~*ward* thither

thift *n.* theft

thilk(e) *adj. demons.* that (same); *pl.* those

thin *pron. poss.* thine, your

thing, thenke *n.* thing, matter; *for no* ~ on no account

thynk(e), thenk(e), thenge *v.* think, think how to, devise, intend, etc.: ~ *on* think of; (impers.) *me/him/us* ~*e(th)/thocht* it seems/-ed to (me, etc.); **thynk(yt)** *pr. 3 sg.*; **thocht, tho(u)ght(en), thowt(e)** *pa.*

thir(e) *pron., adj. demons.* these

thyrlyth *pr. 3 sg.* pierces; **thyrlyt** *p.p.* pierced

this *adv.* thus

this(e) *pron., adj. demons.* this, *fro* ~ *furth* from this time on; *pl.* these; this this is (treated as monosyllable) (6 A 112)

tho; thocht, thoght; thocht, thoff, thoght *see* tho(o); thynk(e), tho(u)ght; though

thoil *v.* endure, suffer; **thoillit** *pa. 3 sg.*

thon *adv.* then, thus

thonke *v.* thank, express gratitude; **thonkid** *pa. pl.*

tho(o) *adv.* then, at that time

tho(o), thoe *pron. demons. pl.* those

thoo(w) *see* though

thopas *n.* topaz

thore *see* ther(e)

thorgh, thor(o)ugh(e), th(o)rou(ght), th(o)row(gh)(e), thrugh, thorw *prep., adv.* through: *where/her* ~ through which/this, ~**out(e)** throughout; throughout, completely, from beginning to end; **thorowly** *adv.* completely

thorpe *n.* village

though, thegh, thocht(t), thoff, thouh, thoo(w), thow(h), thowthe *adv., conj.* though, if

tho(u)ght(e), thocht, thow(gh)t *n.* thought, mind, memory, heed; sorrow, melancholy (sometimes person.); **thowtys** *pl.*; **thoughtful, thoughty** *adj.* sorrowful, pensive, melancholy

thought(e)(n), thowt(e); thouh, thow(h), thowthe; thraly *see* thynk(e); though; thro

thrang *n.* throng, crowd, press, battle

thrang; thrawe *see* thryng; throw

thrawand *pr.p.* rushing; **thrawing** *pr.p.* throwing

thred, thredly *see* thridde

thressed *p.p.* threshed

threste *see* thryst(e)

thretis *n. pl.* threats

thriddle, thred *adj.* third; ~**ly** *adv.* thirdly

thries, thryis, thrise *adv.* thrice

thrif *v.* prosper

thryft(e) *n.* servings, salvation

thryng *v.* thrust, push forward, press, bind; **thringis** *pr. 3 pl.*; **thrang** *pa. 3 pl.*; **thrung** *p.p.*

thryse *n.: at* ~ at a go, at once

thrist *n.* thirst

thryst(e) *v.* thrust; **threste** *pa. 3 sg.*

thritty *num.* thirty; *by* ~ *and* ~ in groups of thirty

thro *adj.* fierce, grim, stubborn in battle; **thraly** *adv.* fiercely

throstles *n. pl.* song-thrushes

throu *see* thorgh

throw, thrawe *n.* time, while

throw(e), throwout, thrugh; **thrung** *see* thorgh; thryng

thuddis *n. pl.* blasts, squalls

thundir *n.* bolt of lightning (20 B 142)

tyd(e) *n.* time, hour, season

tide *p.p.* restrained (from)

tyde *pr. 3 sg. subj.* befall

tydeus *adj.* harmful

tyght *adv.* quickly

til(l), tyl(le) *prep., conj.* to; until, till
tym(e) *n.* time; *by* ~ in (good) time; *on a* ~ once
tyme *n.* thyme
tyndes *n. pl.* antlers
tyne *v.* lose
tynsall *n.* losing
tyse *v.* entice
tissew, tyssue *n.* rich cloth interwoven with gold or silver
tit *pr. 3 sg.* pulls
tythingges *n. pl.* news
tythis *n. pl.* tithes
titil, title *n.* title, claim
tytyll *v.*[1] whisper
tytyll *v.*[2] write
to *see* to(o)
to *adv.* too
to *prep., conj.* to, in order to, for, according to, towards; **to** . . . **ward** *see* **toward**; until, till
tobanne *v.* curse thoroughly
toborch *v.* redeem, rescue
tobrast, tobrest *pa. 3 sg.* broke, burst
tobrent *p.p.* burnt, scorched
toche, tuche *v.* touch, touch on, concern; **touchyng(e)** *pr.p.*; **touchide, towched** *pa.*
tocken *see* token
to-comynge *adj.* future
tod *n.* fox
to-eke *adv.* besides
tofor(e) *adv., prep.* ago, before(hand); before
toforne, toforowe *adv.* before, in front
togeder(ys)/-gedre/-gedir(s)/-gid(d)-er(e)/-gydre/-githers *adv.* together
togloryede *p.p.* over-glorified
toyes *n. pl.* antics
token, tocken, tokyn, takyn *n.* sign, portent, token; **toknes, tookenys** *pl.*
toke(n); told(e) *see* tak(e); tell
tolde *p.p., adj.* taken toll of, taxed, i.e. cut short (16. 671)
tomorne, tomorwe *adv.* tomorrow
ton *n.* tone
ton(e), toon *adj., pron.* one
to(o) *n.* toe
to(o), towe *num.* two
tookenys *see* token
toowne *n.* farm (11 G 2)
toppe *n.* hair on top of head; *in his* ~ harrying him
toragged *p.p., adj.* very ragged

torde *n.* turd; **toordes** *pl.*
torente *p.p., adj.* completely in tatters
tornye *v.* tourney, joust
toschaik *p.p.* shaken off
totare *p.p.* torn to pieces
tother, tothir *adj., pron.* other
touche *n.* trick
touchide, touchyng(e) *see* toche
touchyng(e), towchyng *prep.* touching, concerning
tourment *n.* tempest
to(u)rne *v.* turn, return, ~ *agayne/ayen* return
toward *prep.* to, toward, in respect of; **(on)to** . . . **ward(e)(s)/wart** (divided): ~ *God/me/my deth/Caleys (etc.)* ~ towards God (etc.)
towartly *adj.* docile, tractable
towched; towchyng; towe; towlde *see* toche; touchyng(e); to(o); tell
trace *n.* track(s); measure, dance
trace *v.* dance; **tracyed** *pa. 1 sg.*
tracte *n.* duration, drawing out
tray *n.* grief, affliction, trouble
traine *n.* circumstances, situation, plight
trayne *n.* (?) treachery, stratagem, (?) body of men (10 A 73)
traist *v.* trust, believe, hope; **traistes** *pr. 2 sg.*; **traistit** *pa.*
tranoyntit *pa. 3 pl.* marched (stealthily) on, set upon
translatit *p.p.* changed, transformed
trast *n.* trust
trauthe *see* trouth(e)
travailoures *n. pl.* toilers, workers
traveyle, travell, travayl(e) *n.* toil, labour, trouble, difficulty, travail, voyaging
traveilen *pr. 3 pl.* afflict; **travayle** *imper. sg.* labour; **travaylled** *pa. refl.* struggled, toiled; **travayled, traveiild** *p.p.* afflicted, oppressed
trawth(e) *see* trouth(e)
tre(a)tyse, tretes *n.* narrative, account, treatise; treaty, compact
tre(e) *n.* tree, gallows-tree, wood; *of* ~ wooden; **treys** *pl.*
trepett *n.* tripping up
tresoureye *n.* treasury, treasure-house
tres(ou)ur *n.* treasure
trespace, trespas(s)(e) *n.* transgression, offence, sin; passing, death
tresses, tressis *n. pl.* braids, plaits
trestis *n. pl.* trestles
treté *n.* agreement, covenant, entreaty

tretes, tretyse; treuth(e) *see* **tre(a)tyse; trouth(e)**

trewnchour *n.* trencher, plate

triacle *n.* a medicinal compound made of many ingredients (in high repute as an antidote for bites, poisons, and a variety of diseases)

trybutarie, tributori *adj.* paying tribute, subject

tryden *pa. 3 pl.* put to the test, used; **tried** *p.p., adj.* proved, proven

trillyng *pr.p.* flowing

trymlys, trymmillis *pr. 3 sg./pl.* tremble, quake; **trymmelyth** *pr. 3 sg.*

tryse *v.* pluck, snatch; **trysyde** *p.p.*

trist(e) *adj.* sad, sorrowful

tryst(e) *v.* trust

troche *n.* a cluster of three tines or branches at the top of a deer's horn

tromles *n. pl.* (?) drums

trompettes *see* **trumpettes**

trone *n.* throne; **trones** *pl.* Thrones (the third of the nine orders of angels)

troubleth *pr. 3 sg.* grows dark, becomes disturbed; **tro(u)blid** *p.p.* disturbed, afflicted

troubly *adj.* troubled

trought *n.* trough

trouth(e), trauth(e), trawth(e), tro(w)th(e), tr(e)uth(e) *n.* truth: *of* ~ truly; fidelity, loyalty; troth, pledged word

trowbyll, troble *n.* trouble, affliction, misery

trow(e) *v.* believe, think

trow(y)t(e) *n.* trout

trumpettes, trunmpetts, trompettes *n. pl.* trumpets, trumpeters

trussed, trussid *pa.* trussed; (refl.) took my/yourself off; *p.p.* (?) (of the body) well-knit together (?) (of clothes) trussed up (24 B 67)

trussyng *n.* packing, trussing

truth; tuche *see* **trouth(e); toche**

tuft *n.* hillock, mound

tuik, tuke *see* **tak(e)**

tuilyeour-lyke *adj.* like a brawler

Twelftheday *n.* the twelfth day after Christmas, the Epiphany

twychyde *p.p.* jerked, twitched

twyez, twyes *adv.* twice

twynkelid *pa. 3 sg.* winked

twynne *n.: in* ~ between (the two)

twistis *n. pl.* branches

ugly, owgly *adj.* fearsome, terrible, ugly

umquhile *adv.* sometimes, at times

unable *adj.* unfit, unable

unaspyit *p.p.* unnoticed

unavised, onavysed *(p.p.) adv.* without warning, without preparation

unccyon *n.* anointing with oil; the sacrament of Extreme Unction

uncessable *adj.* unceasing

unconnynge *adj.* ignorant

uncoupled *pa. 3 sg., p.p.* unleashed

uncouth, unkouth(e), unkowthe, unketh *adj.* unknown, strange, unpleasant

uncunnandly *adv.* clumsily, without skill

uncurteis, oncurtes(s) *adj.* discourteous, lacking courtesy, unkind

uncurtesie *n.* discourtesy

undirstonde, undrestonde *see* **wndyrstonde**

undirtake *pr. 1 sg.* affirm, declare; **under-/undirtake** *p.p.* undertaken, decided on

undo(o) *v.* bring to nought; open; cut up (a deer); **ondoth** *pr. 3 sg.*; **ondon, wndon** *p.p.*

undowted *(p.p.) adv.* undoubtedly

unfayned, unfeyned *p.p., adj.* not feigned, sincere, honest

unfair *adv.* untidily, roughly

unfest *p.p.* unfastened

unhappy *adj.* unlucky, disastrous, wretched

uniaunce *n.* union

unketh *see* **uncouth**

unkynde, wn-/onkynde *adj.* ungrateful; **unkyndenes(se)** *n.* ingratitude

unknawin (?) *pr. p.* not knowing, (?) *p.p.* (it being) unknown (5. 108)

unkonyng *n.* ignorance

unkouth(e), unkowthe *see* **uncouth**

unluffit *p.p.* unloved, without being loved in return

unneth(e)(s) *adv.* scarcely, with difficulty

unpropre *adj.* improper, unnatural

unresonable *adj.* irrational, without the power of reason

unresty *adj.* unquiet, restless

unricht *adv.* astray

unshamefaste *adj.* shameless; ~**nes** *n.* shamelessness

unspecable, unspekabyl *adj.* indescribable

unthrifty, onthryfty *adj.* without profit, wasteful, harmful, disreputable; unchaste, wanton untyll(e), ontill *prep.* unto, to, for (sometimes following obj.: *you* ~)

unto, wn-/on(e)to *conj. prep.* until; unto, comparable with, in comparison with; ~ . . . -*ward* towards

untrew *adj.* untrue, faithless; (as n.) unfaithfulness

untro(w)th *n.* infidelity, faithlessness

untwynde *p.p.* destroyed

unware *adj.* unaware, innocent; ~ly *adv.* without warning

unweldynes *n.* weakness, sickness

unwiis *adj.* unwise; unwyseman *n.* fool

unworthie *adj.* worthless

upbullyrris *pr. 3 sg.* boils up

uphald *v.* maintain

uphesit *pa. 3 sg.* raised

uplondyssh *adj.* rustic, rural

uprais *pa. 3 sg.* rose up

up-so-do(u)n/-downe *adv.* upside down

upspredis *pr. 3 pl.* reach up, spread up

upsprent *pa. 3 sg.* sprang up

upsprungin *p.p.* risen up

upstowryng *pr.p.* stirring up, raising up

upstrikis *pr. 3 sg.* rises, springs up

upwarpys *pr. 3 sg.* hurls up

urisonnis *see* orisoun

use(n), usyn *v.* use, employ, practise, be accustomed, be in the habit of; usit *pa. 3 sg.*; usyd *p.p.*

uther, uthir *see* other

utterbrasses *n. pl.* (?) outer braces, outer stays

utt(e)red *pa.* shot, sent flying; said

uttermest *adj. sup.* outer, outermost

uttmyst *adj. sup.* utmost

vayage *see* vyage

vailyeand *adj.* valiant; valyeandly *adv.* stalwartly

valeryane *n.* valerian (a medicinal herb)

valys *n. pl.* veils

valour *n.* value

vane *n.* banner

vane, veyne, wane, weyn *adj.* vain, useless, idle, absent, lacking

vary *v.* wander in mind, rave

varied *pa.* differed; varyinge *pr. p.*: *been* ~ differ, diverge

varlette *n.* servant

vaughtes *see* volt

vaunchace *n.* the front of the hunt

veiling *pr.p.* doffing

veyne *see* vane

veirs *n.* verse(s)

ven *imper.* come

veneger, venegur *n.* vinegar

venge *v. refl.* revenge oneself (on); venged *p.p.* avenged

vengeable *adj.* vengeful, cruel

venter *v.* make trial of

vere *v.* let out, pay out

verjus *n.* verjuice (a sour juice from unripe grapes, crab-apples, etc., used in cooking)

vermyn *n.* vermin, noxious animals (esp. reptiles)

ver(r)(a)y, ver(r)(e)y(e), werray, whery *adj., adv.* true, real, very; (as n.) truth; truly, very; ver(r)ely, ver(r)yly, veraly *adv.* truly

vertu, wertu *n.* virtue, power

vertuus *adj.* virtuous, having the virtue or magical power of precious stones

vexed, vexit *p.p.* afflicted

vhos *see* be

vyage, vayage *n.* voyage, journey

vyces *n. pl.* mechanical devices, pivots

vyolere *n.* violet

vyroned *p.p.* surrounded

visaged *p.p.*: *wel* ~ having a pretty face

vyser *n.* visor

vysytacyon *n.* affliction

vissy *v.* visit

vytayll, vitel *n.* food, victuals; vitayles, vitelys *pl.*

vocatioun *n.* summoning

voce *see* voys(e)

voyde *v.* leave, go (from); expel, do away with; empty, clear, evacuate; avoid; voydyd, voyded *pa., p.p.*; voyde *adj.* deprived, empty, clear; voyder *n.* expeller

voys(e), voce, woce *n.* voice, sound, roar (of artillery); *say his* ~ make his call, crow

volt *n.* vault; vaughtes *pl.*

Voluntyn(e) *n.* Valentine

wa *see* wo

wacch, weche *v.* keep vigil, watch over

wach(e) *n.* wakefulness

wag *v.* shake

wage *v.* wager, stake

waif *v.* wave

waykly *adv.* weakly

waile *v.* choose; *to* ~ which could be chosen; **waillit, walit** *p.p., adj.* chosen, excellent

waill *n.* gunwale

waynd *v.* shrink from, hesitate

wair; wait *see* **be; wete, wyt(e)**

wait, wayte *n.* observation, ambush

wayted *p.p.* watched, spied upon; **waytyng** *pr.p.* watching, waiting

waithman *n.* forest outlaw

wak *adj.* wet

wake(n); wald(e); walit *see* **walk; wyl; waile**

wale *n.* choice; *to* ~ at one's choice, in plenty

walk *n.* cloud

walk, wake *v.* wake, waken, stay awake; **woik** *pa.*; **walk(i)n(n)it** *pa., p.p.*; **waken** *p.p., adj.* vigilant, i.e. ready for use

walkning *n.* waking

walkryfe *adj.* vigilant

wally *adj.* stormy, tempestuous

wallowit *p.p.* withered, faded

walow *v.* wallow, roll, toss; **walwyd** *pa. sg.*

Walsyngham wystyll *n.* a whistle sold to, or used by, pilgrims to Walsingham (a shrine in Norfolk)

walx; wan *see* **wex(e); wyn**

wand *n.* rod, staff, scourge, slender stick, paling

wane *see* **vane**

wane *n.* hope

wanhope *n.* despair

wanne *see* **wyn**

wanne *adj.* dark; pallid, pale, sickly; **wanner** *comp.* more faded

wanrufe *n.* disquiet

wantoun *adj.* unruly, insolent, passionate; ~**ly** *adv.* playfully, lightly

wap *v.* lap

wapper *n.* a weapon with a leaden ball on a strap; **wappred** *pa. 3 pl.* hit with a wapper

warantyse *n.*: *on* ~ of a surety, for certain

ward (*with* **from/(on)to** *earlier in phr.*); **wardly; war(e)** *see* **fro(m)ward(e), toward; worldli; be**

war(e), wer *adj.* alert, watchful, aware, wary, ready, careful; *by/be* ~ take care; *was* ~ *of* saw, noticed

ware *n.* wares, goods, field-produce, plants

ware *pa.* wore

warke, warkis; warld; warldly, warldlynes *see* **werk(e); world(e);**

wordli

warp *p.p.* thrown, tossed; **warpit** *pa.* threw, turned

war(re), wer *adj. comp.* worse

wartake *n.* a kind of rope

wasch *v.* wash; **weshe** *imper. sg., pa.*; **wesshe, wasch(yn)** *p.p., adj.* washed, cleansed

wast *n.* waste; *at* ~ wastefully

watch *n.* vigilance, attention, vigil

wate *see* **wyt(e)**

watt *n.* hare

watur-sokul *n.* (?) water-dock; **water-sokkels** *pl.*

waverynge *pr.p., adj.* changing

waw(e) *n.* wave

waxe(n), waxid/-ith *see* **wex(e)**

webbes *n. pl.* (?) membranes growing in a tree or bush, (?) roots

weche *see* **wacch**

wed *n.* pledge; *in* ~ as pledge; **weddes** *pl.*

wedder *n.* ram, wether

wed(d)er, wed(d)ir *n.* weather, storm, tempest; **wedris** *pl.*

wed(e), weid *n.* weed; **wedys** *pl.*

weed, weid *n.* clothing, garment; **wedis** *pl.*

weel; weenen *see* **wel(e); wene**

weeres *n. pl.* weirs

weerne; weet *see* **werne; wete**

weet *imper. sg.* wet

weid; weyke; weilfa(i)r(e); weil(l)(e), weill-ne(i)r; weyn *see* **weed, wed(e); weke; welfare; wel(e); vane**

weyng *n.* wing; **wengis** *pl.*

weip *v.* weep; **weipit** *pa. 3 sg.*

weyr *see* **wher(e)**

we(i)r, werre *n.* war, strife; **wer(r)is** *pl.*

weir, were *n.* doubt: *withouten/but* ~ certainly, assuredly

weir *v.* ward off, defend

we(i)rd *n.* fate, destiny, lot; *gif my* ~ *wald* if my fate allows it

weiris *pr. 3 sg.* wastes away, fades

weyt(h) *see* **wete**

weyve *v.* avoid

wek(e), wyke *n.* week; **whekys** *pl.*

weke, weyke *adj.* weak, feeble

wele *n.* joy, well-being, good fortune, happiness, wealth; ~ **encomyne** *n.* communal welfare

wel(e), weil(l)(e), weel, w(h)ell(e) *adv.* well; *as* ~ as well, also; ~ *is me* I am delighted; ~ *were him* well were it for him; **weill-ne(i)r** *adv.* almost

welfare, weilfa(i)r(e) *n.* well-being, good condition; abundance; good fortune, happiness

well(e) *n.* well, fountain, source, spring

wellit *p.p.* plunged

weltiris *pr. 3 pl.* stream, flow; **welterit** *p.p.* tossed about, overturned

welth(e) *n.* well-being, happiness; wealth

welwillid *adj.* benevolent

welwillyng *adj.* ready, desirous, eager

wend(e)(n) *v.* go, pass away; turn; **w(h)ent** *pa., p.p.*

wene *v.* think, suppose, expect; **weenen** *pr. 3 pl.*; **wenyng(e)** *pr.p.*: ~ *unto* (impers.) it seeming to; **wend(e)** *pa., p.p.*; **wenyng** *n.* thinking, expecting

wengis; wenyng(e) *see* **weyng; wene**

wentes *n. pl.* openings, passages

wer, wer(e)(n); werchyng; werd; were *see* **be, war(e), war(re), we(i)r, wher(e); werke; we(i)rd; weir**

were *v.* wear

weryit; weris *see* **wer(r)yit; we(i)r**

werk(e), warke *n.* work, workmanship, labour, deed, happening, business; **warkis** *pl.*

werke, wirk(e)(n), worch *v.* work, act, do, make, create; ~ *furthe* work out; work on, torment; ache, hurt; **worchys** *pr. 3 sg.*; **wro(u)ght, wrocht, wrowghte, wrowt** *pa., p.p.*; **werchyng, worchyng** *n.* operation, working, action

werly wherly pyt *n.* whirlpool full of eddies

werne, weerne *v.* order, command; refuse, forbid

werray; werre, werris *see* **verray; we(i)r**

werre *v.* make war

wer(r)yit *p.p.* worried (killed by being bitten and shaken); **worrowyd** *pa. 3 sg. refl.*

werthurgh; wertu; wes *see* **wher(e); vertu; be**

wesant *n.* throat

wes(s)he *see* **wasch**

wete, wait, weet, weyth *adj.* wet, moist

wet(e); wether *see* **wyt(e); whyder**

wethy *n.* willow, withy, willow branch; **wetheis** *pl.*

wetyn, wette *see* **wyt(e)**

wetis *pr. 1 sg.* wet (19 C 29)

wewche *n.* injury, misery

wex(e) *v.* grow; **waxith** *pr. 3 sg.*; **wexe, waxe/-id, walx, wolx** *pa.*; **wexynge** *pr.p.*

wha *see* **who**

whay *n.* way

what, quhat *adj., pron. interrog.* what, what kind of, who; ~ *for then* what of that; ~ *that ever* whatever, ~ *ye be*; ~ *this is a . . .* what a . . . this is, ~ *for* what with; **quhateuer/-ir** *adj.* whatever

whe *pron.* we

whech; wheder/-ir; whekys; whell; whellcwmyd *see* **which(e); whether, whyder; wek(e); wel(e); wyllcwmyd**

whellfavyrd *p.p., adj.* well-favoured, good-looking

whent(e); wher *see* **wend(e)(n); be**

wher(e), we(y)r, wer(e), quha(i)r(e) *adv., conj.* where, in what, wherever; ~ *that* if; ~**as** where; ~**by** whereby; ~**ever** wherever; ~**fra** from where; ~**of** wherewith; ~**on** whereon; ~**so** wherever; ~**thurgh** through which

whery *see* **ver(r)ay**

wherles *n. pl.* pulleys of spindles

whether, whethyr, wheder/-ir, whyther, quhether *pron., conj.* which, whichever; whether; (intro. questions) do . . .?, can it be that . . .?

which(e), whech, whilk(e), wych(e), quhich, quhilk(is), qweche *adj., pron.* which, who; *the* ~

whyder, w(h)ether, wheder *adv.* whither

whyet(e), whyght; whyght *see* **whit; wight**

whyle *n.* wheel

while, wh(h)yll, quhyle, quhill *n.* time, while; *an Ave Marie* ~ for the time of an Ave Maria; *other* ~*s* (at) other times; *oft* ~ often

whilk(e) *see* **which(e)**

whyllys, whils, wilis *conj.* whilst

whilom, quhilom, qwylum *adv.* formerly, once, once upon a time

whynarde *n.* short sword

whyne *n.* wine

whit, whitt, whyet(e), whyght, quhit(e) *adj.* white; **whittist** *sup.*

whyther *see* **whether**

whytt, qwytt *n.* whit, small amount; *no* ~, *the deull have the* ~ not at all, nothing at all

whytty *adj.* clever, wise; **wyttyly** *adv.*

whytty (*cont.*):
cleverly
who, wha, quha, quho *pron. interrog., indef.* who, whoever, if anyone; ~ *that*; **quhais, quhois** whose; **quham, quhom(e)** whom
who *see* **wo**
wholl, wolle *n.* wool, fleece; **wholl getherars** *n. pl.* middlemen who collected wool from the growers
whol(l)d(e); whon; whos *see* **wyl; o(o)n; be**
whoso(e), quhasa *pron. indef.* whoever, whosoever, if anyone
whote; whowldde; whryte; wych(e); wicht, wichtlie *see* **hote; wyl; writ(t); which(e); wight**
wickir *n.* willow, twig, withy
wickit *adj.* wicked, evil, cruel
widdercock *n.* weathercock
widderit, wydred *p.p.* withered
widdy *n.* withy, hangman's rope
wydequhar *adv.* everywhere
wye *n.* man; **wyis** *pl.*
wyer *n.* wire
wyf(fe), wijf *n.* wife, woman; **wyvis, wyffis** *pl.*
wight, wicht, whyght *n.* person, man, being, creature
wight, wi(c)ht *adj.* strong, vigorous, bold, brave; **wightly, wichtlie** *adv.* quickly, valiantly
wyke *see* **wek(e)**
wyl, wille *v.* wish, desire, want, be willing to; ~ *he other nell he* whether he wishes it or not; **wyll(e), wolt, wol(l)(e)(n), wull** *pr.*; **wald(e), w(h)ol(l)d(e), whowldde, woold, wuld** *pa.*
wyldefyre *n.* wildfire (inflammable material used in warfare)
wyle *adj.* vile
wyle, wyll *conj.* while, during the time that, until; ~ *that* as long as, provided that, if
wilis; wyll *see* **whyllys; while**
will *adj.* astray; ~ *of wane* bewildered, hopeless
wyllcwmyd, whellcwmyd *pa. sg.* welcomed
wyll(e) *n.* will, consent; wish, desire, inclination
wylly *adj.* willing
wympled *p.p.* covered with a wimple (a cloth worn on the neck and head)

wyn, wynn *v.* win, get to, reach, gain, fight one's way; **wan(ne)** *pa.*: ~ *on fute* got up; win, **wonne** *p.p.*
wynche *v.* kick impatiently
wynches *n. pl.* wenches
wynde *n.*: *in the* ~ *the weder was clere* it was clear
wynde *v.* wind: ~ *up* hoist, draw up; **wounde** *pa. pl.*; **wond** *p.p.*
wyn(n)yng(e) *n.* gain, profit
wyppit *p.p., adj.* fastened, bound round
wyrin *adj.* made of wire, like wire
wirk(e)(n) *see* **werke**
wirschip, worship(p)(e)/-shepe/-chep, wurship *n.* honour, reverence, glory, good name; **wirchipes** *pl.*; **~ful(l)(e), worschyppull, wyrschepyll, worcheppyll** *adj.* excellent, honourable, noble; **wyrchipfulleste** *adj. sup.*; **~fully** *adv.* honourably, worthily
wirschip, wors(c)hip(e) *v.* venerate, worship, revere, bring glory to; **worschipand, wirchipyng** *pr.p.*; **wirchiped** *pa. 3 sg.*
wis *n.* wish; *at* ~ at (your) wish, as much as you could desire
wyse *n.* manner, way
wyshly *adv.* certainly, steadfastly
wysnyt *p.p.* shrivelled
wystyll; wyt *see* **Walsyngham; with**
wyt(e), wytte *n.* wit, mind, understanding, skill, intelligence: *out of* ~ out of one's mind; **wyttes** *pl.*: ~ *fyve* (the) five senses
wyt(e), wytt(e), wet(t)(e), wetyn, wait *v.* know, be aware of, find out; *it is to* ~ it is to be known, *that is to* ~ that is; **wate, wot(t)(e)** *pr. 1, 3 sg.*, **wotist, wostow** *pr. 2 sg.*, **wottys** *pr. 3 sg.*; **witting** *pr.p.*; **wist(e)** *pa.*; **wittyng** *n.* knowledge
wyte *v.* blame, accuse
wyt(h), witht *prep.* with, by; ~ *us* among us
withal(l) *adv.* moreover, also, indeed, therewith
withdrawin *p.p.* taken away; **withdrow** *p.p. refl.* withdrew
withgang *n.* success, advantage
withhaldynge *n.* holding back
withholde *p.p., adj.* (?) controlled (by), in the service (of)
withinneforth *adv.* within

without(e), wythout(h)e, wythowt(en) *adv., conj., prep.* outside; unless; ~ *that* unless, without; **withouteforth** *adv.* outside

witte, wyttes, wittis, wytt(e) *see* wyt(e)

wittering *n.* knowledge

wyttyly, wittyng *see* whytty; wyt(e)

wndyrstonde *v.* learn, understand; undirstonde, undrestonde *p.p.*

wndyrstondynge *n.* understanding, intellect

wndon; wnkynde *see* undo(o); unkynde

wnlaw *n.* fine, penalty

wnlusty *adj.* not wishing to work, listless

wnther *prep.* under

wnto *see* unto

wo, woo, wa, who *n.* woe, misery, sorrow; *as adj.* grieving, miserable; ~ *is hym/me* he/I is/am unhappy

woce *see* voys(e)

wod(d)(e), woid *n.* wood; ~ *cuntré* wooded country; wodes, woddis *pl.*

wod(e) *adj.* mad, raging, furious; ~ *wrothe* violently angry; wo(o)d(e)nes(se) *n.* madness

wodebynde *n.* woodbine, honeysuckle

wodehouses, wodehowses *n. pl.* woodwoses, wild men of the woods

wodnesse; woid; woik *see* wod(e); wod(d)(e); walk

woir *pa. 3 sg. (out)* ~ (?) carried out, caused to flutter out

wold(e), wol(e), wolen, woll(e), wolt *see* wyl

wolen *n. pl.* woollen things, woollen clothes

wolle; wolx *see* wholl; wex(e)

womanhede, womanheid *n.* womanliness; **womanly** *adj. as n., adv.* woman; in a ladylike manner

womentyng *n.* lamentation

won; wonde *see* o(o)n; wynde

wond(e) *n.* wound

wondere *v.* wonder, gaze at with wonder; wondryng *n.* wondering, wonder

wonder(e), wondre; wonders *adv.* wondrously, very

wondryng; wone *see* wondere; o(o)n

wone *n.* dwelling

wone *v.* dwell; be accustomed to; woned, wonyd *p.p., adj.*

wonne *see* wyn

woo-bistad *p.p.* hard pressed by sorrow

woodenes; woold; worch, worchyng,

worchis; worchep, worchepfull(y), worcheppyll; wordy; wordyn *see* wod(e); wyl; werke; wirschip; worthy; worthe

wordli, war(l)dly *adj.* worldly, of this world, mortal; worldynes *n.* worldly affairs

world(e), word, warld *n.* world, multitude, state of affairs; *it is a* ~ it is a marvel

wormes *n. pl.* dragons

worrowyd; worschipand, worschipe, worschipful(le), worschyppull, worship(p)(e), worshepe, worshypfully *see* wer(r)yit; wirschip

wortes, wortys *n. pl.* vegetables; herbs; pottage

worth *n.: take it of* ~ value it

worthe *pr. 3 sg. subj.* come to, fall on; wordyn *p.p.* become

worthy, wordy *adj.* worthy, worth, noble, excellent, appropriate, proper; worthynes(se) *n.* nobility, honour, virtue

wortwormes *n. pl.* caterpillars that feed on vegetables

wost(ow), wote, wotist, wotte, wottys; wounde *see* wyt(e); wynde

wovun *p.p.* woven

wox(e) *see* wex(e)

wp(pe) *adv.* up, upwards; upright

wrachit *adj.* wretched, miserable

wraik, wrake *n.* revenge, vengeance, mischief; wraikfull *adj.* vengeful

wrait *see* writ(t)

wraith *n.* wrath

wrange *see* wring(e)

wrappit *p.p.* wrapped, enclosed

wraxlynges *n. pl.* wrestlings

wrecche *n.* wretch

wreche *n.* vengeance

wrestyd *pa. 3 sg., p.p.* struggled; twisted

wretchitlie *adv.* in misery

wretyn, wreton *see* writ(t)

wrye *v.* twist, turn

wring(e) *v.* wring, twist; droop; wrange *pa. sg.*

writh *v.* turn, twist round, distort; wrything(e) *pr.p.*

writ(t), whryte *v.* write; wrait, wrotte *pa.*; wretyn, ywhreton *p.p.*

wrocht, wroght *see* werke

wroken, wrokin *p.p.* avenged (~ *towarde us . . .* on us)

wroth(e), wrooth *adj.* angry; sad, despondent

wrotte; wrought, wrowghte, wrowt *see* writ(t); werke

ws *pron.* us

wull; wurship *see* wyl; wirschip

xal(t), xuld(e), xuldist *see* shal(le)

y-/i- (*vocalic*) *see* i-

ya(a); yaf, yave *see* ye; yeve

yate, yeit, yet(t) *n.* gate; **yatis, yettis** *pl.*

yawmeris *n. pl.* yells, outcry

ye, yhe, ya(a), yys *adv.* yes, yea; indeed, to be sure

yearne *adj.* vigorous, eager

yede, y(h)eid, yode *pa.* went; ~ *to* went to work

yeer(e); yef(f); yeff; yeftes; yeir(e); yeit *see* yer(e); yyf(f); yeve; yiftes; yede; yer(e); yate

yelde *v.* yield, render, give, return, surrender; **yelded** *p.p.*

yeman, yemon *n.* yeoman, servant; ~ *at hors* (?) mounted yeoman, (?) title of an officer; **yomen, yemen** *pl.*; **yemandry** *n.* yeomen, commoners

yemit *p.p.* kept, guarded

yender *adj., adv.* yonder

yer(e), yeer(e), yeir, ier *n.* year; ~*day* annual commemoration of a death; **yerely** *adv.* yearly

yerly *adv.* early

yerth *n.* earth

yet, yyt *adv.* yet, still; *as* ~ still

yet(t), yettis *see* yate

yeunge, yewng, yyng *adj.* young

yeve, yeff, yive *v.* give; **yaf, yave** *pa.*; **yiving** *pr. p.*; **yeve, yive, yove** *p.p.*; **yevynge** *n.* giving

yevell; yeven; yevynge; yhe; yheid *see* evyl(l); eve; yeve; ye; yede

yyf(f), yef(f) *conj.* if

yiftes, yiftis, yeftes *n. pl.* gifts

yyng; yys; yyt; yive, yivyng; yode *see* yeunge; ye; yet; yeve; yede

yokkit *p.p., adj.* yoked

Yol *n.* Yule, Christmas

yond *adv.* yonder

yon(e) *demons. adj.* that, those

yongth *n.* youth

yonste *n.* favour, goodwill

youe, yowe *pron.* you; **youer, youris** yours

youtheid *n.* youth, youths

yove *see* yeve

yoxing *n.* hiccuping

SELECT LIST OF PROPER NAMES

Adonay (Old Testament name for) God
Almaigne, Almeyn Germany
Alpies Alps
Arabie Arabia(n)
Arcady Arcadia
Arge Argos
Aries the Ram, a sign of the zodiac
Armynake Armagnac
Artour Arthur; **Artourys** *gen. sg.*
Auster the south wind
Avylyon Avalon
Awrora Aurora, the Dawn
Azyncorte Agincourt

Bacus Bacchus
Barthilmewes, Sainte *gen. sg.* St Barth-
   olomew's
Barwicke Berwick
Bedlem, Bethlem Bethlehem
Bery *see* **Bury**
Blak(e)heth Blackheath
Bordews Bordeaux
Boreas the north wind
Borgoyn *see* **Burgoyn**
Boulonges *gen. sg.* of Boulogne
Bretayn, litle Brittany
Brinston Branxton, near Flodden
Brystow Bristol
Burgoyn(e), Borgoyn Burgundy
Bury, Bery Bury St Edmunds

Cal(e)ys Calais
Cananee, Chanane Canaan
Capricorn the Goat, a sign of the zodiac
Cardros Cardross (Dumbarton)
Cartage Carthage
Chanane *see* **Cananee**
Chepe (the) Cheap(side)
Chirklonde the area of Chirk (in Clwyd)
Cipres Cyprus
Cytheron Mt. Cithaeron (a mountain—
   sometimes confused with the island of
   Cythera, sacred to Venus)
Cloros Claros
Creit Crete
Cupid(o) Cupid, son of Venus; **Cupidis**
   gen. sg.

Dame (the) Damme, near Bruges

Delphé Delphi
Dower Dover

Elycons well the spring on Mt. Helicon,
   sacred to the Muses
Enee Aeneas
Eoye Eous, one of the horses of the Sun
Esax Essex
Ethios Ethous (or Aethon), one of the
   horses of the Sun
Exanthus (the river) Xanthus

Famagust Famagusta
Flete the Fleet, a London prison near a
   body of water called the Fleet running
   into the Thames between Ludgate
   Hill and Fleet St.
Flora(y) Flora, goddess of flowers

Gabryellys, Sent *gen. sg.* St Gabriel's
Genius an attendant spirit, the 'bishop' of
   Venus
Gyle, Sent St Giles
Grewe Greece

Herowde Herod
Hert Hart (Inn)
Hyspalensy supposedly a city in Spain

Inde India
Isodre Isidore of Seville (*c.*560–636)

Jack Napys, Jacke Napes a name for a
   tame ape or monkey
Jaff, Port Jaffa
Jaffrey Geoffrey
Jasoun Jason
Jeremy Jeremiah; **Jeroms** *gen. sg.*
Jones, Sent ~ *day* St John's day (27
   December)
Jony Joigny
Josaphath Josaphat
Jubyter, Jupyter Jupiter; *as name for God*
   (21. 407)
Junoys *gen. sg.* Juno's

Kyllyngworth Kenilworth
Knarsbrugh Knaresborough

575

Lyncome Lincoln
Lysya Lycia (Asia Minor)
Lowes, St Louis IX of France (1215–70)
Lowrence Laurence, a name for a wolf or a fox
Lucyne Lucina, the Moon
Lumbardy(e), Lumberdye Lombardy
Lusseboene Lisbon

Macedoyne Macedonia
Mahownis *gen. sg.* Mahomet's; ~ *men* Saracens
Malkyn Molly
Mary Mawdelyn St Mary Magdalene (who wept greatly)
Marshalsye Marshalsea, a prison in Southwark
Martis *gen. sg.* of Mars
Menatair Minotaur
Mercury(e), Mercurius Mercury, the planetary god; quicksilver, alchemists' mercury
Mychell Michael
Myssyas Messiah
Moyses Moses; *gen. sg.* of Moses

Neptunus Neptune, god of the sea
Newgate a famous London prison
Noy *gen. sg.* Noah's
Northefolke Norfolk

Occyan the greate se the great ocean thought to encircle the world
Olyvete the Mount of Olives
Orchady, the Isles of Orkney
Orleaunce Orléans
Oswaldestree Oswestry (Shropshire)
Oxinfurd Oxford

Parys(ch) Paris
Pernasus (Mt.) Parnassus
Peros Pyrois, one of the horses of the Sun
Phateros Patara
Phebus Phoebus, the Sun
Philogie Philogeus (Phlegon), one of the horses of the Sun
Poil(l) the Pole, pole-star
Portyngale Portugal
Port Jaff *see* **Jaff**

Poule, Saynt St Paul; **Poulis** St Paul's Cathedral

Queneburghe Queenborough (Kent)
Qwyntyn, Sent St Quentin

Raffe Ralph (? with pun on **raff** *n.* refuse)
Ramys Rama (? Ramla)
Rochister, Rouchestre Rochester

Sabaoth: *God of* ~ Lord of Hosts
Salesbyry, Salusbyry, Salysbery Salisbury
Salomon Solomon
Sathan(as) Satan; **Sathanas/-is** gen. sg.
Saturne, Saturnus Saturn
Sesar Caesar
Sevenok Sevenoaks (Kent)
Sycil Sicily
Sydony Sidon (Sayda, north of Tyre)
Southsex Sussex
Suthfolk Suffolk
Suthwerk Southwark

Tamyse (the river) Thames
Tanne, Sent St Anne
Thenedos Tenedos
Thomas, Saint: ~ *eve of Caunterbury* the eve of the feast of the Translation of St Thomas Becket (i.e. 6 July)
Tyborn(e), Tiburne Tyburn, a place of public execution in London (at the junction of the present Oxford St., Bayswater Rd., and Edgeware Rd.)
Tyllbery Tilbury (on the Thames)
Titan the Sun
Tull(y)e (Marcus Tullius) Cicero

Valentynnes, Seynt: ~ *day* St Valentine's day (14 February)
Vesper the evening star

Walys Wales
Wlcanus Vulcan

Yolus Iulus, i.e. Ascanius, son of Aeneas

Zelande Zeeland
Zephirus the west wind

INDEXES

The following Indexes are intended as a guide to the contents of the texts, not to the editorial matter. They list authors, titles of works, first lines of verse extracts, and the majority of the subheadings. In the titles and subheadings definite and indefinite articles have been omitted. In the Index of Verse Titles and First Lines quotation marks are used to differentiate first lines; in the Index of Prose Titles italics are used to differentiate titles of works from other headings.

INDEX OF AUTHORS

For anonymous pieces see Index of Verse Titles and First Lines and Index of Prose Titles

INDEX OF VERSE TITLES
AND FIRST LINES

INDEX OF PROSE TITLES